THE UNITED STATES
IN OUR OWN TIMES

1865-1920

THE UNITED STATES
IN OUR OWN TIMES
1865–1920

BY

PAUL L. HAWORTH, Ph.D.

AUTHOR OF "THE HAYES-TILDEN ELECTION," "AMERICA IN FERMENT,"
"RECONSTRUCTION AND UNION," "GEORGE WASHINGTON: FARMER," ETC.
SOMETIME LECTURER IN HISTORY, COLUMBIA UNIVERSITY, AND
ACTING PROFESSOR OF HISTORY, INDIANA UNIVERSITY

CHARLES SCRIBNER'S SONS

NEW YORK   CHICAGO   BOSTON

A

PREFACE

IF it be true that an important object of history study is to enable one to understand the present, then it is clear that the time has come when greater emphasis than hitherto must be laid on the period since the Civil War. Fifty-five years—almost half the period of our existence under the Constitution—have passed since the close of that conflict, and most of our problems have little or no direct relation to those that troubled Lincoln and his predecessors.

This book is designed to meet the needs of students who desire to know our country in our own times. In it I have devoted a large share of space to social and industrial questions, but I have been on my guard against swinging too far in this direction. After all, the business of government is still of prime importance to the welfare of the nation, and it is essential that our citizens should understand our past political history.

Throughout the book I have tried to bear in mind that history is made by men and not by abstractions. Nor have I forgotten that generalizations about a subject mean little to a student until he has some knowledge of what actually took place.

I am indebted to a number of persons for assistance rendered in the preparation of the volume, but most of all to Professor James A. Woodburn, my old preceptor and later colleague, for reading the proof and making many helpful suggestions.

PAUL L. HAWORTH.

CONTENTS

CONTENTS

MAPS

THE UNITED STATES IN OUR OWN TIMES

CHAPTER I

THE AFTERMATH OF WAR

On a never-to-be-forgotten April day General Robert E. Lee bowed to Grant and the inevitable at Appomattox, and his war-worn veterans in gray scattered, heavy-hearted, to their distant homes, after fighting for four years with a valor to which the world pays willing homage. President Jefferson Davis and a few misguided irreconcilables sought to continue the struggle on other fields, but in vain. Before the end of May the last armed force that had marched beneath the stars and bars had dissolved or surrendered, and Davis himself was a prisoner. The victors participated in a memorable grand review in Washington, and then they too laid down their arms, to take up once more the prosaic tasks of peace.

Collapse of the Confederacy.

The bloodiest civil war in history was over; the work of the soldier was done; but there still remained for solution by statesmen three great problems. The first of these was, What should be the future status of the eleven States that had tried to quit the Union? Second, What should be the status of the individuals who had taken part in creating and upholding the now defunct Confederacy? Third, What should be the status of the more than 4,000,000 ignorant black freedmen, most of whom had hitherto been mere human chattels who could be bought and sold like any other property? Even as they greeted with glad acclaim the glorious news of peace, far-sighted men anxiously considered how these problems could be solved.

Three Great Problems.

I

Five days after Appomattox Abraham Lincoln fell by the bullet of a half-crazed assassin, and after a few hours of unconsciousness his labored breathing ceased and the Emancipator exchanged immortalities. Shortly afterward, in the parlor of the Kirkwood House, Andrew Johnson received the presidential oath of office from Chief Justice Chase. "You are President," said the chief justice solemnly, as Johnson handed back the Bible. "May God support, guide, and bless you in your arduous duties!"

Johnson Becomes President.

Andrew Johnson was born of "poor white" parentage at Raleigh, North Carolina, in 1808. His boyhood was spent in the densest ignorance, and it was not until he was entering manhood that he so much as learned to read. He became a tailor, and at eighteen crossed the mountains to Greenville in eastern Tennessee, where he presently married a capable and ambitious woman, who taught him to write and cipher. Unpromising as was his origin, Johnson possessed a natural genius for politics. He was elected in turn alderman, mayor, member of the State legislature, federal representative, and governor of Tennessee, and when his State seceded he was one of its representatives in the Senate of the United States. His success in politics was all the more remarkable because it was extremely unusual in the South for poor men to be elected to high office; such places were usually grasped by the rich, slave-owning planters. He had many conflicts with the men of that class, whom he once characterized as a "scrub aristocracy," and he repaid their hostility and contempt by hatred and by refusing to follow his State into the Confederacy. By his loyal stand he won high favor in the North, and in April, 1862, Lincoln appointed him military governor of Tennessee, a difficult position, which he filled with marked courage and ability. In 1864 the feeling on the part of many Republican leaders that it would be desirable to put a Southern man and former Democrat on the national ticket resulted in his nomination for the vice-presidency, and in his election to that office. The circumstances of his remarkable rise from ignorance and poverty to position and power were

Johnson's Career and Character.

highly to his credit, just as they were in the case of Lincoln, but unfortunately he lacked much of having attained Lincoln's mental, moral, and intellectual stature. Despite his successes, he remained uncultured, narrow-minded, obstinate, and it was whispered that he had a weakness for strong drink.

Many of the radical Republicans had opposed Lincoln's generous policy toward the South, and some of them regarded Johnson's accession as "a godsend." On Sunday, the day after Johnson took the oath, certain radicals, including Senators Chandler of Michigan and Wade of Ohio, called on the new President. "Johnson, we have faith in you," cried Wade enthusiastically. "By the gods, there will be no trouble now in running the government!" Johnson thanked Wade and responded: "I hold this: robbery is a crime; rape is a crime; *treason* is a crime, and *crime* must be punished. . . . Treason must be made infamous, and traitors must be impoverished."

Radicals Pleased with Johnson.

While in this mood Johnson signed a proclamation that charged Jefferson Davis and other prominent Confederates with complicity in Lincoln's assassination, while to persons who talked with him he harped so much upon punishing "traitors" that even some of the radicals began to fear that he would be too vindictive, that he would carry out a bloody proscription of Southern civil and military leaders.

In the days immediately following the surrender of Lee, Northerners were inclined to feel magnanimous toward the South, but Booth's dastardly deed roused a bitter desire for vengeance. Booth himself was presently hunted down and slain; four of the other conspirators, including a woman, Mrs. Surratt, were convicted and hanged; while others were sentenced to long terms of imprisonment, three of them for life. But many people believed that the wretched assassins were mere tools of Jefferson Davis and other high Southern leaders, and throughout the North an insistent demand arose that the "rebel chieftains" should be hanged. It is now known that Booth had no prominent accomplices, but the contrary view long persisted among

Northern Attitude.

multitudes of men, and the course of events was influenced by this belief, mistaken though it was. Even many persons who scouted the idea that the Southern leaders had stooped to assassination reflected that the bloody deed was a result of secession, and they hardened their hearts toward the South.

On the other hand, it was not in human nature for ex-Confederates soon to display enthusiasm for the Union or for Union men. They had bowed to stern necessity; they smarted keenly under the sense of defeat; their loyalty, as a Northern traveller reported, was simply "disloyalty subdued." Some of them found comfort in asserting that they had been "overpowered" but not "conquered," and for years the vain hope that "the Lost Cause" might yet triumph in a new outbreak lingered in a few breasts. Southern men who had lent aid to the Union cause were regarded as black-hearted traitors, while "Yankee" soldiers and civilians were frequently made to feel that their presence was unwelcome. Women were particularly open in displaying their hatred and contempt. For example, it was commonly remarked by Union officers that women passing them on the street would gather up their skirts as if to avoid touching what they so much abhorred. An officer stationed in a Virginia town complained that whenever he went to church and attempted to enter a pew the ladies seated in it invariably rose to leave. Such manifestations of Southern hostility were viewed in the North with resentment, mingled with amusement, but they were natural under the circumstances and had a pathetic side. The Southern people had experienced bitter losses; in the words of Professor Fleming: "They must have time to bury their dead, and it was long before the sight of a Federal soldier caused other than bitter feelings of sorrow and loss."

In general, however, there was less friction between the garrisons and the people than might have been expected. Now and then white soldiers foolishly forced "noisy and scornful unrepentants" to walk under the stars and stripes, or cut the buttons off Confederate uniforms—often the only

Southern Attitude.

clothing their wearers possessed—or occasionally committed worse excesses; but there were few armed conflicts, and in time

Federal Troops in the South.

many of the soldiers came to feel a certain sympathy for the white population, while their presence came to be regarded by the whites as a guarantee of peace and order. The presence of colored troops was considered particularly humiliating by the whites. They were likely to be insolent, they inoculated the freedmen with ideas of equality, and in some instances they were guilty of serious crimes.

Several theories had been advanced as to the effect of secession upon the status of a State, but, as Lincoln wisely said in his last public speech, made to a crowd of serenaders only three

Lincoln's Reconstruction Policy.

days before his death, all men would agree that such States were "out of their proper practical relation with the Union," and that the sole object of statesmanship should be again to "get them into that proper practical relation." Early in the war he had realized the desirability of restoring the semblance of loyal self-government in the seceded sections, and one result of his policy in this direction was the erection in Virginia of a Union government that consented to the setting up of West Virginia as a separate commonwealth. In Virginia proper the fragmentary political organization that remained after West Virginia had been set apart established itself at Alexandria, under the protection of Federal cannon. Although this government, which was headed by Governor Francis H. Pierpont, was frequently snubbed by Congress and by military commanders, Lincoln recognized it, being hopeful that it would furnish a nucleus for future loyal development. In 1862 he appointed military governors in Tennessee, North Carolina, and Louisiana. An important duty of these governors was to stimulate loyal sentiment among the inhabitants, and considerable success resulted from the experiment in Louisiana and Tennessee. After the surrender of Vicksburg Lincoln appointed a military governor for Arkansas, and near the close of the year he issued a general proclamation in which he offered that if 10 per cent of the male inhabitants in any rebellious State, except Virginia, would take an oath of loyalty, and would organize a State government, he would recognize it. In Louisiana, Arkansas, and Tennessee such "10 per cent governments" were actually formed, and Lincoln carried out his promise regarding them; but the policy displeased the radicals in Congress, and neither house would admit members chosen from these States. When the Confederacy collapsed the net result of Lincoln's reconstruction policy was, therefore, that Virginia, Louisiana, Arkansas, and Tennessee possessed a semblance of a loyal government, but none of them had been definitely readmitted into the Union.

Infinitely more difficult was the problem of the negroes. Even the question of whether they should be slaves or freemen had not yet been settled absolutely, for the Thirteenth Amendment had not been ratified by three-fourths of the States, while the Proclamation of Emancipation did not apply to all sections of the South, and its validity remained a matter of some doubt. It was practically certain that freedom would triumph, but, granted this, there still remained the complicated questions of the freedman's political, social, and economic status. And it could safely be predicted that these questions would continue to plague the country long after the status of the seceded States and of ex-Confederates had been fixed and forgotten.

Question of the Freedman's Status.

During the war slaves in regions remote from the clash of arms had usually remained quietly upon the plantations. Dim notions that the war might bring them freedom penetrated the minds of some, and escaped Union prisoners could generally count upon their assistance, but fears of servile revolts proved groundless. In after years a celebrated Georgia orator, Henry Grady, said gratefully: "A thousand torches would have disbanded the Southern army, but there was not one." However, when a Union force entered a district many of the slaves would flock to it, and when Sherman's victorious columns swept through Georgia to the sea thousands of blacks, fondly believing that "the Day of Jubilee" had come, fell in behind their deliverers, having, as a South Carolinian later complained, been

Behavior of the Slaves during the War.

"seduced from their allegiance" by the prospect of freedom. On foot, on horses or mules, and in every conceivable vehicle, from rough ox-carts to sumptuous carriages taken from their masters' stables, they followed the conquering hosts and often proved a source of no small embarrassment to their liberators. "Ise hope de Lord will prosper you Yankees and Mr. Sherman," said the spokesman of a large number of these refugees to an aide-de-camp, "because I tinks, and we all tinks, dat youse down here in our interests." Another gray-haired "uncle" told Sherman "that he had been looking for the 'angel of the Lord' since he was knee-high," and that he was sure that Union "success was to be his freedom."

When the Confederacy collapsed some of the freedmen willingly hired themselves to their former masters, but hundreds of thousands could not rest content until they had tried out their freedom. A desire to behold the fascinating wonders of the world and fear lest slavery might be suddenly restored and they be caught by their old owners stimulated this tendency, and many freedmen changed their names to disguise their identity or to signify that they had passed from under the yoke. Multitudes swarmed into the towns or tramped aimlessly about the country, and, as they were not accustomed to caring for themselves, thousands died during the next year. Many negro men seized the opportunity to desert their families and get new wives, for it was regarded as a relic of bondage to be tied to an ugly old wife who had been married in slavery. Revivals and camp-meetings were held in many places and aroused much religious fervor. One old negro woman baptized in a river came out screaming: "Freed from slavery! Freed from sin! Bless God and General Grant!" To many negroes freedom meant primarily the chance to escape from work, and they experienced a sad disillusion when they learned that they must still labor for a living. To avoid so disagreeable an alternative, many resorted to stealing; it was not considered sinful to take pigs or chickens from the whites; that was merely "spilin' de 'Gypshuns."

Unrest among Freedmen.

Other freedmen were actuated by more laudable ambitions, notably to acquire the white man's learning in the schools, upon which optimistic Northern philanthropists were expending much money and effort. More than a score of societies were formed to minister to the freedman's material wants and to uplift him morally and mentally, and large sums were subscribed for this missionary work. Yankee schoolmasters and schoolma'ams invaded the South, filled with all the hopeful zeal of crusaders, and were regarded with a mixture of amused contempt and angry hostility on the part of most of the white population. As for the blacks, many had the view that education—best of all, a knowledge of Greek and Latin—was the sesame that would open all doors to them. Children and grown-ups alike were seized with the thirst for knowledge. An officer of the Freedmen's Bureau reported that in a school in North Carolina he saw sitting side by side representatives of four generations: a child six years old, her mother, grandmother, and great-grandmother, the last over seventy-five years old—all studying their letters and learning to read the Bible. Little wonder, therefore, that the results of this educational crusade present an odd mixture of the ludicrous, the pathetic, and the sublime.

Desire for Education.

White men complained that the negroes were demoralized by freedom, that they would not work except under compulsion, that they were "lazy and sassy," that they would not display the old deference. One of Howell Cobb's overseers wrote to his employer that the blacks would remain in their houses for days, feigning sickness or giving other more trivial excuses. "Tha air," he declared, "steeling the green corn verry rapped. Som of them go when tha pleas and wher tha pleas an pay no attention to your orders or mine. . . . You had as well Sing Sams to a ded horse as to tri to instruct a fool negrow." Some white employers resorted to the old methods, such as whipping or hanging up by the thumbs, while more serious offenses were now and then committed against freedmen, either by employers or ordinary ruffians.

Complaints about Freedmen.

From the days when they were imported into America

against their will the negro race had labored for their masters without financial reward, but among both freedmen and many white men there now developed the idea that some recompense should be made for unnumbered years of forced service. In the course of the war freedmen in some parts of the South had been established on confiscated estates, and this fact helped to create a belief that the government would adopt a general policy of seizing the property of the masters and dividing it among the emancipated slaves. In some way the notion got abroad that each negro family would receive "forty acres and a mule," and for years the idea persisted in some black districts. In certain quarters white sharpers reaped a rich harvest by selling to credulous freedmen the painted stakes, or "pre-emption rights," with which each must be provided if he expected to obtain his share on the day of division. The deed sold to one credulous negro read as follows: "Know all men by these presents, that a nought is a nought and a figure is a figure; all for the white man and none for the nigure. And whereas Moses lifted up the serpent in the wilderness, so also have I lifted this d—d old nigger out of four dollars and six bits. Amen! Selah!"

"Forty Acres and a Mule."

There were Northerners who urged that both justice and considerations of the freedmen's future demanded that financial assistance should be given to the emancipated race, but in the end nothing of consequence was done. In the words of a celebrated leader of the race, namely, Frederick Douglass, the negro "was turned loose, naked, hungry, and destitute to the open sky." He was made a freeman, but he was left economically dependent upon his former master.

Little Done for Freedmen Financially.

The fact had an important bearing on the subsequent history of the South. It meant that generally the negroes must continue to work for others, instead of settling down upon their own little plots of ground and leading a lazy, care-free existence. In consequence the problem of obtaining labor has never become so acute in the South as in Guiana and certain West India islands, where the emancipated blacks easily obtained land, and solved the

Effect on Labor Conditions.

question of living by setting out a few banana-trees and cultivating a yam patch. Even to-day the number of negro farmers who own their land is comparatively small.

To act as a guardian for the freedmen, and to stand as a buffer between them and the whites, Congress, by act of March 3, 1865, created an institution called the Bureau of Refugees, Freedmen, and Abandoned Lands. General Oliver

Freedmen's Bureau.

O. Howard, commander of one wing of Sherman's army, a philanthropist of great zeal, a man who had won the title of "the Christian Soldier," was made commissioner of the bureau. Not all the officials were of so high a type, for many were lacking in tact, while some proved to be rascals. There can be no doubt that the bureau did much work that needed to be done, but by Southern white men it was generally regarded with hostility. Many of the bureau agents ultimately organized their black wards politically, and swelled the ranks of the "Carpet-Baggers," as Northern men who entered Southern politics were called.

In weighing the difficulties involved in effecting the transition from a slave-labor to a free-labor system, it should not be forgotten that the task was complicated by unfavorable economic

Economic Condition of South.

nomic conditions. The North was actually richer and more prosperous, despite the war, than it had been in 1861, and the victorious Northern soldier returned to a land full of the busy hum of industry. In the words of Henry Grady, it was far otherwise with "the footsore Confederate soldier, as, buttoning up in his faded gray jacket the parole which was to bear testimony to his children of his fidelity and faith, he turned his face southward from Appomattox, in April, 1865. Think of him as ragged, half-starved, heavy-hearted, enfeebled by want and wounds; having fought to exhaustion, he surrenders his gun, wrings the hands of his comrades in silence, and, lifting his tear-stained and pallid face for the last time to the graves that dot the old Virginia hills, pulls his gray cap over his brow and begins the slow and painful journey. What . . . does he find when, having followed the battle-stained cross against overwhelming odds, dreading death not half so much as surrender, he reaches the home he left so prosperous and beautiful? He finds his house in ruins, his farm devastated, his slaves free, his stock killed, his barn empty, his trade destroyed, his money worthless; his social system, feudal in its magnificence, swept away; his people without law or legal status; his comrades slain, and the burden of others heavy on his shoulders. Crushed by defeat, his very traditions gone; without money, credit, employment, material training; and beside all this, confronted with the gravest problem that ever met human intelligence— the establishment of a status for the vast body of his liberated slaves."

"Everything has been mended, and generally in the rudest style," wrote an observer of Southern conditions. "Window-glass has given way to thin boards, and these are in use in railway coaches and in the cities. Furniture is marred and broken, and none has been replaced for four years. Dishes are cemented in various styles, and half the pitchers have tin handles. A complete set of crockery is never seen, and in very few families is there enough to set a table. . . . A set of forks with whole tines is a curiosity. Clocks and watches have nearly all stopped. . . . Hair-brushes and tooth-brushes have worn all out; combs are broken and are not yet replaced; pins, needles, and thread, and a thousand such articles, which seem indispensable to house-keeping, are very scarce. Even in weaving on the looms, corn-cobs have been substituted for spindles. Few have pocket-knives. In fact, everything that has heretofore been an article of sale at the South is wanting now. At the tables of those who were once esteemed luxurious providers, you will find neither tea, coffee, sugar, nor spices of any kind. Even candles, in some cases, have been replaced by a cup of grease, in which a piece of cloth is plunged for a wick. The problem which the South had to solve has been, not how to be comfortable during the war, but how to live at all."

A Picture of Southern Conditions.

The Civil War had begun as a revolt to perpetuate slavery and the right of secession; it had ended in a revolution that extinguished both. It had been a bitter battle, and both belligerents had fought on until one had been overwhelmed by numbers and material resources. After so protracted a struggle, after so complete an overturn of old institutions, it was inevitable that even the wisest statesmanship should not be able immediately to restore peace and prosperity in the conquered section. And unhappily really wise statesmanship was to prove chiefly conspicuous through its absence.*

No Perfect Solution Possible.

* A list of "Suggestions for Further Reading" is given in the Appendix.

CHAPTER II

PRESIDENT JOHNSON'S PLAN OF RECONSTRUCTION

FOLLOWING the assassination of Lincoln, many prominent Southerners were seized and thrown into prison, but the only person who was tried, convicted, and punished was Wirz, the commander of Andersonville prison, who was sent to the gallows by a military tribunal. The expected trials for treason were indefinitely postponed; most of the prisoners were soon released. Jefferson Davis was kept for about two years at Fortress Monroe, and for a short time was subjected to the indignity of being put in irons, but ultimately he was released on bail, and was never tried; curiously enough two of the men who signed his bond were old abolitionists, namely, Gerrit Smith and Horace Greeley.

Treatment of Southern Leaders.

That events took such a course was largely due to Johnson's dropping his punitive policy toward the South. The main influence in effecting this revolution in the President's mind was probably the cabinet. James G. Blaine, in his *Twenty Years of Congress*, attributes the change to Secretary of State Seward; others reject this view. Though marked for assassination by Booth and his fellow conspirators and dangerously wounded by one of them, Seward retained his naturally generous disposition. To him an enemy who surrendered was an enemy no more. One day he met an old senatorial associate from Virginia, a man with whom he had often clashed in ante-bellum days, but Seward's heart went out to him. "Come and dine with me, Hunter," said he to the ex-Confederate. Hunter accepted, and when he raised his plate at the secretary's hospitable board he found beneath it a "pardon," duly signed and sealed.

Change in Johnson's Policy.

Having decided to follow a liberal course, Johnson virtually adopted Lincoln's plan of reconstruction; but unfortunately, in carrying out the details, he lacked the Emancipator's infinite tact. He soon accorded recognition to the "10-per-cent" governments established by Lincoln in Louisiana, Tennessee, and Arkansas, and to the Pierpont government in Virginia, and on May 29 he proclaimed William W. Holden provisional governor of North Carolina and directed him to call a constitutional convention for the purpose of organizing a new civil government. Holden was a Raleigh newspaper publisher and politician who had given the Confederate authorities much trouble, and had in 1864 come near to being elected governor on a "peace-at-any-price" platform. The President's proclamation provided that only loyal persons could participate as electors or as delegates to the convention; the test of loyalty established was the taking of an oath prescribed in an amnesty proclamation issued the same day. Among those excluded from the benefits of this amnesty proclamation were civil or diplomatic officers of the Confederacy, military officers above the rank of colonel, governors of seceded States, and persons who owned taxable property worth more than twenty thousand dollars. All other persons might take the oath, which required, among other conditions, a pledge to support all laws and proclamations regarding slavery. Even the excepted persons might make special application to the President for pardon, and the proclamation held out the hope that "such clemency will be liberally extended." Within a few weeks the President took similar action regarding the six remaining seceded States. The President let it be known that to secure the restoration of their States into the Union the conventions must accept the results of the war. His fundamental conditions were: (1) Repeal of the ordinance of secession or declaring it null and void. (2) Acceptance of emancipation. (3) Repudiation of debts contracted in aid of the Confederacy.

As Congress would not meet until December, President Johnson for several months had a free hand to carry out his reconstruction plans, and meanwhile the Southern people were

Johnson Virtually Adopts Lincoln's Plan.

given an opportunity to reveal their attitude of mind toward the new order of things. The situation was one that called for wisdom on the part of Southerners; their section was, so to speak, on probation, and common sense dictated that they display a prudent regard for the prejudices of the conquerors. But human nature is apt to be perverse, and unfortunately most of the ablest men of the South, being still under political disabilities, were unable to participate in the work of the constitutional conventions and of the legislatures that followed them; it is not strange, therefore, that prudence was sometimes forgotten and that things were done that proved unfortunate for the country and particularly for the South.

The Southern Opportunity.

Before the end of the year new constitutions had been completed by all the States except Texas, which did not finish the task until some months later. In most respects the conventions showed a reasonable willingness to accept the results of the war and to comply with the wishes of the President. All formally abolished slavery, though not without protests on the part of some delegates; and, with the single exception of South Carolina, all repudiated the State debts contracted in support of the war, though it required strong pressure from Washington to bring about this result in some cases. The secession ordinances were annulled by most of the States, and North Carolina conceded the illegality of her ordinance by declaring that it "at all times hath been null and void." The old States-rights view still flickered feebly in South Carolina and Georgia, however, and their conventions *repealed* the ordinances. In the hope of disarming Northern opposition to his reconstruction policy, Johnson suggested that the Mississippi convention should extend the elective franchise to all freedmen who could read and write, or who paid taxes on real estate valued at not less than two hundred and fifty dollars, but the convention ignored the recommendation.

Work of Constitutional Conventions.

The more detailed work of economic, social, and political reorganization was presently taken up by newly elected legislatures. All these legislatures, except that of Mississippi, ratified the Thirteenth Amendment, which was formally proclaimed a part of the Constitution December 18, 1865, but, generally speaking, the legislatures displayed a more independent spirit than had the conventions. This was especially true with regard to the enactment of laws fixing the status of the freedmen.

Much political controversy has raged over these "Black Codes," as they were called. The task of framing them was one of peculiar difficulty, not only because of the complicated nature of the problem itself but because of the suspicious attitude of the victorious North. Some such legislation seemed necessary, for the old slave codes or the laws concerning free negroes were not applicable to the new conditions. The charge has frequently been made that the Black Codes were passed in a spirit of defiance of the North, but it would be more exact to say that in enacting them the Southern legislators did not take Northern prejudices sufficiently into account. Both sections recognized that the blacks were *free*, but in the North freedom was often interpreted to mean equality of the blacks with the whites, while in the South the prevailing idea was that the freedmen must be assigned to an inferior condition. Even some of the Northern States still denied equality to the negroes, and this fact was not lost sight of by these Southern legislators. In part, therefore, the codes were an honest effort to meet a difficult situation, but it cannot be denied that at times the old Southern belief that the negro was divinely created to be servant to the white man peered through these codes unpleasantly, and furnished proof that their framers had not yet fully realized that the old order had passed away.

Among the least liberal codes were those of South Carolina and Mississippi, States in which the blacks considerably outnumbered the whites. South Carolina designated her former slaves as "persons of color"; prohibited them from engaging in any occupation except "that of husbandry, or that of a servant under contract for labor," except after obtaining a license costing from ten to a hundred dollars; prohibited servants on plantations from being "absent from the premises without the permission of the master"; and gave to masters power to complain of servants to judicial officers, who were authorized "to inflict, or cause to be inflicted, on the servant, suitable corporal punishment, or impose upon him such pecuniary fine as may be thought fit."

The Mississippi Code.
The Mississippi code withheld from the freedmen the right to own or lease land except in incorporated towns, and provided for "apprenticing" negro children whose parents were unwilling or unable to support them, preference being given in such cases to former masters, who were given power to use "moderate corporal chastisement." Any negro over eighteen years of age who should be found on the 2d of January, 1866, or thereafter, without lawful employment or business was made subject to fine and to imprisonment at the discretion of the court, and to being hired out in case he did not pay such fine.

Discrimination against Freedmen.
In some of the codes the words "servant," "master," and "mistress," and other slavery terms were constantly used, while for some offenses freedmen were made subject to heavier penalties than was the case with white persons. In certain States the blacks were prohibited from owning firearms or other deadly weapons, or even from assembling together except under stringent restrictions, and only Tennessee permitted them to testify in legal cases between white litigants. Defenders of the codes have asserted that they were mainly designed to force lazy freedmen to work, but it is clear that one tendency was to set the negroes apart as an inferior and, to some extent, still servile class. The fact that four decades later "peonage" flourished in some Southern communities and was broken up only through the activity of federal courts would seem to indicate that under such laws the freedmen would often have been imposed upon by the unscrupulous.

One matter dealt with in the codes was the matter of the relations between the sexes. Prior to emancipation, marriage between slaves, in the civilized sense of the term, was rare; promiscuity was common. "All freedmen, free negroes, or mulattoes who do now and have here-before lived and cohabited together as husband and wife, shall be taken and held in law as legally married, and the issue shall be taken and held as legitimate for all purposes," ran the Mississippi code, and the same general rule was adopted elsewhere. South Carolina provided that in case a man had two or more reputed wives, or one woman two or more reputed husbands, he or she was to be permitted to select one of them and the ceremony of marriage was then to be performed. Intermarriage between the races was forbidden under heavy penalties, that prescribed by Mississippi being life imprisonment.

Regulation of Relations between the Sexes.

It need hardly be said that the proceedings of Southern conventions and legislatures were closely scanned by Northern men. Opposition to the President's reconstruction policy quickly developed, yet there were many Northerners willing to suspend judgment and to watch what use the South would make of her opportunity. Johnson's right-about-face sorely disappointed the radicals, who had welcomed his advent to power with such enthusiasm, and such leaders as Benjamin F. Wade, Charles Sumner, and Thaddeus Stevens did not long disguise their feelings. In a letter to a friend Sumner accurately forecast what subsequently occurred: "Then comes a collision with Congress, and inseparable confusion and calamity." Under the inspiration of Stevens and Sumner, Republican conventions in Pennsylvania and Massachusetts opposed the President's policy, but other conventions indorsed it, while men like Morton of Indiana, and Andrew of Massachusetts, both great "war governors," spoke out in its support.

Radicals Oppose the Johnson Policy.

The course of events proved favorable to the radicals. Every time that news came up from the South of a tactless or defiant utterance, of a discriminating law or constitution, of the mistreatment or murder of a freedman or white Union man, it meant increased opposition to Johnson's plan of reconstruction. Even the praise that Northern Democrats and Democratic newspapers hastened to shower upon the President

Rising Tide
of Opposition
in the
North.

aroused suspicion in multitudes of breasts. Millions still believed that the assassination of Lincoln had been instigated by Confederate leaders, and the bloody deed tended to make the North less liberal. Most of the Black Codes were not formulated until 1866, but enough had been passed in 1865 to show the drift of such legislation. Upon this and similar matters Northerners were kept well informed by newspaper correspondents, most of whom transmitted stories illustrating Southern contempt for the freedmen and Union men, or describing sporadic instances of conflicts between the two races. "We tell the men of Mississippi," said the *Chicago Tribune* (December 1, 1865), "that the men of the North will convert the State of Mississippi into a frog-pond before they will allow any such laws to disgrace one foot of soil in which the bones of our soldiers sleep and over which the flag of freedom waves."

All over the North men were saying that the Southern States had been in a great hurry to get out of the Union, and that they could have no valid ground for complaint if the nation took its time about letting them back in.

CHAPTER III

CONGRESS TAKES CONTROL

WHEN the Thirty-ninth Congress met for its first session (December 4, 1865), a number of persons elected in Southern States to be senators or representatives appeared to claim their seats; but, under the leadership of Thaddeus Stevens, the Republican caucus had agreed upon a plan that boded ill for such members and for the realization of the President's reconstruction policy. The clerk of the House, Edward McPherson, omitted calling the names of claimants appearing from seceded States, and his action was sustained. A similar course was taken by the Senate. As soon as the House had completed its organization, Stevens introduced a resolution for the appointment of a joint committee of nine representatives and six senators to inquire into the condition of the States recently in rebellion and "report whether they or any of them are entitled to be represented in either house of Congress." The resolution passed both the House and the Senate, and thus originated the celebrated "Reconstruction Committee," which was to play so decisive a part in the coming drama. Stevens became the chairman of the House committee, and Fessenden of Maine, secretary of the treasury under Lincoln, headed that appointed by the Senate.

Reconstruction Committee.

It was significant that the House acted on the Stevens resolution before expressing a willingness to receive the President's message, the reading of which was delayed until the next day. The message reviewed the course of reconstruction, and dealt with the subject with such excellent temper and in so admirable a style that it was a matter of public wonder that a man who had not learned to read and write until he was grown could have composed such a state paper. It was not until forty years later

Johnson's First Message to Congress.

that it was discovered by Professor Dunning that the original draft of the document was in the handwriting of George Bancroft, the celebrated historian, who had been secretary of the navy under Polk.

It is undeniable that many of the President's opponents were genuinely anxious to safeguard the rights of the freedmen, but there was also another motive. The adoption of the Thirteenth Amendment rendered it certain that in the future five-fifths instead of only three-fifths of the former slaves would be counted in apportioning members of Congress and presidential electors, with the result that the political power of the South would be considerably strengthened. Republicans began to fear that if the President's plan were carried out an alliance between ex-Confederates and Northern Democrats might soon succeed in gaining control of the federal government. Sumner had already declared this to be the Southern policy, and that Southerners hoped to win "by covert guile" what they had lost in "open war."

Republican Fears.

Color was lent to such charges by the course of events in the South. That section seemed to be losing some of its spirit of compliance. Stories of the mistreatment of freedmen and Union men heaped fuel on the fire of Northern suspicion, as did the fact that many ex-Confederates were being elected to office. Even Johnson protested against the proposed choice by the Georgia Legislature of Alexander H. Stephens as United States senator, and telegraphed: "There seems in many of the elections something like defiance, which is all out of place at this time." His protest was ignored, and presently the man who, less than a year before, had held the second office in the Confederacy appeared at the capital to claim his seat, in the face of the "iron-clad oath" of 1862, which required all who wished to qualify for federal office to swear that they had never voluntarily given aid or encouragement to enemies of the United States. "In his astounding effrontery," says James G. Blaine, who was then a member of the House, "Mr. Stephens even went so far as to insist on interpreting to those loyal men

Alexander H. Stephens Elected Senator.

who had been conducting the government of the United States through all its perils, the Constitution under which they had been acting." Stephens subsequently became a useful member of Congress, and he might have proved so at this time, but it is not strange that the men who for four bloody years had borne the burden of saving the Union opposed the speedy restoration to places of trust of such men as he.

When such feelings were developing in the North it was inevitable that radicals like Charles Sumner and Thaddeus Stevens should wield great influence. Sumner had long been a prominent member of the Senate and a bitter opponent of what was known as "the Slave Power," and back in the '50's had been almost beaten to death by a Southern representative, Preston R. Brooks. Sumner was a Massachusetts Brahmin, but in theory he was a doctrinaire believer in human equality, anxious to put freedmen and former masters upon identically the same political and social plane. In his opinion the attempt of Southern States to secede was illegal, and the result null and void, but he held that such action was equivalent to "a practical abdication by the State of all rights under the Constitution." In other words, he believed that the seceded States had virtually committed suicide, and he declared that they were now practically territories under "the exclusive jurisdiction of Congress." In a resolution introduced in the Senate on the first day of the session he laid down five conditions that must be accepted by the people of a seceded State before such State could be restored to its former privileges in the Union. One of these conditions was that there should be "no denial of rights because of color or race."

Stevens had long represented a Pennsylvania district in the House of Representatives, and was now a "sharp-faced, grim-looking," lame old man of seventy-three, but he still possessed an iron will, and in practical leadership of men he far surpassed Sumner. When we study his career we are inevitably reminded of Cromwell or the old Covenanters. Though he had a profound sympathy

Sumner's Theory of "State Suicide."

Stevens's "Conquered Province" Theory.

for the oppressed, he was a bitter partisan and a violent hater of the slaveholding South. He bluntly declared that the seceded States were conquered provinces, having no constitutional rights the conquerors were bound to respect. Congress, not the President, was the only power competent to "revive, recreate, and reinstate these provinces into the family of States." He disclaimed a desire for "bloody punishments to any great extent," but he favored stripping "a proud nobility of their bloated estates; reduce them to a level with plain republicans; send them forth to labor, and teach their children to enter the workshops or handle the plough, and you will thus humble the proud traitor. Teach his posterity to respect labor and eschew treason." Like Sumner, he advocated suffrage for the freedmen and wished to give them homesteads carved out of the plantations of their former masters. "The infernal laws of slavery," he declared (December 18, 1865), "have prevented them from acquiring an education, understanding the commonest laws of contract, or of managing the ordinary business of life. We must not leave them to the legislation of their late masters, but we must provide for them protective laws. . . . If we fail in this great duty now when we have the power, we shall deserve and receive the execration of history and of all future ages."

In advocating negro suffrage Stevens and Sumner stood far in advance of many of their party associates. The general feeling even in the North was that the freedmen were too ignorant to use the ballot intelligently. Men like Governors Andrew and Morton at this time declared against negro suffrage, while Lincoln had never gone beyond suggesting that the franchise should be conferred upon the "very intelligent" and those who had "fought gallantly in our ranks." Only six Northern States permitted black men to vote, and in the fall elections of 1865 Wisconsin, Minnesota, and Connecticut voted down negro-suffrage proposals. It was only the course of events, the growth of a feeling that the franchise was a weapon the freedman could use in his own defense, a fear that a combina-

Northern Opposition to Negro Suffrage.

tion of "Southern rebels and Northern copperheads" might gain control of the government and nullify the results of the war, that ultimately brought the Republican party to force through the Fourteenth and Fifteenth Amendments.

Before adopting his lenient reconstruction policy President Johnson had sent Major-General Carl Schurz to the South to report upon conditions in that section.   Schurz was a natural-

Schurz's Report on Southern Conditions.

ized German who had narrowly escaped a Prussian firing-squad in the Revolution of '48, and who had won world-wide fame by gallantly rescuing his friend and preceptor, the poet Gottfried Kinkel, from the Berlin penitentiary.   He was an idealist by tempera-ment, and on his arrival in America had thrown himself ardently into the battle against slavery.   Lincoln appointed him min-ister to Spain, but Schurz soon found that he preferred the tented field to diplomacy, so he entered the Union army and rose to high rank.   At Johnson's behest he visited several of the South-ern States, and at first his reports were well received, but presently he found that the President had lost interest in his work.   Returning to Washington in October, Schurz repeatedly requested the President to permit him to make a formal re-port.   In a personal interview Johnson expressed the view that this was unnecessary, but Schurz persisted that he would do so and a bitter altercation followed.   "I thereupon turned my back on Andrew Johnson," said Schurz many years later, in describing the scene to the author, "and I never spoke to him again."   Subsequently he wrote out a detailed account of his observations and impressions, and the radicals in the Senate, aware that it contained facts tending to discredit the presiden-tial reconstruction plan, passed a resolution calling on Johnson to transmit it.

In the report Schurz conceded that there was no present danger of another insurrection on a large scale, but he declared that Southern submission sprang "from necessity and calcula-tion," that treason did "not appear odious," and that there was "*an utter absence of national feeling.*"   He believed that Southerners realized that slavery in its old form was doomed, but thought they hoped that "some form of serfdom, peonage, or other form of compulsory labor" might be substituted. He found much friction growing out of the new economic relations between former masters and the freedmen, and reported that many crimes had been committed against negroes and white Unionists. For the protection of the freedmen he urged that the right to vote should be given to them before the seceded States were readmitted.

Schurz Favors Negro Suffrage.

Johnson reluctantly complied with the demand for Schurz's report, and, to counteract it, transmitted a report made by General Grant, who had recently made a hasty trip through the South. Grant reported: "I am satisfied that the mass of thinking men of the South accept the present situation of affairs in good faith. . . . Slavery and the right of a State to secede they regard as having been settled forever by the highest tribunal, arms, that man can resort to." He expressed the view, however, that possibly four years of war had left Southerners "in a condition not to yield that ready obedience to civil authority the American people have been in the habit of yielding," and said that military garrisons were still necessary and that "black and white mutually require the protection of the general government."

General Grant's View.

Early in February, 1866, Congress passed a bill enlarging the powers of the Freedmen's Bureau and extending its life for one year, but Johnson vetoed the measure, declaring that it was unconstitutional, and naming as "another very grave objection" the fact that it was passed by a Congress from which the representatives of eleven States were excluded. This last argument was one of which the President's supporters were making much use, and the Democratic *New York World* habitually placed "Rump Congress" at the head of its account of congressional proceedings. As many Republican senators and representatives still hoped to avert a final break with Johnson, an attempt to pass the bill over the veto failed.

The President's opponents commanded, however, a majority

in each house, and, as a reply to the veto, the House of Representatives, at the instigation of Stevens, passed (February

20) a concurrent resolution to the effect that no

Congress Votes to Exclude Southern Senators and Representatives.

senator or representative from a seceded State should be admitted to a seat until Congress had formally declared that the State from which he came was entitled to representation. Two months before this the Senate had rejected such a proposition, but on March 2 it concurred in the resolution. Thus was definitely asserted the right of Congress to be the final authority in the matter of reconstruction.

The President's course was warmly praised by some and attacked by others, but it was noticeable that most of the epistolary and newspaper commendation came from the South

Johnson's Denunciatory Speech.

and from Northern Democrats, and his enemies were careful to point out this fact to the public. On Washington's birthday a mass meeting of his supporters assembled at Grover's Theatre, in the capital, and proceeded to the White House to congratulate their hero. Hugh McCulloch, the secretary of the treasury, advised his chief not to make an address, and Johnson said: "I shall thank them and that's all." But the course of Congress had aroused his naturally strong combativeness, and the appearance of a large and friendly crowd "excited his itch for public speaking." Encouraged by cries of "Give it to them, Andy!" and "Hit them again!" he delivered a wild and incoherent harangue, in the course of which he denounced the Joint Committee on Reconstruction as "an irresponsible central directory" that had usurped "all the powers of Congress"; charged Charles Sumner, Thaddeus Stevens, and Wendell Phillips with laboring to destroy "the fundamental principles of this government"; and even declared that some of his enemies desired to remove the "'presidential obstacle'" by assassination. The speech delighted his enemies, who took care to revive stories of his tendency to inebriety, and it did much to alienate the country.

A month later Congress passed a Civil Rights bill designed

to carry the Thirteenth Amendment into effect and to safeguard the freedmen against the obnoxious features of the
Black Codes. It made the freedmen citizens of
Civil Rights the United States, with all civil rights, prohibited
Bill of 1866.
any one from interfering with such rights under
color of a State law, but did not give negroes the right to vote.
The bill had been submitted to Johnson in advance, and many
people supposed that he would sign it, but on March 27 he returned it with his veto. By so doing he alienated many moderate senators and representatives who hitherto had striven to
avoid a breach between the President and Congress, and after
a hard and close contest the veto was overridden. Feeling ran
so high that when the vote was announced in the Senate the
floor and the galleries burst into a tumult of cheering.

It was the first time in the history of the country that an
important measure had been passed over the veto, and it signified that Congress had seized the helm of state. Johnson's
Congressional plan of reconstruction was promptly shelved, and
Plan of Re- a new one, evolved by the Joint Committee on Reconstruction.
construction, was substituted. This plan took the
view that the seceded States had forfeited their rights and that
they should not be permitted their old rights in the Union
until the results of the war had been written into the Constitution. The essential features of the new plan were contained
in a Fourteenth Amendment, which was approved by Congress
on June 13, and was submitted to the States for ratification.

This amendment wrote into the Constitution the essential
provisions of the Civil Rights Act in order to place that legislation beyond danger of repeal by a subsequent Congress. It
The made the negroes citizens of the United States, and
Fourteenth prohibited the States from abridging their privileges
Amendment.
and immunities as such. It did not give them the
franchise, but it made it to the interest of a State to do so by
providing that representatives should be apportioned among
the States according to population, excluding Indians not taxed,
and that if any State denied the right to vote to any of its
male citizens for other reasons than crime its representation in

Congress, and hence in the electoral college, should be proportionately diminished. It provided that any person who had previously held any office necessitating his taking an oath to support the Constitution of the United States, and had then engaged in rebellion, or given aid or comfort to the enemies of the nation, should be ineligible for office, either State or federal, but Congress might, by a two-thirds vote, remove such disability. It affirmed the validity of the public debt incurred in conducting the war, and forbade the assumption by State or nation of any debt "incurred in aid of insurrection or rebellion," or any claim for loss or emancipation of any slave. The amendment was meant to settle certain issues growing out of the war, but one clause, forbidding any State to "deprive any person of life, liberty, or property, without due process of law," was later used by conservatively inclined courts for very different purposes from those then contemplated.

The Joint Committee also proposed that, when the new amendment should become a part of the Constitution, the seceded States that had ratified it should be accorded representation in Congress. A bill to that effect failed to pass, but the principle was soon followed in the case of Tennessee, whose "Union" legislature disfranchised many ex-Confederates and ratified the proposed amendment (July 19, 1866). Five days later Congress voted to restore Tennessee to "her former proper, practical relations to the Union."

Tennessee Readmitted.

In the same month Congress passed over the veto a bill extending the life of the Freedmen's Bureau for two years. By this time the breach between Johnson and the majority party had become so wide that in the Senate only three Republicans joined with the Democrats to sustain the veto.

Freedmen's Bureau Extended.

If the other Southern States had followed the example of Tennessee and accepted the congressional offer—that is, the Johnson conditions plus ratification of the Fourteenth Amendment—they would have avoided much future humiliation. But the quarrel between President and Congress and the advice of Northern Democrats led them to hope that they might, with their Northern allies, regain control of the government.

The Southern Mistake.

Not another Southern State ratified the amendment at this time; the majorities against it were overwhelming. In the opinion of the historian Rhodes: "It was a sad blunder. Compared with the settlement of other great wars, the plan was magnanimous, for it involved no executions, confiscations, or imprisonments. It restored the ballot to virtually every white man who would take an oath to support the Constitution, and it did not admit the negro to the franchise, though it held out a reward to the States to confer the franchise upon him."

Whether the presidential or the congressional plan should triumph depended on the outcome of the elections in the autumn of 1866. In August friends of the President held at Phila-

Political Campaign of 1866.

delphia what was officially known as the National Union Convention, but which was popularly dubbed the "Arm-in-Arm Convention," because, as a sign of the closing of the "bloody chasm" between the sections, the Northern and Southern delegates dramatically marched into the hall, or "Wigwam," together. Opposition speakers and newspapers were soon calling the "Wigwam" a "Noah's Ark" into which "the animals entered two by two, the elephant and the kangaroo, of clean beasts and of beasts that are not clean, and of fowls and of every thing that creepeth upon the earth." They craftily pointed out that "Rebels" and "Copperheads" attended, and they charged that such persons were not permitted to voice their true sentiments. Furthermore, as a counter-demonstration, Southern Unionists and many Northern men met in Philadelphia on September 3, and, though they wrangled over the negro-suffrage question, they agreed in denouncing the President's Southern policy. On September 17 soldiers and sailors who favored the President assembled at Cleveland, but it was noticeable that none of the great Union generals attended. A week later some thousands of anti-Johnson soldiers and sailors held a convention in Pittsburgh and passed resolutions favoring Congress and its policy.

The President's cause was weakened by outrages committed against freedmen and white Unionists in the South. Outbreaks of this kind occurred at Memphis and elsewhere, but the most notable took place in New Orleans (July 30, 1866). Agitators favoring negro suffrage had arranged for a meeting of the convention of 1864 for the purpose of changing the State constitution. The convention's legal right to do this was doubtful, and the mayor, Monroe, the same bitter secessionist who had held office when Farragut and Butler captured the city, was determined to break up the meeting if possible. A procession of negroes marching to Mechanics' Institute, in which the meeting was to be held, became involved in a conflict with a white mob. The affair ended by the mob, the police, and the city firemen storming the hall and killing 40 or 50 negroes and white radicals, and wounding about 150 more. General Sheridan, who commanded the district, characterized the affair as "an absolute massacre . . . a murder which the mayor and police of the city perpetrated without the shadow of a necessity."

Race Conflicts.

President Johnson took the view that the riot was due to the agitation for negro suffrage, and held that the responsibility rested upon Northern radicals, but his explanation failed to convince the country. The Southern Unionist Convention, which met at Philadelphia some weeks later, charged that "more than a thousand devoted Union citizens have been murdered since the surrender of Lee," and begged that loyal Southern men should not be left at the mercy of their enemies. The number of slain was perhaps exaggerated, but such affairs as that at New Orleans went far toward convincing doubtful Northern voters that the President's generous policy toward the South was unsafe.

Appeal of Southern Unionists.

In August and September an invitation to attend the dedication in Chicago of a monument to Stephen A. Douglas gave Johnson an opportunity to visit some of the chief cities of the country and speak in defense of his course. On this "swing around the circle," as the tour came to be called, he took with him Seward, Admiral Farragut, and General Grant, in order, it was charged, to attract crowds. The trip began auspiciously. The reception accorded the President in Philadelphia was cordial, while in New York City decorative banners bore such inscriptions as, "Thrice welcome, Andrew Johnson, the sword and buckler of the Constitution, the Union's hope and the people's champion," and he was greeted by tens of thousands with real enthusiasm. But Johnson's injudicious words soon proved his undoing. He constantly glorified himself, bitterly denounced Congress, and offended his hearers by references to "Northern traitors" and "foul whelps of sin." At Cleveland he indulged in an unseemly wrangle with some of the audience and, in reply to a rebuke, shouted: "I care not for dignity!" He also demanded: "Why don't you hang Thad Stevens and Wendell Phillips?" In St. Louis, when his egotistical harangue was interrupted by cries of "New Orleans," he cried out that the riot at that place could be traced "back to the radical Congress." At Indianapolis the audience resented his remarks so much that he was silenced and driven from the platform. He returned to Washington much weaker than he had left it. What James Russell Lowell humorously described as an "advertising tour of a policy in want of a party" had failed miserably.

Johnson's "Swing around the Circle."

In his desperation Johnson removed many of his opponents from office, and made use of various other doubtful expedients, but all to no purpose. His opponents gleefully proclaimed that "Copperheads" and "Copperjohnsons" were supporting him with enthusiasm, but that few Union men were following him into the Democratic party. Even three members of his cabinet—Postmaster-General Dennison, Attorney-General Speed, and Secretary of the Interior Harlan—resigned rather than break their party ties, while Secretary of War Stanton openly proclaimed his opposition. The fall elections of 1866 proved a Waterloo to Johnson's hopes. The voters gave his opponents a majority of more than two-thirds in each house of Congress.

Johnson Defeated.

In February following the election a meeting of Southerners in Washington put forward an alternative for the proposed

Fourteenth Amendment, which by this time had been rejected
by every seceded State except Tennessee, but their suggestion
Congress
Proceeds to
Restrict
President's
Powers. passed unheeded. The congressional majority regarded the election result as a mandate to reduce
the President to a cipher and adopt a more rigorous reconstruction policy. Numerous measures
were passed to harass the President and to restrict his powers.
A "rider" to an army appropriation bill forbade (March 2,
1867) his issuing any military orders except through the general
of the army—that is, Grant—to relieve the general of command,
or to station him anywhere except at the capital, unless with
his own consent or with the approval of the Senate. For a
long time there had been unfounded rumors that the President
contemplated gathering the unrecognized Southern claimants
to seats in Congress and his own congressional supporters into
one body, and recognizing it as the legal legislature of the nation,
and this restriction was partly designed to prevent him from
executing any such *coup d'état*.

Another act of the same date, passed, of course, over the
veto, prohibited the President from dismissing civil officers
without the consent of the Senate, but conceded a suspensive
Tenure-of-
Office Act. power when the Senate was not in session. In
case the President made use of this suspensive
power he must, when the Senate reconvened, send
in his reasons for acting in a given case, and, if the Senate refused to concur, the suspended official resumed his position.
Violation of this Tenure-of-Office Act laid the President liable
to fine and imprisonment. Opponents of the measure denounced it as unconstitutional, and pointed out that Washington and every other President since his day had exercised the
power of removal unhampered. The Constitution is silent
upon the subject; it merely stipulates that appointments shall
be "by and with the Advice and Consent of the Senate."

Edwin M.
Stanton. The Tenure-of-Office Act was largely designed to
prevent the dismissal from the cabinet of Edwin
M. Stanton, whose position as secretary of war
was at this juncture a highly important one. Stanton favored
the radical reconstruction plan and opposed that of the

President, and the radical leaders desired to keep him in the cabinet as a check on Johnson.

On the same day that the Thirty-ninth Congress laid restrictions upon the President's removing power it passed over his veto (March 2, 1867) the Great Reconstruction Act. Two days later, in obedience to a law enacted for that purpose, the new Fortieth Congress assembled, and this body enacted two supplementary reconstruction measures (March 23, July 19, 1867). The existing governments in the ten remaining "rebel States" were brushed aside, and the States were divided into five military districts, each to be ruled over by a military officer not below the rank of brigadier-general. Under the oversight of these officers constitutional conventions might be held, but the delegates to these conventions must be elected by the male citizens irrespective of "race, color, or previous condition," the constitution must confirm the right of the freedmen to the suffrage, and the legislature elected thereafter must ratify the Fourteenth Amendment. In order to enable the negroes and white radicals to gain political control, the supplementary act of March 23 provided that all applicants for registration must take an oath that excluded many ex-Confederates. Although he bitterly opposed the congressional plan, President Johnson did not venture to disregard these laws, and he assigned Generals Schofield, Sickles, Pope, Ord, and Sheridan to command the five districts.

Military Reconstruction.

On the day after the passage of the second supplementary act Congress, disregarding the warnings of members who thought it unsafe to leave Johnson unwatched, adjourned until November. Many of the President's supporters had long been urging him to dismiss Stanton from the cabinet, and Johnson took advantage of the adjournment to get rid of his obnoxious secretary of war. On August 5 he wrote Stanton saying that "public considerations of a high character" constrained him to ask for the secretary's resignation. Stanton responded: "I have the honor to say that public considerations of a high character, which alone have induced me to continue at the head of this depart-

Johnson Suspends Stanton.

ment, constrain me not to resign the office of secretary of war before the next meeting of Congress." Johnson then suspended Stanton and appointed General Grant, against Grant's desire, secretary of war *ad interim*. He also removed Sickles from command of the district comprising the Carolinas, and Sheridan from that consisting of Louisiana and Texas, and substituted Generals Canby and Hancock. The removal of these officers pleased the Southern whites, but aroused bitter condemnation in the North, as did also the suspension of Stanton.

For months there had been talk of impeaching Johnson, and when Congress reassembled a resolution to that effect was introduced in the House, but it was lost by a vote of 108 to 57
Johnson Dismisses Stanton. (December 7, 1867). The Senate, however, refused to concur in the suspension of Stanton (January 13, 1868), and Grant willingly relinquished the office to him, thereby angering Johnson, who wished him to hold on, in order to compel Stanton to resort to litigation that would result in a judicial opinion as to the constitutionality of the Tenure-of-Office Act. Johnson bitterly assailed Grant for his course, and presently brought the whole political conflict to a crisis by peremptorily dismissing Stanton and designating (February 21, 1868) a garrulous and convivial old general named Lorenzo Thomas as secretary of war *ad interim*. When Thomas appeared at the department to demand possession, Stanton firmly refused to yield. An amusing colloquy ensued, which ended amicably and with Stanton still in possession.

The attempt to remove Stanton aroused great excitement in Washington and throughout the country. The Senate, by a large majority, denied the President's power to dismiss Stan-
House Impeaches Johnson. ton, and the House, without loss of time, by a vote of 126 to 47, resolved (February 24): "That Andrew Johnson, President of the United States, be impeached of high crimes and misdemeanors in office." Eleven charges were drawn up against the President. Most of the articles dealt with Johnson's alleged violation of the Tenure-of-Office Act. The tenth article, drawn up by the incorrigible Benjamin F. Butler, charged that the President's denunciatory

speeches in 1866 constituted "a high misdemeanor in office." The eleventh article was fathered by Thaddeus Stevens, and was a sort of omnibus charge cleverly designed to catch votes.

The trial proper began on March 30, with Chief Justice Chase presiding over "the Senate sitting as a court of impeachment," and with the chamber crowded with members of the two houses, high dignitaries, and other spectators.

Impeachment Trial. Among those who appeared to represent the House were John A. Logan, George S. Boutwell, Benjamin F. Butler, and Thaddeus Stevens. The President's counsel included Benjamin R. Curtis, ex-justice of the Supreme Court, the brilliant William M. Evarts of New York, and Henry Stanbery, who resigned his position as attorney-general in order to defend his chief. The sittings were not continuous but were strung out through a period of almost two months. The trial afforded the lawyers and politicians concerned a splendid opportunity to display their skill and eloquence for the admiration of court and country, but, in the words of Professor Dunning, "as a revelation to the world of lawlessness and infamy in Andrew Johnson, it soon became farcical." The President's defenders succeeded in showing that in dismissing Stanton he had not intended to start a revolution but had expected to get before the courts a test case as to the constitutionality of the Tenure-of-Office Act. Furthermore, evidence was brought in to prove that certain senators who were now favoring impeachment had taken the view, when the bill was under consideration, that it would not safeguard the places of members of the cabinet who held over from Lincoln's administration, as Stanton had done. In short, all efforts to prove that Johnson was guilty of "Treason, Bribery, or other high Crimes and Misdemeanors," which are the sole offenses specified in the Constitution for impeachment, broke down. But partisan bitterness was so aroused against Johnson that many senators believed that it would be justifiable to remove the President for political reasons or on grounds of public policy, and as a precedent they could point to the impeachment because of drunken insanity of Judge John Pickering in the days of Jefferson's presidency.

The public clamor for conviction was prodigious, and the result was in doubt. The supporters shrewdly managed that the first vote should be taken on the omnibus article. Seven Republican senators—Fessenden of Maine, Henderson of Missouri, Fowler of Tennessee, Van Winkle of West Virginia, Trumbull of Illinois, Grimes of Iowa, and Ross of Kansas—joined with the Democrats to save the President, and the vote stood: "guilty," 35; "not guilty," 19—or one less than the necessary two-thirds. It is now known that at least two other senators—Sprague of Rhode Island and Willey of West Virginia—stood ready to vote against impeachment had their votes been needed. Later ballots on other articles proved equally vain, and, amid the helpless rage of the radicals, the case came to an end.

Failure of Impeachment.

The failure of impeachment caused great disappointment in the North, but it is the general verdict of historians that the outcome was fortunate for the country, that it was well that the independence of the executive should be preserved.

Secretary Stanton at once resigned from the cabinet and retired to private life, being subsequently appointed by Grant a justice of the Supreme Court a few days before his death, in 1869. To fill the vacancy Johnson nominated General Schofield, and the Senate accepted him. The Senate spitefully refused, however, to consent to the return of Stanbery to the office of attorney-general, but ratified the nomination of the brilliant and popular Evarts. The new cabinet members were tactful men who possessed the confidence of Congress as well as of the President, and they helped to establish a truce that lasted until the end of Johnson's administration.

A Truce.

The impeachment controversy did not prevent progress in carrying out the congressional plan of reconstruction. Under the oversight of military commanders elections were held to choose delegates to constitutional conventions, and in these elections negroes participated, while many white men were unable to take the prescribed oath and were excluded. Many of the delegates—in Louisiana and

New Southern Constitutions.

South Carolina a majority—were freedmen fresh from slavery, and of course not conversant with the framing of fundamental laws, but the chief part in the conventions was usually taken by Northern white men who had come South with the army or the Freedmen's Bureau. The main feature of the constitutions was that they gave to negroes civil and political rights. In many matters, notably in the provisions for public education—in which hitherto the South had been backward—the conventions freely copied from the institutions of certain Northern States. Naturally the origin of such provisions did not tend to increase the popularity of the constitutions in the eyes of the white population.

In the winter and spring of 1868 the work of constitution-making was completed in all the States except Texas, and the electorates received an opportunity to pass upon the new fundamental charters. Opponents of the constitutions at
Attitude of the Whites. once raised the cry that "Caucasian civilization" was about to be submerged in "African barbarism." "Continue over us, if you will do so, your own rule by the sword," petitioned a convention of Alabama whites to Congress. "Send down among us honorable and upright men of your own people, of the race to which you and we belong, and, ungracious, contrary to wise policy and the institutions of the country, and tyrannous as it will be, no hand will be raised among us to resist by force their authority. But do not, we implore you, abdicate your rule over us, by transferring us to the blighting, brutalizing, and unnatural dominion of an alien and inferior race, a race which has never exhibited sufficient administrative ability for the good government of even the tribes into which it is broken up in its native seats; and which in all ages has itself furnished slaves for all the other races of the earth."

In six States—Louisiana, Georgia, Arkansas, Florida, and the Carolinas—the voters at once ratified the constitutions. That of Mississippi was rejected by over 7,000 votes. Alabama's constitution was approved by over half the votes cast, but many whites, in accordance with a prearranged plan, remained away from the polls, with the result that less than half of the registered voters participated; as Congress had provided that a majority must participate to make ratification valid, the constitution, in effect, was defeated. In June, 1868, Congress voted that, as soon as the legislatures of the six States that had accepted their constitutions should accept the Fourteenth Amendment, they should once more be considered in full fellowship in the Union. Furthermore, even Alabama was restored with the rest under the constitution which had failed of ratification. In Virginia, through the neglect of Congress to appropriate money for an election, the new constitution was not submitted to the people, so the Old Dominion, along with Mississippi and Texas, continued under military rule.

Readmission of Seven States.

In the States that had been readmitted elections were held for the selection of State and local officers, and the radical party, composed of negroes led by Northern "Carpet-Baggers" and Southern white "Scalawags," proved generally successful. The Fourteenth Amendment was duly ratified by all the legislatures, and on January 20, 1869, it was formally proclaimed a part of the Constitution.

"Carpet-Baggers" and "Scalawags" Seize Control.

In most of the South society had been turned upside down. Those who had been the slaves were now the masters. Consideration of the results of this remarkable state of affairs is reserved for a later chapter.

CHAPTER IV

MEXICO, ALASKA, AND THE ELECTION OF 1868

FROM his predecessor President Johnson inherited a dangerous Mexican problem. In that country, ever since it became independent, revolution and rapine had been the rule rather than the exception. Foreigners were frequently mistreated and even murdered, while both private and public debts were often repudiated. Late in 1861 Great Britain, France, and Spain agreed to intervene in the country, being "compelled" to take this course "by the arbitrary and vexatious conduct" of the Mexican authorities. The three powers disavowed any intention of acquiring territory or special advantages, and agreed not "to prejudice the right of the Mexican nation to choose and to constitute freely the form of its government." The United States was invited to participate in the intervention, but declined.

Vera Cruz was seized by the allies, but Great Britain and Spain soon withdrew from the enterprise. The French remained in Mexico and continued to push preposterous claims for damages and debts, for Napoleon III, Emperor of France, was full of imperialistic notions of restoring French power and influence in the New World. In secret instructions to his commander in Mexico he pointed out the desirability of setting limits to the power of the United States, and emphasized "the duty of marching upon Mexico, there boldly planting our flag and establishing perhaps a monarchy, if not incompatible with the national sentiment of the country." Ultimately, in fact, the French captured the City of Mexico and, with the approval of the Clerical party, set up a throne, upon which they placed as Emperor the Archduke Ferdinand Maximilian, brother of Kaiser Francis Joseph of Austria. Many of the Mexicans refused to recog-

39

nize Maximilian's authority and, under the leadership of Benito' Juarez, waged a bitter guerilla warfare against him and his supporters.

The French course in Mexico was a plain violation of the Monroe Doctrine, but, with the Confederacy on his hands, President Lincoln deemed it wise to confine his disapproval to verbal protests. But the United States was merely biding its time, and when the Southern collapse came many Americans thought the interlopers should be driven out by force of arms. In May, 1865, General Grant sent Sheridan to Texas to assemble a large force along the Rio Grande, and both generals did not hesitate to render, more or less openly, assistance to Juarez. Secretary of State Seward, however, felt confident that he could solve the difficulty by diplomacy, and he and the President held advocates of more forceful methods in check. Through various channels Napoleon III was plainly but politely informed that he must withdraw his forces. The Emperor had found his Mexican experiment unpopular and enormously expensive, and he shrank from a conflict with the victorious fleets and armies of the United States. In April, 1866, an official announcement was made in Paris that the French troops in Mexico would be withdrawn.

The United States Forces French to Withdraw.

In the spring of 1867 the last French troops left Mexico, and the Clerical party had not the strength to uphold Maximilian's tottering throne. The Emperor was captured, was tried and condemned to death, and was shot by a firing-squad at Querétaro, along with two of his generals. His fate served as a grim warning to other European princes who might in future think of setting up kingdoms in America. His queen, Carlota, daughter of Leopold I, King of the Belgians, had gone to Europe in a vain quest for assistance, and during a tragic interview with the Pope her reason fled and she became hopelessly insane. For half a century the demented princess resided in a palace in Belgium, and she was still living there when the German army overflowed that unhappy land.

Defeat and Death of Maximilian.

Relations with Great Britain during these years lacked much of being entirely cordial. Late in 1865 Irish Fenians in the United States met in Philadelphia and organized a "Republic," with a "President," a "Congress," a "Secretary of War," and so on. Large sums were raised, ostensibly to further the cause of Irish freedom, but much of the money was wasted and only a comparatively small part found its way across the Atlantic. One faction of the order favored fighting England in Canada, and in 1866 repeated efforts were made to invade that country. The United States authorities exerted themselves to suppress these filibustering attempts, but millions of Americans did not hesitate to declare their sympathy with the Irish cause.

The Fenian Movement.

The truth was that Americans had not forgotten the attitude of Great Britain during the Civil War, and a strong determination existed to exact satisfaction for damage done by the *Alabama* and other British vessels sailing under the Confederate flag. Charles Francis Adams, our minister at the Court of St. James, insisted upon reparation, but the British Government persistently refused to allow American claims. In August, 1868, Reverdy Johnson succeeded Adams and negotiated what is known as the Johnson-Clarendon Convention, but Americans felt that it failed to satisfy their just demands and the Senate rejected it by a vote of 54 to 1 (April 13, 1869). Sumner, the chairman of the committee on foreign relations, denounced it unsparingly. He estimated that Great Britain owed the United States $15,000,-000 for direct damages inflicted by the *Alabama* and other cruisers, and upward of $2,000,000,000 for indirect damages to our merchant marine and on account of prolonging the war by too hasty recognition of Confederate belligerency and by failure to observe neutrality obligations. In lieu of these vast sums he suggested that Great Britain should cede us Canada. The speech gave Sumner a moment of genuine popularity in America, but in Great Britain it put friends of America in an awkward position, and seemed to diminish the prospect for a peaceable settlement of the dispute.

The "Alabama Claims."

Secretary of State Seward was an ardent expansionist. In 1867 he negotiated a treaty with Denmark for the cession of the Danish West Indies, only to have it come to naught through senatorial opposition, but he won a vaster triumph in an unexpected direction. Russia expressed a willingness to sell to the United States her immense possessions in northwestern America, and on March 30, 1867, Seward and the Russian minister, Baron de Stoeckl, signed a treaty providing for the purchase of the region, the price being fixed at $7,200,000. Considerable opposition to the treaty developed, but expansion sentiment was strong, men remembered that during the Civil War Russia had displayed a friendly spirit, and some thought that the transaction would spite England, that through it we would "cage the British lion on the Pacific coast." Sumner threw his influence into the scale in favor of the treaty, and it was soon ratified almost unanimously.

Alaska Purchased.

Few Americans possessed any definite knowledge regarding the region thus quickly acquired. Some insisted that it was nothing but a barren region of rocks and ice, that the ground was frozen six feet deep throughout the year, that such territory was not worth taking as a gift. Wits delighted in calling the new possession "Seward's Folly" and "Johnson's Polar Bear Garden," and suggestions were made that it should be christened "Walrussia," but Seward fitly named it "Alaska," after its chief peninsula. Time was to show that Seward did a splendid stroke of business for Uncle Sam in buying Alaska, for it was found to be rich in fish, furs, and minerals.

Mistaken Notions about the New Possessions.

On May 20, 1868, four days after the vote on the eleventh impeachment article, the National Union Republican party met in convention at Chicago. The platform condemned President Johnson in unsparing terms, congratulated the country on the assured success of congressional reconstruction, denounced "all forms of repudiation as a national crime," and in rather guarded terms opposed the so-called "greenback" plan of paying the national debt in depreciated paper, a scheme that had many supporters, particu-

Republican Convention of 1868.

larly in the Democratic party. With the subject of negro
suffrage the convention found it expedient to deal very cau-
tiously, for the four Republican States of Ohio, Michigan,
Minnesota, and Kansas had recently refused to give the ballot
to the blacks. The plank on this subject was a model of ingenuity. It read: "The guarantee by Congress of equal suffrage to all loyal men at the South was demanded by every
consideration of public safety, of gratitude, and of justice, and
must be maintained; while the question of suffrage in all the
loyal States properly belongs to the people of those States."

Chief Justice Chase and various other men had been considered for the presidential nomination, but sentiment had crystallized in favor of the victor of Donelson, Vicksburg, and Appomattox, and amid great enthusiasm Ulysses S. Grant
was named unanimously. For the vice-presidency
the convention put forward Schuyler Colfax of
Indiana, speaker of the House of Representatives. Grant accepted the honor in a characteristically short letter, which
closed with the words: "Let us have peace." The phrase
caught the popular fancy and was much used during the campaign. It is now graven upon the tomb that rises so imposingly
over the Hudson in the city of New York.

Grant and
Colfax.

On July 4 the Democratic convention met in Tammany Hall,
in New York City. Among the candidates were President
Johnson, Chief Justice Chase, George H. Pendleton of Ohio,
General Winfield S. Hancock of Pennsylvania, and
Senator Thomas A. Hendricks of Indiana. Johnson had the nominal support of many delegates
from the South, but Democrats generally, though they had applauded his stand against Congress, preferred some other candidate. Chase had hoped to obtain the Republican nomination, but as that had gone to Grant he was willing to accept
that of the Democracy. Lincoln had long before noted Chase's
"insanity on the subject of the presidency." In reality,
Chase's desire to land the coveted prize was in large degree due
to the ambition of his daughter, Kate Chase Sprague, wife of
the senator from Rhode Island, a beautiful and accomplished

Democratic
Aspirants.

woman, who had long looked forward to acting as mistress of the White House.

Pendleton had been McClellan's running mate in 1864. He lived in cultivated and polite surroundings in Cincinnati, and was popularly known as "Gentleman George." He made his campaign for the nomination on what was known as the "Ohio idea," which meant the payment of certain government bonds in greenbacks instead of coin. As business was bad and taxes heavy, the slogan of "The same currency for the bondholder and the plough-holder" proved popular, especially in the West. Those who took this view urged that the bonds had been paid for in depreciated currency and that it was only just that they should be redeemed in the same medium. The letter of the law did not forbid this, though it provided that the interest should be paid in coin. Opponents of the greenback scheme held that the spirit of the law was against such a policy, and that to adopt it would amount to partial repudiation, and would lower the credit of the United States in the future. Some people favored repudiating the war bonds altogether.

The Greenback Craze.

The platform adopted by the convention expressed the view that bonds not expressly made payable in coin should be redeemed in "lawful money," or, in other words, greenbacks, and favored taxing the bonds, which would have been equivalent to reducing the rate of interest. It recognized the fact that "the questions of slavery and secession" had "been settled for all time to come," but it denounced the reconstruction acts "as usurpations, and unconstitutional, revolutionary and void," and charged Congress with having "subjected ten States, in time of profound peace, to military despotism and negro supremacy." All the States should at once be restored to full rights, amnesty should be granted to ex-Confederates, and each State should decide the suffrage question for itself.

Democratic Platform.

The Pendleton forces had dictated the platform, and for fifteen ballots he led in the balloting, but on the sixteenth ballot he was passed by Hancock. On the fifth day of the convention Governor Horatio Seymour of New York, the presiding officer, made a speech designed to bring about the nomination of Chase, but the attempt failed. On the twenty-second ballot Ohio gave Seymour himself twenty-one votes, and started a stampede which ended by his receiving the vote of every delegate present. For the vice-presidency the convention nominated General Francis P. Blair, of Missouri, a soldier who had fought gallantly under Sherman.

Seymour and Blair.

In the campaign the greenback issue played only a minor part. The main emphasis was laid on the Southern question, and Republican orators and newspapers harped constantly on accounts of outrages committed against their political brethren in the South. In the election Grant carried 26 States and received 214 electoral votes, while Seymour carried only 8 States, with a total of 80 electoral votes. Virginia, Mississippi, and Texas, not being reconstructed, did not participate in the election. Of the other seceded States Seymour carried Louisiana and Georgia—it was charged by gross frauds and terrorism.

Grant Elected.

The presidential contest was really much closer than the electoral votes indicated. Grant's plurality of the popular vote was only a little more than 300,000, and the result in several States was very close. When they studied the returns closely Republican leaders realized that if they were to retain control of the federal government in the future they must make use of the negro vote to carry Southern States. When Congress assembled, therefore, the Republicans carried through Congress a Fifteenth Amendment, which decreed that the right to vote should not be denied or abridged "on account of race, color, or previous condition of servitude."

Republican Reflections.

CHAPTER V

THE FRUITS OF RECONSTRUCTION

PRESIDENT-ELECT GRANT felt so bitter toward Johnson that he refused to ride in the same carriage with him on inaugural day; in consequence, the retiring executive absented himself from the ceremonies, and, having issued a farewell address, left the same day for Tennessee, where for several years he lived in "restless obscurity." In March, 1875, he returned to Washington as a member of the body that had lacked only one vote of expelling him from the presidency; but his health was broken and he did not long enjoy his triumph, dying in the following July at his daughter's home in Tennessee. Historians are now almost unanimous in conceding the honesty of his intentions, and many are inclined to praise his plan of reconstruction, but his faults of temper proved disastrous in so critical a period, and his quarrel with Congress made inevitable a more radical Southern policy than would have been followed had a more tactful man held the helm.

Johnson's rise from ignorance and poverty, astonishing though it was, had been less meteoric than that of his successor. Only eight years before Grant had been working in his father's store at Galena, Illinois, at a salary of six hundred dollars a year, and had behind him a practically unbroken record of failure. Beginning life in the army, he had fought bravely in Mexico, but had resigned from the service a few years later. He then tried running his wife's farm and later dabbled in real estate; in neither pursuit did he make good. But hidden under an unpromising exterior he possessed military genius, and the nation's need gave him an opportunity to display it. In less than three years he was leading all the armies of the Union, and now he was Chief Executive. But the most splendid part of his career was already a matter of history, and the years of his presidency tended to diminish rather than to exalt his fame. Nature had created him for the camp rather than the council chamber, for the battle-field rather than the finesse of politics. His notions of statecraft were apt to be vague, and, through a strange paradox, though he displayed remarkable skill in selecting military men, he proved a failure in choosing civil subordinates. Honest and trustful by nature, he could not detect dishonesty in others. Designing men who pretended to be his friends frequently brought him into disrepute, yet even when their rascality was exposed he too often displayed misguided fidelity and refused to desert them "under fire."

In his inaugural Grant said: "The office has come to me unsought; I commence its duties untrammelled." He virtually ignored the party leaders in selecting his cabinet, and the appointments were personal rather than political.

The Cabinet. For secretary of state he nominated Elihu B. Washburne, an Illinois congressman who had been so enthusiastic in advancing Grant's military career that he was said to have "Grant on the brain." But Washburne's appointment was intended as complimentary only and to give him prestige for the French mission, to which he was quickly transferred. In the bloody days of the Red Commune he won renown for himself and reflected high honor on his country. To fill the vacancy Grant named ex-Governor Hamilton Fish, of New York, who proved to be one of the ablest diplomatists that had ever held the office. Grant's selection for secretary of the treasury was Alexander T. Stewart, a celebrated merchant prince of New York City. The nomination had hardly been confirmed before it was discovered that Stewart was ineligible because the act creating the Treasury Department had excluded any one who should "directly or indirectly be concerned or interested in carrying on the business of trade or commerce." As Congress was unwilling to change the law, Grant named George S. Boutwell, a Massachusetts congressman, for the place. For secretary of the navy Grant nominated Adolph E. Borie, a rich Philadelphian who was politically so obscure that both the Pennsylvania senators professed never to have heard of him. For secretary of the interior the President named Jacob D. Cox, an able soldier and politician from Ohio; for attorney-general, E. Rockwood Hoar, a distinguished Massachusetts jurist; for postmaster-general, John A. J. Cresswell, of Maryland; and for secretary of war, his old mentor and chief of staff, General John A. Rawlins. Cabinet changes were so frequent in the next eight years that the seven portfolios were occupied by twenty-four men, and only Hamilton Fish continued in office until the end of Grant's presidency. Rawlins died in the following September, and his loss was irreparable, for he had long been a sort of *fidus Achates* to Grant, and, being a man of good judgment, had exercised a powerful influence for good over his chief. Had Rawlins lived, he would probably have helped Grant to avoid many pitfalls.

Grant early asked to be freed from the restraints of the Tenure-of-Office Act, and when Congress demurred he brought that body to terms by threatening to leave Johnson's appointees in office until his wishes were complied with. The act was radically amended, but it was not finally repealed until the first administration of Grover Cleveland, after having long been in what he called a state of "innocuous desuetude."

Tenure-of-Office Act Modified.

Under Grant, as under Johnson, problems of reconstruction continued to be the most persistent of any that faced the country, and to this complicated but interesting matter we shall first turn our attention.

From the outset the Southern whites had viewed with hostility all efforts to raise the freedmen to a plane of equality with themselves. The view that the negro was divinely created to be a servant to the white man had so long been a matter of faith in the South that his occupying any other position was regarded as an attempt to overturn natural laws. He had been assigned to a distinct "place" as a menial, but now he was the nation's ward, and he was being encouraged to assert equal rights with his former master. Such things were not to be

Southern White Attitude toward the New Order.

borne; the South was determined never to submit to negro equality or negro rule. But the new order was backed up by federal bayonets, and open resistance was hopeless. Some subterranean method must be found. As a result there sprang into being the secret societies variously known under such names as the Invisible Empire, or Ku Klux Klan, the Pale Faces, the White Brotherhood, and the Knights of the White Camelia.

The Ku Klux Klan, the most famous of these organizations, was first formed in the spring of 1866 at Pulaski, Tennessee. Its originators were young men, and it is said that their prime motive was amusement, but the order soon came to have a different purpose. Deep mystery was affected, while the weird potency of the name of the order aroused curiosity and helped the order to spread. In 1868 the various "dens" scattered over the South were said to have a membership of half a million, but the order was never closely organized, and no one knew with absolute definiteness how many persons had joined it. Profound secrecy was exacted from the members, and an elaborate rescript was drawn up providing for officers with such high-sounding names as Grand Wizard, Grand Dragon, Grand Turk, and Grand Cyclops. Any member who should betray the order or reveal its secrets was to suffer death.

The Ku Klux Klan.

Some defenders of the Klan have represented that it sprang into being as a protest against negro and Carpet-Bag rule, but, as noted above, its formation considerably antedated the conferring of suffrage on the blacks. In its early history it seems to have done occasionally some really laudable work. In the disturbed period following the war, thieving and the burning of barns and gin-houses became common, while worse crimes, even murder and rape, were now and then committed by the blacks. The Klan did something to restrain such lawlessness, and also scared lazy negroes into keeping at work. It was only gradually that the "dens" became instruments of political proscription and private vengeance. Ultimately the general objects of the Klan and of the other similar orders came to be to keep the negro in his "place"

Objects of the Klan.

as an inferior, to intimidate him and keep him from voting, to restrain his Scalawag and Carpet-Bag leaders, and otherwise to maintain the supremacy of the white race and the Democratic party. Its operations varied from warning or punishing rascally negroes who richly deserved such attentions, to brutally whipping, maiming, or murdering white and black men whose chief offense was that they were politically active in the interest of the "Radical" party, as the Southern Republicans were called. Many of the crimes charged against the Klan were really committed by irresponsible individuals using its name and regalia as a disguise. The Ku Klux and the Knights of the White Camelia, an order that was strongest in the Gulf States, were exceedingly active in the presidential campaign of 1868, and some of their work did much to convince wavering Northern voters that the South could not be trusted to deal justly with the freedmen. Early in the following year the Ku Klux Klan was disbanded by proclamation of its Grand Wizard (February 20, 1869), but individual members and dens continued their operations long afterward.

In their raids the Klansmen took shrewd advantage of the credulous fears of the superstitious blacks. They usually assumed some awesome disguise and worked only at the most "witching time of night." "A trick of frequent

Methods of the Klan.

perpetration in the country," says a member, "was for a horseman, spectral and ghostly looking, to stop before the cabin of some negro needing a wholesome impression and call for a bucket of water. If a dipper or gourd was brought, it was declined, and a bucket full of water demanded. As if consumed by raging thirst the horseman grasped it and pressed it to his lips. He held it there till every drop of water was poured into a gum or oiled sack concealed beneath the Ku Klux robe. Then the empty bucket was returned to the amazed negro with the remark: 'That's good. It is the first drink of water I have had since I was killed at Shiloh.' Then a few words of counsel as to future behavior made an impression not easily forgotten or likely to be disregarded." Written warnings were often used. These bore rude drawings of skulls and crossed bones, pistols and muskets, or coffins, and the messages were plentifully besprinkled with such terms as "hollow tomb," "bloody moon," "hobgoblins," "hell-a-Bulloo," and "Horrible sepulchre." In the early days of the orders, "a silent host of white-sheeted horsemen parading the country roads at night was sufficient to reduce the blacks to good behavior for weeks or months"; but gradually fear of the mysterious beings wore away, and a time came when more violent methods had to be used. "Uppish" negroes were warned, disarmed, whipped, mutilated, or murdered, while negro schoolhouses in some sections were burned and white teachers of negro children abused and driven out.

Opposed to the Ku Klux and similar societies stood the Union or Loyal League, an organization formed in the North in 1862 and later transplanted in the South as a sort of radical bureau for organizing the negroes in the interest of the Republican party. Its leaders were usually white men, many of them Freedmen's Bureau agents, and they were frequently to be seen in Washington, denouncing Johnson's reconstruction plan and indorsing that of Congress. The conclaves of the league were usually held at night, with awe-inspiring rites, and at these meetings the negroes were taught that their interests were opposed to those of their former masters. The league did much to widen the rift between the races, and to render it impossible for the whites to control the blacks politically. A freedman might come to his former master for advice about every other conceivable subject, but let politics be broached and he would become "as silent as a tombstone," for that was a matter concerning which "Old Massa" could not be trusted. In some cases members of the league were armed, and drilling would take place. After the close of a meeting the members would sometimes, in the words of Professor Fleming, "march along the roads shouting, firing their guns, making great boasts and threats against persons whom they disliked." Such activities naturally provoked counter-demonstrations by the Ku Klux, and the ultimate decline of the league was in part due to the work of the Klansmen.

The Union League.

As already narrated, the process of reconstruction in Texas, Mississippi, and Virginia was delayed. These States were ultimately required to ratify not only the Fourteenth but also the Fifteenth Amendment, and early in 1870 Congress recognized them as being once more in full fellowship in the Union. It was significant of the mighty revolution of a decade that the man who appeared in the Senate from Mississippi to take the seat vacated by Jefferson Davis was a quadroon, Reverend Hiram R. Revells. Georgia had been readmitted some time before, but she had fallen under congressional disfavor for having expelled negro members from her legislature. Acting under authority conferred by Congress, General Terry purged her legislature of twenty-four Democrats who were ineligible under the Fourteenth Amendment, after which the legislature restored the negro members to their seats, ratified the Fourteenth and Fifteenth Amendments, and elected two new senators. Georgia was then again readmitted into the Union.

Completion of Reconstruction.

The Fifteenth Amendment had already received a sufficient number of ratifications before Georgia acted, and it was proclaimed a part of the Constitution on March 30, 1870. Although it was an attempt to carry to a logical conclusion the doctrines of the Declaration of Independence, many historians now regard its enactment as a mistake. Regret has also been expressed that it was not accompanied by some scheme for national education of the new voters. Sumner, Grant, and many other leaders favored the education at national expense of both whites and blacks in the South, in so far as the States of that section were unable or unwilling to provide it. In his announcement of the ratification of the amendment President Grant earnestly recommended such a provision, but the plan failed because of constitutional objections and what the late Senator Hoar called "mistaken notions of economy." Before the war the teaching of negroes to read and write was generally forbidden in the South, while the percentage of illiteracy among the "poor whites" was appalling.

Fifteenth Amendment.

Although the Fifteenth Amendment was ratified by every

Southern
Opposition
to Negro
Suffrage. former seceded State except Tennessee, the white people of the South never really accepted its principle. From the outset they determined to exclude the negro from the suffrage whenever possible, and with every election there recurred scenes of violence, intimidation, and fraud.

The admission of the negroes to voting privileges by the reconstruction acts inaugurated a weird contest for political power that lasted in some States for a decade. On one side,

Character
of the
Contest. in this contest, stood practically all the freedmen, led by Scalawags and Carpet-Baggers; on the other, the vast majority of the white people, including almost all the considerable property-owners. Generally speaking, it was a conflict between black ignorance on the one hand and white enlightenment on the other, made possible by the fact that the negroes and their white leaders professed loyalty to the Union and the results of the war, while the white population was out of harmony with the new order of things.

In Virginia the whites were lucky enough at once to take over the government from the federal military authorities, and that State escaped the harrowing experience of negro domination and Carpet-Bag rule. In Tennessee the con-

Early
Escape of
Certain
States. flict was largely between white men, for white Union men had always been numerous in that State; furthermore, the radicals as early as 1869 lost control in that State. Georgia and North Carolina were "redeemed" by the conservatives in the following year, but all the other former Confederate States were forced to remain for a longer period under the rule of the negroes and their white allies, the Carpet-Baggers and Scalawags.

It was a strange and sinister alliance which was made possible by the belief in the North that the freedmen

A Strange
Alliance. must be given the ballot for their own protection and to safeguard the interests of the Union and of the Republican party. The new voters were wholly without political experience, and most of them were illiterate and unmoral. Some of their white allies were well-meaning men, but many were mere adventurers who took advantage of the situation to enrich themselves. The inevitable result was a lurid carnival of misrule hitherto undreamed of in America.

Large volumes have been written about the experiences of each of the States under radical rule, but here a few characteristic facts regarding the course of events in two of the worst States, South Carolina and Louisiana, must suffice.

In Louisiana wholesale corruption, intimidation of negro voters, political assassination, riots, revolutions constituted the normal condition of affairs for a decade. That this carnival of lawlessness surpassed that in any other State was probably due in part to the character of the population. The negroes, despite the presence of a considerable number of educated "persons of color" in New Orleans, were on the average less intelligent than in most of the slave States; as late as 1874 it was estimated that only 8,597 out of 87,121 negro voters could read and write. Many of them lived on immense plantations where civilizing contact with the white race was slight, while some of them were men of desperate or criminal character who, by way of punishment, had been "sold down the river." Self-government based on such a constituency was foredoomed to failure. Furthermore, even under white rule Louisiana had not been notable as a law-abiding State. Antebellum society, particularly in New Orleans, had been polite and even brilliant, but the custom of the duello still lingered, and many bloody encounters took place beneath the moss-hung "duelling oaks" that are still pointed out to tourists. Now and then this lack of respect for law revealed itself in political matters, as in the notorious Plaquemine frauds of 1844, and in the New Orleans riot of 1855, when for a time the city was a battle-ground between two rival factions, who seized public buildings and barricaded the streets.

As elsewhere in the South, the white people of Louisiana did not take kindly either to emancipation or enfranchisement, but they did not wait to prove the fruits of African rule before

falling upon the hapless freedmen. In July, 1866, before the
negroes obtained the suffrage, occurred the bloody New Orleans
riot that has already been described. In the sum-
Early
Conflicts.   mer and fall of 1868 the Knights of the White Camelia systematically set about terrorizing the new
voters and did the work so thoroughly that a Republican
majority of over 26,000 in the spring election was in November
transformed into a Democratic majority of about 46,000 for
Seymour.

In explaining this remarkable reversal the Republican members of a congressional investigating committee stated that
testimony showed that over 2,000 persons had been killed or
wounded in Louisiana within two weeks prior to
Violence in
the   the election; "that half the State was overrun by
Campaign   violence; and that midnight raids, secret murders,
of 1868.
and open riot kept the people in constant terror
until the Republicans surrendered all claim." In the parish of
St. Landry, on the river Têche, the Republicans had a majority,
in the spring, of 678. "In the fall they gave Grant no vote,
not one—while the Democrats cast 4,787, the full vote of the
parish, for Seymour and Blair. Here occurred one of the bloodiest riots on record, in which the Ku Klux killed or wounded
over 200 Republicans, hunting and chasing them for two days
and nights through fields and swamps. Thirteen captives
were taken from the jail and shot. A pile of 25 dead bodies
was found half-buried in the woods. Having conquered the
Republicans and killed or driven off their leaders, the Ku
Klux captured the masses, marked them with badges of red
flannel, enrolled them in clubs, made them vote the Democratic
ticket, and gave them a certificate of the fact." S. S. Cox, a
Northern Democratic member of Congress, says, in his *Three
Decades of Federal Legislation*, that this statement was "a good
deal exaggerated, especially as to the number killed," but he
concedes that "the failure of the negroes to vote can be explained only on the theory that a reign of terror existed."

During the period of Carpet-Bag-negro rule the value of
property in the State greatly declined, the payment of taxes

fell far in arrears, and the public debt increased many millions of dollars. The decline in property values was in part due to

Disastrous Economic Results.

the ravages of war, to the unsettling effects of the change from a slave-labor to a free-labor system, and to the disastrous panic of 1873, but in large measure it was the result of bad government. There were some legitimate reasons why the State debt should have increased, among these being the cost of repairing levees that had fallen into bad condition during the war, but vast amounts were embezzled. Much of the increase in some of the States was due to the granting of subsidies to new railroads; grave frauds were often connected with these grants. Bond issues were always floated below par, for investors lacked faith in Southern bonds, partly because many States in that section had repudiated their debts in the '30's and '40's.

In course of time the radicals quarrelled among themselves, and Governor Warmoth, an unscrupulous Carpet-Bagger who had amassed a fortune in office, went over to the conservatives.

Carpet-Bag Government Upheld by Federal Bayonets.

The election of 1872 was claimed by both parties, but the Republicans managed to persuade a complaisant federal judge named Durell to issue a "midnight restraining order," and obtained the all-important aid of federal troops, with the result that they were able to install William Pitt Kellogg as governor. McEnery, the conservative claimant, also took the oath of office but soon had to abandon attempts to assert his authority, as this would have brought him into conflict with the federal government. In September, 1874, however, the White League, an armed conservative organization, rose against the Kellogg government, and Kellogg and his supporters were forced to take refuge in the custom-house. But President Grant interfered, and the radical government was reinstated by federal bayonets. A congressional investigating committee arranged a sort of compromise between the opposing parties, but for two years a state of virtual anarchy existed in parts of Louisiana.

Probably never in history has a proud people drunk deeper

from the cup of humiliation than did the white inhabitants
of South Carolina in the period following the conflict begun by
their ordinance of secession and the firing on Fort
Sumter. After four years of desperate warfare they
had at last been forced to accept the inevitable,
after Sherman's army swept through the State,
consuming and destroying, and leaving the capital in ruins.
At intervals thereafter for more than a decade Yankee troops
wearing the hated blue were stationed here and there about
the State, and from their camps there floated not infrequently
the strains of a song dealing with a certain John Brown, whose
body lay "a-mouldering in the grave" but whose soul went
"marching on." No such reminders were necessary to bring
home the fact that the old order had passed away. The pyra-
mid of society had been turned upside down. Those who had
been the slaves were become the rulers. In the government,
in the places of the now impoverished aristocracy, stood black
and brown freedmen, led by hated Yankees and equally hated
Scalawags; and from the panels over the door of the capitol at Columbia the marble visages of George McDuffie and
Robert Young Hayne looked down upon the incomings and
outgoings of a strange legislature, three-fourths of whose members belonged to the despised race once the victims of the institution which had formed the "corner-stone" of the fallen
Confederacy.

Social Overturn in South Carolina.

In 1873 James S. Pike, a Northern observer who recorded
his impressions in a book called *The Prostrate State*, found 101
negro members in the House of Representatives and only 23
white men; the latter sat "grim and silent," feeling themselves "but loose stones, thrown in to
partially obstruct a current they are powerless to
resist." Of the colored legislators the same observer wrote:
"They were of every hue from the light octoroon to the deep
black. . . . Every negro type and physiognomy was here to
be seen from the genteel serving-man to the rough-hewn customer from the rice or cotton field. Their dress was as varied
as their countenances. There was the second-hand black

A "Black Legislature."

frock-coat of infirm gentility, glossy and threadbare. There was the stove-pipe hat of many ironings and departed styles. There was also to be seen a total disregard of the proprieties of costume in the coarse and dirty garments of the field; the stub jackets and slouch hats of soiling labor. In some instances, rough woolen comforters embraced the neck and hid the absence of linen. Heavy brogans and short torn trousers it was impossible to hide. . . . The Speaker is black, the Clerk is black, the doorkeepers are black, the chairman of the Ways and Means is black, and the chaplain is coal black. . . . At some of the desks sit colored men whose types it would be hard to find outside of Congo; whose costume, visage, attitude, and expression only befit the forecastle of a buccaneer. . . . Seven years ago these men were raising corn and cotton under the whip of the overseer. To-day they are raising points of order and questions of privilege."

A large majority of these legislators could not read or write; most paid no taxes. The total sum paid by all the members of the legislature of 1868–72 is said to have been only about

A Carnival of Misrule.

$634 annually. Naturally such a legislature had little fear of extravagance, and, though some of the members had good intentions, misgovernment was certain. As a matter of fact, though the history of South Carolina in this period was not quite so replete with pitched battles as was the case in Louisiana, the financial aspects of negro rule in the Palmetto State were fully as deplorable. In the six years from 1868–74 the public debt was increased by about $14,000,000, while there was a great decline in the value of property.

There were public land-steals, printing steals, railroad-bonus steals, and financial scandals of various other kinds, but perhaps the most striking instances of misappropriation of funds

Some Details.

are to be found under the head of legislative expenses. A free bar was established in the State-house, and thither members of the legislature resorted for expensive cigars, wines, whiskeys, and brandies; some would even come to the room before breakfast for an "eye-opener." In refurnishing the State-house $4 looking-glasses were replaced by $650 French mirrors, $1 chairs by $60 chairs, $5 clocks by $600 ones, 40-cent spittoons by $60 imported china cuspidors, and in four years over $200,000 was paid out for furniture, the appraised value of which in 1877 amounted to $17,715. Under the heading of legislative supplies were included such items as champagne, best Westphalia hams, imported mushrooms, finest plush velvet tête-à-têtes, feather beds, suspenders, ladies' hoods, bonnets, chemises, gold watches, garters, perfumes, palpitators, and a metallic coffin. Needless to say, many of these articles did not long remain in the State-house.

The great mass of the freedmen suffered from this carnival of misrule along with their white neighbors, but fear that conservative victory would mean a return of slavery long kept the negroes voting for their despoilers, and as they Why the Radicals outnumbered the whites by about five to three, Retained they always elected the radical candidates for State Power. office, no matter how incompetent, disreputable, or dishonest. Some of the whites early resorted to Ku Klux methods in order to hold the blacks in check, but years passed before anything was accomplished toward bringing about better government. Many white people openly professed that they saw no way of escape, and grew "gloomy, disconsolate, hopeless."

The first two radical governors were arrant rascals, but fortunately the third, Daniel H. Chamberlain, elected in 1874, was of a different type. A native of Massachusetts and a graduate of Yale, he left the Harvard Law School to Daniel H. become an officer in a black regiment, and at the Chamberlain. close of the war he settled in South Carolina as a cotton-planter. He served for four years as attorney-general of the State, but it was not until he became governor that he really made himself felt. Realizing that "the civilization of the Puritan and the Cavalier, of the Roundhead and the Huguenot" was "in peril," he set his face against the corrupt schemes of his unscrupulous party associates, and with the aid of the conservatives and of honest members of his own political faith, he managed to check the carnival of misrule that had so long disgraced the State. By so doing he won high encomiums not only in the North but also among Southern conservatives. But it was an unequal battle in which he was engaged, and the historian, as he studies the period, cannot but realize that, owing to the ignorance of the freedmen, no permanent good government could be obtained in South Carolina or in any other Southern State until the white people regained control.

In the Southern elections of the period of 1868–70 the Ku Klux Klan and similar orders played so active a part that Republican national leaders realized that unless more effective methods were evolved for protecting the freedmen in their political rights most or all of the reconstructed States would soon be wrested from their party. In an effort to meet the situation, Congress passed a so-called Enforcement Act (May 30, 1870), which provided heavy penalties for infringing upon the rights conferred by the Fourteenth and Fifteenth Amendments, and gave to the federal courts jurisdiction over cases arising under the act. The act was notable as involving an extension of federal authority over a field hitherto left exclusively to the States.

First Enforcement Act.

In the elections later in the year the Democrats not only carried certain Southern States, as already related, but reduced the Republican majority in the House of Representatives from 97 to 35. This result spurred on the Republican leaders to carry through a more sweeping measure whereby a rigorous system of federal supervision over congressional elections was established. The new act was intended to be applied not only in the South but in certain great Northern cities, like New York, where fraudulent practices had come to be common.

Second Enforcement Act.

For special application in the South Congress passed what was commonly called the Ku Klux Act, which conferred greater powers on the federal judiciary to deal with secret conspiracies against the negro's rights, and empowered the President, in certain contingencies, to suspend the writ of habeas corpus and suppress the Ku Klux by military force. Under this act President Grant, in October, 1871, declared nine counties in South Carolina to be in a state

The "Ku Klux Act."

of rebellion, and sent thither federal troops who arrested several hundred persons. More than a hundred persons in South Carolina, and more than a thousand in the South as a whole, were convicted under the act during the next two years. In 1882, however, the Supreme Court adjudged the Ku Klux Act unconstitutional.

In April, 1871, Congress created a joint committee to inquire into Southern conditions, and in particular to investigate the activities of the Ku Klux. This committee took twelve thick volumes of testimony, and added another volume

Ku Klux Investigation. containing majority and minority interpretations of the testimony. Beyond question, the investigation revealed in many Southern communities an appalling state of violence and disorder and of barbarities committed upon freedmen by low-class whites. This aspect of the subject was emphasized by the Republicans in their report.

Although admitting "deeds of violence which we neither justify nor excuse," the Democratic minority members of the investigating committee declared: "We think no man can look over the testimony taken by this committee with-

Report of the Democratic Minority. out coming to the conclusion that no people had ever been so mercilessly robbed and plundered, so wantonly and causelessly humiliated and degraded, so recklessly exposed to the rapacity and lust of the ignorant and vicious portions of their own community and of other States, as the people of the South have been for the last six years. History, till now, gives no account of a conqueror so cruel as to place his vanquished foes under the dominion of their former slaves."

In the matter of ex-Confederates who suffered under political disabilities commendable magnanimity was displayed during these years. Amnesty was granted by the President in many individual cases, and in May, 1872, Congress by a

Amnesty to Individuals. general act relieved all except a few hundred persons. In 1875 an attempt was made to remove all remaining disabilities, but James G. Blaine seized upon the opportunity to fire the Northern heart by making a bitter attack on Jefferson Davis, and the bill failed. In the quarter-century following 1872, however, many individual bills were passed, and finally, amid the good feeling aroused by the Spanish-American War, full amnesty was granted to the few ex-Confederates who had not yet received it (June 6, 1898).

The Amnesty Act of 1872 would have been passed earlier had it not been for the attempts of Northern radicals, especially Charles Sumner, to enact a measure safeguarding the negro's civil rights. Many Southern legislatures passed

Civil Rights Act of 1875. such acts, but it was only in 1875, after Sumner's death, that a law of this sort was adopted by Congress. This federal act guaranteed equal rights to negroes in public conveyances, hotels, and places of amusement, and prohibited excluding them from juries, but did not apply to churches, schools, or cemeteries. The determination of Southern whites not to admit of anything approaching social equality made it difficult to enforce laws of this sort, whether State or federal. In 1883 the Supreme Court held most of the Civil Rights Act unconstitutional. After the overthrow of radical rule in the South, State civil-rights acts were repealed, and ultimately they were supplanted by "Jim Crow" laws, expressly forbidding the mingling of whites and blacks in railroad cars and other specified places.

Despite the Enforcement Acts, the Southern States continued

Whites Gradually Regain Control. to slip away from the Republican grasp. In 1873 Texas, in 1874 Arkansas, and in 1875 Mississippi escaped from Carpet-Bag-negro domination. The methods employed by the whites in these States were more or less lawless, being often a compound of bribery, persuasion, force, and fraud, but they proved effective. By 1876 only Florida, South Carolina, and Louisiana remained in the hands of the radicals.

CHAPTER VI

FOREIGN RELATIONS AND THE LIBERAL REPUBLICAN MOVEMENT

THE greenback craze had played a prominent part in the campaign of 1868, and in his inaugural Grant hastened to declare for sound money. "To protect the national honor," said he, "every dollar of Government indebtedness should be paid in gold unless otherwise stipulated in the contract." A measure designed "to strengthen the public credit" was speedily enacted (March 18, 1869) which "provided and declared that the faith of the United States is solemnly pledged to the payment in coin or its equivalent" of the United States notes and of all bonds, except where it was expressly stipulated that they might be paid in "other currency than gold and silver."

Act "to Strengthen the Public Credit."

The act also promised the earliest possible redemption of the notes, but years were to elapse before the resumption of specie payment. Meanwhile the fluctuation in the price of greenbacks was productive of much inconvenience and speculation. Soon after Grant entered office two unscrupulous New York financiers, Jay Gould and James Fisk, Jr., attempted to "corner" gold, and thereby precipitated the famous financial flurry known as "Black Friday." In less than three weeks (September 2–22, 1869) the conspirators managed to force the price of gold from 132 to 140½. On Friday, September 24, 1869, Wall Street became a maelstrom of wild speculation, surpassing anything ever before known. Gold leaped to 162, but then came word that Secretary of the Treasury Boutwell, after consulting with Grant, had ordered the treasurer in New York City to dump $4,000,000 in gold on the market. At once the bubble burst.

"Black Friday."

Fisk was temporarily ruined, but Gould, who had been warned, had quietly been selling gold and came through almost unscathed.

The speculation had resulted in great harm to legitimate business, and the popular uproar was so great that a congressional investigation was held. It resulted in the disclosure of

Congressional Investigation. the fact that the assistant treasurer at New York and even President Grant's brother-in-law had been members of the plot. Grant's honor was untouched, but his brother-in-law's participation in the affair and the fact that Grant himself had incautiously accepted the hospitality of Gould and Fisk caused much criticism. Unfortunately it was not the last time that he allowed himself to be imposed upon by designing men.

In the February following the Black Friday convulsion a great furor was aroused in financial circles by the Supreme Court's deciding, in the case of Hepburn *vs.* Griswold, that the

The Legal-Tender Cases. Legal-Tender Act of 1862 was unconstitutional so far as concerned debts contracted prior to the passage of the act. A curious feature of the case was that the decision was handed down by Chief Justice Chase, who as secretary of the treasury had been one of the chief promoters of the act. Justices Davis, Swayne, and Miller took a dissenting view of the case, and the majority opinion aroused much opposition throughout the country. On the same day, however, that the decision was handed down President Grant filled two vacancies on the Supreme Bench by nominating Joseph P. Bradley of New Jersey and William Strong of Pennsylvania, both of whom sympathized with the minority view. Two new legal-tender cases presently came before the court, which, by a vote of five to four, reversed the ruling in the case of Hepburn *vs.* Griswold and held the act to be constitutional. As Grant and many other prominent Republicans were much disturbed by the original decision, it was charged that the court was purposely "packed" to secure the reversal, but the charge has received slight credence among historians.

Early in his administration Grant became eager to annex

the black republic of Santo Domingo, and without consulting the leaders of his party procured the negotiation of a treaty to that effect. When the treaty came before the Senate it was defeated (June 30, 1870), largely through the opposition of Sumner, who was chairman of the committee on foreign relations. Sumner

Failure of Attempt to Annex Santo Domingo.

and Grant quarrelled bitterly, and in revenge Grant recalled the senator's friend, John Lothrop Motley, the historian, from the English mission. In organizing the next Congress (March, 1871) the Republican caucus deposed Sumner from the chairmanship of the committee on foreign relations, a position he had held for a decade. Sumner soon drifted out of the party he had helped to found.

In 1868 Spanish misgovernment in Cuba provoked a revolt that occasioned troublesome diplomatic complications during Grant's presidency. Most Americans warmly sympathized with the rebels, and in August, 1869, Grant, under the influence of Secretary of War Rawlins, signed a proclamation recognizing Cuban belligerency.

Cuban Rebellion.

Secretary of State Fish, however, thought that conditions in the island did not justify the step, and realized, furthermore, that recognition would be inconsistent with the stand we had taken toward Great Britain in regard to her attitude toward the Confederacy. Fish pigeonholed the proclamation, and it was never issued. In 1873 a Spanish gunboat captured on the high seas, between Cuba and Jamaica, a filibustering steamer called the *Virginius*,

Virginius Affair.

flying the American flag and bearing arms and men to the insurgents. The vessel was taken to Santiago, and there fifty-three of those on board, among them eight American citizens, were summarily shot. The seizure was contrary to international law. Feeling flamed high in the United States. War seemed almost inevitable. But Spain ultimately agreed to surrender the *Virginius* and to make some other reparation, while American passion was also somewhat soothed by the discovery that the ship had obtained her registry by fraud and was not entitled to fly our flag. But the bloody incident and the cruelties practised by the Spaniards against the rebels were not forgotten by Americans. For ten years the "Pearl of the Antilles" was devastated by war, but finally the Spaniards, partly by force, party by promises of reforms, managed to restore their rule.

A yet more burning international question in this period was that of reparation by Great Britain for failing to enforce strict neutrality during the Civil War. The rejection of the Johnson-Clarendon convention has already been described; also Sumner's radical speech setting forth American wrongs. American sympathy with the Fenian movement helped to reveal to British statesmen the depth of feeling existing in the States, while Americans did not hesitate to say that if Great Britain ever became involved in a war she might expect privateers fitted out in our ports to pay her back in her own coin. Furthermore, the United States might even resort to arms to enforce her claims, and the prospect of being forced to meet the shock of veterans of the Civil War, led by such generals as Sheridan and Sherman, was not one to arouse enthusiasm in Great Britain. The outbreak, in the summer of 1870, of the Franco-Prussian War, and the course of that conflict added point to the arguments of British leaders who felt that it would be wise to reach an amicable settlement with their indignant kinsmen beyond seas.

Anglo-American Relations.

The President's message of December 5, 1870, contained a paragraph, written by Secretary of State Fish, that conveyed a plain warning that the United States intended to push its claims. The passage stated that the British Government had hitherto failed to admit responsibility for the acts complained of, and the President, therefore, recommended that Congress "authorize the appointment of a commission to take proof of the amount and ownership of these several claims, on notice to the representative of her Majesty at Washington, and that authority be given for the settlement of these claims by the United States, so that the Government shall have the ownership of the private claims as well as the responsible control of all the demands

Grant's Recommendation Regarding Claims.

against Great Britain." The menace of this message was not lost on London.

Fortunately a beginning toward a peaceful settlement had already been made (July, 1869) at a friendly interview in Washington between Secretary Fish and Sir John Rose, a member of the Canadian cabinet and a skilful diplomat.

Treaty of Washington.
In a subsequent visit to England Rose used his influence in favor of an amicable settlement with such success that in January, 1871, he arrived in Washington authorized to treat concerning the disputed matters. Sumner, who was still chairman of the committee on foreign relations, drew up a memorandum insisting upon the withdrawal of the British flag from Canada, but Fish favored moderation. Fish, Rose, and Thornton, the British minister, reached an agreement to submit the *Alabama* claims and other disputes to a joint high commission which should meet and formulate a plan of settlement. On February 27 the high commission, composed of five representatives from each country, began its deliberations in Washington, and on May 8 signed the famous Treaty of Washington, which was speedily ratified by the Senate. The outcome was due in part to Secretary Fish's statesmanlike qualities, in part to the friendly spirit displayed by the Gladstone government. In the negotiation free use was made of the new Atlantic cable.

The treaty contained a frank expression of "the regret felt by Her Majesty's Government for the escape, under whatever circumstances, of the *Alabama* and other vessels from British ports and for the depredations committed by those vessels," and it provided for referring the claims resulting therefrom to a tribunal composed of five arbitrators, one appointed by the Queen, one by the President of the United States, one by the Emperor of Brazil, one by the King of Italy, and one by the President of Switzerland. The treaty further provided for referring a dispute regarding North Atlantic fisheries to a mixed commission, and another regarding the northwest boundary to arbitration. It may be said here that the boundary question was ultimately referred to the

German Emperor, who in 1872 rendered a decision favorable
to the United States. The work of the mixed commission was
greatly prolonged, and it was not until 1877 that a decision
was reached that the United States must pay $5,500,000
damages for illegal fishing in Canadian waters.

The *Alabama* tribunal met December 15, 1871, in the Hôtel
de Ville in the city of Geneva. The American arbitrator was
Charles Francis Adams; the British, Chief Justice Alexander
Cockburn; the Swiss, Jacques Staempfli; the Italian,
Count Schlopis; the Brazilian, Vicomte d'Itajubà.
The insistence of the American agent, Bancroft Davis, upon
enormous "indirect claims" aroused intense opposition in
Great Britain and threatened to wreck the proceedings, but
fortunately, after prolonged negotiations between London and
Washington, the commission, on the initiative of Adams, de-
cided to exclude the "indirect claims" from consideration.
The deliberations were then resumed, and on September 2, 1872,
all the arbitrators except Cockburn, who bitterly dissented,
voted to award $15,500,000 for damages inflicted on American
commerce by the *Alabama* and certain other cruisers.

The Award.

The outcome was a glorious triumph of international peace
and good will, and, in the words of Rhodes, "Geneva,
staid chamberlain of mighty issues, has never helped
to crown a worthier undertaking." Two great nations had found a better method than the sword. Well would
it have been for humanity if their illustrious example had always
been followed in future years by the great powers of the world!

A Victory
for
Civilization.

The successful settlement of the *Alabama* dispute reflected
credit on Grant, but unfortunately he was less successful in
many other matters. Starting out with the assumption that the
presidency was a sort of personal possession given
him by the people to manage as he thought proper,
he at first virtually ignored the party leaders, but
this independent policy broke down, and presently
he fell entirely into the hands of the politicians, with disastrous
results. He displayed lack of taste in choosing some of his
personal associates, accepted presents with "Oriental non-

Grant Falls
into the
Hands of
Politicians.

chalance," and appointed some of the givers to public office, was guilty of nepotism, made some half-hearted efforts to reform the civil service but failed to follow them up, forced Cox and E. R. Hoar, two able and honest men, from the cabinet, and in various other ways brought disappointment and dismay to some of his most high-minded supporters of 1868. In his conduct of Southern affairs he usually listened to the radical wing of the party—to such men as Morton, Butler, and Conkling —and turned a deaf ear to the advice of more liberal-minded leaders who favored a more generous policy toward the South.

In course of time there developed within the Republican ranks an anti-Grant movement, the members of which came to be known as "Liberal Republicans." Missouri was the original storm centre of the movement, and a prominent part was taken in it by Senator Carl Schurz, who disliked Grant's radical Southern policy, his attempt to annex Santo Domingo, and certain other features of the administration. In 1870 these Missouri Liberals allied themselves with the Democrats and managed to elect B. Gratz Brown as governor over the regular Republican candidate. In January, 1872, a mass convention of the Liberals met in Jefferson City and issued a call for a national convention to meet in Cincinnati for the purpose of nominating candidates for the coming presidential election. The movement had the powerful support outside of Missouri of several great Republican newspapers, and of such individuals as Samuel Bowles, David A. Wells, William Cullen Bryant, David Davis, Horace Greeley, Jacob D. Cox, Lyman Trumbull, Edward Atkinson, and Charles Francis Adams.

The Liberal Republicans.

When the convention assembled (May 1, 1872) Schurz was made permanent chairman. The platform unsparingly denounced President Grant for having used his power for the "promotion of personal ends" and charged that he had "kept notoriously corrupt and unworthy men in places of power and responsibility, to the detriment of the public interest." It also declared for reform of the civil service and for a more liberal policy toward the South,

Liberal Republican Platform.

but as regards reducing the tariff—a subject that had been much discussed—the views of the delegates were so divergent that the question was remitted to "the people in their congressional districts and the decision of Congress thereon."

Schurz and most of the saner leaders had expected to bring about the nomination of Charles Francis Adams, who was then engaged in the *Alabama* arbitration. But, as not infrequently happens in conventions, the delegates got out of hand, and on the sixth ballot there was a sudden stampede to Horace Greeley and he was nominated. For the vice-presidency the convention then selected B. Gratz Brown of Missouri.

Greeley and Brown.

On June 5 the regular Republican convention met in Philadelphia. The platform "pointed with pride" to the fact that during eleven years of supremacy the party had "accepted with grand courage the solemn duties of the time. It suppressed a gigantic rebellion, emancipated 4,000,000 of slaves, decreed the equal citizenship of all, and established universal suffrage." Taxes had been lowered, yet the national debt was being reduced at the rate of a hundred million dollars a year; menacing foreign difficulties had been "peacefully and honorably composed"; repudiation had been frowned down; prosperity blessed the land. "This glorious record of the past is the party's best pledge for the future. We believe the people will not entrust the government to any party or combination of men composed chiefly of those who have resisted every step of this beneficent progress."

Republican Platform.

Grant was renominated for the presidency amid scenes of great enthusiasm. For the vice-presidency the convention then nominated Senator Henry Wilson of Massachusetts—the "Natick cobbler"—over the incumbent, Schuyler Colfax.

Grant and Wilson.

When the Democratic convention met in Baltimore (July 9) most of the delegates realized that the only hope of beating Grant was to form an alliance with the Liberal Republicans. By large majorities the convention, therefore, accepted the Liberal Republican candidates and platform. A more inconsistent step was probably never taken by a political party. The Liberal Republican platform solemnly declared: "We pledge ourselves to maintain the Union of these States, emancipation and enfranchisement, and to oppose any reopening of the questions settled by the Thirteenth, Fourteenth, and Fifteenth Amendments." By accepting this pledge the Democrats turned their backs on their platform of four years before, and openly confessed defeat on the war and reconstruction issues. Their indorsement of Greeley was no less remarkable, for there was no public man in the country who had said more bitter things about Democrats and the South. For years, in fact, he had been saying in effect that, while not all Democrats were horse-thieves, all horse-thieves were Democrats. Little wonder, therefore, that the *New York Nation* declared that he appeared to be "'boiled crow' to more of his fellow citizens than any other candidate for office in this or any other age"—and thus was the political vocabulary enlarged by the expression, "to eat crow." One fact that helped Southerners to accept Greeley was that he had signed Jefferson Davis's bail-bond. Some Democrats, however, found the dose too strong and considered the party's action "a cowardly surrender of principles for the sake of possible victory." A convention was held at Louisville by Democrats who felt thus, and Charles O'Conor of New York was put forward for the presidency, but he declined to accept. In the election about 30,000 voters, nevertheless, voted for him.

Democrats Indorse Greeley.

Greeley had not only been bitterly anti-Democratic and anti-Southern, but he did not favor either tariff reform or civil-service reform—two of the main tenets of many of the Liberal Republicans. His political judgment was notoriously bad, while his record, personal characteristics, and childlike naïveté, which is discernible even in his portraits and statues, lent themselves to ridicule and caricature. To *Harper's Weekly* Thomas Nast, then at the height of his fame, contributed numerous striking cartoons that did much to bring Greeley's characteristics into high relief. One

Absurdities of Greeley's Candidacy.

cartoon represented the old Abolitionist editor eating with a wry face from a bowl of uncomfortably hot porridge that was labelled, "My own words and deeds." Another pictured Greeley at his country home at Chappaqua, sitting well out on a limb, which he was solemnly sawing off—between himself and the tree! Ultimately some of the very men who had promoted the Cincinnati movement declared for Grant, while others gave Greeley only half-hearted support.

Grant's hold on the great mass of the Republican party remained unshaken. To millions his administration had proven satisfactory, and even those who realized that he had made some mistakes could not forget the thrills with which, in days when patriots despaired of the republic, they had heard the news of his victories. The criticisms uttered by Democrats and Liberal Republicans received scant consideration from men who had marched where "Ulysses led the van."

Grant Still Popular.

In the campaign Republican orators brought the Southern issue to the front and made effective use of stories of Ku Klux outrages and of the cry "Grant beat Davis, Greeley bailed him." In September Greeley caused Republican managers some uneasiness by making a tour through the "October States," for his name had long been a household word in the North and vast crowds assembled to see and hear him, but the results of the early elections in these States showed that many people were drawn by curiosity rather than political sympathy.

The Campaign.

When the returns from the November election came in it was found that Greeley was one of the worst-beaten men who had ever been a candidate of a great party for the presidency. He did not carry a single Northern State, and only six Southern States, while Grant received a popular plurality of over three-quarters of a million and a vast majority of the electoral votes.

Grant Re-elected.

The canvass had been a comedy; it was followed by a tragedy. Chagrin over the result, financial troubles, and the death of his wife proved more than the old journalist could bear, and

Greeley died within the month (November 29, 1872). In that tragic hour men forgot his failings, and over his grave honored him for the good deeds that lived after him.

In this campaign opponents of the use of intoxicating liquors had met at Columbus, Ohio, and had nominated a ticket and framed a platform declaring for prohibition, woman's suffrage, and other reforms. They polled less than 6,000 votes in the election, and their voting strength in later years never rose to 300,000, yet in every presidential campaign thereafter they took the field and made their moral protest against "John Barleycorn." Like the Liberty and Free Soil parties, the Prohibitionists were destined never to win as a party, yet their cause ultimately triumphed.

Formation of Prohibition Party.

CHAPTER VII

THE END OF AN ERA

THE Southern States suffered severely from corruption under Carpet-Bag rule, but they were equalled, if not surpassed, in this respect by the metropolis of the country under the notori-

Tweed Ring.

ous Tweed Ring. William Marcy Tweed, better known as "Boss" Tweed, was an accomplished rascal who won friends by his liberal giving and coarse joviality, held numerous offices, and built up a band of political crooks who controlled Tammany Hall and ruthlessly plundered the city. The ring was greatly aided by the fact that a large part of the voters were ignorant foreigners, destitute of any standards of civic virtue, nor did the ring hesitate to use bribery, fraud, and all the other nefarious tricks common to corrupt politics. The ring included in its membership mayors and even judges, and in 1868, and again in 1870, Tweed managed to place one of his creatures, John T. Hoffman, in the governor's chair at Albany and even groomed him for the Democratic nomination for the presidency. Estimates of the amount of money stolen by Tweed and his associates vary from $45,000,000 to $200,000,000.

For years many New Yorkers realized that they were being robbed, but the ring was so powerful that it long retained control of the city. Finally the *New York Times*, which was con-

The Ring Broken up.

ducted by two courageous, public-spirited men— George Jones and Louis J. Jennings—began a crusade against Tweed and his copartners; and *Harper's Weekly*, which worked effectively through the powerful cartoons of Thomas Nast, presently joined in the hue and cry. Tweed brazenly asked: "What are you going to do about it?" But the end of his power was at hand. Some prominent Demo-

74

crats, among them Samuel J. Tilden and Charles O'Conor, joined in the battle against the ring. Some of the members fled to other countries; others were arrested; a few were convicted and punished. Tweed himself was sentenced (1873) to twelve years' imprisonment and to pay a heavy fine, but was soon released on a technicality. He was arrested again, managed to escape to Spain but was recaptured and brought back, and finally died in the Ludlow Street jail (April 12, 1878). Thus ended the Tweed Ring, but unluckily it was not the end of corruption in New York City politics.

Tweed and his associates were not the only politicians who preyed upon America in this period, but fortunately a young country, like a rhinoceros, can thrive and grow fat and lusty even when fed upon by a multitude of parasites.

Census of 1870.

Nor had the ravages of a great war sufficed to keep the United States at a standstill. The census of 1870 showed that in a decade the population had increased over 7,000,000, or from 31,443,321 to 38,558,371. Only three States had lost in population, and, curiously enough, two of these—New Hampshire and Maine—were in the North, while the decrease of the third—Virginia—was largely due to her western counties having been set apart as a separate State. Every year thousands of settlers were pouring into the trans-Mississippi region, and the centre of population in a decade had shifted forty-two miles westward, to a point forty-eight miles east by north of Cincinnati.

It was a period of almost unparalleled business expansion, especially in the development of transportation facilities. Cities, counties, States, and the nation lavishly voted loans and subsidies to encourage the construction of rail-

Railroad Construction.

roads. The land grants given by Congress to such enterprises exceeded a hundred million acres. In the period 1869–72 more than 24,000 miles of new railroad were built, largely in the West and Northwest, while old lines were improved. This activity in railroad construction enormously expanded the iron-and-steel industry, and greatly stimulated other lines of business, so that labor was kept busy, wages rose, immigration was fostered, and even the South reaped a rich harvest from the cotton crop.

Frenzied speculation inevitably accompanied such activity, and "energy outran available means." Although much European capital was invested in the new enterprises, money gradually grew closer, for there had been "an excessive conversion of circulating capital into fixed capital."

Panic of 1873.

At a moment when investors were still gloating over their paper profits there came the stunning news of the failure (September 18, 1873) of the famous firm of Jay Cooke & Company. This firm had been the chief fiscal agent of the government in the sale of war bonds; it was at this time promoting the construction of the Northern Pacific Railroad; the public supposed it to be as solid as the eternal hills. The failure precipitated a great rush to sell stocks, and the following day, in the New York Stock Exchange, the names of nineteen other firms that could not meet their contracts were announced. From coast to coast wild panic spread, and soon business was more completely paralyzed than at any time since 1837. To quote Rhodes, the next five years form "a long dismal tale of declining markets, exhaustion of capital, a lowering in value of all kinds of property including real estate, constant bankruptcies, close economy in business and grinding frugality in living, idle mills, furnaces and factories, former profit-earning mills reduced to the value of a scrap heap, laborers out of employment, reductions of wages, strikes and lockouts, the great railroad riots of 1877, suffering of the unemployed, depression and despair."

Banks resorted to a new device, namely clearing-house certificates, in the settlement of balances, but these afforded only partial relief, and, as is usual in panic times, a great demand developed for more money. President Grant was implored to reissue greenbacks and "save the country from bankruptcy and ruin," and he complied to the extent of ordering the purchase of bonds with $13,000,000 of surplus greenbacks in the treasury, but refused to trench on the reserve. However, Richardson, Boutwell's

Demand for More Greenbacks.

successor in the treasury department, reissued $26,000,000 of greenbacks that had been retired in Johnson's presidency, and thus brought the total amount in circulation up to $382,000,000.

When Congress met in December, scores of remedies were proposed to cure the financial ills of the country, and presently an "inflation bill" validating Richardson's action, the legality

Inflation Bill Vetoed.
of which had been questioned, and providing that the maximum issue of greenbacks should be $400,-000,000 passed both houses. Many prominent Republican leaders supported the measure, but Grant vetoed it. Rhodes says that the veto served notice "that we should not part company with the rest of the world in finance but that our endeavor would be to return to the recognized standard," and he calls it "the most praiseworthy act of Grant's second administration." Greenbackers, of course, took the view that the veto helped the creditor class at the expense of the debtor class.

It was Grant's misfortune to be President in a period when political morality had fallen to a low ebb. The nation had recently emerged from the greatest civil war known to history,

Administrative Demoralization.
and, even under Lincoln, the tremendous increase in governmental revenues and expenditures had resulted in a vast amount of peculation. In the morally unhealthy atmosphere that almost inevitably follows a resort to arms, it was but natural that the spoils system should produce its most noxious growth and that numerous scandals should dishearten lovers of their country. No President, no matter how capable, could have saved the country from some of the evil consequences of such a situation, and unfortunately Grant, though personally honest, possessed no skill in preventing administrative demoralization and political corruption.

Public Scandals.
By revelations concerning what were known as the "Sanborn contracts" Secretary of the Treasury Richardson was so badly discredited that he resigned, being succeeded by Benjamin H. Bristow, an able and courageous Kentuckian (June 1, 1874). Somewhat earlier our

minister to Great Britain, General Schenck, brought disgrace upon himself by association with a dubious mining concern. But the most famous of the scandals of the day was that connected with the Crédit Mobilier.

The Crédit Mobilier was a company formed by certain controlling stockholders of the Union Pacific Railroad, the history of which will be given in the next chapter. This inner ring of "high financiers," as stockholders of the road, awarded to themselves, as members of the Crédit Mobilier, the contract of constructing much of the road, with the expectation of realizing an immense profit—nor were they disappointed. Prominent among these selfish financiers was a certain Massachusetts member of the House of Representatives named Oakes Ames. The road had received an immense amount of assistance from Congress, and, fearing interference from that body, Ames, back in 1867–68, distributed at a low price among his congressional associates many shares of extremely valuable Crédit Mobilier stock, his object being to put the shares where, in his own words, they would "do the most good." Some of the statesmen to whom the shares were offered were high-minded enough to refuse them, but it is significant of the rudimentary state of political morality regarding such matters that those who accepted included several of the most prominent men in public life, among them being Schuyler Colfax, then speaker of the House and soon after elected Vice-President. For some years the matter remained a secret, but in the campaign of 1872 certain Democratic newspapers made charges which resulted in a congressional investigation that brought to light sensational facts that besmirched Colfax and others. The expulsion of Oakes Ames and James Brooks was recommended by the investigating committee, but they escaped with a formal censure. Both men died, however, within three months, their deaths being hastened by mortification and disgrace. A Senate committee recommended that Senator Patterson of New Hampshire should be expelled, but, as his term would expire in five days, no action was taken.

The same Congress that investigated the Crédit Mobilier

scandal passed an act increasing the salaries of the President, cabinet members, judges of the Supreme Court, and members of both houses of Congress. For the last-named the

The "Salary Grab." measure was made retroactive. Precedents for such action existed, but this "salary grab," or "back-pay steal," as it was called, was "like vitriol on the raw wound of public sentiment"; such an outcry arose that many representatives and senators found it inexpedient to retain their share of the increased pay, while the new Congress that met in December, 1873, hurriedly repealed all the increases except those of the President and justices of the Supreme Court.

Political scandals and hard times combined to create a great revulsion against the party in power. In the summer and fall of 1874 Republican orators continued to harp upon Southern

"Tidal Wave" of 1874. "outrages," but hundreds of thousands of the Republican rank and file refused to hearken to the old cries and voted for Democratic candidates, with the result that the Democrats carried even such States as Ohio, Pennsylvania, and Massachusetts. By this political "Tidal Wave," as it was called, the Republican majority of two-thirds in the House of Representatives was transformed into a minority of only a little more than one-third. It was a rude shock to Republican leaders, who had fallen into the pleasant belief that the question of dispensing the loaves and fishes of patronage was settled forever.

The expiring Congress struck a heavy blow at paper money. Under the leadership of Senator John Sherman of Ohio the Republican majority carried through a bill that provided (Jan-

Resumption Act. uary 14, 1875) for the reduction of the circulation of greenbacks to $300,000,000, for an expansion in the circulation of national-bank notes, and named January 1, 1879, as the day when the government would begin the redemption of greenbacks in coin. Though the measure met with bitter opposition from the friends of greenbacks, who were particularly numerous in the Democratic party, most historians praise it as eminently wise and honorable.

In 1875, by skilful detective work, Secretary of the Treasury

Bristow and able assistants unearthed startling facts regarding what was known as the "Whiskey Ring." In St. Louis and
The "Whiskey Ring." other cities of the Middle West there had long existed a secret understanding between distillers and internal-revenue officers to cheat the government of revenue duties. The government investigators decided that Colonel Babcock, the President's private secretary, was a member of the ring. When a letter to this effect was shown to Grant (July 29, 1875) he wrote on the back of it: "Let no guilty man escape"; and he said: "If Babcock is guilty, there is no man who wants him so much proven guilty as I do, for it is the greatest piece of traitorism to me that a man could possibly practice." But friction between Grant and Bristow, public talk that Grant himself was connected with the ring, and some indiscreet remarks uttered in one of the trials by a government prosecutor, combined to cool the President's prosecuting ardor. He made a deposition in Babcock's behalf that helped to save the secretary, but, though the jury's verdict was "not guilty," that of the public was "not proven." The friction between Grant and Bristow presently resulted in the retirement of the latter from the cabinet (June 20, 1876).

Hardly had the Babcock trial closed when an investigating committee of the House of Representatives created a new sensation by recommending that Secretary of War Belknap should
Impeachment of Secretary Belknap. be impeached for malfeasance in office. For some years the post-trader at Fort Sill, in the Indian Territory, had been paying $12,000 a year to a friend of Belknap's for the privilege of retaining his lucrative business, and the testimony showed that part of this money had been turned over to Belknap or his wife. Belknap hurriedly resigned before the House could take action against him, and Grant foolishly accepted the resignation "with great regret." In consequence the guilty secretary escaped punishment, for, though the House impeached him, some senators took the view that he was no longer subject to the Senate's jurisdiction, and the vote in that body stood 37 to 29, or seven less than the required two-thirds.

There were so many public scandals in these years that one eminent historian has characterized the period as "the high water mark of corruption in national affairs," while another has termed it "the nadir of national disgrace." By a sad irony of fate the year that witnessed the trial of Babcock and the disgrace of Belknap was also the hundredth anniversary of the nation's birth.

"The Nadir of National Disgrace."

For five years vast preparations had been making for a Centennial Exposition in Philadelphia, the city in which independence had been declared. The exposition was formally opened (May 10, 1876) by President Grant in the presence of a distinguished company, including the Emperor and Empress of Brazil, and it proved to be the most remarkable display of its kind seen up to that time in the western world. Visitors flocked thither from every corner of the country and also from foreign lands, and the total attendance was almost 10,000,000. The exposition did much to educate the people in art and taste, as well as in more material matters.

Centennial Exposition.

The year 1876 also proved notable because of a remarkable electoral contest. In the preliminaries of the campaign the Republicans shrewdly sought to distract attention from uncomfortable disclosures of corruption under their rule, the leadership in this manœuvre being taken by the "magnetic" James G. Blaine of Maine. Blaine had for eight years been speaker of the House, was still a member of that body, and was now and for years later an eager seeker after the presidency, but, like Henry Clay, with whom he has often been compared, he was repeatedly to see less brilliant men win the coveted prize and was to die disappointed in his great ambition. In January, 1876, a bill to grant amnesty to all persons still under political disabilities gave Blaine an opportunity to demand the exclusion of Jefferson Davis, to revive the horrors of the war and of Andersonville prison, to point out that there were sixty-one ex-Confederate soldiers then members of the House, and to bait these "Southern brigadiers" into saying things that rasped Northern sensibilities.

James G. Blaine.

By his adroit use of these "waving-the-bloody-shirt" tactics, as this sort of political manœuvre came to be called, Blaine did much to fix the issues of the coming campaign, but his own personal fortunes were soon disastrously affected by charges that while speaker he had held improper relations with the affairs of the Little Rock and Fort Smith Railroad. Having discovered that some letters written by him to a certain Mulligan were about to be produced against him, Blaine regained possession of the letters by a ruse, and later made a dramatic defense in the House, in the course of which he read from some of the letters. The speech was a great histrionic effort, and his admirers claimed that it cleared him of all charges, but his enemies refused to accept this view.

The "Mulligan Letters."

For a time there was talk of renominating Grant, but a great uproar was raised about "dynasties," "dictatorships," and "Cæsarism," and the House of Representatives effectively put an end to the third-term agitation by passing, by a vote of 233 to 18, a resolution declaring that any attempt to depart from the precedent established by Washington and other Presidents "would be unwise, unpatriotic, and fraught with peril to our free institutions."

As the time for the Republican convention drew near it became apparent that Blaine would be the leading candidate. His availability was, however, lessened by the scandal described above, and he also labored under the handicap of having, years before, incurred the undying enmity of a powerful Republican leader, Senator Conkling of New York, by describing in debate "his grandiloquent swell, his majestic, supereminent, overpowering, turkey-gobbler strut." Conkling himself was a candidate, as were also Senator Morton of Indiana, Secretary of the Treasury Bristow, Governor Rutherford B. Hayes of Ohio, and others. Bristow was regarded with special favor by "reformers," some of whom met (May 15–16) in New York City, in what was known as the Fifth Avenue conference, and issued a statement, written by Carl Schurz, in which they declared that they

Republican Aspirants.

would not support any candidate concerning whom there could be any question as to his being "really the man to carry through a thorough-going reform in the government." As regards Hayes, comparatively few, even of his supporters, expected him to be nominated, and it is said that if the Ohio Republicans had really hoped to land the coveted prize, they would have put forward Senator John Sherman.

The Republican convention, which met at Cincinnati on June 14, adopted a platform that temporized regarding resumption, feebly indorsed civil-service reform, commended Grant's administration but promised "that the prosecution and punishment of all who betray official trusts shall be swift, thorough, and unsparing," declared in favor of protection and against polygamy, and denounced the Democratic party as "being the same in character and spirit as when it sympathized with treason."

Republican Platform.

Blaine's name was presented to the convention by Colonel Robert G. Ingersoll, a celebrated orator and agnostic, who characterized his hero as "a plumed knight" who "marched down the halls of the American Congress and threw his shining lance full and fair against the brazen forehead of every traitor to his country and every maligner of his fair reputation." At the conclusion of the speech-making the tide in Blaine's favor was running so strongly that if the voting had begun at once he might have been nominated, but it was found that the lighting equipment of the building was out of repair and an adjournment was taken to the next day. It has since been charged that Blaine's enemies purposely cut off the gas supply in order to procure delay.

The "Plumed Knight."

When the first ballot was taken next morning Blaine received 285 votes, Morton 125, Bristow 113, Hayes 61, and Hartranft 58, with the rest scattered between minor candidates. On the sixth ballot Blaine's vote rose to 308, and his supporters were jubilant. But Hayes had been gaining slowly and had 113 votes, and when the names of Morton and Bristow were withdrawn most of their delegates flocked to the Ohio man, with the result that on the seventh

Hayes and Wheeler.

ballot he received 384 votes, 5 more than a majority. For the vice-presidency the convention then nominated William A. Wheeler, a New York member of the House of Representatives.

The selection of Hayes surprised the country, but he was acceptable to both wings of the Republican party and was probably the strongest candidate that could have been named.

Career and Character of Hayes.

As a Union soldier he had been four times wounded and had won a brevet major-generalcy. The quality of the man was shown when, in 1864, while serving under Sheridan in the Shenandoah valley, he was urged to come home and campaign for a seat in Congress; he replied that any one who would leave the army at such a time to advance his political fortunes "ought to be scalped." He was elected to Congress, nevertheless, and subsequently was three times chosen governor of Ohio. In each of his gubernatorial campaigns he had stood stubbornly for "sound money," and in his letter accepting the presidential nomination he denounced the spoils system and declared for civil-service reform. On this subject the platform was weak and evasive, but Hayes's letter won favor among reformers, and ultimately most of the Liberal Republican leaders, including Carl Schurz, gave him their support.

The Democratic national convention met at St. Louis late in June and adopted a vigorous platform, the key-note of which was reform. "Reform," it declared, was necessary to save the

Democratic Slogan— "Reform."

country "from a corrupt centralism which, after inflicting upon ten States the rapacity of carpet-bag tyrannies, has honeycombed the offices of the Federal Government itself with incapacity, waste, and fraud, infected states and municipalities with the contagion of misrule, and locked fast the prosperity of an industrious people in the paralysis of 'hard times.'" After enumerating a long list of public scandals it contended that "the demonstration is complete, that the first step in reform must be the people's choice of honest men from another party, lest the disease of one political organization infect the body politic, and lest by making no change of men or parties we get no change of measures and no real reform."

Senator Thurman of Ohio, Senator Bayard of Delaware, Governor Hendricks of Indiana, and General Hancock of Pennsylvania competed for the nomination, but the logical man to lead a reform campaign was Governor Samuel J. Tilden of New York, and on the second ballot he was nominated. For second place on the ticket the convention then selected Hendricks.

Tilden and Hendricks.

From boyhood Tilden had taken an active part in Democratic politics, and in his teens was a protégé of that prince of New York politicians, Martin Van Buren. In 1855 he was an unsuccessful candidate for attorney-general on the "soft shell" Democratic ticket, and in 1866 he was chairman of the Democratic State committee. Down to 1871 he was chiefly known as a shrewd lawyer who by his skill in helping financiers to "reorganize" and consolidate railroads had made himself a millionaire. In 1871 he threw himself into a vigorous fight against the Tweed Ring, and by this activity so won public favor that in 1874, though bitterly opposed by Tammany Hall, he won the Democratic nomination for governor and was elected by a plurality of over 50,000. As governor he managed the finances of the State with conspicuous ability and added to his record as a reformer by breaking up a corrupt organization known as the "Canal Ring." The source of Tilden's political leadership lay chiefly in his intellect and in his ability as an organizer; personally he was cold, calculating, exceedingly secretive, and almost totally lacking in the arts that usually arouse popular enthusiasm.

Career and Character of Tilden.

Tilden secretly managed his own campaign, and effectively directed the Democratic artillery against the many vulnerable points in the Republican record. Republicans sought to shift the issue from "reform" by vigorously "waving the bloody shirt," attacking Tilden's war record, and charging him with "wrecking" railroads and failing to make full returns of his income to tax-assessors. In hard-money centres they also pointed to the ambiguity of the Demo-

The Campaign.

cratic platform on the currency question and to the fact that Hendricks was openly a friend of fiat money. For *Harper's Weekly* Nast drew a striking cartoon along this line, representing the Democracy as a "double-headed, double-faced Tiger," one head being that of Tilden, the other that of Hendricks; the collars round their necks were labelled respectively "Contraction" and "Inflation," while the inscription below asserted that the beast could "be turned any way to gull the American people."

The currency question was, in fact, one of the main issues of the campaign. Radical friends of paper money had met in May and had organized the Independent National, or Greenback, party and had nominated Peter Cooper of New York for the presidency. This party polled only 80,000 votes in the election, but these figures by no means represent the strength of the paper-money tide. In the congressional election of 1878 the Greenbackers cast a million votes, but in 1880 their candidate, General James B. Weaver of Iowa, received only a third of that number. Four years later the party took the field for the last time under Benjamin F. Butler, who had left the Democrats in the Civil War period and now turned his back upon the Republicans. Butler made a vociferous campaign, but received only 175,000 votes. The party then disappeared from the political arena, but many of its members later took an active part in the Populist movement and carried with them some of their old principles.

In the South the Democrats made strong efforts to "redeem" South Carolina, Florida, and Louisiana—the three States remaining in Republican hands—and their methods were so vigorous that stories of intimidation and murder were telegraphed to the North and reacted against the Democratic cause in that section. In South Carolina white "rifle clubs," as the Democratic organizations in that State were known, became so active that in October, in response to an appeal from Governor Chamberlain, President

Grant sent more than thirty companies of regulars into the State to restore the peace.

Preliminary elections in the "October States" proved unfavorable to the Republicans, and the returns that came in on the night of the November election ran so strongly Democratic that next morning almost every Republican newspaper in the country conceded a Democratic victory; even the Republican managers in the Fifth Avenue Hotel in New York City early deserted their national headquarters and went to bed in the belief that they were beaten. But the *New York Times* took the view that the result was in doubt, and its news editor, John C. Reid, in the early morning hurried to the Republican headquarters to point out to the managers the possibilities of the situation. In the hotel he fell in with William E. Chandler, a national committeeman from New Hampshire, and the two obtained from Zachariah Chandler, the national chairman, authority to continue the contest. Later in the day Zachariah Chandler sent out a telegram to the effect that "Hayes has 185 electoral votes and is elected."

Tilden Thought to be Elected.

Developments presently showed that Tilden would receive 184 electoral votes, 1 less than a majority, that Hayes was certainly entitled to 166 electoral votes, and that the 7 votes of South Carolina, the 8 votes of Louisiana, the 3 votes of Florida, and 1 vote in Oregon were in doubt.

The Outcome in Doubt.

In Oregon the Hayes electors had received a majority of the popular vote, but one of them was a postmaster, and the Democrats contended that this served to disqualify him and to give a place in the electoral college to the Democratic candidate who received the next highest number of votes. After a prolonged contest two electoral returns were forwarded to Washington, one of them, the Republican return, giving 3 votes to Hayes, and the other, the Democratic return, giving 2 votes to Hayes and 1 to Tilden.

The Oregon Contest.

In South Carolina the campaign had been a disorderly one,

bloody race conflicts had occurred, and many negroes had been intimidated from voting as they desired, but the returns showed

In South Carolina.

small majorities for the Hayes electors. The State returning board certified their election, but the Democrats claimed a victory, took the contest into the courts, and ultimately two sets of returns were forwarded from South Carolina.

In Florida both parties were guilty of illegal campaign methods, but the State returning board, acting under the eyes of "visiting statesmen" of both parties from the North, certi-

In Florida.

fied the choice of the Republican electors. As in South Carolina, the contest was thrown into the courts, and ultimately there were three returns—two Democratic, one Republican—from that State.

In Louisiana the Democrats had a majority of several thousand on the face of the returns, but the State returning board, all of whom were Republicans and most of whom were negroes

In Louisiana.

or mulattoes, proceeded to throw out enough polls in which the Democratic vote predominated to obtain a majority of over 3,000 for the Hayes electors. In this, as in the other disputed Southern States, it was the old story of the kettle and the pot. In the campaign the Democrats employed every conceivable device, from moral suasion to murder, to accomplish their ends; as for the Republicans, a shrewd investigator, Benjamin F. Butler, subsequently remarked that what they "lacked of the lion's skin they eked out with the fox's tail." In the parish of East Feliciana Democratic "bulldozing" tactics were so pronounced that the Republicans, who two years before had cast 1,688 votes, gave up the contest and cast only one ballot and that a defective one. In several other parishes there were almost equally remarkable results. The returning board not only threw out most of the precincts in these parishes, but did much less justifiable work in dealing with returns from other places. As the Louisiana Supreme Court had held that the decisions of the returning board were not subject to judicial review, it was impossible for the Democratic electoral claimants to carry the matter into the courts.

Nevertheless, they, as well as the Republican electors, met and voted, and ultimately, as a result of further complication, four certificates were forwarded to Washington, one of them being a humorous one signed by "John Smith, bull-dozed Governor of Louisiana."

The electoral colleges met and voted on the 6th of December; Congress had assembled two days earlier. Meanwhile the country resounded with cries of fraud and threats of violence, and every rumor, no matter how wild, found ready belief among the credulous. All men realized that the situation was fraught with peril, all the more so because of the vagueness of the Constitution on the matter of counting the electoral votes. Then, as now, the Constitution merely provided that the returns from the electoral colleges should be transmitted sealed to the president of the Senate, and that "the President of the Senate shall, in the presence of the Senate and House of Representatives, open all the certificates, and the votes shall then be counted." But counted by whom? Herein lay the crux of the whole controversy. If by the president of the Senate, then Thomas W. Ferry of Michigan, president *pro tempore*—Vice-President Wilson having died in 1875—would decide between the contesting returns, and, as Ferry was a partisan Republican, there could be little doubt that he would declare Hayes elected. Most Republicans contended that to Ferry belonged the counting power; most Democrats were equally positive that no votes could be counted without the consent of the House of Representatives, in which they had a majority. It was clear to every one that if the decision was left to the two houses voting separately, a deadlock would ensue, and one view was that the choice of a President would then be thrown into the Democratic House, that of the Vice-President into the Republican Senate. All sorts of theories were propounded and debated, but none found general acceptance, nor were there any conclusive precedents that could be invoked.

Much violent talk was heard in Congress and throughout the country, but Americans had so recently passed through the

Who shall Count the Votes?

fiery furnace of civil war that a great majority were anxious for a compromise of some sort. Southern Democrats were less warlike than some of their Northern compatriots. In a Democratic congressional caucus Benjamin Hill of Georgia, an ex-Confederate general, referred cuttingly to a section of his party who were "invincible in peace and invisible in war," and he asserted that Fernando Wood of New York and other fiery Northern members of Congress had "no conception of the conservative influence of a 15-inch shell with the fuse in process of combustion." However, there were men in each party willing to go to any lengths to win. In a number of places Tilden and Hendricks "minute men" were enrolled into companies, and Colonel Henry Watterson declared in a speech made on "St. Jackson's Day" that he would take a hundred thousand Kentuckians to Washington to see that justice was done Tilden. Meanwhile President Grant quietly but grimly prepared to preserve the peace, for he was determined not "to have two governments or any South American *pronunciamientos.*"

Peace or War?

Fortunately the "fire-eaters" of both parties were pushed aside, and a joint committee of both houses, after weeks of wrangling, ultimately presented a plan for a compromise. The plan provided for an electoral commission composed of five representatives, five senators, and five justices of the Supreme Court, who were to consider disputed returns concerning which the two houses could not agree, and their decisions were to stand unless rejected by both houses voting separately. Neither Hayes nor Tilden favored the plan, but the country was eager for a peaceful settlement and the bill passed both houses and was signed by President Grant (January 29, 1877).

Electoral Commission Bill.

In fulfilment of an understanding that was not incorporated into the act, the Senate named two Democrats—Bayard of Delaware and Thurman of Ohio—and three Republicans—Frelinghuysen of New Jersey, Edmunds of Vermont, and Morton of Indiana. The House named two Republicans—Hoar of Massachusetts and Garfield of Ohio—and three Democrats—

Hunton of Virginia, Abbott of Massachusetts, and Payne of Ohio. Two Republican justices—Miller and Strong—and two Democrats—Field and Clifford—were indirectly designated by the act, and it was made their duty to select a fifth. While the bill was under consideration it was supposed that Justice David Davis of Illinois would be the fifth judge. Davis had been appointed to the Supreme Court by Abraham Lincoln, but he now had Democratic leanings and had besides a desire for the presidency. He was an exceedingly fat man, of size so vast that it was said that he had to be "surveyed for a pair of trousers." His disinclination to accept the thankless task of casting the deciding vote fully equalled his dimensions. While the Electoral Bill was still before Congress the Democratic members of the Illinois Legislature, with strange fatuity, combined with five independents and elected Davis to the United States Senate, to succeed John A. Logan. This gave Davis an excuse to decline an appointment on the electoral commission, and the four justices ultimately named Justice Joseph P. Bradley, who had been appointed as a Republican but who was the most acceptable to the Democrats of any of the remaining judges.

The Fifth Judge.

During February the disputed electoral returns from Florida, Louisiana, Oregon, and South Carolina were referred to the commission by Congress, and in every case, on every vital question, Justice Bradley voted with the Republican members, and the commission, by a strict party vote of 8 to 7, decided that all the disputed electoral votes should be counted for Hayes. The House in each case voted to reject the award, but the Senate in each case sustained it, so, under the law, the decision stood.

"Eight to Seven."

Democrats savagely attacked the majority of the commission for their rulings, most of all for refusing to take evidence *aliunde* the certificates, and the charge was then made, and has frequently been repeated, that some of the rulings were inconsistent. The truth, however, is that the majority followed the convenient line of cleavage between State and federal powers, as laid down in

The Charge of Inconsistency.

the constitutional provisions regarding the choice of electors, and, whatever else may be said as to the commission's decisions, they were consistent.

Though bitterly disappointed in the commission's decisions, most Democratic leaders realized that they were bound to accept the result, but in the final days of the count irrecon-

The Wormley Conferences. cilables began a filibuster designed to prevent the completion of the count before March 4, when Congress would expire, and Grant's term would come to an end. Some of the participants were Southerners who cared comparatively little for Tilden, but thought the occasion opportune to force the incoming Hayes administration to promise concessions to the South. In Florida the Democratic claimants to State office had succeeded in gaining control, but in Louisiana and South Carolina there existed rival Republican and Democratic governments, each claiming to be the legal one. Up to this time the Republican claimants had been upheld by federal troops, but it was well understood that if this support were withdrawn the Carpet-Bag-negro governments would quickly fall. In what were known as the "Wormley Conferences" friends of Hayes, though without express authority from him, undertook to guarantee that if the Democrats would permit the count to be completed, the new President would cease to support the Southern Republican claimants.

Despite this "bargain" some Democrats attempted to continue the filibuster, but Speaker Samuel J. Randall suppressed them with an iron hand. After exciting scenes the count was

The Count Completed. finally completed at four o'clock in the morning of March 2, and President *pro tempore* Ferry formally announced that Hayes and Wheeler were duly elected, having received 185 electoral votes to 184 for Tilden and Hendricks. The greatest contest for an elective office in the history of popular government had been peacefully concluded.

There were many rumors that Tilden intended to take the oath of office and assert his rights, but he was in no sense a revolutionist and contented himself with making verbal protests. To the last, however, there was considerable uneasiness, and, as March 4 happened to fall on Sunday, it was thought best by President Grant that Hayes should be inducted into office on the night of the 3d. The oath was secretly administered by Chief Justice Waite in the Red Room of the White House, in the presence of Grant and his son Ulysses. The formal inauguration ceremonies were held on Monday, March 5.

A delicate task which confronted the new President was that of adjusting affairs in South Carolina and Louisiana. Although not formally bound by the promises made at the Wormley Conferences, Hayes seems to have felt himself *Adjustment in the South.* under obligation to carry them out, and besides he had come to believe that it was time for federal interference in the South to end. In April the troops were ordered to cease supporting the Republican claimants in the two States, and in both the Carpet-Bag governments speedily vanished into thin air.

Thus ended the final scene in reconstruction. It had been a lurid drama but perhaps an inevitable one. A frightful war had been fought for certain principles that the world now agrees were just and right. The problem that pre- *Reflections concerning Reconstruction.* sented itself at the close of the conflict was the preservation of the principles that had triumphed on the battle-field. One policy—the milder one—offered some promise of achieving the desired result, but whether or not it would have done so will always be a matter of debate. Had Lincoln lived, this milder policy might have been adopted, though this is by no means certain. A harsher policy, one less magnanimous and more in accord with human passions, assured the result beyond reasonable doubt and seemed to promise certain benefits to the race which the war had freed. The latter policy was adopted. It produced many unfortunate results, but it at least tided the country over the crisis and secured the fruits of the war. It is easy now to point out the faults of reconstruction, and it is reasonably certain that military rule until the rights of the freedmen were fully established would have been better than negro suffrage, but it is beyond question that military rule or any other plan would also have had its failures.

Southerners, with reason, look back to the reconstruction period as a dark one, and yet, comparatively speaking, the treatment of the South was not really very harsh. "Imaginary comparisons with other civilized governments are sometimes useful," says the historian Rhodes, in this connection. "It seems to me certain that in 1865–1867 England or Prussia, under similar circumstances, would not so summarily have given the negroes full political rights. More than likely they would have studied the question scientifically through experts, and therefore could not have avoided the conclusion that intelligence and the possession of property must precede the grant of suffrage. Their solution of the difficulty would therefore have been more in the interest of civilization. On the other hand, with the ideas which prevail in those countries concerning rebellion against an established government, England and Prussia would undoubtedly have executed Jefferson Davis and others and confiscated much of the southern land. The good nature and good sense of the American people preserved them from so stern a policy, and as a choice of evils (since mistakes it seems were sure to be made) the imposition of negro suffrage was better than proscriptions and the creation of an Ireland or a Poland at our very door."

Rhodes on Treatment of the South.

After the withdrawal of federal armed support, the Republican party virtually disappeared in the South. Since 1876 not one of the former Confederate States has ever cast its electoral votes for other than a Democratic candidate. Wherever necessary, the negro vote was eliminated by fraud or force, such methods being excused on the ground that white supremacy must be preserved. The negroes soon found that it was unsafe to persist in trying to assert their political rights, and except in a few districts they practically ceased voting.

The "Solid South."

In course of time, however, the whites discovered that the methods used to eliminate the negro voters were tending to demoralize the white people themselves, and they sought legal or quasi-legal methods for accomplishing the desired result. The problem was a difficult one, for the Fifteenth Amendment

Attempts to Avoid the Fifteenth Amendment. expressly prohibits suffrage discrimination on account of race, color, or previous condition of servitude, and it was clear that straight property or educational qualifications would deprive many poor and illiterate white men of the franchise.

In 1890 Mississippi evolved what is known as "the understanding clause" plan. A provision was inserted into the constitution to the effect that all persons permitted to register

The "Understanding Clause." "shall be able to read any section of the Constitution of the State; or he shall be able to understand the same when read to him, or to give a reasonable interpretation thereof." As the registration officers were practically all white men, it was easy for them, when they deemed it desirable, to enforce a very high standard in the case of negroes and to lower the bars for illiterate whites.

Several of the other Southern States presently adopted this or some other plan for steering between "the Scylla of the Fifteenth Amendment and the Charybdis of negro domina-

The Louisiana Plan. tion." Louisiana, for example, in 1898 adopted educational and property qualifications for voters, but as loopholes for poor and illiterate whites of native birth incorporated a "grandfather clause," and for those of foreign birth a "naturalization clause." No citizen who was on, or prior to, January 1, 1867, a voter, or who was the son or grandson of such a voter could be deprived of his right to vote, even though he could not meet the educational or property qualifications; and similarly no citizen of foreign birth naturalized prior to January 1, 1898, could be excluded from the polls. All persons desiring to take advantage of either of these loopholes must, however, register prior to September 1, 1898, and neither loophole was available for illiterate poor whites who came of age after that date. As only a few Northern States permitted negroes to vote prior to 1867, the number of colored citizens able to register under the "grandfather clause" was negligible. The general effect of the new system was to reduce the number of registered negro voters from 127,000 in 1896 to 3,300 in 1900; many more than the last number were eligible to register but felt that it was useless to do so. The adoption of such restrictions laid States liable to have their representation in the House of Representatives lowered, as provided by the Fourteenth Amendment, but Congress, fearful of reviving sectional antagonisms, never deemed it expedient to impose the penalty.

The federal courts long evaded passing judgment upon the constitutionality of the disfranchising provisions, "Grandfather Clauses" Declared Void. but finally, in 1915, the Supreme Court decided that the "grandfather clauses" were unconstitutional, because the device "recreated the very conditions which the Fifteenth Amendment was intended to destroy." The practical effect of the decision was, however, negligible.

With the final restoration of home rule in the South the era of civil war and reconstruction may be said to have ended. The old issues long continued to play a part in politics, but more and more they were relegated into the background by great social and economic questions, with which we shall deal in future chapters.

Despite the ravages of war and misgovernment in reconstruction days, the South recovered its material prosperity more rapidly than could reasonably have been expected. By The "New South." 1880 the section was growing a greater cotton crop than had ever been "made" under slave labor; by 1911 the number of bales produced was over four times the number of 1860. The courage and energy with which the Southern people set themselves to the task of rehabilitation were worthy of unstinted praise. To be sure, there was some repining, but the mass of the people soon emerged from the dark shadow of lethargy and despair into the sunshine of hope for the future. By 1886 Henry Grady of Atlanta could say to the New England Society in New York City:

We admit that the sun shines as brightly and the moon as softly as it did "before the war." We have established thrift in the city and country. We have fallen in love with work. We have restored comforts to homes from which culture and elegance never departed. We have let economy take root and spread among us as rank as the crab grass which sprung from Sherman's cavalry camps, until we are ready to lay odds on the Georgia Yankee, as he manufactures relics of the battlefield in a one-story shanty and squeezes pure olive oil out of his cotton seed, against any downeaster that ever swapped nutmegs for flannel sausages in the valley of Vermont.

By 1880 the South was producing one-eighth of all the coal mined in the United States; by 1909 more than a sixth. Alabama, Tennessee, and other Southern States contain immense deposits of iron ore, though the ore is not so rich as that about Lake Superior. In 1909 Alabama produced 4,687,000 tons of ore, which was almost 5 per cent of the total mined in the United States, and Birmingham had become a miniature Pittsburg. In the '80's and '90's cotton-mills began to spring up in many parts of the South, and the textile industry developed with astonishing rapidity. In 1909 North Carolina and South Carolina stood second and third respectively in the manufacture of cotton goods, being surpassed only by Massachusetts. Despite industrial progress, however, the South remained primarily an agricultural section, and the value of all products manufactured in all the States south of Mason and Dixon's line and east of the Rockies was, in 1909, only 12.7 per cent of the total manufactures of the whole country. Next to agriculture, lumbering was the most productive of Southern occupations, though many others, including the production of petroleum, especially in Oklahoma, Texas, and Louisiana, were important. The whole section is rich in natural resources, and future years will doubtless behold some marvellous developments in the South.

As in other sections of the country, industrial development in the South produced some trying problems, one of the most notable being that of child labor in the cotton-mills. Children of tender years worked incredible hours in some of the mills, and, as in some Northern States, selfish influences long balked efforts to abolish this hideous wrong. Lazy and shiftless par-

Industrial Progress.

ents of the "poor white" class would often put their children at work and then live off the proceeds. "What all's the use of me workin' when I got three head of gals in the mill?" said such a parent as he leaned over the bar of a Southern saloon. In recent years progress has been made toward regulating child labor, but some States still lag disgracefully behind the procession.

Child Labor.

Gradually the old Southern enmities toward the North have disappeared. Hostility toward "Yankees" in the abstract still lingers in some circles, however, though usually combined with surprising friendliness for individual Yankees in the concrete. The "Lost Cause" is still romantically cherished by Daughters of the Confederacy and other organizations, but few Southerners regret that the nation is united. Even Jefferson Davis, though never really "reconstructed," closed his book on the rise and fall of the Confederacy with the sentiment—"The Union, *Esto perpetua!*"

The "Lost Cause."

The final reconciliation took place during the Spanish-American War. That conflict roused a great wave of patriotic feeling in the South such as had not been experienced since Taylor and Scott led their armies into Mexico. For the first time since the sad days of secession the nation became a real union of hearts. Volunteers came forward as freely in the South as in any other section, and a number of ex-Confederate officers accepted high command. It is said that in the heat of conflict one of these officers forgot himself and implored his men to "give the Yankees hell!" But everybody smiled over such incidents, and felt no desire to criticise. Says Roosevelt, in describing the progress of his Rough Riders from San Antonio to Tampa:

Effect of Spanish-American War on Southern Feeling.

We were travelling through a region where practically all the older men had served in the Confederate Army, and where the younger men had all their lives long drunk in the endless tales told by their elders, at home, and at the crossroad taverns, and in the court-house squares, about the cavalry of Forrest and Morgan and the infantry of Jackson and Hood. The blood of the old men stirred to the distant breath of battle; the blood of the young men leaped hot with eager desire to accompany us. . . .   Everywhere we saw the Stars and Stripes, and everywhere we were told, half-laughing, by grizzled ex-Confederates that they had never dreamed in the bygone days of bitterness to greet the old flag as they now were greeting it, and to send their sons, as they now were sending them, to fight and die under it.

On the fiftieth anniversary of Gettysburg the survivors of the hosts who had fought under Meade and Lee assembled on that famous field and mingled as comrades rather than as enemies. At the appropriate hour a handful of gray-haired Confederate veterans marched slowly up the slope where Pickett had led his gallant column in the long ago. As they reached the top of Cemetery Ridge and "High Tide," they were greeted with cheers and handclasps and embraces by their former foes. The "bloody chasm" was forever closed.

CHAPTER VIII

THE PASSING OF THE "WILD WEST"

A GENERATION ago every American boy knew of Sitting Bull and Geronimo and was full of their bloody exploits on the war-trail. A youth of the present generation, when asked about living Indians, will name such "chiefs" as Thorpe or Bender, and will tell you of how they won championships at Olympic meets or mowed down batsmen in world series. Between the two attitudes of mind lies a wonderful transformation, not only in the status of the Indian race but in the whole of the great West.

At the close of the Civil War the population of the region beyond the Mississippi, excluding the older States of Iowa, Missouri, Arkansas, Texas, and parts of Minnesota and Loui-

A Wonderful Transformation.
siana—constituting about two-thirds of the United States proper—was only a million and a half; and vast areas existed that were peopled only by no-madic savages who won a livelihood by slaying the swarming buffaloes. Forty-five years later the wild buffaloes in the limits of the United States had long since gone the way of the passenger-pigeon and the great auk; the sons and grandsons of their breech-clouted pursuers were attending Carlyle or Haskell and playing football and baseball instead of seeking scalps on the war-trail; and the region above described contained more than 13,000,000 people. This marvellous transformation of the romantic "Wild West" of buffalo herds and "hostiles" into a peaceful land of ranches and railroads, of wheat-fields and fruit farms, of dams and irrigation ditches, of mines and macadam roads, forms one of the biggest facts in American history and is worthy of study.

It is hard for Americans of this generation to realize that for

years after the Civil War most of the Far West continued to be
"Indian country," and that travellers who crossed the Great
Dispossessing the Aborigines. Plains and the mountains beyond ran imminent
risk of leaving their bones bleaching in the buffalo-
grass and of having their scalps swing in the smoke
of wigwams—even in times of so-called "peace." In the West,
as formerly in the East, the history of how the aborigines were
conquered and dispossessed is a long and complicated story of
encroachments upon the Indian's lands, of warfare, of treaties
"made to be broken," a story that does little credit to Americans
and their government. However, in the words of Chittenden:
"It was the decree of destiny that the European should displace
the native on his own soil. No earthly power could prevent it."

Even after the tribes accepted the guardianship of the government they were often mistreated by rapacious Indian agents
and contractors. For years an "Indian Ring" preyed upon
The "Indian Ring." the reservation Indians, cheating them in the
amount and quality of the supplies they were supposed to receive. The blankets given them were
likely to be of shoddy, the cattle fed to the wards of the nation
were apt to be leaner than Pharaoh's kine, and many of the
supplies for which the government paid never reached the red
men at all. More than one bloody outbreak was due to dissatisfaction and hunger caused by such cheating. As already
related, some of the facts regarding this "ring" came to light
in the impeachment proceedings against Secretary of War
Belknap, but a thorough investigation of the abuses was never
made, partly because certain politicians were anxious to preserve the existing state of affairs.

Furthermore, unscrupulous white men encroached upon the
Indians' lands, stole their horses, slaughtered the game upon
which they depended for food, debauched their squaws, cheated
them in trades, sold them "firewater," and taught them all the
vices of civilization but few of the virtues.

However, the Indians were not altogether blameless in most
of the scores of petty wars that occurred in the quarter-century

following 1865. Despite attempts to idealize the red men, their normal existence was a state of warfare. When they were not fighting the palefaces, they were apt to be making bloody forays against other tribes. Indian children were brought up to regard cruelty as praiseworthy, and they delighted in helping to torture captives. The men whom boys took as their models were warriors renowned for ferocity and cunning on the war-trail, for the ponies they had stolen, for the number of enemies they had slain. The prime ambition of a youth was to tear a scalp from the head of an enemy, and to obtain the gory trophy he would murder a woman or a child as remorselessly as he would a man. In peace the Plains Indian was polygamous, lazy, a habitual gambler, and grossly licentious. In war the cruelties he practised upon his captives were of so shocking a nature that they cannot be put down in public print. When we realize that practically every white woman and girl ever captured by war parties of the Plains tribes was subjected to nameless outrages, we need not feel surprise that an implacable feud developed between the two races and that a fixed axiom in the minds of frontiersmen was that "the only good Indian is a dead Indian."

Character of the Western Indians.

It was an inevitable and irrepressible conflict, the kind of conflict that invariably develops when a stronger civilized race is brought into contact with a weaker primitive but warlike people.

Even in those days, however, the red man did not lack friends and defenders. Eastern idealists and the officials of the Indian Bureau usually stood ready to uphold his cause against the army and the men of the frontier. For a long period the army and the Indian Bureau worked at cross-purposes in the management of the tribes, and as a result of divided jurisdiction it not infrequently happened that soldiers of the one fought hostiles who were furnished with repeating rifles and cartridges by agents of the other.

Cross-Purposes.

At the close of the Civil War the whole Western frontier was

ablaze, and nearly every important tribe from the Canadian
border to the Red River of the South was on the
war-path. In the Indian campaigns of that year
about $40,000,000 was expended, yet very few hos-
tiles were either killed or captured.

Indian Wars
of 1865.

The next quarter-century witnessed wars with the Modocs,
Comanches, Nez Percés, Arapahoes, Kiowas, and
other tribes, in the course of which many hundreds
of "contacts" occurred between troops and hostiles, but the tribes that caused the most persistent trouble
were the Apaches of the arid Southwest and the great Sioux
confederacy of the upper Missouri country.

Scores of
Petty Wars.

In August, 1862, the Sioux in the region of the upper Mississippi had risen and massacred nearly a thousand white settlers
on the Minnesota frontier, and had caused 50,000 others to
flee in terror to St. Paul and other places of refuge,
but the hostiles were speedily defeated, many were
captured, and thirty-nine were hanged for murder.
Some of those who escaped joined their wilder brethren, the
Plains Sioux of the Dakota region, and hostile bands kept up a
desultory warfare for years.

Sioux War
of 1862.

One cause of the persistent hostility of the western Sioux
was the opening of a new road from Fort Laramie to the mines
of Montana and Idaho. A few chieftains, mainly from a degen-
erate band known as the "Laramie Loafers," gave
their assent, but the real leaders of the Sioux did not,
and this "Bozeman Road," as it was called, was all
the more distasteful to the aborigines because it led through a
favorite hunting-ground, a charming foot-hill country, where
bears, antelope, elk, buffalo, and other game abounded.

The
Bozeman
Road.

Many travellers along the new road were waylaid and slain,
and in December, 1866, a big band of Sioux, aided by some
warriors from other tribes, surrounded and massacred to the last man a force of eighty-one men under
Captain William J. Fetterman close to Fort Phil
Kearney, near the Bighorn Mountains. A few months later
another detachment of about thirty men, under Major James

The
Fetterman
Massacre.

Powell, were attacked not far from the same place by a vast force of hostiles, but Powell stationed his men behind a breastwork of bullet-proof wagon-beds made of iron and drove off the Indians with great slaughter.

In 1868 the warlike Cheyennes swept through western Kansas like a devastating storm, and in a single month killed or captured over eighty men, women, and children, while again and again they wiped out gangs of workmen employed in the construction of the new railroad to the Pacific. The fate of the captured women and girls was particularly revolting, and the stories of how some of them were finally rescued exceeds in adventurous interest most fiction.

The Cheyenne War of 1868.

General Sheridan, of Winchester fame, personally took the field against the Cheyennes and other bands, but it was generally easy for the hostiles to evade the troops, for the Indians depended mostly upon game for food and were mounted upon swift ponies that were usually able to out-travel the slow-going horses of the troopers, while, when hard pressed, a band could easily scatter and later meet again at an appointed rendezvous. Sheridan, in fact, found the task of catching his enemy so difficult that he compared it to "chasing the *Alabama*." In September a thousand hostiles under Chief Roman Nose made the mistake of attacking a band of fifty scouts intrenched on a sandy island in the Arickaree fork of Republican River, and were beaten off after a desperate struggle, largely because of the determined resourcefulness of Colonel George A. Forsyth. Near the end of the year General George A. Custer, with the Seventh Cavalry, carried out a winter campaign when the snow was deep and the Indian ponies were weak from lack of proper food. By good management he surprised Black Kettle's band of Cheyennes and Arapahoes in camp along the Washita River, killed more than a hundred warriors, took many prisoners, almost a thousand ponies, also hundreds of buffalo-robes and bows, arrows, and other savage paraphernalia. The surviving Cheyennes and Arapahoes made peace soon after.

Custer's Victory on the Washita.

In the previous spring peace had been concluded with the Kiowas, Apaches, Sioux, and certain other tribes by what was known as the Peace Commission. By these treaties the Indians conceded certain rights of transit through their country, but reservations were set apart for their use, and the Bozeman Trail in the Powder River country was given up by the whites.

Treaties of 1868.

Under President Grant a Board of Indian Commissioners was created, and in general better Indian agents were appointed, but dishonesty still lurked in the Indian Bureau, and the Indians were still often cheated in the matter of supplies. Furthermore, encroachments on the Indians' lands continued, with much killing of the game upon which the aborigines largely depended for subsistence. In 1874–76 the discovery of gold in the Black Hills, on the Sioux reservation, precipitated a great rush of prospectors to that region and helped to bring on the last great Indian war.

Rush to the Black Hills.

At that time there were many Indians who refused to remain on the reservations, as provided by the treaty of 1868, but roamed at will over the buffalo country and never visited the agencies except to see friends or relatives, or to trade—preferably for guns and ammunition. These irreconcilables came to be known as the "hostiles," and they habitually waylaid hunters, trappers, and other white men who ventured into the region. Every hunting season other Indians from the reservations would travel to the camps of the hostiles, partly to kill buffaloes for meat and robes, and on such occasions these "agency Indians" were almost as dangerous as their wilder brethren.

The "Hostiles."

The foremost leader of the hostiles was a Sioux of the Hunkpapa Teton tribe, named Sitting Bull. He was not really a fighting leader, but when bullets were flying preferred to remain in his tepee making "medicine"; nevertheless, he wielded great influence and had about sixty lodges of followers upon whom he could always depend.

Sitting Bull.

Early in 1876 the federal government determined to round

up these irreconcilables and force them to settle upon the reserves. With that end in view three expeditions were prepared
Plan of Campaign in 1876. and sent out: General Gibbon with the so-called "Montana column," marched from the west; General Crook, who had won fame fighting the Apaches in Arizona and New Mexico, moved up from the south; and General Terry, who was in supreme command, led a force from the east. It was expected that the hostiles would be found somewhere in the Yellowstone country.

On June 17 Crook's column attacked the hostiles in the valley of the Rosebud River, but were beaten off. About the same time a scouting force from Terry's command discovered
Custer's March. the Indian trail leading up the Rosebud, and Terry ordered Major-General George A. Custer to take his regiment, the Seventh Cavalry, consisting of some 600 troopers, follow the trail, and attack the Indians. Custer had won high distinction under Sheridan in the Shenandoah Valley and elsewhere, and subsequently in Indian warfare; he was a handsome, dashing officer, fond of wearing the buckskin clothing of the border and his yellow hair long and in curls; he was bold even to rashness, and was, in fact, almost the ideal cavalry leader. Custer's little force, travelling mostly at night, in order to conceal their movements, followed the trail and by the 25th of June were in striking distance of the hostiles, whose camps were pitched in the valley of the Little Big Horn River. With some Crow scouts Custer personally reconnoitred the enemy, but the camps were strung out for several miles along the valley, and, owing to some intervening bluffs, Custer, unfortunately, did not see all of them.

The truth was that many lodges of agency Sioux had journeyed into the buffalo country to join their hostile brethren, so that, encamped along the river that day, there were from 2,500
Strength of the Hostiles. to 4,000 warriors—Sioux, Cheyennes, Arapahoes, etc.—under such chieftains as Sitting Bull, Crazy Horse, Crow King, and Rain-in-the-Face. Most of these warriors were armed with breech-loading rifles—many even with repeaters—being better equipped, in fact, than the

troops, who carried Springfield carbines that had been originally muzzle-loaders but converted into breech-loaders; the
extractors of these weapons worked so badly that often, in removing empty shells, it was necessary for the soldiers to use
their knives, which meant, of course, loss of precious time.

According to Captain Godfrey, who survived the campaign
and later wrote an account of it, one of the Crow scouts remarked that there were enough hostiles to keep the troops busy
Custer's
Plan.
fighting several days, but Custer only smiled and
said that he thought the task could be finished in
one day. He was then unaware of the magnitude
of the force confronting him, but even had he known the truth
he would doubtless have attacked, though he would hardly
have employed the plan he adopted. This plan was based
upon the knowledge that Indian fighting was "touch and go
warfare," that ordinarily the great problem was to catch the
Indians. He realized that if he attacked as one force the warriors would rush to confront him and hold him off until the
squaws and other non-combatants could have time to save
their belongings and drive off the valuable pony herds. Therefore he divided his regiment into four parts: he ordered one
troop to guard the pack-train, sent Captain Benteen with
three troops to the left and Major Reno with three troops and
some Indian scouts to cross the Little Big Horn and move up
the valley against the Indian camps, while he personally took
five troops and made a detour to the right in order to cut off
the Indians when they fled toward the fastnesses of the Little
Big Horn Mountains.

Reno soon met so many Indians that, after hard fighting, he
gave up the attempt to reach the village and rejoined Benteen's force, suffering heavy losses, particularly in recrossing
The Custer
Massacre.
the river. Uncertain what to do, the united force
hesitated and thus gave the Indians an opportunity
to concentrate against Custer's five companies.
Practically the whole Indian force, under able war chiefs, surrounded the little band of 200 troopers and slew them to the
last white man; only a half-breed Crow scout named Curly

managed to escape. Later in the day the Indians attacked
Reno and Benteen's force, but, largely owing to the courage
and skill of Benteen, the white men managed to hold them off
until the approach of the combined columns of Gibbon and
Terry. Only then did the survivors of the regiment learn that
Custer had met with disaster.

The hostiles gained little by their victory, for during the
following fall and winter they were continually pursued by
fresh forces, and many found it expedient to surrender. Sitting
Bull and some of his followers managed to escape
into Canada, whence they occasionally sent out
raiding parties over the border, but in 1881 they
were so reduced by hunger that they returned and surrendered.
One result of the war was that the Sioux were forced to cede
the Black Hills country. For almost a decade they resided on
the reservations in reasonable peace and quiet.

About 1888 many of the western tribes began to hold "ghost
dances," and their medicine men were constantly prophesying
the coming of a Messiah who would destroy the white men and
bring back the buffalo herds. The delusion gained
such a foothold that a wide-spread outbreak seemed
imminent. The Sioux became especially uneasy,
and it was known that Sitting Bull was once more engaged in
stirring them up. Indian policemen were sent to arrest him,
but some of his followers defended him, and Sitting Bull was
slain (December 15, 1890). A couple of weeks later a considerable battle took place at Wounded Knee, but the Sioux suffered
heavily, and this defeat and the energetic action of General
Nelson A. Miles sufficed to bring to an end what proved to be
the last of our many Indian wars.

The submission of the Plains tribes to the inevitable was
due almost as much to the disappearance of the
buffaloes as to the campaigns of the soldiers. These
mighty, shaggy, lumbering beasts were to these red
men what manna was to the Children of Israel
during their sojourn in the Wilderness—and more, for from
them the Indians obtained not only most of their food, but

*Sioux
Subdued.*

*Outbreak
of 1890.*

*Importance
to the
Indians of
the Buffalo.*

also clothing, bowstrings, harness for ponies and dogs, and skins for lodges. While the buffaloes were plentiful it was generally easy for bands on the war-path to evade the slow-moving soldiers, but when the herds of "Plains cattle" disappeared, the old system of warfare became impossible. Lack of food was the main factor that forced Sitting Bull and his band to return from Canada.

When white men first settled on the Atlantic coast, the buffaloes ranged over a large part of the United States, Canada, and Mexico, and only five years before the Revolution, George Washington and some companions shot five of them in one day near the Great Kanawha River, in what is now West Virginia. By 1830 they had been driven far beyond the Mississippi, except in the region of Minnesota, yet as late as the early '70's they still numbered millions. In 1868 General Sheridan and an escort rode for three days through one vast herd. The same year a train on the Kansas-Pacific Railroad ran for more than 120 miles through "an almost unbroken herd," and the next year a train on the same road was delayed for eight hours by buffaloes crossing the track ahead of it. Though vast in size and ferocious in aspect, buffaloes were really among the least dangerous of large wild animals, and the comparative safety with which they could be hunted, the value of their hides and flesh, and their intense stupidity all combined to hasten their destruction. Their stupidity was so great that when stampeded they would sometimes plunge by hundreds over cliffs, dash madly into moving railroad trains, wade into quicksands that had already swallowed up multitudes of their companions ahead, or stand foolishly in range of ambushed hunters until literally hundreds had been shot down. Colonel Richard I. Dodge, the author of an interesting book on the Plains, records that he once counted 112 dead buffaloes lying inside a semi-circle of 200 yards, all of which had been slain by one man firing from the same spot.

The Indians annually killed hundreds of thousands of the animals for their meat and hides. Every fall hundreds of Red

River half-breeds from the Lake Winnipeg region journeyed into the buffalo country and returned with their creaking wooden carts (in the manufacture of which not an ounce of iron was used) laden down with hides and jerked meat. Hunters from the East and from Europe sought the plains to gratify their desire for slaughter, and shot buffaloes until their passion was appeased, being usually content to leave the bodies lying undisturbed, or, at most, to take the horns and tails for trophies, with perhaps the tongues and a little of the hump for meat. Not infrequently buffaloes were shot by passengers firing from the windows of moving trains, the sole object being mere slaughter. Sometimes, of course, the killing of buffaloes served a more useful purpose, as, for example, when William F. Cody, in eighteen months, killed 4,280 to furnish food for the builders of the Kansas-Pacific Railroad and thereby won his famous sobriquet of "Buffalo Bill."

Their Enemies.

The number of buffaloes was so vast, however, that the animals would have survived much longer had it not been for the operations of "skin-hunters" seeking "robes" for Eastern markets. This destructive industry, which first attained considerable dimensions about 1872, was rendered practicable by the construction of railroads, which made the buffalo country more easily accessible. The most approved parties for this business were composed of four men—one shooter, two skinners, and one cook, who also stretched hides. Heavy, long-range Sharps or Remington rifles were generally used, and, if buffaloes were plentiful, the hunter had little difficulty in keeping the skinners busy; in fact, he often killed more animals than they were able to take care of. The herds were constantly harried by these skin-hunters, and in places the air for miles would be poisoned by the noxious effluvia from the rotting carcasses. Colonel Dodge estimates that in the three years 1872–74 fully 3,000,000 buffaloes were slain by hide-hunters, and that the total number killed in those years was probably 5,000,000. Practically all the meat was wasted, but years afterward bone-pickers went about the plains and gathered up the skeletons for fertilizer.

The "Skin-Hunters."

As early as 1870 the original range on the Plains had been divided, and there was a northern and a southern herd, which never came together. By the end of another decade the great herds had been wiped out, but a few small ones remained in the Llano Estacado country in the south, and Montana in the north. In 1887 there remained in the whole United States only a few hundred scattered buffaloes, and these were soon exterminated save in Yellowstone National Park, where a small herd is still preserved. In Canada the wild buffaloes lasted longer, and a few so-called "wood bison" still wander through the remote wilderness between the lower reaches of the Liard and Peace Rivers.

Their Extinction.

In the far Southwest the Apaches, an offshoot from the Athabascan family of the far Canadian northland, indulged in frequent bloody forays against scattered ranchers and prospectors, and displayed unsurpassed cunning and a pitiless ferocity that spared neither sex nor age. Although less numerous than the Sioux, they dwelt in a more difficult country, full of mountain and desert fastnesses, while, when hard pressed, they were often able to escape over the border into Mexico. Thither they were frequently followed by American forces, while Mexican troops co-operated against the common foe. Such Indian leaders as Cochise, Victorio, Juh, and Geronimo won fame in these outbreaks, while on the side of the white man the most noted names were those of Generals Crook and Miles. It was not until 1886 that the final outbreak was suppressed. In that year the Chiricahua Apaches, the most incorrigible of all, with their leader Geronimo, were deported to Florida and Alabama, where they were subjected to military imprisonment, being subsequently transferred to Fort Sill, Oklahoma, on the Kiowa reservation. At the last-mentioned place they engaged in successful farming, and developed an ability to make money and to save it.

The Apache Wars.

In 1887 Congress passed the so-called Dawes Act, under the provisions of which many Indian reservations were broken up, part of the land being allotted to the Indians in severalty, while the remainder was opened to white settlement. Most of the tribes of the Indian Territory consented to accept the terms of the act, and ultimately the territory was admitted to the Union as the State of Oklahoma (1907). A picturesque episode in the transformation occurred on April 22, 1889, when more than a million acres were opened to homesteaders. At noon precisely, at the call of a bugle, tens of thousands of frantically eager would-be settlers, on foot, on horseback, in every imaginable vehicle, dashed madly over the border to claim fertile quarter-sections or choice town lots. By nightfall, Guthrie, which six hours before had been only a town site, was thronged with 10,000 people, while Oklahoma City and other places were thickly populated. Many persons who participated in the rush soon sold out their holdings and departed, but most remained, and by the end of 1889 Oklahoma, "the Beautiful Land," which as yet included only a part of the Indian Territory, had a population of about 60,000. Subsequently other reservations were thrown open to settlement, and similar scenes were enacted. The soil proved highly productive, oil and various kinds of minerals were discovered, and the territory and later the State prospered exceedingly, so that by 1910 Oklahoma contained 1,657,153 inhabitants.

The Opening of Oklahoma.

Tribal relationships were broken up so rapidly that by 1910 there remained in the United States only 71,872 Indians who were not taxed as citizens. Those retaining their reservations still held, however, an area twice that of the State of New York, scattered through twenty-six commonwealths.

Number of Tribal Indians in 1910.

In the United States, exclusive of Alaska, the total number of Indians was 265,683, which, strange as it may seem, was probably not much less than the number living in the same limits in the days of John Smith, Powhatan, and Pocahontas. Included, however, were many persons of mixed blood, for miscegenation with Indians has excited comparatively little prejudice, and one President was fond of boasting that he had Indian blood in his veins. Only a few States, such as California and Arizona,

Present Condition of the Indians.

where the aborigines are rather lower in the scale than elsewhere, forbid intermarriage, and in many places the red race
is rapidly being absorbed by the Caucasians. In some instances the Indians who have turned farmers are thrifty and
prosperous, this being especially true in Oklahoma, where a
considerable number have become rich through the discovery
of oil on their lands. Many, of course, are shiftless and degraded, victims often of tuberculosis, "fire-water," and venereal
diseases. In most the primitive love of the woods and waters
persists, but, within the limits of the United States, the really
"wild" Indian is virtually a thing of the past. So far as their
welfare depends upon governmental assistance, they are better
cared for than formerly. Large sums are expended to give
them elementary, secondary, and higher education, and comparatively few of the younger generation are unable to read
and write. The glorious scalp-lifting days are gone forever,
but the young men now play baseball and football, and recently helped their white brethren to fight the "Huns."

A more serious obstacle in the way of settlement of the West
than the aboriginal inhabitants was the problem of transportation. The Pacific coast region could be reached by way of
Panama or the Straits of Magellan, though either
of these routes was long, costly, and dangerous,
but the plains and mountain country required an
overland trip. The usual starting-place for such a journey was
some point on the Missouri River, which offered an inlet for
3,000 miles, by steamer, mackinaw boats, or canoes, for fur
traders, missionaries, trappers, prospectors, or other travellers; but it was a treacherous stream, the Indians along
its upper reaches were often hostile, and sixty or sixty-five
days were required to reach the head of navigation even by
steamer.

Passengers for the interior rode on horseback, in stage-coaches,
or in prairie-schooners; some of the mail for a time reached
its destination by the famous "pony express"; while freight
was carried by pack-trains or wagon-trains, drawn by horses,
mules, or slow oxen. It took from forty-five to seventy-four

days for teamsters to go from Fort Leavenworth to Denver, and freight rates ran as high as twenty-five cents a pound in the Civil War period, though the average was nearer ten cents. The great companies engaged in the transportation of passengers and mails were Wells Fargo & Company and the Overland Stage Line, the latter owned by an aggressive individual named Ben Holladay, who at one time owned 260 coaches, 6,000 horses and mules, scores of stage stations, and other equipment. Except in the heart of winter or when the Indians were too aggressive, a coach set out daily from Atchison to Placerville, and another from Placerville to Atchison, and the trip required on the average five days and four hours of continuous travel. In 1865 the fare to Denver was $175, to California $500. A telegraph line to San Francisco was completed as early as 1862, and remained in continuous operation except when disturbed by storms, Indians, or buffaloes.

Methods of Travel.

Several routes for a railroad to the Pacific coast were surveyed by the federal government in 1853–54, but sectional rivalries and the outbreak of the Civil War delayed the consummation of the project, and it was not until 1862 that Congress formally authorized the construction of a Pacific railroad. In aid of the venture the government granted ten alternate sections of land per mile on each side of the road, and issued bonds to the ultimate sum of over $55,000,000, these last being secured by a mortgage on the road. Construction was begun at both ends of the line, in both Nebraska and California, by companies organized for that purpose.

A Pacific Railroad Begun.

At the end of 1865 the Union Pacific builders, working from Omaha, had finished only forty miles of road, but progress thereafter was more rapid. Meanwhile the Central Pacific was building eastward from Sacramento through the Sierras. At both ends "Hurry!" was the watchword, for each mile constructed meant an added subsidy in bonds. The Western builders were hampered by the necessity of bringing the rails immense distances via Panama or the Horn, and also by lack of labor, but they solved the latter

Difficulties of Construction.

difficulty by employing thousands of Chinese. Those moving toward the sunset were often molested by Indians, but, as many of the workmen were veterans of the Civil War, the construction gangs were usually able to beat off their savage assailants.

Finally, on May 10, 1869, "tracks ends" met at Promontory Point, northwest of Ogden, Utah. When Leland Stanford, president of the Central Pacific, drove the golden spike furnished by California into the last tie of laurel wood,

The Road Completed.

men felt that at last East and West were joined. The occasion was celebrated with noisy demonstrations throughout the United States. A historian who has written extensively on the history of travel in America expresses the view that as the multitudes lifted up their rhythmic shouts in answer to the bells, "It was as though they were chanting the last, triumphant words in a long epic of human endeavor. And if those of future times should seek for a day on which the country at last became a nation, and for an event by virtue of which its inhabitants became one people, it may be that they will not select the verdict of some political campaign or battlefield but choose, instead, the hour when two engines—one from the East and the other from the West—met at Promontory."

At all events, the completion of a railway to the Pacific, by solving the problem of transportation, spelled the doom of the "Wild West" and opened a "new period of national assimila-

A New Period Begun.

tion." Before this to reach the Rocky Mountains or the region beyond necessitated arduous and often dangerous effort; thenceforth the would-be settler could be whirled thither in a day or two, and, furthermore, he would have a means of sending his products to Eastern markets.

By 1884 three other transcontinentals had been added, while many branches from all four had been pushed out

New Transcontinentals.

into regions not traversed by the main lines. The days of the stage-coach and of the slowly moving wagons of the freighters were numbered, and the "Frontier" had vanished.

In the occupation by white men of the Far West east of California a distinct succession is noticeable: first came the trapper and Indian trader, next the prospector and miner, next the cattleman and sheep-herder, and finally the farmer. The trader sometimes carried his goods overland by pack-train, but more commonly he made his slow way up the muddy current of the turbulent Missouri, and established his post somewhere along its upper course.

The Trader.

From such posts the trapper usually pushed out into the haunts of the beaver, taking little except traps and his rifle and ammunition, for he trusted for food almost solely to the game he could kill. Furs weighed little, and if he went in with horses, he brought out his spoil on their backs; if afoot, he might build a boat and descend one of the numerous streams to the great river. Usually he sold his catch to the traders of the country, but occasionally he might float it down to a better market in St. Louis.

The Trapper.

As gold and silver were discovered, the miner followed the trapper into the land. He required more supplies than did the trapper, and to meet his needs trails were opened, and pack-trains, and later wagon-trains, made their slow way to his diggings. Still his product, like that of the trapper, had little weight and bulk in comparison to value, and the placer miner, in rich ground, could operate without the railroad. Quartz-mining and stamping-mills were another matter.

The Miner.

Following the miner and close on the heels of the vanishing buffaloes came the cowboys, with their herds of long-horned cattle ranging free over the plains and through the valleys. The cattleman's product could transport itself, and herds of branded steers were often driven hundreds of miles to the end-of-steel, whence they were carried by rail to Kansas City or Chicago. A rival of the cattleman was the sheep-herder, and many were the bitter battles fought by these two for possession of a choice range.

The Cowboy.

The Western cattle business first attained importance in

Texas, where a wild variety, descended from those brought over by the Spaniards, had long thrived on the nutritious native grasses. Gradually cattle-raising became more and more profitable and spread to the northward.

The "Long Drive."

A day came when some cattlemen annually made the "Long Drive" from Texas to Dakota, Wyoming, or Montana; that is, as the summer sun scorched the grass of the plains they would move their herds slowly northward and thus keep them on fresh grass. In the fall they would sell the cattle to stock up ranches that were being established in the north country or to be killed for beef. Even many of the cattlemen who did not make the Long Drive would move their herds northward from Texas across the "Territory" or the "Panhandle" to some shipping-point on the railroad. Those were the halcyon days of gambling-dens and dance-halls, of cowboys who wore fifty-dollar broad-brimmed hats, enormous spurs, and *chaparajos*, and "shot up" towns; of "rustlers" who altered brands and ran off cattle and horses; of terrors to desperadoes like "Wild Bill" Hickock, marshal of Hayes City.

The prices of horses and cattle often fell so low that ranching frequently was more picturesque than profitable, but the grass on the public domain cost nothing, and the mere romance of the business attracted many men into it, even Easterners and Englishmen. Among the former was Theodore Roosevelt, who for several years owned the "Elkhorn Ranch" on the Little Missouri River in western Dakota. His narratives of his experiences as a rancher and big-game hunter vividly describe certain phases of Western life in that period.

Ranching.

Not far behind the cattleman came the homesteader, with his prairie-schooner, his draught-horses, oxen, and milch cows, his pigs, ploughs, and barbed-wire fences. The last soon put an end to the free ranges, except where the soil was too arid to be cultivated successfully without irrigation. Cowboys, "longhorns," round-ups, and romance gave place to prosaic fields of wheat, oats, alfalfa, and potatoes.

The Homesteader.

Down to the Civil War settlers on the public domain were required to pay for their land, though the price was never large. For many years there was agitation in favor of giving The the land to actual settlers, but this plan aroused Homestead much Southern opposition, and it was not until Law. 1862 that Congress passed the celebrated Homestead law. Under it any citizen of the United States twenty-one years of age, or any one of that age who had declared an intention of acquiring citizenship, might become the owner of a piece of surveyed land up to 160 acres by residing on it for five years and paying certain nominal entry-fees. This Homestead Law, with its future amplifications, constituted an invitation to all the world to come to America and receive free land. In the words of a popular song:

> "Of all the mighty nations in the East or in the West
> This glorious Yankee nation is the greatest and the best;
> We have room for all creation and our banner is unfurled,
> Here's a general invitation to the people of the world.
>
> Come along, come along, make no delay,
> Come from every nation, come from every way;
> Our lands are broad enough, don't be alarmed,
> For Uncle Sam is rich enough to give us all a farm."

Every year tens of thousands at home and abroad accepted the invitation and received millions of rich acres from the public domain. The homestead policy not only hastened the Free Land settlement of the West but—and this point deserves a Safety- emphasis—long served as a sort of safety-valve Valve. whereby men dissatisfied with economic and social conditions in long-settled districts could escape to a new and freer environment. From the moment that free land became practically exhausted industrial and social problems became more acute.

Let us turn now to some of the details of the development of specific Western communities. Following the discovery of gold in California in '48, that region was settled so rapidly that "Jonah's gourd" ceased to be any longer "the symbol of mir-

aculous growth," and by the beginning of our period the State
contained half a million people.   It was still primarily a land
California.   of gold-miners, but wheat-farming was beginning
to take on "bonanza" proportions in some of its
rich valleys, the wine vintage reached 3,500,000 gallons by
1867, lumbering flourished in the incredible forests of immense
trees, and in the south oranges, lemons, figs, English walnuts,
and similar products were "growing in sub-tropical profusion."
Already California was one of the wonder spots of the world,
and after the completion of the Pacific railroad San Francisco
became the main American gateway to the Orient.

As in the case of California, the first important influx of white
settlement into most of the mountain States resulted from the
discovery of mineral wealth. California had developed a pro-
Prospectors   fessional mining class of eager prospectors who were,
and Their   says a historian of the West, Professor Paxson, "mo-
Work.
bile as quicksilver, restless and adventurous as all
the West, which permeated into the most remote recesses of
the mountains and produced before the Civil War was over,
as the direct result of their search for gold, not only Colorado,
but Nevada and Arizona, Idaho and Montana.   Activity was
constant during these years all along the Continental Divide.
New camps were being born overnight, old ones were abandoned by magic.   Here and there cities rose and remained to
mark success in the search. Abandoned huts and half-worked
diggings were scars covering a fourth of the continent."

Small discoveries of gold in the desolate region of the present
Nevada, then a part of Utah Territory, resulted in 1858 in the
founding of Carson City, but it was not until the spring of
Nevada.   1859 that the finding of incredibly rich silver deposits near Gold Hill east of Lake Tahoe produced
a real "stampede" thither.   In five years a hundred million
dollars in ore was mined from the sides of the mountains, and
the "Comstock lode" and bonanza towns like Virginia City
were famous the world over.   Among those who sought their
fortunes in the new country was a young journalist named
Samuel L. Clemens, who subsequently penned a graphic ac-

count of those wild days in *Roughing It.* In 1861 Nevada was made a separate territory, and in 1864 the exigencies of Union politics caused Congress to admit the "child of the Comstock lode" as a State, though the actual population scarcely justified such a step. No other State has been so much dependent upon mining as has Nevada, and the census figures furnish a rough index to the prosperity of the mining industry: in 1870 the population was 42,491, in 1880 it had risen to 62,266, in 1890 and 1900 it had declined to 47,355 and 42,335 respectively, and in 1900 it had risen to 61,875. After yielding more than $300,000,000 in silver and gold bullion the Comstock lode was finally exhausted, but rich discoveries of silver, gold, and copper were made elsewhere, and such camps as Tonopah, Ely, and Goldfield became famous.

In the summer of 1858 rumors reached Missouri that gold had been discovered in the Pike's Peak region, and soon hundreds of prairie-schooners bearing such legends as "Pike's Peak or Bust" were pushing westward across the plains. Groups of delvers in the sands of Cherry Creek combined and took the name of Denver City—named in honor of the governor of Kansas Territory—of which the new gold region then formed a part. Other towns sprang up, but some were short-lived, for not a few of the "finds" proved of trifling importance. Many argonauts, "bitter, disgusted, and poor," returned to the States, and their wagons on the homeward way not infrequently bore such mottoes as "Busted, by Gosh!" Others persevered and prospered either as miners or by turning their hands to farming and other occupations. When Horace Greeley visited the West in 1859, Denver was still composed of Indian lodges and a couple of hundred log cabins, with earth floors and mud roofs, but by 1864 it contained 4,000 inhabitants, and a choice corner lot had been sold for $12,000. The placer diggings soon became exhausted, but rich gold and silver quartz veins were discovered in many places and furnished a more solid basis for prosperity. In 1861 Colorado was formally organized as a separate territory, and in 1876 it was admitted to the Union, being popularly known as "the Centennial State."

Colorado.

About 1861 gold was found in the sands of Grasshopper Creek in what is now Montana. Bannack City sprang up "with mining-camp rapidity," and soon a couple of thousand prospectors were gathered along a crooked street that ran down the narrow gulch. In 1863 a rich strike was made in Alder Gulch between the Beaverhead and Madison Rivers, and Virginia City, at first named Varina in honor of Mrs. Jefferson Davis, came into being, and by 1864 had a population of perhaps 10,000. As early as 1860 gold was discovered in the Clearwater country of what is now Idaho, but the real history of this State may be said to begin with the finding of gold in the Boisé Basin two years later. In 1863 Idaho, which included the present Montana and most of Wyoming, was organized as a territory, but Montana was set apart in 1864, and Wyoming, which for a time had been reattached to Dakota, in 1868, the same year that the Union Pacific reached Cheyenne. The building of the Northern Pacific, completed in 1883, and the discovery of vast copper deposits at Butte greatly aided the development of Montana.

(marginal note:) Montana, Idaho, and Wyoming.

Of the mining camps Professor Paxson has said, in his *The Last American Frontier*, that they developed a type of life unlike any other that America had known. Their picturesque features misled thoughtless people into regarding them as romantic, but at best the dark places were only "accentuated by the tinsel of gambling and adventure." He continues:

A single street meandering along a valley, with one-story huts flanking it in irregular rows, was the typical mining camp. The saloon and the general store, sometimes combined, were its representative institutions. Deep ruts along the streets bore witness to the heavy wheels of the freighters, while horses loosely tied to all available posts . . . revealed the regular means of locomotion. . . . Few decent beings habitually lived in the towns. The resident population expected to live off the miners, either in way of trade, or worse. The bar, the gambling house, the dance-hall have been made too common in description to need further account. In the reaction against loneliness, the extremes of drunkenness, debauchery and murder were only too frequent in these places of amusement.

(marginal note:) The Mining Camp.

In 1875–76 rumors of gold in the Black Hills caused a rush thither, despite the danger of being scalped by the Sioux owners, but the diggings presently petered out, and Dakota was to owe its main development to the discovery that its prairies would grow wheat. In the '80's native Americans and hardy immigrants from the Scandinavian countries and Germany braved the northern blizzards, and the rapidity with which the tough sod was broken and prairie-dog villages gave place to sod huts and waving fields of grain was one of the wonders of the age.

The Dakota Wheat-Fields.

An important factor in the development of the Dakotas, Montana, and the Pacific Northwest was the completion in 1883 of the Northern Pacific Railroad, which had reached Bismarck, on the Missouri, just as the panic of 1873 brought ruin to its promoters, Jay Cooke and Company. In 1879 the road was revived under the presidency of Frederick Billings, but its completion was largely due to the activities of Henry Villard, a German journalist and financier who was a son-in-law of William Lloyd Garrison. The outcome of the venture proved financially disastrous to Villard personally, but the road immensely benefited the whole Northwest.

The Northern Pacific Railroad.

Railroads made the plains more easily accessible, but it is beyond question that settlement of the prairies would have been much slower if it had not been for the development of the labor-saving device known as McCormick's reaper. Cyrus H. McCormick took up, when scarcely more than a boy, the development of an idea that had ruined his father. His first patent for a machine to cut grain was granted in 1834, but it was not until 1840 that the device was placed on the market. He established a factory in Chicago about 1846, perfected self-rakes, mowing-machines, and finally the self-binder, and lived till the whir of his invention was "heard around the world." By using McCormick's devices one man could do the work of many men, and W. H. Seward once expressed the view that owing to them "the line of civilization moves westward thirty miles a year."

Effects of McCormick's Reaper on Settlement of the West.

The passing of the frontier and the Wild West was bewildering in its rapidity. As Whittier wrote:

"Behind the scared squaw's birch canoe,
    The steamer smokes and raves;
And city lots are staked for sale
    Above old Indian graves.

I hear the tread of pioneers
    Of nations yet to be:
The first low wash of waves where soon
    Shall roll a human sea.

The rudiments of Empire here
    Are plastic yet and warm;
The chaos of a mighty world
    Is rounding into form!"

"The West has changed," wrote one who beheld the transformation. "The old days are gone. The house dog sits on the hill where yesterday the coyote sang. The fences are short and small, and within them grow green things instead of gray. There are many smokes rising over the prairie, but they are wide and black instead of thin and blue."

The disappearance of the Wild West meant progress in civilization, yet many people viewed its passing with regret. It is not meet that all the land should be tamed and parcelled out
The National Parks.
into farms and town lots. For the sake of posterity lovers of nature in its primeval forms sought to preserve unspoiled some of the choicest bits of the Western wonderland. In 1872 Congress set apart 3,344 square miles of northwestern Wyoming as the Yellowstone National Park, and this area was subsequently doubled. The spouting geysers and other natural wonders of the region had first been discovered by John Colter, one of Lewis and Clark's men, who had remained in the mountains to trap beaver; but seventy years elapsed before a skeptical world was convinced of their existence. The park was also made a sanctuary for wild animals; and buffaloes, elk, black and grizzly bears, bighorn sheep, and other animals roam there in large numbers. Many other parks have since been created, among them the

General Grant and Sequoia Parks, partly designed to preserve the world's largest living trees; Yosemite and Grand Canyon Parks; Mesa Verde, with its cliff-dwellings; and Mount Lassen Park, with its volcano. In the grandeur and variety of their natural wonders the national parks far surpass the scenery of Switzerland, but it is only recently that the mass of Americans have come to realize their attractions.

CHAPTER IX

AN INTERLUDE

PRESIDENT HAYES was an able, honest man who earnestly sought to live up to the maxim, announced in his inaugural address, that "he serves his party best who serves his country best." He gathered round him an unusually capable group of advisers, including William M. Evarts as secretary of state, John Sherman as secretary of the treasury, and Carl Schurz as secretary of the interior. In the hope of helping to close the chasm that still yawned between the sections, he called to the head of the Post Office Department David M. Key, of Tennessee, an ex-Confederate soldier. He had even considered asking General Joseph E. Johnston to become secretary of war, but gave up the idea when he discovered that the step would arouse wide-spread opposition. "Great God! governor, I hope you are not thinking of doing anything of that kind!" exclaimed one horrified Republican to whom he mentioned the possibility.

The President's wife, Lucy Webb Hayes, exercised an influence on the course of events fully equal to that of a cabinet member. She was a high-minded, energetic, charming woman, who, like Abigail Adams, was a model of the domestic virtues. She did much to restore a wholesome simplicity in the White House, and, being a strong prohibitionist, she banished intoxicating liquors from the President's table. The innovation was bitterly attacked in some quarters and warmly defended in others. On one occasion the witty Evarts was asked how a certain state dinner had gone off, and he replied: "Excellently, the water flowed like champagne!" In course of time, however, it was whispered that the White House chef had taken compassion on thirsty souls and had evolved for their benefit a dessert composed of an orange skin filled with a "delicious frozen punch, a chief ingredient of which was strong old Santa Cruz rum." Thenceforth this dessert was very popular among the knowing, who called it "the Life-Saving Station"; and there was much quiet merriment at the expense of the good hostess, who, it was presumed, was ignorant of the matter. From President Hayes's diary, however, we learn: "The joke of the Roman punch oranges was not on us, but on the drinking people. My orders were to flavor them *rather strongly* with the same flavor that is found in Jamaica rum. This took! There was not a drop of spirits in them!"

Under President Hayes much was done to improve administrative efficiency and to weed out dishonesty, and he made an earnest effort to introduce civil service reform. Back in 1871

Hayes and Civil Service Reform. Congress, under pressure of public opinion, had authorized the President to prescribe rules for the entrance of men into the civil service and to name a body of men to aid him in the work. Grant appointed a commission of seven members, headed by George William Curtis, an eminent editor and reformer. But practical politicians sneered at the "Chinese system," which deprived them of their patronage, and Congress in 1873 failed to make any further appropriation for the work, with the result that the commission, though it still had a nominal existence, could accomplish virtually nothing. Hayes repeatedly urged upon Congress the desirability of the reform, but did not succeed in prodding that body into action.

In 1877 an investigation into the affairs of the New York custom-house resulted in the disclosure of mismanagement and undue political activity on the part of many of the officials,

Conflict with Conkling. who formed part of the "machine" of Senator Roscoe Conkling, the proud Republican boss of the State. Hayes removed Chester A. Arthur, collector of the port, and A. B. Cornell, the naval officer, and thereby precipitated a bitter controversy with Conkling and other senators over the patronage question. A majority of the Senate at first sustained Conkling but later accepted the President's nominees. In New York, however, the "Stalwarts," as one wing of the Republican party was coming to be known, nominated Cornell for governor, and elected him, in spite of considerable defection known as "Young Scratchers."

Temporarily the efforts of Hayes in behalf of civil service seemed almost barren of results, but what he did served to keep the subject agitated. Meanwhile other reformers were at work helping to educate the public as to the need of the reform. In 1877 a civil service reform association was organized in New York and quickly spread to other States. Four years later a national civil service reform league was formed. Thus the seeds were being sown; the harvest was not far in the future.

The President's attitude toward the civil service and his withdrawal of the troops from the support of Southern Carpet-Bag governments aroused bitter hostility among many Republicans, while Democrats criticised him even more vigorously than is the usual custom on the part of the opposition. Favorite Democratic names for him were "the *de facto* President," "Old Eight to Seven," "The Usurper," and "The Boss Thief," while their newspapers never lost an opportunity to refer to the "Great Steal." To a crowd of admirers assembled in front of his house at 15 Gramercy Park, in New York City, Tilden declared that he had been cheated out of the presidency by a "political crime," which the American people would not condone "under any pretext or for any purpose."

Democratic Attitude toward Hayes.

In order to gather political ammunition, the House of Representatives, which was controlled by the Democrats, created (May 17, 1878) what was known as the "Potter Committee" to investigate once more the elections in Louisiana and Florida. The Democratic members of this committee labored with zeal and took much testimony discreditable to their opponents, being greatly aided by several Southern Republicans who were disgruntled because they felt that they had not been properly rewarded by the Hayes administration. Long lists were also made of Repub-

The Potter Committee.

licans connected with the Southern elections who had since been given lucrative federal offices, and an attempt was made to show that the appointments had been made as rewards for corrupt services. One member of the committee, Benjamin F. Butler, who was now an independent, said of the appointments that the most charitable construction was that "*post hoc* is not always *propter hoc*."

The jubilant Democrats broadcasted the Potter Committee revelations over the country, and confidently looked forward to a bountiful political harvest, but an unexpected turn to the investigation suddenly dampened their hopes and revived the spirits of their depressed opponents.

The Cipher Despatches.

It so happened that the New York *Tribune*, a Republican paper, had in its possession several hundred cipher despatches that had been transmitted by Democratic leaders during the exciting days of the disputed election. By using methods more suggestive of Poe's *Gold Bug* than of an event in real life, two ingenious members of the *Tribune* staff managed to discover the "keys" to all except a few messages. The translations of some revealed the fact that Democratic agents had attempted to purchase Southern electors and returning boards, the sums named being enormous; and the sensation created by publication of the despatches was all the greater because many of them were transmitted from or to Tilden's residence, being addressed to or signed by his nephew, Colonel W. T. Pelton. Republican pressure forced the Potter Committee to investigate the cipher despatches. Some of the Democrats concerned admitted their own complicity, but all did their best to shield Tilden. Tilden himself denied having taken any part in the corrupt negotiations, and testified that when the negotiations came to his attention he ordered that they be discontinued. Most historians are inclined to acquit him of blame in the matter. The general effect of the cipher-despatch disclosures was, however, to blanket the other revelations made by the Potter Committee, and to render ineffective the Democratic cry of "fraud."

Throughout the Hayes administration the Democrats controlled the House of Representatives, and during the last two years of it they controlled the Senate also. One of their main efforts was directed toward repealing the federal laws designed to protect the political rights of the Southern negroes. By refusing to appropriate money for the army the House finally forced the Senate and the President to accept a bill (June 18, 1878) prohibiting the use of troops at the polls. Subsequently Hayes vetoed eight measures aimed at the remaining "force bills." The "force" legislation that survived became almost a dead letter, and some of it was declared unconstitutional in 1882. Most of what remained was repealed by a Democratic Congress in 1894.

Struggle over Federal Election Laws.

The currency question continued to excite much controversy during this administration. The country had not yet fully recovered from the effects of the panic of 1873, and the debtor class, to which many Western and Southern farmers belonged, inclined to oppose the resumption of specie payments and to favor a further inflation of the currency. In their opinion it was a hardship that they should be compelled to pay their debts in dearer dollars than those they had borrowed. With this view we ought not to quarrel, though we can hardly sympathize with the desire of many to pay in cheaper dollars than those they had obtained. Honest creditors, on the other hand, thought that they ought to be paid in dollars that were at least no cheaper than those they had loaned, while the grasping were eager for contraction, which would obviously be to their interest.

The Currency Question.

In the elections of 1878 the "Greenback" party, which had had a ticket in the field in 1876, cast a million votes, while inflationist sentiment ran strongly even in the two older parties. During 1877 and 1878 persistent efforts were made to repeal the Resumption Act of 1875, or to postpone its execution, but all came to naught except that a provision for the retirement of the greenback circulation in excess of $300,000,000 was repealed. In preparation for

Resumption Carried out.

the appointed day Secretary of the Treasury Sherman was careful to gather by December, 1878, a gold reserve of $142,-000,000, which was about two-fifths of the amount of outstanding notes. In consequence resumption was effected without creating a financial ripple. The report from the New York subtreasury for January 2 (the 1st, the date fixed by the act, having fallen on Sunday) showed only $135,000 of notes had been presented for coin, while $400,000 of gold had been turned in for notes! Gold and greenbacks had at last been put upon a par, and, as Sherman had predicted, when the public found they could have either gold or notes, they preferred the notes.

Resumption was a great triumph of sound finance, and the credit for bringing it about belongs first of all to Sherman, the author of the act, and the man who put it into execution. In this and in other matters, notably in refunding bonds at a lower rate of interest, he showed himself one of the greatest of our public financiers.

Owing largely to the development of rich silver mines in the Western States and Mexico the world's production of the white metal had for some years been increasing more rapidly than

Silver Demonetized in 1873.

that of gold. As a result the relative value of the two metals was changing in favor of gold. In 1860 the ratio had been 15 to 1, in 1873 it was 16 to 1, and by 1877 it was 17 to 1. In 1867 an international conference that met in Paris recommended the adoption of the single gold standard, and most great nations gravitated in that direction. In 1873 Congress in codifying the coinage laws omitted from the standard list the silver dollar, which had been little used for nearly forty years, and this "demonetization of silver," which attracted little attention at the time, was subsequently denounced as "the Crime of 1873."

The decreasing value of silver served to make that metal attractive to advocates of cheap money, and under Hayes a strong demand arose for the restoration of bimetallism. In 1877-78 debtors and the silver-producing barons of the West rallied enthusiastically in favor of a bill introduced by Richard

P. Bland, a Democratic Representative from Missouri, to restore silver to "its ancient legal equality with gold as a debt-
paying money." Thenceforth any owner of silver
The Bland-
Allison Act. bullion was to have the right to bring it to the
mint and have it coined at the ratio of 15.62 to 1.
The bill passed the House, but the Senate, on motion of Senator Allison of Iowa, struck out the "free and unlimited"
feature, and provided instead that the secretary of the treasury
must purchase monthly not less than $2,000,000 nor more than
$4,000,000 worth of silver bullion and coin it into money.
Finding that they could not pass the original measure, the
radical advocates of silver, on the theory that half a loaf is
better than no bread, consented to accept the Bland-Allison
bill, as it was called, and the measure became a law over the
President's veto (February 28, 1878).

During the next eleven years (February 28, 1878 to November
1, 1889) $286,930,633.64 worth of silver bullion was purchased
under the act and coined into 343,638,001 standard dollars,
but it was found difficult to keep them in circulation, and they
persisted in drifting back into the vaults of the treasury in
payment of government dues and taxes. On November 1,
1889, less than a fifth were in circulation.

The Hayes administration was marked by unrest in many
other matters. A description of the great railroad strike of
1877 will be given in the next chapter. Another manifestation
of discontent was the "Sand-lot" movement, or
Kearneyism. Kearneyism. The originator of this agitation was
an Irishman named Dennis Kearney, who was the prime mover
in founding (September 12, 1877) the "Workingman's Party
of California," an organization that demanded abolition of
land and moneyed monopolies, also shorter hours for labor, but
laid most stress on excluding the Chinese.

In the early years following the discovery of gold these
almond-eyed Celestials had been welcomed on the West Coast,
for they willingly did cooking, laundering, and other work
that white men disliked. In 1868 the Burlingame Treaty
formally recognized their right to enter the United States, and

the census taken two years later showed that they numbered 56,000, all but 467 of whom were west of the Rockies. Already, however, white laborers were beginning to feel their competition, for the Chinese were frugal and hard-working, willing to work for wages on which a white man would starve. Furthermore, their customs were outlandish, their habits repellent, and they gathered in filthy, congested districts where strange and abominable vices were practised. In 1871 a mob in Los Angeles shot or hanged more than a score of Chinese; similar brutal scenes became common over the West. Attacks upon Chinese quarters formed, in fact, a reasonably safe sort of diversion, for the dwellers in such places rarely made any effective resistance, and their government at home was too weak to exact satisfaction for outrages against its citizens abroad.

The Chinese Question.

Kearney's party brought the hostility to the Celestials to a head. Kearney, imitating Cato, habitually ended all of his speeches—which were usually made on the vacant "sand lots" of San Francisco—with the slogan, "The Chinese must go!" In 1879, in alliance with the Grangers, the new party controlled the State constitutional convention and inserted into the new fundamental law clauses aimed at the Chinese, but these and some State laws having the same object were set aside by the federal Supreme Court.

Kearney's Crusade.

For years the East gave scant attention to the Chinese question, but when Celestials began to appear in that section, Eastern workingmen, fearing their "cheap labor," made common cause with their Western brethren. Interested capitalists and disinterested philanthropists vainly strove to quiet the agitation; Western mobs continued to maltreat and murder the "heathen Chinee." In 1879 Congress passed a bill restricting the immigration of the Chinese, but Hayes vetoed the measure on the ground that it was in conflict with the Burlingame Treaty. Next year, however, the United States persuaded China to modify that treaty, and in 1882 legislation excluding Chinese coolies for ten years was enacted. In 1892 the drastic Geary law extended the period

Chinese Exclusion Acts.

for another decade, despite the protests of China. Later legislation continued the prohibition, and in recent years the number of Chinese in the United States has tended to diminish rather than increase. In 1910 there were only 71,531. Only students and certain other designated classes are now permitted to come into the country at all.

Historians are inclined to agree that Hayes ruled firmly and patriotically in a confused and critical period, but he never managed to achieve much popularity. In his letter of acceptance he had declared that if elected he would not be a candidate for a second term, and the "Stalwart" faction of his party were determined to hold "Granny Hayes," as many of them called him, to his word.

Among the candidates for the Republican nomination in 1880 were Secretary Sherman of Ohio, Senator Blaine of Maine, and Senator Edmunds of Vermont, but the name that attracted most attention was that of General Grant, The Grant Third-Term Movement. whom certain Stalwart leaders, notably Conkling of New York, Don Cameron of Pennsylvania, and Logan of Illinois, were bringing forward for a third term. On his retirement in 1877 Grant had made a tour around the world, in the course of which he had been received with high honors that were very flattering to the American people. Many Republicans believed that his added experience would enable him to avoid the blunders of his previous tenure of office, while, to combat the arguments against a third term, it was urged that the precedent applied only to a third consecutive term. His candidacy was greeted with warm approval and equally warm opposition.

The Republican convention, which met at Chicago on June 2, 1880, praised the record of the Republican party and the administration of President Hayes and denounced the Democratic party's "supreme and insatiable lust of office Republican Platform. and patronage" and the methods taken by it to secure a "solid South." The platform, as reported, omitted any reference to civil service reform, but a Massachusetts delegate proposed a "plank" demanding that "Congress shall so legislate that fitness, ascertained by proper practical tests, shall admit to the public service." Thereupon a delegate from Texas, Flanagan by name, won nation-wide notoriety by springing to his feet and proclaiming the old slogan, "To the victors belong the spoils." "What are we up here for?" he demanded, mystified. Probably a majority of the delegates sympathized with Flanagan's view, but they felt it unsafe to go on record to that effect, so the amendment was adopted.

Conkling presented Grant's name in a striking speech which began:

"And when asked what State he hails from, our sole reply shall be,
He hails from Appomattox and its famous apple tree."

The speech of James A. Garfield in Sherman's behalf was also a splendid effort, and it was to have unexpected results. On the first ballot Grant led with 304 votes, Blaine was a close second with 284, Sherman had 93, and Edmunds 34, with the rest scattering. Grant's "phalanx," as his delegates were called, stuck to him to the end, but his vote never rose above 313, which was 65 short of a majority. Sherman's vote rose to 120 on the thirtieth ballot, but he could get no more, while Blaine's number never exceeded 285. On the second ballot one delegate had voted for Garfield, and on several succeeding ballots he received 1 or 2 votes; on the thirty-fourth ballot Wisconsin gave him 16 votes, making him a total of 17. To show his loyalty to Sherman, Garfield sprang to his feet to make a protest, but Senator George F. Hoar, the permanent chairman, who tells us in his *Autobiography* that he secretly hoped that the deadlock would be broken in the way that actually happened, ruled Garfield out of order and commanded him to sit down. On the next ballot Garfield received 50, and on the next a mad rush to him ensued, with the result that he received 399 votes and the nomination. As a sop to Conkling and the disappointed Stalwarts, the convention then named for the vice-presidency Chester A. Arthur, the man whom Hayes had removed from the collectorship of the port of New York.

James A. Garfield, who was thus unexpectedly nominated, was born at Orange, in the Western Reserve of Ohio, in 1831. His parents were poor, and as a boy he drove mules on the tow-

Garfield's Career and Character.

path of the Ohio Canal, but he managed to obtain a college education. When the Civil War came, he was president of a small institution known as Hiram College, but he entered the army and rose to the rank of a major-general, being later elected to the House of Representatives, where he served several terms. At the time he was nominated he had been elected by the Ohio Legislature to the Senate, but had not yet taken his seat. The story of his rise from poverty and obscurity made a strong popular appeal.

Many people supposed that the Democrats would renominate Tilden and under his leadership seek to "right the wrong" of 1876. But he was far from popular with most of the leaders,

Democrats Nominate Hancock and English.

and many believed that the cipher-despatch disclosures weakened his availability. When Tilden wrote a somewhat equivocal letter in which he expatiated upon his bad health and seemed to deprecate proposals to nominate him, most Democrats chose to interpret the missive as a definite declination, and in the convention, which met at Cincinnati (June 22), he received only a few votes. On the first ballot nearly a score of other candidates received more or less support, among them being Thomas F. Bayard of Delaware, Henry B. Payne of Ohio, Allen G. Thurman of Ohio, and Thomas A. Hendricks of Indiana, but General Winfield S. Hancock of Pennsylvania led, and on the second ballot he was nominated. The man thus selected was a veteran of both the Mexican and Civil Wars, and had greatly distinguished himself at Gettysburg and Spottsylvania. His fine appearance and soldierly bearing had won him the nickname of "the Superb." Although he had fought against the South, he had won favor in that section by showing, as a district commander, that he did not sympathize with the Congressional plan of reconstruction. As his associate on the ticket, the convention selected William H. English of Indiana, a former member of Congress in the days of the Kansas controversy.

In the campaign the Democratic orators harped constantly on the "fraud of 1876," an issue which their platform declared "dwarfs every other" and "imposes a more sacred duty upon the people of the Union than ever addressed the conscience of a nation of freemen." Republicans retorted with details of the cipher-despatch disclosures and with stories of the methods used by their antagonists to suppress the negro vote and maintain the "solid South." The tariff, the currency, and Garfield's alleged connection with the Crédit Mobilier scandal also received attention. In the last week of the canvass the Democrats also gave wide publicity to a forged document known as the "Morey letter," in which Garfield was represented as deprecating the agitation against "Chinese cheap labor." The letter was chiefly designed for effect on the Pacific coast, and probably won Hancock five of the six electoral votes of California. On their side, the Republicans caught up a phrase of Hancock's in which he characterized the tariff as "a local issue," and they tried to convince voters that such a statement revealed his abysmal ignorance of public questions. The fact is that in this period of transition the contest was little more than a struggle for office. Old issues were dead or dying, and neither party championed any great cause.

The October election in Maine proved discouraging to the Republicans, but they redoubled their efforts thereafter, and even the silent Grant took the stump in behalf of the ticket. Hancock carried the "solid South," but in the North and West he won only New Jersey, Nevada, and five of the six electoral votes of California—in all, 155 electoral votes. Garfield carried the same number of States but received 214 electoral votes and the presidency. The Republicans regained control of the House of Representatives, while the Senate would stand 37 Democrats, 37 Republicans, with the balance of power resting in the hands of the Vice-President and two independents.

The victory was speedily followed by a quarrel between the victors. Garfield at first sought to conciliate Senator Conkling of New York, but soon incurred his hostility by naming James G. Blaine, one of Conkling's bitterest enemies, as secretary of state, and by nominating W. H. Robertson for collector of the port of New York, a position which carried great weight in politics, as the collector had over a thousand subordinates who were expected to be political workers, according to the spoils system, upon which Conkling was largely dependent for his power. Robertson had repeatedly defied the Stalwart boss, and at the Chicago convention had supported Blaine instead of Grant. Conkling believed that in Robertson's appointment "he saw the fine Italian hand of Blaine." In his insane determination to make the President "bite the dust," Conkling made public a letter written by Garfield to stimulate the collection of campaign contributions from government employees. The disclosure brought discredit upon the President, but it did not enable Conkling to persuade the Senate to reject Robertson. He therefore petulantly resigned his seat in the Senate, and his example was followed by his colleague, Thomas C. Platt, who thereby won the nickname of "Me Too." The two expected and demanded a re-election as a vindication, but, to the delight and amusement of the country, the New York Legislature elected two other men, E. G. Lapham and Warner Miller. Conkling never again held public office, but Platt, a younger man, subsequently regained his power, and, as "the Easy Boss," was long a familiar figure in both State and national politics.

During the campaign Garfield had written to J. A. Hubbell, chairman of the Republican congressional committee, another letter of the same tenor as that which Conkling made public. This letter fell into the hands of Second Assistant Postmaster-General Brady. Brady and confederates had long been involved in corrupt practices in connection with the "star" mail routes, and when James, the new postmaster-general, began an investigation of these

The margin notes read:
The Garfield-Conkling Feud.

The "Star" Route Frauds.

frauds, Brady tried to frighten the President into stopping it. Failing, he published the Hubbell letter, and thus added to the scandal already created by the letter that Conkling had made public. Several prominent men were involved in the frauds, but the prosecution was hampered by all sorts of obstacles, and only one of the offenders, and he a minor one, was finally brought to justice.

Great crowds of office-seekers dogged Garfield's footsteps and crowded his waiting-room. Of course, many were disappointed. Among these was a half-crazed creature named

Garfield Assassinated.

Charles J. Guiteau, who had been at various times preacher, editor, "reformer," and politician. Personal resentment and an insane notion that the death of Garfield would help to close the yawning chasm in the Republican party determined Guiteau to kill the President. On July 2, 1881, Garfield and Secretary of State Blaine were walking on the platform of a railway station in Washington, waiting to take a train in order to attend commencement at Garfield's *alma mater*, Williams College, when Guiteau drew near and fired two bullets into the President's back. For eleven weeks the wounded man lingered between life and death, while optimistic and pessimistic bulletins alternately cheered and depressed his sympathetic countrymen. At last, after a brave fight for life, he died (September 19, 1881) at Elberon on the Jersey coast, whither he had been taken in the vain hope that the ocean breezes would benefit him. His murderer was brought to trial, and, despite a plea of insanity made in his behalf, he was convicted and hanged (June 30, 1882).

During Garfield's long illness the country remained virtually without a President, and various theories were proposed as to what should be done to meet the situation, but fortunately no

Arthur President.

vital questions pressed for a decision. On the day following his death Vice-President Arthur took the presidential oath in his New York home, and a few days later the ceremony was repeated in Washington. "Men may die," said the new President on the latter occasion, "but the fabrics of our free institutions remain unshaken."

Arthur's past record seemed to justify the prevailing impression that he was merely a second-rate politician. Furthermore, as he was a member of the Stalwart faction, which many people held responsible for the tragedy, he incurred a part of the odium. Little wonder, therefore, that millions deplored the fact that this "pot-house politician," as some newspapers called him, must take the place of Garfield, who was already idealized as a martyr. Fortunately Arthur was an abler and better man than most people supposed, and the tremendous responsibility placed upon his shoulders served to bring out the best that was in him, with the result that as President he displayed unexpected firmness and sagacity.

Arthur presently reorganized the cabinet, and only Secretary of War Lincoln, a son of the martyred President, remained in office for any length of time. Before the end of the year Blaine was succeeded by Frederick T. Frelinghuysen of New Jersey, and the "Man from Maine"

Cabinet Reorganized.

retired temporarily from politics, busying himself with the production of his well-known *Twenty Years of Congress*, the first volume of which was published in 1884. Otherwise the new President permitted most of Garfield's appointees to remain in office, and some of them repaid his generosity with ingratitude. The expectant Stalwarts won no special consideration from him, and some of them, including Conkling, soon drifted into hostility to his administration.

The murder of Garfield by a disappointed office-seeker directed the attention of the country in a dramatic way to the evils of the spoils system, and thus the tragedy had one good result. Although once a spoilsman, President Arthur discouraged the assessment of federal officials for political purposes, and in 1881 and again

The Pendleton Act.

in 1882 he urged upon Congress the desirability of civil service reform legislation. Public pressure proved so strong that early in 1883 the Pendleton bill, which had really been drawn by Dorman B. Eaton, a leading reformer, was enacted into law. The measure forbade the assessment of federal employees and provided for the appointment of a Civil Service Commission of three persons, who were to conduct examinations for persons wishing to enter what was known as the "classified service" of the government. The law did not require the appointment of those who passed with the highest grades, and some political manipulation remained possible; nevertheless, a great step forward had been taken. Arthur made Eaton chairman of the commission, with John M. Gregory and Leroy D. Thoman as associates. He also placed 13,780 offices in the classified service.

Spoils politicians long continued to sneer at "snivel service," as they dubbed the reform, and to call its supporters "goody-goodies" and "holier-than-thous," but their ridicule and hostility alike proved unavailing.

Another subject that was attracting considerable attention in these years was that of polygamy in Utah and adjoining territories. Since their migration across the Great Plains to the Salt Lake Basin in the '40's the Mormons had The Edmunds Act. prospered exceedingly, and some of them, as their money multiplied, had made corresponding increases in the number of their wives. This state of affairs had been frequently denounced in party platforms, and that of the Republican party in 1880 had declared "that, slavery having perished in the States, its twin barbarity, polygamy, must die in the Territories." In 1882 Congress enacted the so-called "Edmunds Law," which prohibited under heavy penalties the practice of polygamy in the Territories. Under this law many polygamists were disfranchised, and several hundred were sentenced to imprisonment.

This administration was also notable for beginning the creation of a new American navy. At the close of the Civil War the American navy had been one of the strongest in the world, but practically no new vessels had since been constructed, and ships that were considered powerful then were now antiquated, obsolete hulks that were fit for little except the junk heap. In March, 1883, Congress authorized the construction of three steel protected cruisers and a despatch-boat, and these vessels, which were named the

Boston, *Atlanta*, *Chicago*, and *Dolphin* respectively, were begun before Arthur retired from office. None of them was a vessel of great power, but they formed the beginning of a navy that was to render notable services to America and to humanity.

A subject with which Congress grappled less successfully was the tariff. There had been some tariff tinkering in the early '70's, but the duties in force were practically the exceedingly high ones levied in the Civil War, the primary purpose of which was revenue rather than protection. There was some popular complaint over the operation of these duties, and they had been attacked by certain theoretical political economists, but the tariff had not yet become a political issue of prime importance, and the main cause for the attempted revision was that the high duties were filling the treasury to overflowing, thereby withdrawing money from circulation and increasing the temptation to extravagant expenditure. Thus the surplus in 1881 amounted to $101,000,-000 and in 1882 to $145,000,000.

The Tariff Question.

In May, 1882, Congress created a commission to study the matter, and this body, after an extended investigation, recommended reductions of at least 20 per cent. But Republican advocates of protection joined with certain similarly minded Democrats, notably ex-Speaker Randall, who came from the great manufacturing State of Pennsylvania, and after much debate, in which the spectre of the competition of European "pauper labor" was made to do yeoman service, Congress in 1883 passed a new tariff act which provided for reductions so slight that most were scarcely perceptible, while some schedules were actually raised. In the words of the *Nation*, "the kaleidoscope has been turned a hair's breadth, and the colors transposed a little, but the component parts are the same."

Tariff of 1883.

The Republicans lost control of the House of Representatives in the election of 1882, but in local contests of the next year the pendulum swung back in their direction, hence both parties approached the greater contest of 1884 with some degree of hope. President Arthur desired to be the Republican standard-bearer in that campaign, and if it had not been for the popularity of Blaine, he would probably have been nominated.

Republican
Pre-convention Contest
of 1884. The "Man from Maine" realized that he lacked the confidence of the reform element of his party and hesitated to make the race, for he feared that he could not be elected if nominated. He was determined, however, to defeat Arthur, and, in casting about for another candidate, hit upon General Sherman. But "Old Tecumseh" had noted the bitter political experiences of his friend Grant, and he wrote: "I would account myself a fool, a madman, an ass, to embark anew, at sixty-five years of age, in a career that may at any moment become tempest-tossed." Ultimately Blaine entered the race, as did also Arthur, George F. Edmunds of Vermont, John Sherman of Ohio, and John A. Logan of Illinois.

The convention that assembled at Chicago (June 3) contained a number of delegates who were to be notable figures in the future. William McKinley and Marcus A. Hanna sat

Blaine and Logan. with the delegation from Ohio, Benjamin Harrison with that from Indiana, Henry Cabot Lodge with that from Massachusetts, and Theodore Roosevelt with that from New York. Andrew D. White, George William Curtis, Roosevelt, Lodge, and others strenuously endeavored to defeat Blaine, but failed. The "Man from Maine's" followers neglected no device that might stampede the convention to him, and, among other things, passed a helmet and plume about the hall. On the first ballot he led the field with 334½ votes, with Arthur trailing next with 278; on each succeeding ballot Blaine's strength increased, and on the fourth he received 541 votes and the nomination. The convention then nominated Logan of Illinois for the vice-presidency.

Between Blaine and the reformers there was a bitter feud. Of them he had written: "They are noisy, but not numerous; pharisaical, but not practical; ambitious, but not wise; pretentious, but not powerful." The reformers had an even worse opinion of Blaine, for they believed that he had prostituted official position for pecuniary gain. Conferences of reformers held some months before had issued warnings aimed at his aspirations, and his nomination produced a schism in the party.

The Mugwumps. Some of the reform element, including White, Lodge, and Roosevelt, ultimately gave him grudging support, but many others, among them Henry Ward Beecher, Thomas Wentworth Higginson, George William Curtis, and Carl Schurz, refused to do so. Several prominent Republican newspapers, including the *New York Evening Post* and *Times*, the *Boston Herald* and *Advertiser*, and the *Springfield Republican*, took a like stand. A conference of reformers held in New York City (June 16) declared that Blaine and Logan represented "political methods and principles to which we are unalterably opposed. . . . We look with solicitude to the coming nominations by the Democratic party; they have the proper men; we hope they will put them before the people." Thus originated the political group known as the "Mugwumps," a name coined a few years before by the *Indianapolis Sentinel* but now applied by the *New York Sun*.

Cleveland and Hendricks. Hendricks, Thurman, Bayard, Randall, Tilden, and others were suggested for the Democratic nomination, but the man whom the Mugwumps expected to be named was Grover Cleveland of New York, and they were not disappointed. When the Democratic convention met in Chicago (July 8), Cleveland received a majority on the first ballot and on the second the necessary two-thirds and the nomination. For his associate on the ticket the convention named Hendricks of Indiana, Tilden's running mate in 1876.

Cleveland's Career. Cleveland was a newcomer in the national lists. He had never even seen the city of Washington, and did not see it until he went thither to be inaugurated President of the United States. He was the son of a Presbyterian clergyman and was born in 1837 at Caldwell, New Jersey, but when he was four years old the family moved to Fayetteville, New York. In his teens he "clerked" for a time in a general store; later he taught in an institution for the blind. When still in his teens he set out for the West, but settled instead at Buffalo, worked in a law office, and was admitted to the bar. In 1863 he was assistant district attorney for the county, and from 1870 to 1873 he served as sheriff. In 1881 a combination of Democrats and Independents elected him mayor of Buffalo. By making efficiency rather than politics the key-note of his administration he won such favorable notice that in 1882 he was nominated by the Democrats for governor of New York, and, partly owing to factional strife among the Republicans, he was elected by the unprecedented plurality of over 190,000. As governor he displayed the same hard-headed honesty and independence he had shown as mayor, and incurred the bitter hostility of Tammany Hall. He was not brilliant; he was a persistent plodder. His education had been limited; his outlook at this time was somewhat narrow. In his speeches and writings he was inclined to use ponderous, polysyllabic words—to make "the little fishes talk like whales." Brusque of manner and blunt of speech, primitive in his tastes, few Presidents have been more courageous or more stubborn, but with the latter quality went an energy and power which more tactful politicians were forced to recognize.

In the campaign much oratory was spilled on the subjects of the tariff and the "solid South," but there was no overshadowing issue, and the contest soon degenerated into one of personalities. Right-thinking people were nauseated by the tactics of both sides, and one editor fitly characterized the campaign as "worthy the stairways of a tenement-house."

A Mud-Slinging Campaign.

Both parties realized the importance of the great State of New York and concentrated their efforts in that pivotal commonwealth. Blaine's managers realized that he would suffer in this State from the antagonism of the Mugwumps and the hatred of Conkling, who was feeding fat his ancient grudge. But the Plumed Knight was popular with the Irish, for his mother was of that race, his sister was the superior of a Catholic convent, and he had championed the cause of Ireland; it was hoped, therefore, that he would gain enough Irish votes to more than make up for Republican defections. On the other hand, Cleveland, as gov-

An Alliterative Clergyman.

ernor, had offended the Catholics, the labor vote, and Tammany Hall. However, the loyalty of Tammany was won through the personal intercession of Hendricks, while the Irish Catholics were alienated from Blaine by the rash words of one of his own supporters. On the 29th of October Blaine received in the Fifth Avenue Hotel in New York City a large delegation of Protestant clergymen. Their spokesman, Doctor Samuel D. Burchard, in the course of his address, characterized the Democracy as "the party of Rum, Romanism, and Rebellion." Blaine failed to notice, or at least to rebuke, the alliterative allusion, and the same evening he was dined by many of the richest men of New York, including Jay Gould and other unpopular magnates. The Democratic managers saw their opportunity, and gave wide publicity to Blaine's "Millionaire Dinner" and to Burchard's unfortunate utterance, and, it was believed, managed to turn enough votes to decide the result.

Outside of New York, Cleveland carried three Northern States—Indiana, Connecticut, and New Jersey—and the "solid South," with a total of 183 electoral votes, while Blaine carried the rest of the Northern States, with a total of 182 electoral votes. The result hinged upon New York, and the contest in that State was so close that for days the outcome was uncertain. Meanwhile there was excitement throughout the country and many rumors and threats. At last the official count showed that Cleveland had carried the State by the narrow margin of 1,149 votes.

A Democratic Victory.

For the first time since 1856 the Democrats had won the presidency. Like Webster and Clay, the Plumed Knight was never to be President. Magnetic and popular though he was, the prize he coveted lay beyond his reach.

CHAPTER X

THE CHANGING ORDER

For almost a decade after the Civil War a state of lawlessness reigned in the Schuylkill and Shamokin mining districts of Pennsylvania. The disorders were the work of a mysterious secret order called the "Molly Maguires," whose members levied blackmail, mobbed and murdered mine bosses and "scabs," and in places were even in collusion with the police and county officials. They were so numerous and well organized that for years they were able to defy the law almost with impunity, but their secrets were finally ferreted out. Many of the Mollies were hanged, many others received long terms in prison, and the gang was broken up.

The "Molly Maguires."

Far more wide-spread but of much shorter duration was the famous railroad strike of 1877. In July, 1877, the Baltimore & Ohio Railroad lowered the wages of its employees for the fourth time in seven years, and thus precipitated the greatest strike the country had yet known. The strike began at Martinsburg, West Virginia (July 16, 1877), and spread rapidly to other States and other lines. Transportation and industry were speedily paralyzed. Bloody clashes between the strikers and the police and militia took place at Baltimore, Pittsburgh, and other towns; at Pittsburgh the mob completely controlled the city, pillaged property at will, and destroyed 100 locomotives and 2,000 cars. In many instances the police and even the militia proved powerless to preserve the peace; in a dozen States a situation developed resembling civil war; to many frightened people it seemed as if the very bases of the Republic were suddenly crumbling; excited journalists compared conditions with those in France under the Red Commune. In some places determined citizens

Railroad Strike of 1877.

formed committees of safety and organized special forces to save the country from anarchy, while the governors of several States called on the President for federal troops, and in most instances he complied. Owing to the hard times, many railroads were in the hands of federal receivers, and in several cases federal judges enjoined the strikers from interfering with the operation of such roads. In Missouri and Indiana the Democratic governors, for political reasons, refused to call on the President for troops, but troops were sent to those States on the demand of United States marshals. Though contemptuous of local and State forces, the strikers were overawed by the display of national power, and within two weeks the strike was at an end.

Labor troubles such as these were symptomatic of a great transformation in the life of the people of the United States. Americans had long been almost wholly an agricultural people, The Changing Order. with an abundance of fertile, unoccupied land to serve as a solvent for economic discontent. But in recent decades the nation had made great strides toward a new order of things. As the land filled with inhabitants, as new industries sprang up, the nation drifted away from the simplicity of an agricultural age, and its problems grew more and more complex. Day by day the struggle for existence became more and more like the bitter, grinding struggle that prevailed among the congested populations of Europe. Food, clothing, and shelter were increasingly difficult to obtain, and men found themselves more and more dependent on others for the mere opportunity to earn a living.

A century before there had begun, first in England, a new economic movement which in its influence on the lives and thoughts of mankind was to prove immeasurably more important than any political revolution in history. Hitherto manufacturing had been done almost wholly Industrial Revolution. by hand, laboriously and slowly, but by inventing labor-saving machinery, such as the spinning-jenny, the power-loom, and the steam-engine, man began to free himself from the limitations of his own puny strength and to harness the powers of nature to work for him. The transformation appeared first in textile industries, but gradually machinery came to be used more and more in other manufacturing; inventions multiplied until they became the greatest wonder of the world; electricity, as well as steam, was set to work; and a day came when man did little save direct the gigantic powers that his genius had enslaved.

One result of this Industrial Revolution*—even the name of which, strangely enough, is not to be found in some of our school histories—is that the quantity of goods that man can create and enjoy has been vastly increased. A few men with a cotton-gin can clean as much cotton as could a thousand using the old hand methods; a few hundred men and women with power-looms can weave more cotton cloth than the whole of the old cotton-weaving world put together; one modern printing-press can print more columns of reading matter in a few hours than all the American hand-presses in 1775 could print in a week. In fact, in many industries man's efficiency has been multiplied a hundred fold, a thousand fold, even ten thousand fold. Furthermore, the introduction and development of steam and electric transportation methods has enabled him to reach out to the ends of the earth for raw materials and to send the finished products where he will. The standard of living has been raised far higher among civilized peoples; even day-laborers now enjoy comforts and luxuries undreamed of by the wealthy before the great transformation.

Good Results of the Revolution.

In certain other respects the results have not been so roseate. A comparatively few people have managed to reap an undue share of the rich harvest. The standard of living has been raised for most classes, but the uplift has not been equal along the whole line, as Henry George pointed out in his widely read *Progress and Poverty*, published in 1879. Furthermore, the new order brought with it profound changes in the organization of industry and of society

Doubtful and Evil Features.

* This account of the Industrial Revolution is adapted from the author's *America in Ferment*, pp. 157–162.

in general. Great factories and factory cities, trusts and combines, child labor, and various other doubtful or evil features of contemporary life are all results of the great revolution.

In past ages industries were managed on comparatively simple lines. Under the old guild system, for example, John Treat, apprentice to Abner Dikeham, the weaver of woollens, worked in his employer's little shop alongside Dikeham himself, three or four other apprentices, and perhaps as many grown-up journeymen. His personal relations with Dikeman were close; they not only worked together in the same shop but they lived together in the same house; and if old Dikeham happened to have a pretty daughter Faith who suited John's fancy, the apprentice might dare to hope that he could win her. At all events, he became a journeyman when he grew up, could work for wages for whom he pleased, and if he proved to be a man of business ability, might become a master weaver himself, with his own shop, apprentices, journeymen, and pretty daughter. The guild system, to be sure, had broken down in many trades long before the Industrial Revolution began, but in most industries, however organized, the relations between employee and employer were still likely to be fairly close, and the passage from one class to the other was still comparatively easy.

Close Relations of Employer and Employee under Guild System.

The Industrial Revolution changed all that. Manufacturing came to be done in great factories, and the cost of machinery, tools, and buildings mounted so high that the transition from worker to employer became much more difficult. In the old days the cost of looms and other equipment for woollen weaving did not exceed the amount of a few months or years of a journeyman's wages; to-day the cost of such plants exceeds the combined wages of many men for whole lifetimes, and what is true of the woollen industry is true of many others. John Treat, the American descendant of mediæval John and Faith, if he begins as a laborer in a factory, has to reconcile himself to the probability that he will always remain a laborer. "Born an employee, die an

Transition from Worker to Employer Difficult.

employee" has become the general rule in a great number of industries, and the rule is all the more maddening because it is out of harmony with our ideal of freedom for the individual—an ideal that was being realized in some respects in the very period when the Industrial Revolution was developing. Occasionally, to be sure, a workman does make the passage to the employer class, but where one succeeds a hundred or a thousand fail. Realizing that the chances are so much against them, workers have acquired a class consciousness that did not exist before, and in many places and many industries have organized themselves into unions to protect their interests.

Furthermore, the employer himself has undergone a great transformation. Instead of one man owning a mill or factory, it came to be common for partnerships to be formed, and the partnership in turn often gave way before another idea. In the evolution of industrial society there developed a system of combination called a corporation, having the activities of individuals and infinitely greater power but without an individual's conscience or responsibility. A day came when corporations expanded or united until sometimes one great company would control not merely one factory or group of factories but practically a whole industry, with power to fix prices, to ruin competitors, and to dictate to the workmen in the industry. Employers even in different industries would organize to advance and protect their interests and more especially to enable them to resist the demands of their workers.

The Growth of Corporations.

The gulf between worker and employer thus became complete. In the old days both belonged to the craft guild and viewed matters either as workers or former workers, as employers or prospective employers. To-day each has his organization—to fight the other. It is a rare thing for the modern John Treat to labor alongside his employer, much less to woo and wed his daughter. If the employer is a corporation, the employer has no daughter. Even if he is an individual, he is often a man of vast interests which he commits to the care of

Gulf between Employee and Employer.

others, so that John Treat may not in his whole lifetime so much as set eyes on him. Under such conditions there can be little community of interest or understanding. Instead there is often lack of sympathy, and, too often, downright hostility.

The Industrial Revolution came much later in the United States than in England. It is generally considered to have begun in 1790 when Samuel Slater brought over from England Industrial to Rhode Island plans of textile machinery and set Revolution up a small factory, but it was not until the period in U. S. of the War of 1812 that manufacturing in the modern sense began to be common in the United States. It was later stimulated by protective duties, and grew with ever-increasing rapidity as the Civil War drew near, jumping from $1,000,000,-000 in 1850 to $1,900,000,000 in 1860. The Civil War gave manufacturing a great impetus, and thereafter the United States experienced an industrial development unequalled in history.

This vast growth was due in part to the expansion of old industries, in part to the creation of some that were entirely new. As a type of the former let us take the making of iron Iron and and steel. In colonial times this industry—partly Steel because of hostile British legislation—had attained Industry. only small dimensions. Even in 1791, when Alexander Hamilton made his famous report on American manufactures, the annual production amounted to only a few millions. There were furnaces for smelting ore in almost every State, but they were small, the industry was decentralized, and the making of nails was still "an occasional family manufacture."

In 1810 the total value of the product was only $14,400,000, but the War of 1812, by cutting off imports from abroad, gave the industry a considerable impetus. It still remained, however, The a widely scattered industry, for, owing to the abun-Charcoal dance of wood, American furnaces generally con-Period. tinued to use charcoal long after their British competitors had come almost entirely to coal. Charcoal-made iron, to be sure, was unsurpassed in quality, but the use of charcoal as a fuel tended to dispersion; wherever iron ore was discovered there small furnaces, using charcoal made from the adjoining forest, were likely to spring up.

In time anthracite coal came to be largely used in smelting the ore, and about 1849 a ton of anthracite iron rather than a ton of charcoal iron became the standard in market quota-

The Anthracite Period.

tions. With the growing importance of the new fuel the tendency was for the main production of iron to centre in the anthracite region, that is, on the highlands between the Delaware, Schuylkill, and Susquehanna Rivers. Many of the charcoal furnaces continued, however, to operate prosperously, for charcoal iron was—and still is—best for certain purposes, while the chief fabricators of iron were still the blacksmiths, "whose resounding shops stood at the crossroads in almost every township in the United States," and, owing to high costs of transportation, local furnaces could often profitably supply the smiths of their locality. As late as 1883 there were still two dozen forges of the old primitive Catalan type in western North Carolina, and another dozen across the border in Tennessee. The bar iron produced at these forges served as a legal tender in some places, and the producers brought it to the little country stores and exchanged it for coffee, sugar, and calico.

The reign of anthracite iron proved short; it was dethroned in turn by bituminous iron, that is, iron made with coke. This method had long been in use in England, and it was successfully

The Coke Period.

employed in a few places in the United States in the late '30's, but the anthracite region possessed certain transportation advantages and anthracite long remained low in price; it was not until railroads had revolutionized transportation and anthracite had risen that coke-made iron eclipsed its old rival, the date when the new aspirant triumphed being 1875. From 1880 onward coke-made iron had a twenty-fold increase in less than as many years. Again the centre of iron production shifted, crawling over the mountains into the drainage basin of the upper Ohio, and Connellsville coke and Pittsburgh became famous in the world of iron and steel.

Shortly after the crowning of coke iron there came a great change in the source of ore supply. Hitherto the main dependence had been comparatively low-grade local ores, from Pennsylvania, New Jersey, and New York, but vast deposits of much richer ore existed about Lake Superior, and these became increasingly important.

The New Mines about Lake Superior.

The Lake Superior ore was brought by cheap water transportation to the lower lakes, and thence transshipped to Pittsburgh and other centres, the total price of transportation per ton being lower than that at which the poorer ores could be delivered. A day came when much of the ore moving down the Lakes was met at the water's edge by coal coming up from the mines, and vast smelters arose at Lake ports that became world-famous.

By 1880 the American iron industry had attained large dimensions, but Great Britain was making almost 8,000,000 tons to our 4,000,000. In the coming years, however, America was to outstrip her old rival. The age of steel— thanks to Bessemer and many other inventors— was already supplanting that of iron; and the American iron and steel industry of the '80's, vast and wonderful though it seemed, was but a pigmy compared with the giant of to-day.

The Age of Steel.

Meanwhile in the world of industry the individual proprietor was giving place to partnerships, and these in turn to corporations. In some industries restless and ambitious men could not rest content with a share but were seeking to grasp control of the whole. In iron and steel, production was becoming more concentrated geographically: fewer plants than in the days of George Washington, but vastly greater production; some great companies, but no one great company, virtually controlling the whole industry. That development did not come in iron and steel until after the dawn of the twentieth century.

Concentration both Geographically and into Great Companies.

It came considerably earlier in the petroleum industry, a new business that scarcely antedates the Civil War.

In the Old World petroleum was known even to the ancients,

but it was in America that the possibilities of the product were first developed to an important extent. The Indians and the

Use of
Petroleum as
a Medicine.

early French explorers and missionaries in northwestern New York sometimes found the oil rising in springs of water, and one missionary describes a "fountain of bitumen" which he saw rising from Lake Ontario in 1627. As early as 1791 some enterprising spirit began to collect petroleum from the springs along Oil Creek in Pennsylvania, and to sell this "Seneca Oil" as a wonderful natural remedy for rheumatism and other ills, though seemingly without much success. In the next few decades oil was found in many places, particularly in digging wells to obtain brine for salt, but though several attempts were made to use the oil as an illuminant, the crude product created such intolerable smoke and odor that the experimenters gave up defeated. At that time tallow candles and whale oil formed the main dependence for lighting purposes, but the supply of both was limited and prices high, and it was inevitable that new experiments should be made. Toward the middle of the century a Pittsburgh druggist named Samuel Kier began vigorously to promote petroleum as a medicine, but though he raised the sales to as much as three barrels a day, the supply of "Kier's Oil" far exceeded the demand, and Kier turned his attention to the illuminating possibilities

As an
Illuminant.

of the product. About 1852 he thought of trying the distilling methods that were being used in obtaining oils from coal and shale, and he succeeded in producing an oil that, though not wholly satisfactory, was much better than the crude product. However, improved methods were soon evolved, together with better lamps for burning it, and a great demand was soon created for this "kerosene" as it was presently called, the name being that already used for the oil obtained from coal and shales.

For a time the petroleum was skimmed off springs or taken from shallow pits or dug wells, but the supply thus obtained was inadequate. Presently a company formed in New Haven decided to drill a well, and sent a railway conductor named Edwin L. Drake out to Oil Creek to oversee the work. Drake met with many difficulties, but he was a man of ingenuity, and in 1859 he managed to reach a depth of sixty-nine feet, when on

The Oil Creek Boom.

returning to work one morning the workmen found the well almost full of oil. A great boom at once developed, with the usual accompaniment of wild speculation. In two years the valley of Oil Creek was transformed into a wilderness of derricks, rude engine-houses, and board shanties; farmers owning land in the valley suddenly found themselves immensely rich.

All the early wells were shallow, and the oil had to be got out by pumping, but in 1861 some enterprising spirits drilled four or five hundred feet down to what is now known as the

Deeper Wells.

"third sand." Then "without warning the drilling tools were hurled high above the derrick, followed by a stream of oil gushing out with such force that it could not be controlled for several days." For months this well produced several hundred barrels a day; other new gushers yielded as much as 4,000 barrels a day, which was as much as one of the earlier wells would produce in a year. Production soon outstripped demand, and the price dropped as low as ten cents a barrel, whereas earlier it had been as high as a dollar a gallon.

The market, however, constantly expanded, and soon the industry revived. New discoveries were made in other localities; new waves of speculation followed, even wilder than the

Wild Speculation.

first; and the world was filled with the tales of sudden wealth and the spectacular extravagances of an eccentric individual called "Coal Oil Johnny." In the middle '60's fully a thousand companies, with stocks nominally aggregating over $600,000,000, were formed, and their glowing prospectuses led humorists to satirize them. One pamphlet of the day represented itself to be the prospectus of "The Munchausen, Philosopher's Stone, and Gull Creek Grand Consolidated Oil Company." The capital stock of this company was $4,000,000,000, the working capital $37.50, and dividends were guaranteed semi-daily except Sunday. The company controlled four tracts of land. On the one after which the concern was named a shaft 16,000,000 feet in depth had been sunk, "yielding cooking butter, XXX ale, turtle soup and bounty money, besides other things too numerous to mention." The "Ananias and Sapphira Tract" was small, containing only 65,000,000 acres; the "Moonshine Tract" was heavily wooded; the "China and Hades Tract" was known to be "especially rich in tea!"

Again the bubble burst; again there came a revival. Gradually both producing and refining were placed on a more solid basis, though from that day to this, with the discovery of every new oil-field, the old story of a lucky strike, a stampede thither, sudden wealth to the fortunate ones, wild speculation, and finally the inevitable bursting of the bubble was almost certain to be repeated.

Improved distilling methods were evolved, and a better, safer kerosene was put upon the market, while dozens of by-products were developed, such as benzine, naphtha, gasoline, vaseline, paraffin, and lubricating oils. And the immensity of the whole business surpassed the wildest dreams of its early promoters.

By-Products.

The later history of the oil business is inextricably interwoven with the biography of an individual—John D. Rockefeller. This modern Crœsus was born at Richford, New York, in 1839, but in 1853 the family moved to Cleveland, Ohio. The Rockefellers of that period were poor, and in after years, when he was the richest man in the world, "John D." was fond of telling admiring Baptist Sunday-school classes how he made his first dollars—and set them to work. When still in his teens he became a partner in a commission business, but in 1862, with his partner and an English mechanic named Samuel Andrews, he engaged in the new business of refining oil. The partners prospered, and about 1867 the new firm of "Rockefeller, Andrews, & Flagler" took over a group of refineries in which the various members of the new partnership—which included William Rockefeller, brother to John—were interested.

John D. Rockefeller.

In 1870 the Rockefellers and their associates took an epoch-making step. They transformed their partnership into a corporation, with a capital of $1,000,000, and took the soon-to-be-famous name of the "Standard Oil Company of Ohio." At that time there were probably 250 other refineries scattered from Ohio to the Atlantic coast, with a total daily capacity of perhaps 16,000 barrels, and the Standard, with a daily capacity of 600 barrels, was merely one of the largest. The new company entered upon an aggressive campaign, and won startling successes, largely because of legitimate business efficiency, foresight, better refining methods, pipe-lines, and utilization of by-products, but partly because of ruthless warfare upon its competitors.

The Standard Oil Company.

In 1872 the two Rockefellers and eleven others formed what was known as the South Improvement Company and managed to obtain a secret contract with the oil-carrying roads to transport oil at about half the price paid by other refiners. The signers of this contract on the part of the railroads included Jay Gould and William H. Vanderbilt. The existence of the agreement became generally known, and it had to be given up, but the Standard succeeded, nevertheless, in obtaining secret rebates, which gave it an immense advantage over less fortunate competitors. Furthermore, the Standard managed to gain control of the great pipe-lines, which were rapidly supplanting other means of transporting oil, and thus put the oil producers practically at their mercy. Many independent oil refiners were soon driven to the hard alternative of going out of business altogether or of selling out at a low price to the Standard Oil Company. The business of whole neighborhoods was paralyzed, and many men were ruined. Public opinion was aroused, congressional investigations were made, but the rebates were continued, as the railroads were not under any effective public control, and their managers and magnates often profited by the arrangement. By 1877 the great octopus controlled 95 per cent of all the oil refined in the United States, and could raise or lower prices at will.

Railroad Rebates.

In 1882 the Standard Oil Company was, for various reasons,

transformed into the Standard Oil Trust. The stockholders in the thirty-nine companies composing the new organization assigned their stock to the two Rockefellers and seven other trustees, giving them permanent power of attorney and receiving back "trust certificates," upon which the profits of the combination were divided.

The Standard Oil Trust.

The "trust" idea soon became highly popular among financiers in other lines of industry, and the example of the Standard was widely imitated. A number of firms or corporations engaged in the same business would unite under a trust agreement for the purpose of regulating the supply and price of the commodity which they produced; such "trusts," as they were called, would conduct ruthless warfare against competitors, and would seek to obtain a monopoly of the industry in which they engaged. Thus were created the great business leviathans that bestrode the financial world and seemed to threaten even the liberties of the Republic. But of this more will be said hereafter.

The Plan Imitated.

These decades also beheld rapid strides in the consolidation of railroads. In the early years of railroad construction most of the lines were short, and were built with little relation to other lines. A traveller from New York to St. Louis or Chicago in the Civil War period, or earlier, had to make repeated changes from one road to another, the terminals of which were often miles apart, had to buy a ticket for each road, would likely waste hours waiting for trains, and otherwise was subjected to vexations and delays little known to-day. The economic disadvantages to the railroads themselves of such a state of affairs were enormous; presently far-sighted managers began consolidating the unrelated short roads into great trunk lines. Thus in 1868 Cornelius Vanderbilt, president of the Hudson River Railroad, united it with the New York Central, thereby forming one continuous line from New York City to Buffalo. Five years later he leased the Lake Shore & Michigan Southern and thereby reached Chicago. About the same time the Pennsylvania and the Baltimore & Ohio also established through lines to the

Railroad Consolidation.

metropolis of the Middle West, and the former also reached St. Louis.

Consolidation enabled the railroads to furnish better service, both freight and passenger, at smaller cost, but the process of consolidation was frequently preceded or accompanied by the financial "wrecking" of roads, the "squeezing out" of minority stockholders, stock-watering, and other reprehensible practices. Furthermore, though many of the roads had received large land or money subsidies, their managers usually forgot to be grateful for such favors and displayed a grasping determination "to charge all the traffic would bear." High freight and passenger rates, and stories of the millions that railway lords were piling up, combined to create great hostility among the people; and the men chiefly engaged in the management of railroads—Jay Gould, the Vanderbilts, Thomas A. Scott, John W. Garrett, and others—were indiscriminately condemned as a band of financial pirates.

Reprehensible Practices.

An element hard hit by this unscrupulous mismanagement of the railroads entirely in the interest of a class rapidly growing rich were the farmers of the West. They formed an organization that took the name of the "Patrons of Husbandry" but that was more popularly known as the "Grangers." This society was founded at Washington in 1867, but did not attain much importance until the panic of 1873, when it developed with astonishing rapidity and soon had a membership of a million and a half, mainly in the Middle West and Northwest. Men, women, and children came to the lodges, or "granges," and while the men talked politics and farming the children played and the women gossiped and prepared a picnic supper. The Grangers had many grievances. One of their main objects was to promote direct dealing between producer and consumer, thus eliminating the middleman, but they also directed their attention to securing better and cheaper transportation. Largely through their influence several Northwestern States enacted the so-called "Granger laws" creating railway commissions with extensive supervisory powers, establishing in some

The Granger Movement.

The Granger Laws.

cases maximum rates, and forbidding discrimination in rates between shippers.

The railroads denounced these acts as confiscatory and attacked their constitutionality, but the Federal Supreme Court, in the "Granger Cases," held (1877) that States possessed the power to regulate rates, provided the rates were not made so low as to amount to confiscation of property. In 1886, however, the same court, in the case of the Wabash Railway *vs.* Illinois, denied to the States the power to adopt regulations affecting interstate commerce. The influence of the Grangers had already declined, and the railroads managed to obtain the repeal of most of the obnoxious laws. But the principle that railroads are quasi-public in character and subject to regulation had been definitely established, and the fact was not forgotten.

The "Granger Cases."

For the time being, however, railroads were left virtually uncontrolled. Rebates to favored shippers, differential rates between towns, and extortionate rates for passengers or freight formed almost the accepted order of things. To prevent ruinous competition between roads, resort was had to "pooling" arrangements whereby rates were kept high and business and profits were divided between the contracting roads.

Rebates and Pools.

The prevailing moral tone in both business and politics was deplorably low. The giving of free passes to public officers, editors, and even to their families and friends formed a flagrant abuse; all who could rode "deadhead, and expected to have their hats chalked." Even judges who had to try railroad cases, and members of the legislatures who were asked by farmers and shippers to pass restraining acts, rode on free passes. A *quid pro quo* was expected for such favors, and too often was received. The transportation companies and allied interests had little difficulty in electing their creatures to Congress and to State legislatures, and in bribing legislators, administrative officers, and even judges on the bench. A detailed history of the subterranean activities of these interests would make a revolting story little to the credit of the country or to human nature.

Low Moral Tone in Business and Politics.

Early in the century workers began to form organizations, but the movement did not become pronounced until the sixth and seventh decades. With the rise of the factory system, the growth of great business enterprises, and the decline of the old personal relations between employees and employer, the individual worker, realizing his own insignificance and impotence when standing alone, began to feel the need of uniting with his fellow workers in defense of their common interests. Trades-unions began to spring up like mushrooms, the rift between capital and labor opened wider and wider, and by the '80's strikes had come to be regarded as part of the routine of industrial life. Higher wages and shorter hours formed the unceasing cry of the workers, and every victory won meant a new demand. Open warfare prevailed; there were truces but never real peace. To the employer's "blacklist," designed to prevent labor agitators from obtaining employment elsewhere, the unions retorted with the "boycott," designed to keep the products of hostile establishments from finding a sale. When unchecked, the unions often proved as tyrannical as the employers, for human nature is about the same beneath jeans as beneath broadcloth.

Labor-Unions.

At Philadelphia in 1869 a number of garment-cutters, led by Uriah S. Stephens, formed the Noble Order of Knights of Labor. This organization soon disbanded, but on its ruins Stephens managed to build (1873) a much broader union designed to embrace all branches of honorable toil instead of merely workers in the same trade. For a decade the organization was secret and had an elaborate ritual, but the excesses of the "Molly Maguires," who had brought discredit upon all organized labor, resulted in the policy of secrecy being abandoned. Starting with only twenty-eight members, the union rapidly increased in numbers, particularly under the leadership of General Master Workman Terence V. Powderly; in 1885 and 1886 its membership sprang from 111,000 to 730,000. At a general assembly held at Reading in 1878 the Knights pointed out the alarming development in power and aggressiveness of money and corporations, and declared that the tendency, unless checked, would "inevitably

The Knights of Labor.

lead to the hopeless degradation of the people." They proclaimed their purpose to be "to make industrial and moral worth, not wealth, the true standard of individual and national greatness." They further declared that workers ought to have the right to enjoy the wealth they create, and they advocated the referendum for making laws, the creation of labor bureaus, the passage of laws safeguarding the health and safety of workers, and shorter working hours, that workingmen might have leisure for intellectual, moral, and social development. The characteristic motto of the Knights was, "An injury to one is the concern of all."

Although labor in these years was rapidly becoming conscious of its grievances and special interests, the condition of American workers happily lacked much of being so serious as

American Workers Fortunate.

in Europe. The natural resources of America were as yet comparatively untouched, and the expenditure of a given amount of labor would in most industries produce a much greater return than abroad; in consequence the workers received higher wages, both nominally and really, than did their brethren in Europe. Furthermore, notwithstanding an ever-increasing number of immigrants, the demand for labor, except in hard times, was always greater than the supply, and workers were nearly always sure of employment at competitive prices. Republicans often attributed this state of affairs to the protective tariff, but in large measure they were claiming credit due to a bountiful Providence for having so richly endowed America with natural resources.

In some fields of endeavor the lack of labor rendered necessary entirely different aims from those in Europe. Back in 1791 George Washington had realized the effects upon agriculture

The Aim of American Farmers.

ture of this shortage in workers, and had written to Arthur Young, a scientific English farmer of the day: "The aim of the farmers in this country (if they can be called farmers) is, not to make the most they can from the land, which is or has been cheap, but the most of the labour, which is dear; the consequence of which has been, much ground has been *scratched* over and none cultivated or improved as it ought to have been: whereas a farmer in England, where land is dear, and labour cheap, finds it his interest to improve and cultivate highly, that he may reap large crops from a small quantity of ground." Extensive rather than intensive cultivation still continues the general rule in the United States, and it must continue so until the land is more thickly settled. The consequence is that an acre in France, England, or Holland is made to return much more than an acre in America, but one farmer in America, using all the latest farm machinery, will reap a far greater return from the expenditure of his own toil than would one man in the countries mentioned.

In farming, manufacturing, and almost every line of effort shortage of workers has necessitated a resort to machinery, with the consequent result that invention has been greatly stimulated, and America has led the world in evolving labor-saving devices.

Use of Machinery.

By the middle of the '80's some of the main features of our present-day problems were taking form. Great industries were developing with incredible swiftness, population was moving into urban centres, the simplicity of an agricultural age was passing. A gulf had opened between labor and capital, and consolidation was becoming the order of the day both in the labor world and the industrial world. New maladies called for new remedies, but the tendencies of the time were little understood, and, as we shall see, there was much dim groping after panaceas.

CHAPTER XI

THE RETURN OF THE DEMOCRACY

On March 4, 1885, a vast crowd assembled before the east front of the Capitol to behold the installation of the first Democratic President since Buchanan. Southerners formed a larger part of the throng than long had been customary on such occasions, and conspicuous in the crowd were, in the words of Professor Peck, "not a few gaunt figures of an old-time quaintness, intense and fanatical partisans from remote localities, displaying with a sort of pride the long white beards which, years before, they had vowed never to shave until a Democratic President should be inaugurated." When the "Man of Destiny" from Buffalo took the oath of office from Chief Justice Waite, the assembled clans acclaimed him with joyous shouts, exulting in the thought that after weary years of waiting they had passed out of the Wilderness into the Promised Land.

Inauguration of Cleveland.

Many Democrats had prophesied that when their party came into power and the public books were "opened" great defalcations would be found, but no such discoveries were made. Equally mistaken were predictions by pessimistic Republicans that hard times or even a restoration of slavery would follow the return of the Democracy to office.

The new President did not hesitate to give the South adequate representation in his cabinet. From the farther South he named Senator Augustus H. Garland of Arkansas as attorney-general, and Senator Lucius Q. C. Lamar of Mississippi as secretary of the interior. Garland had sat in the Confederate Congress, and Lamar, a highly talented scholar, had drafted the ordinance of secession in his State, but both had accepted the results of the war

The New Cabinet.

in good faith.   From a border State, namely Delaware, Cleveland selected as secretary of state Senator Thomas F. Bayard, a capable statesman whose family had taken a prominent part in public affairs for five generations.   From the other extreme sectionally came Secretary of War William C. Endicott of Massachusetts, "a very Brahmin of the Brahmins," being descended from Governor John Endecott of Puritan memory; also Postmaster-General William F. Vilas of Wisconsin, who had served in the Union army, reaching the rank of colonel. Secretary of the Navy William C. Whitney and Secretary of the Treasury Daniel Manning were likewise from the North; both were New Yorkers, Manning being an Albany banker who had been recommended by Tilden, while Whitney was a man of wealth who had managed the New York campaign.

Cleveland's sudden rise to prominence helped to create an almost unprecedented interest in his personal affairs, and this interest was heightened by the fact that he was only forty-seven years old, the youngest man, except Grant, who had ever been elected to the presidency, and was still a bachelor.   For a time the White House was presided over by his sister, Miss Rose Cleveland, a woman of intellectual attainments who published at this time a volume entitled *George Eliot's Poetry and Other Studies*.   Presently the rumor spread that the President was about to marry his ward, Miss Frances Folsom, daughter of his deceased law partner. Miss Folsom was a girl of twenty-one who had only recently graduated from college;   her youth and beauty combined with the august position of her intended husband to raise public interest to a high pitch.   The wedding ceremony was performed (June 2, 1886) in the Blue Room of the White House, being the first time that a President had been wedded in that mansion.   For weeks the newspapers were filled with descriptions of the event and of the honeymoon.   The young mistress of the White House proved to be cultured, sensible, domestic in her tastes, and the marriage served to throw an element of romance about the President.

Before attaining the happiness just described President

Cleveland, like all new incumbents of his office, was called upon to satisfy with five loaves and two small fishes the desperate hunger of an unprecedented horde of office-seekers.

The Office-Seekers.

Both before and after election he had repeatedly pledged himself to the principles of civil service reform. "Merit and competency shall be recognized instead of party subserviency," he had announced in his inaugural address, but, in a letter to George William Curtis (December 25, 1884), he had also given warning that "offensive partisans and unscrupulous manipulators of local party management" had "forfeited all just claim to recognition."

Democratic politicians, who almost unanimously wished to make a "clean sweep" of the hundred and twenty thousand offices, smiled knowingly when they read Cleveland's pronouncements on this subject; they did not conceal

Spoilsmen Disappointed.

their disgust when they discovered that he took his pledges seriously. Even prominent leaders like Tilden and Hendricks found him obdurate to their pleas in behalf of friends. It was reported that some weeks after the inauguration the Vice-President, an ardent spoilsman, came away from an interview at the White House shaking his head sadly and saying: "I hoped that Mr. Cleveland would put the Democratic party in power in fact as well as in name, but he does not intend to do it." To a Democratic senator who complained because the President did not "move more expeditiously in advancing the principles of Democracy," Cleveland flashed back: "Ah, I suppose you mean that I should appoint two horse-thieves a day instead of one." Such a Mugwump attitude deeply disappointed politicians who had hoped to see the President put in practice "the good old Democratic doctrines" of Andrew Jackson. Their dissatisfaction is sufficiently indicated by a story that a North Carolina senator told of an old farmer who left a small estate to his two sons. Settlement of the estate was so long delayed by the probate court that in disgust the elder son burst out: "Durned if I ain't almost sorry the old man died!"

On the other hand, Cleveland made so many removals that

the extreme advocates of civil service reform, men who wished
"the millennium right away," were almost equally disappointed.

Cleveland Relaxes Somewhat.
Constant party pressure caused the President to
relax somewhat, and at the end of four years comparatively few Republicans remained in office out-
side the classified service.   Some of the President's subordinates
were especially zealous "in advancing the principles of Democracy" and interpreted the phrase "offensive partisanship"
very liberally.   The first assistant postmaster-general, Adlai
E. Stevenson, displayed such activity in decapitating postmasters that "Adlai's axe" became famous.   One of the arguments most used in defending such acts was that practically
all office-holders were Republicans and that the principle of
"equalization" must now be put in force.

The personnel of the Civil Service Commission degenerated,
and two of the members were little better than political hacks.
Such a body could accomplish little aggressive work.   On the
other hand, despite frequent lapses in practice, Cleveland continued to protest his allegiance to the reform principle, took a
stand against the assessment of office-holders and against their
activity in politics, and toward the end of his term increased
the classified service from 15,573 to 27,830 places.

The fact that some fragments of the Tenure-of-Office Act
still remained on the statute book afforded the Republican
majority in the Senate an excuse for harassing the President on

Contest with the Senate.
the subject of suspensions and removals.   Early
in 1886 the Senate, by calling on the attorney-general
for all papers connected with the suspension of the
district attorney for Alabama, drew from Cleveland a special
message in which he complained because after "nearly twenty
years of almost innocuous desuetude" the remnant of the
Tenure-of-Office Act was brought out to embarrass the executive.   He argued that he possessed the constitutional powers of
suspension and removal, and declared that the documents requested were "purely unofficial and private; not infrequently
confidential, and having reference to the performance of a duty
exclusively mine."   After protracted political skirmishing the

Republican senators discovered that they could not gain the partisan advantages they had hoped for, so they consented to the repeal (March 3, 1887) of the Tenure-of-Office Act; full powers in matters of removal were thus restored to the executive.

Throughout Cleveland's first presidency the Senate continued to be Republican and the House Democratic. Partisan measures were, therefore, impossible, but a number of important laws were passed.

One such act regulated the presidential succession. Hitherto the line of succession had been the President, the Vice-President, and the President *pro tempore* of the Senate. On November 25, 1885, before the Senate had elected a President *pro tempore*, Vice-President Hendricks died.

Presidential
Succession
Act, 1886.

Had Cleveland died or resigned before the meeting of Congress, there would have been no one to take his place. To meet such a possible situation in the future, an act was passed providing (January 18, 1886) that the line of succession should be the Vice-President, the Secretaries of State, Treasury, and War, the Attorney-General, the Postmaster-General, the Secretary of the Navy, and the Secretary of the Interior.

Another weakness that had long been recognized was the lack of definite rules for determining and counting the electoral votes. Beginning with 1800 repeated efforts had vainly been made to remove the defect. Even the dangerous crisis following the election of 1876 had not brought Congress to agree on a remedy. Finally in 1887 an act was passed that in the main followed the lines laid down in the decisions rendered by the electoral commission. Contests regarding the choice of electors were to be left to State authorities, and their decision must be accepted by Congress as final. In case of a conflict of tribunals that return was to be counted which the two houses, voting separately, concurred in receiving. No return was to be rejected except by the vote of both houses. In case of a conflict between the two, that return was to be counted that was certified by the State executive. Unfortunately even this law left possible loopholes for future disputes, though none as yet has arisen.

Electoral
Count Act.

The same Congress that passed the two laws above described also attempted an infinitely more difficult task, namely, to remove some of the evils that had crept into the transportation system of the country. The transportation situation at this time was exceedingly chaotic. There had just been a period of tremendous railroad expansion, and in the five years 1879–1884 the total mileage of the country had increased almost one-half. In many instances the roads had been built in advance of local needs, and time was required to provide adequate traffic to make them profitable. Furthermore, many of the companies were organized on a grossly inflated basis, and capitalization, in bonds and stocks, often greatly exceeded the actual money invested. In fact, many, if not most, promoters and builders were far more interested in stock manipulations than in legitimate construction or operation. It was notorious that much of the money that was supposed to go into construction and equipment was diverted through channels of "high finance" into the pockets of "controlling" stockholders. Lack of business, cut-throat competition, and reckless or dishonest financiering brought many roads to a sorry plight, and in the period 1876–1894 nearly six hundred roads, having a total mileage of 60,000, were sold under foreclosure. But it did not escape the public notice that though the roads became bankrupt, their builders, by some trick of financial legerdemain, generally became rich.

Competition for traffic frequently ran to such lengths that the rates charged were too low to meet the cost of the service rendered. Shippers temporarily profited by such rate wars, but in the end such contests usually reacted disastrously not only on the roads but also on business generally. Keen-sighted men realized that some means should be found of making rates low enough to be reasonable to shippers and high enough to be profitable to the roads. But hostility to railroads often ran so strong that a large section of the public failed to realize that common interests required that the roads should be prosperous.

As a means of preserving themselves from this disastrous

competition the railroads, as mentioned in the last chapter, evolved agreements called "pools," whereby they agreed to charge certain passenger and freight rates and to divide traffic or earnings upon fixed percentages. Unfortunately the railway managers often failed to be content with reasonable returns and combined to exact extortionate rates. Shippers, aware of the outrageous financial manipulations of the roads, asked, with reason, why they should be forced to pay dividends on "watered" stock.

Railway Pools.

Even worse evils than excessive rates were discriminations in rates between different places and different shippers. Discrimination between shippers was the worst evil of all. Secret special bargains were made with favored shippers, who were charged less than the published rates. As we have already seen, these secret rates aided the Standard Oil Company and other growing monopolies to crush out competition.

Discrimination between Places and Shippers.

The story of the "Granger laws" and of the practical failure of State regulation of railroads has already been told. Many reformers realized that the problem demanded federal rather than State legislation. As early as 1873 attempts were made to secure the passage of an interstate commerce act, but in vain. Three years later Representative Hopkins of Pennsylvania introduced a resolution providing for an investigation of railroad abuses, but the matter was referred to the committee on commerce, some of whose members had no desire to ascertain the facts. The investigation was never completed. Even the testimony that had been taken disappeared, and there seems reason to believe that it was stolen.

Early Demands for Federal Regulation.

A decade later, after other abortive attempts, the public clamor became so insistent that Congress enacted the famous Interstate Commerce Law (February 4, 1887). The law prohibited discrimination between persons, higher rates for a short haul than for a long haul over the same line, forbade pooling, and required the carriers to make public their schedules and to file them with a newly created body called the Interstate Commerce Commission.

Interstate Commerce Law, 1887.

This commission was to consist of five members appointed by the President, and to it were given powers to make investigations, collect statistics, and to prosecute offenders against the act.

President Cleveland appointed able commissioners, headed by Judge Thomas M. Cooley, a distinguished Michigan jurist, who had gained much helpful experience as a receiver of bankrupt railways. The commission labored diligently, Partial Failure of the Commission. but unfortunately the powers conferred upon it were not drastic enough. Rebates to favored shippers were continued, pools survived in the shape of traffic associations and informal "gentlemen's agreements," and other old evils persisted or new ones sprang up. Furthermore, many of the commission's acts were reversed by the courts, which interpreted its powers very strictly, thereby aiding railway and corporation managers, who in evading the act displayed truly Machiavellian ingenuity.

Many managers were, in fact, so wanting in honor that they would not live up to the terms of the agreements with each other, and secret violations of such agreements in order to increase traffic precipitated ruinous rate wars. The only really satisfactory method, therefore, of escaping from the evils of competition was consolidation of competing lines, and for this and other reasons consolidation proceeded apace. By 1895 half the mileage of the country was operated by about forty companies.

The passage of the Interstate Commerce Act was largely due to the impression made on Congress by manifestations of public discontent. It was a period of great social and industrial unrest. Socialism and even anarchism had Social and Industrial Unrest. gained a foothold in America. Ignorant agitators and men of education such as Henry George, whose celebrated "single-tax" book, *Progress and Poverty*, has already been referred to, and Edward Bellamy, whose widely read Utopian romance, *Looking Backward*, appeared in 1888, were pointing out inequalities in the existing order and were preaching changes that seemed to threaten the very bases of society. Workers were more thoroughly organized than ever before, and the "walking delegate," who stirred up discontent and called strikes, had become a prominent, often a sinister, factor in industrial life. The Knights of Labor continued to play a prominent part in labor affairs, and, as already related, the years 1885–86 witnessed a tremendous increase in their membership.

In 1886 the labor world seethed with discontent, and there were twice as many strikes as in any previous year. One of the most serious of these occurred on the Gould railways of the Southwest. It was precipitated by the dismissal for cause of a mechanic in the shops of the Texas and Pacific Railroad at Fort Worth, Texas. The man was a prominent Knight of Labor, and his fellow mechanics demanded his reinstatement. When the demand was refused, they struck (March 6, 1886), and, owing partly to other grievances, the strike soon spread to the whole Gould system, so that about 6,000 miles of road were tied up. Master Workman Powderly, head of the Knights, strove to keep the strikers within legal bounds and sought to settle the quarrel, but violent men held sway in some places, particularly in St. Louis, where an ignorant and ruffianly district leader named Martin Irons inflamed the mob to desperate deeds. Both in the St. Louis neighborhood and elsewhere trains were held up by force, railroad and other property was pillaged or destroyed, and a number of persons were slain. For seven weeks the strike continued and then collapsed completely.

Southwestern Railroad Strike.

Still more serious was a strike growing out of the demand of labor for an eight-hour day. May 1, 1886, was the date set by the workers for the new system to go into effect. But most employers refused to accept the plan, and strikes resulted in many places. The most serious of these occurred in Chicago, where 50,000 or 60,000 men and women were soon involved.

Demand for an Eight-Hour Day.

At this time there existed in Chicago a small but very active and violent group of anarchists, nearly all of whom were of foreign origin, chiefly German. In the strike these agitators saw an opportunity to spread their doctrines and to stir up trouble. Their organs, the *Alarm* and the *Arbeiter-Zeitung*, contained highly incendiary articles

The Chicago Anarchists.

counselling violence and praising the "sublime" virtues of dynamite bombs.

On May 3 a collision between the strikers and the police took place at the works of the McCormick Reaper Company, and several of the strikers were wounded. The next evening a great mass meeting assembled in Haymarket Square to protest against this "atrocious attack of the police in shooting our fellow workmen." A. B. Parsons, August Spies, Sam Fielden, and other anarchists spoke; Fielden became so violent in his language that the captain of a battalion of policemen who had just marched into the square ordered the crowd to disperse and arrested Fielden. Some one in the crowd fired a pistol, and almost immediately a gleaming object hurtled through the air and fell among the police, exploding with terrific force and killing or mortally wounding eight of the guardians of the law and injuring over sixty more.

Haymarket Riot.

This dastardly deed shocked the entire country, and a widespread demand arose that drastic steps should be taken against the men guilty of raising the red flag on American soil. Many of the "Reds" were arrested, and their trial proved to be one of the most famous in our history. Eight were convicted of having instigated the attack on the police; seven were sentenced to death; and one—Oscar Neebe—to imprisonment for fifteen years. One of the condemned—Louis Lingg—cheated the gallows by committing suicide; four—Parsons, Fischer, Engle, and Spies—were hanged; while the sentences of two—Fielden and Schwab—were commuted to imprisonment for life. Eight years later a radically inclined Illinois governor, John P. Altgeld, pardoned the three who remained in prison.

The Anarchists Punished.

Industrial arbitration and various other plans for the peaceful adjustment of labor disputes were brought forward, but the action of Congress was confined to the passage of an act providing for the settlement by arbitration of disputes between railroads and their employees. Resort to the plan was not made compulsory, however,

Industrial Arbitration.

and the practical results proved small. A number of States also passed arbitration laws of varying merit.

The failure of most of the strikes supported by the Knights of Labor in this period tended to discredit that order in the eyes of workingmen, while the sympathy of the general public was alienated by the scenes of violence and by the order's passing resolutions asking mercy for the condemned anarchists. The influence of the Knights began to wane, while that of a new organization, the American Federation of Labor, increased. This new order was first formed in 1881, but did not take the name just given until 1886. Unlike the Knights of Labor, it consisted of an alliance of separate trades-unions, and, as the autonomous principle was better suited to the needs of the labor situation, the Federation throve at the expense of its rival and ultimately became the most powerful body of its kind in the world.

American Federation of Labor.

A subject concerning which there was much partisan wrangling during this administration was that of pensions to veterans of the Civil War. A very liberal policy had prevailed in this matter, and by 1885 the pensioners numbered 345,125, annually receiving $65,171,937. Great laxity prevailed in the Pension Office, yet many claims were rejected by it, and a custom had arisen of disappointed claimants persuading members of Congress to present their claims in special pension bills. Many such claims were meritorious, but thousands of these private pension bills were presented, so that often they received little careful scrutiny even in committee; hundreds were sometimes passed in a single session of the House or Senate. Under such circumstances, "influence" or "pull" frequently proved the determining factor rather than truth or merit, while throughout the country there seemed to exist a sort of public conspiracy to aid even the undeserving to get on the pension pay-roll, and it was notorious that physicians and other individuals often swore falsely in affidavits made in behalf of applicants. In consequence, men who had never heard the whistle of a Confederate bullet, men who had been dishonorably discharged, even deserters and ma-

The Pension Question.

lingerers who had shot off their own fingers or hands in order to be discharged from military service, had managed to get their names placed on the pension-roll. This unfortunate state of affairs was largely due to politicians playing for votes, and to the unscrupulous activities of a great body of pension claim agents, who preyed both upon the veterans and the public treasury. Even the Grand Army of the Republic, a veterans' association, the original objects of which were highly praiseworthy, sometimes exercised an influence that laid it open to the charge that it had come to be "an instrument for the procuring of pensions."

With his usual hard-headedness, President Cleveland studied the pension question and reached the conclusion that a reform was needed. He subjected all private pension bills that came to him to a careful scrutiny and vetoed 228 such bills out of a total of 1,871. Some of the claims thus denied were not only fraudulent in character but had a humorous side. One applicant's disability was due to the fact that long after the war he had broken his leg while gathering dandelions in a ditch. A widow of a veteran asked a pension because her husband had been accidentally killed by a neighbor who was trying to shoot an owl. Another widow's husband had been captured by the Confederates and had fought during the remainder of the war in their ranks. "We are dealing with pensions, not with gratuities," wrote the President in vetoing one such bill, and he insisted again and again that the pension roll ought to be kept a roll of honor, not of fraud.

Cleveland Vetoes Many Private Pension Bills.

Pension attorneys and Republicans alert for partisan advantage raised a great outcry over these pension vetoes, which many alleged were due to Cleveland's "Rebel sympathies." The prejudice thus created was much increased when the President vetoed (February 11, 1887) a bill to grant twelve dollars a month to veterans of twelve months' service who were dependent for support upon their daily toil or upon others.

Dependent Pension Bill Vetoed, 1887.

Soon after vetoing the dependent pension bill Cleveland

made the mistake of authorizing Adjutant-General Drum to return to Southern States certain captured Confederate flags that were in the possession of the government. The President doubtless intended the step in the spirit of Charles Sumner's bill of years before, to the effect that "the names of battles with fellow-citizens shall not be continued in the Army Register, or placed on the regimental colors of the United States." But the "Rebel Flag Order" created a great furor throughout the North. Hundreds of Grand Army posts denounced the plan; the "Rebel Sympathizer" was deluged with threats of personal violence. It was pointed out that since the flags were the property of the nation they could not be disposed of without the consent of Congress. In the end Cleveland had to take the humiliating step of issuing (June 16, 1887) an executive order admitting his lack of power and annulling action taken by the adjutant-general. He also deemed it expedient to withdraw his acceptance of an invitation to attend the annual encampment of the Grand Army of the Republic, which was held that year in St. Louis. It is significant that eighteen years later a Republican Congress and President returned the flags without exciting a ripple of protest.

"Rebel Flag Order."

In his annual messages of 1885 and 1886 President Cleveland urged upon Congress the desirability of reducing what he regarded as excessive tariff duties. But the Senate, being Republican, was hostile to such a policy, while even in the House enough protectionist Democrats combined with the Republicans to prevent tariff tinkering.

Not to be turned aside, Cleveland, in December, 1887, against the advice of some of his counsellors, departed from all precedents and devoted the whole of his annual message to arguing the need of revenue reform. He pointed out that every year the treasury receipts exceeded expenditures by many millions, that the vaults were becoming congested with money, that the surplus thus created was an incitement to extravagance, that the withdrawal of so much money from circulation was disturbing to business. He asserted that the high duties enabled certain interests to exact excessive profits at the expense of consumers,

Tariff Message of 1887.

including both laboring men and farmers.   However, he deprecated the "bandying" of such epithets as "protection" and
"free trade"; said that the entire withdrawal of duties should
not be contemplated; and summed all up in the much-quoted
phrase: "It is a condition which confronts us—not a theory."

Few presidential messages ever created such a sensation.
Republicans gleefully asserted that Cleveland had made the
issue for the campaign of 1888, and declared that American
industries were threatened with destruction by free
trade.   From Paris, where he was sojourning,
Blaine sent home a scathing criticism of the message,
and on his return to America contrasted the poverty of the
British worker with the comparative affluence of the American
wage-earner, and attributed the difference to the beneficent
effects of protection.   Congressman William McKinley of Ohio
charged that the assault was "inspired by our foreign rivals."
"Let England take care of herself," said he, "let France look
after her interests, let Germany take care of her own people,
but in God's name let Americans look after America."

The message dismayed many Democrats, but the party
managed to close its ranks and carry through the House (July
21, 1888) the so-called Mills bill, which reduced duties about
7 per cent.   Republicans and independents did not
fail to point out that the measure dealt gently with
certain industries that flourished in Democratic
States but more rigorously with those in Republican States.
The bill received scant consideration in the Republican Senate.
That body reported (October 3, 1888) a tariff measure of its
own, after which Congress adjourned, leaving the tariff controversy before the voters.

The Democratic national convention had met in St. Louis
on the 5th of June.   President Cleveland had antagonized
many of the politicians of his party, but he was renominated
by acclamation.   For his running mate the convention selected ex-Senator Allen G. Thurman of Ohio,
a picturesque "Old Roman" whose habit of carrying and flourishing a red bandanna handkerchief received much
public attention and gave a touch of color to the campaign.

The platform praised the Democratic record, declared its sympathy with the efforts of Ireland to obtain home rule, but devoted most attention to the tariff. By the existing duties, it asserted, "the cry of American labor for a better share in the rewards of industry is stifled with false pretences, enterprise is fettered and bound down to home markets," while the price of nearly everything farmers must buy "is increased by the favoritism of an unequal system of tax legislation." Much was made of the theory that lower duties would cheapen the cost of the necessaries of life.

It had been expected by most Republicans that Blaine would again be their nominee, but early in 1888, while still abroad, he wrote that he would not be a candidate. Ultimately many aspirants sought the honor of leading the Republican party, among them Senator Sherman, Senator Benjamin Harrison and Judge Walter Q. Gresham of Indiana, Senator W. B. Allison of Iowa, Senator Chauncey M. Depew of New York, and ex-Governor Russell A. Alger of Michigan. Of all the candidates Sherman was decidedly the best known, but, though one of the ablest men of his day, he somehow failed to arouse enthusiasm among the people. Gresham had an honorable record as a soldier and had won a large popular following by his attitude as a judge, having shown in his decisions that he realized the evils of monopoly and corruption; he was satisfactory to Mugwumps but he was unpopular with politicians, and his candidacy was weakened by his inability to secure support in his own State, all of whose delegates declared for Harrison.

Republican Aspirants.

The platform adopted by the Republican convention, which met in Chicago on the 19th of June, imitated the reference of their rivals to Irish home rule, charged that the Cleveland administration and the Democratic majority in the House of Representatives owed their existence to the unlawful suppression of the negro vote in the South, and denounced the Democratic attitude on the tariff question and other matters. It declared that Republicans stood "uncompromisingly in favor of the American system of pro-

Republican Platform.

tection. . . . Its abandonment has always been followed by disaster to all interests, except the usurer and the sheriff." Another plank ran: "The Republican party is in favor of the use of both gold and silver as money, and condemns the policy of the Democratic administration in its efforts to demonetize silver." In the light of after events this statement possesses a peculiar interest.

On the first ballot Sherman received 229 votes, Gresham 111, Depew 99, Alger 84, Harrison 80, with the rest trailing. For five more ballots Sherman held the lead, but his strength never exceeded 249, and in his *Recollections* he later attributed his defeat to the purchase by friends of Alger of Southern delegates pledged to his support. At one juncture an appeal that he should consent to be a candidate was cabled to Blaine, who was visiting Andrew Carnegie in Scotland; but Carnegie flashed back: "Too late, Blaine immovable. Take Harrison and Phelps." The despatch had some weight, as did also the course taken by Boss Platt of New York, who offered his influence, on conditions, to Gresham and probably to others, but finally threw it to Harrison. On the seventh ballot Harrison forged into the lead, and on the eighth he was nominated. For second place, the convention ignored Carnegie and Blaine's recommendation and nominated Levi P. Morton, a New York banker who had been a member of Congress and minister to France.

Harrison and Morton.

The Republican candidate for first place was a grandson of the log-cabin and hard-cider President, and a great-grandson of Governor Benjamin Harrison, a signer of the Declaration of Independence. His followers strove to revive some of the enthusiasm of 1840 and held many great rallies and torchlight processions, while trembling old men of Whig antecedents brought out and wore with great pride badges that had been used forty-eight years before when the welkin had been made to ring for "Tippecanoe and Tyler too!" The Democrats ridiculed "Grandfather's Hat" and declared that it was much too big for "Little Ben," the descendant who now wished to wear it. In reality, however, Harri-

Benjamin Harrison.

son was no mean candidate, and though he was not tall nor specially imposing, owing to the fact that both his neck and his legs were almost abnormally short, he possessed a learning and intellectual acumen equalled by few. As a lawyer he surpassed his opponent, but he was not so forceful a personality. He had commanded a regiment in a splendid charge at Resaca and had attained the rank of brigadier-general, facts that his supporters constantly contrasted with the fact that Cleveland had hired a substitute. In 1876 he was the Republican candidate for governor of Indiana but was defeated, and he had recently completed a term in the United States Senate. During the campaign he made scores of short speeches to delegations visiting his home in Indianapolis, and these speeches proved to be so apt and pithy that even his friends were agreeably surprised.

In honorable contrast with the campaign of 1884, personalities played little part in the contest. The main battle raged around the tariff question. Societies were formed to defend protection or to promote tariff reform; thousands of orators discussed the great issue upon the stump; voters were deluged with "literature" as never before. Democratic managers collected all the money they could from office-holders; Republican managers held up the spectre of free trade and persuaded nervous manufacturers and other business men to subscribe as never before. Workingmen were warned that they were in imminent peril of being reduced to the level of the "pauper labor" of Europe; many of them shivered at the thought and voted the protectionist ticket. Much was made of the assertion that the proposal to lower duties was inspired abroad, and it was charged that the British free-trade Cobden Club was contributing to the Democratic campaign fund.

By a clever *coup* the Republicans managed to give color to such stories. Two months before the election Sir Lionel Sackville-West, the British minister at Washington, received a letter dated at Pomona, California, and signed "Charles F. Murchison." The writer represented himself to be a naturalized Englishman. He spoke of Cleveland's Canadian policy and free-trade proclivities and of Harrison's high-tariff and "American" principles, and asked his lordship, "privately and confidentially," for an opinion as to which man, if elected, would be most friendly to British interests. Sackville-West, who was a very dull Briton, responded in language favorable to the aspirations of Cleveland. In reality the letter had been written by a man named Osgoodby, and it came at once into the hands of the Republican managers. They held it until near the end of October, and then published it in the newspapers and in millions of handbills. It filled the Democratic managers with dismay. In their panic they implored the President to do something to save the Irish vote. Cleveland had a cable sent to the British Foreign Office asking for the too trustful minister's recall; Lord Salisbury demurred, whereupon Sir Lionel was handed his passports. But the damage was done; the dish was broken and could not be mended.

The "Murchison Letter."

The main contests centred in New York and Indiana. Both parties threw into these pivotal States all the money upon which they could lay their hands, and neither side was too scrupulous as to methods. Harrison carried his own State by the narrow margin of 2,248 votes. In New York Governor David B. Hill, the "Sage of Wolfert's Roost," an able but exceedingly selfish politician, was a candidate for re-election on the Democratic ticket. Neither Hill nor Tammany Hall liked Cleveland. Hill was fond of beginning his speeches with the emphatic assertion, "I am a Democrat," but his chief concern was that his machine should continue to control the State of New York. It was charged that some of his followers entered into agreements to cast their votes for Harrison in return for Republican votes for Hill. Hill was re-elected by 18,000 votes, while Cleveland lost the State by 13,000. Cleveland carried the "solid South" but only two Northern States, Connecticut and New Jersey, with a total of 168 electoral votes. Harrison carried all the other Northern States and received 233 electoral votes. Cleveland's popular

Indiana and New York the Pivotal States.

Harrison Elected.

vote exceeded Harrison's by 100,000, but Republicans declared that in view of the wholesale suppression of the negro vote in the South, this meant little.

A great scandal was caused by the publication of a letter sent out by the National Republican Committee to party workers in Indiana. The letter bore the name of W. W. Dudley, treas-

The "Blocks of Five" Scandal. urer of the committee, and it contained the following significant instruction: "Divide the floaters into blocks of five and put a trusted man with the necessary funds in charge of these five, and make him responsible that none get away, and that all vote our ticket." "Floaters," of course, were purchasable voters, and Democrats charged that the letter furnished evidence of a purpose to bribe the Indiana electorate on a large scale.

The truth is that in this period political morality stood at a very low ebb in both parties. Bribery of voters took place in nearly every precinct in the country. Even some Republicans

Political Corruption General. and some Democrats demanded pay for voting their own tickets, and in case their demands were ignored would remain away from the polls or perhaps, in revenge, vote for the opposing candidates. As voting was done openly, a party worker could place a ballot in a bribed man's hand, march him to the voting place, and watch him deposit it; or else some bystander or member of the election board could report whether or not the voter had given "value received." Laws against corruption were weak; in some States only the receiver of a bribe could be punished. Defective or non-existent registration laws opened a wide door to wholesale "repeating" and other evils, particularly in cities, where many of the voters were strangers to each other. The author once knew personally a Civil War veteran who admitted that when home on a furlough he voted forty-nine times for Lincoln and Johnson—once for each absent member of his company. Almost any party worker who grew confidential could tell many stories illustrating the corruption that pervaded elections. Some of the men who managed the "dirty work" regretted that such a state of affairs existed, but they considered it a necessary evil because the other party resorted to such practices. Most men despaired of being able to improve such conditions and agreed with Senator Ingalls of Kansas when he flippantly exclaimed: "The purification of politics is an iridescent dream; the Decalogue and the Golden Rule have no place in a political campaign."

Prior to the election of 1888 Massachusetts had adopted the secret or "Australian" voting system, and before the next presidential election more than thirty other States imitated her

The Australian Ballot System.
example. The new system did much to eliminate bribery and other election evils, but it proved less successful than reformers had hoped. Ingenious and unscrupulous party workers often devised ways of finding out whether a "floater" had fulfilled his bargain, while unfortunately it is a trait of human nature that a man may be dishonorable enough to accept a bribe and "honorable" enough to abide by the terms of the corrupt bargain. With the secret ballot, more stringent laws against bribery, the adoption of registration requirements, and the growth of a healthier public sentiment, however, corruption in elections gradually became less prevalent in most parts of the nation.

CHAPTER XII

THE SECOND HARRISON

REPUBLICANS rejoiced exceedingly over the result of the election of 1888 and fondly believed that the most dangerous antagonist who had faced them for many years was disposed of forever. On the night before the inauguration a crowd of gleeful victors gathered near the White House and warbled discordantly a ditty that had been exceedingly popular during the campaign:

Cleveland in Retirement.

"Down in the cornfield hear that mournful sound,
All the Democrats are weeping—Grover's in the cold, cold ground."

As for Cleveland, he took the result of the contest philosophically, good-naturedly held an umbrella over the bared head of his successful rival as he took the oath of office in a dashing rain, and then retired to private life and the practice of law in the city of New York. Subsequent events were to show that he was not buried so deep politically as his enemies supposed.

Almost of necessity the new President named Blaine as secretary of state, a post the Plumed Knight had held under Garfield and one that suited his tastes. Of the other cabinet appointees, the best-known was Postmaster-General John Wanamaker, the celebrated Philadelphia merchant prince. To the recently created Department of Agriculture Harrison called ex-Governor Jeremiah M. Rusk of Wisconsin, a soldier and farmer; and "Uncle Jerry," as he was familiarly called, proved well fitted for the task of organizing the new department. Thomas C. Platt of New York claimed that Harrison's managers at Chicago promised that he should be secretary of the treasury, but Harrison had not been a party to the bargain and named William Windom of Minnesota, formerly a member of Garfield's cabinet, instead. Platt, how-

The New Cabinet.

ever, was given a large share in the disposal of patronage, but ultimately drifted into opposition to the President.

In his inaugural address Harrison promised that he would "fully and without evasion" enforce the civil service law, but hastened to add that "honorable party service will certainly not be esteemed by me a disqualification for public office." He kept his pledge regarding the classified list, but outside that list there was a rather clean sweep, and the guillotine of First Assistant Postmaster-General Clarkson became as famous as "Adlai's axe." In a year the new "headsman" decapitated 30,000 office-holders. In his dealings with favor-seekers Harrison, in self-defense, adopted a cold and repellent demeanor. According to Senator Hoar, "Blaine would refuse a request in a way that would seem like doing a favor. Harrison would grant a request in a way which seemed as if he were denying it." With members of his family and a few chosen friends the President was genial and warm-hearted, but politicians and the general public thought him very reserved and dignified, and it was popularly said that " Harrison sweats ice-water."

Harrison and Civil Service Reform.

Harrison's course regarding appointments disappointed some civil service reformers, but it should be said to his credit that he extended the classified list and strengthened the civil service commission by appointing to it men of force and zeal. One such appointee was Theodore Roosevelt. This young man, then thirty years of age, had served two terms in the New York legislature soon after graduating from Harvard, had been the Republican candidate for mayor of New York City in 1886, had run a cattle ranch in Dakota, and had shot grizzlies and other big game in the Far West. Roosevelt threw himself into the work with characteristic vigor and aggressiveness. In speeches in various places he explained to the people the needs of the reform, exploded the myths by which politicians had sought to discredit the commission, and put the spoilsmen on the defensive. "No longer was there an air of apology; blow was given for blow." In a report concerning the political assess-

Theodore Roosevelt Brings New Life to the Civil Service Commission.

ment of office-holders he charged that much of the money thus obtained was retained by "the jackals who have collected it." When Clarkson published an attack on the commission, Roosevelt properly characterized it as a "loose diatribe equally compounded of rambling declamation and misstatement." Harrison thought that Roosevelt wanted to go too fast with the reform, but ultimately he dismissed Clarkson and broke with other spoilsmen.

During the first two years of Harrison's administration the Republicans controlled both houses of Congress and were able to put through party measures. Their majority in the House, however, was small, and the minority frequently sought to block proceedings by determined filibustering; never before had there been so boisterous a session. The Speaker at this time was Thomas B. Reed of Maine, a big man physically and mentally, gifted with keen wit and the ability to utter striking and incisive phrases, one who was not afraid to take the bull by the horns. Reed repressed the Democratic efforts at obstruction so ruthlessly that he was nicknamed "Czar" Reed and for a time was the most talked of man in the country. The stringent rules adopted by the House were called the "Reed Rules." It is beyond question that Reed often used his power in a partisan manner, but it was an anomaly that a minority should be able to block business indefinitely, and even the Democrats recognized this fact when they came into power. Thenceforth in the House it was possible for a majority to expedite business, but in the Senate, owing to the absence of closure of debate, it remained possible down to our war with Germany for a few recalcitrants to hold up a measure indefinitely.

The great fight of the session came over a determined effort on the part of the Republicans to pass legislation to protect Southern negroes in their right to vote. The Democrats raised the spectre of black rule, and a movement was even begun in the South to boycott Northern products if the "Force Bill," as it was called, became a law. After bitter and protracted debates the bill passed the House, but in the Senate it was defeated by a coalition of Democrats and Silver Republicans (January, 1891).

Among the measures passed by this Congress were an act for the admission of Idaho and Wyoming—the Dakotas, Washington, and Montana had been admitted near the close of the previous session—an anti-lottery law, aimed at the notorious Louisiana Lottery Company, an "original package" law, which regulated interstate shipment of liquors, a law forfeiting land grants made to railways that had failed to fulfil the terms of their contracts, and a dependent pension act, under the operation of which the annual expense of pensions leaped in four years from $89,000,000 to $157,000,000. This Congress also passed a silver act, an anti-trust act, and a tariff act, and these measures require more detailed consideration.

New States.

During Cleveland's administration the silver-coinage question had attracted increasing attention. Silver dollars were regarded as a cumbrous nuisance in the East, and flowed back to the treasury in such streams that the vaults were choked with white metal coined under the Bland-Allison Act of 1878. In 1886 provision was made for the issue of silver certificates in denominations of one, two, and five dollars, but throughout Cleveland's term attempts to increase silver coinage failed, and by 1887 the relative value of silver and gold had declined to 22.10 to 1. Meanwhile the prices of corn, wheat, cotton, and other farm products fell to low levels, and many people attributed the decline to an insufficient supply of money. Such persons pointed out that the world's output of gold was decreasing, that the circulation of national-bank notes was contracting, that meanwhile the volume of business done was rapidly increasing. Silver-miners, debtors, the generally discontented, and many others, led by such men as Representative Bland of Missouri and Senator Stewart of Nevada, were insistently urging free coinage, and toward the end of 1889 the demand for a greater use of the white metal had become acute.

The Silver Question.

As we have seen, the Republican platform in 1888 contained

a declaration favorable to silver and a denunciation of Democrats for their alleged effort to demonetize that metal. Unlike Cleveland, Harrison found it expedient to display a friendly attitude toward silver, and Windom, his secretary of the treasury, in December, 1889, presented to Congress a report favoring an increase in the use of silver. After a protracted struggle Congress in 1890 repealed the Bland-Allison Act and enacted in its stead that the secretary of the treasury should every month purchase four and a half million ounces of silver bullion and issue in payment therefor, at the old ratio of 16 to 1, legal tender notes redeemable on demand in "gold or silver coin at his discretion." The act satisfied neither the partisans of free silver nor those who favored the single gold standard, but was a compromise resulting from the anxiety of Republican leaders to prevent a split in their party. Senator Sherman had a good deal to do with the details of the act, and it received his name, but he did not really believe in it and supported it merely to prevent worse from befalling. Some friends of silver accepted the bill on the half-a-loaf theory, but the radicals denounced it unsparingly. Bland characterized the measure as a "masterpiece of duplicity and double-dealing." Agitation for free coinage continued. Meanwhile the value of silver declined; by 1893 the market ratio between silver and gold bullion had fallen to 26.49 to 1.

The Sherman Silver-Purchase Act of 1890.

The famous Sherman Anti-Trust Act (July 2, 1890) resulted from the tendency to concentration of industry described in a previous chapter. Besides the Standard Oil Company, combinations had been formed in the cordage, meat, cottonseed, sugar, whiskey, and other industries. Centralization of business management, avoidance of duplication in many things, large-scale production, utilization of waste products, and other advantages often enabled the great organizations to effect many economies, but the trusts displayed little tendency to permit the public to share in the benefits resulting from increased efficiency; instead they were more likely, having stamped out competition, to raise the price of articles they controlled. Some prominent men insisted that

The Savings of Combination.

trusts were only a temporary phenomenon, that presently they would fall of their own weight, that they were only dangerous to their own stockholders. Even so keen a man as Speaker

Speaker Reed on Trusts.

Reed insisted that, aside from articles controlled by patents, there were no monopolies and never could be; "there is no power on earth that can raise the price of any necessity of life above a just price and keep it there." But thousands of business men who had felt the heavy hand of monopoly, and millions of consumers who were paying monopoly prices, did not accept this optimistic view. A congressional investigation (1888–89) had brought to light some startling facts regarding the operations of the Standard Oil Trust, the meat trust, and the sugar trust, and in his first annual message President Harrison asked for legislation on the subject.

The measure finally adopted was passed by a non-partisan vote, though some sleek senators of both parties affected to doubt its constitutionality. Its most important clause pro-

The Sherman Anti-Trust Act, 1890.

vided that "every contract, combination in form of trust or otherwise, or conspiracy, in restraint of trade or commerce among the several States, or with foreign nations, is hereby declared to be illegal." Few sentences have ever been so variously interpreted or have caused so much controversy. The penalties for violation of the act were fine or imprisonment, or both.

Some persons contended then, and the number thinking thus is greater now, that the act did not approach the problem from the right view-point. In their opinion the trusts were a natural

Should the Trusts be Broken up?

development, a manifestation of a tendency toward combination and closer social co-operation discernible the world over, and one of the logical outgrowths of the Industrial Revolution. To enact legislation to break them up would be to try to turn the clock backward; the proper remedy was to control them in such a way as to give society in general some of the benefits resulting from the savings and efficiency of combination.

The act did not solve the trust problem, nor did it break

up the trusts. When called on to interpret it the courts displayed, in the opinion of many, greater tenderness for private interests than for the public welfare. Of eight cases under the law during Harrison's administration the courts decided adversely to the government's contention in seven, and not a single person was actually tried on the facts. The trusts "changed their clothes" by substituting in place of the trust agreement such devices as "communities of interest" and "holding companies" chartered in complaisant States like New Jersey. The Standard Oil Trust, for example, in 1892 dropped the trust agreement and resorted to a "community of interest" between nine controlling stockholders, of whom John D. Rockefeller was one; seven years later the device of a holding company was adopted.

The Act is Evaded.

The Republicans interpreted the result of the election of 1888 as a mandate to revise the tariff. When the new Congress met, the committee on ways and means, headed by William McKinley of Ohio, took over a bill that had been reported to the Senate in the previous session and made it the basis of a measure the avowed object of which was to perfect the system of protection. For many months this McKinley Bill was debated, amended, and fought over, and not until October 1, 1890, was it finally enacted into law.

McKinley Tariff Bill, 1890.

Some articles that did not come into competition with home productions—or very little—were placed on the free list. The most important of these was raw sugar, which had been the most remunerative item of the old tariff. For the sake of Louisiana producers a bounty of two cents a pound was promised, while the bill also provided that on sugar imported from countries paying a bounty a duty of one-tenth of a cent a pound must be paid. On certain other articles, such as woollen cloths, dress-goods, carpets, and tin-plate, duties so high as to be almost prohibitive were imposed. The net result of all these changes was, of course, to reduce revenues and solve the problem of the surplus. To conciliate farmers, some of whom were beginning to doubt the

Terms of the Act.

blessings of protection, exceedingly high duties were imposed on potatoes, barley, wheat, eggs, and other farm products. In those days shipping such products as these into the United States was like "sending coal to Newcastle," hence the practical benefits which the agricultural population derived from such protection were little more than nominal, but the duties helped Republican politicians to keep the bucolic population satisfied.

Some Republicans, among them Secretary Blaine, who had never been accused of being a free-trader, thought the bill amounted to "protection run mad," but its framers defended it on the theory that high duties and high prices are a distinct advantage to a country. Prior to the meeting of Congress McKinley had said: "I do not prize the word cheap. It is not a word of comfort; it is not a word of cheer; it is not a word of inspiration! It is the badge of poverty; it is the signal of distress. . . . Cheap merchandise means cheap men and cheap men mean a cheap country; and that is not the kind of government our fathers followed, and it is not the kind their sons mean to follow."

Theories of Its Framers.

While the bill was still before Congress Blaine wrote to Senator Frye (July 11, 1890): "There is not a section or line in the entire bill that will open the market for another bushel of wheat or another barrel of pork." He was anxious to have "reciprocity" features incorporated into the measure, for the sake of increasing American foreign trade, particularly with South American countries. He was shrewd enough to see that, with wise management, a vast commerce could be built up with the states to the south of us. During his previous incumbency as secretary of state, he had tried to arrange for a Pan-American Congress, and in October, 1889, such a congress, composed of delegates from nineteen nations, at last actually convened at Washington. Better trade relations was one of the main topics considered by the congress, and Blaine was anxious to take advantage of the opportunities thus opened. The high priests of protection opposed the reciprocity plan, but the feature was finally incorporated, though not in the form Blaine desired. Instead

Blaine and Reciprocity.

of offering, as he proposed, to lower the protective bars to countries offering concessions to American goods, the Aldrich reciprocity amendment authorized the President to raise still higher bars against countries that refused such concessions.

Blaine expressed a belief that the McKinley type of protection would "protect the Republican Party into a speedy retirement." Events justified his prediction. Even before the McKinley bill was passed prices rose in anticipation; after it became a law they soared far beyond what the increase in duties justified, for profiteers seized upon the act as an excuse for extortion. Millions of people speedily felt the pinch of the increased cost of living, while, on the other hand, wages rose little or not at all. Furthermore, the Democrats made much of the lavish expenditures by the government, and filled the air with denunciations of "the Billion-Dollar Congress." To such arguments Speaker Reed retorted, "Yes, but this is a billion-dollar country."

The Act Causes Increased Prices.

Republican explanations were in vain. In the congressional election of 1890, which took place a month after the passage of the McKinley Act, the Democrats swept the country. Two hundred and thirty-five Democrats and only 88 Republicans were elected to the House, while in the Senate the Republican majority was reduced from 14 to 6. There had been no such political "tidal wave" since 1874. Even McKinley himself was beaten, though chiefly because a Democratic legislature had gerrymandered his district.

Political Reaction, 1890.

In this election a new party, which ultimately became known as the "People's Party" or "Populists," played a striking part. Its membership was chiefly composed of former Greenbackers and Grangers, and of members of a new and widely extended organization called the Farmers' Alliance. In some places it received aid from the Knights of Labor. It was chiefly active in the West and South; Kansas, "the mother of radical movements," was the cyclone centre. Hard times prevailed in both sections; the prices of cotton, corn, wheat, and other agricultural products were low; mortgages were more common than bank-accounts. The new party

The Populists.

demanded the free coinage of silver and supported other radical proposals. It denounced both the old parties as corrupt political oligarchies whose leaders were owned by the rich. Democrats and Republicans affected to laugh at its activities, but it elected two senators and nine representatives, and by its subsequent aggressiveness gave sleepless nights to leaders of both the old parties.

With the Democrats in control of the House of Representatives, very little except routine legislation was enacted by the new Fifty-Second Congress. Much of the time was wasted in partisan wrangling for political advantage in the coming presidential campaign.

When Blaine became secretary of state, the United States was in the midst of a controversy concerning our rights in the Samoan Islands. The earliest navigators in the South Seas had found these tropical islands and their picturesque people irresistibly attractive, and at the time of which we speak the celebrated romanticist Robert Louis Stevenson was spending the last years of his life there. The German Empire was entering upon that grandiose policy of world domination that was to prove so disastrous to herself and to humanity, and her leaders, having entered late into the struggle for colonies, coveted for commercial and strategic reasons this rich but still independent archipelago. But Great Britain and the United States also had interests in Samoa, and back in 1878 we had concluded an agreement whereby we obtained the fine harbor of Pago-Pago for a coaling station. With rival chieftains contending for supremacy, and with Germany intriguing for possession, the situation in Samoa was fraught with explosive possibilities.

The Samoan Question.

In April, 1886, the arrogant German consul, Herr Stübel, raised the German flag over Apia, the capital, and proclaimed that thenceforth only Germany should rule in that portion of the islands. The American consul, Greenebaum, retorted by proclaiming a protectorate over the whole archipelago. Both Germany and the United States disavowed the acts of their consuls, and a conference of

German Pretensions.

the three powers was held (1887) in Washington over Samoan affairs. The conference agreed that the native government was incompetent but disagreed as to what form of government should be substituted. The *status quo* was temporarily maintained, but German intrigues for possession continued.

In 1888, taking as a pretext a drunken brawl between some German sailors and a few Samoans, the Germans landed marines in Apia, deposed and deported King Malietoa, who was friendly to the Americans and the British, and set up a creature of their own named Tamasese. The American consul, Harold M. Sewall of Maine, vigorously protested against this high-handed course and received typically German answers. Many Samoans refused to recognize the authority of the German puppet, and, taking to the bush, conducted a guerilla warfare against the Teutons, receiving more or less aid and comfort from the American and British residents. Opportunely there arrived in Samoan waters the American gunboat *Adams*, under Commander Richard Leary, whose Irish name, as Stevenson remarks in his account of these stirring times, was diagnostic. Leary set himself energetically to thwarting the German plans, and once ran his ship directly between the German corvette *Adler* and a Samoan position at Apia that the Germans were about to bombard. Somewhat later, when the *Adams* had gone to Hawaii with despatches, German marines attempted to surprise a force of Samoans but fell (December 18, 1888) into an ambush and were driven back to the beach after losing fifty men. Furious over this defeat, the Germans began bombarding indiscriminately, endangering American property and killing Samoan women and children. Their armed boats also seized an American flag in the harbor of Apia; the hated bunting was trampled on and torn to shreds. The American vice-consul sent word of these happenings home, and added: "Admiral with squadron necessary immediately."

The American people did not want Samoa, but news of these insults aroused their wrath. The Cleveland government hurried war-ships to the island, and early in March, 1889, the *Trenton*, *Vandalia*, and *Nipsic*, under Admiral Kimberly, lay at anchor

German Intervention in 1888.

in the harbor of Apia, confronting an equal number of German ships, the *Adler*, *Eber*, and *Olga*, while Great Britain was represented by the cruiser *Calliope*. A conflict seemed

Rumors of War.

likely, and four days after Harrison's inauguration a rumor was circulated in Germany that the *Nipsic* had fired on the *Olga;* a little later a cablegram from Kiel, transmitting a report that was supposed to have come by way of Australia, repeated the rumor and added that the American vessel had been sunk by a German torpedo. American anger flamed high; the fighting spirit was aroused; our government even made tentative preparations for war. But presently the truth regarding events in Samoa arrived, and it was found that there had only been a terrific battle of the elements. A tropical hurricane had swept over the archipelago, and of all the war-ships at Apia only the *Calliope* escaped.

The disaster helped to slacken the warlike tension, and Chancellor Bismarck proposed that a conference should be held to settle the Samoan question. When the conference

Berlin Conference, 1889.

met in Berlin (April 29, 1889), Bismarck sought to secure recognition of Germany's political predominance in Samoa and adopted his usual arrogant, domineering tone toward the American representatives. The Americans cabled home that the Chancellor was very irritable, but Blaine, in no wise daunted, flashed back: "The extent of the Chancellor's irritability is not the measure of American right." The British representatives united with the Americans in opposing the German pretensions, and ultimately Germany receded from her advanced position and agreed to the restoration of King Malietoa and to the establishment of a protectorate

Islands Divided.

in which all three powers should participate. Ten years later Great Britain withdrew entirely from Samoan affairs, the United States received Tutuila, with its valuable harbor of Pago-Pago, and a few smaller islands, while Germany was allowed the rest.

At home the Samoan quarrel served to direct public attention to the urgent need of a greater navy; some new vessels had been added under the Cleveland administration, and now under Harrison many ships, including several battleships, were authorized. Abroad our bold stand against German aggres-

Results of the Samoan Quarrel.

siveness attracted wide-spread and favorable comment, particularly in England and France. For the first time the United States departed from its traditional international policy and insisted on participating in affairs outside America. For the first time the Republic of the West collided with the ambitions of the grasping, ruthless House of Hohenzollern. There were to be other clashes, notably in Manila harbor in 1898, and regarding Venezuela in 1902, and finally an armed conflict.

Early in 1891 a revolt broke out in Chile against the authority of President Balmaceda, who was accused of attempting to set up a dictatorship. The United States refused to accord bellig-

The Chilean Difficulty.

erent rights to the Congressionalists, as the rebels were called, and this party attributed the refusal to the influence of the American minister, Patrick Egan, whom they accused of undue friendship for Balmaceda. In May a Congressionalist merchant vessel called the *Itata* was seized at San Diego, California, for attempting to carry munitions of war to the rebels contrary to our neutrality laws. The crew overpowered the United States officials and sailed southward, escaping the cruiser *Charleston*, which was sent in pursuit. The fugitive vessel reached Iquique safely but was finally surrendered on demand to a United States squadron under Rear-Admiral McCann. The hard feeling created among the Congressionalists by this episode was increased when their forces triumphed and some of the Balmacedists were accorded a safe refuge in the American legation at Santiago. While feeling was still bitter a party of sailors on shore leave from the American cruiser *Baltimore* were set upon in the streets of Valparaiso by a mob of Chileans aided by policemen, and two were killed and nearly a score more were wounded. The United States at once demanded an explanation, but the new government procrastinated. In his annual message of December, 1891, President Harrison discussed the matter, whereupon Señor Matta, Chilean minister of foreign affairs, cabled to Chilean representatives

throughout the world declaring that the statements on which
the President's discussion were based were "erroneous or deliberately incorrect" and "that there is no exactness or sincerity
in what is said in Washington." The Chilean explanation,
which reached Washington soon after, proved unsatisfactory.
The United States made preparations for war and presented
(January 21, 1892) an ultimatum demanding of Chile that the
Matta despatch should be withdrawn and an apology offered
for it, that the refugees in the legation at Valparaiso should be
given safe-conduct out of the country, and that an indemnity
should be paid to the injured sailors of the *Baltimore* or their
heirs. Chile found it expedient to comply.

In March, 1891, a number of Italians accused of having
assassinated the chief of police of New Orleans were lynched
by a mob, which broke into the city prison to accomplish that

A Quarrel
with Italy.

purpose. Italy at once demanded that the mob
should be punished and that an indemnity should
be paid. Secretary Blaine stated in reply that he regretted the affair, but he pointed out that under our federal system criminal proceedings against the mob lay within the sphere
of the local Louisiana authorities, that the national government
had no power in the matter. He urged upon Governor Nicholls,
however, that the mob should be brought to justice, but this
was a difficult thing to do, for the public believed that the dead
Italians were members of a secret blackmailing organization
known as the Mafia, and the lynching was generally approved.
After further diplomatic exchanges Italy withdrew her minister,
Baron Fava, from Washington, and the United States recalled
Minister Porter from Rome. The judicial proceedings against
the mob came to nothing, but Congress, not as a matter of right
but as an expression of the regret felt by the United States,
voted $25,000 to the families of the murdered Italians, while
President Harrison in a message referred to the matter in tactful words that soothed Italian pride. In April, 1892, Minister
Porter and Baron Fava returned to their respective posts and
normal diplomatic relations were resumed.

The episode is chiefly important because it revealed a defect in our governmental system that has more than once involved us in difficulties with foreign states and might some day cause

A Dangerous Defect.
us to be involved in war. It is clear that the federal government, which has charge of diplomatic relations, ought also to possess the power to safeguard foreigners sojourning in the United States and to punish persons injuring them. We shall see later how the same lack of authority complicated relations with Japan under Presidents Roosevelt and Wilson.

The Harrison administration inherited from its predecessor a troublesome dispute with Great Britain over fur-seals. These interesting animals, the pelts of which are extremely valuable,

The Fur-Seal Question.
were then, and are still, in the habit in the spring and summer of landing on the Pribyloff Islands near the centre of Bering Sea in order to rear their young. Leaving their "pups" upon the beach, the grown-up seals swim far out to sea in search of food; and later in the year young and old alike take to the water and rove hundreds of miles southward far out of sight of land. In 1870 the United States Government gave, for a consideration, a concession to the Alaskan Commercial Company to kill every year on the Pribyloffs a certain number of "bachelor seals," as the males are called. Attracted by the great value of the fur, other sealers, especially Americans, Canadians, and Russians, pursued the animals in the open sea, killing males and females indiscriminately, causing many of the helpless "pups" on shore to die of starvation, and even threatening the total extinction of the species. These hunters contended that they had a perfect right to carry on such operations in the open sea outside the three-mile limit to which international law says a nation's sovereignty extends.

In 1881, however, the United States set up the claim that the whole of Bering Sea belonged to the United States and that it, therefore, had the right to regulate or prohibit sealing therein. Five years later three vessels of British register engaged in sealing operations in the forbidden waters were seized and condemned. Further seizures were made in 1887, and a federal district court in the condemnation proceedings held that the rights transferred by Russia in 1867 included control of Bering Sea as a *mare clausum*, or closed sea.

Vigorous protests were made against such seizures, and in 1887–88 Secretary Manning conducted negotiations with Great Britain, Russia, Japan, and other nations in the hope of reach-

The "Closed Sea" Contention.

ing an international agreement whereby the fur seals would be protected against extermination. The negotiations failed because of the objections of Canada. In March, 1889, Congress officially sanctioned the doctrine of *mare clausum*, and during the following season eight more vessels were seized. Great Britain vigorously protested, and a long argument ensued between Secretary Blaine and Lord Salisbury, the British Premier and Foreign Minister. Blaine not only advanced the doctrine of a closed sea and argued that the seals should be saved from destruction, but he even contended that the United States had a property right in the seals, wherever they might go, just as if they were domestic animals. Salisbury denied the force of such arguments, and insisted that there must be no more seizures. At one time the controversy reached the danger-point, for Canadians felt bitter about the confiscated vessels, while there were Americans who enjoyed the hazardous game of "twisting the lion's tail."

Finally the two nations, with their usual good sense, agreed (February 29, 1892) to submit the dispute to arbitration. The tribunal met in Paris in the following year. The United States

Question Arbitrated.

was represented by eminent counsel, but international law was against them. The arbitrators rejected the doctrine of *mare clausum*, accepted the British contention that the seals were *feræ naturæ* and not, as the Americans contended, practically domestic animals, and awarded damages to owners whose vessels had been seized outside the three-mile limit. The tribunal also recommended a set of regulations for the future protection of the fur-seals, and this desirable object was ultimately accomplished by international agreement.

The only other important diplomatic complication of Harrison's administration resulted from a revolution in Hawaii. These beautiful islands, the gems of the central Pacific, were first visited more than a century before by the celebrated navigator Captain Cook, and the native inhabitants displayed such little sense of appreciation for his efforts that they killed and ate their discoverer. But many missionaries and other white settlers, largely Americans, had since settled in Hawaii and had wrought a great transformation. A prosperous sugar-planting industry had been built up, and the islands were much visited by travellers, both because of their natural charm and because they formed a half-way house on the way to the Orient. The native Kanakas had dropped their cannibal practices and had adopted many civilized institutions, including a liberal constitution.

The Hawaiian Islands.

In 1891 King Kalakaua, a royal wastrel, died and was succeeded by his sister, Queen Liliuokalani, a woman of education and charm but a stickler for the divine right of rulers. In January, 1893, exasperated by the restraints imposed upon her by the old constitution, she tried to set it aside and substitute another, more favorable to royal prerogatives. This attempted *coup d'état* precipitated a revolution, which resulted in the deposition of the Queen and the substitution of a provisional government, headed by Sanford B. Dole, who was judge of the supreme court. Dole was of American descent, and many of the other revolutionists were of foreign antecedents, though natives also participated. No blood was shed, but there was much excitement in Honolulu, and the provisional government asked the American minister, John L. Stevens, for help in maintaining order. At that time there was no cable to the islands, so Stevens, without waiting for instructions from Washington, landed marines from the cruiser *Boston*, formally recognized the new republic, raised the American flag over the government building, and proclaimed Hawaii under the protection of the United States. For half a century there had been more or less desire in the United States to annex the islands; Stevens himself was eager for such a consummation; and he was probably aware that his superiors

Revolution and American Intervention.

at Washington had similar views. "The Hawaiian pear is now fully ripe," he wrote to his government, "and this is the golden hour for the United States to pluck it."

A Hawaiian commission hastened to Washington to ask for annexation. They found both President Harrison and John W. Foster, who had succeeded Blaine as secretary of state, in a receptive mood. The protectorate proclaimed by

Annexation Treaty Negotiated but Not Ratified.

Stevens was disavowed, but a treaty of annexation was speedily negotiated and signed (February 15, 1893). Those who favored the treaty urged the great commercial and strategic value of the islands, and pointed to the danger that they might be seized by some other power. Opponents of annexation declared that the American minister had taken too active a part in the overthrow of the Queen, and asserted that the provisional government represented the foreign rather than the native population. Many senators felt that the acquisition of territory outside America was too momentous a step to be taken hastily, and for this and other reasons action on the treaty was delayed until after the Harrison administration came to an end.

The circumstances which had brought about that administration's defeat remain to be told. As President, Harrison displayed integrity and ability, but he never succeeded in becoming the real master of his party. He antag-

Harrison Unpopular.

onized some of the great Republican chieftains, notably Quay of Pennsylvania and Platt of New York, while he failed to arouse much enthusiasm among the rank and file. Ex-President Hayes humorously records in his diary that one observer explained Harrison's lack of popularity on the ground that "he is a deacon in the Presbyterian Church. They are never liked by the people. They are stiff, cold, distant. They are the elect of God—by faith, not works, to be saved."

Enemies of the President persistently besought Blaine once more to enter the presidential lists. But political usage estopped a member of the cabinet from seeking a nomination against his chief, and Blaine long rejected all overtures. The two men, however, had never been really cordial; political differences had multiplied; a feud had developed between their wives; while

Blaine Resigns.

Blaine had become a brooding invalid. Only three days before the meeting of the national convention he yielded to the pleadings of his wife and others, and in a curt note, containing no explanations, resigned from the cabinet (June 4, 1892).

It was too late. The Harrison delegates, a large proportion of whom were federal office-holders, controlled the organization of the convention and renominated Harrison on the first

Harrison and Reed.

ballot, giving him 535 votes, 82 more than a majority. Blaine and William McKinley each received 182 votes. For second place on the ticket the convention nominated Whitelaw Reid, editor of the *New York Tribune*. Sick and disillusioned, the Plumed Knight retired to his home in Maine, where he died early in the following year.

When Grover Cleveland retired from office in 1889, he stepped into a lucrative law practice in New York City, but he made it his custom to spend a generous portion of his time at "Grey

Cleveland's Stand on Public Questions.

Gables," on the Massachusetts coast, where he entertained his friends and indulged his fondness for fishing. His enemies hoped that his political career was ended, nor did he seemingly make much effort to disappoint them. He continued, however, to take an interest in public questions, and when his opinion on such matters was sought, he was accustomed to give plain, straightforward answers. His party was becoming more and more divided upon the currency question, but, instead of temporizing and trying to win favor with both factions, Cleveland (February 10, 1891) boldly voiced his uncompromising hostility to "the dangerous and reckless experiment of free, unlimited, and independent silver coinage." Instead of ending his political prospects, as many observers predicted, this statement ultimately helped him, while the fact that he was the main exponent of tariff reform created a wide-spread demand for his renomination.

The opposition to Cleveland rallied around David B. Hill,

who was now a United States senator. In February, 1892, long before the usual time, Hill made use of his control of the

Cleveland and Stevenson.

Democratic machine in New York to hold a packed or "snap" convention, which named delegates favorable to him. But this sharp practice by one whose alleged treachery in 1888 had not been forgotten proved a boomerang. Friends of Cleveland held an "anti-snap" convention and sent a contesting delegation. Elsewhere the Cleveland tide set in so strongly that when the national convention assembled in Chicago (June 21) he was renominated on the first ballot. As a concession to the free-silver and spoils elements, Adlai E. Stevenson of Illinois, the former "headsman," was named for the vice-presidency.

The platform denounced the McKinley Act as "the culminating atrocity of class legislation," and declared that since the act went into effect there had been ten reductions of wages to

Democratic Tariff Stand.

one increase. The "constitutional power to impose and collect tariff duties except for the purposes of revenue only" was boldly denied. In his letter of acceptance, however, Cleveland did not take so radical a stand, but stated that no exterminating war would be waged against any American interest and that the Democracy merely contemplated "a fair and careful distribution of necessary tariff burdens rather than the precipitation of free trade."

A formal organization of the People's Party, or Populists, had been effected in 1891, and on the 2d of July a national convention assembled at Omaha. General James B. Weaver, a

Populists Nominate Weaver and Field.

former Greenback chieftain, was nominated for President, and James G. Field of Virginia was named for Vice-President. The platform denounced both the old parties as the tools of capitalists, and declared "they propose to drown the outcries of a plundered people with the uproar of a sham battle over the tariff." The general state of the country was portrayed in the following pessimistic passage:

We meet in the midst of a nation brought to the verge of moral and material ruin. Corruption dominates the ballot-box, the legislature, the Congress, and touches even the ermine of the bench.

The people are demoralized; most of the States have been compelled to isolate the voters at the polling-places to prevent universal intimidation or bribery. The newspapers are largely subsidized or muzzled; public opinion silenced; business prostrated; our homes covered with mortgages; labor impoverished; and the land concentrating in the hands of the capitalists. The urban workmen are denied the right of organization for self-protection; imported pauperized labor beats down their wages; a hireling standing army, unrecognized by our laws, is established to shoot them down, and they are rapidly degenerating into European conditions. The fruits of the toil of millions are boldly stolen to build up colossal fortunes for a few, unprecedented in the history of mankind; and the possessors of these, in turn, despise the republic and endanger liberty. From the same prolific womb of governmental injustice we breed the two great classes of tramps and millionaires.

Among the remedies proposed were the free and unlimited coinage of silver at the ratio of 16 to 1, direct election of senators, the initiative and referendum, shorter hours for labor, the establishment of postal savings-banks, a graduated income tax, and the governmental ownership and operation of railroads, telegraphs, and telephones. Such proposals excited much ridicule in conservative circles, but as the historian reads this Populistic platform he is forced to reflect upon how much it reflected actual conditions and foreshadowed the future.

Populist
Remedies.

When Cleveland retired from office four years before, exultant Republicans had gleefully sung:

> "Grover! Grover!
> All is over!"

Now confident Democrats were constantly chanting:

> "Grover! Grover!
> Four more years of Grover.
> In he comes,
> Out they go,
> Then we'll be in clover!"

The course of events helped to make good this hopeful prediction. There was much economic discontent, and Democrats pointed out that, despite roseate protectionist promises, many protected industries were cutting the wages of employees.

In June such a reduction made by the Carnegie Steel Company provoked a strike at Homestead, Pennsylvania; in bloody clashes between the strikers and Pinkerton detectives hired by the company nearly a score of persons were killed and many more were wounded. This and other events reacted against the party in power.

The Course of Events Favors Democrats.

Most veteran political observers predicted that the election would be close; it proved to be unexpectedly decisive. Cleveland carried the Solid South and New York, Indiana, California, Connecticut, Illinois, New Jersey, West Virginia, and Wisconsin, and received 5 electoral votes from Michigan and 1 each from North Dakota and Ohio, his total electoral vote being 277. Harrison received only 145 electoral votes, Weaver 22. The divided vote in Michigan was due to the fact that a Democratic legislature had temporarily established the old method of choosing electors by congressional districts. In five States—Colorado, Idaho, Kansas, North Dakota, and Wyoming—the Democrats had nominated no electors, but voted for the Populist candidates, their idea being that if the electoral result should be close and these States should be carried by the Populists, the election might be thrown into the House of Representatives, which was controlled by the Democrats. Weaver, in fact, won three of these States— Kansas, Colorado, and Idaho. He also carried Nevada and received one electoral vote in Oregon and North Dakota; in these three States there had been partial fusion with the Democrats. Of the popular vote Cleveland received 5,556,543, Harrison 5,175,582, Weaver 1,040,886. For the first time since 1859 the Democrats would control the presidency and both houses of Congress.

Cleveland Re-elected.

The Democrats rejoiced exceedingly over the result, but if they could have foreseen what the future had in store they would not have felt so much elated over their triumph.

CHAPTER XIII

HARD TIMES AND FREE SILVER

FOR some years vast preparations had been making for holding in Chicago an exposition in honor of the quadricentenary of the discovery of America by Columbus. The enterprise was pushed with customary Western energy and with a taste that surprised the skeptical East. Almost every nation in the world was represented, and about $35,000,000 was expended in gathering the exhibits and transforming a tangled stretch of swamp and sandy plain along Lake Michigan into "a shimmering dream of loveliness under the magic touch of landscape gardener and architect and artist." Between May 1, 1893, when the exposition was opened by President Cleveland, and the last of October, when it was closed, there were 21,477,213 paid admissions. The Duke of Veragua, a lineal descendant of the discoverer, attended as an official guest; likewise the Spanish Infanta Eulalia. Full-sized reproductions of the caravels *Santa Maria*, *Pinta*, and *Niña* were brought from the port from which Columbus sailed to the lake shore, where there was also exhibited a model of a Viking ship. Another exhibit that recalled events of the past and paid honor to the immortal dead was a reproduction of the convent of La Rabida, so intimately connected with the career of Columbus. There were also a monster Ferris Wheel, a Babel-like Midway Plaisance, and a multitude of other wonders. But the real importance of the celebration lay in the fact that the exposition broadened the outlook of millions of Americans whose lives had been narrow and colorless, and opened their eyes to the power of beauty in art and nature.

American pride in the marvellous achievements of four centuries was marred by hard times, and, even as multitudes were journeying to and from the magic "White City" beside Lake Michigan, the financial affairs of the nation were falling into a confusion that brought ruin and misery to millions.

A drop of $50,000,000 in customs duties under the McKinley Act and the expenditures authorized by the "Billion Dollar Congress" had transformed a troublesome surplus into a much more trying deficit. The financial stringency proved all the more embarrassing because of a peculiar situation relating to the currency. At the end of Harrison's presidency there were outstanding $346,000,-000 of greenbacks, and, in addition, since the passage of the Sherman Silver Purchase Act of 1890, there had been annually added $54,000,000 of "coin certificates." The greenbacks were, of course, redeemable in gold. The Sherman Silver Purchase Act had provided that the secretary of the treasury should redeem the "coin certificates" "in gold or silver coin at his discretion, it being the established policy of the United States to maintain the two metals on a parity with each other upon the present legal ratio or such other ratio as may be provided by law." Under both Harrison and Cleveland the secretaries of the treasury chose to redeem the certificates in gold—a policy that was bitterly criticised by the friends of silver. Usage had established a rule that the treasury must keep on hand a gold reserve of not less than $100,000,000. During 1891 and 1892 there was an insistent demand for gold to be sent abroad to meet unfavorable trade balances (a condition partly due to prohibitive schedules under the McKinley Act), and there was a net loss of over $90,000,000, much of which was drawn from the treasury. A circumstance that made the situation all the more serious was that the coin certificates, even when redeemed, must be reissued again and again, and thus they formed a sort of "endless chain" for the depletion of the gold reserve. Even before Harrison's retirement the reserve fell so low that the Treasury Department was forced to borrow $6,000,000 of gold on call, and resort to other temporary expedients in order to avoid the necessity of issuing bonds. Preparations for such an issue were actually made.

The Currency Situation and the Gold Reserve.

The government's financial difficulties were partly due to unwise legislation, but the country was caught in a business depression that was world-wide. Hard times were probably inevitable, even had the Republicans remained in power, but the Democratic victory, foreshadowing tariff revision and perhaps changes in the monetary system, served to deepen the dark cloud of doubt and apprehension.

Hard Times Inevitable.

It is a commonplace of financial history that hard times follow flush times as the trough of the sea follows the crest of the wave. In the United States periods of great depression have come about every twenty years. There were such depressions in 1819, 1837, 1857, 1873, 1893, and 1913–14, while smaller flurries have usually taken place between each pair of these dates. Why this periodicity of panics should occur at such regular intervals has never been satisfactorily explained, but the fact is undeniable. By some it is contended that under our present currency laws panics are impossible, but only time will show whether or not their view is correct.

The Periodicity of Panics.

Even before Cleveland's inauguration securities fluctuated violently, bankers grew conservative regarding loans, money rates rose, the Philadelphia & Reading Railroad went into bankruptcy (February 20, 1893), and a sharp stock panic shook the exchanges. As spring passed and summer came on conditions gradually grew worse. The Erie Railroad and a great trust called the National Cordage Company followed the Reading into bankruptcy, banks began to resort to clearing-house certificates, the mints of India were closed (June 26) to the private coinage of silver, thereby still further depressing the value of that metal, many Western silver mines closed, people began to hoard gold, prices of agricultural products, already excessively low, continued to decline, and a chain of nearly fifty Western banks that had been founded by a certain Zimri Dwiggins went down in one grand crash. During the year hundreds of banks failed, and the total liabilities of mercantile failures amounted to

Premonitory Symptoms and then the Grand Collapse.

$347,000,000; railway construction almost ceased, and 22,500 miles passed into the hands of receivers; the production of iron, the best barometer of business conditions, fell off almost a fourth; debtors found it increasingly difficult to meet their obligations; property often had to be sacrificed at low prices; and ruin came to many thousands of honest, toiling people.

All sorts of remedies, sensible and otherwise, were proposed to meet the emergency, and an almost universal demand arose that the President should call an extra session of Congress. He complied and summoned it (June 30) to meet on the 7th of August. In his opinion one of the main causes of the panic was the Sherman Silver Purchase Act, and in a special message he demanded its unconditional repeal. The friends of silver fought repeal to the bitter end. They declared that what the country needed was not less but more money. It was only through the aid of many "gold" Republicans and by vigorous use of patronage that Cleveland obtained his wish (October 30). In the Senate 26 Republicans voted for repeal, and only 22 Democrats. A chasm was opening in the Democracy that did not close for years.

Sherman Silver- Purchase Act Repealed.

The situation in which the Democracy found itself proved all the more serious because as an executive Cleveland had at least one great fault: he lacked tact in dealing with lesser Democratic chieftains. He was patriotic, he was conscientious, he was courageous, but he did not know how to lead. As ours is a government by parties, unity of party action is essential to successful administration, but this unity Cleveland was often unable to secure. Having once decided that a given course was the right one, he was inclined to be intolerant of those who differed with him, for coercion came to him more naturally than conciliation. This trait in his character was more pronounced in his second administration than his first, and even before the quarrel over silver he had alienated many Democratic leaders by his impatience at their advice regarding appointments. However, even had his skill as a political leader been far greater than it was, he

Cleveland's Defects as a Leader.

would hardly have proved equal to piloting his party past the rocks that rose in its course.

New differences speedily developed over an attempt to revise the tariff, the great task to which the party stood pledged. Soon after the opening of the regular session William L. Wilson of West Virginia, chairman of the Committee on Ways and Means, reported (December 19) to the House a bill upon which that committee had been working since August. The bill did not entirely fulfil the platform pledge of a tariff for revenue only, but it provided in many cases for substituting *ad valorem* for specific duties, reduced the almost prohibitory duties of the McKinley Act on such articles as silks, cottons, woollens, and glass, and placed lumber, coal, iron ore, wool, and other raw materials that form the basis of production on the free list. It was estimated that the customs receipts would be reduced about $50,000,000 annually, so a slight increase was made in the internal-revenue taxes on distilled spirits, and a tax of 2 per cent was levied on incomes of over $4,000.

Wilson Tariff Bill.

The bill failed to command united Democratic support. It was again the old story of the London fishmonger who favored "free trade in everything but herring." Seventeen Democrats voted against the bill in the House, but it passed that body by 204 to 140. In the Senate the Democrats had a majority of only three over the Republicans and Populists combined, and this narrow margin enabled Democratic malcontents to work their will with the measure. The senators from Louisiana disliked the sugar schedule; the senators from Maryland, West Virginia, and Alabama wished to retain protection for iron ore and coal; others, like Hill of New York, wished to eliminate the income-tax provision. Under the leadership of Brice of Ohio and Gorman of Maryland—both protectionists—the Democratic insurgents, with Republican aid, made over six hundred changes in the measure, and so mangled it that it was almost unrecognizable. Coal, iron ore, and sugar were taken off the free list; specific duties in place of *ad valorem* were restored on some imports; and the

Senate Amends the Bill.

rates on many articles were raised. It was charged that the
sugar trust secured favorable changes by corrupt means, and
one senator, Quay of Pennsylvania, openly admitted that he
had purchased sugar stock for a rise.   Cleveland denounced
the Senate bill as involving "party perfidy and
party dishonor."   The House at first refused to
accept it, but in the end Gorman and his associates
triumphed (August, 1894).   The President let the
bill become a law without his signature, but he wrote to a representative concerning it: "The livery of Democratic tariff
reform has been stolen and worn in the service of Republican
protection."

*"Party
Perfidy and
Party
Dishonor."*

The contempt with which the act was regarded by the public
was presently increased when early in 1895 the Supreme Court,
by the narrow margin of 5 to 4, held that the income-tax
feature was unconstitutional.   The ground taken
by the majority was that the income tax was a
direct tax, and that it had not been apportioned
according to population, as the Constitution required with regard to such taxes.   As the court fifteen years
before had unanimously upheld an income tax levied during
the Civil War, the new decision aroused much criticism.   The
decision cut off a large source of revenue and greatly added to
the financial difficulties of the government.

*Income Tax
Adjudged
Unconstitu-
tional.*

These difficulties had already caused grave embarrassment.
The repeal of the Sherman Silver Act had brought little or no
relief either to the country or the government.   Many people
contended, of course, that its repeal made matters
worse.   By the middle of January, 1894, the gold
reserve fell to $70,000,000, a "feeble prop" with
which to support $500,000,000 in paper, most of
which was in circulation.   In desperation Secretary
of the Treasury Carlisle offered to sell for gold $50,000,000 of
5 per cent bonds, redeemable in ten years.   The proposal
aroused strenuous opposition from the friends of silver, and the
Knights of Labor even applied for a judicial order to restrain
the secretary from making the issue.   As the premium de-

*Bonds
Issued to
Maintain
the Gold
Reserve.*

manded was 17 per cent, bids came in slowly; it was only by going to New York and making a personal appeal to bankers that Carlisle finally placed the loan. The net proceeds realized amounted to $58,661,000, but the treasury "was chasing a phantom," for subscribers to the bonds presented $24,000,000 in notes and drew from the treasury gold with which to pay their subscriptions. There seemed to be no way of stopping the operations of the "endless chain," whose buckets were automatically dipping into the treasury. Congress wrangled continually over what should be done and could agree on no sensible remedy, while business conditions had become so bad that people were constantly drawing gold from the treasury and hoarding it. By August 7 the reserve had fallen to $52,189,000.

The "Endless Chain."

A second issue of $50,000,000 in bonds in November again afforded only temporary relief. The "endless chain" continued in operation, and in a single month $45,000,000 in gold was drawn from the treasury. In a special message Cleveland proposed (January 28, 1895) that fifty-year gold bonds should be issued in sufficient quantity to provide for the redemption and cancellation of all the legal-tender notes, but Congress continued to quarrel about the respective merits of gold and silver and did nothing.

New Difficulties.

The reserve speedily dropped to $41,000,000, and Cleveland found it expedient to call to the White House J. Pierpont Morgan, the most astute and influential of New York financiers. The upshot of this famous conference was that the banking-houses of Morgan, Belmont, and Rothschild agreed to sell the government three and a half million ounces of gold ($65,118,000), taking in exchange thirty-year 3¾ per cent bonds at 104½. The lenders also agreed to use their influence to protect the treasury against the withdrawal of gold. Silver men of all parties went wild when they heard that Cleveland had made such a bargain with the "Gold Bugs of Wall Street." In the House William Jennings Bryan, a fluent and rising young member from Nebraska, declared that the President had attempted to inoculate the Democratic

The Bargain with J. P. Morgan.

party "with Republican virus, and blood poisoning has set in."
The fact that Morgan and his associates soon sold the bonds
at a big advance over the price paid, helped to fan the flame of
criticism. But Cleveland never ceased to believe that he did
right in the matter, and it is beyond question that his critics
failed to give due weight to the provision whereby the bond
syndicate undertook to protect the treasury against the withdrawal of gold.

It was not until January, 1896, that the reserve again ran so
low as to necessitate a new issue of bonds. The amount was
fixed at $100,000,000, the rate at 4 per cent, and, as a conces-
sion to popular criticism, the loan was thrown open
to public subscription. The whole issue was sold
at prices averaging about 7 per cent higher than
that paid by Morgan and his associates for the previous loan.
In some circles this was interpreted as proving Cleveland's
mistake in dealing with Morgan.

Popular
Loan of
1896.

Again the "endless chain" was set in motion; the reserve
once more fell below the hundred-million mark. But the momentous political campaign of 1896 was being fought, and many
bankers and other moneyed men feared that a new
issue of bonds might react in favor of Bryan and
his free-silver associates. These business men,
therefore, co-operated to protect the treasury, and
in a single week more than $25,000,000 in gold was
paid in for paper legal-tenders. The result of the election assured the maintenance of the gold standard, gold came out of
its hiding-places, and thereafter an adequate gold reserve was
easily maintained.

Business
Men Unite
to Protect
the Reserve,
1896.

The financial troubles of the government were only one
phase of the prevailing hard times. The year 1894 surpassed
any other in the history of the United States in the number of
workers out of employment. Many plans were
proposed to meet the needs of the hour, but the
most startling was that brought forward by an
agitator named J. S. Coxey, of Ohio. Coxey announced that
he would lead an army of the unemployed to the capital to ask

Coxey's
Army.

Congress to pass a good-roads law and a non-interest-bearing bond law, and thereby furnish work for the needy and expand the monetary system. The "army," consisting of about 100 men, "escorted by forty-three reporters," started from Massillon, Ohio, on March 24 and depended for food mainly on contributions along the way. In Europe certain newspapers gravely likened the movement of Coxey's nondescript force to the march of the mob from Paris to the palace at Versailles, but at home the press treated the whole affair as a huge joke, and the public were daily regaled with burlesque descriptions of "General" Coxey and his subordinates and of their doings. On the last day of April the army, then numbering about 300, reached Washington, and on May day they marched to the Capitol in the presence of thousands of curious spectators. When Coxey and two of his lieutenants walked on the Capitol lawn, they were arrested for trespassing on the grass, and for this offense and for displaying a banner without a permit they were imprisoned for twenty days. By the time they were released their picturesque followers were scattered to the four winds.

In certain Far Western States other leaders, notably Kelly and Frye, imitated Coxey, and led ragged bands of "Industrials" or "Commonwealers" toward the East. Many of the men who participated in these marches had been stranded in the West and took advantage of the opportunity to get back home; others were mere tramps; some were criminals. These armies proved less law-abiding than that under Coxey: in some cases they seized railway trains; now and again they engaged in violent encounters with the police. But, like Coxey's force, none of these armies ever became large; and they were important only as being symptomatic of hard times and the prevailing unrest.

Eleven days after Coxey's band reached Washington a strike began at the plant of the Pullman Palace Car Company, near Chicago, as a result of a reduction in wages. Many of the strikers belonged to the American Railway Union, an organization with a membership of more than 100,000 and headed by Eugene V. Debs, a shrewd and determined yet kindly labor leader who was later several times the Socialist candidate for President. Opposed to this union stood the Railway Managers' Association, representing more than twoscore railway corporations. The members of the railway union refused to handle Pullman cars; the Managers' Association held that contracts with the Pullman Company must be carried out; and thus labor and capital stood aligned against each other for one of the most titanic struggles the country had seen. The strike quickly spread into twenty-seven States and Territories, involving roads all the way from Cincinnati to San Francisco, but the main storm centre was Chicago. In that city mobs, composed in part of strikers, in part of hoodlums and professional criminals, who were all the more numerous because of the exposition of the previous year, stopped trains and gathered in freight-yards and looted and burned hundreds of cars. The police and the other local peace officers were utterly unable to control the situation, but Governor Altgeld of Illinois sympathized with the strikers and delayed calling out the militia.

The strike might have succeeded had not the strikers made the serious mistake of stopping trains carrying the United States mail. On the 2d of July Federal Judge Woods, by request of the United States district attorney, issued a "blanket" injunction forbidding Debs and his associates and "all other persons whomsoever" from interfering with the transportation of the mail or obstructing interstate commerce. The mobs jeered at the writ when it was read to them, but the President, against the protest of Governor Altgeld, backed it up, sending troops under General Miles to the scenes of disturbance. Rioting, pillage, and destruction continued for some days, but the vigorous use of the troops restored order. On July 10 Debs and three associates were arrested on a charge of having been guilty of conspiracy contrary to the terms of the Sherman Anti-Trust Act. They were speedily released on bail, but were soon arrested again (July 17) charged with contempt of court in having disobeyed Judge Woods's injunction.

A Federal Injunction.

Debs and Associates Imprisoned.

The strike collapsed. In December Debs was sentenced to six months in jail for contempt of court; his associates received three months each.

The part taken by the courts in the whole affair provoked a great outcry, even outside labor circles. Injunctions had never before been used in this way, and the fact that in the case of

Labor Agitation against Injunctions.

Debs and his associates the judge was also the accuser, and that the defendants had not the right of trial by jury, was declared to violate the spirit and practice of Anglo-Saxon jurisprudence. The Supreme Court, however, unanimously upheld the sentences and refused a writ of *habeas corpus*. "Government by injunction" was frequently resorted to in subsequent strikes, and thus a new grievance was added to those of which labor complained. It was not until the first administration of Wilson that the injunction powers of federal judges in the matter of strikes were circumscribed.

Hard times, labor troubles, the currency controversy, and Democratic discontent with Cleveland's leadership combined to produce in the autumn of 1894 a political overturn compara-

Political Reaction in 1894.

ble with that of four years before. In the Northern States the Democrats carried hardly a dozen congressional districts, and their total membership in the House was reduced to 104, as against 248 Republicans. The Republicans were jubilant, and boasted that in 1896 they could "nominate a rag-baby or a yellow dog and elect it."

Before describing the events of that notable election we must turn for a few moments to two diplomatic questions.

For secretary of state Cleveland named Walter Q. Gresham, a prominent candidate for the Republican presidential nomination in 1888 but a recent convert to Democracy. The appoint-

Secretary of State Gresham.

ment displeased many Democrats, who thought that the place should have gone to a man older in the faith, while Republicans considered Gresham a renegade and regretted that he had been rewarded. Furthermore, though a man of intellectual ability, Judge Gresham had never made any special study of international law, while his personal manners were regarded as too informal by punctilious representatives of foreign powers. His attitude on certain diplomatic questions inherited from the previous administration was colored by dislike for his old rival and personal enemy, Benjamin Harrison.

At a conference between Gresham and Cleveland prior to the inauguration Gresham urged a reversal of policy toward the Hawaiian Government, and the two reached an agreement on

Hawaiian Policy Reversed. the matter. The treaty of annexation was speedily withdrawn (March 9) from the Senate "for the purpose of re-examination." A few days later Cleveland sent a special representative, one James H. Blount of Georgia, to Hawaii to investigate existing conditions and how the revolution had been brought about. His authority was made "paramount." On the day after his arrival in Honolulu Blount ordered the American flag to be lowered from the government building and sent the marines on shore back to the *Boston*. Later Blount made an elaborate report (July 17, 1893) in which he pictured the revolution as due to a conspiracy managed by aliens, chiefly Americans, and countenanced by Minister Stevens, whose support had overawed the Queen and her supporters.

Secretary Gresham and President Cleveland decided that a wrong had been done and that it must be righted by putting Liliuokalani back in power. Albert S. Willis, the new minis-

Attempt to Restore the Queen Fails. ter to Hawaii, was directed to secure from the Queen a promise of amnesty for the revolutionists, after which he was to notify the provisional government to relinquish its power. But the vindictive Queen declared that she meant to behead the ringleaders and confiscate their estates, and some time elapsed before she could be persuaded to drop her plans for vengeance. Furthermore, President Dole, having a force of well-drilled troops, politely but firmly declined to comply with the Cleveland-Gresham programme.

Meanwhile the administration's Hawaiian policy had provoked a great popular outcry. Many critics declared that in sending Blount to the islands without obtaining the Senate's ratification of his appointment Cleveland had exceeded his powers; a few even demanded that the President should be impeached. The idea of making war on the white revolutionists and overthrowing their republic in order to restore a bloodthirsty and—report said—immoral Polynesian Queen to her throne failed to arouse enthusiasm in the United States. Aware that the executive department could go no farther alone, Cleveland submitted the Hawaiian problem to Congress. The House condemned (February 7, 1894) the course of Minister Stevens, but neither that body nor the Senate would authorize the use of force against the Dole government, and Cleveland's policy was strongly criticised even by members of his own party. Ultimately the Senate voted (May 31, 1894) unanimously that Hawaii should manage its own governmental affairs and that the United States should not interfere. This outcome was very humiliating both to Cleveland and to Secretary Gresham.

The Administration's Policy Unpopular.

Annexationist sentiment both in the islands and the United States persisted, and when the war with Spain broke out the Hawaiian authorities permitted American war-ships to use Honolulu practically as a naval base. The war made the desirability of the islands more than ever manifest, and annexation was accomplished (June 15 to July 7, 1898) by joint resolution, as in the case of Texas. The United States thus obtained far out in the Pacific a possession having considerable natural resources and immense strategic and commercial value. Two years later Hawaii was formally organized as a Territory (April 30, 1900), and the Hawaiians were admitted to citizenship.

Hawaii Annexed in 1898.

Another diplomatic complication with a much greater power threatened for a time to have more serious consequences. For more than fifty years Great Britain and Venezuela had differed regarding the boundary between the latter and British Guiana. The disputed region was long thinly inhabited, some of it, in fact, hardly explored, but in course of time gold was discovered there, and thus a

Venezuelan Boundary Dispute.

different aspect was given to the quarrel. After finding that the territory might have great value Great Britain even extended her claims by thousands of square miles, and many of her subjects settled in the disputed tract. More than once Venezuela appealed to the United States, as "the oldest of the republics of the new continent," to prevent British aggressions on the soil of a sister American state; but our government long continued to limit its activities to tenders of our good offices and to proposals that the dispute should be arbitrated. Great Britain, however, persistently refused arbitration, and in 1887 the controversy became so acute that diplomatic relations between the disputants were broken off.

In his second administration President Cleveland came to believe that Great Britain was unduly aggressive toward a smaller and weaker power, and was threatening the Monroe Doctrine. Political conditions in Great Britain and international conditions throughout the world doubtless had something to do with forming this opinion.

Cleveland's View of the British Attitude.

Most of the European powers—Great Britain included—were engaged in a mad scramble for colonial possessions. The British Government was controlled by the Conservatives, notoriously more grasping and imperialistic than the Liberals; and the premier was Lord Salisbury, a cynical Briton inclined to believe that in international affairs might made right.

President Cleveland referred to the dispute in his annual messages of 1893 and 1894. The idea of arbitration was again and again suggested to Great Britain, and early in 1895 Congress passed a joint resolution to the effect that the quarrel ought to be settled in that manner. Lord Salisbury soon after instructed the British minister in Washington to say that his government was willing

Great Britain Refuses Arbitration.

to arbitrate regarding part of the territory but that it "could not consent to any departure from the Schomburgk line." This was a line surveyed by the British many years before, and it had been characterized by Lord Aberdeen, then foreign minister, "as merely a preliminary measure open to further discussion."

Such an answer severely tried the patience of the American Government. In the opinion of the President, Great Britain was trying to extend her sovereignty over territory belonging to an independent American state, and he held the view that this constituted a clear violation of the Monroe Doctrine, which declared that the American continents were not to be considered subject to future colonization by any European power.

In July, 1895, Richard Olney, who had become secretary of state after the death of Gresham in May, transmitted a long despatch asserting the application of the Monroe Doctrine to the Venezuelan controversy and once more suggest-
Olney's Despatch.
ing arbitration as a solution of the question. The United States, he bluntly declared, is "entitled to resent and resist any sequestration of Venezuelan soil by Great Britain." Even then Lord Salisbury failed to realize the seriousness of the situation, perhaps because he had often before seen American secretaries of state vigorously "twist the lion's tail" yet prove to be amenable in the end. He took his time about answering Olney's note, and finally (Novem-
Salisbury's Answer.
ber 26) replied cavalierly to the effect that the Monroe Doctrine was not a part of international law, that Great Britain and Venezuela only were concerned in the dispute, that his government was willing to arbitrate concerning part of the territory but must hold fast to the Schomburgk line.

Believing that only extraordinary methods would bring the British Government to reason, President Cleveland made a bold decision. He startled both nations by sending (De-
Cleveland's Bold Message.
cember 17, 1895) to Congress a special message asking that body to authorize the appointment of a special commission to determine the true boundary, and saying that it would be the "duty of the United States to resist by every means in its power, as a wilful aggression upon its rights and interests, the appropriation by Great Britain of any lands or the exercise of governmental jurisdiction over any territory which after investigation we have determined of right belongs to Venezuela." He added the following signifi-

cant words: "In making these recommendations I am fully alive to the responsibility incurred, and keenly realize all the consequences that may follow." The message precipitated a panic on the stock exchanges and was severely criticised by "occasional dissidents," but it met with favor among the people generally, and Congress speedily empowered the President to appoint the commission. The persons named were all men of eminence, without any tendency to jingoism, and they presently set about their work in a tactful manner.

Meanwhile British public opinion made itself heard in unmistakable fashion. It is true that the American army numbered only 25,000 men, that we had not a single completed first-class battleship, that there was hardly a modern gun mounted on the Atlantic coast; yet Great Britain, partly for selfish, partly for humanitarian reasons, had no desire to go to war with us. Furthermore, on December 29 Doctor Jameson and his band began their sensational raid into the Transvaal, and the Kaiser soon transmitted his celebrated cablegram to President Krüger. These spectacular events threw the Venezuelan dispute into the background, and gave the British other topics for talk and reflection.

Attitude of the British Public.

Manifestations in both countries of a desire to settle the dispute amicably encouraged the American Government once more to suggest the desirability of arbitration. Salisbury, in chastened mood, informed Bayard, the American minister in London, that he had empowered Sir Julian Pauncefote, British Minister at Washington, "to discuss the question either with the representative of Venezuela or with the Government of the United States acting as the friend of Venezuela." He thus conceded the whole American contention. A general arbitration treaty was signed at Washington in January, 1897, by Pauncefote and Secretary Olney, and though the Senate refused to ratify this agreement, it subsequently accepted (February 2, 1897) another providing for the arbitration of the Venezuelan dispute. The decision of the tribunal to which the controversy was referred proved

The Dispute Arbitrated.

(October 3, 1899) to be favorable in the main to Great Britain but awarded to Venezuela some territory east of the Schomburgk line.

The outcome of the whole matter was a notable example of the triumph of reason in international affairs and also deserves careful study because of its bearing on the Monroe Doctrine.

The Significance of the Controversy. According to the *London Times*, Great Britain admitted "that in respect of South American Republics the United States may not only intervene in disputes, but may entirely supersede the original disputant and assume exclusive control of the negotiations." In insisting on the application of the Monroe Doctrine the United States had, in effect, proclaimed her hegemony in the New World, and Great Britain had conceded it. Grasping European powers, including Germany, which had territorial aspirations in Brazil and elsewhere, were made to understand that the Monroe Doctrine meant, "You must not seize American soil," and that violation of the doctrine spelled war with the United States.

Business conditions improved somewhat during 1895, yet tens of millions continued to feel the pinch of hard times. In cities many men still sought work in vain and were dependent upon charity for the wherewithal to sustain themselves and their families. Western farmers and their wives and children worked long hours, yet could not sell their wheat and corn, their hogs and cattle, for enough to meet expenses and pay the interest on the mortgage. In both town and country disappointment and misery bred despair, discontent, and a demand for a change.

Most Republicans cast the blame on the Democratic tariff, but throughout the country and especially in the West there was an increasing number of persons who proclaimed the view that the country's troubles were due to "the crime against silver." *Coin's Financial School*, a plausible propagandist book written by a man named Harvey, was sold by hundreds of thousands, and was studied as devoutly as if it were a new dispensation from Sinai. The demand for the free coinage of the white metal became a craze,

Free Silver Movement.

an obsession, in the minds of multitudes. In the words of William Allen White:

It was a fanaticism like the Crusades. Indeed, the delusion that was working on the people took the form of religious frenzy. Sacred hymns were torn from their pious tunes to give place to words which deified the cause and made gold—and all its symbols, capital, wealth, plutocracy—diabolical. At night from ten thousand little white schoolhouse windows, lights twinkled back vain hope to the stars. . . . They sang their barbaric songs in unrhythmic jargon, with something of the mad faith that inspired martyrs going to the stake. Far into the night the voices rose,— women's and children's voices, the voices of old men, of youths and of maidens, rose on the ebbing prairie breezes, as the crusaders of the revolution rode home, praising the people's will as though it were God's will and cursing wealth for its inequity.

As the campaign of 1896 drew near it became clear that the money question would be one of the main issues. The Populists were already enthusiastically committed to free silver, and both the old parties contained a large freesilver wing. The Republican party was less infected with free-silver doctrines than the Democracy, yet in Congress many Republican senators and representatives had joined Democratic and Populist colleagues in supporting various schemes for securing free coinage in the United States or forcing the world to bimetallism. In the Republican State conventions held in 1896 ten openly came out for free silver, about half opposed free coinage, some straddled the issue or evaded it, and only a few declared uncompromisingly for the gold standard. In all parties men felt so strongly upon the issue that they were unwilling to keep silent upon it for the sake of party solidarity. Even the Prohibitionist national convention, held in Pittsburgh near the end of May, split into two factions over the silver question, and these factions framed two platforms, and nominated two tickets. Their action was ominous.

Among the men put forward for the Republican nomination were Levi P. Morton of New York, William B. Allison of Iowa, and Matthew S. Quay of Pennsylvania, but the leading candidates were Reed of Maine and McKinley of Ohio. Reed had many enthusiastic friends, who were attracted by his record as speaker and by his forceful personality and great intellectual gifts, but he lacked an efficient organization to promote his candidacy. McKinley was peculiarly acceptable to the "old soldiers," a powerful factor, for he had fought in the Civil War and had attained the rank of brevet major. He had been a member of the House of Representatives almost continuously from 1877 to 1891, and his name had become practically synonymous with extremely high protection. Defeated for re-election in 1890, as a result of the reaction against his tariff bill and of the gerrymandering of his district by a Democratic legislature, he had speedily been elected governor of Ohio and later was re-elected. In 1888 and again in 1892 he had been seriously considered by many Republicans for the presidential nomination. He was now an avowed candidate. Calculating and rather cold, yet suave and courteous, he had few personal enemies; and fortunately for him the panic of 1893 had done much to rehabilitate his political reputation, which had been temporarily tarnished by popular disapproval of his tariff measure. Public opinion had veered regarding the tariff, and it was now possible to arouse enthusiasm for "Bill McKinley and the McKinley Bill."

Reed's Candidacy.

McKinley's Candidacy.

McKinley was fortunate in having as his manager one of the most forceful personalities that had yet come to the front in American public life. This was Marcus Alonzo Hanna, a Cleveland business man, who had made a fortune in coal and iron and the Lake carrying trade, and had entered politics partly because he enjoyed it as a game, partly because he owned street railway and other franchises and found politics a helpful adjunct in such business. Hanna did not seek office for himself; he wanted to be a Warwick—to make a President. He first took up Sherman and strove ardently to secure his nomination in 1888 but failed. Later he turned to McKinley. It was largely through his efforts that the "High Priest of Protection" became governor.

"Mark" Hanna.

And when McKinley, through indorsing a friend's paper, became involved in financial difficulties to the extent of more than $100,000, Hanna, with a little help from others, rescued him from bankruptcy and political oblivion. Hanna knew the power of money in influencing elections; he was perhaps inclined to underestimate the value of sober appeals to the sense and conscience of the people. Personally he was a blunt, coarse-fibred man, yet one who possessed many likable traits. For McKinley he entertained a sincere admiration and a devoted friendship.

Hanna set about the task of nominating McKinley with vast energy and skill. He furnished ample money for the work, and spent it lavishly, particularly in the South. The combination of Hanna's management with McKinley's popularity proved irresistible. When the Republican convention met at St. Louis in June, "the Advance Agent of Prosperity" was overwhelmingly nominated on the first ballot, receiving 661½ votes to 84½ for Reed, his nearest competitor. Garret A. Hobart, a wealthy New Jersey lawyer and business man, was named for the vice-presidency.

Hanna's Campaign Succeeds.

The real struggle in the convention took place over the currency question. McKinley's record regarding silver was by no means a consistent one, and for this and other reasons he and Hanna had paraded the tariff as the important issue. But in the convention Senator Teller of Colorado and other friends of silver were insistent in their demands, while, on the other hand, Eastern business men were clamoring that the platform must declare for the gold standard. Hanna shrewdly kept his own views and those of McKinley secret, yet he cannily managed that the platform as reported should declare against "the free coinage of silver, except by international agreement with the leading commercial nations of the world, which we pledge ourselves to promote."

The Free-Silver Issue in the Republican Convention.

Senator Teller moved to substitute a plank favoring free coinage, and he supported his amendment in a speech in which he referred with much feeling to the fact that he had been a

Republican since the formation of the party and now he feared that he must sever the old ties. The audience listened to his plea in sympathetic silence, but his substitute was voted down by 818 to 105, after which the platform was adopted by 812 to 110. Teller then rose and dramatically left the hall. He was followed by thirty-three other delegates, including two members of the House of Representatives and three other senators.

Withdrawal of Free-Silver Delegates.

Other planks of the platform declared for American control of Hawaii, for a firm policy with regard to the revolt in Cuba, for a stronger navy, and for a restoration of "the policy of protection" to home industries. The "calamitous consequences" of Democratic rule were pictured with heavy strokes, and the Cleveland administration was charged with responsibility for "a record of unparalleled incapacity, dishonor, and disaster."

The Democratic convention met in Chicago on the 7th of July. The silver men immediately took control and elected their candidate for temporary chairman. The platform, as reported, did not commend the administration of President Cleveland, neither did it expressly attack it, but it denounced "the issue of interest-bearing bonds of the United States in time of peace and . . . the trafficking with bond syndicates," condemned "arbitrary interference by federal authorities in local affairs," and characterized "government by injunction" as "a new and highly dangerous form of oppression by which federal judges become at once legislators, judges, and executioners." It contained other bids for the support of labor and iterated the doctrine of 1892 regarding a tariff for revenue. But by far its most important pronouncement was that upon the currency question. The demonetizing act of 1873 was appropriately denounced; monometallism was declared to be a British policy that had "locked fast the prosperity of an industrial people in the paralysis of hard times"; and an unqualified demand was made for "the free and unlimited coinage of both silver and gold at the present legal ratio of sixteen to one without waiting for the aid or consent of any other nation."

Free-Silver Men Control Democratic Convention.

A minority report from the committee on resolutions proposed an amendment commending the Cleveland administration and another opposing free coinage. A bitter debate followed. Senator "Pitchfork" Tillman of South Carolina in passionate words assailed Cleveland as "a tool of Wall Street." The main conservative argument was made by David B. Hill, who began by saying, "I am a Democrat, but I am not a revolutionist." But the one memorable speech, one of the most memorable in American history, was that delivered by a young man of thirty-six from Nebraska—William Jennings Bryan.

A Bitter Debate.

Bryan was then a comparatively unknown man whose experience in public position was limited to two terms in the federal House of Representatives. He had come to the convention at the head of a contesting silver delegation from Nebraska and had been seated. In his college days and afterward he had cultivated the art of oratory, and he had brought to the convention a carefully prepared speech, which he had committed to memory. At an opportune moment, when the assemblage had been wrought up to a pitch of madness by the "gold" arguments of Hill and others, he stepped upon the platform to plead the cause of silver.

William Jennings Bryan.

All who heard him that day are unanimous in agreeing that it was a notable performance. His presence was pleasing and magnetic; his marvellous mellow voice penetrated easily to every corner of the great hall; his first sentences caught the attention of the throng and held that attention to the final, overpowering end. It was not presumptuous, he asserted, for him to speak, for this was not a mere measuring of abilities, not a contest between persons. "The humblest citizen in the land, when clad in the armor of a righteous cause, is stronger than all the hosts of error. I come to speak to you in defence of a cause as holy as the cause of liberty—the cause of humanity."

A Notable Performance.

He told how the advocates of silver, with a zeal approaching that which inspired the crusaders who followed Peter the Hermit, had marched on from victory to victory until now they

"were assembled not to discuss, not to debate, but to enter up
the judgment of the plain people. . . . When you [turning

The Plain
People's
Cause.

to the gold delegates] come before us and tell us
that we shall disturb your business interests, we reply that you have disturbed our business interests
by your action. We say to you that you have made too limited in its application the definition of a business man." The
wage-earner, the country lawyer, the crossroads merchant,
"the miners who go a thousand feet into the earth or climb
two thousand feet upon the cliffs, and bring forth from their
hiding-places the precious metals"—all these are "as much
business men as the few financial magnates who, in a back room,
corner the money of the world. . . .

"It is for these that we speak. We do not come as aggressors.
Our war is not a war of conquest. We are fighting in the defense of our homes, our families, and posterity. We have petitioned, and our petitions have been scorned. We have en-
treated, and our entreaties have been disregarded. We have
begged, and they have mocked when our calamity came. We
beg no longer; we entreat no more. We defy them!"

With each sentence the vast crowd had grown more and

An
Oratorical
Triumph.

more enthusiastic. After each passionate passage
there came thunderclaps of applause from 20,000
throats. When the young orator flung out the
sentence, "'We defy them!' the leaderless Democracy of the
West was leaderless no more. In that very moment, and in
that burst of wild applause, it was acclaiming its new chief."*

He closed by proclaiming: "We care not upon what lines the
battle is fought. If they say bimetallism is good but we cannot have it until other nations help us, we reply that, instead

The
Peroration.

of having a gold standard because England has, we
shall restore bimetallism and then let England have
bimetallism because the United States have. If
they dare to come out and in the open defend the gold standard
as a good thing, we shall fight them to the uttermost. Having
behind us the producing masses of this nation and the world,

* Peck, *Twenty Years of the Republic*, page 500.

the laboring interests, and the toilers everywhere, we will answer their demand for a gold standard by saying to them:
'You shall not press down upon the brow of labor this crown
of thorns—you shall not crucify mankind upon a cross of
gold!'"

Few speeches have had such important results. The proposed amendments to the platform were voted down overwhelmingly, and the thoughts of the delegates were turned
toward the young orator as the proper person to
lead the new crusade. Next day "Silver Dick"
Bland, the "Father of Free Silver," and all the
other candidates were cast aside, and on the fifth ballot William
Jennings Bryan was nominated for the presidency.

Bryan Nominated.

For the vice-presidency the convention named Arthur Sewall
of Maine. The selection was a rather remarkable one, for
Sewall was president of a ship-building firm and of a national
bank, was a protectionist, and lived in a State so
"impregnable in its Republicanism" that the Democrats could have little hope of carrying it. However, Sewall possessed "the saving grace of recent conversion
to free silver."

Sewall for the Vice-Presidency.

Among conservative Democrats, most of whom resided in
the East, the nomination of Bryan was received with dismay.
"Are you still a Democrat?" a friend inquired of David B.
Hill upon his return to New York. "Yes, I am a
Democrat still," replied the senator—then added
after a significant pause, "*very still.*" Early in
September a considerable number of gold Demo-
crats held a convention in Indianapolis, assumed
the name of "National Democratic Party," and nominated
General John M. Palmer of Illinois for the presidency and
General Simon B. Buckner of Kentucky, one-time commander
at Fort Donelson, for the vice-presidency. Many other gold
Democrats openly announced that they would support McKinley, while a yet greater number secretly gave him their ballots.

Gold Democrats Nominate Palmer and Buckner.

On the other hand, the National Silver party declared for
Bryan and Sewall, and the Populists for Bryan but named

Thomas E. Watson of Georgia for the vice-presidency in place of Sewall.

The Republicans sought to make the tariff the leading issue, but the money question soon dwarfed all others. Republican orators sang the praises of gold, and dwelt with unction upon the contention that they stood for "an honest dollar." Democrats retorted that a contracted currency, such as the "Gold Bugs" desired, was as dishonest as an inflated currency and also bore most heavily upon debtors, who were least able to bear it. One of their campaign ditties ran:

Money Question the Leading Issue.

> "You may say what you will of the fifty cent dollar,
> But I tell you it beats none at all, all holler."

Few campaigns have been so animated. Bryan swept through many States, travelling over 18,000 miles and speaking to probably 5,000,000 people. McKinley remained at his home in Canton and greeted enthusiastic delegations from all over the Union. His managers, in particular "Mark" Hanna, hoisted on high the "full dinner pail" to catch the labor vote, and, by picturing the dangers of free silver and free trade, succeeded in collecting from manufacturers and others the largest campaign fund ever gathered. Bryan and his lieutenants also raised a considerable fund, and they managed to arouse wild enthusiasm in the West. But they were handicapped by the burden of hard times under Democratic rule, and a majority of the voters took the view that the country would be more prosperous under the Republicans. In the election Bryan carried all the States south of Mason and Dixon's Line, except Delaware, Maryland, West Virginia, and Kentucky, and many of the Western States, with a total of 176 electoral votes; but McKinley won the New England States, the Middle States, and all the Middle Western States, with some of the Border and Western States, and received 271 electoral votes and a popular plurality of more than 600,000. "The Boy

The Campaign.

McKinley Elected.

Orator of the Platte" had failed to convince the country of the virtue of his panacea.

The election thus closed had been far more than a mere struggle over a metallic standard.   For the first time on a large scale since Andrew Jackson's day, there had been some-
Real Significance of the Contest. thing approaching a class alignment.   The promi- nence given the money question had served to ob- scure more serious ills from which the country was suffering.   By striving to establish a doubtful eco- nomic principle the free-silver advocates unwittingly postponed many much-needed reforms.   In the words of Theodore Roose- velt, in his *Autobiography:*

The fear of Mr. Bryan threw almost all the leading men of all classes into the arms of whoever opposed him. . . .   Good and high-minded men of conservative temperament in their panic played into the hands of the ultra-reactionaries of business and politics.   The alliance between the two kinds of privilege, political and financial, was closely cemented; and wherever there was any attempt to break it up, the cry was at once raised that this merely represented another phase of the assault on national honesty and individual and mercantile integrity.   As so often happens, the ex- cesses and threats of an unwise and extreme radicalism had resulted in immensely strengthening the position of the beneficiaries of reaction.

CHAPTER XIV

THE WAR WITH SPAIN

AMID more than usual pomp and display William McKinley was duly inaugurated on March 4, 1897. For secretary of state he named Senator John Sherman of Ohio. Sherman was now

Sherman and Hanna.

an old man, whose once keen mind was beginning to show the ravages of age. It was generally believed that he was "kicked up stairs" in order to make a place in the Senate for "Mark" Hanna, McKinley's efficient political mentor and manager. At all events, Hanna was soon appointed by the governor of Ohio to fill the vacancy thus created, and the following year, after an exceedingly close and bitter fight, he was elected by the legislature. Judged in the light of after events, the other important cabinet appointments were those of General Russell A. Alger of Michigan as secretary of war, and of John D. Long of Massachusetts as secretary of the navy. Theodore Roosevelt, who for some time had been a police commissioner of New York City, became assistant secretary of the navy.

Under the administration just beginning, "business" sat enthroned in the government. This is not to say that President McKinley and his advisers were without other ideals or aspira-

A "Business Administration."

tions or that they had not the interests of their country at heart. But their training and surroundings had been such that to make business prosperous seemed to them the prime object of statesmanship; they expected all other blessings to follow naturally in the wake of prosperity. It was the man of affairs, the hard-headed, practical money-maker, whose counsels were welcomed at the White House in these years; the theorist, the idealist, received scant consideration.

The main conflict of the campaign had been over the currency question, but legislation on the subject was long delayed. It was not until March 14, 1900, that President McKinley

Gold Standard Act of 1900. signed the measure known as the Gold Standard Act. That act made the dollar containing 25.8 grains of gold, nine-tenths fine, the standard of value, and provided that the secretary of the treasury must maintain all forms of money issued or coined at a parity with that standard. For that purpose he was authorized to set aside $150,000,000 in gold coin and bullion as a redemption fund, and if at any time this fund should fall below $100,000,000 and he should be unable to replenish it in the usual manner he could sell bonds and restore the fund to $150,000,000. The act did not affect the legal-tender quality of silver dollars, but it provided for the retirement of the treasury notes issued under the act of 1890 as rapidly as the silver bullion on hand should be coined and silver certificates issued in amounts equal to the notes so retired. The act in no sense met the views of advocates of silver. But business conditions were prosperous; increased production of gold, particularly in the Yukon region and South Africa, had greatly enlarged the world's stock of the yellow metal, thereby lessening the stringency in the medium of exchange, and the Gold Standard Act consequently excited little popular protest.

There was no such delay in regard to the tariff. One of McKinley's first important official acts was to call Congress in extra session on March 15. Even before the inauguration it

The Dingley Tariff Act, 1897. had been arranged among Republican members of the House that Thomas B. Reed should be reelected Speaker, and Reed had indicated that he would appoint Nelson Dingley of Maine and certain others as the majority members of the Committee on Ways and Means. In advance of their actual appointment Dingley and his associates began work on a new tariff bill. As a result of this forehanded work the bill was reported to the House and passed by that body in less than two weeks after Congress assembled. The Senate considered the measure more leisurely and adopted several hundred amendments. The bill passed the Senate on

July 7, went to a conference committee, the report of the conference committee was accepted by both houses, and the Dingley Act became a law by the President's signature on July 24.

The new act was drawn primarily in the interests of producers rather than consumers, and in it many of the big contributors to the Republican campaign fund reaped their reward.

Nature of the Act.

In some respects it resembled the McKinley Act, but the average rate of duties was somewhat lower, and, as a deficit not a surplus was now the problem of the Treasury, it contained some duties levied solely to produce a revenue. Defenders of the act made much of its reciprocity feature. The President was empowered to enter into certain limited reciprocity agreements with foreign powers and to proclaim them without the action of the Senate. He

Reciprocity Feature Proves a Delusion.

might also negotiate more formal treaties providing for a reduction of not more than 20 per cent of the Dingley rates or for placing natural articles not produced in the United States on the free list. In the next two years seven formal reciprocity treaties were negotiated, but protectionist sentiment was so strong in the Senate that not one was ratified.

Business conditions had improved even before Cleveland retired from office, and prosperity blossomed in wonderful luxuriance under McKinley. As the main explanation, protectionists triumphantly pointed to the Dingley

An Era of Prosperity.

Act. For some years arguments favoring free trade or a tariff for revenue only fell upon stony ground. To a majority of voters it seemed that experience proved that Republican spell-binders were right in proclaiming that free trade meant "free soup houses," while protection assured a "full dinner pail."

For a long period internal economic questions had chiefly absorbed American attention. America had led an

A Broader Stage.

almost hermitlike existence, caring little for events beyond her borders. At intervals diplomatic disputes with other powers had flared up for a moment, only to die down like a fire that has little on which to feed. But the period of isolation was drawing to a close. Events were under way that were to force the United States out upon the broader stage of world affairs.

Following the Ten Years' War in Cuba, a short account of which was given in an earlier chapter, many of the insurgents had taken refuge in the United States; but they and other patriots who remained upon the island never ceased to plan a renewal of the struggle for liberty when times should be more propitious. Continuance of the old selfish Spanish policy of exploitation, and failure to carry out reforms promised at the end of the previous revolt made the patriots all the more determined that some day Cuba must be free.

The Cuban Question.

In February, 1895, a leader named José Marti landed in eastern Cuba and began a revolt that soon swept westward past the outskirts of Havana and into the province of Pinar del Rio. A republic was proclaimed, and Thomas Estrada Palma, who for years had been a school-teacher in the State of New York, became provisional President. To suppress the insurrection Spain sent a large army to Cuba. Unable to meet these better armed and trained soldiers in the open field, the *insurrectos*, led by such partisan chieftains as Maximo Gomez, Antonio Maceo, and Calixto Garcia, resorted to guerilla warfare, cutting off a detachment here, capturing a town there, then vanishing into the jungle. Under Governor-General Martinez Campos the Spaniards conducted the war in accordance with civilized usages, but these methods failed, Campos was recalled, and in February, 1896, he was succeeded by General Valeriano Weyler, whose ferocity and ruthless methods won for him the name of "the Butcher." Weyler carried out a policy of *reconcentration*, whereby the peasants in many districts were forced to assemble in the fortified towns in order that they might not give any assistance to the insurrectionists. Lack of food and poor sanitation caused suffering and death among these unfortunate *reconcentrados*, and the policy excited the indignation of the world.

The Cuban Revolt.

Weyler's Harsh Policy.

From the outset the great mass of the people of the United States heartily sympathized with the rebels and wished them success, but for a long period our government preserved a strict

The United States Neutral.

neutrality. Cubans in the United States and American sympathizers frequently managed, nevertheless, to evade our neutrality regulations and send arms and supplies to the insurgents; while a considerable number of adventurous Americans secretly made their way to the island and enlisted in the Cuban cause.

One of these soldiers of fortune was Winchester Dana Osgood, another was Frederick Funston. Osgood was the son of an American army officer and had won fame as a football player

Osgood and Funston.

at Cornell and Pennsylvania. He became chief of artillery in General Garcia's army, and was shot through the brain while sighting a cannon in the siege of a small town called Guaimaro. He was succeeded by Funston, an Ohioan by birth but long a resident of Kansas, who had been a student at Kansas University and subsequently had travelled in Alaskan wilds for the Department of Agriculture. Funston reached Cuba on the famous filibustering vessel *Dauntless*, commanded by picturesque "Dynamite" O'Brien. Unlike Osgood, he survived the Cuban War, performed notable exploits in the Philippines, rose to high command in the American army, and left a book describing in vivid language his adventures in two hemispheres.

Early in 1896 American sentiment in favor of putting a stop to the conflict became so strong that both houses of Congress, by large majorities, passed a concurrent resolution favoring

Cleveland's Attitude.

the recognition of Cuban belligerent rights and offering our good offices to Spain for the recognition of Cuban independence. But President Cleveland held that he was not bound by this resolution and refused to act in accordance with it. Secretary Olney did, however, offer to mediate between Spain and the insurgents for the restoration of peace on the basis of a larger autonomy, but Spain turned the tender aside. In his last annual message President Cleveland took the view that the time had not come to recognize either the belligerency of the insurgents or their independence. But he added that a time might come when our obligations to the sovereignty of Spain might be superseded by our higher obligations to humanity.

The Republican platform of 1896 took strong ground with regard to the Cuban question, but neither President McKinley nor his mentor, Hanna, wanted war. The President managed

McKinley Anxious for Peace.

to secure the release of certain American citizens who were held by the Spaniards for alleged participation in the revolt, and he also secured from Congress an appropriation to be used in feeding the starving *reconcentrados*. On June 27, 1897, Secretary Sherman transmitted through Hannis Taylor, the American minister at Madrid, a despatch protesting against the policy of General Weyler, particularly his *reconcentration* order. The Spanish Government adopted procrastinating tactics, but finally replied (August 4) to the effect that the situation in Cuba was not so dark as pictured. It sought to justify Weyler's measures by comparing them with those of Hunter and Sheridan in the Shenandoah Valley, and complained of the activities of the Cuban Junta in New York City and of the assistance rendered the rebels by American citizens.

On September 13, 1897, General Stewart L. Woodford, who had succeeded Taylor at Madrid, once more tendered the good offices of the United States to end the war, and intimated that

Spain Concedes Autonomy.

American patience was approaching an end. A few days later the existing Spanish ministry resigned, and a new one was formed under Señor Sagasta. The brutal Weyler was soon superseded, and a decree was published granting autonomy to Cuba. In his annual message (December 6, 1897) President McKinley expressed the view that the new policy should be given a fair trial.

But autonomy pleased neither the rebels nor the Cuban loyalists. The latter indulged in riotous outbreaks (January

The *Maine* Sent to Havana.

13, 1898) at Havana by way of protest, and were so denunciatory of Americans that Consul-General Fitzhugh Lee, nephew of the famous Confederate leader, advised his government that it might become necessary to send war-ships to Havana to protect our interests. The second-class battleship *Maine* was actually ordered to Havana, while, to preserve the appearance of amity, it was arranged that the Spanish cruiser *Vizcaya* should visit New York.

A few days after the *Maine* dropped anchor in Havana harbor the *New York Journal*, a Hearst paper that had long been advocating intervention, published a letter written by Señor

De Lome's Letter.

Dupuy de Lome, Spanish minister at Washington, in which he characterized President McKinley as "weak and a caterer to the rabble . . . a cheap politician who wishes to leave a door open to himself and to stand well with the jingoes of his party." The letter had been obtained surreptitiously, but Señor de Lome admitted its genuineness. His recall was demanded, but the Spanish Government accepted his resignation before the demand arrived.

Excitement over this episode had not yet subsided when the world was startled with the news that on the night of February 15 the *Maine* had been blown up in Havana harbor, causing

The *Maine* Blown up.

the death of 260 of her officers and crew. Captain Sigsbee of the ill-fated ship cabled home, asking the public to suspend judgment until the facts could be ascertained, but most Americans jumped to the conclusion that the loss was due to treachery. A Spanish court of inquiry reported that the explosion was an internal one; an American court held (March 2) that first there had been an external explosion which had set off two of the forward magazines. When the shattered hulk was raised from the muddy harbor bottom, more than a decade later, the American experts again held that the American contention was sustained. The real facts concerning the affair remain unknown to this day, but historians acquit the Spanish Government of complicity. The deed may have been the work of hot-headed subordinates.

Throughout the United States the vengeful cry resounded:

America's Ultimatum.

"Remember the *Maine!*" Yet President McKinley still held back, partly because he wanted time to put the country on a war basis, partly because he hoped that delay might bring some peaceful solution. But further negotiations proved fruitless, and finally, on March

29, Minister Woodford presented the following statement: "The President instructs me to say that we do not want Cuba. He also instructs me to say, with equal clearness, that we do wish immediate peace in Cuba. He suggests an armistice, lasting until October 1, negotiations in the meantime being had looking to peace between Spain and the insurgents, through the friendly offices of the President of the United States."

Spain made various counter-proposals, but the President deemed them insufficient. An attempt on the part of Germany, Austria-Hungary, and France to intervene in Spain's behalf was balked by the friendly attitude of Great Britain and by McKinley's own diplomatic deftness. On April 11 the President sent to Congress a special message favoring forcible intervention to put a stop to the conflict. Eight days later, on the anniversary of Concord and Lexington, Congress adopted by great majorities resolutions declaring "that the people of the island of Cuba are, and of right ought to be, free and independent," demanding that Spain withdraw from the island, and directing and empowering the President to use our forces to carry the resolutions into effect. In a "self-denying ordinance" that followed, Congress disclaimed any intention of exercising "sovereignty, jurisdiction, or control over said island except for the pacification thereof," and pledged the United States, as soon as this object was accomplished, "to leave the government and control of the island to its people." Rupture of diplomatic relations and formal warfare speedily followed. In American eyes the conflict thus begun was a crusade for humanity.

The United States Determines to Free Cuba.

On March 8 Congress had appropriated $50,000,000 as an emergency fund for national defense, and three weeks later had added $39,000,000 more for the navy. Much of this money was spent abroad for guns and ships before the outbreak of hostilities.

In the War Department Secretary Alger and the bureaucrats under him had been slow to awake to the crisis. Our military status on April 1, 1898, may be summarized as follows: a reg-

ular army of 28,183 officers and men; a larger force of ill-trained
State militia, who could not be taken into the federal service
Military
Unprepared-
ness. without their consent; 53,508 Krag-Jorgensen rifles
and 14,895 Krag-Jorgensen carbines, both good
weapons for that day; a large number of antiquated 45-calibre Springfields, using black powder, whose
smoke would betray to the enemy the position of troops using
these weapons; a scanty supply of smokeless-powder cartridges;
considerable coast-defense artillery but few field-guns, and all
of these using black powder; great dearth of clothing, tents,
and other necessary equipment. Congress authorized the
President to call for more than 200,000 volunteers, and about
182,000, many of them militiamen, were actually enlisted.
Among these volunteers were many former Union and Confederate officers, among the latter being Fitzhugh Lee and
"Fighting Joe" Wheeler, the celebrated cavalry leader.

According to her army lists, Spain had at this time under
arms 492,000 men, of whom 10,000 were in Porto Rico, 51,000
in the Philippines, and 278,000 in Cuba. But many of these
The Spanish
Army. men were poorly trained and equipped; others had
been forced into the service against their will and
their hearts were not in the work. Spain had not
in her whole army a force to match the American regular army,
which, though small, was composed of well-drilled, straight-
shooting men, commanded by officers most of whom were West-
Pointers and many of whom had seen service in the great civil
conflict or in the wild warfare against the Indians of the West.

Ships rather than armies were to prove the main factor in
deciding the war. The new American navy, though a pygmy
beside that of Great Britain, contained some formidable ves-
The New
American
Navy. sels, manned by officers and men filled with the
traditions of a service that had produced a Paul
Jones, a Decatur, a Macdonough, a Perry, two
Porters, and a Farragut. The main fighting strength was concentrated in four first-class battleships: the *Iowa*, of 11,340
tons, with a primary battery of four 12-inch rifles, and the
Oregon, Massachusetts, and *Indiana*, of 10,288 tons, and armed

with four 13-inch rifles. Besides these vessels there were a second-class battleship, the *Texas*, numerous cruisers of various classes, gunboats, torpedo-boats, and nearly a score of antiquated monitors, most of which last were available only for coast defense.

At the head of the Navy Department stood a capable man, John D. Long, and he had an even more capable assistant—Theodore Roosevelt. Roosevelt had foreseen that war was inevitable and had energetically prepared for it.

The Navy Ready. He had written the best history of the naval war of 1812 then extant, and he possessed a keen knowledge of naval requirements. In the words of Admiral Dewey: "He was impatient of red tape, and had a singular understanding both of the importance of preparedness for war and of striking quick blows in rapid succession once war was begun." Knowing that it is "only the hits that count," he had kept the gunners busy at target practice, had managed that Commodore George Dewey should be put in command of the Asiatic squadron, and otherwise had prepared the navy for the test of war. The whole service was permeated with a keen professional spirit, and the department could command the advice of many able officers, among them Captain Alfred T. Mahan, the great authority on the influence of sea power in history.

Some European writers assumed that the Spanish fleets would sweep the American ships from the seas, but in reality the Spanish navy was much the weaker, both in material and

Weakness of the Spanish Navy. morale. Spain had only one first-class battleship, the *Pelayo*, but she was smaller than the American ships of the same class, was thirteen years old, and was in a bad state of repair. The main Spanish strength lay in a number of armored cruisers, and one of these, the *Cristóbal Colon*, would have been a really formidable antagonist had she not lacked her heavy guns. Spain also had many lighter vessels, notably seven destroyers, a valuable type, of which the United States had none. In general, the Spanish ships were poorly equipped and poorly manned. Rear-Admiral Cervera probably did not exaggerate when, two months before the war began, he wrote to the minister of marine that the Spanish navy was only one-third as strong as that of the United States and that he thought it improper to cherish "illusions which may bring about terrible disappointments." Most Americans supposed that Spanish sea power was much more formidable than it really was, and fear of bombardment caused uneasiness in Atlantic coast cities.

The first blow was not long delayed. The American Asiatic squadron had been concentrated at Hong Kong in readiness to strike at Spanish power in the Philippine Islands. It was com-

Dewey Ordered to the Philippines.
posed of the 5,870-ton protected cruiser *Olympia*, three smaller cruisers, two gunboats, a revenue vessel, a collier, and a supply ship, and was commanded by Commodore George Dewey, an officer who had fought under Farragut. Forced to leave Hong Kong by the British proclamation of neutrality, the fleet rendezvoused at Mirs Bay, on the coast of China, and there (April 25) Dewey received the following cablegram from Washington: "War has commenced between the United States and Spain. Proceed at once to the Philippine Islands. Commence operations, particularly against the Spanish fleet. You must capture vessels or destroy. Use utmost endeavors."

The fleet waited until the next day (April 26) for the arrival of Williams, the American consul at Manila. Then, in the afternoon, the ships weighed anchor and steamed across the South China Sea on their fateful errand.

The Spanish fleet at Manila, commanded by Rear-Admiral Montojo, was decidedly inferior to Dewey's force, nor did the Spaniards display any skill in making use of their shore de-

Battle of Manila Bay.
fenses. On the last night of April the American ships passed through the broad entrance of Manila Bay, exchanging a few harmless shots with the batteries, and in the early morning of May Day came in sight of Montojo's vessels lying off Cavite arsenal. Within a few hours the Spanish fleet had been annihilated, while the Americans lost not a single ship and had only eight men slightly wounded. The victory put Manila completely at Dewey's mercy, but, as

CUBAN AND PORTO RICAN CAMPAIGNS

SCALE OF MILES

0   100   200   300   400   500

CUBAN AND PORTO RICAN
CAMPAIGNS

he had no troops with which to garrison the city, he decided not to take it until the arrival of troops from the United States.

Nearer home the American naval forces at the beginning of the war were distributed as follows: the North Atlantic Fleet, commanded by Rear-Admiral William T. Sampson and composed of the battleships *Indiana, Iowa,* the armored cruiser *New York,* some sea-going monitors, and many other vessels, lay at Key West, or in the vicinity, in readiness to blockade Cuba. A Northern Patrol Squadron, under Commodore J. A. Howell, was guarding the coast from eastern Maine to the Delaware capes. A Flying Squadron, under Commodore Winfield S. Schley, and composed of the battleship *Massachusetts,* the second-class battleship *Texas,* and the cruisers *Brooklyn* and *New Orleans,* was at Hampton Roads in readiness to go wherever needed. The battleship *Oregon,* Captain Charles E. Clark, was making a 14,000-mile voyage from the Pacific coast round South America to the coast of Florida. Much anxiety existed for her safety, but on May 26 she reached Jupiter Inlet on the coast of Florida in splendid condition, ready for any duty.

The North Atlantic Fleet.

The Flying Squadron.

Voyage of the Oregon.

Immediately after the declaration of war Sampson's fleet proceeded to blockade the Cuban coast from Cardenas to Bahia Honda. Sampson wished to attack the defenses of Havana, and it is now known that such a bombardment might have succeeded, but the Washington government, fearing further European complications, especially with Germany, ordered him to conserve his ships. For some days his activities were confined to capturing an occasional prize and to exchanging a few long-distance shots with the batteries at Cardenas. Then the important news came that the main Spanish fleet, under Rear-Admiral Cervera, had sailed from the Cape de Verde Islands, presumably for West Indian waters.

The Cuban Blockade.

An interesting game of hide-and-seek followed. Thinking that Cervera might call for coal at San Juan, Porto Rico, Sampson sailed thither, towing the slow monitors, but on his arrival off that port (May 12) he did not find the prey he sought; so, after subjecting the defenses to a short bombardment, he turned back toward Havana. On the previous day Cervera's squadron, which had been much hampered by defective machinery, arrived off Martinique, and thence proceeded to Curaçoa, where it stopped (May 14) for coal. News that the Spaniards were off Martinique reached Washington on the night of the 12th and resulted in Commodore Schley, with the *Brooklyn*, *Texas*, and *Massachusetts*, being sent to Charleston and then to Key West. There his squadron was strengthened and was sent to Cienfuegos, a port on the south coast of Cuba, connected by rail with Havana and thought to be the most likely destination of Cervera. In reality, however, Cervera took refuge in the bottle-shaped harbor of Santiago, and days passed before the Americans finally succeeded in locating him. Here he was safe from immediate danger, for the narrow entrance to the harbor was strongly defended by batteries and mines. He was also in telegraphic communication with Havana, but there was no communication by railway, and neither troops nor supplies could be sent to his aid. His fleet now consisted of four armored cruisers—the *Infanta Maria Teresa*, the *Cristóbal Colon*, the *Vizcaya*, and the *Almirante Oquendo*—and two destroyers—the *Furor* and *Pluton*. A third destroyer, the *Terror*, because of disabled boilers, had put in at Fort de France and later sailed to San Juan.

On May 28 Schley's squadron established a close blockade of the harbor. Three days later Sampson arrived and took command of the blockading fleet, which now consisted of the greater part of the American navy. The shore batteries were subjected to occasional long-range bombardments, and on the early morning of June 3 Naval Constructor Richmond Pearson Hobson and seven volunteers attempted to block egress from the harbor by sinking an old collier, the *Merrimac*, across the channel. The vessel drifted too far in before sinking, and the attempt to "cork the bottle" failed, but the effort was a gallant one, and Hobson and

Seeking Cervera's Fleet.

Cervera Takes Refuge in the Harbor of Santiago.

Hobson's Exploit.

his comrades, all of whom were captured, won enthusiastic applause from a world-wide audience.

Our military authorities had not intended to land any considerable force in Cuba until after the tropical summer, with its deadly fevers, had passed, but the plight of Cervera's fleet offered a tempting opportunity to strike a decisive blow. In the middle of June a force of 17,000 men sailed on about thirty transports from Tampa, Florida, bound for Santiago. Much confusion attended the embarkation; some of the supplies furnished were bad; the clothing of the soldiers was better suited to the snows of Wyoming than to the sultry climate of the West Indies; the commander, Major-General William R. Shafter, was so stout and so badly afflicted with the gout that he could not mount his horse; but, so far as underofficers and men were concerned, no better force was ever assembled under the American flag. It was composed entirely of regular troops, with the exception of the Second Massachusetts Regiment, the Seventy-First New York, and eight dismounted companies of the First Volunteer Cavalry.

A Land Force Sent to Santiago.

This last force was composed of Western cowboys, ranchmen, big-game hunters, and Indians, with a few Eastern football players and other adventurous spirits. It was commanded by Colonel Leonard Wood, an army surgeon who had seen active service against the Apaches. Its chief creator was its lieutenant-colonel, Theodore Roosevelt, who resigned his post in the Navy Department to organize it. He was offered the colonelcy, but insisted that the first place should be given to his more experienced friend, Wood. Altogether the regiment was a picturesque assemblage, and Americans watched eagerly to see how "Roosevelt's Rough Riders"—or "Teddy's Toughs," as they were sometimes called at first—would behave in battle.

The Rough Riders.

On June 22, under the guns of the fleet, the army began disembarking at Daiquiri, to the eastward of Santiago, and by nightfall, despite inadequate landing facilities, about 6,000 men were ashore. Next day General Lawton seized Siboney, eight

miles nearer Santiago, and the rest of the army landed there.
On the 24th an advance detachment, commanded by Brigadier-General S. M. B. Young, and including
La Guásima. the Rough Riders, struck a Spanish force at La
Guásima and chased it pellmell toward Santiago. The next
week was devoted to concentrating the army at Sevilla, to bringing up food and munitions, and to getting in touch with a
ragged army of insurgents under General Garcia. Officers and
men alike suffered from rain and heat, poor rations, and inadequate shelter, while fever began its deadly ravages. During
much of the time General Shafter was too ill to leave his headquarters. Though a really capable officer, his great size and
other bodily infirmities rendered him unfit to conduct a campaign in such a country.

At the end of June, despite Shafter's illness, it was decided
to make a general attack. Major-General Wheeler's division
of dismounted cavalry, which included the Rough Riders, and
Kent's division of infantry, were to move toward the Spanish
defenses on and about the low elevation known as San Juan
Hill, while 6,000 men, under Major-General H. W. Lawton,
were to carry the fortifications at El Caney and take position
on Wheeler's right. Both forces had a few light field-guns, all
firing black powder, the smoke of which betrayed their position to enemy sharpshooters.

Lawton attacked on the early morning of July 1, but the
Spanish troops at El Caney, protected by barbed wire, trenches,
and block-houses, held out stoutly, and it was late in the afternoon before their resistance was overcome. Mean-
Lawton at while the movement against San Juan had gone
El Caney.
forward in a haphazard manner. An observation-
balloon raised above the ford of the San Juan River drew the
enemy's fire thither, causing heavy losses to the troops crossing
the stream; lack of any general authority caused doubt and
hesitation; and for a time the troops lay inactive under a gall-
ing fire. Finally some fighting subordinates, namely, Brigadier-
General Hawkins, a gallant white-haired veteran of the Civil
War, and Colonel Roosevelt, who was now head of his regiment,

Wood having been promoted, led spirited charges that swept the Spaniards out of their defenses. In this work, and in holding the positions thus taken, a battery of Gatling guns, under Lieutenant John H. Parker, rendered effective service. Even after the San Juan positions were captured, the Spaniards kept up so hot a fire from works nearer Santiago that some officers in the rear wanted to retire; but the men and officers at the front protested, and "Fighting Joe" Wheeler, though so ill that he could hardly be about, refused to order a retreat. The victors dug themselves in on the captured heights; but, even as late as July 3, General Shafter, depressed by his bodily condition, cabled Washington that he could not take Santiago by storm, and that he was "considering withdrawing about five miles and taking up a new position." The American losses in three days had been about 1,100 men.

San Juan Hill.

On the very day that Shafter sent his depressing despatch, an event occurred that dissipated all thoughts of withdrawal. The Spaniards believed that the capture of Santiago was imminent. In obedience to telegraphic orders from General Blanco at Havana, Admiral Cervera, about half-past nine o'clock in the morning of July 3, steamed out of the harbor with his squadron and attempted to escape to the westward. Admiral Sampson, in the cruiser *New York*, was temporarily absent on an errand to eastward, but he had long before issued instructions to cover such a contingency, and the other war-ships dashed in pursuit. Within a few hours every Spanish vessel was a blackened, sunken wreck on the coast of Cuba. The *Cristóbal Colon* was the last afloat, but being hotly pressed by the *Oregon* and *Brooklyn*, she turned toward the shore, surrendered, and sank soon afterward. The American loss was only one man killed and one seriously wounded. Sampson in the *New York* did not arrive in time to participate in the engagement, and as Schley was the senior officer present, a bitter controversy later developed over the question of who was in command. In reality, the battle was "a captains' fight."

The Spanish Fleet Destroyed.

Though subjected to a bombardment from land and sea,
Santiago held out until the 14th, when General
Toral agreed to capitulate. The actual surrender
took place three days later. The prisoners numbered about 10,000.

Santiago Surrenders.

By this time the American army was suffering severely from
the ravages of malaria and yellow fever. As only a few men
would be needed to hold Santiago, the officers felt
that heavy losses could be avoided only by sending
most of the regiments to a healthier climate. The
War Department had other plans, but a "round robin" signed
by many of the officers had the desired effect, and early in
August most of the army was sent to Montauk Point on Long
Island.

The "Round Robin."

Several minor naval operations took place in the West Indies
in the course of the war, but the only other land operation was
an invasion of Porto Rico. On July 25 about 3,000 men, under
Major-General Miles, landed at Guanica on the
south coast, and within a few days this force was
augmented to nearly 17,000. In about two weeks
the invaders, with a loss of only 3 men killed and 40 wounded,
overran the southern and western portions of the island. Complete conquest was imminent when news arrived that a protocol
had been signed suspending hostilities.

Invasion of Porto Rico.

On the other side of the world, Dewey, now a rear-admiral,
had patiently awaited the arrival of troops from home. Meanwhile important internal developments had taken place in the
Philippines.

As in Cuba, many of the native inhabitants had long been
dissatisfied with Spanish rule, and there had been frequent
uprisings against it. The last of these had broken out in 1896,
the causes being partly racial, partly the oppressive civil and economic power wielded by the friars,
who held vast areas of land. The revolt was organized by the "Katipunan," or Patriots' League,
and the chief leader was a young Tagalog named Emilio Aguinaldo. After much bloodshed, the insurgents were brought to

The Philippine Revolt of 1896-97.

such straits that Aguinaldo and other leaders accepted an agreement called the treaty of Briac-na-bato (December 15, 1897),
in which the Spanish governor-general, Primo de Rivera, promised to carry out certain reforms and to pay the leaders $800,-
000 to lay down their arms and go into exile. The reforms were
never carried out, and only three-fourths of the money was paid.

Shortly before Dewey left Hong Kong he was informed by
the American consul at Singapore that Aguinaldo was at that
place and was anxious to co-operate in an attack upon the
Spaniards. Dewey sent word for him to come on,
and the Tagalog leader hurried northward, but
when he reached Hong Kong Dewey was gone.

Aguinaldo Begins a New Revolt.

However, nineteen days after the destruction of the Spanish
fleet the American despatch-boat *McCulloch* brought Aguinaldo
and thirteen associates to Manila Bay. The Americans lent
them some moral and material aid, and the Filipinos rose in a
new revolt that soon extinguished Spanish authority in a large
part of the Philippines. A rebel force under Aguinaldo even
laid siege to the city of Manila.

Meanwhile Dewey had been subjected to an unexpected an-
noyance. Several neutral powers, as is not uncommon in such
cases, sent war-ships to Manila to protect their citizens and
commercial interests. For some reason Germany,
whose interests were small, sent five ships, a force
more powerful than that commanded by Dewey
himself. All the other neutral war-ships observed

Dewey Clashes with German Admiral.

the proprieties demanded by the situation, but the German
ships ignored the rules of blockade and interfered with the
operations of the insurgents, while some of their officers openly
proclaimed their sympathy with Spain. Whether the Germans had any ulterior purposes has never been revealed, but
their behavior finally became so obnoxious to Dewey that he
lost patience and sent word to the German commander, Vice-
Admiral von Diederich, that if he wanted a fight he could "have
it right now." This blunt message, joined with the fact that
Captain Edward Chichester, the commander of the British
naval force in the harbor, declared in no uncertain terms that

he would support the Americans, brought the insolent Teutons to terms. Afterward the monitor *Monterey*, armed with powerful 12- and 10-inch guns, arrived (August 4), and so strengthened Dewey's force that he had no reason to fear either the Germans or any Spanish fleet that might be sent out against him.

In this matter, as in that of the attempted intervention at the beginning of the war, the United States had reason to feel grateful to Great Britain. British friendship in this period was largely due to the personal influence wielded by John Hay, our ambassador at London, who as a young man had been assistant private secretary to Abraham Lincoln. Thenceforth Anglo-American relations became increasingly cordial.

Great Britain Friendly.

At the end of June a force of 2,500 American troops, under Brigadier-General Thomas M. Anderson, reached Cavite, having, in an *opéra bouffe* attack, taken the little island of Guam on the way. Two other contingents, under Brigadier-General Francis V. Greene and Major-General Wesley E. Merritt, arrived before the end of July, making a total of almost 11,000.

Arrival of an American Army.

The position of the Spanish forces defending Manila was hopeless. Back in June a third Spanish fleet under Admiral Camara had set out from Spain for the Philippines by way of the Suez Canal, but an announcement that Rear-Admiral Watson would lead a squadron to ravage the Spanish coast caused great uneasiness at Madrid, and after the destruction of Cervera's fleet Camara was ordered home, just as he was about to set out down the Red Sea. Deprived of all hope of relief, the Spanish leaders at Manila nevertheless refused to capitulate, for they feared court-martial and punishment in Spain. Secretly, however, they arranged with the Americans to make only a show of resistance and then to surrender. On August 13 the American land and naval forces made a joint attack. After a short fight, in which only a few men were killed or wounded, a white flag went up, and Manila surrendered.

Manila Surrenders.

The destruction of Spanish sea power at Manila and Santiago had put both the Philippines and Cuba at American mercy. Spain was almost bankrupt. Castilian honor had been satisfied. The Spanish Government bowed to the inevitable, and on July 18 requested the French Government to authorize the French ambassador at Washington to arrange for preliminary terms of peace. On August 12, the day before the capture of Manila, Ambassador Cambon and William R. Day, who had succeeded John Sherman as secretary of state, signed a protocol providing for a suspension of hostilities, for the relinquishment of all Spanish claims to Cuba, for the cession of Porto Rico and one of the Ladrone Islands, in the Pacific, to the United States, and for the appointment of peace commissioners to meet in Paris not later than October 1. In the meantime the Spanish forces were to evacuate Cuba and Porto Rico. The question of what disposition would be made of the Philippines was left an open one to be decided by the peace conference.

The American delegation at the peace conference was headed by William R. Day, who resigned the post of secretary of state for that purpose, being succeeded by John Hay. The Spanish delegation was headed by President of the Senate Don Eugenio Montero Rios. The Spanish representatives devoted most of October to a fruitless attempt to saddle the big Cuban debt either upon Cuba or the United States. They wasted most of November in an equally fruitless effort to save the Philippines. American public opinion was divided as to what should be done with the archipelago. McKinley himself hesitated, and his letter of instructions merely directed our representatives to ask for Luzon. Some prominent men wished no more than a coaling station; others, including Senator Gray of the commission, favored withdrawing from the Philippines altogether. In the end McKinley decided to demand the whole archipelago, and the Spanish commissioners, as is usually the case with the defeated party, had to give way on this and every other important question. Spain had to withdraw from all her possessions in the West Indies, thus surrendering the last of her once imperial domain in the New World, and to cede the Philippines and the island of Guam. The United States, however, assumed the claims of its citizens for damages done in Cuba during the insurrection, and in consideration of the cession of the Philippines, agreed to pay $20,000,000, and for ten years to admit Spanish ships and merchandise into the islands on the same terms as American ships and goods.

The Philippine feature of the treaty provoked strong opposition in the United States. Opponents of annexation contended that owing to their remoteness and the character of their in-

Opposition to the Treaty.

habitants the islands could never be admitted to statehood, and must always remain colonies. Senator Vest, a prominent Democrat, introduced a resolution to the effect "That under the Constitution of the United States no power is given to the federal government to acquire territory to be held and governed permanently as colonies." Senator Hoar of Massachusetts, a prominent Republican, declared that to acquire and hold the Philippines would be not only a violation of the Constitution and the Declaration of Independence, but of the whole spirit of American institutions. Friends of annexation denied the force of such contentions, while others pointed out that to refuse to ratify the treaty would result in a renewal of the war, and that the question of the ultimate disposition of the Philippines could be threshed out later. The fate of the treaty was in grave

Bryan's Attitude.

doubt when William Jennings Bryan came to the capital and urged ratification. The question of imperialism, he told his followers, would be an issue in the next presidential campaign. Ten Democratic senators voted for the treaty, and it was ratified (February 6, 1899), with but one vote in excess of the required two-thirds. Ratification by the Queen Regent of Spain was delayed six weeks longer (March 19, 1899).

There were Americans dishonorable enough to advocate that we should break our solemn pledge and annex Cuba, but the great majority insisted that the island should be given its independence. A provisional government was established to manage affairs temporarily, and this was headed during most

American Rule in Cuba.

of the period of American tutelage by Governor Leonard Wood, who displayed great tact and high administrative abilities under difficult circumstances.

Many improvements in law, education, and sanitation were introduced, roads were improved, and financial affairs were so well handled by General Tasker H. Bliss that a balance of $1,792,109.52 was accumulated in the treasury. An important achievement under this régime was that of an army surgeon, Major Walter Reed, who conducted investigations that resulted in the discovery that yellow fever, one of the most deadly of tropical diseases, is transmitted by a species of mosquito. To control the disease became thereafter a comparatively simple matter, and the discovery has already resulted in the saving of many thousands of lives, not only in Cuba but also in the United States and other countries.

Late in 1900 a constitutional convention, composed of elected delegates, met in Havana and proceeded to frame a constitution modelled after that of the United States. Under pressure

The "Platt Amendment."

from the United States the convention added (June 12, 1901) an appendix to the constitution embodying the so-called "Platt Amendment," which had

been inserted in the American army appropriation bill of March 2, 1901. Of the eight points to this amendment the most important were that Cuba must not contract a public debt of unreasonable dimensions, that the United States might intervene to protect Cuban liberty or to maintain "a government adequate for the protection of life, property, and individual liberty," that the Cuban Government would carry out and, as far as necessary, extend plans devised or that later might be agreed upon for the sanitation of the cities of the island, and that Cuba would sell or lease to the United States lands necessary for naval stations at certain points to be agreed upon. It was further stipulated that Cuba would embody these provisions in a permanent treaty with the United States, and this was done, though final ratifications were not exchanged until 1904.

The general effect of the Platt Amendment was to make Cuba a protectorate of the United States. The United States could intervene to protect Cuba's independence or to restore domestic order, and could enforce sanitary regulations that were highly important to American coast cities, which in the past had frequently suffered from diseases carried thither from Cuban ports. Ultimately only one naval base, namely, at Guantánamo on the southeast coast, was occupied and developed; but this gave the United States a foothold on the island, as well as a strategic strong point on the Caribbean Sea, and conveniently near the channel between Cuba and Haiti. The United States has never, however, exercised its protectorate in a manner contrary to the interests of the Cuban people.

An American Protectorate.

On the last day of 1901 a general election was held in Cuba, and resulted in the choice of electors who named (February 24, 1902) for first President the fine old revolutionist Thomas Estrada Palma. On May 20, 1902, General Wood and the last American troops sailed from the island, and the new republic formally entered upon her independent existence. Thus closed one of the most admirable chapters in human annals.

American Withdrawal, 1902.

The rich island of Porto Rico, the fourth in size of the Antilles, was retained by the United States. The population at that time consisted of 589,426 whites, mostly of Spanish descent, 304,352 mestizos, and 59,390 negroes. Under the Foraker Act (April 12, 1900) Congress established a civil government in which the people were allowed some participation, but the inhabitants were described as "citizens of Porto Rico, and as such entitled to the protection of the United States." The Porto Rican was thus neither a citizen of the United States nor an alien. In the words of Professor Ogg, "he was left, like Mohammed's coffin, dangling between earth and heaven." In March, 1917, however, a new act conferred full citizenship upon the Porto Ricans, and increased their participation in the local government.

Porto Rico.

The management of the War Department during the Spanish-

American conflict aroused such severe criticism that in September, 1898, President McKinley appointed a commission

Investigation of the War Department.

to investigate the charges. Among other things, the critics alleged that the department had displayed incompetence in providing weapons and munitions; that chemically treated beef—"embalmed beef," it was popularly called—had been fed to the soldiers, thereby injuring their health; and that some of the instruction camps had been badly managed, resulting in unnecessary loss of life by disease. The commission's report "whitewashed" the War Department, but admitted that Secretary Alger had "failed to grasp the situation." The report did not allay the criticism, but McKinley, for political reasons, retained Alger in the cabinet. A coolness developed between the two men, however, and the President ultimately asked for Alger's resignation. He was succeeded (August 1, 1899) by Elihu Root of New York, a keen lawyer and able administrator, who carried out a reorganization of the department.

In glaring contrast with the War Department, the Navy Department was managed in a manner well-nigh beyond praise, and the fighting efficiency of the ships and crews added new

Admirable Strategy.

lustre to American laurels. The soldiers, too, though handicapped by politics and mismanagement in the War Department, fought bravely and performed every feat required of them. Nor should sight be lost of the fact that in its larger strategical aspects the war was managed with consummate skill. The Naval War Board, of which Captain Mahan was the most eminent member, unerringly discerned where and when to strike, and decisive results were accomplished with a minimum expenditure of blood and effort.

Measured by the amount of blood shed, the war was, in fact,

America a World Power.

a petty affair. Fewer Americans had been slain in it than had been killed in combats of the great civil conflict that had not risen above the dignity of skirmishes. Measured by its effects upon the United States and the world, it was one of the most important wars in which we have been engaged. For better or for worse, the United States dropped its traditional policy of isolation and stepped out upon the broad stage of international affairs. The restless energy that had conquered the continent westward to the Pacific had now carried the flag beyond the too narrow confines of the western hemisphere. Doubtfully, almost unwillingly, the nation fronted its fate, stooped to take up "the White Man's burden," and undertook to govern strange peoples, "half devil and half child," in lands beyond the seas.

CHAPTER XV

"IMPERIALISM"

THE Philippines, ceded to the United States by Spain, consist of 3,141 islands, seven-eighths of which have an area of less than one square mile each, while 9 contain over 10,000 square

The Philippines and the Filipinos. miles each, the largest being Luzon, with 40,969 square miles, and the next largest Mindanao, with 36,292 square miles. The total land area is 115,026 square miles, and the total native population in 1899 exceeded 7,000,000. In race they varied from brown Malays to black, woolly-headed Negritos, in religion from Christians to Mohammedans and pagans, in civilization from college graduates to naked savages whose favorite dainty was dog meat and whose chief delight was hunting human heads. For three hundred years the islands had been subjected to Spanish rule, and most of the Filipinos, who constituted about seven-eighths of the whole population, were at least nominally Christians and civilized, but slavery, peonage, polygamy, and other barbaric practices still flourished in places, especially among the fierce Mohammedan Moros. Large numbers of Chinese had settled in the islands, but the total white population, even as late as 1903, was only 14,271, with 15,419 mestizos, or persons of mixed native and Chinese blood.

The course of events in the Philippines proved much less happy than in Cuba. By treaty the United States acquired Spain's title to the archipelago, but we had captured only the

McKinley Decides to Hold the Islands. city of Manila, and, in the words of Admiral Dewey, "we were far from being in possession of the territory we had bought." It was only after much hesitation that President McKinley decided not only to exact the cession of all the islands but also to hold them, at least for a time. A desire to extend American power and commerce in the Orient, an unwillingness to lower the American flag where it had once been hoisted, and doubts as to the ability of the heterogeneous native population to govern themselves appear to have been the chief reasons that caused him to reach these momentous decisions.

Before the United States declared its purpose regarding the islands, Aguinaldo and his followers hoped and expected to be treated on the same basis as the Cuban revolutionists. They proceeded, with some slight aid from the Americans, to overrun a large part of the archipelago. On June 12 Aguinaldo, as dictator, declared the independence of the Philippines. Later in the same month he proclaimed a revolutionary government, "with a paper organization of executive, congress, and courts." Aguinaldo continued in power as "President," but the Americans usually referred to him as "General," nor did they ever in any formal way recognize the Filipino government.

Aguinaldo's Government.

Even before the capture of Manila the insurgents began to doubt American intentions, and there was more or less friction between the besieging forces. After the capitulation the Filipinos occupied part of the city, but in the middle of September General Elwell S. Otis informed Aguinaldo that he must withdraw his men or force would be used. Aguinaldo complied with this ultimatum, but kept it a secret from the rank and file, who "marched out in excellent spirits, cheering the American forces."

Insurgents Ordered out of Manila.

The capital of the insurgent government was established at Malolos, twenty miles north of Manila. A congress of somewhat irregular character met there, and a constitution was framed and adopted by this body (January 20, 1899).

The dictator and his close associates were well aware that differences of opinion existed in the United States regarding the Philippines. More than one American newspaper was hailing Aguinaldo as the "savior of his country" and "the Washington of the Orient"; enterprising American editors were soliciting his "views on the issues of the day"; and it is alleged that political managers were even

American Praise of Aguinaldo.

hinting that "his influence would be of material value in the coming presidential election in the United States."

After the withdrawal from Manila the insurgents continued to hold positions close to that city. Believing that a conflict with the Americans was inevitable, Mabina, a paralytic young lawyer who was the ablest of Aguinaldo's advisers, urged that matters should be brought to a crisis at once, but he was overruled. Realizing that the situation was becoming tense, Admiral Dewey advised President McKinley to define the intentions of the United States in order to put an end to uncertainty, and McKinley (December 21, 1898) transmitted a proclamation asserting the "supremacy" and "sovereignty" of the United States, and stating that its authority would be enforced over the islands until legislation "shall otherwise provide." The proclamation declared that the Americans came "not as invaders or as conquerors, but as friends," and that the American mission was "one of benevolent assimilation, substituting the mild sway of justice and right for arbitrary rule." But the Filipinos had long been accustomed to the flowery rhetoric and hollow promises of their Spanish masters, and paid little heed to anything but the fact that their independence was not conceded. The bad effect of the proclamation was heightened by the fact that at Manila General Otis published it in expurgated form, omitting some of the objectionable phrases, while General Miller at Iloilo issued it (January 6) as originally written. The Filipinos saw in the discrepancy a proof of American duplicity.

An armed conflict became inevitable. It was precipitated on the night of February 4, two days before the Senate ratified the treaty, by four Filipino soldiers approaching an American outpost near Manila and ignoring a command to halt. The sentry fired at them, and a Filipino detachment stationed not far away returned the fire. A general battle soon developed, in which the navy played an effective part. The Filipinos were soon thrown back, with losses estimated by General Otis at 3,000, while those of the Americans amounted to only 50 killed and 184 wounded. It is

McKinley's Proclamation, Dec. 21, 1898.

A "Revolt" Begins.

believed that the incident that precipitated the clash was not premeditated by the Filipino leaders, but for some time they had been making ready for an attack on the Americans, and Aguinaldo had the draft of a declaration of war in readiness.

The conflict thus begun was a most uneven one. The Filipinos had few cannon and comparatively few rifles; the supply of ammunition was scanty; and many of the soldiers were so inexpert with rifles that they did not even know how to aim them. The Filipinos were, in fact, often more effective when armed with spears, bolos, and other primitive weapons. Opposed to them stood in the beginning about 14,000 Americans; many of these were volunteers who lacked thorough training; but regulars and volunteers alike were far more than a match, individually or collectively, for "the little brown men" who had thrown down the gauge of battle to them. Furthermore, the war-ships were able to render much assistance, while an endless supply of men, money, and munitions could be sent out from the United States. Nevertheless, the Filipinos at first fought pluckily, and from one to half a dozen men would often be standing ready to snatch up the precious rifle of a killed or wounded man and turn it once more against the enemy. The bitter experience gained in a few battles soon taught them, however, that they could not withstand the stalwart, straight-shooting Americans in open battle, and many of the later conflicts resembled foot-races rather than fights.

Character of the War.

Toward the end of March General MacArthur took the offensive and soon captured Malolos, the insurgent capital. During the next few weeks he and General Lawton defeated the insurgents in numerous engagements, and took many towns. Meanwhile other forces, aided by the navy, took Iloilo and Cebu, and extended American authority over the Visayan and Sulu archipelagoes. The rainy summer season caused military activities to languish, but in the fall Generals Lawton and Wheaton once more took the field and defeated the Filipinos in numerous engagements, in one of which Lawton was slain (December 19, 1899).

Americans Take the Offensive.

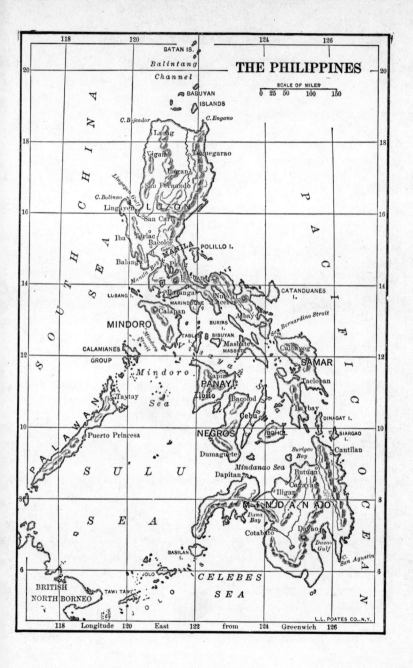

Aguinaldo went into hiding in the mountains of Luzon. Many of his followers surrendered; others broke up into small bands and waged a guerilla warfare that was far more trying to the Americans than organized tactics had been. Fields were laid waste, the rhinderpest swept away thousands of the tame carabaos, a sort of buffalo, which is the chief beast of burden in the Philippines, and it has been estimated that during three years of warfare some hundreds of thousands of Filipinos perished from famine and pestilence.

Guerilla Warfare.

In America the course of events in the Philippines caused much searching of hearts. There were, to be sure, persons of gross mould who swept sentiment aside and frankly favored keeping the islands because of the gold they could be made to pour into our lap. But some men doubted whether our treatment of the Filipinos squared with the precepts of the Declaration of Independence. To many it seemed that we had entered the war with Spain to free a people, and were ending by enslaving one. Others, though believing it necessary to establish American control for the good of the inhabitants, felt, nevertheless, the tragedy of the situation; like Admiral Dewey, they were "deeply affected by the necessity of the loss of life and the misery which the pacification of the islands imposed."

Opposition to the Philippine Policy.

While public opinion still hesitated, a powerful influence was cast in favor of retaining the islands by the publication (February, 1899) of a remarkable poem. "In winged words which circled the earth in a day, and by repetition became hackneyed in a week," Rudyard Kipling stripped the imperial vocation of its tinsel and glitter, and "revealed it as a necessary but thankless task to be performed by the white race under the restraints of conscience." He called upon America to

Kipling's "White Man's Burden."

> "Take up the White Man's burden—
> Send forth the best ye breed—
> Go bind your sons to exile
> To serve your captives' need;

To wait in heavy harness,
On fluttering folk and wild—
Your new-caught sullen peoples,
Half devil and half child.

. . . . . .

Take up the White Man's burden—
Ye dare not stoop to less—
Nor call too loud on Freedom
To cloak your weariness.
By all ye will or whisper,
By all ye leave or do,
The silent sullen peoples
Shall weigh your God and you."

At the outset, opposition to retaining the Philippines was mostly non-partisan in character; anti-imperialist leagues, which sprang up in many parts of the country, but particularly in New England, drew members from all parties. The Anti-Imperialists. Andrew Carnegie, Senator George F. Hoar, George S. Boutwell, ex-President Harrison, Speaker Reed, and other prominent Republicans disliked the administration's policy in the Philippines; Reed even resigned from Congress because of it. On the other hand, some Democrats and Democratic newspapers at first favored expansion. Less than a week after the ratification of the treaty with Spain, William Jennings Bryan, who expected once more to be the Democratic presidential candidate in 1900, issued a manifesto opposing "imperialism." The disposition of the Philippines Democrats Make Imperialism a Political Issue. speedily became a political question, and the Democrats displayed a determination to make it a leading issue in the campaign of 1900. The prosperity of the United States was very great, and Republicans charged that Democratic leaders, seeing that free silver was unpopular, realized that their only hope of winning would be to inject a new issue into politics.

When the Republican convention met at Philadelphia (June 19, 1900) its leaders were full of confidence. The platform pointed to the financial transformation wrought under Republican rule, and lauded many other achievements. The Philippines and their people were referred to as "a new and noble responsibility." Having destroyed Spain's sovereignty in the

Republican Platform of 1900.

islands, we were bound to "provide for the maintenance of law and order," to put down insurrection, and to "confer the blessings of liberty and civilization" upon the people. One plank dealt with the trusts. These were now multiplying with great rapidity, but this fact did not give the Republican leaders much anxiety. Mark Hanna, the "political prime minister" of the administration, wrote the trust plank, which recognized "the necessity and propriety of the honest co-operation of capital to meet new business conditions" but condemned "all conspiracies and combinations intended to restrict business, to create monopolies, to limit production or to control prices."

As had long been foreseen, McKinley was unanimously renominated, and the only question that aroused any real curiosity was the choice of a vice-presidential nominee. Vice-

McKinley Renominated.

President Hobart had died in office, hence the ticket of 1896 was impossible. Among those mentioned were Secretary of the Treasury Bliss, Secretary of the Navy Long, Representative Jonathan P. Dolliver of Iowa, Timothy L. Woodruff of New York, and Theodore Roosevelt. Roosevelt's foresight and energy in preparing the navy for the war, his valor as leader of the picturesque Rough Riders, and his well-known reforming zeal had combined to make him one of the most popular men in the country. In the fall of 1898 he had been elected governor of New York and his vigorous course in that office had increased his reputation, but he had incurred the opposition of certain great corporations and of Senator Thomas C. Platt, the Republican boss of the

Roosevelt Nominated for the Vice-Presidency against His Wishes.

State. Platt decided to bring about Roosevelt's nomination as Vice-President in order to prevent his re-election as governor. In this scheme he was greatly aided by the enthusiastic desire of a multitude of Republicans, especially in the West, to put the Rough Rider on the ticket. Neither McKinley nor Hanna wanted him nominated, and Roosevelt himself, desiring to be governor again, declared that he could not accept a nomination; but the strange alliance of Platt and Republican sentiment won the day. Roosevelt received every vote in the convention except his own, and bowed to the will of his party. As no Vice-President since Martin Van Buren had been elected President, it was supposed by Roosevelt's friends and enemies alike that he was "shelved" politically.

The Democratic convention met in Kansas City on July 4, the date being specially chosen to emphasize the reaffirmation by the platform of the Declaration of Independence, "that immortal proclamation of the inalienable rights of man." "We assert," the platform continued, "that no nation can long endure half republic and half empire, and we warn the American people that imperialism abroad will lead quickly and inevitably to despotism at home." The Republican Philippine policy had been dictated by "greedy commercialism"; the war was one of "criminal aggression." The Filipinos must be given, "first, a stable form of government; second, independence; and third, protection from outside interference." "Imperialism" was pronounced "the paramount issue of the campaign," but the gold standard act of 1900 was denounced, and a demand was made for "the immediate restoration of the free and unlimited coinage of silver and gold at the present ratio of 16 to 1, without waiting for the aid or consent of any other nation." Many delegates had wished to omit any reference to the currency, but the Bryan influence had been too strong. The platform also pledged the Democracy to "an unceasing warfare . . . against private monopoly in every form," and denounced the Dingley Act as "a trust-breeding measure."

Democrats Declare Imperialism the "Paramount Issue."

There had been some talk of Admiral Dewey as the presidential candidate, but Bryan was renominated by acclamation. Adlai E. Stevenson, Vice-President from 1893 to 1897, was named as his associate on the ticket.

Bryan and Stevenson.

The "Fusion Populists," the "Liberty Congress of the

American League of Anti-Imperialists," and the "Silver Republicans" also indorsed Bryan, but the Populists put

Minor Parties. forward Charles A. Towne of Minnesota for the vice-presidency instead of Stevenson. The "Anti-Fusion," or "Middle-of-the-Road" Populists, nominated a separate ticket, but they played little part in the campaign.

The Social Democrats. The Prohibitionists, the Socialist Labor party, and the Social Democratic party also put tickets in the field. That of the Social Democrats was headed by Eugene V. Debs, leader of the railroad strikers in 1896. A Socialist Labor Party had nominated candidates in 1892 and 1896, but many of its members now joined the Social Democrats; others nominated candidates of their own and have had a presidential ticket in every campaign since, but have never polled a large vote.

During the campaign the Democrats tried to persuade the people that the Republican policy in the Philippines would result in the destruction of liberty at home. Many Republicans were, it is true, dissatisfied with our course

The Campaign. in the islands; but the suppression of the political rights of Southern negroes by Democrats did not harmonize well with their enthusiasm for Filipino independence, while the nomination of Bryan and the continued demand for free silver repelled many voters. On all questions the Republicans refused to accept the defensive, and as regards the Philippines they asserted that Democratic agitation of the subject encouraged the insurgents to persist in their "rebellion," and resulted in the death of many American soldiers.

As usual, Bryan swept through many States, speaking to immense audiences, but he met an equally determined cam-

"The Full Dinner Pail." paigner in Roosevelt, who aroused great enthusiasm wherever he went. Senator Hanna managed the Republican campaign with skill, and by hoisting on high "the full dinner pail" as the emblem of Republican prosperity, he won many labor votes.

The result proved even more decisive than that of 1896. McKinley carried nearly every Northern and Western State,

and also Delaware, Maryland, and West Virginia, with a total

of 292 electoral votes to 155 for Bryan; the popular vote stood 7,219,525 for McKinley, and 6,358,737 for Bryan. The Populist vote was reduced to 50,599, being exceeded by that of the Prohibitionists, with 209,157, and the Social Democrats with 94,864.

Meanwhile the Filipino insurgents had continued to carry on guerilla warfare. To meet these tactics the American commanders found it necessary to divide their forces into several

hundred detachments to hold villages and other posts, and the insurgents found it comparatively easy to surround and massacre weak detachments, though usually only after heavy losses to themselves. When hotly pursued, they would frequently hide their weapons and, mingling with the population of a village, comport themselves as smiling "*amigos*," or friends. From May 5, 1900, to June 30, 1901, a period of fourteen months, 1,026 "contacts" occurred between the hostile forces, in which over 700 Americans and about 5,000 insurgents were killed or wounded.

For a time the insurgents were buoyed up by the hope that the Democrats would win the presidential election. The rank and file were told of the Democratic platform pronouncement

regarding the Philippines, and insurgent agents in Canada even wrote home that they had established confidential relations with Bryan. No tale of the alleged course of events in the United States was too wild to be believed. The Republican victory proved a bitter disappointment to the insurgents, and thereafter their cause declined.

In March, 1901, Brigadier-General Frederick Funston, the enterprising Kansan whom we have already met with the Cuban

insurgents, managed to penetrate, with a few Americans and a party of Macabebe scouts, into the wilderness of northern Luzon, and, by a clever stratagem, captured Aguinaldo and some of his chief officers. The insurgent leader was taken to Manila, was well treated, and soon issued a proclamation to his followers advising them to give up the struggle.

Sporadic resistance continued for many months, however, and many cruel deeds were done on both sides. Even before Aguinaldo's surrender, American troops, exasperated by insurgent treachery and by the frightful cruelties inflicted upon captive comrades, resorted in some cases to what was known as the "water cure" and other modes of torture, in order to obtain information from prisoners. Such methods were happily not general, but their occasional use persisted until the end of the insurrection. Furthermore, the Americans, especially in Batangas, imitated Spanish "reconcentration" methods, but treated the people in such camps humanely. One brigadier-general, popularly known as "Hell Roaring Jake Smith," ordered his men to make the island of Samar "a howling wilderness. . . . Kill everything over ten." For issuing this order, and for having been indirectly responsible for the shooting of prisoners without trial, he was convicted by a court martial and was placed on the retired list by the President.

Gradually the insurgents recognized the inevitable and bowed to it, but it was not until July 4, 1902, that President Roosevelt officially declared the islands pacified. Even afterward there were sporadic outbreaks, especially among the warlike Mohammedan Moros and other "non-Christian tribes."

On January 20, 1899, President McKinley appointed a commission of five persons, including President Jacob G. Schurman of Cornell University, Rear-Admiral Dewey, and Professor Dean C. Worcester, to investigate conditions in the Philippines and assist in pacifying the islands. The commission issued a proclamation to the Filipinos and held conferences with insurgent agents, but their peace efforts proved only partly successful. In regard to the people of the islands they reported that "lack of education and political experience, combined with their racial and linguistic diversities, disqualify them, in spite of their mental gifts and domestic virtues, to undertake the task of governing the archipelago at the present time."

In April, 1900, the President appointed a new commission, consisting of Judge William H. Taft, Dean C. Worcester, Luke E. Wright, Henry C. Ide, and Professor Bernard Moses, to organize a civil government for the Philippines. The instructions for the guidance of the commission were drawn up by Secretary of War Root, whose department supervised Philippine affairs. All the commissioners were men of ability and good intentions, and they were able to make real progress. They were also all men of large size physically, their average weight being 227 pounds. As they did much travelling about the islands, their great avoirdupois often proved trying during the hot season, but the Filipinos, who are a tiny people physically, considered them "an imposing spectacle."

Second Philippine Commission.

On July 4, 1901, the military régime in the islands was brought to an end, and Judge Taft was inaugurated civil governor. Two months later three Filipino members were added to the commission, and native judges and other public officials were also appointed. As rapidly as military conditions would permit, local civil governments were established, and a great scheme of public education was formulated and carried out. Hundreds of American young men and women were induced to go to the Philippines and teach the Filipino children, while the normal school already existing at Manila was greatly expanded, and many native teachers were trained there. It was an educational crusade the like of which the world had never before seen, and, though some of the results were disappointing, the effort, as a whole, proved a great success.

Taft Becomes Civil Governor.

An Educational Crusade.

Strange as it may seem, the teachers accomplished much good by introducing outdoor sports. Hitherto the Filipinos had had practically no athletic games, but were fond of cockfighting, while gambling was their "besetting sin." The effort to introduce such games as baseball had some amusing results.

For example, Moro men quickly grew eager to bat, but insisted for a time that the vigorous work of base-running ought to be done by their servants! Real enthusiasm for the new sports soon spread through the islands. The resultant physical development of the participants has been remarkable, cock-fighting is less popular than formerly, and a spirit of sportsmanship and fair play, hitherto lacking, has sprung into existence. Villages which in 1898 habitually indulged in head-hunting forays against each other now engage in friendly "tugs of war" and games of baseball. "It is indeed a startling sight," says Dean C. Worcester, in his book *The Philippines, Past and Present*, "to see two opposing teams of youthful savages in Bukidnon or Bontoc 'playing the game,' with obvious full knowledge of its refinements, while their ordinarily silent and reserved parents 'root' with unbridled enthusiasm!"

Effect of Outdoor Games.

Opponents of the retention of the Philippines put forward as one of their main arguments the contention that our system of government was not suited to the government of distant dependencies inhabited by "inferior peoples." They asserted that "the Constitution follows the flag" and argued that its provisions safeguarding individual rights—such as freedom of speech, trial by jury, and habeas corpus—would hopelessly hamper colonial administrators. But the expansionists declared that the United States had always been a colonial power, that it had repeatedly acquired new possessions, that it had governed the Indians as subject peoples. They denied that the Constitution extends of its own force (*ex proprio vigore*) to new territory, and they pointed to a long series of acts of Congress expressly extending the Constitution and statutes to recently acquired possessions. In support of their view they also quoted the constitutional clause which provides that "Congress shall have power to dispose of and make all needful rules and regulations respecting the territory or other property belonging to the United States"; they contended that this clause was broad enough to meet all emergencies.

Does the Constitution Follow the Flag?

In deciding what are known as the "Insular Cases" the Supreme Court, though badly divided in opinion, in effect held (May, 1901) that the Constitution does not extend *ex proprio vigore* to new possessions. The federal government was, therefore, left unhampered in its work of governing the Philippines and Porto Rico. The court also held that the United States could impose tariff duties on goods coming from the islands.

The "Insular Cases."

One of the main causes of the Filipino revolt against Spanish rule was the enormous political and economic power wielded by the friars, who owned much of the best land and controlled the local government. The natives hated the friars so bitterly that they tortured and even murdered some of them, and drove out the rest. After the American occupation the religious orders continued to lay claim to their lands, but the natives generally refused to pay rent. It was decided that the claims should be extinguished by purchase, and Governor Taft visited Rome in person to negotiate the sale with the papal authorities. In 1903 the purchase was consummated, the price agreed upon being $7,239,000 for 410,-000 acres. Religious and agrarian questions continued, however, to be sources of trouble in the Philippines.

The Friars Land Question.

By act of July 1, 1902, Congress declared the inhabitants of the archipelago to be "citizens of the Philippine Islands, and as such entitled to the protection of the United States." It extended to them most of the constitutional guarantees for the protection of life, liberty, and property, but withheld trial by jury. It also provided for the creation of a legislature to be composed of the commission and an elective assembly. Certain conditions must, however, first be fulfilled; and, as a large part of the population was illiterate, some being, in fact, savages, educational and property qualifications were imposed for the suffrage, and it was found that only about one-tenth of the adult males could qualify. Congress also retained the right to veto all insular legislation, and provided that appeals might be taken from the Philippine supreme court to the Supreme Court of the United States.

A Frame of Government Provided, 1902.

The necessary conditions having been complied with, a general election was held in the islands on July 30, 1907. The Nationalist, or independence, party won the largest number of

First Legislature Meets, 1907.
seats in the assembly. The first session met on the 16th of the following October. Neither this assembly nor any later one was notable for business sense, and all refused to pass bills proposed by the commission for stamping out slavery and peonage, the last of which, in particular, still exists in the islands.

Some Republicans put forward the theory that when the people of the Philippines had been sufficiently educated to govern themselves they should be given their independence, but no

The Question of Independence.
definite date was ever fixed by Republicans for the relinquishment of American control. The usual assumption was that a long time would necessarily elapse before the thing could safely be done. The Democrats, on the other hand, repeatedly declared in favor of early independence for the archipelago. Their platform of 1912 said: "We favor an immediate declaration of the nation's purpose to recognize the independence of the Philippine Islands as soon as a stable government can be established, such independence to be guaranteed by us until the neutrality of the islands can be secured by treaty with other powers."

When the Democratic party came into power, however, it proved less radical in deed than in word. In his first annual message to Congress (December 2, 1913) President Wilson conceded

President Wilson's Attitude.
ceded that our duty toward the Philippines is a "difficult and debatable matter. . . . We must hold steadily in view their ultimate independence, and we must move toward the time of that independence as steadily as the way can be cleared and the foundations thoughtfully and permanently laid. . . . Step by step we should extend and perfect the system of self-government in the Islands, making test of them and modifying them as experience discloses their successes and their failures."

For three years the Senate and House were unable to agree upon a Philippine policy. Early in 1916 the Senate added to a bill already passed by the House an amendment providing that the islands should be given complete independence within two, or at the discretion of the President, four years. But

An Indefinite Promise. the House rejected the amendment, and the two bodies ultimately agreed (August, 1916) upon a measure that merely provided that independence should be conceded "as soon as stable government can be established"—which was much more indefinite.

President Wilson had already given the Filipinos a majority of the Philippine Commission, which formed the upper house of the insular legislature, and had otherwise extended the partici-

Further Extension of Self-Government. pation of natives in their government. The new act substituted a senate for the commission, and twenty-four of the twenty-six seats in it were made elective. The educational qualification for voting, which had been limited to males who spoke, read, and wrote English or Spanish, was broadened to include males who spoke and wrote a native dialect; the total number of voters was thereby increased from about 225,000 to over 800,000. The post of governor-general was retained, and to him was given an independent veto power and also large powers of appointment. The governor-general, the justices of the supreme court, and certain other officials were to be appointed by the President.

It is greatly to the credit of the United States that the government of the Philippines has mainly been conducted in the interest of the native inhabitants, and that ruthless exploita-

An Unselfish Policy. tion of the islands by outside capital has been prevented. For some years our tariff policy toward the Philippines was narrow and grasping, but a more generous policy has since been adopted. Most of the natives have been convinced that American intentions are beneficent, but many are not content to be wards; they prefer to be free from all tutelage, and to manage their own affairs. It is, however, exceedingly doubtful whether they could maintain a stable government. Recent world events, in Mexico and elsewhere, have undoubtedly tended to increase the number of Americans who believe that a long interval must elapse before it will be safe to withdraw from the islands and leave the inhabitants to their own devices.

For a time expansionist orators were fond of drawing gorgeous pictures of the great wealth that possession of the islands would bring to the United States. But the dream that bearing An Unprofitable Policy. "the White Man's burden" would prove profitable has been dissipated. According to official estimates made by the War Department, the United States during 1898–1902 expended on the islands about $190,000,000, including the purchase price. Later expenditures brought this sum up to fully $300,000,000, and this estimate does not include the value of lives lost, pensions, and other indirect expenses. In time the insular government came to be nearly self-sustaining, except for the cost of defense, which amounted in peace times to from $10,000,000 to $14,000,000 yearly. Trade with the islands has increased considerably, but the profits thereon have been a bagatelle compared with the great sums expended. At present little is said about the economic value of the islands to the United States, and the main arguments of those favoring retention centre around the alleged incapacity of the natives for self-government.

At the time the Americans entered the Philippines, European powers were engaged in grabbing Chinese territory, marking out "spheres of influence" for themselves and extorting concessions for mines, railways, and commercial privileges. Attempt to Partition China. The United States did not participate in this unseemly scramble, but the perilous state of the Celestial Kingdom was undoubtedly a factor in causing President McKinley to decide to retain the Philippines, for he believed they would serve as a base from which we could exercise an important influence on Oriental affairs.

The United States was anxious to preserve the territorial integrity of China, and also to safeguard American Hay's "Open Door" Policy. commercial interests in the endangered empire. On September 6, 1899, Secretary of State Hay despatched notes to Great Britain, Russia, and Germany, asking them formally to declare that they would respect existing treaty ports, and would not discriminate against other foreigners—in short, that they would not interfere with what came to be called the principle of the "open door" in China. Great Britain acceded to the request; the other two powers pretended to be in accord with the principle, but avoided committing themselves formally. Hay adroitly announced, however, that he regarded their acceptance as "final and definitive." Subsequently he sent notes to France, Italy, and Japan.

For about a decade the principle of the "open door" was reasonably well observed, but in the presidencies of Taft and Wilson American influence in Chinese affairs waned, and there were encroachments by Russia and Japan. During the Great War Japan was permitted to gain a paramount position in China, but the exact extent of her control is not yet fully disclosed.

Waning American Influence.

Soon after Secretary Hay succeeded in establishing the principle of the "open door," Chinese resentment over the exploitation of their country culminated in what was known as the "Boxer" movement. The Boxers—more literally the *I Ho Chuan,* or "Righteous Harmony Fists" —maltreated and murdered native Christians, missionaries, and other foreigners in many parts of China. Both the Empress Dowager and Prince Tuan, commander-in-chief of the army, sympathized with the anti-foreign movement, no real effort was made to put down the disorders, and the Boxers were joined by many of the imperial troops. To safeguard the foreign legations at Peking, some of the powers sent reinforcements to the guards stationed in the legations, and early in June, 1900, an international force of sailors and marines, including some Americans, marched toward the capital, but were held back by immense masses of Boxers and troops. On June 20 the German ambassador, Baron von Ketteler, was murdered in the street by a Chinese soldier in uniform. The whole foreign colony, including many women and children, would probably have been murdered had they not taken refuge within the compound of the British legation. There for two whole months they heroically held at bay an immense mob of Chinese.

The Boxer Movement.

While an international relief force was being gathered at Tientsin, seemingly authentic news reached the outside world that the Boxers had captured the legation and massacred or

The March
to Peking. captured all the defenders. But Secretary Hay, by shrewd management, succeeded in getting a cipher despatch from Conger, the American minister, through Wu, the Chinese minister at Washington. The despatch stated that the legation still held out, but that "Quick relief only can prevent general massacre." Only about 20,000 men, including 2,500 Americans under Brigadier-General Adna R. Chaffee, were ready, but these marched from Tientsin and battled their way desperately to Peking, which they captured in time to save the beleaguered little band from annihilation.

In punitive expeditions against the Boxers some of the allied troops, especially the Germans and Russians, behaved with great barbarity toward the Chinese population, and were guilty

Emperor
William's
Instructions
to German
Soldiers. of carrying off immense quantities of loot. In sending out soldiers Emperor William instructed them to give no quarter and to behave like "Huns," so "that no Chinese shall ever again dare even to look at a German askance." The Americans displayed greater humanity, though some, including members of the legation, were guilty of at least purchasing loot. Many of the Boxers were executed, and an indemnity, amounting to about $333,000,000, was exacted from the country. In fact, had it not been for the restraining influence of the United

The United
States
Remits Part
of the
Indemnity. States, China might have been broken up altogether. In course of time it was discovered that the share to be paid the United States far exceeded the amount of damage done, and in Roosevelt's presidency more than half, amounting to about $16,000,000, was remitted, and is being used for the education of Chinese youths in America. This honorable action immensely increased American influence in the Celestial Kingdom.

President McKinley did not live to see the restoration of peace in the Philippines. In the September following his second inauguration he visited the Pan-American Exposition in the city of Buffalo, and delivered a notable address in which he paid a tribute to Blaine, "whose mind was ever alert and thought ever constant for a larger commerce and a truer fraternity of the Republics of the New World."

McKinley's Speech at Buffalo.

He seemed also to forecast a modification of the extreme policy of protection. "We must not," he declared, "repose in fancied security that we can forever sell everything and buy little or nothing. . . . The expansion of our trade and commerce is the pressing problem. . . . Reciprocity treaties are in harmony with the spirit of the times; measures of retaliation are not."

The next day (September 6) while holding a public reception in the Temple of Music, he was shot and mortally wounded by a young Polish anarchist named Leon F. Czolgosz, who was later executed for the deed. For several days hopes were held out for the President's recovery;

The President Assassinated.

then he grew suddenly worse, and on the early morning of September 14 he died. He was buried in a cemetery at Canton, his old Ohio home. At the hour that the simple ceremonial was "proceeding a great hush came over every city and hamlet in the land. The streets were deserted. The activities of 70,000,000 of people ceased. Men and women of every type and class felt the shadow touch for a moment their own lives, and they let their sorrow find supreme expression in the solemnity of a reverent silence. It was very human and it was very wonderful."

History will not assign to the dead man a place among the foremost of our statesmen, yet he was a man of abilities, and in both his public and private life there was much to commend. He was religious, temperate, kindly, gentle. Though not endowed with much originality or an intellect of the keenest type, he was shrewd, tactful, and knew how to profit by advice. He was not a great orator, yet he always managed to secure a hearing. As a politician he knew how to hold his ear close to the ground. He was particularly successful in his dealings with Congress, and this was due largely to his having been so long a member of the

McKinley's Character and Place in History.

House. He was charged with being too complaisant toward men of great wealth, and interests representing wealth, but in his behalf it should be said that the dangers of plutocracy were not so apparent then as later, and it may well be doubted whether he understood some of the economic tendencies of his time.   It was his good fortune to be President in an epoch-making period, when the United States definitely forsook its time-honored policy of isolation and became a world power, and his place in history will, therefore, be larger than that of some abler men.

CHAPTER XVI

"BIG BUSINESS" AND THE PANAMA CANAL

ON the afternoon of September 13 Vice-President Roosevelt climbed Mount Tahawus, in the heart of the Adirondacks, and in the descent had reached a little lake not far from the summit,

Roosevelt Takes the Oath.

when he was met by a guide bearing a telegram, to the effect that McKinley was much worse, and that it would be well to hurry to Buffalo. In the night he made a forty-mile drive over rough mountain roads, and on reaching the railway at dawn next morning learned that the President was dead. A special train carried him swiftly to Buffalo, and there, in a private house and in the presence of several members of the cabinet, he took the oath as twenty-fifth President of the United States. He at once announced that he would continue McKinley's policies unbroken, and he insisted upon each member of the cabinet remaining in office. Senator Hanna voluntarily promised his powerful political support, but was careful to state that he would not commit himself to Roosevelt as a candidate in 1904. As Roosevelt wrote in after years, "His ideals were in many ways not my ideals, and there were points where both by temperament and by conviction we were far apart. Before this time he had always been unfriendly to me; and I do not think he ever grew to like me, at any rate not until the very end of his life."

The new President was not yet forty-three, and was the youngest man who had attained that exalted office. Few men, however, ever came to the position so well equipped to shoulder

A Remarkable Personality.

its responsibilities. He was born in New York City, and on the paternal side was descended from a long line of Knickerbocker ancestors. His mother was a Bulloch of Georgia; one of her brothers, as Confederate naval agent in England, had arranged for the building of the *Alabama*, and another brother had fired the last shot from that famous cruiser when she was sunk by the *Kearsarge*. As a boy, Roosevelt was sickly and delicate; it was only by careful and persistent exercise that he managed to grow up a sturdy, robust man. A Harvard graduate, a political reformer, a historian of distinction, naval administrator, rancher, big-game hunter, faunal naturalist, and Rough Rider, his interests were world-wide; of all the Presidents, he was the most versatile, the nearest approach to him being Thomas Jefferson. In temperament, however, he more nearly resembled Jackson than Jefferson, and had all of Old Hickory's restless energy, combativeness, frankness, ability to lead, and skill in winning popular applause, combined with far greater educational advantages, culture, and breadth of view. Some critics said that he acted too impulsively, but, in reality, he worked and thought more rapidly than most men, and rarely, if ever, decided any really important question without first having made a careful investigation and formed a well-reasoned decision. Not infrequently during his presidency opponents pounced upon a supposed mistake only to find themselves involved in a maze of circumstances which justified his course. His capacity for work was, in fact, truly prodigious. His desk was always kept clear of business, so that he had time for the long look ahead. In part, this was due to his abounding vitality, which enabled him to meet the demands of an office whose duties had become so exacting that only a physically strong man was capable of filling it. All in all, no cannier or firmer hand ever held the helm of the ship of state.

In his earlier career Roosevelt had actively promoted the cause of civil service reform, and he continued to uphold the principle as President. In most cases he permitted senators to

His Faculty for Selecting Efficient Assistants.

name men for offices of a routine kind, but would himself select men for the more important posts; in either case he insisted that the appointees should be capable and honest. Of course, some mistakes were made, but Roosevelt had an unusual faculty for selecting efficient and devoted public servants, and instilling into them an enthusiastic *esprit de corps*.

There were in the South comparatively few white Republicans, and where honest and capable men of that party could not be found the President usually appointed Democrats. This policy pleased Southern white men and friends of good government everywhere, but the good feeling caused thereby was dissipated by what most Northerners considered an unimportant episode.

Policy toward Southern Appointments.

At this time the most prominent American negro was Booker T. Washington. Born a slave, Washington had managed to work his way through Hampton Institute, and subsequently founded the Tuskegee Institute in Alabama. He made this a wonderful school, at which thousands of colored boys and girls not only acquired book-learning but practical training that fitted them to earn a livelihood. He constantly preached to his race the much-needed doctrines of thrift, sobriety, and labor. It was his view that the negro should not be too insistent upon his rights until he was fitted to exercise them. Professor Washington was one of the most eloquent speakers in the country, and had charmed multitudes by his humor, his homely common sense, his appeal to universal brotherhood. His books, especially his autobiographical *Up from Slavery*, were read by millions. His influence for good was so great that a prominent Southern historian had stated that, with the exception of Robert E. Lee, he was the greatest man born in the South in a hundred years. Soon after Roosevelt became President, Washington came to the White House on business, and at the end of the interview accepted an invitation to dinner. When the news spread through the South that the President had entertained a member of the "inferior race" at his table there was a great outburst of anger; for many Southerners saw in the episode an attempt to practise "social equality," and some considered it a deliberate affront to their section.

The Booker Washington Episode.

Democratic politicians made much of the matter, and also criticised the President for his policy with regard to negro office-holders. There were comparatively few such officials, and most of these were in localities where the negro population outnumbered the whites. The most discussed cases were those

Southern Objections to Negro Office-holders. of a negro collector of the port of Charleston, and of a negro postmistress at Indianola, Mississippi. The former was appointed by Roosevelt; the latter had been in office for a decade. Both incumbents were efficient public servants; the only objection was to their color. White residents of Indianola even threatened the postmistress with mob violence, and, as the local authorities could not guarantee her protection, the President ordered the delivery of the mail at Indianola suspended. A fact that added to Northern bewilderment was that the patrons themselves then hired a colored man to carry their mail from the nearest office, so that they received it from black hands as before. In reply to objections to the appointment of negroes to office Roosevelt emphatically declared that he could not consent to "close the door of hope—the door of opportunity" to any one because of race or color. Like most sudden effervescences, Southern wrath soon subsided, and ultimately Roosevelt had a host of warm admirers in that section.

Roosevelt not only sought to appoint capable men to office but he insisted on holding incumbents to a high standard of honesty and efficiency. Early in his presidency he carried out

Rooting out Corruption. a searching investigation into corrupt conditions in the post-office department, and relentlessly prosecuted the offenders. Several of the accused were convicted and served terms in prison. Some of the men implicated were influential Republicans, and the secretary of the national committee escaped prosecution only because of a statute of limitations. The President also broke up a Western land ring that was engaged in fraudulently obtaining public lands; a United States senator, a representative, and many smaller thieves were given penitentiary sentences. Another senator was prosecuted and convicted for having illegally used his influence with the post-office department to prevent the issue of a fraud order against a company of questionable character. In these, as in numerous other cases, it was made plain that even men of great influence could not violate the law with impunity.

Such prosecutions were viewed with misgivings by some Republican leaders. In later years, in his *Autobiography*, Roosevelt wrote that at the time of the post-office investigation,

Honesty
Good
Politics.

"Several Senators came to me—Mr. Garfield was present on the occasion—and said that they were glad I was putting a stop to corruption, but they hoped I would avoid a scandal; that if I would make an example of some one man and then let the others quietly resign, it would avoid a disturbance that might hurt the party. They were advising me in good faith, and I was as courteous as possible in my answer, but explained that I would have to act with the utmost rigor against the offenders, no matter what the effect on the party, and, moreover, that I did not believe it would hurt the party. It did not hurt the party. It helped the party. A favorite war-cry in American political life has always been, 'Turn the rascals out.' We made it evident that, as far as we were concerned, this war-cry was pointless; for we turned our own rascals out."

The greatest problem confronting the country when Roosevelt came to power was that of the trusts. Hard times during Cleveland's second administration had brought about a lull

The Trust
Problem.

in industrial consolidation, but the return of prosperity after McKinley entered office had been followed by a new rush toward the formation of monopolies, or attempted monopolies. Prior to 1897 only sixty-three such combinations had been formed; within the next three years almost three times that number had been organized. By 1903 the total capitalization of all the trusts amounted to about $7,000,000,000.

Wherever there was an industry in which it seemed probable

How Trusts
were
Formed.

that even the semblance of a monopoly could be built up, some promoter would set about forming an organization. This was usually done by inducing some of the great companies engaged in the business to agree to a consolidation; such companies would put their property into the common undertaking and would receive stock in the trust. Those companies or individuals who refused to enter the combination would then be subjected to bitter competition, and would generally be crushed out or reduced to accept terms dictated by the trusts.

Exaggerated ideas as to possible profits were spread abroad by the promoters, or "Captains of Finance," as they were usually called, and nearly every trust formed was greatly over-capitalized. Comparatively little attention was paid to the actual investment in an industry. Good-will, the savings of combination, the profits accruing from tariff protection, even those due to the evasion of the laws against restraint of trade—these and other equally intangible assets were capitalized, along with the actual invest-ment. And such was the fever for speculation that the gul-lible public bought these watered securities with the avidity of hungry gudgeons. Thus the promoters who floated the schemes not only made untold millions, but the people actually supplied money for their own undoing.

Excessive Capitaliza-tion.

The bigness of the sums involved in these vast transactions, and the rapidity with which the promoters piled up great for-tunes, "dazzled men's minds, so that they became drunk with the passion of money-getting, and blind to all other standards and ideals. They thought and spoke in millions; and the Napoleons of Wall Street became, in a sense, heroes and demigods. Men and women and even children all over the country drank in thirstily every scrap of news that was printed in the press about these so-called 'cap-tains of industry,' their successful 'deals,' the off-hand way in which they converted slips of worthless paper into guarantees of more than princely wealth, and all the details concerning their daily lives, their personal peculiarities, their virtues and their vices. To the imagination of millions of Americans, the financial centres of the country seemed to be spouting streams of gold into which any one might dip at will; and every Wall Street gutter figured as a new Pactolus."*

Frenzied Finance.

* Peck, *Twenty Years of the Republic*, page 634.

The greatest trust of all was formed in the steel industry. That industry had been striding ahead with incredible rapidity. New processes, new methods, efficient business organization had worked miracles, not only in cheapening the cost of production, but also in multiplying the output.

The Steel Industry.

For example, by 1901 ore was being unloaded from the ore boats at a cost of seven cents per ton, a sum that was soon after lowered to two cents; the Carnegie Steel Company was carrying ore from Lake Erie to its mills near Pittsburgh at the rate of one mill per ton mile; in everything machinery ruled supreme, and in the most up-to-date establishments the ore was smelted at one end and the resultant mineral was never allowed to cool until it came out a finished steel product at the other end.

Thanks to favorable natural conditions, business ability, the protective tariff, and other factors, the iron and steel business was generally immensely profitable, yet at times there was ruinous competition which diminished or destroyed profits and disorganized industry. In 1901 such a war impended between the great Carnegie Steel Company and its rivals. Through the management of the astute J. Pierpont Morgan, of New York, who in those days figured as a sort of modern Midas, at whose touch everything turned to gold, a combination known as the United States Steel Corporation was formed that included the Carnegie Company and ten others of the leading steel and iron concerns, controlling about two-thirds of the total steel output of the country.

Formation of the Steel Trust.

Each of these eleven concerns was already a combination of smaller companies, representing a total of more than two hundred in all. The tangible value of the investment in the plants absorbed by the trust was estimated by the bureau of corporations at $682,000,000, but their combined stock-and-bond capitalization amounted to $911,-700,000. It was assumed that the practical elimination of competition would make the steel-and-iron business more than ever profitable, and the promoters of the new trust soon issued securities amounting to the enormous sum of $1,404,000,000. The

"Watered Stock."

common stock was nothing but "water," that is, it had no real present value but merely value in prospect, yet immense blocks of it were sold; it soon went beyond 50, and a day was to come when it rose above par.

A great number of Americans viewed the rush to consolidation with grave misgivings. Thousands were ruined by the ruthless competition of the trusts; millions felt the pinch of monopoly prices. It had been our proud boast that "America" was synonymous with "opportunity," but the rapid concentration of the resources of the country in a few hands seemed likely to deprive future generations of the chance of obtaining a fair start in life. It was notorious that Machiavellian methods pervaded "Big Business" and that the fortunes of some of the great magnates had been built up by reprehensible practices. It was even believed by many that the federal and State governments were sometimes dominated by a plutocracy of special privilege.

The
Dangers of
Plutocracy.

The problem was complicated by the fact that many of the trusts were more or less intimately connected by cross directorates, interlocking directorates, and control of banks and trust companies. A community of interest was thus created that tended to destroy competition throughout its range, and to render the position of a trust almost impregnable. Thus John D. Rockefeller, the dominant figure in the Standard Oil Trust, was not content to deal merely in oil, but obtained control of the great Amalgamated Copper Company, and practical control of more than half a hundred banks, besides engaging in gas and various other industries. Much the same situation obtained regarding J. P. Morgan and other trust magnates. In 1904 John Moody, a recognized authority on financial matters, wrote of the Rockefeller and Morgan interests in his *The Truth about the Trusts:*

Interlocking
Interests.

Around these two groups, or what must ultimately become one greater group, all other smaller groups of capitalists congregate. They are all allied and intertwined by their various mutual interests. For instance, the Pennsylvania Railroad interests are on the one hand allied with the Vanderbilts, and on the other with the Rockefellers. The Vanderbilts are closely allied with the Morgan group, and both the Pennsylvania and Vanderbilt interests have recently become the dominating factors in the Reading system, a former Morgan road, and the most important part of the anthracite coal combine which has been dominated by the Morgan people. . . . Viewed as a whole, we find the dominating influences in the trusts to be made up of an intricate network of large and small capitalists, many allied to another by ties of more or less importance, but all being appendages to or parts of the greater groups which are themselves dependent on and allied with the two mammoth, or Rockefeller and Morgan, groups. These two mammoth groups jointly . . . constitute the heart of the business and commercial life of the nation.

The Rockefeller and Morgan Groups.

Men came to call this great financial octopus, with its wide-reaching tentacles, "The System," and it was hated and feared by millions.

"The System."

The trusts, however, did not lack defenders. Such organizations were, it was alleged, a natural outgrowth of the Industrial Revolution and of modern business conditions. Great emphasis was laid upon the increased efficiency of production under a trust. A trust had need of only one set of highly paid executive officers instead of many; it could obtain raw materials more cheaply, make greater use of by-products, obtain markets with less advertising and fewer travelling men, and in a great variety of ways could eliminate the many "wastes of competition." The claim was also advanced that, owing to efficiency of production under the trust system, the general public would share some of the benefits in decreased prices.

Defenders of the Trusts Emphasize Their Greater Efficiency.

Many enemies of the trusts denied the validity of such arguments; more discriminating critics admitted the force of some of them, but doubted whether the good aspects of combination outweighed the bad. For example, they pointed to the flagrant overcapitalization of most of the trusts as sufficient evidence of the fact that captains of finance did not form combinations from altruistic motives. It was evident, they alleged, that the magnates expected to pay dividends on "watered stock" by exacting great

Arguments of Enemies of the Trusts.

sums from consumers, and had no intention of allowing the general public to reap any of the much-vaunted benefits resulting from combination. In fact, it frequently happened that soon after a product "went into a trust" the price was raised rather than lowered.

Many persons contended that the trusts were an unnatural development resulting from artificial advantages such as the protective tariff; in their opinion the trusts ought to be broken

Were Trusts a Natural Development? up by rigorous legislation, and the old era of competition restored. Others thought the trusts in the main a natural development, but differed as to how they ought to be dealt with. The trust magnates, of course, wished to be left unfettered and unchecked. Other thinkers contended for government control. The Socialists raised the cry that the nation should own the trusts.

The Sherman Antitrust Law of 1890 was a halting effort at repressing the trusts altogether. It had doubtless served to render combinations somewhat more moderate in their aggres-

The Sherman Antitrust Law Practically a Dead Letter. sions, but most of the cases begun under it had had a disappointing ending, and it seemed hardly more than a dead letter. The McKinley administration made no effort to enforce the law; McKinley himself seems to have felt some uneasiness over the progress of consolidation, but his mentor, Hanna, viewed it with complacency. Trust magnates contributed heavily to the Republican campaign fund in 1900, and, in the words of Herbert Croly, Hanna's biographer, "When Mr. McKinley was re-elected, big business undoubtedly considered that it had received a license to do very much as it pleased." In fact, the great captains of finance were rapidly coming to feel that they formed a privileged class, above and beyond the reach of restraint from any source.

They were destined to a rude disillusionment. Many Americans were coming to believe that big business was rotten at the core, and that something must be done in the interest of the common man. The *laissez-faire* policy (let business alone), crowned a century before by Adam Smith, was still powerful, but a revolt was brewing against the principle. For many generations the Anglo-Saxon race had been plodding along the road to political equality, and in theory had reached that goal. But men were beginning to see that political equality is a poor thing unless accompanied by something approaching equality of economic opportunity. For the new battle men now began to gird themselves. Most demanded not equal wealth but a fair start.

A Battle for Equality of Opportunity.

President Roosevelt held the view that the trusts were in a measure a natural development that must be controlled in the public interest, and he drew a distinction between business done on a large scale, which he considered legitimate, and monopolistic combinations, which he sought to destroy. In his first message to Congress (December 3, 1901) he discussed railroad and trust questions, conceded that industrial concentration could not be prevented, and expressed the view that if properly regulated it was highly desirable. State control, he asserted, was no longer adequate, and federal control must be increased. Therefore, he urged federal control over all combinations engaged in interstate trade, the elimination of overcapitalization, railway rebates, and other abuses. Congress paid little heed at first to his recommendations. Their reception in the Senate, some of whose members were rather the paid attorneys of powerful financial interests than representatives of the States they were supposed to serve, proved particularly cold. The President determined to arouse public opinion to his support, and in the summer and autumn of 1902, in speeches made in New England and the Middle West, he vigorously propounded his views regarding the trusts. In a speech at Cincinnati (September 20, 1902) he said:

Roosevelt's Distinction between Large-Scale Business and Monopoly.

He Favors Federal Control.

In dealing with the big corporations which we call Trusts, we must resolutely purpose to proceed by evolution and not by revolution. . . . The evils attendant upon overcapitalization alone are in my judgment sufficient to warrant a far closer supervision and control than now exists over the great corporations. . . . We do not wish to destroy corpo-

All Must Obey the Law.

rations; but we do wish to make them subserve the public good. All individuals, rich or poor, private or corporate, must be held to the law of the land . . . and the Government will hold them to a rigid obedience. The biggest corporation, like the humblest private citizen, must be held to strict compliance with the will of the people as expressed in the fundamental law. The rich man who does not see this is indeed short-sighted. When we make him obey the law, we insure for him the absolute protection of the law.

There was nothing revolutionary in such utterances, but they aroused apprehension and anger in the minds of trust magnates. The President had already taken action which showed that he did not mean to stop with words. In the preceding March he had instructed his attorney-general, Philander C. Knox, to bring suit under the Sherman Antitrust Act to dissolve the Northern Securities Company, a so-called "holding company," organized in hospitable New Jersey by the Hill and Morgan interests for the purpose of "merging" the Great Northern, Northern Pacific, and Burlington railways, and eliminating competition. This company would have dominated the transportation of the Northwest, and it might have been the beginning of a movement to consolidate all the railways of the country. The governors of some of the Northwestern States had protested, started suits in the local courts, and appealed to the President for aid. In the so-called Knight case, decided in 1895, the Supreme Court had taken so narrow a view of the Sherman Act that most lawyers believed that the federal suit against the Northern Securities Company would fail. Attorney-General Knox thought otherwise. He had himself been a great corporation lawyer, and he knew all the weak joints in the trusts' armor. Under his capable management of the case the government won a decision in a federal circuit court (April 9, 1903), and the decision was sustained by the Federal Supreme Court (March 14, 1904). The company was forced to dissolve.

Meanwhile the East had received an object-lesson in the evils of unrestrained monopoly. Most of the anthracite coal mines of Pennsylvania were in the hands of a combine that controlled both the mines and the coal-carrying railroads. The magnates were exceedingly grasping in their dealings with both their employees and consumers. The employees were not only poorly paid but were often compelled to buy their supplies at the company's stores, to live in the company's houses, even to employ the company's physicians. In the middle of May, 1902, after vainly asking for better terms, the men struck for higher wages, shorter hours, recognition of their union, the United Mine Workers of America, and abolition of the "pluck-me stores" and other grievances. The strikers numbered about 150,000, and under the capable leadership of John Mitchell, head of the United Mine Workers, they succeeded in practically paralyzing the anthracite industry. Largely through the influence of Mitchell, the strikers indulged in comparatively little violence, and, as they had real grievances, they won the sympathy of a large part of the general public.

The Anthracite Coal Strike, 1902.

The strike continued during the summer and early fall, and as cold weather came on a wide-spread coal famine developed. In the great cities of the East prices soared; often coal could not be obtained at any price. All classes suffered, but the poor most of all. Even hospitals sometimes had to go without fire. The situation created great alarm, and a wide-spread demand arose that the strike must be settled at any cost. The strikers expressed a willingness to arbitrate the differences, but the coal barons arrogantly turned a deaf ear to any suggestions that they make concessions, and actually withheld some of the coal mined in the hope that the suffering for lack of fuel would react against the strikers.

The Public Suffers.

From all sides appeals were sent to President Roosevelt that he should intervene to stop the strike. Though without definite constitutional authority, the President considered the situation to be so serious that he summoned representatives of both parties to the White House and appealed to them to settle their differences for the public good. Mitchell and other representatives of the miners had already agreed to submit the dispute to a commission which the President should name, and they renewed the offer; but

An Unavailing Conference.

the operators displayed a studied insolence of manner, refused to talk arbitration or accommodation of any kind, and used language that was insulting to the miners and offensive to the President.

The President almost despaired of reaching an agreement. He formed a secret plan to appoint an investigating committee to look into the rights of the case, and obtained a promise from ex-President Cleveland to serve as head of the com-

Roosevelt's Secret Plan.

mission. He also arranged to send a force of regulars into the anthracite district and to have their commander keep order, "dispossess the operators and run the mines as a receiver," until the commission could report and some better plan could be put into effect.

Fortunately it did not prove necessary to resort to such a radical step. Public indignation and an inkling as to what might follow if they remained obstinate forced the operators to

The Strike Settled.

give way, and at a new conference (October 15) they agreed to accept arbitration. Mining was speedily resumed, suffering from lack of coal was soon alleviated, and when the arbitration commission appointed by the President brought in its award (March 18, 1903), the terms were generally favorable to the strikers.

The strike thus ended is notable from many points of view: for its magnitude, the arrogant behavior of the coal barons, the extraordinary method taken by the President to force a

Aspects of the Conflict.

settlement, recognition of the fact that in the mighty battles between labor and capital in the present day there is a third party concerned, namely, the great general public, whose interests in the last analysis must be paramount to those of either or to those of both combined.

The problem of industrial peace had become of primary importance. In the period 1881–1905 there occurred 36,757 strikes and 1,546 lockouts, involving almost 200,000 establish-

The Problem of Industrial Peace.

ments and over 9,000,000 employees. The total direct and indirect losses resulting therefrom can only be guessed at, but they probably exceeded the direct cost of any war in which the United States had then been engaged. Many of the strikes were peaceable in character, yet hardly a month passed in which, in some part of the country, destruction of property, and beating and murder of "scabs," conflicts between rioters and the police or militia, secret assassinations, dynamiting, bomb-throwing, and other manifestations of lawlessness and violence did not combine to produce a condition which, if reported from a Spanish-American country, would be dignified with the name of "revolution." Thinking men were asking whether such a recurring condition of violence, with its accompaniments of great economic loss, bloodshed, starvation of women and little children, should be allowed to continue forever.

Various solutions had been proposed, and of these arbitration was the most promising. Many of the States had enacted laws providing for conciliation and arbitration, and some good results were accomplished under these laws, but in general the results proved disappointing. In 1898 Congress passed the so-called Erdman Act, but for some years it remained practically a dead letter. Ultimately resort was had to it, and in the five years preceding 1913 it was invoked in forty-eight cases, some of them important. The act was amended in 1911, and again in 1913. The last-mentioned amendment established a permanent federal board of conciliation and arbitration, but resort to it remained a matter of choice. Both capital and labor have generally shown themselves hostile to any system of compulsory arbitration, and there are so many other difficulties involved that most authorities regard arbitration in labor disputes to be a palliative rather than a panacea.

The Erdman Act, 1898.

President Roosevelt's interference in the coal strike intensified the dislike which some financial magnates were beginning to feel toward him. Through newspapers controlled by them, and through many other agencies, an effort was made to discredit him with the people, and to inculcate the view that he was a "dangerous man," that he had a "lawless mind," that he was "revolutionary," if not "anarchical." All their efforts proved vain. The President had bitter critics, and not a few enemies, but he

Vain Effort to Destroy Roosevelt's Popularity.

captured the confidence of the great mass of the people. No other President since Jackson was so generally applauded. His vigor, his denunciation of wrong-doing, his fondness for life in the open, his frankness, and even some of his faults won him multitudes of friends. It was his proud boast that the doors of the White House swung as easily to the poor man as to the plutocrat. Authors, scholars, artists, journalists, laborers, business men, ranchmen, Rough Riders, and even prize-fighters were freely admitted to his office, and many were entertained at his table. Throughout his presidency his remarkable popularity remained the despair of his enemies.

By 1903 confiding investors in the stocks of some of the trusts discovered how poorly performance matched promise, and awoke to the painful discovery that some of the demigods of finance were no better than vulgar swindlers. This disillusionment, combined with the attitude adopted by the administration, brought an end to the financial frenzy, and stopped the wild rush to consolidation. Stock exchanges were bloated with "undigested" and "indigestible" securities. Inflated values dropped like the barometer before a cyclone. Some trusts failed altogether. Even the preferred stock of United States Steel, which had risen as high as 101⅞, fell to 49, and the common stock, which had been quoted as high as 55, dropped to 8¾. The slump in stocks of this character proved only temporary, however, and in later years some of them rose to much higher levels.

Almost from the beginning some of the leaders in Congress of Roosevelt's own party were either openly or covertly hostile to him, but on important measures he was usually able to obtain the support of a number of progressively minded Democratic senators and representatives. In his *Autobiography* Roosevelt later paid a high tribute to Democrats who, like Senator Clark of Arkansas and Senator Cockrell of Missouri, refused to permit loyalty to party to interfere with loyalty to the interests of the country.

In 1902 the President secured the passage of the important Reclamation Act, described in a later chapter; and in December, 1903, he managed, against the bitter opposition of the beet and cane sugar interests and other high protectionists, to force through favorable reciprocity concessions to Cuba. Both these measures received large Democratic support, and the first was fathered by a Democrat, namely Francis G. Newlands, a broad-gauge representative from Nevada.

Cuban Reciprocity.

In the direction of trust control the President also secured the creation in 1903 of a Department of Commerce and Labor, with a bureau of corporations, whose business should be to collect information concerning combinations engaged in interstate and foreign trade. In the same year Congress also passed the Elkins Act forbidding railroads granting rebates to favored shippers, but the measure was less drastic than the President desired and the needs of the situation demanded.

New Department of Commerce and Labor.

The Elkins Act.

A number of important international questions engaged the President's attention in these years. In this field he possessed unsurpassed abilities, and in the person of John Hay he enjoyed the capable assistance of one of our greatest secretaries of state. Together the two made a combination rarely equalled in our history.

A Great Combination.

At this time Venezuela was ruled by a mongrel named Castro, a Spanish-American dictator of the worst type. Under him Venezuela fell behind in her financial obligations to the citizens of many nations, and large claims were also put forward against her for the alleged seizure or destruction of property during civil wars. In 1901 the governments of Germany, Italy, and Great Britain took steps to compel Venezuela to make payment to their citizens. The validity of some of the claims and debts was doubtful, the right of a nation to exact payment of sums owed to its citizens was dubious, and for these and other reasons the government of the United States watched the undertaking closely. In the initial stages the enterprise resembled the intervention of France, Great Britain, and Spain in Mexico in the time of our Civil War. Germany was the moving spirit in

The Venezuelan Debt Question.

the new combination, and in view of her well-known hunger for territory, and of the fact that she had recently tried to obtain naval bases in Lower California, and off the coast of Venezuela, there seemed to be reason to fear that the Kaiser might aspire to play in Venezuela some such rôle as that attempted by Napoleon III in Mexico.

After much diplomatic sparring, Germany, which, in Roosevelt's words, was "rather feebly backed by England," declared (December 8, 1901) what was called a "pacific blockade" of Venezuelan ports. Secretary Hay repeatedly protested that such a blockade was a contradiction in terms, and that its enforcement against the rights of neutral states could not be tolerated. He urged that the dispute should be referred to arbitration. Italy and Great Britain expressed a willingness to come to an understanding, but Germany refused. In December, 1902, Germany and Great Britain severed all diplomatic relations with Venezuela, and declared a formal blockade. It was certain that the bombardment of Venezuelan ports and the seizure of Venezuelan territory were imminent.

Germany Refuses to Arbitrate.

Neither Roosevelt nor Hay desired to protect Venezuela from the payment of just debts, but both statesmen understood German ambitions in South America. Though Germany professed that if she seized territory, occupation would be only "temporary," they knew that such possession might easily become permanent, and they decided that the time had come to uphold the spirit of the Monroe Doctrine. Luckily both men understood the arguments that appeal to the Prussian mind; luckily, also, the United States had at that time a navy that was more than a match for the one that flew the flag of the Hohenzollerns. Quietly, and as if merely for "manœuvres," the President gathered the American fighting fleet in West Indian waters. The commander of this fleet was Admiral George Dewey. "I was at Culebra, Puerto Rico, at the time," wrote Dewey many years later, "in command of a fleet consisting of over fifty ships, including every battleship and every torpedo-boat that we had,

Roosevelt and Hay Determine to Call a Halt.

with orders from Washington to hold the fleet in hand and be ready to move at a moment's notice."

Roosevelt had ascertained that Great Britain "was merely following Germany's lead in rather half-hearted fashion," and that she would not back Germany in case of a clash with the United States. He therefore determined to force the issue with the Kaiser's government. One day he summoned to the White House Herr von Holleben, the German ambassador, and informed him that he could not acquiesce in the seizure of Venezuelan territory, and that the dispute must be arbitrated. The ambassador replied that his government would not arbitrate, and reiterated that Germany had no intention of taking "permanent" possession of any territory. The President responded that Germany's "temporary" occupations had a way of becoming "permanent," and that he did not intend to have another Kiauchau on the approach to the Panama Canal. He also informed Herr von Holleben that unless by noon ten days later Germany had agreed to arbitrate, he would send Dewey's fleet to Venezuelan waters to see that the German forces did not take possession of any territory. The ambassador attempted to argue the question, but Roosevelt stated that it was not a matter of argument but of information, which it would be well for the ambassador to convey to Berlin.

A week later Von Holleben again had an interview with the President on various topics, and rose to go without having said anything about the Venezuelan matter. The President inquired whether he had heard from his government regarding arbitration. The reply was that he had received no word. "In that case," said the President in substance, "it will be useless to wait as long as I intended, and I shall instruct Admiral Dewey to sail a day sooner." Much perturbed, the diplomat expressed deep apprehension, and again said that his government would not arbitrate; the Kaiser had said he would not arbitrate and, of course, would not recede from his stand. However, less than twenty-four hours before the ultimatum expired word came from Berlin that

Germany would accept arbitration. Thereupon President Roosevelt, who had withheld the real facts from the world, publicly complimented the Kaiser on his friendship for arbitration! But, says the biographer of Hay, "the humor of this was probably relished more in the White House than in the Palace at Berlin." More than a dozen years elapsed before the full story was given to the world.

The claims of the citizens of ten powers were submitted to
The Outcome. the Hague tribunal, and all were scaled down, the amount ordered paid to German citizens being less than a third of what they had demanded.

Having failed to impose his will in America by rattling the scabbard, the Kaiser resorted to blandishments to win influence in the United States. He ordered a yacht built in this
German Preparations in America. country, and sent his brother, Prince Henry, to attend the launching—also "to solidify the German-American movement in behalf of the Fatherland." In a great variety of ways—by the gift of a statue of Frederick the Great, by organizing German-American societies, by exchanging professors, even through pacifist propaganda—an effort was made to insert the pan-German poison into American veins, for already the great Plot that was to bring disaster to mankind, and misery and death to millions, was in preparation.

The situation of Venezuela as regards debts and damages owed to foreigners was a common one among the rebellion-ridden Latin-American states, particularly those in tropical
The Problem of Intervention in Latin-American States. regions. Furthermore, some of these states, or revolutionary parties in those states, were not infrequently guilty of grave infractions of international law that called for redress. In a message to Congress (December 3, 1901) at the beginning of the Venezuelan squabble, President Roosevelt had taken the view that the coercion of an American State did not violate the Monroe Doctrine, provided that such action did not "take the form of the acquisition of territory by any non-American power."

Señor Drago, the Argentine minister of foreign affairs, took a different view of the question, and in a note dated December

29, 1902, restated in modified form the "Calvo Doctrine," named after an Argentine publicist who formulated it. Accord-

The Calvo-Drago Doctrine.

ing to this doctrine a government has no right to insist, even by diplomatic action, that the pecuniary claims of its citizens against another state be paid. As regards forcible collection of loans by military means, Drago contended that it "implies territorial occupation to make them effective, and territorial occupation signifies the suppression or subordination of the governments of the countries on which it is imposed." The "Calvo Doctrine," or as it came to be usually called, the "Drago Doctrine," was indorsed by most of the Latin-American states, and in part was adopted by the Hague Conference of 1907. The powers bound themselves not to employ force for the recovery of contract debts, but the undertaking was not to be binding in case the debtor state refused or neglected to reply to an offer of arbitration, or, having accepted arbitration, failed to accept the award.

Complications arising in 1904-05 in connection with Santo Domingo led President Roosevelt to evolve a new plan in regard to such questions. Affairs in that "black Republic" were

Santo Domingo.

in a state of chronic disorder. In the words of Roosevelt, in his *Autobiography:* "There was always fighting, always plundering; and the successful graspers for governmental powers were always pawning ports and custom-houses, or trying to put them up as guarantees for loans. Of course the foreigners who made loans under such conditions demanded exorbitant interest, and if they were Europeans expected their governments to stand by them. So utter was the disorder that on one occasion when Admiral Dewey landed to pay a call of ceremony on the president, he and his party were shot at by revolutionists in crossing the square, and had to return to the ships, leaving the call unpaid." There was default in the interest due to foreign creditors; certain nations—especially France, Belgium, and Italy—arranged for concerted action; and the United States was notified that the powers interested intended to occupy several of the ports in order to collect the customs. President

Morales appealed to the United States to save his country from the disaster of foreign occupation.

At this juncture President Roosevelt adopted the view that the United States could not undertake to protect delinquent American nations from punishment for the non-performance of their duties unless she would also undertake to make them perform their duties. In a message to Congress (December 6, 1904) he said: "Chronic wrong-doing, or an impotence which results in a general loosening of the ties of civilized society, may in America, as elsewhere, ultimately require intervention by some civilized nation, and, in the Western hemisphere, the adherence of the United States to the Monroe Doctrine may force the United States, however reluctantly, in flagrant cases of such wrong-doing or impotence, to the exercise of an international police power."

America's Obligation.

In the following February a protocol was arranged with the existing Santo Domingan Government, whereby the United States undertook to take charge of the custom-houses, collect the customs, and turn over 45 per cent to Santo Domingo, and put the remainder in a sinking fund for the benefit of the creditors. For two years the United States Senate refused to ratify the treaty, but the President proceeded under a *modus vivendi* to carry the plan into execution. Finally, in February, 1907, the Senate consented to ratify a revised treaty, which, however, continued the financial arrangement. Since that time it has several times been necessary for our sailors and marines to fight petty battles to preserve order, but, upon the whole, the arrangement has worked well.

The U. S. Assumes the Management of Santo Domingan Finances.

The principle that the United States may exercise "an international police power," and act as the agent in the collection of debts from irresponsible American states, has sometimes been called the Roosevelt corollary of the Monroe Doctrine. In view of the increasing importance of our relations with Latin America, the problem it attempts to solve is likely to attract much attention in the future.

Roosevelt Corollary to the Monroe Doctrine.

During these years, relations with Great Britain became increasingly friendly. A long-outstanding dispute over the

Relations with Great Britain.

Alaskan boundary was settled (October 20, 1903), and by consenting to abrogate the Clayton-Bulwer convention of 1850 Great Britain good-naturedly removed a diplomatic obstacle that stood in the way of our constructing an isthmian canal.

For centuries men had dreamed of digging through the narrow isthmus that separates the Atlantic from the Pacific, and opening a highway for ships between the two oceans. The discov-

The Dream of an Isthmian Canal.

ery of gold in California and the desirability of a shorter water route to the new El Dorado first caused the people of the United States to consider the thought of an isthmian canal seriously. But the time was not yet come. A Panama railway was, however, constructed by American capital for use in carrying passengers and freight from one ocean to the other. The United States also concluded with Great Britain the Clayton-Bulwer convention, which contemplated the construction of a canal by private capital, and pledged each party never to "obtain or maintain for itself any exclusive control over the said ship canal." This convention was later a source of much embarrassment to the United States.

The completion in 1869 of the Suez Canal, and the great success of that venture, revived interest in the American project. In 1872 an interoceanic canal commission, created by Con-

De Lesseps Seeks New Laurels.

gress, began to survey possible routes, and about the same time Ferdinand de Lesseps, the famous builder of the Suez Canal, decided to add to his Old World laurels fresh ones won in the New. De Lesseps and his associates considered a number of routes, among them that across the Isthmus of Tehuantepec, that by way of Lake Nicaragua, and that across the Isthmus of Panama. The last was the shortest, and it was ultimately chosen. A great company was formed in France, a concession already granted by Colombia to a Frenchman named Wyse was taken over, and other preparations were made to transform a dream into a reality.

The plan for a canal under French auspices aroused much antagonism in the United States, for the interference of Napoleon III in Mexico had not been forgotten, and the idea that any canal constructed at Panama must be under our control had taken deep root. But in 1880 De Lesseps came to the United States and did much to disarm his critics by pointing out that his company was a private enterprise, in no sense an affair of the French Government, and that by subscribing to a majority of the stock Americans could obtain control. He also managed to obtain considerable financial support, and even induced a member of Hayes's cabinet, namely Richard W. Thompson, to accept the presidency of an American advisory committee, a circumstance which led Hayes to ask for Thompson's resignation. In a message to Congress Hayes himself had declared (March 8, 1880): "The policy of this country is a canal under American control. The United States cannot consent to the surrender of this control to any European power, or to any combination of European powers." Such a canal "would be the great ocean thoroughfare between our Atlantic and our Pacific shores, and virtually a part of the coast-line of the United States."

American Opposition.

Early in 1881 the De Lesseps company began work on the great enterprise. De Lesseps estimated the cost at only $120,000,000. He even fixed upon 1888 as the year for opening the canal, and issued invitations for the ceremonies! But the natural obstacles at Panama were far greater than at Suez, labor problems were more difficult, and, as the deadly character of mosquitoes was then unknown, yellow fever and malaria swept away the workmen by thousands. Furthermore, the company's financial affairs were grossly mismanaged; vast sums were deliberately stolen. In 1884 De Lesseps' estimate had already been exceeded by $10,000,000, and the real work was hardly begun. Five years later the company collapsed. Investigations revealed a vast amount of corruption. Some of the culprits were sentenced to prison; the scandal shook France to its foundations, and threatened the life of the republic. Only a fraction

Failure of the French Company.

of the excavating work had been done, and costly steam-dredges, engines, and other machinery lay rusting for years in the muddy ooze of tropical swamps.

Meanwhile many plans had been formed for digging a purely American canal. In 1889 Congress granted a charter to the Maritime Canal Company, which proposed to use the Nicaraguan route. Some construction work was done by this company, but in 1893 its limited funds became exhausted, and work was practically suspended. A strong effort was made to induce Congress to subsidize the company, but the hostility of the transcontinental railways, which dreaded competition by water, and doubts as to the feasibility of the enterprise combined with other causes to prevent favorable action.

The
Nicaragua
Route.

In 1898 the spectacular voyage of the *Oregon* focussed public attention upon the need for a canal, and helped to develop an insistent demand that the United States should construct and control such a waterway. In the way stood the Clayton-Bulwer treaty. In the early '80's Secretary of State Blaine and his successor, Frelinghuysen, had repeatedly tried to secure modifications of the treaty, but had found Great Britain obdurate. When John Hay became secretary of state he took up the task, and in 1900 negotiated with Lord Pauncefote, the British ambassador, a treaty removing some of the objectionable features of the pact, but retaining others. The Senate amended the treaty, and Great Britain refused to accept the amendments. Finally, soon after Roosevelt became President, Hay and Pauncefote reached a new agreement formally abrogating the Clayton-Bulwer convention, and this was duly ratified. The new treaty made it possible for the United States to construct, fortify, and operate a canal. The only important limitation was that the canal must be open to the vessels of all nations "on terms of entire equality."

Clayton-
Bulwer
Treaty
Abrogated.

Before this time the New Panama Canal Company, successor to the old De Lesseps Company, had offered to sell its rights on the isthmus to the United States for $100,000,000. The

sum was excessive, and a canal commission had reported in favor of building a canal by the Nicaragua route. But on Janu-
Nicaragua
vs. Panama
Route. ary 4, 1902, the French company reduced its price to $40,000,000, a reasonable amount. The alarmed friends of the Nicaragua route managed a few days later to carry through the House, almost unanimously, a bill providing for a canal by that route. But the Senate, after a long fight, adopted an amendment authorizing the President to accept the French company's offer, to acquire control at Panama of a strip of land not less than six miles in width from sea to sea, and to dig the canal at that place; provided, however, that in case he found it impossible to do these things, within "a reasonable time and upon reasonable terms," then he should turn to the Nicaragua route. The main influence in bringing the Senate to make this decision—an eminently wise one—was wielded by Senator Hanna, whose keen business brain discerned the many advantages of Panama over Nicaragua. In a speech championing his view he made use of the argument that the Nicaragua region was much subject to seismic disturbances—an argument that was especially effective because recent volcanic eruptions on the island of Martinique, resulting in frightful loss of life, had made a deep impression in the United States. The House subsequently accepted the Senate's amendment, and President Roosevelt, who himself favored the Panama route, signed the bill (June 28, 1902).

An agreement with the French company was reached without difficulty, and on January 27, 1903, Secretary Hay and Doctor Thomas Herran, Colombian *chargé* at Washington, signed a
Treaty with
Colombia. treaty whereby the United States agreed to pay Colombia $10,000,000 for her consent to our purchase of the French company's rights, and for leasing in perpetuity a strip six miles wide across the isthmus, and that after nine years Colombia was to receive an annual bonus of $250,000. The Senate of the United States promptly ratified the treaty.

The government of Colombia at this time was the usual South

American "dictatorship," with all that this word implies. "President" Maroquin, under whose authority the treaty had been negotiated, called a Congress to consider the treaty—the first that had met for five years. After long delay the Senate unanimously rejected the treaty. It is alleged that before this was done efforts were made to compel the French company to pay $10,-000,000 for the privilege of selling. There is no doubt that the Colombian authorities hoped to force the United States to raise the price. Furthermore, some of them wished to wait and confiscate the property of the French company, whose concession, they contended, would soon expire.

Colombian
Senate
Rejects
Treaty.

The people of the isthmus had looked forward to deriving great benefits from the canal, and were deeply disgruntled by the rejection of the treaty. The French company also felt chagrined, and feared that its rights would be confiscated. Agents of the company and of the people planned a revolution in Panama. Such a conspiracy, it may be remarked, was not unusual in Colombia, for in fifty-three years there had been at least fifty-three revolutions, or attempted revolutions, in that distracted country. Maroquin himself had in 1900, when he was Vice-President, gained control by the simple expedient of seizing and imprisoning his superior, and then claiming to be chief executive because of "the absence of the President!" Doctor Manuel Amador Guerrero, one of the isthmian leaders, and M. Philippe Bunau-Varilla, chief engineer of the company, met in the United States and perfected the arrangements for the uprising. Guerrero tried to learn from Secretary Hay what course the United States would pursue in case of an outbreak on the isthmus, but Hay would only say guardedly that the United States would enforce the treaty of 1846. By this treaty the United States had bound itself to keep peace and order along the right of way of the Panama Railroad. Six times the United States had landed sailors and marines for that purpose, one of these instances being in the first administration of Grover Cleveland.

Panama
Plans to
Revolt.

President Roosevelt himself was aware of the ferment on the

isthmus. He was deeply exercised by the failure of Colombia to ratify the treaty. In later years he declared: "You could no more make an agreement with the Colombian rulers than you could nail currant jelly to a wall."

But in a letter to the editor of the *Review of Reviews* he wrote (October 10, 1903) that he cast aside the proposition "to foment the secession of Panama. Whatever other governments can do, the United States can not go into the securing, by such underhand means, the cession." He frankly admitted, however, that "privately . . . I should be delighted if Panama were an independent state, or if it made itself so at this moment." Feeling thus, he did not, in his own words, "lift my finger to incite the revolutionists. . . . I simply ceased to stamp out the different revolutionary fuses that were already burning." And "I directed the Navy Department to station various ships within easy reach of the Isthmus, to be ready to act in the event of need arising."

The arrival on November 3 of 450 Colombian soldiers at Colon on the Atlantic side precipitated the uprising a day sooner than the revolutionists had intended. Some of the officers, who had hurried across the isthmus to the town of Panama, were seized by the revolutionists, and the officer left in command of the troops was bribed to re-embark his men and depart. About fifty American sailors and marines were landed at Colon to maintain order and protect American lives and property. Colombian authority on the isthmus was speedily overthrown without any blood being shed, except that a shell fired by a Colombian gunboat in the harbor of Panama killed a Chinaman and a dog. The people supported the uprising almost unanimously.

The Revolt
Succeeds.

American naval officers in isthmian waters had already received orders from Washington to keep the line of transit open, and to "prevent the landing of any armed force with hostile intent, either Government or insurgent, at either Colon, Porto Bello, or other point." Enforcement of this order practically estopped Colombia from attempting to reconquer the revolted province, for an over-

Naval
Orders.

land march through the mountains and tropical jungles was impracticable.

Our government hastened to take advantage of what the gods had brought. Three days after the revolt began, Secretary Hay cabled the American consul at Panama to recognize the *de facto* government, and a week later President Roosevelt formally received M. Bunau-Varilla as envoy extraordinary and minister plenipotentiary of the republic of Panama. A few days later (November 18) Hay and Bunau-Varilla signed a treaty by which Panama promised to cede perpetual control of a zone ten miles wide across the isthmus, while the United States agreed to pay therefor $10,000,000 down and an annuity of $250,000, beginning nine years thereafter. The example of the United States in recognizing the independence of Panama was quickly followed by most other powers. Colombia vehemently protested, but was too weak to venture beyond protests. Her rulers had grasped for too much and had lost all.

Panama Recognized and a New Treaty Negotiated.

The administration's course in the Panama affair provoked much criticism, mainly but not wholly from Democratic sources. The United States, the critics declared, had taken advantage of a weaker power, and had violated principles of international morality. They alleged that by the treaty of 1846 the United States had guaranteed the sovereignty of Colombia over the isthmus. They denounced the speedy recognition of Panama as "indecent." Some even openly charged the President with having fomented the revolution. On the other hand, the administration's course found warm defenders. The President himself denied having fostered the revolt, and justified his recognition of Panama and the negotiation of the new treaty on the ground of Colombia's grasping conduct, and her powerlessness to preserve order. In support of the latter argument he emphasized the fact that Colombia was then under the rule of a dictator, and that the constitution of the country was suspended. He further declared that Colombia had no right "to bar the transit of the world's traffic across the

Criticism of the Panama Policy.

Roosevelt's Defense.

Isthmus," and he contended that "intervention was justified by the treaty of 1846, by our national interests, and by the interests of civilization at large."

Most critics thought that his defense was not conclusive, but Colombia had behaved in such a dog-in-the-manger fashion, and the prospect of a canal was so fascinating, that Americans generally applauded the accomplished fact, and did not scrutinize too closely the means by which it had been brought about. As a canal would greatly benefit the South, most Democratic senators voted for the treaty, though some criticised the way in which it had been obtained. The treaty was, therefore, ratified (February 23, 1904) by the overwhelming majority of 66 to 14.

The Treaty Ratified.

The purchase of the rights of the French company was consummated, and the way was thus finally cleared for digging the "big ditch." Many practical problems, however, had to be solved before the work could be completed. Yellow fever and malaria began their old-time ravages among the canal workers, but under the energetic direction of the chief sanitary officer, Colonel William C. Gorgas, who had already performed notable work of the same sort in Cuba, a vigorous campaign was waged against filth and the deadly mosquitoes, and the Canal Zone was made "as safe as a health resort." Difference of opinion existed as to whether it would be better to construct a lock or a sea-level canal. In November, 1905, a board of American and European engineers, by a vote of 8 to 5, declared in favor of a sea-level canal. But it was certain that a canal of that type would involve greater expense and increased engineering difficulties, and would require a much longer time. After careful investigation President Roosevelt wisely decided in favor of a lock canal, and Congress ratified the decision.

Preliminary Preparations.

Congressional insistence upon having the construction work managed by a commission delayed the enterprise. Certain selfish interests, including some of the transcontinental railroads, covertly tried to discredit the undertaking, while, of course, the political opponents of the administration sought with their probes to find party capital. Late in 1905 a well-known journalist spent twenty-eight hours and ten minutes on the Isthmus,

Attempts to
Discredit the
Enterprise. and subsequently published an extremely critical article, entitled "Our Mismanagement at Panama." Some criticisms had a better basis than those contained in this article, but, upon the whole, the enterprise was conducted on a high plane, without corruption or notable waste. Even in the least satisfactory period much valuable preliminary work was done in sanitation, and the assembling of material and men. In February, 1907, President Roosevelt announced that he had decided to put the undertaking in charge of army engineers. Lieutenant-Colonel George W. Goethals

Colonel
Goethals. was appointed chief engineer, with Majors William L. Sibert and David Du B. Gaillard as assistants, and the President managed matters in such a way as to give Goethals ample powers.

Thenceforward the enterprise moved forward more rapidly. Labor problems were solved, the Chagres River was controlled by building a great dam, the famous Culebra Cut was excavated, the Gatun locks were built, the dirt was really

The Canal
Completed. made "to fly." On October 10, 1913, not quite a decade after the Panama revolt, water was turned into the Culebra Cut, and soon after small boats were able to navigate the whole length of the canal. The first commercial use of the waterway was made on May 19, 1914, when three barges, loaded with sugar from Hawaii, passed through from the Pacific to the Atlantic. The formal opening to traffic occurred on August 15 of that year. For a considerable period slides in the Culebra Cut caused much trouble, and on one occasion the canal was closed to traffic for months, but trouble of this kind had been anticipated and the difficulty was finally solved. The greatest engineering enterprise in all history had been completed. Goethals, Gorgas, Sibert, and Gaillard were appropriately rewarded by promotions for their splendid work, which had really been beyond praise. In 1915 the opening of the canal was fitly celebrated at great expositions at San Francisco and San Diego. The total cost of the canal, including appropriations for the fiscal year 1915, was $361,874,861.

The opening of the canal to traffic was almost coincident with the outbreak of the Great War. That war demoralized the commerce and water transportation of the world, and delayed the realization of some of the benefits expected from the canal. Still, in the first eleven and a half months of its operation 1,258 vessels passed through the waterway, and the tolls collected almost sufficed to cover the costs of operation and maintenance. With the return of peace it may confidently be predicted that the canal will play an increasingly important part in the transportation of goods between the eastern and western parts of the United States, and that it will do much toward revolutionizing our commercial relations with western South America, Australia, and the Orient.

Future Importance of the Canal.

The revolt of Panama occurred only a few months before the opening of the presidential campaign of 1904. President Roosevelt frankly desired a nomination and election in his own right, and by the rank and file of his party his ambition was regarded with enthusiasm, for, unlike Tyler, Fillmore, Johnson, and Arthur, he had succeeded both as a statesman and as a politician. By some financial interests, and by certain Republican leaders his candidacy was looked upon with strong hostility, and through newspapers and other agencies they sought to convince the public that he was "rash," "impulsive," "overconfident of his own judgment," and generally "unsafe." The man selected to oppose the President for the nomination was Senator Hanna. A political fund was raised and tentative steps were taken toward controlling delegates. Hanna himself disclaimed any purpose of becoming a candidate, but, on the other hand, he held back from indorsing Roosevelt. It is possible that he might ultimately have been persuaded to enter the contest, but his health was bad, and in February, 1904, he died.

Opposition to Roosevelt's Nomination.

His death removed the only person who would have had the slightest chance of defeating Roosevelt. Already the ground swell of disapproval of the plan to thrust aside the popular idol was making itself felt in unmistakable fashion, and soon all op-

Roosevelt and Fairbanks.

position to his nomination utterly collapsed. When the national convention met in Chicago (June 21–23), its orators vied with one another in praising the President's personality and achievements, and he was nominated by acclamation. For Vice-President the convention named Senator Charles W. Fairbanks, a conservative from Indiana.

Two decisive defeats had tended to discredit the Bryan, or free-silver, wing of the Democracy; and when the national convention met in St. Louis on July 6, the conservatives, who

Conservatives Control Democratic Convention and Nominate Parker.

were dubbed the "safe and saners," managed to control it. The leading candidate put forward by the conservatives was Judge Alton B. Parker of New York, and his candidacy was astutely managed by David B. Hill, who here appeared for the last time on the national stage. Among the other candidates for the nomination were Arthur P. Gorman of Maryland, ex-Governor Pattison of Pennsylvania, Senator Francis M. Cockrell of Missouri, Richard Olney of Massachusetts, and William R. Hearst, formerly of California but then a resident of New York. Hearst was the foremost exponent of "yellow journalism," and his candidacy was promoted by his numerous newspapers and by leagues formed in his favor. Bryan preferred either Pattison or Cockrell, but his wishes were disregarded, and Parker was nominated on the first ballot. Ex-Senator Henry Gassaway Davis, an octogenarian millionaire of West Virginia, was named for the vice-presidency.

The platform iterated former Democratic pronouncements on the tariff, trusts, and imperialism, condemned the Roose-

Parker's Telegram Regarding Gold Standard.

velt administration as "spasmodic, erratic, sensational, spectacular, and arbitrary," and charged it with a long series of unlawful and unconstitutional acts. As originally drafted, the platform contained a declaration to the effect that the great increase in the production of gold had removed the currency question "from the field of political contention," but the Bryan element managed to eliminate this plank, and the platform as adopted did not mention the money question. Before the convention adjourned, a telegram was received from Parker stating that he regarded "the gold standard as firmly and irrevocably established," and adding that if this view was unsatisfactory to a majority of the convention, he would decline the nomination. The telegram created much consternation and drew a bitter speech from Bryan, but after an acrimonious debate the convention replied that the money question had been ignored because it was not considered an issue in the campaign.

Judge Parker, who had thus been selected to lead the Democratic hosts, had seen long years of service on the New York bench and was then chief judge of the court of appeals. His

Parker's Career and Principles.

views on public questions were little known, but some of his supporters had urged that this fact rendered him more "available," an argument which had drawn from Bryan the retort that "it is the first time in recent years at least, that a man has been urged for so high a position on the ground that his opinions are unknown." In reality, Parker was decidedly conservative in his opinions, but he had not deserted the party in 1896 nor 1900. About all the public knew of Davis, the vice-presidential nominee, was that he was in his eighty-second year, and was a rich ex-senator. Altogether, the ticket justified the statement of a colored Republican orator when he said that the Democrats had "nominated an enigma from New York, and a reminiscence from West Virginia."

Both Cleveland and Bryan announced that they would support the ticket, and, to outward appearances, the schism in the party seemed healed. But immediately after the conven-

Radical Democratic Discontent.

tion Bryan had said that little could be hoped from the Democracy so long as it remained "under the control of the Wall-Street element," and he opined that Parker's nomination "virtually nullifies the anti-trust plank." His support was largely perfunctory and for the sake of regularity. Hundreds of thousands of other radical Democrats openly or secretly determined that they would not accept

Parker and the conservative elements that were most conspicuous in his support.

Their defection alone would have been enough to render the result certain, but in addition the Democratic managers committed the monumental blunder of making Roosevelt's personality one of the main issues of the campaign. At that time the President was almost at the zenith of his popularity. The great mass of the people were convinced of his honesty and nobility of purpose. His many-sidedness was such that he appealed to all manner of men. His character was held up as a shining example to young men, and the "strenuous life," the title of one of his essays, became a sort of fad. The newspapers and magazines were filled with pictures showing him in all manner of costumes—as Rough Rider and ranchman, "sitting on his porch at Sagamore Hill, hunting the grizzly in the Far West, or taking a fence on a fine mount." His admirers even enjoyed the cartoons of their idol, representing him as "Terrible Teddy," at the sight of whose big teeth the trusts and other "malefactors of great wealth" went into hysterics. At a celebration "under the Oaks at Jackson" of the fiftieth anniversary of the Republican party, John Hay drew the following portrait of his chief:

Roosevelt's Popularity.

Of gentle birth and breeding, yet a man of the people in the best sense; with the training of a scholar and the breezy accessibility of a ranchman; a man of the library and a man of the world; an athlete and a thinker; a soldier and a statesman; a reader, a writer, and a maker of history; with the sensibility of a poet and the steel nerve of a rough rider; one who never did, and never could, turn his back on a friend or on an enemy.

When the mass of Americans were willing to subscribe enthusiastically to such an eulogium, it is evident that the Democrats could make no headway by raising their voices in behalf of a Constitution endangered by an irresponsible dictator. On the contrary, the people generally felt well pleased with a President who would go to the limits of his authority—or even a little beyond—in their behalf.

Democratic Attack Ineffective.

As for the great financial interests, some of them supported Roosevelt from the beginning. Others would have preferred to see him beaten, but most of these soon decided that he was

Attitude of "Big Business." certain of election, and not a few of them ultimately subscribed to the Republican campaign fund in the hope that the Republicans would prove grateful. These were old "Big Business" tactics. Years before, Henry O. Havemeyer, president of the sugar trust, had testified that the trusts contributed to both parties, placing their money where it would do the most good.

The original Democratic plan of campaign was that Judge Parker should remain, with dignity befitting a judge, at his

Parker Emerges from Retirement. summer home at Esopus on the Hudson. Presently, however, the party managers found that their cause was losing ground, and, as a forlorn hope, they sent their candidate out to make some speeches. But Judge Parker did not possess the art of winning popular applause, nor did he have the knack of sounding clarion calls.

The closing days of the contest saw one sensational incident. In speeches at Madison Square Garden and elsewhere Judge Parker insinuated that the President had placed George B.

Parker's Charge and Roosevelt's Reply. Cortelyou in charge of the Republican campaign because Cortelyou, having been secretary of the new Department of Commerce and Labor, possessed information that would enable him to blackmail the trusts into making contributions to the Republican fund. Three days before the election Roosevelt denounced the charge as "unqualifiedly and atrociously false." He admitted that some corporations were contributing to the Republican fund, as others were to the Democratic fund, but he said that the Republican fund was the smallest for twelve years. He also pointed out that the Department of Commerce and Labor had been so recently organized that as yet it had no corporation secrets, and he stated that he had selected Cortelyou to direct the campaign only after other men had refused to serve. He closed by saying that, if elected, he would be unhampered by any promise or pledge except to "see to it that every man has a square deal, no less and no more."

The election returns showed that Roosevelt's personality and the administration's record had won an overwhelming victory. Judge Parker was the worst-defeated candidate of a major party since Horace Greeley, in 1872. He carried none except States south of Mason and Dixon's Line, and of the border States he lost Missouri, Delaware, and West Virginia, and one of the electoral votes of Maryland. His total electoral vote was 140; that of Roosevelt, 336. Of the popular vote, Parker received 5,084,491, Roosevelt 7,628,834; in other words, the plurality of the exponent of "the square deal" was more than 2,500,000.

A Roosevelt Triumph.

The Populists' party, which had nominated a candidate in the person of Thomas E. Watson of Georgia, polled 114,546 votes. A more notable feature of the election was the great increase in the Socialist vote. The Social Democratic party had now taken the name Socialist party, and Debs, who was again the candidate, received 402,460 votes, as against only 94,768 in 1900. In Minnesota, Montana, Colorado, Massachusetts, and Missouri, all of which gave Roosevelt big pluralities, Democratic governors were elected. This phenomenon was due in part to Roosevelt's popularity, in part to dissatisfaction with local Republican machines, in part to growing independence of the voters, more and more of whom were becoming willing to "split a ticket."

Political Independence Displayed by Voters.

In later years much light was thrown on the subject of financial contributions during this campaign. In 1905 an investigation of the management of certain great life-insurance companies disclosed the fact that some of them had contributed heavily to the Republican fund. In 1907 it was revealed that E. H. Harriman, the great railroad magnate, raised $250,000 for use in New York. In 1912 it became known that many other large interests, including perhaps the Standard Oil Company, had made contributions to

Later Revelations.

the Republican fund. Roosevelt admitted having been aware of Harriman's activities, but asserted that the money thus raised was for the purpose of aiding the local ticket in New York, as his own success in that State had been beyond doubt. In support of this statement he pointed out that his own plurality in New York proved to be 175,000, while Higgins, the Republican candidate for governor, was elected by only 80,000. Before a congressional investigating committee in 1912 he stated that he expressly instructed Chairman Cortelyou to reject contributions from Standard Oil. Cortelyou bore out this testimony, but, as the Republican national treasurer was dead and his records were destroyed, it was impossible to ascertain what his course had been.

The course of the administration during 1905–09 was such that no one ventured to accuse the President of displaying any undue friendship for either Harriman or Standard Oil, but some Parker's critics asserted that the revelations proved the Charge Not truth of Parker's charge. To this, Roosevelt's Proved. friends responded that in his denial of Parker's charges he had expressly admitted that corporations were contributing to the Republican fund; they said that the essence of Parker's charge was that Cortelyou had been made chairman in order to blackmail the trusts into making contributions, and they pointed out that no evidence had ever been brought forward to prove this charge.

In his reply to Parker, Roosevelt had asserted that corporations were also making contributions to the Democratic fund, and this statement received ample confirmation. In 1905 one Corporations of the great insurance officers testified: "My life also Aided was made weary by the Democratic candidates Democrats. chasing for money in that campaign. Some of the very men who to-day are being interviewed in the papers as denouncing the men who contribute to campaigns—their shadows were crossing my path every step I took." In 1912 August Belmont and T. F. Ryan, great corporation magnates, testified that they gave many hundreds of thousands of dollars to aid Parker.

Patriotic men in all parties recognized the danger in such gifts and deeply deplored the practice. In 1907, after the insurance revelations, Congress passed an act forbidding corporations to contribute money to be used in federal elections. Later federal statutes required the publication of campaign contributions, whether made in primaries, conventions, or elections.

Federal Legislation Regarding Contributions.

Canal a Tolls in the new congress.

On the night of the election, and as soon as the outcome was certain, Roosevelt gave out a statement in which he said: "On the 4th of March next I shall have served three and a half years, and that three and a half years constitutes my first term. The wise custom which limits the President to two terms regards the substance and not the form, and under no circumstances will I be a candidate for or accept another nomination." The statement was intended as a reply to critics who had alleged that he meant to perpetuate himself in power, and as a declaration of independence from the Republican bosses. However, it was to prove a source of embarrassment to him in the future.

Roosevelt's Statement Regarding a Renomination.

By the time that Roosevelt entered upon his second term his conception of the presidential office was clearly manifest. He believed that the President should have definite policies, a coherent programme, and should lead the country. He held that the executive, in a sense, should even "manage Congress," and he did not hesitate to force through legislation distasteful to many of the leaders of his party. In after years he wrote, in his *Autobiography:*

Roosevelt's Theory of the Presidency.

The course I followed, of regarding the executive as subject only to the people, and, under the Constitution, bound to serve the people affirmatively in cases where the Constitution does not explicitly forbid him to render the service, was substantially the course followed by both Andrew Jackson and Abraham Lincoln. Other honorable and well-meaning Presidents, such as James Buchanan, took the opposite and, as it seems to me, narrowly legalistic view that the President is the servant of Congress rather than of the people, and can do nothing, no matter how necessary it be to act, unless the Constitution explicitly com-

The Buchanan Method and the Jackson-Lincoln Method.

mands the action. Most lawyers who are past middle age take this view, and so do large numbers of well-meaning, respectable citizens. . . . There are many worthy people who reprobate the Buchanan method as a matter of history, but who in actual life reprobate still more strongly the Jackson-Lincoln method when it is put into practice. These persons conscientiously believe that the President should solve every doubt in favor of inaction as against action, that he should construe strictly and narrowly the constitutional grant of powers both to the National Government, and to the President within the National Government. In addition, however, to the men who conscientiously believe in this course from high, although as I hold misguided, motives, there are many men who affect to believe in it merely because it enables them to attack and to try to hamper, for partisan or personal reasons, an executive whom they dislike.

There can be no question that the Presidents generally regarded as most successful have taken a broad view of their powers. Roosevelt's successor adopted the legalistic view, with results not altogether happy. In general, the people undoubtedly desire the President to lead, and they applaud an executive who gets results, whether with "a Big Stick" or by the milder methods of moral suasion. Under our system of division of powers between the executive, legislative, and judicial branches, unity of action, which is requisite to any real efficiency, can often only be obtained by the President's assuming control, and even taking an active hand in the work of Congress, though party discipline may sometimes accomplish this result in an imperfect way when the executive and legislative branches are in harmony politically. A President who does not lead Congress, or at least work in harmony with it, is certain to be a weak President, and the country is likely to suffer under him.

Necessity of Leadership.

During Roosevelt's "first" term there were certain changes in the cabinet, but the personnel remained the same from one term to the other. Secretary of State Hay was, however, sinking toward the grave, and in the middle of March he sailed for Europe in a vain search for health. He returned in June, spent a week in Washington, and died (July 1, 1905) at his summer home at

Death of John Hay.

Newbury, New Hampshire. His death was greatly regretted both at home and abroad, for few American diplomats had ever won so enviable a reputation. His relations with President Roosevelt had long been intimate, even affectionate, for, though unlike in many respects, and differing on some points of domestic policy, they were a unit on foreign affairs, had many tastes in common, and each understood and respected the great qualities of the other. To fill the vacancy created by Hay's death, Elihu Root was transferred from the War Department to the State Department, and our international relations continued to be conducted with the same firmness and success. William H. Taft, governor of the Philippines, succeeded Root as secretary of war.

In his first administration President Roosevelt had remarked that the sum of wisdom in international affairs was "to speak softly and to carry a big stick." By this motto he meant that a nation should deal courteously with other powers, but should be so well prepared to defend its interests that no one would deem it safe to trample them under foot. Under both Hay and Root, Americans, in whatever country they might happen to be, could safely rely upon being fully protected by the long and powerful arm of the United States. A good example of this occurred in 1904, when a Moroccan chieftain named Raizuli kidnapped Ion H. Perdicaris, an American citizen, and held him for ransom. After vain negotiations, Hay cabled to Morocco this ultimatum: "We want Perdicaris alive or Raizuli dead." In two days Perdicaris was free. Roosevelt believed such a policy to be the only one that a self-respecting nation can follow, and that it is far safer in the end. He held that a government that will not protect its citizens when abroad in the exercise of all their legitimate rights is unworthy of the name, and can expect to retain neither the confidence of its people nor the respect of the world. Acquiescence in encroachments, according to his view, usually means repetition of the offense in one form or another, and far greater danger of war in the end.

The "Big Stick" Policy.

Roosevelt believed that wars were still possible, at times

perhaps even necessary, the world being such as it is. He pursued a policy of "steady preparedness," and insisted upon a programme of "two battleships a year," for he had no desire that the United States should become another China, "the helpless prey of outsiders because it does not possess the power to fight." In his *Autobiography*, published in 1913, he wrote: "It is folly to try to abolish our navy, and at the same time to insist that we have a right to enforce the Monroe Doctrine, that we have a right to control the Panama Canal which we ourselves dug, that we have a right to retain Hawaii and prevent foreign nations from taking Cuba, and a right to determine what immigrants, Asiatic or European, shall come to our shores, and the terms on which they shall be naturalized and shall hold land and exercise other privileges. We are a rich people, and an unmilitary people. But I know my countrymen. Down at bottom their temper is such that they will not permanently tolerate injustice done to them. In the long run they will no more permit affronts to their national honor than injuries to their national interest. Such being the case, they will do well to remember that the surest of all ways to invite disasters is to be opulent, aggressive, and unarmed."

His Belief in "Preparedness."

Roosevelt's insistence upon preparedness led some people to believe that he was a rampant jingo, bent upon involving the United States in war. In reality, he favored what he was fond of calling "the peace of righteousness," and he was a friend to arbitration, though he held the view that there were some disputes that could not be arbitrated. Through his management and that of Hay a dispute with Mexico over the "Pious Fund of the Californias" was referred (1902) to the Hague court, being the first case referred to that tribunal. The second case before the court was that of the claims against Venezuela, already described. The dispute with Great Britain over the Alaskan boundary was settled by a joint tribunal. Roosevelt also wished to issue the call for the second Hague conference, but stood aside in favor of the Czar, at whose instance the first had

A Believer in "the Peace of Righteousness."

met. With his consent, John Hay devoted almost his last public efforts to negotiating limited compulsory arbitration treaties with France, Great Britain, and other countries, but the Senate refused to ratify them. Under Secretary Root treaties drawn after the model recommended by the first Hague conference were negotiated with most of the great powers, and were duly ratified. These treaties did not bind the contracting parties to submit to arbitration questions affecting their territorial integrity, national honor, or vital national interest.

Roosevelt's most conspicuous service to the cause of international peace was performed in 1905, when, through his initiative, delegates from Russia and Japan met at Portsmouth, New Hampshire, and agreed upon a peace that brought to an end the bloody war that had been raging between those two nations. The President's part in the affair was managed with consummate skill, and won for him not only the coveted Nobel peace prize, but the enthusiastic applause of an admiring world.

Helps to End the Russo-Japanese War.

In August of the following year a revolt broke out in Cuba against the government of President Palma, who, feeling himself too weak to preserve order, asked the United States to intervene under the Platt Amendment. President Roosevelt was reluctant to do so. He issued an appeal to the Cuban people to save their country from "the anarchy of civil war," and sent Secretary of War Taft and Assistant Secretary of State Bacon to Havana to investigate the situation. Palma resigned, and the investigators found conditions so hopeless that, acting on instructions from Washington, Secretary Taft issued a proclamation taking temporary control. Six thousand regulars were hurried to the island under Brigadier-General Frederick Funston, who, as a former filibuster and comrade-in-arms of many of the Cuban leaders, was peculiarly fitted for the task. No attempt at resistance was made. Under the rule of Governor Charles E. Magoon, who was transferred thither from the Canal Zone, peace and order were restored, numerous reforms were inau-

Intervention in Cuba, 1906.

gurated, and two years later (January 28, 1909) control was once more turned over to a rehabilitated Cuban government, headed by President José Miguel Gomez. President Roosevelt had given warning that it was out of the question for the island to continue independent if the "insurrectionary habit should become confirmed," yet in the next decade intervention was more than once imminent, and early in 1917 it became necessary to land marines at Santiago and other ports for the protection of life and property. There is reason to believe that the disorders on this occasion were due to the machinations of German agents.

Pregnant with more dangerous possibilities was a controversy with Japan. Ever since the days when Admiral Perry persuaded the Japanese to open their ports to foreigners, warm friendship had existed between America and the Land of the Rising Sun. America had sent hundreds of teachers to Japan and had received many Japanese young men and women into her own colleges. America proudly regarded Japan as a sort of protégée, grew enthusiastic over her art and literature, and was her best commercial customer. Most Americans sympathized keenly with the Japanese in their war with Russia, but soon after the close of that war a change took place. It was due in part to the clash of American and Japanese interests in China, but mainly to an increased influx of Japanese immigrants into the Pacific coast States. In 1900 there were only 24,326 Japanese in the whole United States, but after 1903 the number increased rapidly, and white laborers, small shopkeepers, and truck farmers began to feel and resent the competition of Orientals accustomed to a lower standard of living. Race prejudice flared up—race prejudice sharpened by economic competition. The people of the Far West transferred to the Japanese their old hatred for the Chinese, and raised the new slogan, "The Japanese must go!" But the new game was infinitely more dangerous than the old. Unlike the Chinese, the Japanese are a proud people, who had just beaten a great power. They are as touchy and susceptible to affront "as Sir Walter's

The Japanese Problem on the Pacific Coast.

Hieland laird, walking the streets of Edinboro, hand on basket hilt, and sniffing the air for an affront." When the San Francisco school board, urged on by the labor element, passed an ordinance (October 11, 1906) segregating "Chinese, Japanese, Koreans, and other Mongolians" in separate schools, Japan vigorously protested. All sorts of wild stories were set afloat regarding alleged designs of Japan against the peace and safety of the United States, and were given wide publicity in the sensational press. It is now known that some of these stories owed their origin to secret attempts of Germany to embroil the two countries—for Japan was allied to Great Britain, Germany's rival and future enemy.

Most Americans deeply deplored the anti-Japanese agitation, yet it was clear to most thinking men that the teeming millions of Japanese must not be permitted to immigrate freely. As in the case of the Italians lynched by the New Orleans mob in Harrison's administration, the federal government was greatly hampered by its lack of control over State and local authorities. However, President Roosevelt personally took a hand in the matter, and succeeded in preventing the California legislature from passing threatened anti-Japanese legislation, and in persuading the San Francisco authorities to modify the school segregation order on the understanding that he would try to secure an agreement with Japan to prevent further immigration. A sort of "gentlemen's agreement" was reached with the Mikado's government, whereby Japan promised not to grant passports to laborers bound for the United States, except returning residents and members of their families, while our government took steps to prevent Japanese from coming to the United States from the insular possessions, or from foreign countries other than Japan. This solution temporarily stilled the anti-Japanese agitation, but, as we shall see, trouble broke out afresh a few years later.

Toward the end of 1907 President Roosevelt came to the conclusion that it would be well to show the world that we were prepared to protect our interests in the Pacific. Our battle fleet at that time was kept in the Atlantic; to have divided it and sent part to the Pacific would have been bad strategy, for, in Cruise of the case of sudden war, there would have been danger Battle Fleet of being beaten in detail. The President decided to around the World. send the whole battle fleet to the Pacific. The plan aroused much opposition along the Atlantic coast and from some who feared that the move might precipitate a war with Japan. But on December 16 sixteen battle-ships, six destroyers, and six auxiliary vessels under command of Rear-Admiral Robley D. Evans—better known as "Fighting Bob"—sailed from Hampton Roads. The fleet visited the ports of several of the South American states, passed through the Straits of Magellan, and reached the coast of California. There Rear-Admiral Sperry took command, and under his leadership the fleet visited Hawaii, Australia, Japan, and other Oriental countries, passed through the Mediterranean Sea and the Straits of Gibraltar, and on February 23, 1909, once more dropped anchor at Hampton Roads, being welcomed home by the President in person. Before this time foreign naval officers had doubted whether a battle fleet could be taken round the world, yet not a single accident had marred the voyage, and the ships returned in better fighting trim than when they set out. The success of the voyage greatly increased the naval prestige of the United States, and the demonstration served the purpose for which it was designed.

Ever since the days of Clay and the younger Adams some men had realized the desirability of closer relations between the United States and other nations of the Western Hemisphere. Pan- Blaine had sought to arrange in 1881 for a meeting American of a Pan-American Congress, and such a body actu- Congresses. ally assembled at Washington in 1889, when he was secretary of state under Harrison. In 1901 another congress met in the City of Mexico; there was a third meeting at Rio Janeiro in 1906, and a fourth at Buenos Ayres in 1910. Secretary of State Root attended the meeting at Rio, and later visited other South American countries, being everywhere received with great cordiality. These congresses did much to promote better relations, both politically and commercially, between the nations of the two Americas, and to create a feeling of solidarity against encroachments from the outside. In 1890 an International Bureau of the American Republics was established at Washington, and proved mutually useful. In 1906 its scope was broadened to include the compiling and distribution of legal and commercial information, and in 1910 it was renamed the "Bureau of the Pan-American Union." A fine building was erected at Washington for the Bureau with funds mainly contributed by Andrew Carnegie, and under the energetic and enthusiastic management of John Barrett, who became director in 1907, much work of value was accomplished.

Throughout his presidency Roosevelt constantly preached a higher standard of citizenship in both private and public life. In an age when business and public morality were at a low ebb, when the word "graft" was taken from the argot of tramps and thieves to fill a felt want in the language, the President's vigorous deeds and his denunciations of dishonesty came like a fresh ocean breeze, driving away the noxious vapors that were poisoning American public and private life. Under his courageous leadership honest men took heart, and a reforming impulse made itself felt throughout the land.

Roosevelt's Moral Leadership.

A whole literature sprang up exposing the nefarious workings of crooked politics and crooked business. The lead in this crusade was taken by *McClure's Magazine*, which in 1903 began the publication of Ida Tarbell's history of the Standard Oil Company. In it she revealed the methods whereby that great trust had built up and maintained its mastery of the oil trade, and she also showed the intimate connection between transportation and monopoly. In the same magazine Lincoln Steffens wrote of "The Shame of the Cities," exposing municipal misgovernment and the corrupt "plunderbund" between Big Business and political rings for obtaining street railway and other franchises. In a series of articles on "Frenzied Finance," published in *Everybody's*, Thomas W. Lawson, a

Exposure of Corruption in Business and Politics by the "Muck-Rakers."

Boston financier, described in sensational language the alleged inner workings of "The System," and explained the methods whereby it fleeced the public. *Collier's* specialized on the exposure of the frauds in the patent-medicine trade. Even novelists took up the cry. In *Coniston* Winston Churchill told the story of a State controlled by a corrupt railroad magnate. In *The Jungle* Upton Sinclair exposed the disgusting horrors of Chicago meat-packing plants. The craze for such literature went so far that it became a sort of hysteria, and Roosevelt himself sought to put a halt to indiscriminate abuse. Taking his text from Bunyan's "man with the muck-rake," he made a speech urging that efforts be turned from destruction to construction. Thereafter writers who stirred business and political cesspools were popularly known as "muck-rakers."

Much that was good came out of the ferment. Citizens rose up in indignation. Political rings were smashed on every hand, and, though some cities and States remained "corrupt and unashamed," there was promise of better things. In St. Louis, for example, a courageous young circuit attorney, Joseph W. Folk, exposed a vast amount of graft and corruption, and, despite bitter business, political, and even judicial opposition, succeeded in sending some of the offenders to the penitentiary. The people of Missouri elected him governor. In New York a legislative investigation of the great life-insurance companies uncovered an appalling lack of business honesty. The chief inquisitor was Charles E. Hughes. The people of New York twice made him their chief magistrate.

Uprisings against Political Rings.

Yet even where reform triumphed selfish interests still lurked in the shadows, watching covertly for the first signs of public indifference in order to regain their power. But the moral atmosphere of the country had been cleared. The years of Roosevelt's rule will always be notable for a revolution in the attitude of Americans toward financial and political matters. Honesty in such matters came into fashion. By no means all the credit for the transformation belonged to him. Other men labored earnestly and effectively

A Moral Revolution.

in the same great cause, but the victory was largely due to his powerful influence.

For years well-informed people had been aware that unscrupulous manufacturerers of food and drugs were accustomed to adulterate their products, to use chemical preservatives that were harmful to health, to make use of diseased animals unfit for human food, to conduct their business amid filthy and unsanitary surroundings. An ever-increasing demand arose for federal legislation to safeguard the people against such abuses. The publication of Upton Sinclair's book, above referred to, did much to bring the agitation to a crisis, and the influence of the President and the pressure of public opinion forced Congress in 1906 to enact sweeping legislation providing for rigorous inspection of meat-packing plants engaged in interstate business, and for the proper labelling of foods and drugs in interstate trade, and prohibiting the use of dangerous preservatives. No better acts were ever passed by Congress, yet selfish interests sought to nullify them; and the Department of Agriculture and its chief chemist, Doctor Harvey W. Wiley, administered the laws "mid the proddings of consumers and the protests of manufacturers."

Pure-Food Laws.

In the long session of the Fifty-ninth Congress, President Roosevelt managed, with the aid of many Democrats, to secure the passage of a more stringent railway-regulation law known as the Hepburn Act (June 29, 1906). By it the membership of the Interstate Commerce Commission was increased from five to seven, and the commission was empowered to fix maximum rates of transportation when complaints were made against the existing rates, but the carriers were given the right to appeal to the courts. The act provided heavier penalties for rebating and made express companies, sleeping-car companies, and interstate oil-pipe lines subject to its provisions. It also forbade the granting of free passes to any except specified classes of persons, and thus struck a heavy blow at a custom whereby transportation companies had been accustomed to influence administrative officers, legislators, and even judges. One clause forbade inter-

The Hepburn Act, 1906.

state or foreign transportation, except for the carrier's own use, of any commodity, other than timber, mined or produced by the carrier. This "commodity clause" was aimed chiefly at the combination between anthracite producers and coal-carrying railroads, but in 1909 the Supreme Court handed down a decision practically annulling this clause of the act.

In this period most of the States also enacted legislation—similar to the Granger Laws of the '70s—regulating common carriers as to rates, liability for damages to injured employees, and other matters. Some of the acts were admirable, but most erred in being too severe. In some States passenger rates were fixed so low as to hamper the roads in making needed repairs and extensions. Where the rates were so low as to amount to actual confiscation, they were, of course, set aside by the courts.

Some State Legislation too Radical.

President Roosevelt repeatedly recommended legislation requiring all corporations engaged in interstate commerce to take out federal charters, but his efforts in this direction failed. He also urged that the Sherman Antitrust Act should be amended and made "more efficient and more in harmony with actual conditions," but again Congress held back.

Trust Recommendations.

Under the President's direction a vigorous campaign was waged against rebating, and many shippers and transportation companies were prosecuted and convicted. In August, 1907, the Standard Oil Company was found guilty on 1,462 counts of rebating, and Judge Kenesaw M. Landis, of the federal district court at Chicago, fined the offender $29,240,000. The verdict was later set aside on a technicality by a higher court, and when the case was brought up for retrial, it was dismissed.

A Record Fine.

In 1907 the government instituted suits under the Sherman Antitrust Act against the Standard Oil Company and the American Tobacco Company, popularly known as the Tobacco Trust. Four years passed before the Supreme Court handed down its final decisions in these cases. The court then ordered the two trusts to dissolve, but the judgments were far from radical, and by taking the view that the law applied only to "unreasonable" restraints of trade, the court, in the opinion of many critics, emasculated the Sherman Act. The decree in the case of the Standard Oil Company ordered that the trust should be broken up into thirty-eight separate companies. There were to be no common officers or directors, but shares in the various companies were distributed ratably to the old stockholders. It was the theory of the court that the new companies would compete with each other, but critics of the decision laughed at the idea that the thirty-eight companies, all commonly owned by the Rockefellers and their associates, would ever compete with each other very vigorously. Soon after the decision was announced Standard Oil stock almost doubled in value, while the prices of gasoline and kerosene were increased. A similar decision was handed down in the case of the Tobacco Trust.

Antitrust Suits, 1907–11.

President Taft and his attorney-general, Wickersham, hailed the decisions as judicial victories, but the general public was inclined to consider them "judicial jokes." It was clear that the Sherman Act was not a satisfactory solution of the trust problem. President Roosevelt had so contended, and had refrained from indiscriminate prosecutions under it. After the above-described decisions the country realized that the act must be repealed or amended, and the work was taken up by the Wilson administration.

Outcome Unsatisfactory.

In the period of Roosevelt's presidency there was an ever-increasing agitation in favor of social justice for workers: for shorter hours, sanitary working conditions, compensation for injuries and deaths received in industrial accidents, minimum-wage laws, prohibition of child labor, and other reforms. The need for legislation regulating such matters, particularly to safeguard the health of women against overwork and unsanitary surroundings, to secure compensation for accidents to workers, and to abolish the hideous wrong of wearing out the lives of little children, was urgent; but selfish exploiters fought regulations that were obviously not only humane but in the interests of the people

Social Justice for Workers.

as a whole. In interpreting laws of this sort passed by the nation and the States, the courts, in the opinion of many, often displayed a narrow view and laid themselves open to the charge that they were more tender of property rights than of human rights—that, in the words of Roosevelt, they "knew legalism but not life."

Many States passed child-labor laws, but some of these laws were defective. In 1908 Congress enacted a satisfactory statute regulating child labor in the District of Columbia, but

Federal
Child-Labor
Law Held
Unconstitu-
tional.

Congress rejected a proposal championed by Senator Beveridge of Indiana to exclude from interstate commerce all goods produced in factories or mines in which children under fourteen years of age were employed. This bill was opposed not only by exploiters of child labor but also by champions of State rights. Woodrow Wilson, for example, characterized it as "manifestly absurd"; when he became President he changed his view and signed an act along these lines, but it was adjudged unconstitutional.

An act passed in 1906 making interstate commerce carriers liable for injuries received by their employees while at work was held unconstitutional by the Supreme Court. A new

Employer's
Liability
Legislation.

measure, passed in 1908, stood the judicial test, partly because it was more carefully drawn, partly because the attitude of the court had changed. Railroads were also compelled to use air-brakes and other safety appliances on trains, and the hours of labor of train crews were restricted. This legislation was badly needed and saved many lives, not only of trainmen but of the travelling public.

America
Lags behind
Europe.

Notwithstanding these beginnings, democratic America lagged behind monarchical Europe in legislation designed to safeguard the interests of those whose only capital is their ability to labor and who, when they have lost that, have lost all.

One of the most praiseworthy movements begun under the Roosevelt administration was that for the conservation of natural resources. Up to that time wastefulness had been the

most glaring of American faults. The land had been ruined
by failure to prevent erosion, or by persistent cultivation of ex-
hausting crops; coal was wastefully mined and
American
Wastefulness. wastefully burned; natural-gas wells were left to roar
unchecked for months, or to flame to the heavens
for years; the forests were ruthlessly cut down, and each year
fires swept away thousands of square miles, leaving worthless
wastes where blasted trunks stood amid the blackened stumps
and prostrate bodies of comrades half consumed. In a variety
of other ways Americans seemed bent on despoiling posterity
of its heritage. As regards the national domain, the accepted
policy had been to give it away as rapidly as possible, and,
though millions of acres had been taken up by desirable and
deserving settlers, immense areas had fallen into the hands of a
comparative few.

George Washington and other far-sighted individuals early
realized the importance of conserving our natural resources,
but for generations their voices of warning were as little heeded
Need of   as those of prophets crying in the wilderness. The
Forest
Conserva-   need of forest conservation was first to be realized,
tion.   both because of the failing supply of timber and because men came to see that, if the destruction of forests covering
watersheds was allowed to proceed unchecked, stream flow
would be disastrously affected: there would be "low water or
no water at all during the long dry periods, and destructive
floods after heavy rains." In 1891, largely as a result of agitation conducted by the Boone and Crockett Club, of which
Theodore Roosevelt was a moving spirit, and by the American
Forestry Association, Congress passed the eminently wise
Forestry Reserve Act. Under that act Presidents Harrison,
Cleveland, and McKinley set apart a total of 35,000,000 acres
of forest, the first tract thus reserved being the Yellowstone
Park Timberland Reserve.

In other lines a beginning was made, and many men bore an
honorable part in advancing the movement, but to Gifford
Pinchot is due the title of "Father of the Conservation Movement." After graduating at Yale in 1889 Pinchot studied sci-

entific forestry in Europe, and in 1892 began at Biltmore, North Carolina, the first systematic forestry work ever at-
Gifford Pinchot's Work.
tempted in this country. Later, under the auspices of the National Academy of Sciences, and with the approval of Cleveland's secretary of the interior, he made a study of the national forests and formulated a policy for their management. In 1898 he became chief of the Division of Forestry, which had been created by Congress in 1881. In this position he did good work, and gathered about him a body of trained foresters, who made a scientific study of forestry problems and helped to promote forestry on private lands. But, strangely enough, these men did not have charge of the public forests; these were under control of a division of the general land office, which was in a separate department, that of the interior, and were under the management of clerks who had no practical knowledge of forestry. In 1901 Pinchot's Division of Forestry became the Bureau of Forestry, and in 1905, through the insistent efforts of Roosevelt, Congress made it the "Forest Service," and Pinchot's trained men were at last given control over the national forests.

Roosevelt and Pinchot were warm friends, and were in hearty
Roosevelt Increases the Forest Reserves.
agreement as to the needs of forest conservation. Roosevelt added about 150,000,000 acres to the forest reserves, and by 1909 Pinchot, as forester, headed an efficient force of over 3,000 men, who protected against fires and thieves a timbered area greater than the total acreage of all Germany.

The new policy toward the forests was bitterly attacked by men whose selfish interests had been balked by it. Every year a fight was made in Congress to cut off the appropriations for
Opposition to Forest Policy.
the Forest Service, and to prevent the setting aside of further reserves. In 1907, while the agricultural appropriations bill was before the Senate, an Oregon senator managed to add an amendment providing that the President could not set aside any additional national forests in the six Northwestern States. This meant the retention of many million acres to be exploited by private interests at the

expense of the public interest. But the Forest Service knew just what tracts ought to be reserved, so Roosevelt issued a proclamation setting aside 16,000,000 acres of timberland, and two days later signed the agricultural bill. In his own words, "the opponents of the Forest Service turned handsprings in their wrath" when they heard the news.

After Roosevelt's administration some additions were made to the national forests, while certain tracts that were found to be fitted for agriculture were opened to settlement. In 1919 there were more than 160 national forests, with a
The National Forests.
total area of 162,000,000 acres. Nearly all these were west of the Mississippi, but there were important national forests about the headwaters of certain streams in the White Mountains and the Appalachians. The forest service not only sought to protect the forests, but set out millions of young trees. The forests were not locked up so that they would be of no use, but timber that was ready to be cut was marketed. A policy was also adopted of exacting charges from stock-raisers who pastured their sheep, cattle, or horses on the public lands.

Being greatly interested in natural history, Roosevelt established fifty-one national reservations in seventeen States and
Bird Refuges and New National Parks.
Territories, from Porto Rico to Hawaii and Alaska, as refuges for birds. By so doing he saved some species that were threatened with extinction. He also created a number of new national parks and a few special game preserves, and withdrew from entry vast stretches of mineral lands.

The President soon became an ardent advocate of conserving all natural resources that are limited in amount. In 1902 he secured the passage of the Great Reclamation Act, a subject
Great Conservation Conference, 1908.
described in detail in the next chapter. In 1907 he induced Congress to authorize an Inland Waterways Commission to study the interlocking problems of waterways and forest preservation, and to investigate the possibilities of inland transportation by water. In May, 1908, to fix the attention of the country upon the im-

portance of conservation, he summoned to Washington an epoch-making conference of governors, scientists, and other prominent men. The discussions took a broad range, and the educational value of the conference proved immense. As the President had hoped, the movement caught the popular fancy, and conservation became a settled policy in the minds of the American people. The conference recommended, among other things, protection of the source waters of navigable streams, prevention of forest fires by both national and State action, extension of practical forestry, the granting of separate titles to the surface of public lands and to the minerals beneath, retention of mineral lands until some system of development by carefully regulated private enterprise could be developed, and appointment by the individual States of conservation commissions to co-operate with one another and with the federal authorities.

Within eighteen months forty-one such commissions had been created, while a National Conservation Commission was established, consisting of one member from each State and Territory, with Gifford Pinchot as chairman. In 1909 Spread of the Idea. a North American Conservation Congress was held, to which came delegates from Newfoundland, Canada, and Mexico, as well as from the United States. This congress formulated a programme designed to make the natural resources of North America of greatest use to present and future generations. The National Conservation Commission collected an immense amount of valuable information, but the hostility of certain Congressmen resulted in 1909 in its being denied an appropriation for further activity. Its place was partly taken by an unofficial National Conservation Commission, whose first president was ex-President Charles W. Eliot of Harvard.

Another organization which did excellent work was the Country Life Commission, designed not so much Country Life Commission. to promote better farming as to improve living conditions in rural districts and render country life more attractive. This commission also was bitterly opposed by certain congressmen.

President Roosevelt's reforming activities aroused bitter antagonism among ultraconservatives and selfish interests, but his popularity among the people increased rather than diminished. In the congressional elections of 1906 his administration again received an overwhelming vote of confidence. Included in the majority membership of Senate and House, however, were many men who were either openly or covertly hostile to the President, and this hostility became more and more manifest as his term drew toward its close.

Late in 1907, soon after the imposition of the great fine against the Standard Oil Company, a financial stringency, amounting in some centres to a panic, developed. There were runs on many banks and trust companies, but the financial interests combined for mutual protection, clearing-house certificates were issued as an emergency currency, and only a comparatively few institutions went to the wall. Basically the business of the country was sound, and the flurry was mainly a "money panic"; it was often referred to as the "rich man's panic." In some of the great industrial centres lack of employment developed, but the West suffered comparatively little and the farming class were not much inconvenienced.

Panic of 1907.

One result of the panic was the passage of the Aldrich-Vreeland bill, authorizing national banks to issue emergency notes in times of financial stress. The act was intended as merely a temporary measure, and was to expire June 30, 1914. It provided for a National Monetary Commission, composed of nine representatives and nine senators, with Senator Aldrich of Rhode Island as chairman. This commission investigated currency and banking questions and ultimately brought in a report, but legislation was delayed until after Wilson came into power.

Aldrich-Vreeland Act.

Some of the President's enemies charged that the panic was due to the activities of "Theodore the Meddler," but many of his friends declared that the flurry was "manufactured" by trust magnates in order to discredit the attempts of the President to subject them to the law.

As fairly good business conditions soon returned, Roosevelt's popularity suffered no serious diminution, and, as the time for the political campaign of 1908 drew near, an insistent demand arose that he should accept a "second elective term."

Roosevelt Selects Taft to Carry out His Policies.
He pointed to his self-denying statement of 1904, but the demand was so strong that it was only by setting his face firmly against it that he prevented his renomination and probably his re-election. He was anxious, however, that his successor should be some one who would carry out his policies. Among the candidates were Senator Knox of Pennsylvania, Governor Hughes of New York, Governor Cummins of Iowa, Vice-President Fairbanks, Senator La Follette of Wisconsin, Speaker Joseph G. Cannon of Illinois, Senator Foraker of Ohio, and Secretary of War Taft. Roosevelt's choice fell upon Taft, and he threw his influence strongly to him. As governor of the Philippines, member of the cabinet, and in the conduct of numerous special missions Taft had displayed abilities of a high order. There was no great enthusiasm for him personally, but he received extensive financial assistance from his half-brother, Charles P. Taft, a multimillionaire of Cincinnati, while Roosevelt's support rendered his success certain. When the Republican convention met in Chicago in the middle of June, he was easily nominated on the first ballot. His nomination was considered a victory of the progressive element of the party. For the sake of harmony the vice-presidential nomination was given to the conservatives, and Representative James S. Sherman of New York became Taft's running mate on the ticket.

In its platform the party confidently asked for its continuance in power on the basis of past performance. The achievements of the Roosevelt administration were lauded in resounding periods. "In no other period since national sovereignty was won under Washington, or preserved under Lincoln," ran one sentence, "has there been such mighty progress in those ideals of government which make for justice, equality, and fair dealing among men." Among the measures promised for the future were amendment

The Platform.

of the Antitrust Act, currency reform, modification of the power of federal courts to issue injunctions in labor disputes, and revision of the tariff. This last task was to be carried out "by a special session of Congress immediately following the inauguration of the next President." "In all tariff legislation," so ran the platform, "the true principle of protection is best maintained by the imposition of such duties as will equal the difference between the cost of production at home and abroad, together with a reasonable profit to American industries." This language was not very specific, and the platform said nothing as to whether revision would be up or down, but in speeches made during the campaign Taft explained that revision would be downward. This pledge later rose up to plague him.

Tariff Revision Pledged.

In the Democratic party the "safe and sane" wing had lost prestige in the disastrous campaign of 1904 and the radicals were again in the saddle. Bryan had kept before the country by lecturing and by publishing a political paper called the *Commoner*, and had laid plans for again leading the party in 1908. Other men were mentioned for the honor, but when the national convention met at Denver (July 7, 1908) Bryan was nominated by a great majority, with John W. Kern of Indiana as the vice-presidential candidate. The platform contained the usual criticisms of the party in power, and, among other things, favored tariff and currency reform and a more stringent antitrust act, and promised changes in the power of federal judges to issue injunctions in case of strikes.

Bryan and Kern.

Both Taft and Bryan made extended speaking tours, but the campaign proved even duller than that of 1904. With returning prosperity the people were well satisfied with Republican rule and evinced small desire for a change. In the election Bryan received 1,323,000 more of the popular vote than had Parker, yet Taft's popular plurality amounted to about 1,270,000, while the electoral vote stood 321 for Taft, 162 for Bryan. Debs, who was once more the Socialist candidate, received 420,820, which was an increase

Taft Elected.

of only 18,000 over that of four years before. The Populists, who appeared for the last time, polled only 29,146, being surpassed by an ephemeral organization known as the Independence party.

In the final session of the Sixtieth Congress the breach which had long been perceptible between President Roosevelt and certain conservative Republicans in the House and Senate became decidedly wider. The leaders of this "stand-pat" element in the Senate were Aldrich of Rhode Island and Hale of Maine; in the House, Speaker Cannon. Of these men Roosevelt later wrote in his *Autobiography:* "I made a resolute effort to get on with all three and with their followers, and I have no question that they made an equally resolute effort to get on with me. We succeeded in working together, although with increasing friction, for some years, I pushing forward and they hanging back. Gradually, however, I was forced to abandon the effort to persuade them to come my way, and then I achieved results only by appealing over the heads of the Senate and House leaders to the people, who were the masters of both of us. I continued in this way to get results until almost the close of my term; and the Republican party became once more the progressive and indeed the fairly radical progressive party of the Nation. When my successor was chosen, however, the leaders of the House or Senate, or most of them, felt that it was safe to come to a break with me, and the last or short session of Congress, held between the election of my successor and his inauguration four months later, saw a series of contests between the majorities in the two houses of Congress and the President,—myself,— quite as bitter as if they and I had belonged to opposite political parties." Dire consequences to the party in power were ultimately to result from the divergencies thus revealing themselves. But at the moment the sun of Republicanism seemed to shine out of practically a clear sky, while Democratic prospects had rarely seemed darker.

The administration thus closing was undoubtedly one of the most remarkable in American annals, and Roosevelt retired amid the enthusiastic plaudits of an admiring people. As an administrator he had displayed remarkable foresight and wonderful ability to get things done. He was not content to wait until a situation became desperate; he acted in accordance with a favorite aphorism, to the effect that nine parts of wisdom is being wise in time. His success in bringing things to pass was partly due to careful planning and remarkable driving force but also in large measure to a rare talent for picking efficient men and inspiring them with an enthusiasm for public service. No American of his time had so many admiring friends or so many bitter enemies. It was highly creditable to be assailed by some of the men who sought to pull him down, yet it must be said that he alienated and antagonized—often on small matters —some men as well meaning as he. This was largely due to what was probably his chief weakness, namely, an excessive tendency to controversy and denunciation. It was proper enough, perhaps, for him to put certain individuals into his "Ananias Club," or to classify some others as "nature fakers" or "malefactors of great wealth," but not infrequently he scorched with vitriolic language persons who hardly deserved such treatment. Furthermore, he often engaged in wordy controversies when silence would have been the better course. It was like gunning for flies with an elephant-rifle. But these were minor blemishes on a great and noble character. Judged merely as an individual, as a specimen of the *genus homo*, he was the most remarkable man of his age, one of the few most remarkable of all ages. A celebrated Englishman, John Morley, said that he had been impressed by two great natural phenomena in America—Niagara Falls and Theodore Roosevelt.

For more than a quarter of a century he fought in the forefront of good causes, standing where the fighting waxed fiercest, giving and receiving mighty blows, and exulting in the joy of conflict. No one preached patriotism and civic righteousness so effectively as he, or taught so many to scorn what is base and ignoble. He brought into public life an inspiration that will abide for generations.

Roosevelt's Achievements and Characteristics.

A Great American.

Long ago it was written that without vision the people perish. Theodore Roosevelt wrote:

We, here in America, hold in our hands the hope of the world, the fate of the coming years, and shame and disgrace will be ours if in our eyes the light of high resolve is dimmed, if we trail in the dust the golden hope of men.

CHAPTER XVIII

THE NEW WEST

RECENT decades have continued to behold a marvellous transformation in the West. In 1870 Idaho, Washington, and Oregon combined had a white population of only 130,000; of these, 91,000 were in Oregon, largely in the wonderful Willamette Valley. Seattle, founded in 1852, had only 1,100, and Tacoma, founded in 1868, only 73. In ten years the population of the region more than doubled, while the decade of 1880–90 witnessed an even greater increase. By 1910 Idaho contained 325,594 people, Oregon 672,763, Washington 1,141,990. Seattle had multiplied over two hundred times, and had 237,194; Tacoma over a thousand times, and had 83,743. Portland, an older city than either, had 207,214. The acquisition of Alaska and the expansion of trade with Hawaii, Australia, and the Orient were important factors in building up all the Pacific States, and San Francisco Bay and Puget Sound had come to be among the busiest waters in the world.

By 1910 California had added $2,000,000,000 to the world's gold supply, but mining was then only one of many industries. A great diversity of manufactures had sprung up. Even petroleum had been discovered, though the fact that California oil has an asphaltum, not a paraffin, base renders it better fitted for fuel than for illuminating or rapid-combustion purposes. Lumbering and the growing of a wide variety of agricultural and horticultural products, including oranges and grapes, employed great numbers of people, as did stock-raising and many other occupations. Tens of thousands of people of wealth had been drawn thither to make their homes by the wonderful natural beauty of the country, and the agreeable climate. With an area larger than that of some empires, with populous cities, great universities, celebrated authors, and wonderful natural advantages as regards climate, location, and otherwise, California possessed an individuality all her own and was famous throughout the world.

Democratic fear of increasing Republican strength long delayed the admission of some of the northwestern States, but in 1889 an omnibus bill conferred statehood upon Montana, Washington, and North and South Dakota, the last two being formed by dividing the immense Dakota Territory. Wyoming and Idaho were admitted the next year. Utah, the "child of the desert," had prospered under the patriarchal reign of Brigham Young, and had a population double that of Idaho and three times that of Wyoming, but, owing to popular hostility to Mormonism, had to wait for statehood until 1896. Oklahoma, after vainly knocking for years, was admitted in 1907; Arizona and New Mexico, whose large Mexican population long kept them out, were finally admitted in 1912. From the Atlantic to the Pacific not a single Territory remained.

Railroads continued to be a vital factor in the life and development of the West. New trunk lines and "feeders" were constructed, and roads were consolidated into great systems, in which process many spectacular fights took place between rival magnates. These magnates were often unscrupulous as to methods; they bent governors to their will, corrupted judges and State legislatures, dominated whole States.

Such a railway-empire builder was Edward H. Harriman, who gained control of the Union Pacific when it was tottering financially, built it up, and used it as a lever to extend his power. In a titanic conflict in 1901 for the control of the Northern Pacific he was beaten by the combined strength of J. P. Morgan and James J. Hill, but he gained possession of the Southern Pacific, and east of the Mississippi controlled the Illinois Central and the Georgia Central, with their branch lines. At his death in 1909 he controlled about 25,000 miles of road, had a strong influence in the management of roads aggregating 50,000 miles more, and also controlled important banks and steamboat lines. He used this great power ruthlessly; his word had practically the force of law in certain States, including California; he defied even the federal government.

A magnate of a different type was James J. Hill, who came to control transportation in the Northwest much as Harriman did that of the Southwest. Born in Ontario in 1838, he settled in

James J. Hill.

St. Paul, which was then a small frontier town, worked in steamboat offices, and finally engaged in fuel and transportation enterprises for himself. In 1878, with three associates—two of them later prominent in the building of the famous Canadian Pacific—he managed to obtain control of "a pitiful heap of unrelated scraps" known as the St. Paul and Pacific Railroad, though its lines extended only a few hundred miles west of the Mississippi. Hill soon became the dominant figure in the enterprise, reorganized the road under a new name, pushed out extensions, and greatly aided in the rapid settlement of Minnesota and Dakota. But his great dream was a transcontinental of his own. Critics sneered at the thought of constructing a new line between the Canadian Pacific, in the building of which he had played a part, and the Northern Pacific; they called the project "Hill's folly." But Hill persevered, and in 1893 completed a road connecting St. Paul and Lake Superior with Seattle and the Pacific coast. Branch lines were thrown out to north and south, and a line of steamships was established to Japan and China, thus realizing the old dream of John Jacob Astor, the founder of Astoria on the Columbia. Not only did Hill by his transportation activities contribute immensely toward the settlement of the Northwest, but he was a pioneer in promoting many ideas which that section and the whole country needed. He encouraged diversified farming, introduced better breeds of stock, urged the use of better seed, established model farms, and preached the conservation of natural resources. A generation passed before he succeeded in hammering his ideas into the bucolic brain, nor was he alone in the work, but the ultimate results justified his labors. In an age when railway magnates and other millionaires were objects of well-nigh universal suspicion, most people made an exception for "Jim" Hill, as he was affectionately called, and he was rightly regarded as one of the real statesmen of the country.

There are many persons still living who studied in their youth geographies containing maps on which a large part of the West bore the inscription, "Great American Desert."

The "Great American Desert." Shortly before the Civil War an eminent scientist of the Smithsonian Institution emphatically declared that the region west of the 98th meridian, which runs through eastern Nebraska and central Kansas, "is a barren waste . . . a wilderness, unfitted for the use of the husbandman, although in some of the mountainous valleys at Salt Lake, by means of irrigation, a precarious supply of food may be obtained." Even as late as 1870 it would have been difficult to find any one to contradict General Hazen when he said that there could be no general agriculture between the 100th meridian, the Sierra Nevada Mountains, Canada, and Mexico.

There was an element of truth in these old views of the West, but not the whole truth. Approximately at the 97th meridian "the region of assured rainfall ends and the arid region begins." To eastward of that line droughts are not

The Arid Region. uncommon, but generally the rainfall is sufficient for the production of crops; to westward droughts are so much the rule that special methods must be resorted to in order to render the production of crops at all certain. Long before the American conquest the mission fathers in California had brought water to their land by artificial means, and prior to 1850 Brigham Young and his Mormon followers had begun to transform the arid region of Salt Lake by irrigation, but elsewhere Americans were slow to realize the possibilities thus disclosed.

The first Easterner of prominence to champion irrigation was Major John Wesley Powell. This soldier and scientist was best known for an adventurous descent of the Colorado River through the great canyon, now a Mecca for tourists. He was

long director of the federal geological survey, and as such carried out extended investigations in the West, the results of which
Work of
Major
Powell. were published in 1879 in his great report on *The Lands of the Arid Region*. It is not too much to say that he "organized the work that laid the foundation for the great irrigation development." From first-hand observation he knew that in the arid West were vast plains and great valleys, fertile of soil but bearing little more than cactus or sage-brush, to which it would be only necessary to bring the vivifying power of *water* in order to make such land as productive as any in the world.

In the decade following the publication of Powell's report Congress authorized some investigations into the possibilities of irrigation, but the only actual development of irrigation projects was done by private individuals or companies.
The Carey
Act, 1894. In several States enterprises due to private initiative were carried into successful operation, and considerable tracts of land were redeemed from the desert. In 1894 Congress gave a great impetus to such work by passing the Carey Act, offering to each of the States in the arid region a million acres of public land, provided the States would see to it that such land was reclaimed and settled. Several States accepted the proposal, and then gave to private corporations the rights to irrigate the land and sell it to settlers.

But private initiative was not equal to the vast task of reclaiming the arid lands, and men began to ask that the nation itself should take up the work of making such lands fit for
The Recla-
mation Act,
1902. settlement. An important factor in developing public sentiment along this line were the Irrigation congresses, the first of which was held at Salt Lake City in September, 1891. The platforms of both the great parties in 1900 declared in favor of federal aid for reclamation work, and in the following year, in the person of Roosevelt, there came into the presidency a man who really understood the West, its needs and its possibilities. In his first message to Congress Roosevelt declared that "forest and water problems are perhaps the most vital internal problems of the United

States," and largely as a result of his energetic support Congress (June, 1902) passed the Newlands Reclamation Act, fathered by Francis G. Newlands, a Democratic representative from Nevada. The act appropriated for reclamation purposes 95 per cent of the money received from the sale of public lands in the West, and put the work in charge of the Department of the Interior. Future generations will probably regard the act as one of the most beneficent ever passed by Congress.

The reclamation work was at first in charge of the Geological Survey, but in 1908 a special Reclamation Service was established, and for the post of director a man of great competence was selected in the person of Frederick H. Newell, who was already chief engineer of the work and who, with Gifford Pinchot, had been largely instrumental in inducing the President to take up the subject. Many great projects were begun, and vast sums were expended under the Reclamation Act and under another act of 1910, which authorized the issuance of $20,000,000 in certificates of indebtedness for use in the work. Private initiative also continued to accomplish important results, and a decade after the passage of the Reclamation Act a member of the Reclamation Service could write:

Irrigation canals representing an investment of one hundred and fifty million dollars, and long enough to girdle the globe with triple bands, have spread oases of green in sixteen arid states and territories. An annual harvest valued at not less than two hundred and fifty million dollars is the desert's response to the intelligent application of water to her sun-burned valleys. Practically all of this stupendous miracle has been wrought within the past quarter of a century, and a large part of it by individual enterprise. The Great American Desert no longer calls up a vision of desolation and horrors. With the westward march of settlers, its boundaries have shrunken. Railroads have thrust its barriers aside. Its flowing streams and its underground waters are being measured and studied, and we are beginning to grasp faintly a little of its potential greatness. Conservative engineers, on the basis of our present knowledge, estimate that not less than thirty million acres are yet reclaimable by water from the streams which drain it.

Since the above was written many million more dollars have been expended, both by individuals and by the government. By 1918 the total amount expended by the Reclamation Service amounted to about $125,000,000. Water had been provided on the government projects for about a million and a half acres, and about a million acres were under cultivation. Some of the dams built to impound the water are wonderful structures; among the most notable are the Engle dam on the Rio Grande River, the Roosevelt dam on Salt River in Arizona, and the Shoshone dam in Wyoming, the last-named being the loftiest in the world. The land irrigated by the Reclamation Service is sold to settlers, and the money invested thus forms a sort of "revolving fund" that can be used in developing future projects.

Later Progress.

The success of reclamation has been so great in the arid region that it is probable that in course of time irrigation will be used in more humid regions. Even in the Middle West hardly a summer passes in which there is not a dry period that damages crops, while every few seasons a drought occurs that causes an almost total failure.

The West has been transformed in fifty years, yet its real development has hardly begun. Sight should not be lost of the fact that two-thirds of the total area of the United States lies to westward of the Mississippi River. Of what immense populations may not this region be the home in generations not far distant!

Future Possibilities.

In the early portion of our period the West was poor and radical. Populism and many another "ism" came out of Kansas and other Western States. Now the West is prosperous and more conservative. Western statesmen have ceased to boast of being "sockless" or of the length of their whiskers. In sections in which, in the early '90's, farmers were burning corn for fuel, and knew not where the money was to come from with which to pay the interest on the mortgage, the same men or their sons ride in high-power motor-cars, clip coupons from government bonds, and grow indignant over the proposals of wild-eyed agitators in Chicago or New York.

The West Less Radical than Formerly.

The progress of Alaska under American rule long continued to be exceedingly slow, and the white population remained so small that it was not until 1884 that the new possession was given a civil government, and not until 1912 that it was permitted to have an elective legislature. Owing to remoteness and transportation difficulties, to high mountains and unfordable rivers, to swarming mosquitoes in summer and frightful cold in winter, years passed before large stretches of the vast interior were even explored. In 1883 Lieutenant Frederick Schwatka, who had had experience as an Arctic explorer, led a party which floated down the Yukon from its headwaters, and Schwatka's book describing the trip made this great waterway better known to the world. Other exploring expeditions gradually unlocked Alaska's geographical secrets and disclosed, for example, that Denali, or Mount McKinley, an immense snow peak 20,300 feet high, forms "the top of the continent."

From a financial point of view, outside interest in Alaska was long chiefly confined to trading with the Indians for furs and to the interesting and highly profitable fur-seal industry. In 1869 the federal government leased the sealing rights on the Pribyloff Islands, where the seals chiefly congregated, to the Alaska Commercial Company for twenty years, and in 1890 made a new contract with the North American Company. Both the companies and the government obtained large financial returns from the fur-seal industry, but pelagic sealing in Bering Sea by Canadians and others resulted in international complications that have been described in an earlier chapter. About 1878 enterprising Americans began to establish canneries near the mouths of the rivers, in order to take advantage of the vast "run" of salmon, which leave the sea and ascend the streams to spawn. In a few years the industry was annually producing immense quantities of food valued at many millions of dollars.

When Alaska was purchased optimists predicted that it would be found to contain vast mineral resources. In 1880 quartz veins were discovered in the region about Juneau, near

the southern extremity. Most of the ore was low grade, yielding only a few dollars in gold per ton; but working conditions
were favorable, and one mine, the famous Tread-
The Gold well, on Douglas Island, soon became one of the
Rush.
most productive in the world. As early as 1873 a
few prospectors began operations in the upper Yukon country.
But the region was exceedingly remote, the working season
was short, food and transportation difficulties were enormous,
and it was not until the finding in 1896 of fabulously rich placer
deposits along Klondike Creek that the world at large learned
of the mineral possibilities of the Yukon country. The "Klondike" lies over the boundary in British America, but rich au-
riferous deposits were soon found on streams emptying into the
Yukon in the true Alaska and even around the head of Cook
Inlet and about Nome, near Bering Strait. Hordes of gold-
seekers hastened from all over the world toward the diggings,
and braved incredible hardships in a hyperborean land of tall
mountains, muskegs, swift rivers, snow, and bitter cold to reach
the region of their hopes. Many died on the way, thousands
turned back, many more thousands found only disappointment,
a few "struck it rich" and dug out great sums in gold dust.
The camps were picturesque and lively, but more orderly than
those of California in '49; there were comparatively few rob-
beries and murders—little need for lynch law. The battles
fought were mostly with hostile nature, but it was not a life
for weaklings. The "sour-dough" poet, Robert Service, wrote
truly:

"This is the law of the Yukon, and ever she makes it plain:
  'Send not your foolish and feeble; send me your strong and your
    sane—
  Strong for the red rage of battle; sane for I harry them sore;
  Send me men girt for the combat, men who are grit to the core.'"

Most of the gold-seekers soon returned to their homes, and
during the first decade of the new century Alaska gained only
about a thousand in population, the number of inhabitants in
1910 being 64,356, of whom 25,331 were Indians. Vast coal,

copper, and other mineral deposits were known to exist; interior valleys were even thought to possess great agricultural and grazing possibilities; reindeer raising had been successfully introduced; but the further development of the country waited on the construction of better methods of transportation and a more definite governmental policy regarding the natural resources of the country. Even so, however, "Seward's Folly" was annually producing, in minerals, fish, furs, and other products, more than five times its purchase price.

Other Resources.

The mighty Yukon affords entrance for 2,000 miles to the heart of the country, and by 1913 a few short railway lines had been built by private companies, but otherwise inland transportation was mostly carried on by dog-sledge, pack-train, and on the backs of men. The great cost of railway construction and the unlikelihood of early profits discouraged private initiative in the development of better transportation facilities, and in 1912 a railroad commission appointed by President Taft reported in favor of the government's taking up railway-building in Alaska. Early in 1914 Congress authorized the President to construct and operate not to exceed 1,000 miles of railroad in Alaska, at an expense not to exceed $35,000,000. A route extending from Seward to Fairbanks, with a branch to the Matanuska coal-fields, was selected in 1915, and work was soon afterward begun. Operation was to be by the government.

The Government Takes up the Transportation Problem.

Many difficulties remain to be overcome before Alaska's resources can be fully developed, but there can be little doubt that the region is a great natural storehouse from which for ages to come our people can draw for use and enjoyment.

CHAPTER XIX

THE PROGRESSIVE REVOLT

On the eve of March 3, 1909, a hundred thousand visitors had gathered in the capital to witness the installation of a President whose administration, it was confidently expected, would be prosperous and successful. The broad equipment and varied training of William H. Taft for the high position to which he had been called were admitted on every hand, and his genial good nature was so pronounced that he had few personal enemies even among his political opponents. The weather bureau forecast fair weather for the great day, but an unexpected "flare-back" swept down upon the city, bringing such a fierce storm of wind, snow, sleet, and rain that for the first time in over a century the inaugural oath had to be administered indoors. In after years men who looked back to that stormy day felt that it foreshadowed coming events—an administration that seemed likely to pass calmly and serenely yet that, in reality, proved full of turmoil and ended in disaster.

From his predecessor's cabinet the new President retained only two men, namely, George von L. Meyer, who was transferred from the post-office to the navy, and James Wilson, secretary of agriculture. Wilson had taken that position in 1897, and he remained in office until 1913, the longest term of a cabinet member in the history of the country and a period in which a vast amount of progress was made in developing scientific agriculture. For secretary of state President Taft chose Senator Philander C. Knox of Pennsylvania, who had been attorney-general in 1901–04; and for attorney-general he named George W. Wickersham, a New York lawyer. In general, it was a cabinet that was notable for legal learning rather than for political sagacity or breadth of view. In some quarters it was assumed that the

President chose so many lawyers because he believed their training would be helpful in translating into effective enactments the sentiment in favor of reform aroused by the agitation under his predecessor.

Soon after his retirement that predecessor sailed for the wilds of East Africa to indulge his fondness for natural history and big-game hunting. With him he took his son Kermit and a staff of scientists from the Smithsonian Institution. The party reached Mombasa in April, and soon plunged into the remote interior, where for many months Colonel Roosevelt and his son hunted rhinoceroses, lions, elephants, and other savage beasts with great success. Meanwhile President Taft was left free to make or mar his administration, without suggestion or dictation from his former chief.

Roosevelt Goes to Africa.

In reality Taft's position was much more difficult than was popularly supposed. Within his party there existed a progressive and a conservative wing. The progressives enthusiastically favored the "Roosevelt policies" and would be bitterly disappointed at any faltering in upholding or promoting them. The conservatives, who were more powerful than numerous, bitterly disliked those policies and were determined to put an end to them. In the beginning Taft appears to have hoped to steer a course which would enable him to obtain the support of both factions. But to do so successfully was beyond his or any other man's powers. Furthermore, as perhaps he failed to see, the political situation was such that unless he worked with the progressive element he really served the purposes of the conservatives, for they were satisfied to stand still, and if the President did not aid the progressives to drive the wagon forward, the conservatives gained their object.

Taft's Difficult Task.

The first important task taken up was the revision of the tariff. In accordance with the platform promise, the President summoned Congress in extra session (March 15, 1909), and the Solons set to work upon a new tariff bill. It quickly developed that neither Republicans nor Democrats would be able to present a united front on the issue. Some Republicans opposed any reductions in the schedules, or even wished to build the tariff wall still higher; others favored carrying out their candidate's pre-election pledge to lower it. Even many Democrats forgot their free-trade principles in their eagerness to secure the highest possible protection for articles produced in their States or districts. As usual, the pressure from protected interests proved tremendous, and the capital swarmed with lobbyists.

As the Senate was controlled by a coterie of extremely high-tariff Republicans, headed by Senator Aldrich, and the House by another, headed by Speaker Joseph G. Cannon, it was clear that decided downward revision was unlikely unless the President forced it by aggressive action. But Taft took the ground that the executive ought not to dictate to the legislative branch, and merely used his influence in a mild way. He succeeded in securing free entrance into the United States for Philippine products in limited amounts, and in substituting a tax on the net earnings of corporations in place of an inheritance tax, but most of his suggestions for downward revision were ignored. After months of jockeying Congress finally passed what is known to history as the Payne-Aldrich Bill, and the President signed it. Twenty Republican representatives and seven Republican senators denounced the measure and refused to vote for it. Among these "insurgent" senators were Dolliver and Cummins of Iowa, Beveridge of Indiana, Bristow of Kansas, and La Follette of Wisconsin. President Taft confessed that the woollens schedule was unsatisfactory, but in a speech delivered at Winona, Wisconsin, in September, 1909, he pronounced the bill, as a whole, the best tariff law ever made. This view found few supporters except among reactionary Republicans and the protected interests.

The "insurgents" who revolted against the Payne-Aldrich Bill were mostly men who had ardently supported the Roosevelt policies. Their number was soon increased by a scandal in the Department of the Interior. As head of that department

Taft had appointed Richard Achilles Ballinger, a Seattle lawyer and politician, who for a time had been commissioner of
the general land-office under Roosevelt. While not
in the public service he had become attorney for
the "Cunningham claims" to valuable coal deposits
in Alaska. The legality of these claims was doubtful, and many
persons believed them fraudulent and part of a plan on the
part of the Morgan-Guggenheim Syndicate—popularly known
as the "Morganheims"—to gobble up the rich natural resources
of Alaska. Among those who believed the claims fraudulent
were Chief Forester Gifford Pinchot and Messrs. Shaw, Glavis,
and Price, of the Forestry Service. All of these men were officials in the Department of the Interior, and hence were subordinates of Ballinger. Believing that Ballinger was betraying
conservation, they ignored bureaucratic red tape and appealed
over his head to the President and people. Taft deemed them
guilty of insubordination and dismissed them from the service; at the same time he declared his confidence in Ballinger.
The controversy caused a great uproar, and many newspapers
and magazines of progressive sympathies upheld Pinchot and
attacked Ballinger. It was charged that Taft had not sufficiently investigated the matter, and, though both he and Ballinger were warmly defended, many people felt that he had
put too much emphasis upon mere official punctilio and too
little upon public efficiency. Later a representative of the
Morgan-Guggenheim Syndicate admitted that his company
held options on many of the Cunningham claims, all of which,
it may be added, were finally held by the courts to be void. A
congressional investigating committee "whitewashed" Ballinger, but he continued to be a target for bitter criticism, and
ultimately (March 6, 1911) he resigned.

Whatever may have been the merits of his course in the
Pinchot-Ballinger controversy, it is beyond question that Taft
remained loyal to conservation. He appointed ardent con-
servationists to fill the vacancies created by the dismissal of
Pinchot and his associates, secured important legislation to

safeguard the movement, and withdrew from entry many million acres of water-power sites and of coal, petroleum, and mineral lands. He also secured legislation providing for the purchase of forest reserves in the White and Appalachian Mountains, already referred to.

But it was beyond his power to close the rift that had opened
A
Republican
Crisis.
in Republican ranks. Before a year of his administration had passed, and while Roosevelt was still in the African jungles, it was clear to keen observers that the party was facing the greatest crisis in its history.

The crisis was all the graver because of the character of the times. It was an age of unrest, of striving after things unattained, perhaps unattainable. Men were not only demanding
A Period
of Unrest.
social and industrial reforms, but were beginning to contend that our whole political system, including even the Federal Constitution, needed overhauling. That document, the critics asserted, was framed in the eighteenth century for a decentralized society, chiefly agricultural in character and as yet untouched by the transforming influences of the Industrial Revolution. There were then no steamships, no railroads, no telegraphs, no factories, no stock exchanges, no tenement-houses, no trusts, no labor-unions, no cities of even 50,000 people, nothing virtually, except Mother Earth and human nature, that entered into the transformed world and its problems. Conditions change, and political institutions must change with them, else countries become petrified, as did China. "Broad construction" and certain amendments had helped to adjust the Constitution to the demands of a new age, but further changes were needed, and fundamental amendments were virtually impossible because the process prescribed is so difficult that conservative influences intrenched in a few States could block changes. As things stood, the critics complained, legislators must devote a large share of their attention to considering not whether a law was needed, but whether, if passed, the courts would adjudge it constitutional.

Criticism of the courts was wide-spread and often virulent.

Even fairly conservative people, including many lawyers, said that they were dilatory, that they were often swamped by technicalities and hide-bound by precedent. More radical critics declared that they were dams to the progress of social justice, gave too much weight to property rights and too little to human rights, that they served as bulwarks of privilege, that the judges themselves lacked an "understanding heart."

Criticism of the Courts.

In all parts of the country, and particularly in the West and Middle West, it was felt that conservative and even reactionary influences too often controlled courts, executives, and legislative bodies; and a wide-spread demand developed for more "direct government." Four devices for checkmating the nefarious designs of "bosses" and special interests were considered especially promising: namely, primary elections, the initiative, the referendum, and the recall.

Demand for More "Direct Government."

Until recently it had been customary for the law to ignore the operations of parties and to regulate only elections. The nomination of persons for office had been left to extra-legal rules drawn up and administered by parties themselves. But parties frequently fell into the hands of "rings," which controlled conventions and put up men likely to betray the public interests. When both the great parties in a city or State nominated such candidates, citizens could only take a choice between two evils—or else resort to the doubtful device of nominating an independent ticket. Political observers had long realized that one of the greatest weaknesses in the American political system was this unsatisfactory method of selecting candidates; and an increasing number of men were insisting that nominations, like elections, must be put under legal restrictions. Prior to 1908 laws regulating primary elections were enacted in a number of Western and Middle Western States, including Wisconsin, Oregon, Washington, Nebraska, and the two Dakotas; and a strong demand for similar legislation arose elsewhere. The innovation was opposed by political bosses and special in-

Primary-Election Laws.

terests, and by some well-meaning men of conservative tendencies.

The demand for the initiative, referendum, and recall grew out of conditions that had long created wide-spread dissatisfaction. Legislatures would frequently refuse to pass legislation which the public desired, or would enact bad laws, while corrupt or incompetent officials would cling to power because the process of impeachment was unwieldy and uncertain. By the initiative voters could themselves propose laws and enact them at elections. By the referendum they could prevent or annul unpopular or unsatisfactory laws. By the recall they could remove dishonest, incompetent, or unpopular officials. Reduced to their lowest terms, these devices constituted an attempt to adapt the principles of the old town meetings of New England to the complicated conditions of a great and populous republic. At the time that the Taft administration came into power all of these three devices were in use in Oregon, and a few other States had adopted the referendum and recall. Agitation in favor of the new "direct democracy" was spreading elsewhere, but encountered bitter opposition in conservative and reactionary quarters.

Initiative, Referendum, and Recall.

By way of anticipation it may be said here that primary-election laws of one sort or another were ultimately adopted in most of the States, but ignorance of the requisites of a good law and underhand work on the part of enemies of the system combined to make many of these laws more or less unsatisfactory. Political machines and the selfish interests back of the machines naturally fought the primary plan and, when forced to concede such laws, often contrived to make them imperfect. To be really effective, a primary law should be as stringent as for an election. Furthermore, it should be combined with what is known as the short ballot, for it is useless to expect the voter to be able to display much discrimination if he is called upon to name a great number of officers. Many political scientists believe that we elect too many officers. In their opinion it would be better to diminish the number of elective positions,

General Adoption of Primary System.

to elect only a few men, to let them appoint the rest, and thus concentrate responsibility. The voter would then be able to form an intelligent opinion as to the character and abilities of the candidates, either at the primary or at the election. The ordinary voter cannot do this when there are a score or more of positions to be filled and the aspirants number hundreds. The amount of money which can be expended by a candidate should be strictly limited. Some authorities are inclined to believe that a majority rather than a plurality of votes should be required; otherwise, a well-organized minority may win. In order to secure such a majority, a system of preferential voting has been evolved whereby the voter can express not only his first but also his second and third choices. But no system can be evolved that will beat the bosses unless a majority of the citizens are fully awake to their responsibilities. After all, the great advantage of the primary is that it enables an aroused public sentiment to take the party organization away from a political ring more easily than where the old convention system prevails.

The initiative, the referendum, and the recall have been less

Initiative, Referendum, and Recall Still on Trial.

widely adopted than the primary system, and their use is still mainly confined to the West and Northwest. Final judgment cannot yet be passed on these devices. Where they have been tried they have scored some successes and some failures.

Americans are too much inclined to lay the blame for misgovernment on faulty systems when some of the causes lie deeper. Improved governmental devices may prove helpful, but, no

Defective Institutions Less to Blame than Defective Citizenship.

matter how ingenious, they cannot neutralize ignorance, nor make up for the indifference which allows what is everybody's business to be nobody's business except the politician's. Better political systems are needed, but, above all, a higher sense of righteousness and responsibility among voters. Most of our misgovernment results not from defective institutions but from defective citizenship. A stream cannot rise higher than its source, and thus far no political hydraulic ram which will raise the best men in a democracy into office has been devised. Before we can have any real regeneration in our governmental affairs there must be a regeneration of the American people.

The demand for reform helped to accentuate the differences in the Republican party. On the one hand stood men of a conservative or reactionary type who thought that the reforming impulse had already gone far enough, or even too far. On the other hand stood the progressively inclined, who believed that only a beginning had been made, that the world is a changing world, that institutions must be overhauled and modified to meet new conditions. As already stated, President Taft, though advocating some progressive measures, seemed to stand with the conservatives. His defenders assert that thereby he showed his greatness. In their view the things for which his critics clamored were not the things the people ought to have had. Taft, they contend, stood up for the old and sound order, and sacrificed himself to save the foundations of constitutional government against ruthless innovation.

Progressives vs. Conservatives.

As time passed Taft became increasingly unpopular. This was due partly to his policies, partly to his personality, partly to the very nature of the situation in which he found himself. It was his misfortune to follow one of the most brilliant political leaders who ever lived—a veritable superman, who possessed a wonderful capacity for doing and saying interesting and impressive things. Throughout, Taft continued to have defenders, but, after Roosevelt, he seemed to many people to be unimaginative, unromantic, prosy, and dull.

Taft's Misfortune.

At first, however, the main wrath of progressives was directed not at Taft but at the body of conservative Republicans who controlled Congress. These men were so powerful that they had arrogated to themselves practically all legislative power. Almost nothing could be accomplished against their opposition. In the House, for example, Speaker Cannon and his fellow stand-patters controlled procedure so thoroughly that Republicans who were

The Stand-Pat Ring in Congress Overthrown.

out of sympathy with them found it almost impossible to obtain the floor in order to speak. Cannon was a picturesque old man from the Danville district of Illinois, much given, despite his Quaker origin, to the use of fine-cut tobacco and profanity. He was generally called "Uncle Joe," and was always cartooned with a tip-tilted cigar between his teeth. He was a man of ability and had once enjoyed decided popularity, but his enemies declared that he was so conservatively inclined that "if he had attended the caucus on Creation he would have remained loyal to Chaos." Most of his popularity had now vanished and an urgent demand had arisen that he should be shorn of his autocratic powers. After frequent parliamentary skirmishes a number of insurgent Republicans, headed by Norris of Nebraska and Murdock of Kansas, united with the Democrats, in March, 1910, and wrested control from Cannon and the stand-patters. Cannon was permitted to retain the speakership, but the power of appointing committees was taken from him and his authority was otherwise circumscribed. This revolution in the House foreshadowed a greater one that was impending.

The public was eager to learn what attitude ex-President Roosevelt would take toward the Taft administration. In the spring of 1910 Colonel Roosevelt, his son Kermit, and the accompanying scientists returned to civilization from the African jungle by way of Victoria Nyanza and the Nile. At historic Khartoum the party was met by many newspaper men; thenceforth the ex-President's journey resembled a triumphal procession. In Italy he was joined by Gifford Pinchot, whom Taft had discharged from the forestry service, and from Pinchot he doubtless heard something of the course of politics at home, and in particular about the Ballinger scandal. In Europe he was received with enthusiasm by people and crowned heads alike, and delivered a series of notable addresses that attracted world-wide attention. On June 18, 1910, he reached New York City and was accorded a spontaneous, enthusiastic, and universal reception. In a speech made on landing he said that he was ready and eager to do his part in helping to solve problems which must be solved, if the

Return of Roosevelt.

people were to see the destinies of the republic "rise to the high level of our hopes and its opportunities. This is the duty of every citizen, but it is peculiarly my duty, for any man who has ever been honored by being made President of the United States is thereby, forever after, rendered the debtor of the American people." Upon the subject of the breach in the Republican party he long remained discreetly silent, but it was noticed that his relations with the Taft administration were slight, and that in his speeches and in his writings as associate editor of *The Outlook* he advocated progressive measures.

The congressional and State elections of 1910 attracted more than usual attention. In response to a wide-spread public call, Colonel Roosevelt, not long after his return, took a vigorous part in the Republican State convention in New York and wrested control of the party organization from the reactionary Barnes machine. He also made a long speaking tour through the country, but his efforts were mainly directed in favor of "insurgent" candidates, and he refrained from saying much in praise of the Taft administration. The Democrats, however, accused him of "straddling" in the interest of party solidarity.

At Ossawatomie, Kansas, at a celebration in honor of John Brown, he delivered (August 31, 1910) a notable address which attracted wide-spread attention. In it he set forth his creed of "New Nationalism." After advocating certain reforms which he considered necessary to meet changed conditions—such as tariff-revision, conservation, a graduated income tax, labor legislation, direct primaries, and recall of elective officers—he urged that federal authority should be increased in order to make it strong enough for every national purpose. In particular he advocated the elimination of what he had long called "the twilight zone" between State and federal authority, which served "as a refuge for lawbreakers, and especially for lawbreakers of great wealth, who can hire the vulpine legal cunning which will teach the way to avoid both jurisdictions. . . . The American people are right in demanding that New Nationalism without which we cannot hope to deal with new problems. The New Nationalism puts the national need before sectional or personal advantages. It is impatient of the utter confusion that results from local legislatures attempting to treat national issues as local issues. It is still more impatient of the impotence which springs from the overdivision of government powers, the impotence which makes it possible for local selfishness or for legal cunning, hired by wealthy special interests, to bring national activities to a deadlock. This New Nationalism regards the executive power as the steward of the public welfare. It demands of the judiciary that it shall be interested primarily in human welfare rather than in property, just as it demands that the representative body shall represent all the people rather than one class or section of the people."

The Democrats entered the campaign full of hope, and fought vigorously. They were aided by discontent in the Republican ranks, and for the first time in eighteen years they won the popular verdict. They carried such States as New Jersey, Indiana, Ohio, New York, Massachusetts, and Connecticut, secured a majority of over sixty in the House of Representatives, and greatly reduced the Republican majority in the Senate. Many "progressive" Republican candidates escaped the cataclysm, which was especially disastrous to "stand-patters," many of whom were defeated in the election or in the conventions that preceded it. This outcome was humiliating to the administration, for Taft had taken his stand with the "stand-pat" wing and had even tried to read some of the progressive leaders out of the party. A minor but significant feature of the election was that the Socialist vote was greatly increased and that for the first time this party elected a member of Congress, in the person of Victor L. Berger of Milwaukee.

Democratic Victory, 1910.

Realizing that the Payne-Aldrich Act had been one of the main causes of Republican defeat, President Taft sought to retrieve that political blunder. The act had authorized him to appoint a tariff board to assist him in applying maximum and minimum rates; he now set it to work collecting information to be used in some future revision of schedules. He also negotiated a reciprocity pact with Canada (January, 1911),

Canadian Reciprocity, 1911.

whereby it was agreed that the duties on such Canadian products as wood-pulp, rough lumber, paper, and wheat should be abolished or lowered, while corresponding concessions should be made to American agricultural implements and certain other commodities. The measure had much to recommend it, but American farmers and lumbermen raised the cry that it sacrificed their interests to those of manufacturers. Many Republicans opposed the pact; most Democrats supported it. By use of whip and spur Taft forced through the House a bill embodying the terms of the agreement, but the Sixty-First Congress came to an end before a vote was taken on it in the Senate. Taft, therefore, called an extra session of the new Congress, and after a long and bitter fight the measure was finally forced through. In times past Canada had vainly begged for reciprocity, but conditions had changed in the Dominion, which now had "infant industries" of its own desiring protection. In September, 1911, a general election was held to ascertain the attitude of the voters on the question. It resulted in the overwhelming defeat of the Laurier government, which had negotiated the agreement, and in the consequent rejection of reciprocity. The outcome still further weakened the Taft administration.

In the new Congress the House of Representatives was, of course, controlled by the Democrats. Champ Clark of Missouri succeeded Cannon as speaker, while Oscar W. Underwood of

"Pop-gun" Tariff Bills.

Alabama became chairman of the Committee on Ways and Means. The Democrats and "insurgent" Republicans combined to carry through both houses a farmer's free-list bill, which removed the duties on such articles as boots and shoes, wire fencing, and agricultural implements; a bill revising the notorious "Schedule K"; and a bill reducing the duties on cotton manufactures, chemicals, and certain other articles. Taft vetoed all these "pop-gun" measures, as they were called. Next year he dealt similarly with an iron-and-steel bill and a new woollens bill. The tariff, therefore, became a leading issue in the campaign of 1912, and Democrats raised the cry that they would reduce duties and lower the cost of living.

Despite its failures, the Taft administration could point to a number of constructive achievements. Numerous arbitration treaties were concluded with foreign powers, New Mexico and

Constructive Achievements.

Arizona were admitted to statehood, and in 1910 a postal-savings system and in 1912 a parcels-post were established. This last innovation had long been successful abroad, but the great express companies had hitherto prevented its adoption in the United States. It was operated in connection with the post-office, and the business quickly assumed mammoth proportions, 700,000,000 parcels being carried the first year.

The period of Taft's presidency also saw the submission by Congress of two long-advocated constitutional amendments. The first of these empowered Congress to levy an income tax

Sixteenth and Seventeenth Amendments.

without the necessity of apportioning it among the States according to population. The second provided for the election of United States senators by popular vote instead of by the legislatures. Both amendments were ratified. The income-tax amendment was proclaimed a part of the Constitution on February 25, 1913; the other on the 31st of the following May. Submission of the income-tax amendment had been agreed upon while the Payne-Aldrich tariff act was under consideration. The other amendment was the outcome of a wide-spread belief that selfish special interests too often controlled the choice of senators in legislatures.

Five vacancies occurred in the Federal Supreme Court during Taft's administration. Thus it fell to him to appoint a majority of that august tribunal. On the death of Chief Justice

Changes in the Supreme Court.

Melville Fuller, who had presided over the court for twenty-two years, Taft promoted Associate Justice Edward D. White of Louisiana to fill the vacancy. Of the other appointees the most notable was Charles E. Hughes, whom we have already met as governor of New York. White and two other appointees were Democrats. In naming them the President showed that he wished to avoid packing the court with Republicans. Bryan and other critics charged, however, that Taft was careful to select jurists who, whatever their political affiliations, were of a conservative cast of mind.

In June, 1910, at the request of the President, Congress created a new Commerce Court, whose main duty should be to consider appeals from decisions made by the Interstate Commerce Commission. This tribunal's career proved short and stormy. It assumed powers that the Supreme Court held to be beyond its jurisdiction, some of its decisions were unpopular, and one of its judges, Robert W. Archbald, was impeached by Congress for having had improper financial relations with certain railway corporations. In 1913 Congress abolished the court altogether.

Commerce Court.

As set forth in an earlier chapter, the Supreme Court in 1911 decided long-pending suits against the Tobacco trust and the Standard Oil Company, and ordered the "dissolution" of those companies. The administration hailed the decisions as great judicial victories. But the general public expressed skepticism regarding the practical value of the decisions, and failed to wax enthusiastic over the filing of other suits. As Roosevelt and others had long held, the Sherman Act was not a satisfactory solution of the trust problem. It exercised a restraining effect that was doubtless wholesome, but suits brought under it tended to unsettle business, and when cases were won the practical results often proved disappointing. As one commentator on the trusts wrote: "Combinations are Protean, and we are baffled by shadowy communities of interest which seem to have no bodies we can grasp. Our lawyers perform inscrutable incantations, making many stock certificates grow where one grew before, but the people are not satisfied that these ceremonies have exorcised the spirit of monopoly from the body of large business."

The Sherman Anti-Trust Act Defective.

Long before 1912 it became certain that any attempt to renominate Taft would meet with bitter opposition. Many Republicans, including some who had been most ardent in his support in 1908, were deeply dissatisfied with his course and believed that the interests of the country demanded a change; others, fearing that it would be impossible to re-elect him, felt

Taft Desires a Renomina-tion. that it would be better to put forward a stronger candidate. But Taft and his friends made light of the opposition, and determined to force his renomination as a "vindication." They controlled the party machinery in most of the States, could obtain ample funds, and could depend upon receiving the aid of most of the Republican leaders. Few of these had any special admiration or love for Taft, but in the progressive movement against him they recognized a menace to their power.

The movement against Taft began to take definite shape early in 1911. Senators La Follette, Bourne, Clapp, Cummins, and Poindexter, Representatives Norris, Murdock, and Lenroot,

The Progressive Movement. and others, both in and out of Congress, formed a definite Progressive Republican organization, whose main objects were to promote progressive measures and beat Taft. Some of the leaders encouraged La Follette to seek the nomination. As the presidential bee had long been buzzing in La Follette's bonnet, it did not require much persuasion to induce him to enter the lists. In the summer of 1911 he began an active campaign for the nomination. In the follow-

La Follette's Candidacy. ing October his candidacy was indorsed by a national conference of Progressive Republicans; and yet, as time passed, it became clear that, despite dissatisfaction with Taft, La Follette was making small headway, and would not be able to defeat the President. In Wisconsin, in the Senate, and through the pages of a weekly newspaper which he owned and edited, La Follette had fought vigorously for progressive measures and was one of the pioneers of the movement. He had attracted much attention by going about the country and reading the "roll-call" of the votes of reactionary senators and representatives on public measures. He had a small following in almost every section of the country, but he lacked the confidence of some even of the Progressive Republicans, and few of his friends and admirers knew how to translate public sentiment into delegates to conventions. Practical progressives soon perceived that there was only one man in the country who stood a chance to turn President Taft and his supporters out of their intrenched position, and he was not Senator La Follette. On February 2, 1912, while under a great mental and physical strain, the senator made a long and injudicious speech in Philadelphia before a meeting of publishers, and this, with other developments, soon resulted in wholesale desertions from his banner.

For months there had been developing an insistent demand that Colonel Roosevelt should enter the race, and his disinclination to answer the call only increased the clamor, which ultimately reached cyclonic proportions. The Colonel's position was peculiarly difficult, not to say embarrassing. A large section of the party of which he had once been the idolized chief had risen in revolt against the man he had set over them, and were now demanding that he should come from retirement and aid them in driving the incumbent from power. He had little to gain, perhaps much to lose, in returning to public affairs. His position in history was assured. The honors he had received at home and abroad were sufficient for the most ambitious of men. He had disclaimed any intention of again being a candidate, though he later explained that his announcement in 1904 referred only to a renomination in 1908. If he entered the contest, he would certainly be assailed with the bitterest virulence by old enemies; it was equally certain that he would alienate many former friends. It was doubtful whether he could be nominated, and yet more doubtful whether, if nominated, he could be elected. But he was deeply dissatisfied with the course of his former protégé. His sympathies lay with the insurgents, who, in times of need in many a bitter fight, had always stood unflinchingly at his back. Doubtless he felt that to refuse their call would be equivalent to deserting them in their extremity. Furthermore, there can be little question that a desire to see written into law his plans for "a New Nationalism" was a strong factor in his ultimate decision. If he could wrest control of the party from the stand-pat leaders and set its feet

The Call for Roosevelt.

anew on the progressive road, he believed that he would accomplish something worth while, even should he be defeated in November. Therefore, after long consideration, in reply to the appeal of seven Republican governors, he announced that his hat was "in the ring." He made the fight on a platform of progressive principles, including the initiative, the referendum, and the recall of elective officers, but, as a substitute for the recall of judges, he suggested a recall of judicial decisions.

The announcement of Roosevelt's candidacy precipitated the greatest pre-convention battle ever seen in American politics. The contest was an even one, for, though Roosevelt had a far larger personal following than had Taft, the President's supporters controlled the party machinery in most of the States. In the Southern States especially, none of which had chosen a Republican elector since 1876, the party was almost synonymous with the federal office-holders, most of whom shaped their political course according to the wishes of the powers in Washington. Protests had often been made against this vicious state of affairs, and some proposals had been made to diminish Southern representation, but nothing had been done, and in 1908 Taft, apparently with Roosevelt's acquiescence, had profited by the situation. In all the Southern States and in many of the Northern States the old convention system, uncontrolled by law, was still in vogue, and this greatly simplified the task of the Taft managers, who hurriedly began to grind out Taft delegates with precision and despatch. The old-line politicians, in their desperation, displayed no squeamishness as to means and methods, for their backs were to the wall and they knew that their own power, as well as that of the President, was at stake.

Had the convention system existed everywhere, Taft's nomination would soon have been assured, but it chanced that in a number of Northern and Western States a system of preferential primaries, safeguarded by law, had recently been established. In some districts where the convention system still prevailed the Roosevelt managers succeeded in choosing the delegates; from many others they

The Fight for Delegates.

The Primary Elections.

sent contesting delegations; but they concentrated their chief efforts on the States having primaries. The first election of this sort took place in North Dakota and resulted in favor of La Follette, with Roosevelt second and Taft trailing far in the rear. Roosevelt then took the stump in his own behalf and attracted vast crowds. Taft followed his example, and the fight soon grew bitter. The President denounced the Roosevelt supporters as "political emotionalists or neurotics," and declared that their success would mean the downfall of our institutions. In reply Roosevelt charged Taft with having fallen under the control of reactionary bosses, and said that though Taft often meant well he meant well feebly. With but few exceptions the preference primaries resulted in Roosevelt's favor. In Wisconsin his supporters left the field open to La Follette, who carried the State over Taft; Taft secured a small plurality in Massachusetts, but lost the 8 delegates at large and 10 of the district delegates. Roosevelt swept Illinois by 138,000, and carried Nebraska, Oregon, Maryland, California, Pennsylvania, New Jersey, South Dakota, and even Taft's own State, Ohio, in most cases by enormous majorities. Out of 360 delegates elected in primaries safeguarded by law, La Follette obtained 36, Taft 46, and Roosevelt 278. In most of the States where a real Republican party existed Roosevelt secured the delegates; Taft controlled all the Territorial and insular delegates and most of those from the Southern States, with a considerable number from New York and other Northern States whose political machinery was controlled by his friends. In Iowa, where the convention system was still in existence, Senator Cummins was a candidate. Roosevelt did not oppose him, and the delegation was about evenly divided between Cummins and Taft.

Roosevelt's supporters declared that so clear an expression of the preference of the Republican rank and file ought to be decisive. Under ordinary conditions this might have been the case, but the bitterness aroused was exceedingly great, and many conservatively inclined Republicans, who stood aghast at the idea of breaking the "third-term" precedent or feared such innovations as the recall of judicial decisions, encouraged the Taft managers to persist in their plan of renominating him

The Contested Seats.
at any cost. Therefore the Taft men retorted that they were under no obligation to change the rules of the game while the game was in progress, and proceeded with their programme. As they controlled a big majority of the national committee, they were able to dictate the decisions regarding the more than two hundred contests heard by that body. Less than a score of these contested seats were awarded to the Roosevelt claimants.

The national convention met at Chicago (June 18) amid intense bitterness and with the Roosevelt supporters openly crying "Steam-roller!" and "Fraud!" In response to a call from

Taft Supporters Control the Convention.
his friends, Roosevelt himself went to Chicago and helped to manage his campaign from outside the convention hall. He was received with great enthusiasm by his followers and said that he felt as strong as "a bull moose." The Taft forces showed signs of wavering and a few delegates went over to the Roosevelt side; it was only by heroic work that Taft's lieutenants managed to hold the rest in line. Many of the contests were brought before the convention, but the Taft contestants who had been seated by the national committee were permitted to vote on one another's right to retain their seats, and after a riotous and dramatic contest the Taft forces managed to organize the convention and to elect Senator Elihu Root as temporary chairman over Governor Francis McGovern of Wisconsin, the Roosevelt nominee, by 558 to 502. The bitterness of the contest may be inferred from the fact that when Root rose to deliver his "key-note" address, he was greeted with derisive cries of "Receiver of stolen goods!"

After further vain efforts to secure a reversal of the convention's stand regarding contested seats, Henry J.

The Protest of the Roosevelt Delegates.
Allen of Kansas read (June 22) a statement to the effect that the national committee had stolen a great number of seats, that the convention no longer represented the party, and that the Roosevelt delegates would decline to vote.

"We shall sit in protest," said Allen, "and the people who sent us here shall judge us." Many of the Roosevelt delegates left the hall and most of those who remained refused to take part in the proceedings. Amid these depressing circumstances what was left of the convention proceeded to adopt a platform and to renominate Taft and Sherman.

Taft and Sherman.

That night Roosevelt's supporters met in Orchestra Hall and, amid tumultuous scenes of excitement and enthusiasm, informally nominated Roosevelt. The Colonel himself appeared in the hall and declared that he had been defrauded, and that, if such practices as had prevailed were condoned and should meet with permanent success, it would mean the downfall of the republic. He asked that a more formal convention be held later and promised that he would accept a nomination tendered by that body or would support any other man it might select.

Roosevelt Nominated Informally.

Meanwhile a vigorous but less spectacular contest had been waged for the Democratic nomination. In that party, as among the Republicans, there was a conservative and a progressive wing that was anxious to control, while many candidates were eager to lead their party to expected victory. Among these were Governor Judson Harmon of Ohio, Congressman Oscar Underwood of Alabama, Speaker Champ Clark of Missouri, and Governor Woodrow Wilson of New Jersey. Harmon and Underwood were most favored by the conservative element; Wilson was regarded as the leading progressive candidate; while Clark's lieutenants flirted with both factions. In both conventions and primaries Clark won the greatest number of delegates, with Wilson second. Clark would undoubtedly have been nominated had it not been for the Democratic rule requiring a two-thirds majority.

The Democratic Contest.

The determining influence in the convention was exercised by William Jennings Bryan. Bryan was determined not to permit reactionary control, and would undoubtedly have precipitated a breach in the party rather than submit to defeat on this vital matter. In the pre-convention contest he had opposed Harmon's candidacy on the ground that Harmon was a friend of Wall Street, and he had even taken the stump in Ohio against him. When the national convention met at Baltimore (June 25), Bryan assumed the leadership of the progressive forces. At first the conservatives controlled, and elected Judge Parker as temporary chairman over Bryan by 579 to 510. But Bryan appealed to the rank and file of the Democracy at home, and in consequence so many protesting telegrams came pouring in to the convention that many of the delegates who had been supporting the conservatives changed their allegiance and enabled the progressives to have their way both as to platform and candidates. On the third day of the convention Bryan precipitated a great uproar by presenting a resolution declaring the convention opposed to the nomination of any candidate for President who was the representative of, or under obligations to, any "member of the privilege-hunting and favor-seeking class," and demanding the withdrawal from the convention of certain capitalist delegates whom he considered as members of that class. In support of his resolution, which he admitted was "extraordinary," Bryan declared that there was not a delegate in the hall who did not know that an effort was being made "to sell the Democratic party into bondage to the predatory interests." After a sensational debate Bryan consented to withdraw the last part of his resolution, and what remained was adopted by a great majority; even many reactionaries voted for it as a matter of policy.

On the first ballot Clark received 440½, Wilson 324, Harmon 148, Underwood 117½, with 56 scattering. For many ballots thereafter Clark had a plurality, and on the tenth ballot Tammany Hall threw its support from Harmon to Clark, and Clark received a small majority. But Bryan, who had been voting for Clark because under instructions to do so from the Democrats of Nebraska, viewed this development with a wintry eye, and in the course of the fourteenth ballot he declared that he would with-

Bryan's Course.

Bryan Secures the Nomination of Wilson.

hold his vote from Clark as long as New York's plutocratic influence was thrown to him. He therefore threw his vote to Wilson, in whose behalf he had been working for some time. Bryan's defection proved a death-blow to Clark's candidacy. The balance began to incline toward Wilson, who sprang into the lead on the twenty-eighth ballot, and on the forty-sixth received the needed two-thirds. For the vice-presidency the convention named Governor Thomas R. Marshall of Indiana.

The Democratic presidential nominee was a newcomer in politics. He was born at Staunton, Virginia, December 28, 1856, of Scotch-Irish ancestry, and was the son of a Presbyterian minister. After graduating from Princeton and from the law school of the University of Virginia, he practised for a short time at Atlanta; then he took graduate work in Johns Hopkins University, and, after receiving the degree of Ph.D., taught history, political science, and kindred subjects at Bryn Mawr College, Wesleyan University, and Princeton University, becoming president of Princeton in 1902. He wrote a popular history of the United States, and a number of other works dealing with history or political science. His entrance into practical politics was partly due to the efforts of his friend and admirer, George Harvey, who persistently advertised Wilson's merits in the pages of his magazines—*Harper's Weekly* and *The North American Review*. In 1910 Wilson was nominated for governor of New Jersey, and was swept into power on the tide of reaction against the Taft administration. As governor he became involved in some bitter quarrels with the reactionary Democratic machine, but managed to secure the enactment of a number of progressive laws.

Woodrow Wilson.

On the 5th of August a great convention of Progressives met at Chicago. The delegates, among whom were eighteen women, displayed an earnestness and enthusiasm which impressed even hostile newspaper correspondents; and delegates and audience sang with the fervor of crusaders such songs as the "Battle Hymn of the Republic" and "Onward, Christian Soldiers." Ex-Senator Beveridge fired the hearts of his hearers with a "key-note" address, and Roosevelt

The Progressive Party.

himself appeared and made a powerful "Confession of Faith," filled with pleas in behalf of social and industrial justice. The convention formally nominated Roosevelt, with Governor Hiram Johnson of California as his running mate. The new party took the name of "Progressive," and adopted the "Bull Moose" as its emblem. Members of the party were popularly known as "Bull Moosers." The name had been suggested by Roosevelt's words on his arrival at Chicago in June; it was first used by enemies as a term of derision, but Progressives perceived its possibilities and adopted it.

In their platform the Progressives combined the Hamiltonian system of nationalism with the Jeffersonian principle of popular rule. The new party's mission was declared to be
Nationalism and Popular Rule. to destroy "the invisible government" that sat enthroned behind the "ostensible government," and "to dissolve the unholy alliance between corrupt business and corrupt politics." The platform favored direct primaries, the short ballot, the initiative and referendum, the recall of executive and legislative officers and of judicial decisions, woman suffrage, conservation, downward revision of the tariff, a non-partisan scientific tariff board, and federal control of industrial corporations engaged in interstate commerce; and laid great stress upon a sweeping programme for social and industrial justice, including workmen's compensation, a minimum wage for women workers, and prohibition of child labor.

Many Republican leaders professed to believe that the Progressives would cut little figure in the campaign, but time quickly showed the hollowness of such predictions. Many of
Progressive Leaders. the most influential men in the old Republican party, including ex-Senator Beveridge of Indiana, Senator Dixon of Montana, Senator Clapp of Minnesota, Senator Poindexter of Washington, Gifford Pinchot, Hugh Hanna, Oscar S. Straus, George W. Perkins, Medill McCormick, James R. Garfield, and Charles S. Bird, enthusiastically took up the Progressive cause. The Progressive platform appealed strongly to idealists and social reformers, and many such persons, including Judge Benjamin B. Lindsey, Raymond Robbins,

Antoinette Funk, and Jane Addams, declared themselves for the new party. Many Republican nominees for presidential electors and other offices withdrew from the ticket in order to support Roosevelt; in several States the Republican organization went over to the Progressives almost intact; and in South Dakota and California the Roosevelt electors ran as Republicans. In Wisconsin, McGovern remained on the Republican ticket as a candidate for governor, but stated that he would vote for Roosevelt. Senator Cummins of Iowa announced that he would continue a Republican, but said that Taft had been nominated by such fraudulent means that he would support Roosevelt. Hadley of Missouri, one of the seven governors who had asked Roosevelt to become a candidate, finally announced that he would vote for Taft, though he expressed disapproval of the methods used to nominate him. Senator La Follette, who had been deeply disgruntled by the desertion of his candidacy, made verbal warfare on both Taft and Roosevelt, particularly on the latter. He accused the Progressive nominee of unbounded ambition and egoism and of being subservient to trusts, and declared that Roosevelt had become progressive only at the eleventh hour. In reply the Progressives republished an article written by the senator in 1909, fulsomely praising Roosevelt, who was then retiring from the presidency.

The Progressives threw themselves into the conflict with the enthusiasm of crusaders, and won converts by the very ardor of their canvass. By November the Bull Moose call was echoing in every forest, and great herds were pouring through every valley and dale. If the Democrats had nominated a conservative candidate, it is possible that the Progressives would have won over enough progressive Democrats to have achieved the seeming impossible; but the selection of Wilson precluded any wholesale desertions from the banner of Democracy. Even as it was, however, a number of rather prominent Democrats, including W. Bourke Cockran of New York, and John M. Parker of Louisiana, supported Roosevelt, while the election figures seem to indicate that some hundreds of thousands of the Democratic rank and file did likewise. On the other hand, it is certain that some Republicans voted for Wilson in order to beat Roosevelt.

Almost from the beginning clear-sighted men saw that Wilson's election was certain, and that the only real doubt concerned whether Taft or Roosevelt would be second in the race.

A Bitter Canvass.

The bitterness that developed between Republicans and Progressives surpassed anything of the sort since the Civil War. Republicans called the Progressives "renegades," "traitors," "disappointed office-seekers," "visionaries"; their leader was a "neurotic," a "demagogue," a "boss boss," seeking to make himself "dictator"; and, strangely enough, an effort was made to convince the people that he was in league with Wall Street. Progressives looked upon the campaign as a new Armageddon, a battle between right and wrong; Taft's nomination was a "steal" managed by a "gang of crooks," and it was put through by an alliance of "crooked business and crooked politics." Their most charitable judgment of Taft was that he was "well-meaning but weak," and that he was surrounded by men who "knew what they wanted," and were "neither weak nor well-meaning."

The Republicans covered dead walls with posters declaring that "prosperity" was in danger and reminding voters that "It is better to be safe than sorry." Their orators denounced

The Republican Plea.

Roosevelt and the Progressives, and appealed to their hearers to remain loyal to the "Grand Old Party." Having learned in the primary contests that he was not a vote-making campaigner, Taft made only a few speeches, but in his few messages to the country he defended his nomination as fair and honorable, declared the Progressives had split off "not for any principle, but merely to gratify personal ambition and vengeance," characterized their platform as "a crazy quilt," and predicted his own election. In notifying Taft of his renomination Senator Root had declared that the action of the Chicago convention had been in accord "with the rules of law governing the party, and founded upon justice and common sense."

Being confident of success, Wilson campaigned somewhat

leisurely, speaking with dignity and perspicacity to large audiences. He dwelt upon the evils of the protective tariff, talked much of the "New Freedom" that he was advocating for business and the people, and accused the Progressives of seeking to legalize monopoly. On the other hand, Bryan, who as usual made an immense number of speeches, thought the Progressive trust remedy socialistic.

The Democratic Campaign.

As befitted the "Bull Moose" candidate, Colonel Roosevelt swept through many States, and everywhere he went the extent of his personal following was revealed in the vast crowds who met to hear and cheer him. On the evening of October 14, when starting from a hotel in Milwaukee to the Auditorium, in which he was to speak, he was shot by John Shrank, a half-crazed fanatic of Bavarian birth, who had long cherished a grudge against Roosevelt for having, when police commissioner of New York, closed a saloon owned by Shrank's uncle. Fortunately the bullet struck a manuscript and spectacle-case in the ex-President's pocket, thereby weakening its force, but the missile entered his breast, causing a deep wound and fracturing a rib. Without waiting to ascertain the extent of his injury, Roosevelt proceeded to the hall and spoke for more than an hour to a large and excited audience. Holding up the manuscript and showing the hole through which the bullet had gone, he said: "It takes more than that to kill a Bull Moose!" Subsequently he was taken to a Chicago hospital and later to his home at Oyster Bay. Thanks to his temperate habits and iron physique, he recovered rapidly, and was able shortly before the election to appear at two monster meetings in New York City. His opponents sought to minimize the political results of the episode, some even criticised his course after the shooting, but it is beyond question that sympathy and admiration for his "gameness" won him many votes.

Roosevelt Wounded.

Most voters went to the polls believing that the main result was a foregone conclusion, and the outcome justified this view. Wilson carried 40 States, and won 2 of the electoral votes of California, receiving a total electoral vote of 435 and a popular vote of 6,286,214. Roosevelt received 11 electoral votes in California, and carried Pennsylvania, Michigan, Minnesota, South Dakota, and Washington, his total electoral vote being 88 and his popular vote 4,126,020.

Wilson
Elected.

Taft carried only Utah and Vermont, with 8 electoral votes, and received a popular vote of 3,483,922. The Democrats also elected a great majority in the House of Representatives and a working majority in the Senate. The Socialist vote increased to 898,296, but that party lost its seat in the House. In one sense the Democratic victory was not so overwhelming as it seemed, for the combined popular vote of Roosevelt and Taft exceeded that of Wilson by 1,323,728; and the combined vote of all the minority parties exceeded Wilson's vote by 2,458,741. In fact, owing to the peculiarities of our electoral system, if 250,000 voters in the right States had transferred their ballots from Wilson to Roosevelt, the latter would have received a majority of the electoral votes and the presidency. Wilson had won, as Lincoln had won in 1860, as a result of division among his opponents.

The Progressives felt that they had gained a moral victory, and declared that the large majority of Roosevelt's popular vote over Taft's set at rest any question as to which man had been the real choice of the Republican party.

What of
the Future?

Most Progressives went further and proclaimed the view that the Republican party was doomed to disappear and that the Progressive party had a glorious future before it. In reality, however, dissatisfaction with Taft and enthusiasm for Roosevelt had been important factors in the great Progressive showing, and many voters had cast their ballots for Roosevelt without ceasing to consider themselves Republicans. Serious as was the split—and the historian has to go back to 1860 to find anything to equal it—it was not so complete as it seemed. In many States and smaller divisions Republicans and Progressives, though differing as to the heads of the ticket, supported the same candidates for Congress and local offices. This state of affairs proved chiefly to the advantage of the Republicans, and, though badly outvoted by the

Progressives in the presidential contest, they won many more local offices and seats in Congress.

For the time being, however, decidedly the most interesting political question was: Will the Progressive party or the Republican party survive? The answer depended in large measure upon whether the course of the victorious Democrats proved progressive or reactionary.

CHAPTER XX

On March 4, 1913, a great crowd assembled before the east front of the Capitol to witness the inauguration as President of the first Democrat who had taken that solemn obligation in twenty years. The day was pleasant, the arrangements were well made, and the multitude had an excellent opportunity to see and hear the man who, in little more than two years, had sprung from the presidency of a university to the presidency of the nation. Woodrow Wilson's inaugural address was pitched on a high plane, and its sentiments were decidedly "progressive" in tone. The new President had a gift for language, and the speech contained passages that were much admired. One of the most quoted was as follows:

"This is not a day of triumph; it is a day of dedication. Here muster not the forces of party, but the forces of humanity. Men's hearts wait upon us; men's lives hang in the balance; men's hopes call upon us to say what we will do. Who shall live up to the great trust? Who dares fail to try? I summon all honest men, all patriotic, all forward-looking men, to my side. God helping me, I will not fail them, if they will but counsel and sustain me."

In selecting his cabinet Wilson fulfilled most predictions and pleased millions of Democrats by naming William Jennings Bryan, Democracy's thrice disappointed leader, as secretary of state. Bryan's immense influence in the party made some such offer almost compulsory; to have ignored him would have been to alienate a great section of the party at the very outset; furthermore, Wilson owed the "Commoner" a great political debt for decisive work done in the Baltimore convention. Bryan had never made any profound study of the practices of diplomacy, but it was not expected that the duties of the position would be very difficult, and one of the ablest authorities on international law in the country was called to the State Department as counsellor.

The other cabinet appointees were much less prominent. The best known was probably Secretary of the Treasury William G. McAdoo, who had won a reputation by building the first tunnel under the Hudson River. In the following year he married one of Wilson's daughters, and he proved to be the man upon whom the President leaned most. Of the other members probably the most capable was Franklin K. Lane of California, a former member of the Interstate Commerce Commission, who became secretary of the interior. In the closing days of Taft's administration the Department of Commerce and Labor had been divided, and to the new Department of Labor the President called William B. Wilson of Pennsylvania, a Scotchman by birth, one of the founders of the United Mine Workers of America, and a member of the Sixtieth, Sixty-first, and Sixty-second Congresses. Upon the whole it was a cabinet that was distinguished neither for ability nor for the lack of it.

Other Cabinet Members.

Five of the cabinet appointees were Southerners by birth, though McAdoo, like the President himself, had settled in the North. The chief justice of the Supreme Court, the Democratic leaders in the House and Senate, even twelve members of the Senate chosen from Northern and Western States, were likewise Southern-born; there were more Confederate than Union veterans in Congress; the chairmen of most of the great committees could sing "Dixie" much better than "Marching through Georgia." It was truly said that the South was "back in the Union and in charge of the Union."

The South in Control.

To many Democrats the change in administration was chiefly interesting because it afforded a prospect for offices. But time and civil service reform had worked great changes. Presidents Roosevelt and Taft had placed the consular service, many subordinate positions in the diplomatic service, and practically all post-office employees except first, second, and third class postmasters under

The Question of Offices.

civil service rules, and had otherwise extended the merit system. The incoming administration stood pledged to civil service reform, and Wilson was himself a vice-president of the Civil Service Reform League. Upon the whole, the President seemed inclined to uphold the merit system, and early in his second administration he took a step forward by extending the competitive system to all first, second, and third class postmasterships. However, there were backward steps—the diplomatic service was somewhat demoralized by substituting, in certain cases, raw men for experienced diplomatists; and in this and other departments Democratic spoilsmen found many ways of rewarding "deserving" party workers.

The new administration hastened to take up the task of writing into law its legislative programme. During the campaign Wilson had said much regarding economic evils and the remedies he proposed to apply, and some of these speeches, in revised form, had been gathered into a book entitled *The New Freedom*, so called after a phrase that recurred in it again and again. Many readers of the book thought it vague in concrete proposals, but the gist of it was that American economic conditions had been transformed, great monopolies had sprung up, and the federal government had become "a foster-child of special interests." Wilson said that he was for honest business, no matter how "big," but he proposed to destroy monopoly, which he assumed had been built up, not by economy, intelligence, or efficiency, but by special favors and reprehensible practices; he constantly insisted upon the "restoration" of older liberties, and by this most people inferred that he meant to restore the era of competition. Many political economists doubted the virtue of his panacea.

In accordance with a determination announced soon after his election, the new President speedily summoned Congress to meet in extra session on April 7. When the two houses had organized he revived a custom that had been disused since the days of the elder Adams, and appeared before them in person and read his message. This revival caused much com-

ment, some of it unfavorable; Wilson himself explained that
it enabled him to enter into closer relations with the legislative branch. The fact was, he had decided to follow the Roosevelt rather than the Taft conception
of the presidential office; to assume the position of
a leader, even in legislative matters. In view of
the lack of coherence in his party, it is probable that
his decision was wise. Some Democratic legislators resented
his interference, but most, realizing how often their party had
failed because of lack of unity, submitted with surprisingly good
grace.

Wilson
Revives
Custom of
Addressing
Congress in
Person.

As the first steps in his programme, Wilson asked for the
passage of a new tariff act, a new currency-and-banking act,
and for new trust legislation.

The tariff was the first of these subjects taken up. In due
course a bill was reported from the House Committee of Ways
and Means by Chairman Underwood. It was based in large
measure upon the "pop-gun" bills vetoed by Taft.
The measure quickly passed the House by a vote
of more than two to one, but in the Senate deliberation proved much more extended. In both houses there
were the usual attempts at "trading," and agents of the protected interests flocked to Washington in such droves that Wilson issued a public statement denouncing the "extraordinary
exertions" of an "insidious and numerous lobby." Both
houses investigated the lobby evil, and the House committee's
inquiry, which reached back for thirty years, laid bare some
startling facts regarding the use of underhand and corrupt influences in determining legislation in the past.

The Tariff
Lobby.

The Underwood bill, as amended by House and Senate, was
finally enacted into law early in October. It was by no means
a free-trade measure, but it reduced duties on over nine hundred
articles, especially on necessities, such as food and
clothing, and it placed raw wool, iron ore, steel rails,
and rough lumber on the free list. The sugar rates
were reduced a fourth, and that commodity was to be placed
on the free list from May, 1916. This sacrifice of the sugar-

The
Underwood
Bill.

growing interests of the country aroused much opposition in the sugar-producing sections; both the senators and some of the representatives from Louisiana voted with the Republicans in opposition to the act. In that State the sugar schedule provoked such an uprising against the Democratic party that in April, 1916, the clause putting sugar on the free list was repealed. The act also contained a clause designed to prevent the "dumping" of foreign goods into the United States at ruinously low rates; it established absolute free trade with the Philippines; and it remitted 5 per cent of the duty on goods imported in American ships, the idea being to encourage the development of our merchant marine. The act did not provide for a tariff commission of any sort, but subsequently agitation in favor of such a body became so strong that in September, 1916, Congress created a bipartisan Tariff Commission of six members to gather information on tariff problems.

It was certain that the new tariff schedules would prove considerably less productive in taxes than the old, so an income-tax feature was added. A tax of 1 per cent was levied on the profits of corporations and on individual incomes in excess of $3,000 in the case of single persons, or $4,000 of married persons. On large individual incomes a graduated surtax was levied, running from 1 per cent on incomes between $20,000 and $50,000, to 6 per cent on incomes in excess of $500,000.

An Income Tax.

On June 23, while the tariff bill was still under consideration in the Senate, President Wilson again appeared before Congress and urged the enactment of a new banking-and-currency law. The need of some such measure had long been recognized by both the great parties. Under Taft the National Monetary Commission, headed by Senator Aldrich, had reported a tentative scheme for reform, but no legislation resulted. A measure known as the Glass-Owen bill was introduced in the House three days after President Wilson's appeal, and after long consideration and some amendments it was enacted into law in December, after the regular session had convened. The main objects of the act were to

Federal Reserve System.

provide a more elastic circulating medium, to reorganize banking in such a way as to render funds better available to meet unusual demands, and to destroy the so-called "money trust," a gigantic concentration of money power the menace of which had been emphasized by facts brought to light by a House committee late in the Taft administration. The act established a system of reserve banks under the central control of a Federal Reserve Board, consisting of the secretary of the treasury, the secretary of agriculture, and the comptroller of the currency *ex officio*, and of four other members appointed by the President with the approval of the Senate. It also authorized the issuance of "federal reserve notes" on the security of commercial paper instead of government bonds, as in the case of the old national-bank notes, for which the new notes were gradually to be substituted. During the next few years the new system proved equal to the needs of most unusual situations, though at present (1920) some critics assert that it tends to a dangerous inflation of the currency. It is not improbable that the act will be considered the most notable achievement of Wilson's first administration.

Early in 1914 Congress took up the trust problem. Five bills, popularly known as the "five brothers," were introduced, and after many months of deliberation two acts were passed. One of these created a Federal Trade Commission, modelled somewhat after the Interstate Commerce Commission. The new commission was given wide powers of investigating matters connected with interstate trade and the management of corporations engaged in interstate trade, and more restricted powers of enforcing antitrust regulations forbidding unfair methods. The other measure, the Clayton Act, prohibited interlocking directorates of banks and other corporations and forbade discrimination in prices when the effect would tend to produce monopoly, and placed under the ban various other practices used by monopolists. Labor and agricultural organizations, "lawfully carrying out the legitimate objects thereto," were exempted from the provisions of the act, and, as a special concession to labor, the injunction powers of the federal courts in labor disputes were greatly curtailed. A bill to regulate the issue of stocks and bonds by common carriers and designed to strike a blow at the plundering practices connected with "watered stock" caused so much opposition that it was dropped.

In some quarters the new trust measures were hailed as a final solution of the great problem. Only time can tell whether or not such predictions were well founded. It should be said, however, that price manipulation and other evils continue, in some cases to an extent hitherto unheard of. It would be unsafe, therefore, to assume that the last word has been said on the trust question.

In the enactment of all these laws President Wilson's influence was insistent and powerful. He gained his ends partly by prodding but largely by persuasion. The docility with which the Democratic factions submitted to his driving was surprising, because for years that party had seemed like a balky team, never willing to pull together. Now and then Democratic pupils displayed signs of restiveness, but "the schoolmaster" always proved his mastery and enforced his discipline. "Mr. Wilson is the whole thing at this juncture," wrote a veteran political observer in *Harper's Weekly* early in 1914. "He dispenses the high and the low and the middle justice. He has suffered no notable rebuff in putting into effect his plans and his ideas. The processes of government reflect his will. The members of Congress do not love him, but they do not doubt the quality of the man. . . . He is, indeed, chief magistrate to the uttermost fringe of his authority."

Wilson's Influence.

Both Wilson and Bryan came to their respective offices with a passion for peace and with theories as to how it could be maintained. Under Roosevelt more than a score of limited arbitration treaties had been concluded with as many nations, and under Taft the arbitration principle had been still further advanced. Bryan plunged into this sort of work with eagerness. In his opinion wars usually result from action taken too precipitately, and he

Bryan and Arbitration.

believed, with much truth, that some plan for delaying action until passions had cooled would be helpful. Less than two months after assuming office he laid before the diplomatic corps at Washington a proposal that each foreign nation should enter into an agreement with the United States to submit to an international tribunal for investigation and report any dispute upon which an agreement could not be reached. During the interval—the period suggested was one year—neither power concerned should declare hostilities or increase its military programme. The plan was cordially received in most foreign capitals, and before the end of the year thirty-one nations signified a willingness to accept. Ultimately treaties embodying the delay principle were concluded with most of the powers of the world, including England and France. Germany and Austria, long the chief stumbling-blocks in the way of international conciliation, held aloof. It was fortunate they did so. It is easy to see that it would have been highly embarrassing in February, 1917, for the United States to have been bound by such a treaty with either.

As set forth in an earlier chapter, President Roosevelt expressed the view that in flagrant cases of "wrong doing or impotence" on the part of other American states, it might become necessary under the Monroe Doctrine for the United States to exercise "an international police power." Acting on this theory, he established a virtual protectorate over Santo Domingo. His successor sought to make a similar arrangement with regard to Nicaragua, which for years had been a scene of disorder and revolution, but he met with much opposition in the Senate, which rejected one treaty and failed to take action upon another. Notwithstanding, Taft sent a representative to Nicaragua to take charge of the customs. The opponents of the treaty were mainly Democrats, some of whom contended that American activity in the Caribbean region was chiefly due to selfish "dollar diplomacy," a name also bestowed upon American policy in the Orient. But the logic of events, in the shape of continued disorders, proved too strong for the Wilson administration. A new treaty was negotiated in 1914 with Nicaragua and this was finally ratified. Furthermore, anarchical conditions in Haiti forced the United States in 1915 to impose a more radical protectorate over that country than any yet arranged. By the treaty concluded with Nicaragua the United States acquired exclusive and perpetual right to construct an interoceanic canal across that country, and also the right to use Fonseca Bay on the Pacific coast and the Corn Islands on the Caribbean side as naval bases.

By payment of $25,000,000 to Denmark the United States in 1916 acquired the Virgin Islands, to the eastward of Porto Rico. The United States had long desired the islands for strategic reasons, and both Seward and John Hay had negotiated treaties of cession, only to see the Danish Parliament reject them—probably in the last instance because of hostile German influence. But the Great War had brought financial embarrassments to the Danes, and they at last proved willing to dispose of their West India possessions.

Purchase of the Danish West Indies.

Ever since the Panama revolution Colombia had nourished a grudge against the United States. To promote better relations, and, critics asserted, to display disapproval of Roosevelt's course in the matter, the Wilson administration negotiated a treaty with Colombia expressing "sincere regret that anything had occurred to mar the relations of cordial friendship that had so long subsisted between the two nations." The treaty further bound the United States to pay Colombia $25,000,000. But all the administration's efforts to pacify Colombia were balked by opposition in the Senate.

Colombian Treaty.

Soon after Wilson's inauguration a renewal on the Pacific coast of anti-Japanese agitation produced a serious diplomatic controversy and gave the country some anxious moments, but a much more persistent source of trouble was the state of Mexican affairs. In that country for many years Porfirio Diaz had maintained peace with a hand of iron, and Mexico had witnessed great national progress. The prosperity of the common people, the peons,

Mexican Revolution.

had not kept pace with mines, railroads, telegraphs, and other signs of civilization. Most of the peons were poor and degraded, few of them could read or write, and many lived on vast estates in a condition comparable to that of serfdom in the Middle Ages. In 1910 the hundredth anniversary of Mexican independence was celebrated with much ceremonial, and Diaz received congratulations from all over the world upon the success of his rule. But the nominal President and actual dictator was now an old man, and had lost much of his once great mental and physical vigor. Hardly had the echoes of the celebration died away when uprisings broke out in Chihuahua and Durango, and soon spread to other provinces. The chief leader among the revolutionists was Francisco I. Madero, a member of a wealthy and powerful family, who seems to have sincerely desired to uplift his people. Finding resistance hopeless, Diaz, in the following May, resigned and sailed for Europe. In October Madero was formally elected President, and a better day for Mexico seemed to have dawned. But outbreaks against his authority soon occurred, and in February, 1913, he was treacherously overthrown, taken prisoner, and assassinated. General Victoriano Huerta, commander-in-chief of the army and one of the conspirators responsible for Madero's destruction and death, seized power as provisional president.

From the outset American property in Mexico had been destroyed and American lives imperilled, but President Taft, though often urged to intervene, confined himself to protests, to concentrating (March, 1911) 20,000 regulars along the border, and to establishing (March 14, 1912) an embargo against the shipment of arms to factions opposing Madero, whose authority he had recognized. President Wilson also pursued a policy of what he later designated as "watchful waiting." He refused to recognize the Huerta government.

"Watchful Waiting."

Huerta's authority was never submitted to by all of Mexico, and an armed movement against him was soon under way. The party opposing him called themselves "Constitutionalists"; they were most active in the northern provinces, and their

most noted leaders were Venustiano Carranza and Francisco
Villa. Carranza, who assumed the title of "provisional President," came of good family and was well educated,
being a lawyer by profession. Villa sprang from the
peon class, had learned to write his name only after
attaining manhood, and had been and remained a bandit. But
he was a bold man, of rough, primitive force, with a natural
gift for leadership.

Carranza and Villa.

Though ostensibly giving aid to neither party President
Wilson desired the success of the Constitutionalists
and made no secret of his wish to eliminate Huerta.
Negotiations designed to persuade Huerta to efface
himself failed. Outrages against Americans and other foreigners
continued, but, in spite of a growing demand for intervention, Wilson held to his policy of "watchful waiting." The
cost of intervention in blood and money, fear that once in
Mexico we would either have to annex it or declare it a de-
pendency, unwillingness to interfere in the internal affairs of
other peoples, and a belief that intervention would antagonize
Latin-American sentiment were among the arguments put forward by the President's supporters in behalf of the "hands off"
policy. Those favoring a more vigorous course pointed to the
vast investment of American capital in Mexico and to the many
outrages committed against our citizens, and argued that, in
view of the inability of Mexicans to govern themselves, intervention was inevitable in the end and might as well come at
once.

Demand for Intervention.

In February, 1914, in the interest of the Constitutionalists,
the President revoked the embargo on arms, thereby, of course,
further antagonizing the Huerta faction. Two months later
some bluejackets from an American war-ship landed
at Tampico, the outlet of the great Mexican oil-
fields, and were arrested by a local Huerta military
officer. They were speedily released by order of a superior
officer, and expressions of regret, in which Huerta joined, were
tendered. There had been other exasperating "incidents,"
and Admiral Mayo, who commanded the American vessels off

Seizure of Vera Cruz.

the port, demanded a salute to the flag, and he was backed up by the President. Huerta refused, and the Gulf fleet, on wireless orders from Washington, thereupon bombarded and seized (April 21, 1914) the city of Vera Cruz. Nineteen Americans were killed, while the Mexican losses, including some noncombatants, were several times greater. Six thousand regulars under General Funston were hurried to Vera Cruz to hold the city. The capture of Vera Cruz was fiercely resented by Mexicans of all factions, even by Carranza. The American Congress passed resolutions justifying the step, but many persons doubted the wisdom of what had been done. Because of Huerta's attitude the embargo on the shipment of arms was restored.

The diplomatic representatives in Washington of Argentina, Brazil, and Chile now tendered (April 25, 1914) their good offices to arrange a peaceful adjustment. As a result a so-called "A B C Conference," in which representatives of the mediators, of Carranza, and of the United States met at Niagara Falls, Canada, and remained in session for some weeks, but without accomplishing anything of much consequence. However, Wilson's acceptance of mediation helped convince Latin America that the United States did not desire to conquer Mexico.

Meanwhile Huerta's position had steadily grown weaker. In the middle of July, 1914, he resigned and fled to Europe. The Constitutionalists soon entered the capital. Some Americans believed that peace and order would soon be restored in the distracted country. The triumph of "watchful waiting" was proclaimed. Such assumptions were premature. Villa and Carranza soon quarrelled, and a new war broke out, fully as frightful as the old. In September Wilson ordered the evacuation of Vera Cruz, but conditions were so threatening that the actual evacuation did not take place until November 23. The maltreatment of Americans in Mexico continued, and lawless bands of marauders even extended their operations to American soil.

Meanwhile the struggle for survival between Republicans

and Progressives had given piquancy to politics at home. The disaster in 1912 had proved a stunning blow to the "Old Guard" Republican leaders. Conciliation, not coercion, became their watchword. All over the land the Progressives were implored to "come back" and help defeat the common enemy, the Democrats. Nor did the appeal lack potency with many of the Progressive rank and file and even with some of the chief leaders. Furthermore, a mild reconstruction of Republican national convention machinery was carried out, and the excessive representation of Southern States was somewhat reduced, but not to a basis of the actual voting strength of Republicans in those States. Most Progressives continued, however, to insist that they intended to remain with the new party and scornfully repelled Republican overtures.

Republican Overtures to Progressives.

The local and State elections of 1913 proved distinctly encouraging to Republicans and discouraging to Progressives, but it was clear that the decisive test would come in the autumn of 1914. Meanwhile an industrial depression settled down on the land. The winter of 1913–14 saw business dull in many lines, and an increasing number of men out of work. Conditions grew slightly worse during the spring and summer, and the outbreak of the Great War in Europe for a time threatened to precipitate a business cataclysm. Political opponents of the administration cried, "I told you so!" and attributed the hard times to the Democratic tariff and general Democratic incompetence. In the fall elections there was a decided reaction against the Democrats, and they were saved from disaster only by reason of the fact that the opposition was still divided. As it was, they managed to carry a number of former Republican States, such as Massachusetts, Michigan, and Nebraska, and to increase their majority in the Senate by two, but their House majority fell from 147 to only 29. The Democratic loss inured almost wholly to the advantage of the Republicans, who carried many of their former strongholds, and also New York. The Progressives, in spite of vigorous campaigning by Colonel Roosevelt, ex-Senator Beveridge, and other prominent leaders, carried only one State,

A Republican Revival.

namely California, where they re-elected Governor Johnson. Their popular vote fell to about 1,800,000, less than half that in 1912, while their representation in the House was cut from 15 to 7. It was clear that the Progressives were doomed.

In this election the choice of senators by direct vote received a trial, in accordance with the new amendment. Another feature was that the Socialists again elected a member of Congress, in the person of Meyer London of New York City.

In the following year anarchy continued to reign in most of Mexico, the capital changed hands repeatedly, and many of the unhappy people were reduced to a state of starvation. Toward the end of the year Carranza's power increased, and in October the United States and several of the Latin American states accorded him recognition as the *de facto* ruler. The embargo on arms, which had been lowered, was reimposed in order to weaken the Villa forces. The Carranza government was also permitted to transport troops across American soil in order to attack rebel forces that could not readily be reached otherwise.

These measures greatly angered Villa. Furthermore, he was worked upon by German agents, who were anxious to embroil the United States with Mexico and thus distract American attention from submarine outrages. It is now known that large sums of money were sent to the bandit leader by these agents. Soon Villa began murdering Americans wherever found. As a culminating act he swooped down one night (March 9, 1916), with several hundred followers, upon the little town of Columbus, New Mexico, and killed eight soldiers and nine civilians, and wounded several others. Some of the raiders were themselves shot down in the attack, while a detachment of cavalry pursued the party for miles, killing many and capturing others.

Villa's Raid on Columbus.

It was announced that a punitive expedition would be sent into Mexico in pursuit of Villa, but that it would be conducted "with scrupulous respect" for Mexican sovereignty. Lack of proper transport facilities and other necessary equipment caused the loss of valuable time, but on March 15 a force of 6,000 men under Brigadier-General John J. Pershing crossed the border on a "cold trail." It was popularly assumed that they meant to get Villa "dead or alive." The Villistas retreated into a wilderness of deserts and mountains, and long managed to evade their pursuers, but on March 29 a cavalry force under Colonel Dodd defeated and dispersed a band at San Geronimo. Villa was severely wounded in this fight, and long remained in hiding. This did not, however, bring the trouble to an end, and early in May there was a new raid into Texas.

A Punitive Expedition.

Many of the Mexican people viewed the expedition as a "Gringo invasion," and Carranza repeatedly protested against the continued presence of the troops on Mexican soil. In the middle of June General Trevino announced that he would not permit the movement of American troops in any direction except toward the border. Soon afterward a clash took place at Carrizal, and a force of American colored cavalry were defeated and scattered, with a loss of about twenty killed and seventeen captured. The immediate release of the prisoners was demanded and was soon conceded. In view of the threatening state of Mexican affairs, President Wilson had ordered out practically all of the National Guard, and he sent most of them to the border to do patrol duty. The mobilization was badly conducted, and the weakness of the American military system was again revealed. It was expected by many that vigorous action would at last be taken in Mexico, but the administration resumed its "watchful waiting." General Pershing was condemned to inaction, and early in 1917 his force was withdrawn from Mexico altogether. The affairs of that unhappy country continued to be distracted, and American lives and property in Mexico and along the border continued to be unsafe. In May, 1920, Carranza was overthrown and slain. After more than nine years of revolution, there seemed no immediate prospect that peace and quiet would be restored. In fact, anarchy, not order, seems to be the normal state of affairs in Mexico, as a study of her his-

Pershing's Force Withdrawn.

tory during the last century reveals. The state of peace under the Diaz régime was abnormal.

From the summer of 1914 onward Mexican affairs were largely overshadowed by the Great War. This tremendous struggle, which was begun by Austria's declaration of war on Serbia (July 28), and Germany's declaration of war against Russia four days later, spread with amazing rapidity, and soon most of the great powers were involved in it. For years well-meaning but short-visioned pacifists had been assuring the world that there would never be another serious war, and yet, almost in the twinkling of an eye, most of the civilized nations were locked in the bloodiest conflict of the ages.

The Great War.

The responsibility for precipitating the war is already fixed. In general it rests upon the houses of Hohenzollern and Hapsburg—two mediæval anachronisms in a modern world—upon the war lords surrounding them, and lastly upon their deluded people. In the final analysis, it rests upon Kaiser Wilhelm II, for it could never have come without his consent, approbation, and instigation. For hundreds of years, by conquest, purchase, marriage, and other methods, his ancestors had built up their dominions until the nation over which they ruled was one of the most powerful in the world. But the Kaiser was not content. In half a century Prussia had waged three wars, none of which had been costly in blood or treasure, and all of which had been enormously profitable. The war lords believed that Great Britain was so distracted by her Irish troubles that she would stand aside. They expected an easy and speedy victory over Serbia, Russia, and France. The German people had been taught to believe in the justice of might and to look forward to the day when Germany would force her *Kultur* upon the world. With few exceptions Germans cheerfully plunged after their war lords into the bloody vortex. Every proposal to adjust the controversy by diplomacy, by an international conference, or by arbitration was pushed aside. The naked sword was to rule. Germany struck for "*Weltmacht oder Niedergang,*" for "world power

The Responsibility.

or downfall." From the outset she followed a deliberate policy of *Schrecklichkeit*, or "frightfulness." She began by making a dastardly attack upon the neutrality of a little nation she was bound by treaty to protect. It was not long before she cast all international law to the winds, and was violating most other laws, both human and divine.

From the beginning many Americans realized that the Entente Allies were fighting for civilization, but the attitude of some others was determined by prejudices rather than by the merits of the case. Both belligerents presented their cases and asked the sympathy of our people. Unfortunately not all Americans were well enough informed to be able to discriminate between the true and the false, and it is well known that fiction is often more convincing than fact. Furthermore, the German Government had long had agents at work in America preparing for the day that had now come. Many people, therefore, took the German side in the controversy. Many others remained indifferent. Not a few assumed that it was a conflict in which no vital principle was at stake on either side. But the ruthless violation of innocent Belgium and the long train of Teutonic barbarities gradually swung the great mass of Americans into antagonism to the powers guilty of such offenses against humanity.

American Sympathies Divided.

Very early in the conflict the American Government proclaimed a policy of strict neutrality. On August 18 President Wilson went further, and issued an appeal in which he said that "Every man who really loves America will act and speak in the true spirit of neutrality, which is the spirit of impartiality and fairness and friendliness to all concerned. . . . I venture, therefore, my fellow countrymen, to speak a solemn word of warning to you against that deepest, most subtle, most essential breach of neutrality which may spring out of partisanship, out of passionately taking sides. . . . We must be impartial in thought as well as in action." But he asked the impossible. Men who knew what was back of the war could not feel "friendliness" toward those guilty of plunging the world into such

Wilson Asks Americans to be Neutral in "Thought and Action."

a disaster. Three years later, looking back to that time, Vice-President Marshall publicly confessed that he had been at fault for having even attempted to be neutral when such issues were at stake.

The effect of the war on American economic interests was at first unfavorable. Business conditions were already bad, and they grew much worse during the fall and winter of 1914–15.

Effect of the War on American Business. Stock exchanges were closed for a time, foreign commerce was demoralized, and gold flowed toward Europe to an alarming extent. Then, though commerce with the Central Powers soon practically ceased, the Entente Allies began to draw supplies of many sorts from America, and thereby gave business a great impetus. The volume of this export business became so vast that the excess of exports over imports, which was only $324,000,000 in 1914, was $1,768,000,000 in 1915, and about $3,000,000,000 in 1916. The Allied powers were forced to send gold to the United States to meet the unfavorable balance of trade, and presently there was actually a plethora of gold in this country. Unable to continue sending gold, the Allies pledged American securities held by their people. Ultimately large loans were floated in the United States, and the money thus obtained was used to pay for goods bought by the Allies. The first foreign loan raised here was, however, a German loan, and some of it was used in instigating measures against the peace and safety of the United States. From being a debtor nation owing $4,000,000,000 or $5,000,000,000 abroad, the United States was soon transformed into a creditor nation.

But as America's economic situation improved, dangerous international complications developed. At the very beginning of the war, by invading neutral Belgium Germany committed one of the grossest violations of international law recorded in history. She immediately followed this up by sowing the high seas with mines that were, of course, dangerous to neutral shipping. Germany sought to justify such acts on the ground that "necessity knows no law"; her defenders must make use of every

German Violations of International Law.

available weapon in order to save their country from annihilation. But such arguments came with ill grace from aggressors.

At first, however, it seemed possible that America's most serious difficulties would be with the Allies. In their efforts to destroy German commerce the Allies resorted to measures that drew protests from our government. Pressure The Allied Blockade. was put by them upon neutral nations, such as Holland and the Scandinavian countries, to prevent them from re-exporting goods brought into their ports, and the list of contraband articles was greatly enlarged. However, international law on many of the points involved had not yet been crystallized, and in defense of the "ultimate destination" rule, that is of stopping the sending of contraband, or conditional contraband, to Germany through neutral countries, England was able to quote a decision of our Federal Supreme Court upholding the right to seize goods going into the Confederacy by way of Mexico. Furthermore, in adopting and enforcing their measures, the British were tender of American susceptibilities, and usually purchased at high rates the cargoes diverted from their destinations. Most important of all, however, the questionable acts of the Allies endangered only property, and not human lives, as was the case with German violations of the law of nations. For this reason, American protests to Great Britain and France were less vigorous than those to Germany. Certainly no acts were committed by these governments that would have justified the United States in doing anything that would aid nations that were engaged in a deadly assault upon civilization.

In all great world wars the side that has been able to gain and hold command of the high seas has emerged victorious from the conflict, or at least has not been defeated. As Mahan pointed out, sea-power has been the determining Importance of Sea-Power. factor in such conflicts from the days of the duels between Athens and Sparta, and Rome and Carthage, down to the time when British fleets foiled the efforts of Napoleon, and finally made possible his downfall.

On land, in the Great War, the Teutonic powers were long

able to set their enemies at defiance, but on the water their war-ships were soon swept off the high seas, and their ocean-borne commerce was paralyzed. As Germany was mainly a manufacturing and commercial country, the loss of most of her foreign trade was very serious. Her war lords realized that unless they could strike a counter-blow on the water their ultimate defeat would be only a question of time. With their submarines and mines they managed to sink a number of enemy war-ships, but the losses thus inflicted made no real impression upon the vast British fleet, while the efforts of their above-water ships proved even more futile. Meanwhile British yards were turning out war-ships much more rapidly than they were destroyed. It was clear that some means must be taken for overcoming this handicap, and in their desperate determination to rule the world or ruin it, the German war lords decided upon the most ruthless step ever taken by a nation calling itself civilized. First, however, they sought a suitable occasion.

The German Dilemma.

On February 2, 1915, Great Britain gave notice that henceforth all shipments of foodstuffs to Germany would be considered as absolute contraband. In justification she pointed out that Germany had just confiscated all grain in private hands and that thenceforth any food going into Germany would very probably be used for the support of the German armies. The Germans at once violently protested against this order, which, they asserted, was meant to doom their whole population to starvation. But their arguments would have had more weight with the neutral world had it not been known that the German armies in 1870–71 blockaded Paris, and reduced the people to eat dogs and cats, and that German soldiers in Belgium and northern France were even then taking food from the starving people. Those who knew Germany felt confident that had Germany, and not England, controlled the seas she would long since have imposed a far more rigorous blockade than any the British had attempted. There was, in fact, a concrete instance of the German policy in such matters. In March, 1915, it was

German Protest against Seizure of Foodstuffs.

learned that the German raider, *Prince Eitel Friedrich*, had, late in January, seized the American sailing-ship, *William B. Frye*, bound from Seattle to Queenstown with a cargo of wheat, and had sunk her on the ground that the wheat was contraband. All German protests sounded hollow after that.

On February 4, 1915, Germany took the drastic step of declaring that after the 18th of that month all waters around the British Isles would be considered a "war zone," and that "all "Frightful- enemy vessels encountered in these waters will be ness" on the destroyed, even if it will not always be possible to Seas. save their crews and passengers." Neutrals were warned not to intrust their people or merchandise to such ships; even neutral vessels entering the zone would expose themselves to grave danger. As the German above-water war-ships rarely dared to venture out of their own harbors, it was evident that Germany had decided to use her submarines in warfare against merchant vessels. It was a well-established principle of international law that such vessels must not be sunk until after all on board had been taken off. But submarines were too small to take on board a considerable number of captives; it was evident that the Germans meant to force passengers and crew to take to open boats, that submarines might even torpedo vessels without giving warning.

The German announcement aroused grave apprehension among neutrals. On February 10 the United States warned the German Government that the proposed measure violated international law, and that should any harm result America's to American ships or citizens, Germany would be Warning. held to "a strict accountability." In reply the German Government insisted upon the necessity of meeting British naval policy with "sharp counter-measures," and disclaimed responsibility for "any unfortunate accidents" that might occur. Acting upon a hint in this note, Secretary Bryan proposed that Great Britain should permit foodstuffs to reach Germany for the use of the civil population, and that Germany should abandon her submarine campaign against merchant vessels, but nothing came from this proposal.

One of the main German objects in attempting this campaign of submarine "frightfulness" was to prevent the shipment of munitions of war to the Allies from America. At the same time an effort was being made in this country

The Trade in Munitions. to bring about the imposition of an embargo on such shipments. Pro-German agents made much of the argument that by permitting the trade in munitions the United States was becoming responsible for prolonging the war. Certain pacifists who exalted peace over justice were taken in by such arguments and aided German sympathizers in their campaign for an embargo. But the movement made small headway. The right of private individuals to sell arms to belligerents was well established under international law, and all well-informed Americans were aware that German firms, notably Krupp's, of which Germans were inordinately proud, had sold munitions in practically every war of recent times.

Notwithstanding the protests of the United States and other neutrals, Germany on the appointed day (February 18, 1915) began ruthless submarine warfare. Within a few weeks the U-boats sank a large number of ships of their en-

The Germans Persist. emies, and of neutrals as well. In some instances warning was given before the fatal torpedo was sped; in others the vessels were torpedoed without warning, with the result that great numbers of persons were slain by the explosions, or were drowned when the ships sank. In either case the survivors, including frequently women and children, were almost invariably compelled to take to small open boats, often when the sea was running high. Many such persons were drowned, or perished of thirst, starvation, or cold.

Late in March the British passenger steamer *Falaba* was torpedoed, and more than a hundred persons lost their lives, among them being an American named Leon C.

Early Outrages. Thrasher. On May 1 the American steamer *Gulflight*, bound for France with a cargo of oil, was torpedoed without warning, and two of her crew were drowned, while her captain died soon after of nervous shock. Other incidents more or less grave took place, but the most terrible was yet to come.

On the day that the *Gulflight* was torpedoed the great British passenger steamer *Lusitania*, one of the largest and finest ships afloat, sailed from New York for Liverpool, with 1,959 souls on board. Not long before her departure the German embassy published advertisements in certain newspapers warning Americans against the dangers of entering the war zone, and it is said that some intending passengers even received telegrams to the same effect. Little heed, however, was paid to these warnings, for the American Government had solemnly protested against the German purpose, and passengers believed Germany would not dare to carry out her threat.

The German Warning.

The voyage proved prosperous until about two o'clock on the afternoon of May 8, when, off the Old Head of Kinsale on the southeast coast of Ireland, the great ship, without the slightest warning, was struck by a torpedo and, according to some accounts, almost immediately by another. Only the pen of a Dante could do justice to the scene of horror that followed—a scene that will forever be remembered with shudders, along with the massacre of St. Bartholomew and the Black Hole of Calcutta, as one of the most dastardly deeds in human history. In that awful moment officers, crew, and passengers—British, Canadians, and Americans alike—displayed heroic qualities in keeping with the best traditions of their race. The cry of "Women and children first!" was raised and heeded. But the stricken ship speedily listed heavily to starboard, so that the decks inclined upward like steep roofs, preventing easy movement, and rendering impossible the launching of some of the boats. Soon she sank, carrying down with her those remaining aboard and many who struggled in the sea about her. In all 1,198 persons lost their lives, including 286 women and 94 children, 34 of the last being babes in arms. The American citizens thus foully done to death numbered 114, among them being Charles Klein, dramatist and author of *The Music Master*;

The Sinking of the *Lusitania*, May 7, 1915.

Charles Frohman, famous theatrical producer; Justus Miles Forman, author; Elbert Hubbard, author and lecturer; Lindon Bates, vice-chairman for relief in Belgium; and Alfred G. Vanderbilt, capitalist. "Save the kiddies!" exclaimed Vanderbilt, while Frohman, a philosopher to the last, said as the ship was about to plunge into the depths: "Why fear death? It is the most beautiful adventure in life."

In Germany the news of the sinking of the *Lusitania* was received with glee. Special medals were struck by way of commemoration, and in places school-children were given a holiday.

German Rejoicings. But the German Government hastily instructed Count von Bernstorff, its ambassador in Washington, "to express its deepest sympathy at the loss of lives on board the *Lusitania*. The responsibility rests, however, with the British Government, which, through its plan of starving the civilian population of Germany, has forced Germany to resort to retaliatory measures." To these crocodile tears German agents added lying statements to the effect that the main damage was done by the explosion of munitions on board, while one of their creatures in New York falsely made affidavit that the ship was armed with naval guns. These tactics were, of course, designed to confuse the issue and divide American sentiment.

In the United States the news was received with a thrill of horror, even by many persons who hitherto had upheld the German cause. Ex-President Roosevelt denounced the deed as "not merely piracy, but piracy on a vaster scale of murder than old-time pirates ever practised."

American Sentiment. Few people ventured openly to justify the deed, but some argued that America should bow before the "mailed fist," and endure the violation of her rights. President Wilson was determined to protest, but hoped that Germany would prove amenable to reason. In a speech at Philadelphia before an audience of newly naturalized citizens he said: "There is such a thing as a nation being too proud to fight. There is such a thing as a nation being so right that it does not need to convince others by force that it is right." These words were severely criticised as unfortunate. In the opinion of the critics Germany had thrown justice and mercy to the winds and cared nothing for the good opinion of the world, if she could only terrorize it. Force, they were convinced, was the only argument the Hohenzollerns respected, and they believed that any suggestion that the United States would not resort to force to uphold its rights rendered future outrages more probable.

The note of protest sent to Germany (May 13, 1915) was signed "Bryan," but it had really been written by the President himself. It emphasized the previous friendly relations between the two powers, upheld the right of Americans to travel on the high seas, pointed out the practical impossibility of using submarines in the destruction of commerce "without an inevitable violation of many sacred principles of justice and humanity," and specified the *Lusitania* and other cases in which American rights had been violated. It expressed a confident belief that Germany would disavow the outrages, would prevent a recurrence of such attacks, and would "make reparation so far as reparation is possible for injuries which are beyond measure." It closed by saying that "the Imperial German Government will not expect the Government of the United States to omit any word or any act necessary to the performance of its sacred duty of maintaining the rights of the United States and its citizens and of safeguarding their free exercise and enjoyment."

The First Lusitania Note.

The German Government took its time about replying, and not until May 28 did it transmit its answer. Reparation was promised for the attack on the *Gulflight*, on the ground that a mistake had been made by the submarine commander, but ruthless submarine warfare and the sinking of the *Falaba* and *Lusitania* were defended on the ground of "just self-defense." The evidence seems to show that the Germans did not take our protest very seriously. In his book, *My Four Years in Germany*, Gerard, American ambassador at Berlin, states that Zimmermann, German undersecretary for foreign affairs, told an American woman not to worry about the breaking of diplomatic relations, as word had

Germany's First Reply.

just been received from the Austrian Government that Doctor Dumba, the Austrian ambassador in Washington, had cabled that Bryan had told him that "the *Lusitania* note from America to Germany was only sent as a sop to public opinion in America, and that the Government did not really mean what was said in that note." It is known that Bryan had an interview with Dumba, but it is unbelievable that an American statesman should have been guilty of such an amazing indiscretion. Gerard himself says that he is sure "that Dr. Dumba must have misunderstood friendly statements made by Mr. Bryan." But Bryan had such a desire for peace that he was opposed to bringing matters to a crisis, and it is possible he did not conceal this view from Dumba. Furthermore, the Germans were well aware that Senator Stone of Missouri, chairman of the Senate Committee on Foreign Relations, and next after Bryan in importance in international matters, was not only a peace-at-any-price man, but a German sympathizer. German-Americans in Germany and in the United States were constantly assuring the Kaiser's government that American public sentiment would not countenance a vigorous policy; "watchful waiting" in Mexico and Wilson's "too-proud-to-fight" speech were not without their influence; therefore, the Imperial Government felt it safe to return a defiant answer. They did not misjudge the situation, for President Wilson had not yet determined to bring the controversy to extremities.

Many Americans and the world at large assumed that the United States would now transmit a real ultimatum. This expectation was strengthened by the sudden resignation (June 8) of Bryan as secretary of state. The explanation given out was that the note in preparation might involve the United States in war. Bryan was succeeded by Robert Lansing, counsellor of the State Department. When the note was given out, however, it was found that it did little more than reiterate the American position; it was not an ultimatum in any sense. The German Government procrastinated a month and then transmitted a reply that was evasive and that made a number of unacceptable suggestions. It was

Resignation of Bryan.

evident that Germany was merely playing for time. Meanwhile she had continued her submarine activities. On May

Second American Note and Second German Reply. 25th an American vessel, the *Nebraska*, was torpedoed off the Irish coast, though fortunately she did not sink. Germany long denied responsibility for the attack, but her guilt was clearly established. American public opinion had grown restive under the long delay, and President Wilson's note-writing proclivities had become a subject of sarcastic and bitter comment both at home

Third American Note. and abroad. The third American note (July 21) proved somewhat more drastic. It characterized the German replies as "very unsatisfactory," and gave warning that a repetition of the acts complained of would be regarded as "deliberately unfriendly." This phrase, in the language of diplomacy, has a special meaning, and connotes an act that will lead to war. Germany vouchsafed no reply to this communication.

Meanwhile German agents spent vast sums of money subsidizing newspapers, forming "leagues" and "societies," and bribing men of influence in order to secure an embargo against

Protests against Munitions Trade. the exportation of munitions of war. On April 4 and on June 29 Austria-Hungary protested that the traffic was unneutral, but our government replied that such trade was fully sanctioned by international law, and pointed to frequent instances in which Germans had engaged in it. The United States stood ready to sell to the Central Powers, and was in no sense responsible for their inability to avail themselves of the privilege. To impose an embargo would be an act of which the Entente Allies could justly complain. Furthermore, the United States, being largely dependent in case of war upon the purchase of munitions from abroad, could not afford to establish such a precedent.

Unable to secure an embargo, German and Austrian agents, working, partly at least, under the oversight and instigation of their ambassadors, Von Bernstorff and Dumba, resorted to violent methods to prevent goods from reaching their enemies. Explosions and incendiary fires damaged munitions plants, bombs were placed aboard vessels carrying cargoes to the Allies, and much property was destroyed and many lives

taken. The whole land was filled with spies, strikes were instigated, and Mexicans were encouraged to murder Americans. In July, 1915, a crack-brained German-American college professor named Erich Muenter, who had disappeared some years before while under suspicion of having murdered his wife, placed a time-bomb in the Supreme Court room in the national capitol, and the explosion did considerable damage. The same man shot and seriously wounded J. P. Morgan, Jr., the fiscal agent of the Allies in America, but was overpowered, and committed suicide in jail. To what extent the government was then aware of Von Bernstorff's nefarious activities has not yet been revealed, but in September, 1915, the President demanded and secured the recall of Dumba, and later of the German naval and military attachés, Captains Boy-Ed and Von Papen. The intrigues and murderous activities of Teutonic agents in this period made up a story so incredible that many trustful Americans, not yet awake to the desperate methods of the war lords, were loath to believe that such things were actually taking place.

While America was protesting, the Germans continued to torpedo merchant vessels, and in August, 1915, two Americans lost their lives in the sinking of the British liner *Arabic*. At

this point, Count Von Bernstorff made vague promises (August 24) of reparation, and on September 1 delivered a memorandum to Secretary Lansing stating that thenceforth "liners will not be sunk by our submarines without warning and without safety of the lives of non-combatants, provided that the liners do not try to escape or offer resistance." Later it was explained that the attack on the *Arabic* had been made by mistake, and regret was expressed, yet Germany refused "to acknowledge any obligation to grant an indemnity." She proposed to submit the particular dispute to The Hague tribunal, but expressly stated that this tribunal should not have the right to make a general decision on the legality of submarine warfare. Early in Oc-

tober, however, Von Bernstorff promised an indemnity for
the lives lost on the *Arabic*, but Germany still continued to
refuse settlement for the *Lusitania* outrage.

In some quarters the German concession was hailed as a
great diplomatic victory, but critics pointed out that the victory was subject to important qualifications in that nothing was
said regarding the safety of the crews of torpedoed
cargo-boats. Furthermore, many Americans were
gravely suspicious of the good faith of the German
Government, and doubted whether it would keep its pledges.
In their opinion, the German civil government did not possess
the real power. They believed that the German Ministry of
Foreign Affairs did not determine international relations, but
merely acted as a mask for the war lords, who were in actual
control. The war lords violated international law, and then put
forward the diplomatists to excuse the violations and to make
adjustments, which might or might not be carried out. Of this
state of affairs our ambassador, Gerard, was well aware at the
time.

The scene now shifted to the Mediterranean. On November 7 the Italian liner *Ancona* was sunk off the coast of
Tunis by a submarine flying the Austrian flag, and several
Americans lost their lives. The United States was
thus forced to take up the whole controversy anew
with Austria, and to demand indemnity for the
victims and punishment for the submarine commander. After
much procrastination, Austria promised (December 3, 1915)
to comply with the demands. Yet attacks on vessels in the
Mediterranean continued, and on December 30 the British
passenger steamer *Persia* was sunk without warning off the
coast of Crete. In this disaster two Americans, one a missionary, the other the United States consul to Aden, were
drowned. In this case the submarine remained submerged,
but the wake of the torpedo was seen. Both Austria and Germany denied responsibility for the act. Later facts came to
light which seemed to prove that the submarine which sank
the *Ancona* was really a German vessel masquerading under

American Doubts.

The Ancona and Persia Cases.

the Austrian flag—a fact that had been suspected from the beginning.

Very early in the war prominent Americans, among them Theodore Roosevelt, Congressman Augustus P. Gardner of Massachusetts, and General Leonard Wood, began urgently to advocate the need of a stronger army and navy to protect American rights. But the mass of the people proved apathetic, while pacifists and pro-Germans strongly opposed preparedness. Secretary Bryan declared that in case of need "the United States could raise a million men between sunrise and sunset." In his annual message of December 4, 1914, President Wilson argued at length against the need of special preparation, though he favored the development of the militia and the extension of voluntary training. "We must depend," said he, "in every time of national peril, in the future as in the past, not upon a standing army, nor yet upon a reserve army, but upon a citizenry trained and accustomed to arms."

The Question of Preparedness.

But Germany's ruthless submarine warfare and the destruction of American lives aroused millions of Americans who deplored "militarism" to a realization that in the last analysis brute force, not right or reason, rules the world, and that America was comparatively defenseless. Despite the threatening state of our relations with Germany, the summer and fall of 1915 passed without anything of much consequence being done save the opening by General Wood of voluntary reserve officers' training camps at Plattsburg. Meanwhile, however, President Wilson had changed his views. In his annual message of December, 1915, he advocated "preparedness," and even made a speaking tour in the Middle West to arouse public sentiment on the question. He declared there was "not a day to be lost," but in speaking of possible dangers he displayed a vagueness that weakened the strength of his appeal. Pro-German influence was thrown unanimously against the preparedness programme, and pacifists ably aided the pro-Germans. In Congress neither party was willing strongly to support preparedness measures. In the

Wilson Changes His View.

face of this opposition and public apathy, Wilson displayed less than his usual decision, and Secretary of War Garrison, who was an ardent advocate of preparedness, resigned (February 10, 1916) because he felt the lack of presidential support. He was succeeded by ex-Mayor Newton D. Baker of Cleveland. Baker was an able man, an exceedingly plausible politician, but the friends of preparedness charged that he had no special qualifications for the post, that he was a pacifist, almost a non-resistant, and they questioned the wisdom of his appointment.

Thereafter the question dragged slowly along. There was much parade of appointing boards and commissions for purposes of defense, and large appropriations were made for both the army and navy, but the concrete results in added fighting strength were disappointing. The most important piece of legislation, the Hay Act (June 3, 1916), provided for increasing the normal peace strength of the regular army by five annual accessions to 175,000 officers and men, though in case of need the number might be raised at once by executive order to 220,000. The State militia, estimated to number 125,000, were to be put under federal control, and were to be increased by five annual accessions to a total of about 425,000. The measure was severely criticised by military experts, and it was largely because he deemed the plan inadequate that Garrison had resigned.

The Hay Act.

Meanwhile the country was flooded with proposals and methods to end war and insure peace. Great numbers of reformers were convinced that they had panaceas that would make war impossible. Societies to eliminate the economic causes of war, world's court leagues, organizations for durable peace, leagues to enforce peace, and similar organizations sprang up. Speakers toured the country—some of them beyond question in German pay —propounding their favorite peace nostrums. A well-known manufacturer even took (December, 1915) a ship-load of pacifists to Europe for the purpose of getting the soldiers "out of the trenches by Christmas." But war stubbornly continued to rage in Europe and even in near-by Mexico.

Pacifist Absurdities.

A constantly increasing number of Allied vessels were being armed with guns as a protection against submarines. The right to do so was well established under international law, but in February, 1915, Germany declared that thenceforth the U-boats would sink such vessels without giving warning. In Congress pro-Germans and pacifists made a strong effort to pass a resolution to keep Americans off such boats, but President Wilson threw his influence against the measure, and it was defeated.

During the winter there had been occasional violations of the pledge made after the *Arabic* sinking, and in April occurred a flagrant case. The British unarmed steamer *Sussex* was torpedoed without warning in the English Channel, and, though she managed to make a French port, many persons were killed by the explosion, and others, including several Americans, were wounded.

Wilson
Threatens
to Sever
Relations.

Germany at first disclaimed responsibility, but pieces of the torpedo were found and they were of German make. The United States thereupon declared that the limit of patience had been reached, and informed Germany that it would sever all diplomatic relations unless Germany "should now immediately declare and effect an abandonment of its present methods of submarine warfare against passenger- and freight-carrying vessels."

Finding further denial useless, Germany somewhat vaguely promised to observe "the general principles of visitation and search." She also promised to punish the guilty submarine commander, but later inquiries regarding the nature of his punishment remained unanswered, and it is improbable that he was treated very rigorously.

The New
German
Promise and
Reservation.

Germany reserved the right to withdraw her concession in case the United States would not persuade the Entente Allies to abandon certain practices of which she complained. The United States accepted Germany's declaration, but stated that it could not consent to the reservation. Upon this point Germany made no further answer.

The outcome was hailed by friends of the administration as

another bloodless diplomatic victory, illustrating the virtue of the President's policy of patience. Many Americans, however, expressed doubt as to whether the victory was so great as was contended. They pointed to Germany's reservation of the right to renew ruthless warfare, and expressed the view that she would keep her pledge only so long as suited her purpose. From Germany Ambassador Gerard warned his government that he "believed that the rulers of Germany would at some future date, forced by the Von Tirpitzes and the Conservative parties, take up ruthless submarine warfare again, possibly in the autumn, or at any rate about February or March, 1917." He renewed this warning when he visited the United States in the autumn. In reality, of course, Germany was merely lulling the United States into a fool's paradise of false security. Meanwhile she kept her shipyards busy day and night building a great fleet of submarines with which to renew her piratical performances on the high seas when her attack would be more irresistible.

Gerard's Warning.

During the greater part of 1916 the international situation was more or less overshadowed by the presidential campaign. It had become apparent by this time that the Progressive party's tenure of life could not be greatly prolonged, and in both the Progressive and Republican camps there existed a strong desire to formulate some plan for united action against the common enemy. By agreement between the two national committees the national conventions of both parties assembled in Chicago on the same day (June 7). They met in separate halls, but protracted negotiations were carried on in the hope of agreeing upon a platform and a fusion ticket.

Progressive and Republican Conventions.

Among the Republican candidates for the nomination were Justice Charles E. Hughes, Elihu Root, Charles W. Fairbanks, Senator Theodore E. Burton of Ohio, and Senator John W. Weeks of Massachusetts. Some Republicans favored naming Roosevelt, and the Progressives insisted that they would accept no other man.

Roosevelt had long been a biting critic of the administration, more especially of its foreign policy, both with regard to Mexico and Germany. He ardently advocated thorough military preparedness as the best insurance against war, and favored a vigorous enforcement, in the old-fashioned way, of American rights. Of our course in regard to the *Lusitania* he said that "the President wrote note after note, each filled with lofty expressions and each sterile in its utter futility, because it did not mean action, and Germany knew it did not mean action." He declared that Wilson was strong in words but weak in action, that he had "met a policy of blood and iron with a policy of milk and water," that his course was "worthy of a Byzantine logothete —but not of an American statesman."

Roosevelt's Criticisms of the Administration.

In a public statement issued upon returning from a trip to the West Indies, Roosevelt announced that he did not care to be President unless the country was in an "heroic mood."

In the Republican convention he received a considerable number of votes, but Hughes was nominated on the third ballot. For the vice-presidential nominee the Republicans once more selected Fairbanks of Indiana. After the second ballot the Progressives, who had been watching the course of events, realized that the Republicans would not take Roosevelt, so they nominated him at about the time that Hughes was named by the Republicans. For the vice-presidency the Progressives put forward John M. Parker of Louisiana, a former Democrat. But Roosevelt realized the hopelessness of the situation, and after considering the matter he declined to run and urged the Progressives to support Hughes. Parker continued in the contest, but he received little support, and the Progressive party virtually disappeared.

Hughes and Fairbanks.

Roosevelt Supports Hughes.

The Republican platform demanded the protection of all American rights, at home and abroad, by land and sea, and charged that in its foreign policies the Wilson administration had resorted to shifty expedients, to phrase-making, and to performances in language only. It gave a vivid description of horrors and outrages in Mexico, denounced the administration's "shameful failure to discharge the duties of this country as the next friend to Mexico," and pledged the Republican party to aid in restoring order in that distracted country. Preparedness was emphasized, as was also the policy of protection. The Underwood Tariff Act was declared to be " a complete failure in every respect."

Republican
Platform.

The Democratic convention assembled in St. Louis on June 14 and renominated Wilson and Marshall by acclamation. The platform pointed to a long list of constructive achievements, favored preparedness and the protection of American rights abroad, condemned organizations that were seeking in America to advance the interests of foreign powers by intimidating the government by threats of reprisal at the ballot-box, and emphasized the diplomatic "victories" of the Wilson administration. On this last subject Senator Ollie James of Kentucky declared that "without orphaning a single American child, without widowing a single American mother, without firing a single gun or shedding a drop of blood, Woodrow Wilson wrung from the most militant spirit that ever brooded over a battlefield a recognition of American rights and an agreement to American demands."

Democratic
Platform.

In the pre-convention campaign pro-German influences had sought to control both parties. The German-American Alliance, an organization dominated by the friends of Germany, had fought Roosevelt's candidacy with particular bitterness. In both the Republican and Democratic parties there was a strong tendency to conciliate the pro-German vote. In the Republican platform and in the speeches of many Republican orators the Wilson administration was denounced for its weak foreign policy, but most emphasis was laid upon Mexican outrages, and comparatively little was said about the *Lusitania* and the other submarine horrors. Colonel Roosevelt, however, did not hesitate to denounce Germany. He characterized Wilson's diplomacy both in Mexico and Europe as weak and pusillani-

Foreign
Policy as an
Issue in the
Campaign.

mous, and declared that his policy made not for peace but for war. Justice Hughes was in no sense pro-German, but at first was more reserved in his language in regard to submarine warfare, though he spoke out vigorously shortly before the election. Toward the end of the campaign a pro-German agitator named Jeremiah O'Leary wrote an offensive letter to the President predicting his defeat, to which Wilson replied: "I would feel deeply mortified to have you or anybody like you vote for me. Since you have access to many disloyal Americans and I have not, I will ask you to convey this message to them." This defiance of alien influence unquestionably won the President many votes. As between the two candidates, Von Bernstoff wrote home after the election that he considered "Wilson as the lesser evil."

In the midst of the campaign the demands of railway engineers, firemen, conductors, and trainmen for an eight-hour day and other concessions precipitated a serious crisis. Suggestions were made that the dispute should be submitted to the Federal Board of Mediation and Conciliation, a body created in 1913, but the brotherhoods refused. Late in August President Wilson called a conference of the brotherhood chairmen and railway managers, but he was unable to persuade them to compromise. On August 28 the brotherhood representatives left the capital bearing orders for a strike to begin on September 4. On the 29th Wilson asked Congress for remedial legislation. A hundred hours later a measure known as the Adamson Eight-Hour Law was ready for his approval. It provided that after January 1, 1917, employees engaged in the operation of trains on interstate steam roads over 100 miles in length should work an eight-hour day, and should receive extra pay for overtime. The wage scale was temporarily to be on the basis of the existing pay, but a commission was to study the question and bring in a report, and a permanent settlement was then to be made. The measure did not apply to switchmen, trackmen, or other employees. Opponents of the law severely criticised the haste with which it was passed. They declared that the government

Adamson Eight-Hour Act.

had been coerced into enacting it, and predicted that the precedent thus set would cause much trouble in the future.

The election proved to be the closest since the Blaine-Cleveland contest of 1884. The early returns which came into New York City seemed to indicate the election of Hughes by a large majority in the electoral colleges, and many

Wilson Re-elected. Democratic newspapers conceded defeat. The Republicans had, in fact, carried Indiana, New York, and other "pivotal" States, but Wilson carried the solid South and Ohio, and ran better than had been anticipated in the West, winning Kansas and almost all of the States in which women voted. The outcome finally hinged upon California, and days passed before the vote in that State could be tabulated. Early in the campaign Hughes had made a tour in California, and while there had consorted with the reactionary Republican leaders and had failed to meet Governor Johnson, former Progressive nominee for the vice-presidency, who was seeking the Republican nomination for senator. For this fatal mistake the Republican national managers were primarily to blame rather than Hughes himself. Subsequently Johnson was nominated, and in his speeches he supported Hughes—at least nominally —but, though Johnson carried the State by almost 300,000 Hughes lost it by 3,773, and with it the presidency. The electoral result finally stood 277 votes for Wilson and 254 for Hughes. The discrepancy between the vote of Johnson and that of Hughes was, however, only partly due to the failure of Hughes to recognize Johnson. In California, as in all other States,

"He Kept Us out of War." the cry, "He kept us out of war," won Wilson many votes. The slogan was particularly effective with women voters, and Wilson carried almost all the States in which women balloted. As regards the Progressives, a large majority undoubtedly followed Roosevelt's leadership and voted for Hughes, but a considerable minority refused to return to the old allegiance. It was the general judgment of political observers that the Republican campaign had been badly managed, and that the Republicans had thrown away what might have been an easy victory.

The Democrats won a considerable plurality of the popular

vote and retained control of the Senate. In the House of Representatives the balance of power would be held by a few Progressives and other independents, and upon them depended which party would be able to organize that body and elect the speaker. The Socialist vote was considerably less than in 1912, being about 590,000. The Socialists retained, however, a seat in the House of Representatives. For the first time a woman, Miss Jeannette Rankin of Montana, was elected to Congress.

During the summer and fall German submarines repeatedly violated, though not in a spectacular way, the pledge given after the sinking of the *Sussex*, but our government ignored these violations. The year had been a hard one for the German army and the German people. The attack on Verdun had been beaten off by the French, and the British had inflicted great losses upon the Germans in the terrific push along the Somme, while the Russians had won a great victory in Galicia. Roumania had finally thrown in her lot with the Allies, but a German drive had resulted in the overrunning of about two-thirds of that country. This victory revived Teutonic spirits, but the people of the Central Powers were in serious distress, and it was necessary to hold up before them another will-o'-the-wisp. On December 12 the German Government surprised the world by transmitting to neutral powers a proposal for a peace conference. But the language used was that of a conqueror, and keen observers believed that the main Teutonic hope was to sow dissensions among the Allies; that, failing to dictate a peace, Germany would resort to a new policy of "frightfulness."

Peace Proposals.

From the beginning of the conflict President Wilson had eagerly sought to play the rôle of peacemaker and had made repeated overtures to that effect. On the subject of peace and regarding our differences with the belligerents there had been many interchanges of opinion of which the general public knew nothing. The confidential agent of the President in these negotiations was often Colonel Edward M. House of Texas, who came and went to Europe on mysterious missions. President Wilson's idea at this time was that there must be a peace by compromise. But the Allies and millions even of Americans believed that an unbeaten Germany would be a world menace and that there must be no peace until those who were guilty of having precipitated civilization into the abyss were forced to make restitution for wrongs done and were deprived of power to offend again in the future. Compromise, therefore, was impossible.

Even before Germany made her peace proposal President Wilson had decided upon a new effort. On December 18, 1916, he asked that all the belligerent powers should state "their respective views as to the terms upon which the war might be concluded, and the arrangements which would be deemed satisfactory as a guarantee against its renewal." In explaining this note, Secretary Lansing said "that we are drawing near the verge of war ourselves." His pessimistic words precipitated a serious stock panic, nor was the country reassured by a second statement issued by him. The note drew replies from both sides but did nothing toward ending the war; neither did a homily delivered (January 22, 1917) by the President before the Senate on world peace, and the methods whereby it could be obtained and observed. In this speech he declared "that it must be a peace without victory," and he emphasized "freedom of the seas," the limitation of armaments, and the adoption of some method of guaranteeing permanent peace.

Nine days later the great blow fell. At six o'clock on the evening of January 31, 1917, Ambassador Gerard was informed by Zimmermann, the German foreign minister, that at midnight the German U-boats would begin unrestricted warfare in a zone surrounding the British Isles and off the western coast of France, and in another zone that included most of the Mediterranean. At four o'clock of the same day a note of the same tenor was handed to Secretary of State Lansing by Ambassador Von Bernstorff. Any ship entering the barred zones, no matter what its cargo, port of departure, or destination, would be ruthlessly sunk without regard to the safety of passengers or crews. As a special concession, however, the war lords gra-

Germany Declares Unrestricted Submarine Warfare.

ciously offered to permit America to send one passenger-ship a week to the port of Falmouth, but the ships must follow a specified route, our government must guarantee that the vessels bore no contraband of war, and the hulls must be painted in alternate stripes of red and white, or as one patriot indignantly declared, "like a barber's pole."

Many explanations have been offered as to why Germany made this astonishing decision to defy not only the United States but the rest of the neutral world. Beyond question the German war lords realized that their plight was desperate, Motives and and that only desperate methods could break the Hopes. strangle hold of the Allied blockade and enable them to win the war. They seem to have hoped that the United States would take no action beyond sending the usual diplomatic notes. Gerard tells us: "The Germans believed that President Wilson had been elected with a mandate to keep out of war at any cost, and that America could be insulted, flouted, and humiliated with impunity." He says that Zimmermann declared that "everything will be all right. America will do nothing, for President Wilson is for peace and nothing else." At the worst, they expected that the United States would not go beyond breaking diplomatic relations. Furthermore, they knew that even if we declared war a long period must elapse before we could become a formidable factor in the conflict. The military weakness of America was much better understood in Berlin than in Washington, and the war lords knew that more than a year must pass before the United States could put an army of any consequence at the fighting front. They hoped to win the war in that interval. In a speech soon after he returned to America, Gerard declared: "If we had a million men under arms to-day, we would not be near the edge of war."

There were pacifists and pro-Germans who insisted that America should meekly bow before the Hohenzollern fist, but the great mass of Americans thought otherwise. President Wilson realized that forbearance had ceased to be a virtue, and that the German declaration closed for the present his altru-

istic endeavors and policy of idealistic hopes. On February 3
he ordered that Ambassador von Bernstorff should be handed
his passports and that our representatives in Germany should return home. On the same day, in a
speech before Congress, he stated that only "actual
overt acts" could make him believe that Germany
would persist in her determination, but he said
that in case his "inveterate confidence" should prove unfounded
he would ask authority to protect our seamen and people on
the high seas. Even yet, however, he had not determined
upon actual war.

Diplomatic Relations Broken, February 3, 1917.

Germany persisted in her piratical course, and several violations of American rights occurred, but for a time nothing took
place that the President thought it wise to consider an "overt
act." On February 26, six days before the end
of the session, the President appeared before Congress and announced that he desired that the United
States should assume a position of "armed neutrality." He
said that he believed that he already had power to authorize
the arming of merchantmen, but he expressed a wish that
Congress would specifically authorize him to do so and thus
support his action. Even as he was speaking, word reached
the capital that a submarine had murdered on the high seas
two American women. On March 1 a despatch from Zimmermann which had come into the hands of our secret service
was published throughout the country, and revealed the fact
that Germany was endeavoring to persuade Mexico
to attack the United States. Germany promised
Mexico "general financial support," while to Mexico
was assigned the simple task of reconquering "the
lost territory in New Mexico, Texas, and Arizona"! The President of Mexico was also to persuade Japan to make peace with
Germany and declare war on the United States. Some pacifists and pro-Germans denied the authenticity of this despatch,
but Zimmermann admitted having transmitted it. The most
skeptical Americans were at last convinced that the war lords
would stop at nothing, no matter how treacherous or dastardly.

"Armed Neutrality."

German Overtures to Mexico and Japan.

A great patriotic uprising occurred. A resolution granting the President what he asked for passed the House by an enormous majority, but in the Senate a little knot designated by the President as "wilful men," among whom were Stone of Missouri and La Follette of Wisconsin, started a filibuster against the measure, and the session closed before a vote could be taken.

The Senate Filibuster.

Thus ended the first administration of Woodrow Wilson, with the country irresistibly drawn into the bloody maelstrom of the greatest war in history.

The events leading up to our entering the conflict will doubtless long continue to be a subject of controversy. President Wilson's course in international affairs will be bitterly criticised and as warmly defended. His admirers justify his policy by such arguments as that for two years he kept the United States out of the war, and that he waited until the people were ready to back up a vigorous course. His critics point out that he got into the conflict in the end, and deny that he prepared the country either mentally or materially for war.

Students of history will not fail to see a close parallel between Wilson's policy in 1914–16 and that of Jefferson and Madison in the period preceding the War of 1812. In each instance a great world war was raging; in each instance America's rights as a neutral were trampled upon. In each instance our government protested but for a long time did not go beyond protest. And in each instance the United States was finally drawn into the struggle unprepared. Once again America had been forewarned but had failed to forearm.

CHAPTER XXI

AMERICA ENTERS THE GREAT WAR

THE submarine dangers proved so great that most American ship-owners refused to send their vessels to Europe unless the government would furnish guns and trained men to operate them. President Wilson had already asserted a belief that he had the power to arm merchantmen, and, despite the failure of the bill expressly granting him that authority, he issued orders a few days after his second inauguration that naval guns should be mounted on the ships. Regular naval officers and men were put in charge of the guns, with orders to fire at submarines on sight. This policy was fully justified by the German declaration that the U-boats would torpedo without warning vessels entering the "war zone."

Merchant Ships Armed.

The filibuster in the Senate had resulted in the failure of needed appropriation bills, and the President, therefore, summoned the new Congress to meet in special session on April 16. But in the middle of March it became known that submarines had sunk three of our ships without warning, causing the death of three Americans. The President realized that his "armed neutrality" policy did not meet the needs of the situation, and he therefore convoked Congress to meet two weeks earlier in order "to consider grave matters of international policy."

"Armed Neutrality" a Failure.

At the moment the President issued the new call, the country was again threatened with a great railroad strike. The Adamson law, passed the previous September, was supposed to go into effect on January 1, 1917, but a federal district court held it unconstitutional. The railroads entered into an agreement with the attorney-general to continue on the old basis but to give the men the back pay due them in case the Supreme Court upheld the law. The

New Railway Troubles.

422

men were dissatisfied, and on March 15, in the midst of the crisis with Germany, the brotherhoods called a nation-wide strike to begin on the 17th, but consented to postpone it until the 19th. On that day the managers, following an appeal to their patriotism, yielded, and on the same day the Supreme Court, by a vote of 5 to 4, upheld the act. Later in the year the men began an agitation for radical increases in their pay and again were victorious.

In the new House of Representatives the two great parties were so evenly matched that doubt existed as to which would be able to organize that body and elect the Speaker. But a feeling developed that it would be better for the legislative and executive branches to be in accord politically. Some independents and a few Republicans threw their votes to Champ Clark, and he was re-elected Speaker over Mann of Illinois. In the executive session of the Senate, which had met after the inauguration, the rules of that body had been modified, and a system of closure of debate had been adopted in order to prevent future filibustering. The ease with which a few senators could block legislation in that body had been a great evil, and a change in rules had long been agitated. Most of the heads of committees in both houses continued to be Southerners.

Democrats Organize the House.

The final crisis with Germany had come. Pacifists and pro-Germans made a last effort. They flooded Congress and the President with telegrams and letters advocating a policy of submission, and thousands hurried to Washington in person to present their views. But America's patience was at last exhausted. The great mass of intelligent people saw that the time for words was past, the time for action come. A great surge of feeling swept over the land, bearing down all opposition, and bands of militant "Pilgrims of Patriotism" visited the capital to demand that the nation should vindicate its rights and those of civilization.

The Crisis Come.

By evening of the day of meeting Congress was ready to listen to the President, and he appeared before a joint session and delivered a momentous message. He said that submarine warfare had proved so destructive and unrestrained that it had become "a warfare against mankind." Armed neutrality, he confessed, was "impractical" and "ineffectual"; he therefore asked Congress to declare that the recent course of the German Government constituted war against the United States, and to take the necessary steps to employ all our resources to force the German Government to terms and end the conflict. This would involve, he said, the closest possible co-operation with the other nations at war with Germany, and the extension of liberal financial credits to those countries. The material resources of the country must be organized and mobilized, the navy must be strengthened, especially with the best means for dealing with submarines; and he recommended that to the armed forces already authorized an immediate addition should be made of at least 500,000 men, "chosen upon the principle of universal liability to service."

Wilson's War Message.

He asserted that we had "no quarrel with the German people," but only with their despotic government. This government, the Prussian autocracy, "was not and never could be our friend." From the very outset of the war it had "filled our unsuspecting communities and even our offices of government with spies and set criminal intrigues everywhere afoot against our national unity of counsel, our peace within and without, our industries and our commerce. Indeed it is now evident that its spies were here even before the war began." "This natural foe to liberty" must be beaten, and "the world must be made safe for democracy."

Autocracy the Enemy.

"There are, it may be," he said in conclusion, "many months of fiery trial and sacrifice ahead of us. It is a fearful thing to lead this great peaceful people into war, into the most terrible and disastrous of all wars, civilization itself seeming to be in the balance. But the right is more precious than peace, and we shall fight for the things which we have always carried nearest our hearts—for democracy, for the right of those who submit to authority to have a voice in their own governments, for the rights and liberties of small nations, for a universal dominion of right by such a concert of free peoples as shall bring peace and safety to all nations and make the world itself at last free. To such a task we can dedicate our lives and our fortunes, everything that we are and everything that we have, with the pride of those who know that the day has come when America is privileged to spend her blood and her might for the principles that gave her birth and happiness, and the peace which she has treasured.   God helping her, she can do no other."

Even while President Wilson was on his way to address Congress, word was being passed about Washington that the American armed merchantman *Aztec* had been sunk without

War Declared, April 6, 1917.

warning, with probable loss of life, and this new example of German "frightfulness" helped to emphasize the demand for war.   A resolution recognizing a state of war, authorizing the President to employ the entire naval and military forces against the Imperial German Government, and pledging all the resources of the country to bring the conflict to a successful termination, was introduced in both houses.   In the Senate it was opposed by such men as Stone and La Follette, but it was passed by a vote of 82 to 6. In the House Kitchin of North Carolina, Democratic floor leader, took a prominent part against it, but it passed by a vote of 373 to 50.   The United States and Germany were definitely at war.

The Central Powers sought to make light of America's entry into the conflict, sneered at the American army and navy, and declared that the Allies would be brought to their knees before

Effect of America's Entry.

the United States would be ready to take an active part.   In reality, however, America's decision to enter the conflict reverberated around the world. It vastly heartened the Allies, put at their service the resources of the richest and potentially the most powerful nation on the globe, and influenced numerous other nations, among them Cuba, China, Brazil, Panama, and Bolivia, either to break diplomatic relations with Germany or to declare war upon her. And, disguise their opinions as they would, the Germans and their allies were unable to view with real equanimity the adhesion of so powerful a country to their foes.

When America threw her sword into the scale, the Great War had been raging two years and eight months. At the outset the Germans had sought to win a speedy decision, but after getting in sight of Paris they had been turned back at the Marne by the genius of Joffre, Foch, and Gallieni. A later drive for the Channel ports had been foiled by the French and British, and the year 1914 ended in the West with the Germans in possession of almost all of Belgium, and an important part of industrial France, but balked of their main object. In the meanwhile the Russians had inflicted tremendous defeats upon the Austrians in Galicia, but they had been hurled out of East Prussia by Von Hindenburg.

Summary of Preceding Events.

In 1915 the Teutons changed their strategy and made their main effort in the East. Accepting the defensive on the western front, they began under Mackensen and Hindenburg a great drive which moved forward triumphantly through the spring, summer, and autumn, and gave them all of Poland, Courland, and other Russian provinces west of the Dvina River, and rewon most of Galicia. Meanwhile the French and British "nibbled" at the German lines on the western front and won some minor successes, but accomplished nothing decisive. The most promising undertaking on the part of the Allies during the year was the attempt to open the Dardanelles, capture Constantinople, reduce Turkey, and obtain a highway for bringing Russian wheat to Western markets and carrying munitions of war to the Muscovites. But the attack was conducted in too leisurely a fashion; not enough troops were thrown into the enterprise; and finally the Allies had to confess failure and withdraw their troops from the Gallipoli Peninsula. In the autumn the Teutonic powers persuaded Bulgaria to enter the conflict as an ally. Caught between two forces, Servia and Montenegro were overrun, and dilatory efforts at rescue conducted by Great Britain and France through Salonica proved unavailing. In Mesopotamia, a British expedition approached Bagdad, but was repulsed by overwhelming forces, was forced to retreat. and after a long siege was compelled to surrender at Kut-el-Amara.

Campaigns of 1915.

In 1916 the Germans once more turned to the West, resolved "to bleed France white" and put her out of the war.   In February they attacked Verdun, and for month after month kept battering away at that great fortification.   It was like the meeting of an irresistible power with an immovable body.   But the French said, "They shall not pass," and French valor, aided by developments elsewhere, foiled the Teutonic efforts.   Early in June the rejuvenated Russians, under Brusiloff, began a new drive which recovered much Russian territory, reconquered part of Galicia, and was finally brought to a standstill only after months of desperate fighting.   On the 1st of July the new British army began its first great effort on the Somme, and there ensued in that region a long-continued battle which equalled, if it did not surpass, the titanic conflict at Verdun.   The Germans were driven slowly back, and were only saved from an extensive retreat by the opportune arrival of wet autumn weather.   Meanwhile the Italians, who had entered the conflict in the spring of 1915, had been slowly pushing their way against stupendous natural obstacles toward Trent and Trieste, and had absorbed much of the Austrian strength.   By the end of the summer it seemed as if the collapse of the Central Powers might not be far off, and the hopes of those who desired this were heightened when Roumania threw herself into the conflict.   But the failure of the Allies to carry out an effective drive northward from Salonica gave Falkenhayn and Mackensen an opportunity to overrun two-thirds of Roumania and to revive Teutonic hopes.

Campaigns of 1916.

In Europe and Asia Minor, therefore, the Central Powers still bade defiance to their foes, and could point to large conquests of territory as proof of the fact that they "had won the war."   But their commerce had long since been swept from the high seas, and each day that passed Germany was losing in foreign trade more than the price of a *Lusitania*.   All of Germany's colonies had been overrun, with the exception of a small stretch of German East Africa.   Arabia was in revolt against Turkey.   The British were once more in the ascendant in Mesopotamia, and early in 1917 they recap-

The Balance.

tured Kut-el-Amara and soon after took Bagdad. In May, 1916, the German High Seas Fleet had ventured to challenge British supremacy in the North Sea, but after the greatest engagement in naval history it had stolen back to port in the night. Though proclaiming a "victory," the German above-water navy never again ventured to try conclusions with its enemies. But the German U-boats waged incessant and destructive warfare against Allied merchant shipping, and even before the announcement of unlimited warfare had sunk several millions of tons, mostly of vessels flying the British flag.

At the moment that America entered the war two circumstances combined to raise Teutonic hopes. In March a sudden uprising in Russia resulted in the dethronement of the Czar and the setting up of a revolutionary govern-ment. In some Allied countries this revolution was greeted with joy, but men of insight foresaw that not improbably it would paralyze Russian military efforts, and so the result proved. In July Kerensky, the minister of war, succeeded in galvanizing the Russian army into making an attack which temporarily proved successful, but defeat soon followed; the army became completely demoralized, German secret agents succeeded in confusing Russian counsels, the vast empire broke up into fragments, and Bolshevism rose amid the ruins. The collapse of Russia freed the Central Powers from the necessity of maintaining great armies along the eastern front, and enabled them to devote their main attention to the western and Italian fronts. As many months must elapse before the United States could supply an army to fill the vacancy left by Russian faltering, the military situation from the Allied point of view was most serious.

But the Germans pinned their main hopes upon the U-boats. Never before had the world witnessed such a carnival of destruction upon the high seas. Ships were sent down by the hundreds, and the waters around Great Britain and off the coast of western France were filled with floating wreckage. In a single week of April, 1917, perhaps the blackest week of all modern history, the submarines sank nearly fifty vessels of more than 1,600 tons, and many smaller ones. The Germans boasted that in three months they would reduce the British to submission, and it was evident to all who had eyes to see that unless some means could be found of checking this warfare, Great Britain, dependent upon the outside world for most of her food supply, would indeed be forced to accept any terms that the war lords might dictate. She might even be compelled to surrender her fleet to the victors. With it the war lords could sweep the seas and reduce all the world, America included, to a state of vassalage.

It was clear that the United States must play a large part in the war in order to secure victory. It was equally clear that we were almost totally unprepared for the task. Let us America's first consider the army. The appropriations for the Military Un- War Department for the fiscal year 1915 had been preparedness. $150,000,000, and for the year 1916 $203,000,000, and the last sum was about $30,000,000 in excess of the whole sum expended by the German Empire in 1913 upon its army of about 800,000 men, well armed, well officered, and well equipped with all the latest military devices. Yet our regular army on April 1, 1917, numbered less than 128,000 officers and men, and some thousands of these had enlisted during the last few months. The National Guard in federal service numbered about 80,000 men. Although part of the Guard and much of the regular army had been on the Mexican border, little or no effort had been made to train either officers or men in the methods of the new warfare. In the new Springfield rifle, adopted in 1903, we had perhaps the best military rifle in the world, but we had only about 600,000. Pains had not been taken to provide the necessary machinery for turning the rifles out in vast quantities, and we were ultimately forced to supply many of our troops with a British model rifle, rechambered to carry the Springfield cartridge. The first few months of the Great War had shown the vital importance of motor-trucks in the new warfare, yet our army had only a few motor-trucks. It had shown the vital need of great numbers of machine-guns, but we had only a few machine-guns. The aeroplane is an American invention, and in 1908 our army had begun experimenting with such craft, but the work had not been pushed vigorously, and when we declared war we had not a single aeroplane fit to meet German planes in battle in the skies. The new warfare was largely a war of artillery, yet we had not a single really up-to-date field-piece. Worst of all, the War Department had made no plans as to what type of motor-trucks, machine-guns, aeroplanes, and artillery should be adopted, and many precious months were spent in planning and experimenting before even construction could begin.

The great immediate need was for weapons with which to fight the submarine, and happily the navy, though its management has been both criticised and defended, was at least more forehanded than the army. Since 1912 our navy had The Navy. fallen in relative strength until it was much below that of Germany, but it contained eleven completed dreadnoughts, and more than a score of pre-dreadnought battleships, though it did not contain a single battle-cruiser, a type of ship that had been found to be of immense value during the war. Luckily Great Britain was amply supplied with dreadnoughts, battle-cruisers, and other large vessels, and our greatest contribution to Allied success on the sea took the form of lighter ships. Of these our destroyers, of which we had more than fifty completed and others in the process of construction, proved to be of greatest value, and they were supplemented by light cruisers and great numbers of yachts and submarine-chasers, which were soon put into commission.

Comparatively few Americans had any definite conception of the difficulties of creating a modern military machine. Talk about a million men springing to arms overnight had Popular Delusions. lulled many into a feeling of false security, while others had the cheerful notion that American inventive genius, if confronted by a crisis, would speedily perfect weapons with which to defeat our enemies. A Naval Consulting Board composed of inventors and men of science had been formed before the war began, and for months the newspapers were filled with speculations concerning the experiments which Edison and other men of genius were conducting in secrecy; more than once the country was heartened by vague announcements that wonderful weapons of warfare had been evolved. Gradually, however, the belief that some way would be found of "inventing" us out of the war evaporated, and the stern fact came home to the people that the conflict could be won only by lavish expenditure of blood and treasure, properly organized and directed. Not a single new American invention that was revolutionary in character played a considerable part in ending the war. The only new inventions of large importance that contributed to that end were the tank and the depth bomb, both of which were produced by our supposedly less nimble-witted cousins, the British.

It was clear that we were confronted with the greatest task of improvisation in all our history, and that to get ready it would be necessary to pour out money in floods hitherto undreamed of. Yet there was much for which to be grateful. Thanks to the Allied armies and the British navy, we could carry out our preparations practically unmolested by the enemy. It would not be necessary for us to sacrifice our regular army, as the British had been compelled to sacrifice theirs, in order to gain time in which to train a new one. Furthermore, our allies gladly supplied hundreds of experienced officers to teach our officers and men the new warfare. Yet we must not be too dilatory, for, as was well said, "time and Von Hindenburg waited for no man," and the disastrous results of failure on the part of the Allies to take sufficiently into account the time element in warfare—more important than ever before—had repeatedly been sadly revealed.

The German hope that the United States would not take an active part in the war was soon dispelled. Congress speedily appropriated (April 27) the immense sum of $7,000,000,000, and authorized the secretary of the treasury to advance loans to nations at war with our enemies. In accordance with the President's wishes, a selective service bill was introduced in Congress. It met with considerable opposition not only from pacifists and pro-Germans, but also from patriotic men who preferred depending entirely on the volunteer system. Even Speaker Clark bitterly opposed it, declaring that in his State, Missouri, "conscript" was considered the same as "convict." But volunteering was slow, there was need of raising men rapidly, and a belief that conscription was the fairest way of doing it created so strong a public sentiment in behalf of the measure that in the middle of May it passed both houses by great majorities. It authorized the President to raise the regular army to the maximum number provided by the act of June, 1916, and to draft into the service members of the National Guard and of the National Guard Reserves, and it required men between the ages of twenty-one and thirty, inclusive, to register. From those thus registered the President was empowered to call out 500,000 men, and then an additional 500,000. The raising of still larger forces was subsequently authorized, and the age limit was extended to forty-five years. The total number of men registered exceeded 24,000,000. Ultimately about 4,000,000 men served in the American army, and about 800,000 more in the navy, the marine corps, and other services.

The Conscription Act.

To supply the officers required for this great expansion of the army many men were commissioned from the ranks or from civil life, but the chief dependence was placed upon officers' training camps. These were opened in many parts of the country, and were conducted upon a plan used by General Leonard Wood at Plattsburg in 1915. Both England and France sent over some of their ablest officers to assist in the training process. Considering the shortness of the time available, the plan worked well. In all, 96,000 officers, about two-thirds of the line officers, were graduates of these camps. Like most of our war effort, however, it was improvisation, and justifiable only on grounds of sheer necessity.

Officers' Training Camps.

One section of the original draft law was inserted against the wishes of the administration. Even before the break with Germany Colonel Roosevelt had applied to the secretary of war for permission, in the event of hostilities, to raise a divi-

sion of volunteers, and he later offered to raise two, or possibly four. He did not ask chief command but expressed a willingness to go as a junior brigadier. The spec-
Roosevelt's
Offer. tacular success of the Rough Riders, enthusiasm for Roosevelt personally, and other considerations caused more than 300,000 hardy spirits—more than the number of men then in the regular army and the National Guard combined—to offer their services. When the proposal came before Congress many Democrats opposed the plan, and friends of the plan charged that these opponents feared that the enterprise would be "carried through in characteristic Rooseveltian fashion," and would have unfavorable results in the presidential election in 1920. Other Democrats, however, heartily supported the plan, and there was finally incorporated into the bill a section authorizing the President to raise not to exceed four divisions of volunteers, none of the men to be under twenty-five years of age. Supporters of the plan urged that it would result in the raising of a powerful fighting force, and that the appearance in France of the most famous of living Americans would greatly hearten the Allied world. But Secretary Baker objected to the proposal from the first, and President Wilson, alleging military reasons, announced that he would not make use of the volunteer forces for the present at least.

It was vitally important that we should increase our merchant marine. Fortunately there were in ports of the United States about ninety German merchant vessels of a total tonnage of over 600,000, and these vessels, together with
Seizure of
German and
Austrian
Ships. a few interned warships, were seized. As Austria-Hungary speedily broke off diplomatic relations (April 8), 14 Austrian ships, having a gross tonnage of 67,807, were taken over. The machinery of nearly all the German ships had been badly damaged by their crews, who supposed that thereby they had put the ships out of commission for many months. But by skilful use of the new method of electric welding, American mechanics put the ships into working order in astonishingly short time. Most of the vessels were rechristened. Thus the *Vaterland*, the biggest ship afloat,

became the *Leviathan*, while others were named after Schurz, Steuben, Sigel, and other Germans who had played noble parts in American history. Subsequently these ships carried many hundreds of thousands of men to France.

The construction of merchant ships did not proceed so smoothly. Back in September, 1916, Congress had created a Shipping Board of five members to regulate the rates and practices of water-carriers in foreign commerce, or in interstate commerce on the high seas or on the Great Lakes. Our entry into the war brought to this board new and vastly important duties, among these being the building of ships. For this purpose the board organized an Emergency Fleet Corporation, with a capital of $50,000,000, all subscribed by the government, while Congress appropriated vast sums for its use. The Shipping Board commandeered all ships being built in American yards, and a vast programme of new construction was undertaken. The need of ships was so vital that plans for great numbers of wooden ships were made. Major-General George Goethals, builder of the Panama Canal, became general manager of the Emergency Fleet Corporation, and the public expected ship construction to move forward rapidly. But shipyards and ways were lacking, the supply of skilled workmen was limited, strikes and other troubles were frequent, and optimistic forecasts, issued by Chairman Denman of the Shipping Board, were not only not realized but even the completion of the ships commandeered was delayed. General Goethals opposed the building of wooden ships, and became involved in a controversy with Denman which resulted in the retirement (August, 1917) of both men.

The Question of Ships.

It was important to be constructing merchant ships, but the war on the sea could not be won merely by setting up new targets for German torpedoes. The really effective policy was to fight the submarines. Shortly before we entered the war, Vice-Admiral Sims was sent to England to arrange co-operation between our navy and those of our allies. Sims was a highly talented officer who had done a great deal to make the American navy efficient. When still

Vice-Admiral Sims.

a lieutenant, he became convinced that the shooting of our naval gunners was poor, and that new methods ought to be adopted. His superiors ignored his recommendations, and it was only when he wrote to President Roosevelt in person that he was given an opportunity to prove his contentions. Having shown that he was right, he was put in charge of effecting reforms in gunnery, and ultimately became known as "the Father of Target Practice." In 1910, in a speech in the Guildhall in London, Sims had declared: "I believe that if the time ever comes when the British Empire is menaced by an external enemy, you may count upon every man, every drop of blood, every ship, and every dollar of your kindred across the sea." For this speech he was reprimanded by the home authorities, but a day came when he was able to remind the British and his own people of his prediction. Admiral Sims held command of our naval forces operating abroad in Atlantic waters throughout the war, and co-operated with our allies in a manner that won their regard and admiration.

The work of patrolling a large part of the Atlantic was soon taken over by our navy, thereby releasing British vessels for use in the North Sea and other waters close at home. Early in May a considerable number of destroyers were sent to British waters, and arrived at Queenstown in such good trim that they were able to set to work as soon as they had taken on fuel. Later their number was considerably augmented, and many cruisers, converted yachts, submarine-chasers, and a few battleships were sent abroad. Hydroplanes and dirigible balloons were also provided in course of time. Even in the autumn of 1918, however, our vessels engaged in anti-submarine work in European waters amounted to only about three per cent of the total Allied effort.

American Destroyers in the War Zone.

Meanwhile American armed merchantmen had continued to make voyages through the war zone. On April 19, 1917, a gun crew on the merchant steamer *Mongolia* fired the first American shot of the war against a submarine, and, it was believed, seriously damaged or destroyed the U-boat. Similar duels, mostly at long range, occurred from time to time, in some of which the

American vessels were sunk, while in others they drove off or sank their assailants. The U-boat captains speedily discovered that it was hazardous to attack armed American merchantmen with gun-fire, and after a few months such conflicts became less common. This was partly due to the fact that the Allies wisely adopted a policy of gathering merchantmen into fleets convoyed by war-ships.

Fighting the U-Boats.

The Entente Allies had planned an early renewal of the offensives which they had been forced to discontinue by the approach of winter. The Russian revolution did much to disarrange the plan, but the French and British persevered in the undertaking. The British successes along the Somme in the preceding year had left the Germans in so perilous a position that early in February, 1917, Von Hindenburg, who had taken over the command in the West, began a great strategic retreat from the Somme region, and fell back to what became known as the Hindenburg Line, running from Lens through St. Quentin and La Fère to the Aisne River near Soissons. The retreat was managed with skill, and the French and British, hampered by the muddy, shell-torn terrain of two former campaigns, and by German destruction of the roads, were unable to inflict heavy losses on the retiring foe. By this withdrawal the Germans gave up over a thousand square miles of French soil, but they reduced it practically to a desert by destroying the towns and villages, filling up or polluting the wells, and even cutting down the vines and fruit-trees.

Hindenburg's Strategic Retreat.

This prudent retreat was a play for time, for the Germans knew that it would take the British and French a long while to build roads up to the new line, bring up artillery, shells, and other supplies, and make the necessary approaches. The British and French persevered, however, in the plan of undertaking the offensive. On April 9 the British began a great "push" against the point where the new line joined the old, namely, about Lens and Arras. The attack was preceded by a stupendous bombardment, and the assaulting forces were aided by low-flying aeroplanes and

British and French Offensive, 1917.

tanks. The Canadian troops won immortal glory by carrying
Vimy Ridge, the chief buttress of the German line in that
sector, and many other positions were taken elsewhere. German
counter-attacks were hurled back with great slaughter, and in a
few days the British were astride the Hindenburg Line, which
the Germans had boasted was invulnerable, and had forced the
defenders back upon a reserve line some distance in the rear.
In a week's time the British captured more territory and more
guns than in the whole of the previous year's offensive. On
April 16 General Nivelle, who had succeeded General Joffre as
commander-in-chief of the French armies, began a great drive
against the German line along the Aisne on a front of twenty
miles between Rheims and Soissons. The attack won much
ground, and resulted in the capture of many guns and prisoners,
but the French losses were heavy, and after some days the
French Government called a halt. General Nivelle was relieved of command and was succeeded by General Pétain, one
of the heroes of Verdun, while General Foch became chief-of-
staff. The slackening of the French attack enabled the Germans to concentrate before the British and to bring them to
a standstill. In June the British launched a furious attack
against Messines Ridge east of Ypres, and they continued battering their way slowly forward in this sector until the approach
of winter once more made operations on a great scale impossible.
The failure of the April drive, together with the course of events
in Russia, cast a cloud of gloom over France. "Defeatism,"
instigated by German gold, reared its head and threatened to
undermine French morale. During the remainder of the year
the French undertook no great offensive, though they managed
to wrest the Chemin des Dames ridge from the Germans and
to threaten Laon. The Russian collapse had frustrated all
hope of decisive victory in 1917, and France and the other
Allied countries felt that the German hosts could not be overcome until a great American army was in the field.

In April British and French commissions arrived in America
to arrange plans of co-operation against the common foe. The
British commission was headed by Foreign Secretary Balfour,

that of the French by ex-Premier Viviani and the immortal General Joffre. The French commission also included the Mar-

French and British Missions. quis de Chambrun, a lineal descendant of Lafayette. Memories of the days when France had stretched out a helping hand to the weak republic in the West arose in every mind and helped to arouse a fervor of enthusiasm wherever the French commission went, while patriots rejoiced that the two great branches of the Anglo-Saxon race, enemies in the long ago, were now fighting shoulder to shoulder for civilization against a common foe. The commissions laid the foundation for effective co-operation between the United States and the other enemies of Germany. They were later followed by missions from Russia, Italy, Belgium, Roumania, and Japan.

France had grown war-weary and her statesmen and military men were anxious to do something that would restore the faith of the French people in ultimate victory. General Joffre and

French Plea that Troops be Sent. his colleagues, therefore, urgently requested that American troops should be sent to France as soon as possible, as concrete evidence that American aid would be forthcoming. We had no troops that were ready to enter the firing line, but for the sake of the moral influence, announcement was made that a force would be sent over as soon as possible.

To command this force the President selected Major-General John J. Pershing, the man who had led the expedition into Mexico after Villa. General Pershing had seen active service

Major-General Pershing. against the Apaches, in the Santiago campaign, and later in the Philippines, particularly against the Moros. As a military observer he had been attached to one of the Japanese armies in the Japanese-Russian War and had there witnessed modern warfare on a large scale. His work in the Philippines was of so high a character that President Roosevelt, a keen judge of men, promoted him from captain to brigadier-general, jumping him over the heads of 862 other officers.

On June 8 General Pershing and his staff landed at Liverpool,

and after a few days in England passed over to Paris.   In both England and France he was greeted with great enthusiasm,

The First Division Lands in France.

but he and those with him soon settled down to the stupendous task of arranging for America's participation in the war on a grand scale.   In the middle of June an American division, which included some marines, set sail for France.   On the way over the transports were attacked by submarines, but the convoying war-ships drove off the enemy, and the troops reached France without the loss of a man.   They were greeted with indescribable enthusiasm by the French people.   On the 4th of July a battalion paraded through the streets of Paris amid a demonstration perhaps never surpassed in the history of that famous capital.   Many of the men in the division were, however, new recruits, and months of weary work lay ahead of the units before they were privileged to take part in an actual battle.

The Germans had boasted that their U-boats would make the transportation of American troops to France practically impossible, and much uneasiness existed in the United States

Convoying the Troop-Ships.

lest the boast might be made good.   Every effort was made by both the American and British navies to protect the troop-ships.   They were convoyed all the way over by war-ships, and as they drew near European shores, where the danger was greatest, they were surrounded by destroyers and other anti-submarine craft, while hydroplanes and balloons kept a careful watch from aloft.   These tactics were successful beyond what even optimists had hoped.   In all, only four transports were sunk, while two others were torpedoed but were able to make port.   Most of these vessels were attacked on the homeward voyage, when less care was taken to safeguard them.   Only 396 men were lost at sea, an infinitesimal loss considering that over 2,000,000 were carried over.

Of the regular naval vessels, the cruiser *San Diego* and the destroyer *Jacob Jones* were sunk by the enemy, the

American Naval Losses.

former by striking a mine laid by a German submarine off the Long Island coast.   Another destroyer, the *Cassin*, was hit by a torpedo but managed to make port, while a few minor craft were sunk. That these losses were so small was partly due to the fact that the German submarines concentrated almost all their efforts against merchant vessels.

Throughout the war by far the greater part of the anti-submarine work continued to be performed by the British, but the American navy co-operated effectively. In all, our ships were credited with certainly destroying one submarine and possibly destroying or damaging about two dozen others. Furthermore, our navy, with some British assistance, laid a great mine barrage from the Norwegian coast to the Orkney Islands, thereby rendering it increasingly difficult and dangerous for the German submarines to reach the high seas.

Services. American

When the United States entered the war, the submarine campaign was at its height. Ships were being sunk in such appalling numbers that when Admiral Sims arrived in London he found many Britons who secretly feared that the war was lost. But the adoption of the convoy system and increased use of depth bombs and other devices proved effective, and gradually the peril diminished. As the destruction of vessels decreased the rate of construction increased, until finally, in May, 1918, tonnage constructed by the Allies surpassed the tonnage sunk by the enemy. This favorable showing was due in no small measure to the activity of American shipyards, which had been put under the energetic direction of Charles M. Schwab. Many disappointments had been experienced in our shipbuilding campaign, but our efforts at last bore fruit. By the autumn of 1918 American yards were delivering more ships than were British yards.

The Submarines Beaten.

The task of mobilizing the country's resources for the war was one of the greatest that had ever faced a nation. It would have been difficult in any circumstances, and it was rendered doubly so by reason of the fact that comparatively little of a practical nature had been done before our entry. As a result everything had to be improvised in haste and at enormous cost, in order to get American troops to the front in time to play their part.

A Stupendous Task.

The country displayed commendable eagerness to assist in the great work, and willingly co-operated with the government. Congress appropriated money in sums hitherto undreamed of,
and enacted many sweeping war measures, including the Selective Draft Act, an Espionage Act, a Food and Fuel Act, a War Risk Insurance Act, and a Daylight-saving Law. The people subscribed hundreds of millions of dollars for the Red Cross, the Y. M. C. A., the Knights of Columbus, the Salvation Army, and other agencies doing volunteer war work. Thousands of business men of large experience dropped their private enterprises and offered their services free of charge or for a nominal wage to their country.

The Nation Puts Its Shoulder to the Wheel.

Yet for reasons upon which men are not yet agreed some aspects of our war preparations moved forward slowly, and in consequence there was much dissatisfaction and criticism.
Toward the end of 1917 a majority of the Senate committee on military affairs, after investigating the alleged shortcomings of the War Department, reported that they had discovered many instances of mismanagement, such as failure to provide blankets, uniforms, arms, and adequate hospital facilities. The leadership in the investigation was taken by Senator Chamberlain of Oregon, a member of President Wilson's own party. An insistent demand was made by many newspapers, and by such men as Colonel Roosevelt, that our war activities must be speeded up. Responsibility for alleged shortcomings was placed in large measure on Secretary of War Baker and certain bureaucrats in his department, but many people felt that the ultimate responsibility rested on the shoulders of the President. In January, 1918, Secretary Baker defended his department in glowing terms, but Senator Chamberlain and other members of the committee and a considerable section of the general public declined to accept his picture of conditions and insisted that it created a wrong impression. In a speech delivered in New York City Senator Chamberlain declared that the military establishment had "almost stopped functioning. Why? Because of inefficiency in every bureau and every department of

Alleged Shortcomings of the War Department.

the Government of the United States." This speech moved President Wilson to issue a counter-statement defending Baker as a capable administrator and denouncing Chamberlain's remarks as "an astonishing and unjustifiable distortion of the truth."

Senator Chamberlain, in a subsequent speech (January 4, 1918), admitted that much had been accomplished, but he charged that the United States Army was almost wholly with-

Senator Chamberlain's Charges.
out ordnance, was insufficiently supplied with rifles, that shortage of clothing and inadequate hospital facilities had caused unnecessary deaths in the army cantonments, and that our whole war effort was lagging. Next day Surgeon-General Gorgas, before the Senate committee on military affairs, confirmed some of Chamberlain's charges regarding inadequate hospital equipment. A few days later Senator Hitchcock, like Chamberlain a Democrat, severely attacked the administration for short-sightedness and failure to prepare for war activities. He painted a gloomy picture of the existing situation and insisted that in many matters America's preparations were far behind schedule.

To remedy the evils he believed existed, Senator Chamberlain introduced two bills, one to create a new department of munitions and another to establish a war cabinet to direct war

War Activities Reorganized.
activities. The Republicans and a few Democratic senators supported these measures, but President Wilson and Secretary Baker bitterly opposed them, and they failed. However, the President recognized that something must be done, and he procured the introduction and passage of what was known as the Overman Bill, authorizing him to reorganize our war activities. Furthermore, he appointed Edward R. Stettinius, an able business man, as surveyor-general of army purchases, and also brought General Goethals back into responsible service.

The airplane situation was one of the matters that caused deepest concern among Americans anxious to win the war. In July, 1917, the government had formulated a plan for the building of 22,000 airplanes. The plan appealed to the imagination of the country, and before the public mind arose a picture of vast fleets of planes darkening the sky and carrying destruction to the heart of Germany. Some persons declared that airplanes were the weapon with which to win the war, and another slogan was added to the many already in existence. Congress unanimously voted $640,000,000 for the aerial service, and subsequently increased this sum. It was confidently asserted that by the opening of the campaign of 1918 thousands of American planes would be at the front.

The Airplane Programme.

Some experts advocated that we proceed at once to manufacture the best types of planes already in existence, but the War Department followed a policy of having some planes built in France, and of seeking to evolve a new type for construction in America. Experts were set to work evolving a new aircraft engine which ultimately became known as the "Liberty Motor." In September, 1917, Secretary of War Baker issued an optimistic statement declaring that the new engine "had passed the final test" and that "in power, speed, serviceability, and minimum weight the new engine invites comparison with the best the European war has produced." Later developments showed, however, that in reality the motor was still in an experimental stage, and many months elapsed before its defects were corrected and it was really ready for war service.

The "Liberty Motor."

Meanwhile America's airplane programme halted, and a serious feature of the situation was that the Germans, stimulated by the news of our aircraft efforts, largely increased their production of planes. A great outcry arose in America. Gutzon Borglum, a well-known sculptor, was permitted by President Wilson to make an investigation of the aircraft situation, and he brought in a pessimistic report in which he attributed the delay in airplane production to gross mismanagement and even treachery. At the President's request ex-Justice Hughes, his late opponent, made a more exhaustive investigation, which showed that there had been some mismanagement, but the Hughes report was much less sensational in its charges.

The Aircraft Investigation.

The aerial service was reorganized, and ultimately, after

many discouraging delays, the production of the Liberty Motor proceeded rapidly, and the motor proved to be of value, especially for training and bombing planes. However, production of both engines and planes in this country was so much delayed from various causes that most of the aircraft actually used by American flyers at the front came from French sources.

Ultimate Progress.

Fortunately the training of American aviators proceeded more satisfactorily. With the aid of foreign instructors, over 8,000 men graduated from elementary flying courses, and about half that number from advanced courses. More than 5,000 pilots and observers were sent overseas, and a considerable number saw active service.

It early became clear that America could render much aid by furnishing larger supplies of food to the Allies. The cry of "Food will win the war!" was raised. Like most other slogans this cry was not literally true, but food would beyond question *help* to win the war, and without it the war would be lost. The need of the Allies was very great, and at the time the United States entered the conflict the whole world's food reserve was very low. Even in the United States the reserve stock of wheat was said to be proportionately lower than at any other time in our history.

The Food Question.

The food campaign took two chief forms: conservation of the existing supply and increased production. A great campaign, partly governmental, partly voluntary, was launched to save such things as sugar, meat, flour, and fats. The general public co-operated with astonishing cheerfulness and loyalty in carrying out a system of rationing whereby immense quantities of foods needed overseas were saved. Another campaign for increased production was conducted with equal energy and resourcefulness. Farmers were encouraged to produce more grain and vegetables, and to raise more cattle and hogs; great emphasis was laid on the importance of good seed; everybody was urged to cultivate a "war garden"; canning clubs were organized; and in a really remarkable manner the public generally and the

Conservation and Increased Food Production.

farmers in particular rallied to the call.   In order to stimulate
the raising of wheat, a minimum price of $2.20 a bushel was
fixed by the government for No. 1 northern spring wheat at
the principal interior markets, with a system of differentials
between zones and different grades.   This and other price-
fixing on other articles was done under authority conferred by
the Food and Fuel Control Act of August 10, 1917, which gave
the government sweeping powers over the sale and distribution
of foods and fuels.   Under the act President Wilson called to
the post of federal food administrator Herbert C. Hoover,
whose services as head of Belgian relief had already won him
international fame.

The railway situation in the United States had long been bad.
Railway magnates had too often been interested in manipulating
the stocks and bonds of their roads in such ways as to fleece
the general public and even their own stockholders,
A Bad
Railway   while their attitude toward the public was often
Situation.   the reverse of obliging.   In consequence, a feeling
of hostility had developed toward the roads, and this was sometimes translated into restrictive legislation that fixed passenger
and freight rates at so low a figure that the roads were unable
out of their receipts to make needed repairs and extensions.
Furthermore, the roads for a long time had found it difficult to
borrow sufficient money for this purpose.   Their equipment had
deteriorated in consequence.   The situation grew worse after
the United States entered the war, and there was great congestion of freight and inability of the roads to perform the transportation work of the country.

The traffic congestion ultimately became so great that, on
December 26, 1917, the federal government abruptly assumed
full control of the railroads under an act of August 29, 1916,
which authorized such a step in time of war.   Over
The
Government   400 separate corporations, 650,000 shareholders,
Takes   260,000 miles of road, property valued at $17,500,-
Control.
000,000, and about 1,600,000 employees were affected by this order.   To manage the roads, the President designated Secretary of the Treasury McAdoo as director-general of

railroads. The property rights of stockholders and others were guaranteed, and in a message to Congress, January 4, 1918, the President recommended as a basis of compensation the average net income of the three years ending June 30, 1917, which, according to the returns of the Interstate Commerce Commission, was $1,049,974,977. Legislation for managing and financing the railroads and compensating the owners was passed by Congress.

Various steps were taken to render the railroads more efficient. Unnecessary trains were taken off, competition between different lines was reduced, and the most direct lines were used in transporting freight, irrespective of the ownership of the lines. The experiment proved less successful, however, than had been hoped. Wages were greatly increased, and from this and other causes the cost of operating the roads rose to unheard of heights. Passenger and freight rates were raised, but, though the roads did an enormous business, receipts lacked much of meeting expenditures, and it was necessary for the government to expend hundreds of millions of dollars to meet the deficit. Thus the general public was forced to pay out of both pockets. Out of one they paid the increased price of passenger and freight rates; out of the other they paid taxes to be used in meeting the extraordinary railroad expenses.

A Great Deficit.

The seizure of the railroads was in large measure due to an alarming shortage in the supply of coal. Toward the middle of January, 1918, in the midst of one of the coldest periods the country had ever experienced, the shortage became so serious that Fuel Administrator Garfield, with the approval of President Wilson, ordered a general shut-down of industry throughout the United States east of the Mississippi for five successive days, and the limitation of the working week to five days during the nine weeks following. Exceptions were made for industries engaged in war work. This drastic order resulted in the loss of hundreds of millions of dollars to manufacturers and other business men, but bore hardest, of course, upon the working class, several million of

A Coal Shortage.

whom were rendered temporarily idle. The five days passed,
and for several Mondays the "heatless" order was carried out;
much fuel was thereby saved, and the coming of milder weather
also helped to relieve the situation, so that the order was suspended before nine weeks had elapsed.

One of the great problems which faced the government was
that of finance. It was clear that the war would be enormously
costly, for not only must we spend vast sums upon our own
preparations but it was vital that we should advance
The Question money to our associates in the contest. New taxes
of Finance. were imposed, but it was clear that most of the
money must be obtained by loans. Congress authorized the
issuance of certificates of indebtedness, war-saving certificates
(better known as thrift stamps), and government bonds. Certificates of indebtedness were intended to run for only a few
months and bore interest at comparatively low rates. Large
sums were temporarily obtained by this means, and over $800,-
000,000 was realized from the sale of thrift stamps. But by
far the greatest amount of money was obtained through the
sale of bonds.

In all, five loans were floated and sold before the signing of
the peace treaty. The first four were known as Liberty Loans;
the last, which was floated after the armistice was signed, was
called the Victory Loan. The bonds of the First
The First Liberty Loan were announced on May 14, 1917.
Liberty Loan. They were dated June 15 of that year, and were to
bear 3½ per cent interest from that date, payable semi-annu-
ally. They were to mature 30 years later but were made
redeemable at the end of 15 years. These bonds were made
exempt both as to principal and interest from all taxation except
inheritance taxes. Holders were accorded the privilege of con-
verting them into bonds bearing a higher rate of interest that
might be issued subsequently. The bonds were issued in denominations as low as $100 for registered bonds, and $50 for
coupon bonds. A partial-payment scheme was adopted, and
other devices were used to encourage small investors to subscribe. When the lists were closed, it was found that over

4,000,000 persons had bought bonds, and that the subscriptions totalled $3,035,226,850, which was 50 per cent more than the amount offered. Allotments were made in full to those who had subscribed $10,000 or less. Those subscribing for larger amounts were allotted from 60 to 20 per cent of their subscriptions.

A second loan of $3,000,000,000 was offered on the 1st of the following October. The rate was fixed at 4 per cent, and the bonds were made payable in 25 years, but the government might at its option redeem them in 10 years. They The Second Liberty Loan. were also made convertible into subsequent issues bearing a higher rate of interest, but they were not exempt from graduated income taxes and excess profits and war profits taxes levied by the federal government. Almost 10,-000,000 persons subscribed a total of $4,617,532,300. This was an excess of 54 per cent, but the government accepted one half of the excess.

A third Liberty Loan of $3,000,000,000 was offered on April 6, 1918, and the selling campaign closed on May 4. The rate of interest was fixed at 4¼ per cent, with about the same exemptions and privileges as was the case with the second Third Liberty Loan. issue except that the bonds were not made convertible into later issues. The date of maturity was fixed at September, 1928. The campaign took place in the dark days of the German drive in Picardy and Flanders, and the result was again a tremendous success. There were over 18,000,000 subscriptions for a total of $4,176,516,850, an oversubscription of nearly 40 per cent.

The fourth Liberty Loan was floated in the fall of 1918 in the midst of Allied victories. The offering was for the enormous sum of $6,000,000,000, the rate was fixed at 4¼ per cent, and the bonds were made payable on October 15, 1938, Fourth Liberty Loan. but were redeemable five years earlier. The patriotic spirit of the nation was so fully aroused that there were over 21,000,000 subscriptions for a total of $6,989,-047,000, making the loan the greatest financial operation in the history of any nation.

Soon after the fourth Liberty Loan was closed the Teutonic collapse took place, but expenses continued to be so enormous that a fifth loan, known as the Victory Loan, became necessary.

The Victory Loan.

The sum asked for was $4,500,000,000. The bonds were issued for the short term of four years, with the privilege to pay in three, and the interest rate was fixed at 4¾ per cent for partially tax-exempt bonds, which were convertible into 3¾ bonds wholly exempt from all except estate and inheritance taxes. By this time war enthusiasm had largely abated, yet there were 12,000,000 subscriptions for a total of $5,249,908,300.

The wonderful success of these loans was in large measure due to the patriotism of the people. Although the bonds were generally considered to be a safe investment, the interest return

The Bonds Fall below Par.

offered was comparatively low, and beyond question a very large majority of the subscriptions were made with the prime object of helping to win the war rather than to obtain a large financial return. In fact, the bonds soon fell below par; by the spring of 1920 those of some issues were quoted below 85. Because of their special income-tax-exemption features, those of the first loan, although for a lower rate of interest, held their own better than any of the other issues except the Victory bonds. The decline in the price of bonds was in large measure due to the fact that many people bought bonds and then found it necessary to dispose of them, even at a sacrifice. It was greatly to the credit of Americans that when bonds of old issues were selling much below par, they were willing to buy new bonds at par.

It was felt, however, that posterity ought not to be made to bear the entire financial burden of the conflict, so an elaborate system of war taxation was adopted. The first measure of

Increased Taxation.

this sort was the so-called War Revenue Act approved by the President on October 3, 1917. Increased income taxes and internal duties, new excise taxes, and a heavy excess-profit tax of from 20 to 60 per cent formed the chief bases of the new act. The individual income tax, which had been increased in September, 1916, was amended so that single persons with a net income of over $1,000 must pay 2 per cent on all beyond that sum, while all married persons having net incomes of $2,000 must pay an excess beyond that sum, provided, however, that an exemption was allowed for each dependent child under eighteen, and for other dependents physically or mentally defective. A graduated surtax rising from 1 to 50 per cent on large incomes was added to the existing rates. It was estimated that the act would produce a revenue of $2,500,000,000 during the fiscal year 1918.

After our declaration of war with Germany, Austria-Hungary severed diplomatic relations with the United States, but formal hostilities did not immediately follow. Many Americans urged

War Declared on Austria-Hungary.

that we should also declare war against the Dual Monarchy, but the President and a majority of Congress thought otherwise. One of the reasons advanced for not doing so was that there were many hundreds of thousands of Austro-Hungarian subjects in the United States and that a declaration of war against their country would tend to make them more dangerous. But the great victory of the Austrians and Germans over the Italians in the fall of 1917 created a new situation. The United States hastened to send money and supplies to the hard-pressed Italians, and the government also prepared to send troops, who would, of course, fight Austrian soldiers. It was also felt that a formal declaration of war would help to improve Italian morale. At the request of the President, Congress, therefore, declared in the middle of December that a state of war existed with Austria-Hungary. Among the grievances specified against the Dual Monarchy were the meddling of former Ambassador Dumba with our domestic affairs, and the sinking of American vessels by Austrian submarines.

The United States was never, however, formally at war with Turkey and Bulgaria, Germany's other allies. Diplomatic relations with Turkey had already been broken, but those with Bulgaria were continued throughout the conflict.

It was, of course, necessary for the American authorities to keep close watch on the immense numbers of enemy aliens resi-

dent in the United States. Acts of Congress required that
Germans and Austro-Hungarians must register as enemy aliens
and carry certificates of identification. They were
Enemy
Aliens.
forbidden to go near army camps, navy-yards, and
other military and naval establishments without
special permits; they were not permitted to reside in, or visit,
certain districts. These provisions at first only applied to
men, but it was soon discovered that women subjects of enemy
countries were, if anything, more dangerous than the men,
and by a bill approved by the President the provisions of the
espionage act were extended to them. The registration revealed the fact that there were about 500,000 German "enemy
aliens," and between 3,000,000 and 4,000,000 Austro-Hungarian
enemy aliens in the United States. In addition, there were
some Bulgarians and Turks, to say nothing of millions of naturalized citizens from the Central Powers, and millions more
of their descendants. There had been much uneasiness lest
trouble might be caused by this population, particularly by the
German alien enemies. Germans in Germany had even boasted
that the United States dare not go to war because to do so
would provoke a civil conflict at home.

Beyond question there were many disloyal utterances, and
some actual damage was done by German spies and sympathizers in the way of blowing up munition plants and causing
"accidents" of one sort or another. Still there were
The Work of
Spies and
Teutonic
Sympathizers.
fewer such outrages than many people had expected.
In fact, there were not so many after we entered the
war as there had been before. That this was so
was due largely to the effective work of the federal secret service, which nipped in the bud many dangerous plots of which
the general public remained in ignorance.

Altogether it was found necessary to arrest about 6,000 persons under personal warrants. Many of these per-
Number of
Arrests.
sons were arrested on suspicion rather than because actual proof had been obtained that they were
dangerous. Some were ultimately released from internment
camps on parole. In the way of criminal prosecutions, 1,532

persons were arrested under the Espionage Act, which prohibited disloyal utterances, enemy propaganda, etc. Sixty-
five persons were arrested for making threats against the President, 10 for committing sabotage, and 908 indictments were
returned under the penal code relating to conspiracy, most of
these being against Industrial Workers of the World.

There were thousands more enemy aliens, and even some
citizens of the United States who secretly sympathized with
the Central Powers, but when the final test came it is to the
credit of citizens of German and Austro-Hungarian origin that
the vast majority, whatever their sympathies had been before
the United States entered the war, whole-heartedly decided
that America was their country, and gave her their loyal support. Hundreds of thousands fought valiantly in battle, and
many laid down their lives in the contest.

The entrance of the United States into the war caused a
split in the Socialist party. Some leaders, such as Charles
Edward Russell and John Spargo, believed that Germany must

Socialist
Attitude
toward the
War.

be beaten, and supported the war. Others opposed
the war, and some seemed really to sympathize
with Germany. At a meeting in St. Louis on
April 14, 1917, Socialist delegates addressed an
open letter to the Socialists in other belligerent countries, to
the effect "that the people of the United States have been
forced by their ruling class into this world cataclysm, as you
have been heretofore by your own rulers." They pledged
themselves to make any sacrifice that might be necessary "to
force our masters to conclude a speedy peace." Many Socialists disavowed the statement, but some persisted in their
unpatriotic course. A few, including Eugene V. Debs, several
times candidate for the presidency on the Socialist ticket, and
Victor Berger, former congressman from Milwaukee, were convicted and sentenced to prison for seditious utterances. Berger
was re-elected to Congress in November, 1918, shortly before
his conviction, but was not permitted to take his seat. In
December, 1919, while out on bail he was again elected.

A set of men who caused the United States more serious

trouble were the Industrial Workers of the World, who had their counterpart in the European Syndicalists. The ideas of

The Industrial Workers of the World.

the Industrial Workers of the World were to the last degree anarchical. They advocated that workers force the owners of factories to turn their possessions over to the employees. To bring about that object they favored strikes and all manner of damage to property—in short, what is known as "sabotage." This word is said to have been derived from the custom of French Syndicalists of throwing their wooden shoes, or *sabots*, into machinery in order to injure it. A favorite form of sabotage in the United States was the putting of emery dust or carborundum into the bearings of machinery. Some of the I. W. W.'s were really in German pay, and did all they could to hamper American war efforts. They put bombs in munition factories, injured machinery, incited strikes, especially among shipbuilders, and set fire to forests, grain elevators, and crops. Many of the I. W. W.'s were arrested, and some, including one of their chief leaders, William D. Haywood, were sentenced to the penitentiary. Others, of foreign origin, were interned as dangerous to the peace and safety of the country. After the armistice was signed, many foreign I. W. W.'s and other radicals, including Emma Goldman and Alexander Berkman, were arrested and deported.

CHAPTER XXII

CAMPAIGNS OF 1918

THE collapse of Russia and the defeat of Italy created a situation of which the Central Powers sought to take full advantage by launching a new peace offensive, the success of which would leave them victors in the war. They redoubled their efforts to negotiate a separate peace with Russia, and at the same time endeavored to detach other belligerents from the alliance against them. During the lull in military operations in the course of the winter, repeated speeches were made by the governmental heads of the chief warring powers on the subject of peace and peace terms. In March, 1918, Russia, which was then under the control of the Bolsheviki, definitely withdrew from the war and accepted the humiliating treaty of Brest-Litovsk. Russia's treachery forced Roumania to accept harsh terms, but all the other peace efforts failed.

Teutonic Peace Efforts.

Even while talking peace the Germans were boasting that in the spring they would launch a resistless offensive on the western front. In Allied countries some military observers supposed that these announcements were designed to hearten the people at home and to terrify France and Great Britain into making peace, or that they were intended to cover a drive against Italy or Salonica. Comparatively few people believed that the Germans would so openly advertise their purpose.

German Boasts.

Yet the war lords meant what they said. The collapse of Russia had enabled them to transfer hundreds of thousands of men and thousands of pieces of artillery to the western front, and to divert thither shells and other munitions that otherwise must have been used against the Muscovites. German industries were combed of every man who could be spared, and the war lords "robbed the cradle and the grave" to obtain the human material with which to make the final supreme effort.

Vast Preparations. Thanks to these preparations, they succeeded in massing on the western front forces about 20 per cent superior in fighting men to the armies of France and Great Britain. As yet the American forces in France were negligible, and the war lords hoped to win before we could turn the scale. Like a pugilist in the prize-ring, Germany realized that the time had come when she must win or admit defeat. Therefore, she made a final effort to score a knockout.

Every preparation which Teutonic military ingenuity could suggest was made. The best men in the German army were put into special units and were carefully drilled as shock troops.

New Tactics. Tactics which had succeeded in Italy and before Riga were to be tried out on a grand scale. The blow was to be the heaviest delivered in all history. The Kaiser himself assumed nominal command and announced after the conflict had begun that the supreme moment was at hand.

At five o'clock on the morning of March 21, German artillery, aided by some Austrian guns, began a terrific bombardment on a front of about sixty miles, in the region between Arras and La Fère. Long-range guns shelled roads and concentration points as far back as twenty-eight miles behind the lines, while thousands of medium and lighter pieces poured millions of projectiles into the British trenches and battery positions, drenching them with clouds of poison gas. After several hours of this hurricane fire the German storm troops moved forward under cover of a mist to the attack, taking with them great numbers of mobile trench mortars that could be pushed forward by hand. Thus began one of the great epic conflicts of history.

The Blow Falls, March 21, 1918.

The British had expected to be attacked, but they were not prepared for a storm so heavy as that which burst upon them. General von Ludendorff had assembled about a hundred divisions, or approximately a million men, and he launched this great force, like a gigantic spear, full at the breast of his enemy. As one division was exhausted another moved forward to take its place. The outnumbered British fought gallantly, but their line was broken in many places, and they were forced backward. The Fifth British Army was practically cut to pieces. For a time a gap was opened, but the determined efforts of Brigadier-General Carey, who hastily organized a scratch force, which included some Americans, closed the gap and saved the situation. In a little more than a week, however, the Germans retook practically all the ground lost in the battle of the Somme, and in the "strategic retreat" of 1917; they claimed to have captured 90,000 prisoners and 1,300 cannon, and they were within a few miles of the vitally important town of Amiens. But in front of Arras and along Vimy Ridge General Byng's Third Army had held firm, containing the German flood on the north, while French reserves poured up on the south and with machine-guns and 75's inflicted frightful losses on the Germans, who had advanced beyond the protecting fire of their own artillery.

A German Tactical Victory.

During those fateful days the whole world watched the conflict with a tensity of suspense probably never before equalled in human annals. The Germans had neglected nothing to make this "Kaiser's Battle" spectacular and terrible. In the hope of helping to break French morale they began on March 23 to bombard Paris with super-guns, firing from the almost incredible distance of seventy-eight miles, while their aeroplanes made raid after raid upon the city, dropping many bombs and sometimes descending so low as to rake the streets with machine-guns. But the shells from the long-range cannon were comparatively small, did not contain a large bursting charge, and though they killed over 200 civilians, they did comparatively little damage. Because of the bombs and shells, and fear of the Germans taking the city, almost a million people left Paris and took refuge in provinces more remote from the seat of war.

The Super-Guns.

By the early days of April the lines seemed once more to be becoming stabilized, but the Teutonic storm had not yet spent its force. On April 9 the Germans attacked in great strength

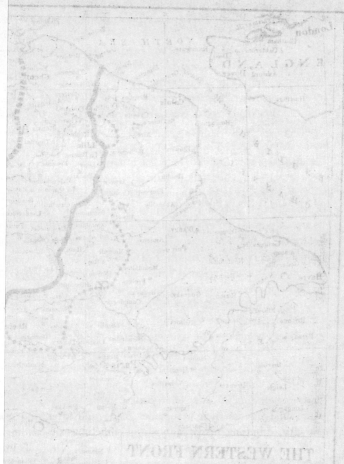

THE WESTERN FRONT
IN 1915

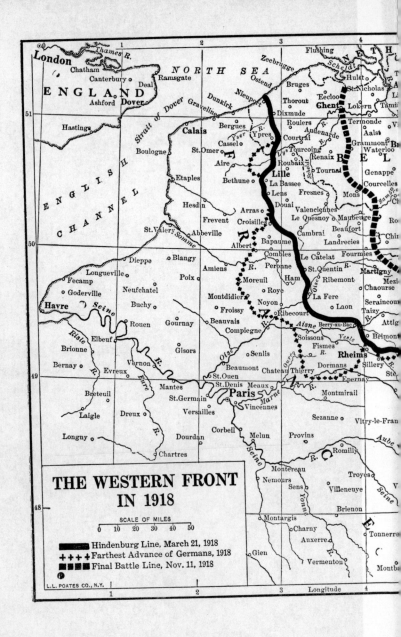

THE WESTERN FRONT
IN 1918

SCALE OF MILES

0   10   20   30   40   50

▬▬▬ Hindenburg Line, March 21, 1918
+ + + + Farthest Advance of Germans, 1918
▰▰▰▰ Final Battle Line, Nov. 11, 1918

L.L. POATES CO., N.Y.

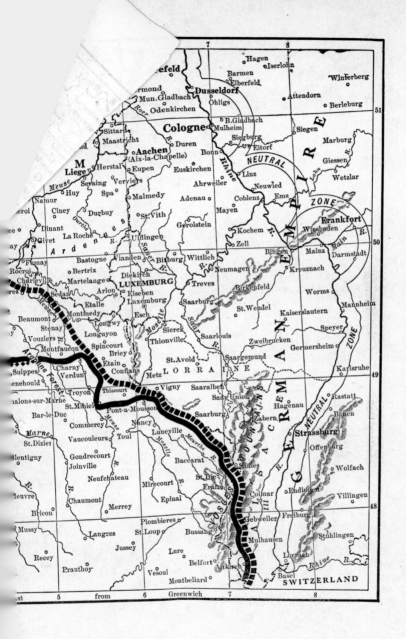

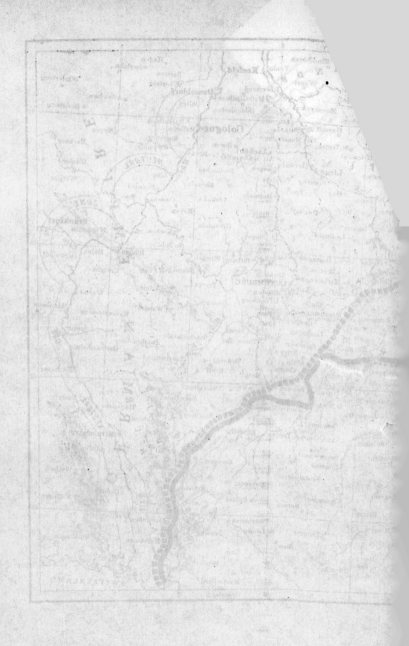

in the region of Armentières and the La Bassée Canal. They
broke through at a point where the line was held by a Portu-
guese division and drove another great wedge into
the Allied front, taking many more prisoners and
guns. By April 12 the situation had become so
desperate that General Haig issued a proclamation in which he
told his men that the enemy were seeking "to separate us from
the French, to take the Channel ports, and to destroy the British army." "Victory," he said, "will belong to the side which
holds out the longest. . . . Every position must be held to
the last man. There must be no retirement. With our backs
to the wall, and believing in the justice of our cause, each one
of us must fight to the end. The safety of our homes and the
freedom of mankind depend alike upon the conduct of each
one of us at this critical moment."

A Desperate Situation.

Extending their attack still further north, the Germans recaptured Messines Ridge and all ground gained by the British
in 1917 in their Flanders offensive. They took Kemmel Hill
and other strong points. Ypres itself was in
danger, no one could say where the flood would go,
but the dogged fighting qualities of the British soldiers and the opportune arrival of strong French
reinforcements once more saved the situation. Repeated German assaults were repulsed with stupendous slaughter, and
again the battle died down.

British and French Valor Check the Drive

The Teutons had won two great tactical victories. They
had taken more than 100,000 prisoners, great numbers of cannon, many tanks, millions of shells, and immense quantities of
other booty, and they had overrun great stretches
of territory. They had brought the Allied cause
to the brink of disaster, and yet they had met a
strategic defeat. They had not divided the British
and French armies. They had not hurled the former back in
irretrievable rout and disorder upon the Channel ports. They
had not won the decision they set out to win. They had lost
time, and time was everything. Other crises were to develop
in the next few months, but never again so grave a one as in

Tactical Victories but a Strategic Defeat.

those weeks of March and April, when British and French valor saved the world in Picardy and Flanders.

Happily the great offensive had some good results. For one thing, it resulted in unity of Allied command. Since the beginning of the war, disaster after disaster had befallen the Allied armies because there was no one man to make decisions. Divided counsels had resulted, and though the final decision might be right, it was often delayed until it was too late. Long before this time Kaiser Wilhelm is reported to have said to King Constantine of Greece: "I shall beat them, for they have no united command." After the Italian disaster a Supreme War Council had been set up at Versailles, but "it was only a body which sought unity of effort through the compromises of conferences." Hitherto international jealousies had prevented the consummation which all clear-sighted men realized was desirable, but in the presence of this supreme crisis selfish thoughts were put aside, and on March 26 the War Council appointed General Ferdinand Foch generalissimo of all the Allied armies. Foch later attributed his appointment to the efforts of Premier Lloyd George, but there can be no doubt that General Pershing, General Bliss, who was our representative on the Council, Secretary of War Baker, who was then in France, and President Wilson exerted their influence in behalf of unified command, and that their influence was helpful in causing the Allied governments to confirm the appointment of Foch as commander-in-chief.

The moment when Foch took command was a critical one, but he was a man made for crises. A scholar and a keen student of military science, he was also a man of action. Before the war, as an instructor at the Ecole de Guerre, he constantly declared: "Battles are won or lost in the minds of those who fight them. No battle is lost until it is believed to be so." At the first battle of the Marne he had commanded the army to whose lot it fell to meet the German effort to break through the French centre. On the decisive day, though hard pressed, he threw forward the immortal Forty-second Division, broke the German line, and helped win the victory. Later in the year he co-ordinated the

French and British forces that fought the first battle of Flanders, and held back the Germans from the Channel ports. He was now condemned temporarily to the defensive, but he had often said in the past that "to make war is to attack," and those who knew him best predicted that when the hour came, he would strike hard and resistlessly. In General Pétain he had an admirable lieutenant, while to Premier Clemenceau, "the Tiger" and crusader for humanity, fell the work of managing civil affairs and keeping up the courage of the people—tasks which, despite his seventy-eight years, he performed like a hero out of Plutarch.

On March 28 General Pershing went to Foch's headquarters and said to him: "I come to say to you that the American people would hold it a great honor for our troops were they engaged in the present battle. I ask it of you in my name and in that of the American people. There is at this moment no other question than that of fighting. Infantry, artillery, aviation—all that we have are yours to dispose of as you will. Others are coming which are as numerous as will be necessary. I have come to say to you that the American people would be proud to be engaged in the greatest battle in history."

Pershing's Offer.

Another result of the offensive was that it showed the Allied peoples the impossibility of peace by compromise. Some men had begun to hope that Germany would be amenable to reason. The idea that the German people were not back of the war had taken fast hold in some circles. But even dreamers were forced to realize that the Germans were mad with the lust of power, and that the downfall of Russia and their victories in the west had revived their hope that they could dictate a conqueror's terms to a vanquished world. Furthermore, many Americans, including some in high position, hugged the vain delusion that Germany would be so deeply impressed by our preparations—by our vast loans, by our aeroplane and shipping programmes, by our military preparations—that she would beg for peace without our being actually forced to fight. We were to march in procession around Jericho, sound the trumpets, and the walls would fall flat. The

Peace Delusions Dissipated.

thing was attempted. The march was made. The trumpets were sounded. But the walls obstinately refused to crumble. Instead of easy-bought victory, the vital question was, Could hard-pressed France and Britain hold back the German horde until America was ready to do her part? Plans for peace were reluctantly tucked away in pigeonholes. With all the people of Germany deliriously applauding victory, even the most optimistic dreamer saw at last that "nothing could unsaddle the men who rode her war-horses, except the thrust of steel." Words counted for nothing; the sword must decide.

General Pershing, with a spirit that did him honor, offered all he had. But as yet he had little. On April 1 less than 370,000 men, of whom about half were non-combatants, had reached Europe. Only four divisions—about 108,000 men, combatants and otherwise—had had experience in the trenches, and some professional observers doubted whether even the most seasoned of these, the First, was ready "to be thrown into the vortex of a violent battle." Only the First, in fact, was at once sent to the active front, being placed opposite the apex of the German salient close to Montdidier. Two other divisions were practically formed but had not yet received their artillery. This artillery must come from French arsenals, as must also aeroplanes, tanks, and most or all of the machine-guns. Over-optimistic officials and press agents had informed the world that by April 1 America would fill the air with a fleet of aeroplanes that would darken the sky. But not a single fighting plane had yet been delivered.

America Not Yet Ready.

In almost every particular the United States was far behind her schedule. For various reasons, there were not in France the number of divisions which, in the words of Lloyd George, "every one had confidently expected would be there." But fortunately, in training-camps at home, there were a million and a half men, and men were sorely needed. They were not thoroughly trained. To organize them into a separate army would take many months. Generals Foch and Pétain had for some time been urging that the Americans should be incorporated with the

Americans to be Brigaded with the British and the French.

French and British armies, but hitherto the Americans had insisted upon acting independently. Now it became clear that as parts of a new machine they would be too late. As new cogs in an old machine they might perform wonders. Lloyd George and Clemenceau submitted to Secretary Baker and to President Wilson a plan for brigading the Americans with the British and French. Acceptance meant sacrifice of American pride, but it was not a time to think of pride. In the words of Lloyd George: "President Wilson assented to the proposal without any hesitation."

Then began the greatest long-distance troop movement in the history of mankind. America had not the ships with which to transport so many men. Great Britain threw her commerce to the winds, drew in her ships from all the seven A Vast Troop seas, and built a bridge of boats across the Atlantic. Movement. American vessels, especially the former German liners, did their part. The French were able to do a little. The British and American navies undertook the work of protecting the transports against the under-water wasps. In April 120,072 men embarked for France; in May 247,714; in June, 280,434; in July, 311,359; in August, 286,375; in September, 259,670; in October, 184,063; in November, 12,124. In all, more than 2,000,000 soldiers were transported through the war zone, with a loss of only 396 men from submarine activities. It was a record of which both navies had good reason to be proud, and it gave the lie to German boasts that they would prevent our men from reaching France. Of those transported, 49 per cent were carried in British ships, 45 per cent by American ships, and the remainder by French and Italian ships, and by Russian ships under British control.

The troops landed in both France and Great Britain, and the people of these countries had concrete evidence of the American Will "invasion," for Americans in uniform were every- Americans where. Their coming worked wonders in keeping up Fight? British and French morale, and yet one vital question had not been definitely answered. It was, Will the Americans fight? Hitherto only the French and the British—including colonials—had shown themselves able to meet the Germans on equal terms. There were pessimists in both France and England who feared lest the newcomers, most of them comparatively fresh from civil life, would not measure up to the bloody work. Up to June there had been no conclusive test. On quiet sectors the Americans had acquitted themselves with credit; and on May 28, in a local counter-offensive, the First Division, commanded by Major-General Robert L. Bullard, retook the town of Cantigny in gallant fashion. But no American division had yet attempted the supreme task of stopping a determined German "drive."

On the day before the American exploit at Cantigny, Ludendorff began a third offensive. Once more the German purpose was carefully concealed, and the surprise was complete. French A New and British forces were sent reeling back from the German Chemin des Dames. The Germans crossed the Offensive. Vesle and the Ourcq. They took Soissons and Fère-en-Tardenois and scores of smaller places. They captured hundreds of guns and many thousands of prisoners. And they came flooding down once more into the valley of the Marne. Foch needed troops badly. Both he and Pershing felt that the time had come to test the real mettle of the men from beyond the seas. The Americans were eager to go in. For months they had been waiting impatiently, like eager hounds straining on the leash.

Two American divisions, the Second, under Major-General Omar Bundy, and the Third, under Major-General Joseph Dickman, were rushed by trains and motor-trucks to the region The of Château-Thierry on the Marne—the point where Americans the Germans were nearest Paris. The Second was Go in. one of the first four divisions in France, and it had had trench experience. The Third had arrived more recently, had not yet received its artillery, and was to have gone to a quiet sector under the support of French guns, when the change of plan placed it in the path of the enemy. One of the brigades of the Second was composed of splendidly drilled, straight-shooting marines, under Brigadier-General Harbord. All the other units of both divisions were regular troops, though a great majority of the men had volunteered since the war began. The motorized machine-gun battalion of the Third was sent at once to the firing line; the other units of the two divisions were put in position to support the French troops ahead, though the 5th machine-gun battalion and some of the marines were sent almost at once into the fight. The sight of so many thousands of Americans rushing to meet the enemy vastly heartened the civilian population, including the crowds of fleeing refugees, and word that the "Sammies" were "going in" stiffened the whole French battle line.

The American machine-gunners and some units of infantry were soon sent to the firing line, and with their aid the French held back the enemy until the early morning of June 4, when Bouresques, Belleau Wood, and Vaux. the Second Division took over a twelve-mile front on both sides of the Paris road. Not content with merely holding, the marines, aided by some regulars, retook the village of Bouresques and Belleau Wood, waging for days a bitter battle with German machine-gunners for the last. In it they captured 700 Germans, and by their valor so impressed the French that the name of the wood was changed to "Bois des marines." Meanwhile machine-gunners from the Third were helping to hold back the enemy in the western outskirts of Château-Thierry, and units from that division were used to replace worn-out units of the Second. On July 1 the 3d Brigade of the Second Division, under Brigadier-General Lewis, recaptured the village of Vaux in a most workmanlike manner, taking 500 prisoners. Elsewhere on the western front more and more Americans were going into the trenches. At Cantigny on June 20 the First Division made another advance, while still farther north (July 4) American infantry brigaded with the British Army aided Australians to perform a notable exploit at Hamel.

After Cantigny and Château-Thierry there could no longer be doubt that Americans would fight, and fight well. The last doubts of the Allies disappeared; French and British spirits soared skyward. In Paris and London startling stories were

told of American valor, of their accuracy of aim, of the panther-
ish fury with which the men went into action, resolved to slay
The
Americans
Will Fight. or be slain. It was hinted that they did not bother
to take prisoners, and it was reported that the Aus-
tralians, who were notorious for not being too gentle
in their methods, conceded that Americans were good soldiers
but a "bit rough"! No one any longer doubted that, given
adequate training and equipment, the Americans would fight
as well as any troops in the war. Even the Germans, who had
invariably made light of American fighting qualities, were finding out their mistake, and the discovery was disquieting.

The claim sometimes made that the Americans in the Château-
Thierry region saved Paris is, however, much too sweeping. It
would be more correct to say that they *helped* to save Paris.
They stood across the Paris road, but the Germans made no
really powerful effort at this time to advance farther in this
region. Farther northward French troops, by employing a new
"yielding defense," baffled all German efforts to widen the
salient, and, particularly in the region of Compiègne, beat back
their assaults with tremendous slaughter. These were the conflicts that really brought the drive to an end.

Thus far the moral, rather than the material, results of our
participation had been most important. But 300,000 Americans were landing in France a month, and the time was near
Allied Rifle
Strength
Passes that
of the
Teutons. when we could strike really weighty blows. Only
a fraction of the Americans in France were yet on
the battle line, but already the "rifle strength" of
the Allies on the western front had passed that of
the Teutons. The Allied total on July 1, according to figures compiled by the Allies, was 1,556,000; of the
Teutons, including a few Austrians, 1,412,000. The evil consequences of putting the best German soldiers into select organizations of "storm troops" were beginning to appear. The
"storm troops" had suffered immense losses, and the fighting
quality of the ordinary divisions, which had been robbed of
their best fighting material, was greatly lowered. By the time
that the Allies took the offensive the German army, though

still powerful, was in the condition of a fighter who after vainly striving to knock out his antagonist finds his own strength badly depleted.

Furthermore, the submarine situation was greatly improved, and glorious events had just taken place on the Italian front. It had been practically a foregone conclusion that at some time the Teutons would launch another "drive" in an attempt to capture Venice and overrun the Lombard plain. If such an attack succeeded, it would practically put Italy out of the war. In view of what had happened in the previous autumn, Allied leaders could not but feel anxious. Foch had not only to hold back the enemy in France but also to keep in mind the possibility of being obliged to furnish men to succor the Italians. But considerable French and British forces, and even a few Americans, were now on the Italian front, while the spirit of Italy had rallied magnificently to meet the crisis. On the 15th of June the long-impending blow fell. On that day the Austrians launched a great offensive along a hundred-mile front from the mountains to the sea. In some places they forced their way over the Piave, but the Italians, French, and British met them with high determination, torrential rains raised the river in their rear, and they were beaten back with great slaughter. The victors took thousands of prisoners, many guns, and much other booty. The failure of the Austrian offensive lifted a great load from Foch's shoulders. The Italian front was safe. He could safely throw all his resources in France against Ludendorff. There can be no doubt that military historians will say that this Austrian defeat marked the beginning of the end.

An Italian Victory and Its Effects.

The great immediate question was, Will the Germans attack again? It was clear that they must either go forward or go back, for the great salients they had driven into the Allied lines, though dangerous to the Allies, were also perilous to themselves. But to retreat would be a confession to their own people and to the world that their great offensive had met defeat. For political reasons, if no other, a new effort must be made. And, still keeping to the

The Germans Prepare a Friedensturm.

policy of holding up a will-o'-the-wisp to hearten their people, the war lords named the new drive a "*Friedensturm*," that is a "storm to bring peace."

Some military critics on the Allied side assumed that the blow would be delivered against the British. But the British had made good their losses in men and material, and had built
They Select the Rheims Salient. so many lines of defense that the prospect in that quarter was not promising. The sector chosen by the Germans was the Rheims salient, and they planned to attack on both sides of Rheims, from Château-Thierry on the Marne almost to the Argonne Forest. Their immediate objectives were Rheims, the so-called "Mountain of Rheims," Epernay, and Châlons. Success might have been followed by a drive on Paris. This time they failed to conceal their intentions, and some days before the attack came the Allied leaders had divined the German plan. Careful preparations were made, and not only were great numbers of French and some Italians concentrated in the threatened sectors, but about 300,000 Americans were on the Marne front or in immediate support.

On the night of July 14 a raiding party of five Frenchmen under a lieutenant named Balestier penetrated the German lines and captured prisoners from whom it was ascertained
The Drive Checked. that the drive would begin next morning. An hour before midnight the Allied artillery opened a furious bombardment, which decimated many of the waiting German units and otherwise played havoc with German plans. The Germans, too, were prodigal with shells, but when the infantry attacked they met a hot reception. East of Rheims General Gouraud's army, which included the famous American "Rainbow Division," yielded the front line according to plan, and then stopped the drive almost immediately, though only after desperate fighting. To the southwest of Rheims French and Italian forces had to cede some ground, but gave up nothing vital. Farther south half a dozen German divisions forced their way over the Marne. In front of the French the assailants made good their foothold. The American forces in this region

belonged to the Third and Twenty-eighth Divisions. Both fought well, though the Third played the larger part. Its artillerymen and riflemen slaughtered the Germans by hundreds as they sought to cross the river, and one regiment, the 38th, under Colonel McAlexander, won immortal glory by holding its position, though surrounded on three sides. It practically annihilated the 6th German Grenadier Regiment, and took 400 prisoners. In some other places the defenders temporarily were driven back from the river, but the Americans counter-attacked, and by noon next day there were no living Germans except prisoners on the south side of the Marne west of Jaulgonne. The Americans had not only repulsed the assailants but had taken over 600 prisoners—news that greatly heartened defenders in other sectors. In some places along the battle front the Germans continued to make efforts to press forward, but by the end of the third day of battle it was clear that the German drive had failed.

For months the Allied leaders had eagerly looked forward to the time when they could snatch the initiative away from the enemy. Foch's hour had struck. The Austrian sword no longer hung threateningly over Italy, while from overseas was pouring an inexhaustible reserve of hardy fighters. Furthermore, Foch had a surprise ready for the enemy. In the preceding November the British had won a striking victory before Cambrai by using tanks. The Allied General Staff decided that the tanks were the long-awaited solution for breaking through the German lines. They decided to build vast fleets of them, especially light, swift tanks, which would be less easily hit by shells than the bigger kind. Some of the new tanks were ready when the Germans launched their March offensive, yet, in spite of the critical moment, Foch refused to use them and thus reveal his hand. Now, however, he had great numbers of tanks, both of the heavier sort and of the lighter variety, called "whippets" by the British and "mosquitoes" by the French. In the words of General Malleterre: "On July 18 General Foch was ready, with his tanks, his cannon, his shells, his Americans. Then began the battle of liberation."

Foch's Opportunity.

With Pétain and Pershing, Foch arranged a great counter-blow at the Marne salient. Two powerful armies under Generals Mangin and Degoutte were secretly assembled on the west side of the salient, and with these armies were two American divisions, the First and the Second.

The Counter-Blow.

At dawn of the 18th, without a preliminary bombardment, these armies, aided by French tanks, suddenly dashed forward behind a rolling barrage. The Germans were completely surprised. Thousands of prisoners and many guns were taken. By nightfall the invaders had been swept back several miles. Caught at a disadvantage, the German High Command threw in hosts of reserves, but in vain. The Allies, including more Americans and even some British, attacked the salient from three sides. The Germans fought stubbornly, but day after day they were forced back. Soissons and Fère-en-Tardenois were retaken, and the invaders were driven over the Ourcq and then over the Vesle. More than 30,000 Germans, 700 cannons, and vast quantities of war material had been captured. The First and Second American Divisions alone took 7,000 prisoners and over 100 guns.

"To make war is to attack," Foch had always contended. He lived up to his maxim now. Hardly were the Crown Prince's forces back over the Vesle, when British and French forces, under Haig, launched (August 8) a new offensive against the point of the salient projecting toward Amiens. Great numbers of tanks were used, and with comparatively small losses the Allies won a great victory. In his book on the war Ludendorff calls this "Germany's Black Day." In less than a week more than 40,000 Germans and several hundred guns were taken. The victors pushed forward relentlessly after the enemy.

Haig's Great Victory.

Meanwhile other strokes were preparing, for Foch was determined not to give the enemy breathing time. His system differed from that of Ludendorff. Ludendorff's plan was to gather all available resources for a stupendous, smashing blow. His system had won victories, but it had a weakness in that several weeks were required to prepare a new blow, and in the interval his enemy had opportunity to recuperate. Foch, like a skilled boxer, struck now here, now there, and the Germans were kept constantly on the run. The war had become one of movement, and Foch was resolved to harry his enemies to the utmost before they could return to their intrenched lines. Though making no promises and even deprecating high hopes, he was striving for a final decision.

Foch's Strategy.

Late in August the British under Byng smashed through the Hindenburg Line, southeast of Arras, while in the same period General Mangin swept the Germans out of high ground north of the Aisne. Early in September the British under Horne broke the famous Drocourt-Quéant switch line on a front of six miles. Up in Flanders the Germans evacuated the Lys salient, closely followed and harassed by the Allies. All along the battle front, from Verdun to the sea, the Allies were pressing the enemy hard, and in most of these movements Americans took part. By the middle of September the Germans were once more virtually back in the old Hindenburg Line, from which they had launched their great offensive in the spring. But in two months they had lost nearly 200,000 prisoners, immense numbers in killed and wounded, over 2,000 pieces of artillery, and vast quantities of supplies. Furthermore, the Hindenburg Line east of Arras and the switch line behind it were already breached. The great question was, Could the Germans hold the Hindenburg Line until winter gave them respite? If they could, they might still obtain favorable terms from a war-weary world.

Germans Driven Back to Hindenburg Line.

Meanwhile General Pershing had been organizing an army under his own immediate command. Long ago it had been settled that our first independent effort should be made against the St. Mihiel salient, which projected southeast of Verdun like an arrow pointed at the heart of France. To erase it was a necessary preliminary to a more ambitious effort. General Pershing gathered a force of about 600,000 men, mostly Americans but including some French. The French and British lent many guns,

Americans Erase the St. Mihiel Salient.

airplanes, and tanks. On the night of September 11 a tremendous bombardment was opened upon the salient, which the Germans were beginning to evacuate. In the early morning the infantry and tanks "went over the top." Twenty-seven hours later the salient was only a memory. Sixteen thousand prisoners, 443 guns, much war material, and valuable territory were taken. Our total casualties were only 7,000. In the words of Pershing: "The Allies found they had a formidable army to aid them, and the enemy learned finally that he had one to reckon with."

The victory also enabled our forces to threaten Metz and the rich Briey iron-fields, from which Germany drew most of her all-essential iron ore. But for the moment these were not
A New American Objective. the American objectives. On the very day after the reduction of the salient artillery and fresh troops began moving toward the line between the Meuse River and the western edge of the Argonne Forest. The immediate object of attack would be the German zone of defense in this region, but twenty-five miles to the northward, at Mézières and Sedan, lay the main enemy artery of communication between Germany and Belgium and northern France. This was Pershing's real goal.

But Foch, the master of all Allied forces, did not confine his plans to the western front. On September 19 General Allenby began an offensive which speedily resulted in the practical
Allenby's Great Victory in Palestine. annihilation of the Turkish army in Palestine. Furthermore, his victorious forces pushed forward, and in the middle of October cut the Berlin to Bagdad Railway near Aleppo, thus isolating the Turkish forces in Mesopotamia and compelling their ultimate surrender. Allenby's spectacular blow practically put Turkey out of the war.

Bulgaria Beaten. Almost simultaneously the Allied army at Salonica, under General Franchet d'Espérey, began (September 14) an offensive northward from Salonica. In a few days the lines of the enemy were broken, and Bulgaria, threatened with annihilation, signed an armistice which was practically a surrender at discretion. This great victory insured the early capitulation of Turkey. It enabled the Serbians to return to their homeland, and it made certain, barring an early peace, the re-entry of Roumania into the war and an invasion of Austria-Hungary from the south and southeast.

The news from the Balkans and Palestine sounded the death-knell to Teutonic hopes. The whole Teutonic edifice was collapsing like a house of cards. Many hundreds of thousands of seasoned Allied troops would be freed for operations against Austria-Hungary and Germany, while an endless stream of Americans continued to pour across the Atlantic. The U-boat campaign was breaking down, Allied construction of ships had passed submarine destruction, and it was clear that the U-boats could not win the war. A speedy peace was the only way whereby the Teutons could save anything from the wreck. Already, on September 15, the Austro-Hungarian Government, with the secret approval of Germany, had asked for a preliminary and "non-binding" discussion of war aims with a view to the possible calling of a peace conference. Happily the Allies avoided the trap.

The Teutons See the Writing on the Wall.

In the last days of September the Allies began the epic struggle that will probably be known as the battle of the Hindenburg Line. An American army, aided by French forces on its left, began a drive down the Meuse Valley, while far to the northwest in Flanders British, Belgians, and French struck in the region of Ypres. Both drives made valuable gains, and since the first was mainly an American venture, more space will be given it in subsequent pages. A little later the French, aided by some Americans, assailed the enemy defenses before Rheims, while the British struck squarely at the Hindenburg Line in the region of St. Quentin and Cambrai. Of all the great hammer-strokes that won the war this was the mightiest, and participating in it were American divisions, notably the Twenty-seventh New York and the "Wildcat Division," the latter largely composed of straight-shooting Southern mountaineers, under Major-General

Battle of the Hindenburg Line.

Lewis. The blow broke the Hindenburg Line on a wide front, and, for the first time since the beginning of trench warfare in the West, the Allies were through the maze of defenses and were fighting in the open. In all these operations great numbers of prisoners and guns were taken, while the Germans were forced to sacrifice immense quantities of supplies. By the end of the third week in October the Hindenburg Line had passed into history, the Germans had evacuated the Belgian coast, and their government was seeking an armistice. But while the negotiations were proceeding, the Allies continued to push ahead, and victories were becoming as monotonous as defeats had once been.

Let us now return to Pershing's army. The task set the Americans was an appalling one. They must make a direct frontal attack in rough, difficult country upon line after line The American of carefully prepared intrenchments, and, as the Drive down holding of these lines was absolutely vital to the the Meuse. safety of most of their army, the Germans might be depended upon to defend them with the courage of despair. On the night of September 25 the Americans quietly took the place of French troops on the sector. Next day they charged through the barbed-wire entanglements and the sea of shell-craters across No Man's Land and mastered all the first-line defenses. The assault was continued on the next two days, against increasing resistance, and gains of from three to seven miles were made, while 10,000 prisoners were taken. Meanwhile French forces on the other side of the Argonne Forest made good progress.

Thus began the bloodiest battle in American history, a conflict somewhat resembling that in the Wilderness fifty-three years before, but on a larger scale and more prolonged. The enemy speedily flung reserve divisions into the fray, The Greatest Battle in and Pershing did likewise. By the 4th of October American the American artillery had been brought up, and History. the infantry again surged forward. Bitter fighting took place all along the line, and not least of all in the gloomy recesses of the almost impenetrable Argonne Forest. The German machine-gunners fought for every foot of ground, and exacted a heavy toll of the assailants, most of whom were taking part in their first great battle. But by October 10 the Americans, with French assistance, had cleared the forest. The great obstacle was now the second zone of German defense, the Kriemhilde Line, but with dogged determination the Americans slowly battered their way forward through this line. Every day thousands upon thousands fell, and the whole battle zone was an inferno of machine-guns, shells, and deadly gas, but Pershing was determined to play his part in the great drama, and sent division after division, some of them without any fighting experience, into the maw of war. To do so was the truest mercy, for the German reserves were rapidly becoming exhausted, each victory made the next easier, the end of the war was in sight, and a quick push and a strong push would be infinitely cheaper in blood than a long-drawn-out conflict.

On November 1 the final advance was begun. After heavy fighting the Germans were flung back, and on the 6th the Rainbow Division reached a point on the Meuse opposite Sedan. In the words of Pershing: "The strategical goal which was our highest hope was gained. We had cut the enemy's main line of communications, and nothing but surrender or an armistice could save his army from complete disaster." Between September 26 and November 6 the American army in the Meuse-Argonne battle had beaten 40 German divisions, most of which, however, were far below normal strength, had taken 26,059 prisoners, and 468 guns. Its own losses had, however, been enormous, exceeding 100,000 men killed, wounded, or missing.

The Goal Reached.

During the whole war the American losses in killed, wounded, missing, and dead of disease, numbered 302,612. The total number of dead was 77,118, including 34,248 killed and 13,700 mortally wounded. The Americans captured about 44,000 prisoners and 1,400 guns, howitzers, and trench mortars. The French and British losses, even for 1918, were much heavier, and they captured several times as many prisoners and guns. During 1918 the British alone captured on the west front 201,000 prisoners and 2,850 guns.

It will no doubt be the final verdict of history that the American army played the decisive part in the final campaign, though its part in the actual fighting was smaller than that of France or Great Britain. American food and money were also vital factors in the fortunate out-come. Comparisons with commonplace things are sometimes illuminating. America played the part of a strong man who, in passing down the street, sees half a dozen men struggling to put a heavy piano into a van. The weight promises to be a little too much for them, but with the aid of the newcomer the piano is lifted in. Perhaps the volunteer does not lift so hard as do the others, certainly he is not so badly exhausted, yet his aid was essential to the performance of the task.

America's Part in the Victory.

The work done by our forces in the field is all the more creditable to them because America was not yet really ready. Many divisions were thrown into the vortex of battle before they had finished their training, and for artillery, airplanes, and tanks our armies were largely (in the matter of tanks wholly) dependent upon the French and British. At the moment the armistice was signed America's prodigious effort in the making of war material was just beginning to bear fruit in a large way, and had the contest lasted until the spring of 1919 there would have been no lack of equipment. As it was, American pluck and determination to win triumphed over all obstacles and achieved victory, though at bloody cost. Some military critics assert that American losses were double what they would have been had the armies been better equipped and the men and officers thoroughly trained.

America's War Effort Just Beginning to Bear Fruit.

By the end of the first week in November the cause of the Central Powers was absolutely hopeless. Bulgaria was out of the war; Turkey was negotiating for surrender; parts of Austria-Hungary were virtually in revolt. A sudden Italian offensive resulted in the absolute ruin of the Austro-Hungarian army and the capture of 300,000 prisoners and 5,000 guns. The French, British,

Hopeless Situation of the Central Powers.

Belgians, and Americans were pressing relentlessly after the remnants of Ludendorff's beaten army, the "rifle strength" of which had been reduced to less than 900,000 men. Foch was on the point of launching in Lorraine a new offensive, which would doubtless have gone through the German lines like water through a sieve. An attempt to send out the German High Seas Fleet had provoked a mutiny. Furthermore, the German "home front" had broken down.

Before the end of September the Germans had realized that they must make peace. Prince Maximilian of Baden succeeded Count von Hertling as imperial chancellor. In a few days he transmitted (October 4) through the Swiss Government a request that President Wilson should invite all the belligerents to send plenipotentiaries for the purpose of opening peace negotiations. The note added that Germany accepted "as a basis for peace negotiations" the programme set forth by President Wilson in a speech he had made to Congress on January 8, 1918, and in later pronouncements, especially in a speech made on September 27. In his speech of January 8 Wilson had set forth fourteen points he considered essential to peace. In general, these points summarized the terms Allied statesmen were demanding, but added some others. They included a stipulation for "open covenants of peace openly arrived at" and no secret diplomacy in future; freedom of the seas in both peace and war; reduction of armaments; impartial adjustment of colonial claims, with due regard to the interests of the native inhabitants; evacuation of all territory conquered by the Central Powers, with reparation and restoration for Belgium, France, Serbia, etc.; Alsace and Lorraine to be given to France; readjustment of the frontiers of Italy along lines of nationality; the peoples of Austria-Hungary to be given opportunity for autonomous development; the Dardanelles to be opened permanently as a free passage to the commerce of the world, and the subject peoples in the Turkish Empire to be given an opportunity for autonomous development; an independent Poland; and the formation of a general association of nations

Germany Asks for Peace.

The Fourteen Points.

to safeguard the political independence and territorial integrity of great and small states alike. In his speech of September 27 the President had dwelt in more general terms upon what he considered the essentials of a just peace and had declared that no peace could be made "by any kind of bargain or compromise with the Governments of the Central Empires. . . . They have convinced us that they are without honor and do not intend justice. They observe no covenants, accept no principles but force and their own interest." To avoid further bloodshed, the German Government also asked for an immediate armistice.

A few days later the imperial chancellor announced changes in the German system of government, and an effort was made to convince the world that there had been a real transforma-
Changes in German Government.
tion. The changes were designed to satisfy home demands and to persuade the world that the war lords were no longer all-powerful. The world, however, displayed some skepticism as to whether the revolution had been as thorough-going as Prince Max pretended.

In reply President Wilson queried (October 8) whether acceptance of his peace terms meant that Germany's "object in entering into discussions would be only to agree upon the prac-
American Reply.
tical details of their application?" He also inquired "whether the imperial chancellor is speaking merely for the military authorities of the empire who have so far conducted the war." He further informed Germany that he would not propose a cessation of arms to the governments with whom the United States was associated so long as the armies of Germany were upon their soil.

The German Government responded that it accepted the President's peace programme, and added that both it and
The German Response.
Austria-Hungary were ready to evacuate occupied territory. It also stated that the existing government had been "formed by conferences and in agreement with the great majority of the Reichstag," and that the chancellor, "supported in all his actions by the will of this

majority, speaks in the name of the General Government and of the German people."

These interchanges aroused profound interest throughout the world. In Berlin the people shouted "Peace at last," and even strangers, meeting on the streets, would kiss one another and shout peace congratulations. In the outside world wide differences of opinion developed. In some circles it was believed that, realizing she was beaten, Germany was seeking to avoid the consequences of defeat. Many people feared that the President, in his enthusiasm for peace, would be too lenient. The almost universal opinion was that if the Germans desired an armistice they should make a proposition to Field Marshal Foch. A strong sentiment developed that the only terms granted should be "Unconditional Surrender." Fresh devastations in France and Belgium and new submarine atrocities served to increase the demand for rigorous dealing.

In a note of October 14 the President stated that the conditions of an armistice must be left to the military authorities. He also quoted from a speech in which he had laid down, as one of the terms of peace, "the destruction of every arbitrary power anywhere that can separately, secretly, and of its single choice disturb the peace of the world; or, if it cannot be presently destroyed, at least its reduction to virtual impotency." He had referred, of course, to the Hohenzollerns and the Hapsburgs, and he now stated that the passage quoted constituted "a condition precedent to peace, if peace is to come by the act of the German people themselves."

An Armistice a Matter for the Military Authorities.

A week previously Austria-Hungary had made a similar proposal for an armistice and peace negotiations. The President replied (October 19) that many things had happened since he laid down his fourteen points, and that the principle of "autonomy" for the Czecho-Slovaks and other subject peoples could no longer serve as a basis of peace. The inference was that only complete independence for these peoples would now suffice.

In a third note, dated October 20, the German Government

defended its military and naval forces against charges of inhumanity brought in the President's preceding communication,

The Third German Note. and continued to insist that a real change in government had taken place, and that the offer of peace and of an armistice had come from a government "free from any arbitrary and irresponsible influence," and "supported by the approval of an overwhelming majority of the German people."

In a third answer (October 23) the President reiterated that the granting of an armistice lay within the province of the military authorities, and he bluntly pointed out reasons why extraordinary safeguards must be demanded. He

Wilson Demands Safeguards. declared "that the nations of the world do not and cannot trust the word of those who have hitherto been the masters of German policy." He added that if the United States "must deal with the military masters and the monarchical autocrats of Germany, or if it is likely to have to deal with them later in regard to the international obligations of the German Empire, it must demand, not peace negotiations, but surrender."

Meanwhile the Allied armies had pressed onward, and every day the military situation from the Teutonic point of view had grown more desperate. Field-Marshal von Hindenburg him-

Hindenburg for an Armistice. self realized the necessity of peace, and supported the attempt to secure an armistice. A session of the German war cabinet and of the crown council took place in which the Kaiser and the Crown Prince participated. General Ludendorff resigned, and on October 27 the German Government once more informed President Wilson that it represented the people and that the military powers were subject to its authority. It closed by saying that it awaited proposals for an armistice.

In the meantime the Allies had conferred with each other regarding the terms of the armistice, and an agreement was reached. On November 5 the President transmitted a final note in which he stated that the Allies took exception to some of the principles enunciated by him. For example, they must reserve to themselves complete freedom as to the subject of "the freedom of the seas." They would also insist that the

Important Allied Amendments. stipulation that "invaded territories must be restored as well as evacuated" must be interpreted to mean "that compensation will be made by Germany for all damage done to the civilian population of the Allies and their property by the aggression of Germany by land, by sea, and from the air." This last reservation was very sweeping and was susceptible of very broad interpretation. The President closed by saying that on application to Foch the Germans could secure the terms of armistice.

The Teutons were beaten. They had struck for "world power or downfall" and had achieved the latter. Austria, her army overwhelmed, had already signed an armistice in the field on November 3. On the morning of November 8 German representatives appeared at Foch's

Foch Presents the Terms. headquarters, which were in a railway train near Rethondes, and the field-marshal whose genius had, in four months, transformed defeat into overwhelming victory, gave them the terms of the armistice. The Germans had been prepared by semiofficial communications for the stipulations as a whole, but the concrete demands seemed to bring to them for the first time the full realization of the extent of German defeat.

The terms were severe, but not too severe. They included the immediate evacuation of all invaded territory, the surrender of 5,000 cannons, 25,000 machine guns, 1,700 airplanes,

Terms of the Armistice, November 11, 1918. all the German submarines, and practically all the fighting forces of the German above-water navy. All of Germany west of the Rhine was to be occupied by Allied troops, who were also to hold bridgeheads at Mayence, Coblenz, and Cologne. A neutral zone ten kilometers wide was to be drawn on the right bank of the Rhine. A German courier carried the terms to the German headquarters at Spa. A revolution had already broken out in Germany. The Kaiser abdicated (November 10), and he and the Crown Prince fled to Holland. At five o'clock A. M.,

Paris time, on November 11 the armistice was signed, to take effect at eleven o'clock A. M. that day. The Allied armies continued to fight up to the last minute of time. The Great War, the most stupendous in history, was over.

As rapidly as possible the German forces were withdrawn from France and Belgium. Allied troops followed them as far as the Rhine. There were some delays in fulfilling other terms of the armistice, but all the essential ones, Fulfilling the Terms. together with some subsequently imposed, were ultimately complied with. The submarines were surrendered at intervals, and on November 21 the main force of the German High Seas Fleet sailed over the North Sea and surrendered to Admiral Beatty and the Allied armada off the Firth of Forth. Included in that armada were some American battleships. A surrender on so gigantic a scale had never before occurred in naval history. *"Der Tag"* had come, but the day brought no satisfaction to those who had toasted it.

CHAPTER XXIII

THE PEACE CONFERENCE

SIX days before the end of hostilities the congressional elections took place in the United States. The campaign had been one of the quietest in recent history, for a deadly plague of influenza had, to a large extent, prevented public meetings, and, furthermore, a strong desire existed to avoid awakening party animosities lest they interfere with the prosecution of the war. President Wilson himself had deprecated political discussion and had declared that "politics is adjourned." There was, however, a decided current of opposition to the party in power, and the Republican managers quietly made the most of it. Republican speakers and writers contended that their party had been more energetic in carrying on the war than had the Democrats. They criticised the alleged incompetence of the party in power, emphasized its failure to prepare for the conflict, and referred sarcastically to the Democratic slogan of 1916, "He kept us out of war." On October 24 President Wilson precipitated a more active contest by issuing an appeal to the country asking that if it approved his "leadership" and wished him to continue to be its "unembarrassed spokesman" it should return "a Democratic majority to both the Senate and the House of Representatives." He declared that the election of a Republican majority in either house would be interpreted abroad as a "repudiation of my leadership." He admitted that the Republicans had been pro-war, but asserted that they were anti-administration and wished to take control away from him. Many Democratic speakers and newspapers contended that a Republican victory would encourage the Germans and would prolong the war. Ex-Presidents Roosevelt and Taft, who were now reconciled, issued a joint statement appealing to the country to elect a Republican Congress, while Republican speakers and newspapers insisted that the Germans would derive cold comfort from the success of a party of which Colonel Roosevelt was the main leader. The truth was that, thanks to Foch's soldiers, the German fighting power was at its last gasp and the result of an American election could have no influence upon the outcome of the struggle.

Speedy victory in the war was now a certainty, and victory in war almost invariably results in political victory for the party in power. But conditions were peculiar, and, rightly or wrongly, the majority of Americans were dissatis-
A Republican Victory. fied with Democratic rule. The elections resulted in a sweeping Republican victory. Out of thirty-one governors elected twenty-one were Republicans. The considerable Democratic majority in the Senate was transformed into a Republican majority of two. The Republicans won a majority in the House of over forty. Meyer London, the Socialist representative in the old House, lost his seat, but in Milwaukee Victor Berger, who was under indictment for sedition, was elected.

For six years the Democrats had controlled the government, and Wilson's wishes and policies had prevailed. After March 4, 1919, the Wilsonian predominance would be at an end, and
Democratic Predominance at an End. with Republican majorities in Congress, it was certain that the next two years would witness bitter struggles between the executive and legislative branches. There would be searching investigations into the management of the war, and the Republicans would participate in the handling of the after-the-war problems.

The war had proved to be expensive beyond all precedent. By April, 1919, the government in two years had expended $30,700,000,000, which was about $4,000,000,000 in excess of
Vast Expenditures. the expenditures of the national government from Washington's day down to 1917, including all civil expenses and the cost of all our other wars. For a period of two years disbursements averaged $1,500,000 an hour. In fact, even since the signing of the armistice the government had spent more than it had expended in the Civil

War. Eight billion eight hundred and fifty million dollars had been advanced to our Allies, and further loans were subsequently made; part, though probably not all, of the loans will doubtless be repaid. Great expenses still loomed ahead, and a tax bill designed to raise $6,000,000,000 the first year had just been passed.

The economic condition of almost the whole world was bad. Some of the European belligerents had gone into debt to the extent of half their national wealth. It was certain that for many generations their people would stagger under stupendous financial burdens. In fact, repudiation seemed certain in some cases, and the Bolshevist government in Russia had already taken that method of escaping irksome obligations. The debt of the United States, though enormous, could be paid, though it would require skilful management. But the immediate financial future of the country gave thoughtful men much anxiety. Prices were high beyond all precedent, as were also wages. The whole business of the country was on stilts. It was doubtful whether it could be lowered to a normal level without a catastrophe. The sudden ending of the conflict had found the country as unprepared for peace as the beginning had found it unprepared for war. The closing of munition plants threw millions temporarily out of work, and the return of discharged soldiers increased the labor problem. The railroad situation was very bad, and, though passenger and freight rates had been largely increased and business had been exceptionally good, the cost of operation exceeded the receipts by hundreds of millions of dollars. Never since the Civil War had the United States faced so many difficult problems of readjustment.

A World in Ferment.

On November 18 it was officially announced that President Wilson would himself attend the peace conference, which was to meet at Paris. The announcement created much discussion. Some critics asserted that it would be illegal for him to leave the country, and in both houses of Congress Republicans introduced resolutions to the effect that the office of President would be vacated during his

Wilson to Go to the Peace Conference.

absence. As a matter of fact, neither the Constitution nor the laws limit the President in this matter, and, though a sort of tradition had arisen that the President should not leave the country, it had not always been observed. President Roosevelt visited the Panama Canal during his administration, though, to be sure, he went on an American war-ship and while in the Canal Zone was on American territory. President Taft, however, in his administration held a meeting with President Diaz on Mexican soil. President Wilson continued to be chief executive while abroad, but during his absence, in obedience to a request on his part, Vice-President Marshall presided over the cabinet meetings. Mr. Marshall did not, however, attempt to exercise any other functions of the presidential office.

On November 29 it was announced that the representatives of the United States at the conference would be the President himself, Secretary of State Lansing, Henry White, former ambassador to France, Colonel Edward M. House, and The American Delegation. General Tasker H. Bliss. Opponents of the administration criticised the make-up of the commission, alleging that some prominent Republicans should have been given places on it, for, though White was a member of that party, he was not high in its councils. Some members of the Senate were also inclined to feel that that body, which is a part of the treaty-making power, should have been represented.

The peace commission and a large corps of expert advisers sailed from New York on December 4, on board the *George Washington*, a former German liner, and reached Brest nine days later. In France, and also in Italy and England, both of which he visited before the conference assembled, President Wilson was accorded a popular reception rarely equalled in its enthusiasm, the homage paid him being partly personal, partly a tribute to America. During these visits he had an opportunity to meet and confer with the statesmen of the three countries concerning the work ahead.

Perhaps never before, and certainly not since the Congress of

Vienna, had there been a peace conference that was confronted by so many complex problems. There was the question of the

Complexity of Peace Problems.

future peace of the world, that of reparation for injuries done, new boundaries to be fixed, new nations claiming independence and recognition, punishment of the guilty—all complicated questions regarding which there were certain to be grave differences even between the victors.

The victors proceeded on the assumption that the vanquished should have no part in formulating the terms of peace. In fact, representatives of the vanquished were not even allowed

Victors Draw up the Terms.

to come to Paris until the terms were ready. The real work of drawing up the terms was chiefly done by the representatives of Great Britain, France, the United States, Italy, and, to a lesser degree, Japan. The weaker nations were allowed little real participation except in matters directly affecting them, but all, great and small alike, were accorded an opportunity to pass upon the completed work.

The first great question to which the conference turned its attention was that of inventing some means for preventing future wars. The subject was one to which many men in all

The Prevention of War.

civilized countries had devoted much attention. The plan finally adopted may be said in a sense to have had its origin in the League to Enforce Peace, a body formally organized in Independence Hall, Philadelphia, in June, 1915, with William H. Taft as president. The programme of the league had been approved by statesmen in most of the warring nations, and President Wilson, in particular, had become an ardent advocate of the general idea. It was largely through his insistent advocacy that the matter was taken up by the conference before what many considered the more immediately pressing problem of bringing the existing war to an end was solved. The attitude of other members of the conference varied from enthusiastic support through various shades of doubt to open hostility. Most seem to have been somewhat skeptical as to the success of any plan that might be adopted, but even many of the skeptics were willing that the experiment should be made.

After months of discussion and amendment the conference finally adopted a "covenant" based upon a plan submitted by General Smuts, the representative of South Africa. The cov-

The League of Nations Covenant. enant provided for the creation of a league of nations, the main object of which was "to secure international peace and security by the acceptance of obligations not to resort to war." The machinery of the league was to consist of an assembly, a council, and a permanent secretariat. The assembly was to consist of representatives of members of the league and was to meet at stated intervals, or from time to time at the seat of the league, or at such other place as might be decided upon. It was to deal with any matter within the sphere of action of the league or affecting the peace of the world. With a single exception, each power was to have one vote in the assembly, and could not have more than three representatives, but five of the British colonies were given membership, so that the British Empire, as a whole, had six votes.

The council was to consist of representatives of the United States, the British Empire, France, Italy, and Japan, together with four other members of the league. These four were to

The Council. be chosen from time to time by the assembly at its discretion. With the approval of the assembly, the council might name additional members of the league, whose representatives should be members of the council. The council was to meet as occasion might require, and at least once a year. At its meetings it might consider any matter within the sphere of action of the league or affecting the peace of the world. At meetings of the council each member of the league represented on the council should have only one vote, but might have more than one representative. Any member of the league not represented on the council should be invited to send a representative to sit as a member during the consideration of matters especially affecting its interests.

A permanent secretariat was to be established at the seat of

the league, and was to consist of a secretary-general and such
secretaries and staff as might be required. The
The Secretariat. first secretary-general was to be named by the
peace conference. Thereafter he was to be appointed by the council with the approval of a majority of the
assembly.

The covenant recognized the importance of reducing national
armaments, and provided that the council should take account
of the geographical situation and circumstances of each state,
and formulate plans for such reduction for the con-
Reduction of Armaments. sideration and action of the several governments.
Such plans were to be subject to the reconsidera-
tion of the council each year. The members of the league undertook to give full and frank information as to the scale of their
military and naval preparations.

Members of the league undertook to respect and preserve
as against external aggression the territorial
Mutual Guarantee of Territories. integrity and political independence of all the
members.

Any war or threat of war, whether or not it immediately
affected members of the league, was to be considered a matter
of concern to the whole body, and the league was to take any
step deemed wise to safeguard the integrity of the
Preventing War. nations. In case such an emergency should arise,
the secretary-general, on the request of any member
of the league, could forthwith summon a meeting of the council. Any member of the league should have the right to bring
to the attention of the assembly or the council any circumstance
which should threaten to destroy either the peace or the good
understanding of the nations.

All members of the league should agree that in case of a mis-
understanding likely to lead to a rupture they would submit
the matter either to arbitration or to an inquiry by the council,
and in no case resort to war until three months after
Arbitration. the award by the arbitrators or the report by the
council. The members agreed, furthermore, that whenever
any dispute should arise which they might recognize as suitable

for submission to arbitration, and which could not be satisfactorily settled by diplomacy, they would submit the whole subject to arbitration.

The council should formulate and submit to the members of the league plans for the establishment of a permanent court of international justice, which should be competent to hear and determine any dispute of international character.

Permanent Court of Arbitration.

In case any member of the league should resort to war in disregard of its covenants, it should, *ipso facto*, be deemed to have committed an act of war against all other members of the league, which should undertake immediately to bring it to terms by cutting off all relations, financially and otherwise, with the offending state. It should also be the duty of the council in such case to recommend to the governments concerned what forces of the league should be contributed to be used to protect the league's covenants.

International Boycott.

In case of a dispute between a member of the league and a state not belonging to the league, or between states neither of them members of the league, the state or states not members of the league should be invited to accept the obligation of membership in the league for the purpose of such dispute upon such conditions as the council might deem just. In case a state so invited should refuse, the council might take such measures and make such recommendations as would prevent hostilities and would result in the peaceful settlement of the dispute.

States Outside the League.

One article of the covenant established a system of mandatories for the conquered German colonies. Another bound the members of the league to secure fair conditions of labor for men, women, and children.

Mandatories and Labor.

Still another article, adopted to conciliate opposition in the United States, was to the effect that nothing in the covenant should "affect the validity of international treaties of arbitration or regional understandings like the Monroe Doctrine for securing the maintenance of peace."

The Monroe Doctrine.

Amendments to the covenant were to take effect when ratified by all the members of the league whose representatives composed the council, and by a majority of the members of

Amendments. the league whose representatives composed the assembly. No such amendment should bind any member of the league which refused to accept such amendment, but in case of refusal it should cease to be a member of the league.

In settling the terms of peace grave differences inevitably developed between the victors. One of the most serious arose over the disposition of the port of Fiume on the eastern Adriatic.

Fiume Dispute. The Italian delegates claimed that under the principle of self-determination Fiume must be assigned to Italy because most of the inhabitants were Italians. The Jugo-Slavs insisted, however, that the whole region about Fiume must belong to them, because a majority of the people outside the city were of their race, and also because they needed the city as a convenient outlet upon the Adriatic. President Wilson strongly opposed the Italian claims, and a quarrel developed which resulted in the temporary withdrawal of the Italian delegates from the conference. Presently the Italian poet and patriot, Gabriel d'Annunzio, with a force of volunteers, seized Fiume in Garibaldian fashion and held it for Italy. Thereafter the dispute dragged along for many months.

Another serious controversy arose over the disposition of the peninsula of Shantung, which had been redeemed from German rule by Japanese and British forces in 1914. China claimed

Shantung Dispute. that, as the original owner, Shantung should immediately be handed back to her, but Japan demurred. Ultimately the conference, partly because of secret treaties made during the war, accepted the Japanese view. Japan was to restore the peninsula at some future time to China, but she was to obtain railroads and other concessions, including the right to make a settlement at Tsing-Tao, south of Kiao-Chau. In many quarters the feeling existed that Japan had been too grasping, and that her policy with regard to

Shantung afforded new evidence of her intention of transforming China into a vassal state.

The completion of the treaty required so much time that it was not until May 7 that the document was delivered to the German delegates, who had been summoned to Paris for that

Germany Accepts.

purpose. Its terms aroused great opposition in Germany, and a cry was raised that the treaty went beyond the "fourteen points" and the other principles which, according to the agreement at the time of the armistice, were to form the basis for negotiations. However, the world knew that the terms were less severe than those which Germany would have imposed upon her enemies had she been victorious, and little heed was paid to German outcries regarding "a peace of violence." The conference consented to modify some of the terms, and then insisted that Germany take the irreducible minimum. Rather than endure invasion, the German National Assembly at last voted to accept.

The treaty is a document of about 80,000 words, but in this book we need consider only the broader outlines. Germany gave up her claims to all her colonies, ceded Alsace-Lorraine to

The Territorial Terms.

France and a small district to Belgium, and on her eastern border resigned much territory to the re-created state of Poland. The port of Dantzig was internationalized, while plebiscites were to be held in certain Prussian districts to decide whether they would remain part of Germany or would join Poland. Plebiscites for a similar purpose were also to be held in districts of Schleswig to decide whether the people wished to be reunited to Denmark. As part compensation to France for the damage wrought to her mines, the Sarre Basin, with its rich coal and iron mines, was to be at the service of France for fifteen years, under international rule, after which the inhabitants were to decide upon their political future.

The German army must be reduced to 100,000 men, including officers, and conscription was to be abolished. In a region extending to fifty kilometers east of the Rhine all importation, exportation, and nearly all production of war material was to be stopped. One object of this stipulation was to safeguard France against a future German invasion. The fortifications of Heligoland must be destroyed, and the German navy was to be reduced to six battleships, six light cruisers, and twelve torpedo-boats. Its personnel must not exceed 15,000 men, and it must have no submarines. Germany was forbidden to build forts controlling the Baltic and must open the Kiel Canal to all nations.

Military Terms.

Germany accepted responsibility for damage done to the Allied nations and their peoples, and agreed to reimburse all damage done to civilians. She must within two years make an initial payment of 20,000,000,000 marks, about $5,000,000,000, and must issue bonds to secure subsequent payments. She must make good illegal damage done to merchant shipping by submarines by turning over a large part of her merchant fleet and building new vessels. She must devote her economic resources to rebuilding the devastated regions in France, Belgium, and elsewhere. She also agreed to the trial of the former Kaiser and other Germans for offenses against international morality and the laws of war. Holland, however, subsequently declined to give up the Kaiser, while the German Government, on the plea that public sentiment would not permit the surrender of the alleged offenders, obtained the concession that the accused should be tried before a German federal court at Leipsic.

Financial Indemnities.

By treaties later concluded Bulgaria was forced to cede territory and to pay an indemnity, while Austria-Hungary was broken up. Parts of the Dual Empire were ceded to Italy, Roumania, and Poland; Czecho-Slovakia and Hungary became independent republics; the territory inhabited chiefly by Jugo-Slavs was combined with Serbia and Montenegro into a Greater Serbia. Of Austria there remained only a small state, of a few thousand square miles, whose 5,000,000 or 6,000,000 people were chiefly of German blood and whose form of government was republican. In the negotiations regarding Turkey the United States did not directly participate. The terms finally

Settlement with Austria-Hungary, Bulgaria, and Turkey.

handed to the Turkish representatives in May, 1920, reduced
the Sultan's domains to Constantinople and to part of Asia
Minor, and an international force is to be kept permanently
in the former. The Dardanelles and the Bosporus are neu-
tralized and passage through them is made free to all nations.
Arabia is to be independent; Mesopotamia and Palestine are
to be under British rule; Thrace and the region about Smyrna
under that of Greece; while France and Italy were given
spheres of influence in Syria and Anatolia, respectively. The
mandate over Armenia was offered to the United States.
President Wilson had said at Paris that the offer would be
accepted, but in this, as in some other matters, he promised
more than he could perform. A commission sent out by him
to Armenia estimated that acceptance would necessitate the
use of 59,000 troops as a police force and that five years' occupation would cost $756,000,000. Congress considered that
these and other objections outweighed humanitarian arguments,
and voted to reject the mandate.

Unfortunately the conclusion of the treaties did not bring
peace and prosperity to the world. At the time of the signing
of the German treaty a score of other wars, or conflicts amount-

The War
Fever Still
Rages.

ing to a state of war, were still raging. Poland, for
example, was fighting the Ukrainians, the Ru-
thenians, the Germans, the Jugo-Slavs, and the Russian Bolsheviki. Poland, Ukrainia, Finland, and other portions of the old Russian Empire had set up as independent states,
while in what remained a bitter struggle was being fought out
between the Bolsheviki and their enemies.

The programme of Bolshevism gave the whole world reason
for apprehension. The movement failed in Germany and in
Austria, but it was dreaded even in the Allied countries. During

The
Menace of
Bolshevism.

part of the peace conference the danger that Bolshevism would sweep over much of western Europe
caused more concern than the question of settling the
treaty of peace. In Italy, France, and even England economic
conditions were such that there was real danger that there
might be a social revolution, but all these countries, for the

time being at least, escaped the menace, partly, it is believed, because of financial assistance rendered by the United States.

In the United States there was never any real danger that such a movement would succeed, and yet attempts were actually made. The most serious effort was made in the city of Seattle, but its courageous mayor acted so vigorously as speedily to suppress the agitation. Other manifestations of a revolutionary spirit took the form of attempts to murder a number of public men by means of bombs. Several persons were killed or injured by the explosions, but among them there was no one of prominence. Toward the end of 1919 the Department of Justice made public the fact that a conspiracy had actually been formed to overturn the government and set up one on the Bolshevist model, but the conspirators were chiefly foreigners and the movement had no chance of success. A campaign to rid the country of undesirable aliens resulted in the deportation of many of the worst leaders.

In the United States.

Meanwhile an animated debate was taking place in the United States over the league of nations. Practically all Americans were eager to prevent war in the future, but many doubted whether the league would secure that desirable result. The issue was also confused by political considerations. Many Democrats forthwith declared themselves favorable to the league without having actually studied the covenant. Many Republicans took an exactly contrary course. However, some Democrats opposed the league, while a number of Republicans, the most notable of whom was ex-President Taft, ardently favored it. Those who opposed the league made much of the fact that it would involve us in European affairs and meant throwing away forever Washington's advice against entangling alliances. Many men did not oppose the general idea of a league, but criticised various features of the one proposed. Amendments adopted by the peace conference removed some of these objections. The most notable of these amendments was the one affirming the continued validity of the Monroe Doctrine.

Contest over the League of Nations.

To be ratified by the United States the treaty must receive the votes of two-thirds of the senators voting upon it. A majority of the senators were Republicans, and feeling in the Senate against Wilson had come to be very bitter. A contest between the President and a majority of the Senate ensued, the leadership in the Senate being taken by Senator Lodge of Massachusetts, chairman of the committee on foreign relations. Early in September, 1919, President Wilson set out on a tour of the country for the purpose of rallying public sentiment in favor of the League without amendments. He spoke to large crowds, but a number of senators, including Johnson and Borah, who opposed the League altogether, followed a few days behind him, speaking at the same places, and they also were greeted by large crowds. On his way back from the Pacific coast the President had an apoplectic stroke and was forced to give up the rest of his tour. For several months he was confined to the White House and was able to see only a few persons and to consider only extremely important public questions. Meanwhile the mass of the people were kept in ignorance of his exact condition.

Wilson's Tour.

For many weeks the struggle over the treaty dragged along in the Senate. All amendments to the League of Nations Covenant were voted down, but the committee of the whole adopted fourteen "reservations" limiting America's liability under the Covenant. President Wilson strongly opposed the reservations, and a situation developed which resulted (November, 1919) in the defeat of the treaty by a vote of 55 to 39. Four Democrats voted for ratification with reservations and 13 Republicans against ratification. The special session of Congress then adjourned. Each side to the controversy sought to throw the blame for the failure upon the other. Meanwhile the United States continued to be technically at war with Germany.

The Treaty Fails.

When Congress met in December the treaty was again submitted to the Senate, and a new struggle ensued. As in the special session, the main battle raged over the reservation to Article X of the Covenant. This

Struggle over Article X.

article bound members of the League "to respect and preserve as against external aggression the territorial integrity and existing political independence of all members of the League." On March 15, 1920, after days of debate, the Senate, by a vote of 56 to 26, voted the following reservation to Article X:

The United States assumes no obligation to employ its military or naval forces, its resources or any form of economic discrimination to preserve the territorial integrity or political independence of any other country, or to interfere in controversies between nations—whether members of the League or not—under Article X, or to employ the military or naval forces of the United States under any article of the treaty for any purpose unless in any particular case the Congress, in the exercise of full liberty of action, shall by act or joint resolution so declare.

Supporters of the reservation contended that it did little more than reaffirm the Constitution of the United States, which reserves to Congress the right "to declare war." But

President Wilson took the view that Article X must

The Treaty Fails Again. not be touched. Of a milder reservation adopted the previous autumn he had declared that it was a "knife-thrust at the heart of the covenant," and he now reiterated the view that any reservation which sought "to deprive the League of Nations of the force of Article X cuts at the very heart and life of the covenant itself." In a letter addressed to his party on January 8, 1920, he said that, if the treaty could not be adopted as it stood, it should be submitted to a solemn referendum at the coming election. Not all Democrats took this view. William Jennings Bryan, for example, declared in favor of compromise, and many Democratic senators refused to support the Wilsonian stand. Fourteen joined the Republicans in adopting the reservation, and 23 voted for the ratification of the treaty with reservations, of which there were 15 in all. The final vote on ratification (March 19, 1920), counting pairs, stood: for ratification, 34 Republicans, 23 Democrats; against ratification, 15 Republicans, 24 Democrats. The vote for ratification lacked seven of the necessary majority, and thus the treaty again failed. A joint resolution declaring the war at an end passed both houses in April and May but was vetoed by the President.

In February a great political sensation was created by the resignation from the cabinet of Secretary of State Lansing under circumstances that were equivalent to his abrupt dismissal.

Resignation of Secretary Lansing. President Wilson, in letters to Lansing, seemed to base his action mainly upon the fact that during his illness Lansing "had frequently called the heads of the executive departments of the government into conference," intimating that he regarded such proceeding as unconstitutional. It was believed by many people, however, that Lansing's disapproval of some features of the peace treaty was the real reason for his fall. Lansing defended his course regarding the cabinet meetings in forceful terms and by a majority of the press was thought to have the better of the controversy. He was succeeded by Bainbridge Colby, of New York, a former Progressive. The incident served to emphasize the fact that for months the President had been too ill to give much attention to public business, and the question was seriously raised as to when a President's "inability to discharge the powers and duties" of the presidential office should devolve the same upon the Vice-President. Fortunately considerable improvement in President Wilson's health prevented the matter from reaching a crisis.

At the same time that the official summary of the treaty had been issued by the peace conference the following statement had been made public:

In addition to the securities afforded in the Treaty of Peace, the President of the United States has pledged himself to propose to the Senate of the United States, and the Prime Minister of Great Britain has pledged himself to propose to the Parliament of Great Britain, an engagement, subject to the approval of the Council of the League of Nations, to come immediately to the assistance of France in case of unprovoked attack by Germany.

Pledge to France.

This agreement was designed to assure the French of future protection against a German attempt at revenge, and to induce them to forego demands for more radical peace terms. Great Britain ratified the agreement, but up to June, 1920, President Wilson had not submitted it to the Senate, nor does there seem much likelihood that the Senate will ever accept it. The President's enemies asserted that in this, as in some other matters, he promised too much. In France a feeling prevailed that she had been left in the lurch, and the feeling was accentuated by the failure of Germany to carry out some of the terms of peace. In March an abortive uprising of German monarchists was followed by revolts of a Bolshevist nature in parts of that country. Under pretext of suppressing this last revolt the German Government sent large bodies of troops into the Ruhr district, which includes the famous Krupp works at Essen. France declared this a serious breach of treaty agreements, and, as a warning to Germany, seized the city of Frankfort and other places beyond the Rhine.

Meanwhile hectic conditions prevailed in the United States. Shortage of commodities of almost all kinds had soon stimulated industry and solved the problem of unemployment, but prices

Labor Troubles and Profiteering.

soared to heights hitherto undreamed of, profiteers reaped rich harvests at the public expense, and there was great unrest among laborers. Increased prices provoked demands for increased wages and vice versa, and no one could say when this pyramiding would end. Great strikes among steel-workers, bituminous-coal miners, and railway men deranged industry and threatened the welfare of the country. It was clear that the question of industrial peace was one of the most serious that confronted the country. Our industrial society had become so complicated and the parts so interdependent that it was possible for a comparatively small minority of workers to bring want and misery to the whole country.

CHAPTER XXIV

A GOLDEN AGE IN HISTORY

THERE have been, as Voltaire long ago pointed out, certain periods in the history of mankind in which the human spirit has risen to unusual heights. In Greece there was the age of Pericles, in Rome that of Augustus, in England that of Elizabeth, in France that of Louis XIV. There can be little doubt that our own generation is living in a period which men in future ages will look back upon as marking an epoch of unusual interest and brilliance. We have beheld the discovery of radium and the X-ray; the invention of the telephone and the talking-machine, of wireless telegraphy and the moving picture; the application of electricity to rapid transit and to propelling machinery; the submarine perfected and the air conquered by the airplane; the last great geographical problems solved by the discovery of the poles; unexampled expansion in higher education and in material wealth; the emancipation of woman; and we have experienced the greatest war in history. In nearly all the manifestations of this wonderful age America has played a part, and in many a leading part.

Let us consider first America's material progress. The census of 1910 emphasized the fact that the nation had been transformed in fifty years. Its area had increased more than 700,-000 square miles, and its population of 101,000,000, including Alaska and the insular possessions, was almost treble the number who had welcomed peace at the close of the great civil conflict. The number of inhabitants per square mile in the United States proper had jumped from 13 to 30.9, and the centre of population had shifted westward from forty-eight miles east by north of Cincinnati to a point within the limits of Bloomington, Indiana.

Wealth had multiplied even more rapidly than population.

Increase in Population.

498

In 1870 the total value of all property approximated $24,000,-000,000 (gold); the average per-capita wealth was about $600.

Wealth.   In 1920 the national wealth was estimated at $200,000,000,000, or even more, while the per-capita wealth was three or four times that of 1860. Sight should not be lost of the fact that the purchasing power of a dollar had greatly declined, but, when all due allowance is made, the fact remains that in no other country had there ever been such a stupendous heaping up of material possessions.

The nation had prospered, yet not all its people had prospered. One of the most alarming features of the times was the tendency to concentration of wealth in a few hands. In

Unequal Distribution.   America, as in all other countries, there had been inequality in wealth, but never before such startling extremes. When George Washington died, in 1799, he was probably the richest citizen of the republic, yet his estate fell below three-quarters of a million. For six decades thereafter, though there were many men of wealth, there were few men of great wealth. The Civil War produced a considerable crop of millionaires, and in the industrial expansion of the next half-century vast fortunes sprang up like mushrooms after a warm spring rain.

Since then individual fortunes have been piled up to heights hitherto undreamed of, and with a rapidity so marvellous that the beholder is reminded of Aladdin's wonderful lamp. The

An Incredible Fortune.   fortune of the richest American of all is variously estimated, but it is safe to assume that, including the vast sums he has given away, he has amassed more than $360,000,000, probably much more. The mind can scarcely grasp what such a sum means. To acquire it by ordinary means would take a long time. If Adam on the day of his creation in the Garden had begun working for some generous employer at a salary of $200 a day and all expenses, including those of his side-partner and the little Cains and Abels, if he had lived and worked 300 days in every year until the present time, if he had deposited every dollar in some vault where neither rust could corrupt nor thieves break through and steal, he would now, after the expiration of 6,000 years of unexampled industry, be worth less than the sum acquired in a single lifetime by our fellow citizen of Pocantico and Forest Hill.

It would be a great mistake to assume that most millionaires have misused their wealth. Rockefeller has given away over $300,000,000, mostly to higher education; Carnegie built libraries and peace temples, established a hero fund and a fund for pensioning college professors, and before his death in 1919 his total benefactions also exceeded $300,000,000. Other men of great wealth have given immense sums to all manner of good causes and in other ways have shown that they regarded themselves only as "stewards" of their possessions. Nevertheless, thinking men could not but deplore the fact that a few men can amass such incredible wealth, while great numbers can scarcely secure a roof to shelter them or clothes to hide their nakedness.

Some years before the Civil War the historian Macaulay wrote to an American friend regarding American conditions: "Your fate I believe to be certain, though it is deferred by a physical cause. As long as you have a boundless extent of fertile and unoccupied land, your laboring population will be far more at ease than the laboring population of the Old World. . . . [A day will come when] wages will be as low and will fluctuate as much with you as with us. You will have your Manchesters and Birminghams, and in those Manchesters and Birminghams hundreds of thousands of artisans will assuredly be sometime out of work. Then your institutions will be fairly brought to the test."

Before the close of the last century events had already begun to justify the great historian's remarkable prediction. Free land, long the great solvent for poverty and social unrest, was practically exhausted; Chicago and Pittsburgh and other industrial centres had surpassed Manchester and Birmingham; and, though wages, measured in terms of money, were not so low as in England, they fluctuated more, the cost of living was higher, and it was by no means uncommon for even millions of artisans to be out of work. Already

American institutions were being subjected to close scrutiny, and voices were heard declaring that the old order must give way to a new one, evolved to meet the changed conditions of a new age.

In the '80's and '90's radicals like Henry George and Henry D. Lloyd began to talk of the "plutocracy," and to cry out against the dangers of "wealth against commonwealth." Gradually discontent spread. For a score of generations Anglo-Saxons had been travelling the stony road to political equality, and in theory at least the goal had been attained. But men were beginning to realize that political equality was a poor thing unless through it they could obtain something approaching equality of economic opportunity. Thus the old question of equality came to the front again, but with a new face. Populism, progressivism, socialism, Bolshevism, were all manifestations of this new struggle for human rights.

A New Battle.

Many plans were propounded for preventing the future concentration of wealth, and for breaking up already existing fortunes. The income taxes imposed by States and nation resulted from the feeling that men of wealth should bear an extra share of public financial burdens. Inheritance taxes, whether State or federal, have thus far been levied merely for the sake of raising revenues; but some men—among them Andrew Carnegie, Justice Brewer, Theodore Roosevelt, and Vice-President Marshall—have advocated heavier taxes of this sort to break up the great fortunes. Some believe that the amount of money that can be transmitted to a descendant should be limited to a comparatively small amount. According to their view we should not fail to cherish the praiseworthy sentiment that has an affectionate regard for the future welfare of those dear to and dependent upon us, but this should not be done in such a way as to tolerate a concentration of wealth that discourages exertion and creates a class of drones who consume immense quantities of wealth and contribute little or nothing to the support of the race. Even to heirs themselves the bequest of

Plans for Breaking up Great Fortunes.

great wealth is likely, in the words of Carnegie, to prove an "almighty curse." Inasmuch as probably about a fiftieth of the wealth of the United States each year would become subject to taxes on inheritances exceeding $10,000, it is apparent that herein lies an immense source of possible income and one likely to be more and more used, especially now that the nation's financial needs have been multiplied by the war.

During half a century many notable changes had taken place in the distribution of population. Vast areas in the West that in 1870 did not contain a single white inhabitant were now well

Distribution of Population.

settled. Almost three-fourths of all the people, however, still lived in the region east of the Mississippi, although that region constituted less than a third of the whole area. A third of the total population resided in the six States of Massachusetts, New York, Pennsylvania, New Jersey, Ohio, and Illinois, whose total area was only 204,-822 square miles. Rhode Island, the smallest of all the States, was also the most thickly populated, having an average of 508.5 persons per square mile; while arid Nevada, the least thickly settled, had only .7 per square mile. It was, of course, natural that the older States should be most thickly populated, but the inequalities had been greatly increased by the fact that most immigrants entered the land through eastern gateways. Lacking money for a longer journey, millions of immigrants did not penetrate far from tidewater. Though a large proportion were accustomed to agricultural life and should have gone, therefore, to the broad reaches of the boundless West, most had to settle down in the industrial regions of the East, thus adding to the congestion of population in centres like New York City's East Side.

At the close of the Civil War the United States was still

Increase of Urban Population.

mainly an agricultural country, though manufacturing had made great progress. In 1870 only 20.9 per cent of the population lived in towns of 2,500 or over. In the next four decades manufacturing made wonderful strides and the urban population increased correspondingly, rising to 46.3 per cent in 1910. In all, 42,623,383 people lived in cities, or 4,000,000 more than the whole population in 1870. In New England the urban dwellers outnumbered the rural population by more than three to one. In the South, however, the cities contained only 25.4 per cent of the inhabitants of that section.

The rush to cities became so great that some rural localities actually decreased in population. During the first decade of the new century seventy-one of the ninety-one counties of Iowa showed such a decrease. The tendency to rural depopulation was so pronounced that a movement was launched to counteract it, the slogan being "Back to the farm!" President Roosevelt was one of the promoters of this movement, and he appointed a special Country Life Commission to investigate rural needs. Rural free delivery, telephones, better roads, better schools, more scientific farming methods, and the automobile have done much to make country life more attractive and profitable, and to transform the mental outlook of farmers, many of whom in the past have been too content to vegetate like their own potatoes, parsnips, or pumpkins. The movement to the cities is, however, not yet checked, and is stimulated by the fact that urban manufacturers even of luxuries are able to pay higher wages than can rural producers of necessities.

Rural Problems.

Immigration had attained such proportions that the very blood of the nation was being changed by it. In prosperous times the horde which in a single year poured into New York harbor several times exceeded the total number of Visigoths who in 376 crossed the Danube and began the barbarian invasion of the Roman Empire. Repeatedly the number of immigrants exceeded 1,000,000, the greatest number being 1,285,349, in 1907. In the decade 1904–14 more than 10,000,000 came in, which was about a third of the total population in 1860. Great numbers, however, perhaps almost a half, ultimately returned home.

The Horde of Immigrants.

In the early part of our period the tide that flowed through Castle Garden was mostly made up of Irish, English, and Germans. In the '70's and '80's other peoples began to turn their faces westward in increasing numbers. Danes, Norwegians, and Swedes made up much of the swarm that settled the wheat lands of the Northwest. Later more southerly peoples—Poles, Magyars, Slovaks, Russian Jews, Italians, Greeks, and Syrians—came flocking in, and, when free land was practically exhausted, they herded for the most part in congested centres of great cities and lowered wages and the standard of living. In the period 1860 to 1910 the number of Austrians in the United States increased from 25,061 to 1,174,924; of Hungarians from a figure so small that they were not enumerated to 495,609; of Italians from 11,677 to 1,343,125. On the other hand, there were more Irish-born inhabitants in 1860 than in 1910. The number of German-born sprang from 1,276,075 to 2,501,333, but in the later years immigration from the Kaiser's domain greatly decreased, being only 27,788 in 1912. There were, in fact, in the United States 300,-000 fewer German-born in 1910 than in 1900.

The influx of immigrants tended not only to change the blood of the nation but also its customs and even its religion. In no section were such changes more marked than in New England. Even in colonial times New York and Pennsylvania had been meeting-grounds for many races, but New England was settled almost wholly by Englishmen, and even as late as 1800 probably 98 per cent of the blood was English. But the sons and daughters of New England followed Horace Greeley's advice to "go West." Their places were taken by French Canadians and Irish, and later by Italians and other southern Europeans, so that by 1910 two-thirds of the people of Massachusetts were of foreign birth or recent foreign extraction, while the same thing was true of over half the population of all New England. It is one of the curious ironies of history that the original settlers, the Puritans, fled from overseas to escape the relics of "popery" in the Anglican Church. They persecuted Antinomians, Baptists, and Quakers, and when in Boston, in 1686, a clergyman of the Church of England, under the protection of the King's agent, performed

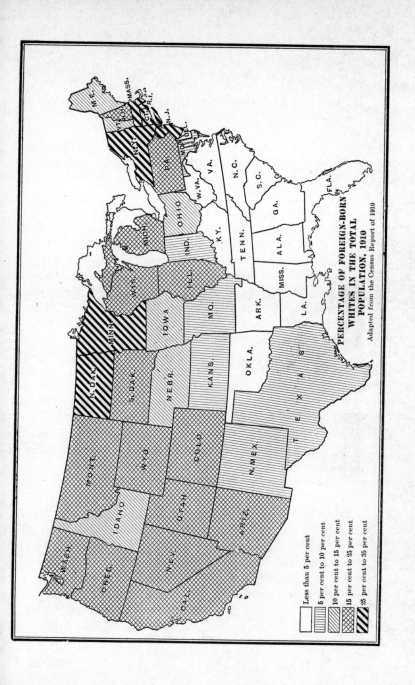

PERCENTAGE OF FOREIGN-BORN
WHITES IN THE TOTAL
POPULATION, 1910
Adapted from the Census Report of 1910

Less than 5 per cent
5 per cent to 10 per cent
10 per cent to 15 per cent
15 per cent to 25 per cent
25 per cent to 35 per cent

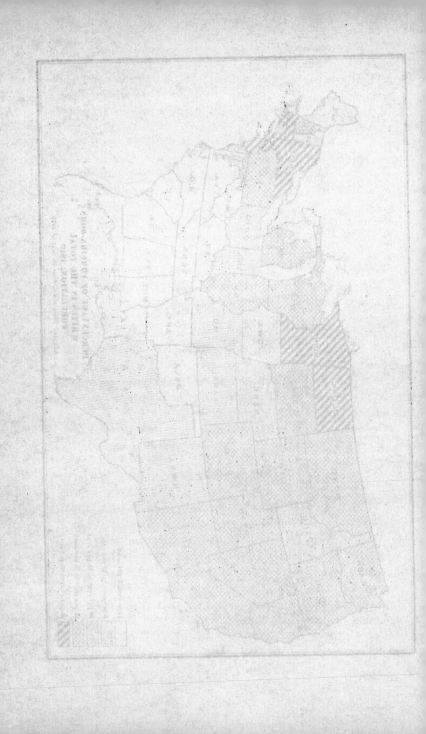

the Episcopal service with the prayer-book and the usual accessories, it caused great scandal, and some of the people called the clergyman "Baal's priest," while one of their own ministers from his pulpit denounced the "praiers" as "leeks, garlic, and trash." To-day New England is the most Catholic section of the country, with the exception of the Mountain States, and in 1910 the Catholic inhabitants outnumbered the Protestants two to one. Boston was a Catholic city. Its mayor and most of its public officers were Catholics. The spires of a cross-crowned cathedral rose high over the tower of the Old South Church, and cassock-clad priests said their prayers within ear-shot of the most sacred precincts of the Puritans.

As for New York City, which was cosmopolitan almost from the beginning, it is a modern Babel. It contains more Jews than ever lived in Jerusalem except during the feast of the Passover, more persons of German extraction than inhabit any German city except Berlin, more Italians than in Venice or Naples, more Irish than reside in Dublin. There are more Cohens than Smiths in its directory, and the Hebrew population about equals the native stock, which in 1910 numbered less than 1,000,000 out of 4,800,000.

In New York City.

Opposition to foreigners was one of the cardinal principles of the Know-Nothings in the '50's, and from that time to this warning voices were often raised against the danger of permitting the influx of immigrants to continue unrestricted. But Americans had long regarded their country as a haven in which the oppressed could find a home, and were loath to raise the bars. Furthermore, industry desired cheap labor, and steamship companies made vast sums transporting immigrants to American shores, while Catholic influence was naturally against restrictions. Exclusion laws were passed against the Chinese, and, beginning with 1882, a series of acts debarred criminals, paupers, and certain other undesirables, forbade the importation of contract laborers, and laid down other regulations. An act of 1907, passed under Roosevelt, made entrance somewhat more difficult and also

Restriction of Immigration.

created an immigration commission, which made an exhaustive study of the problem and recommended further restrictions, including a "literacy test." A bill providing such a test had passed Congress in 1897 but was vetoed by Cleveland. New bills to exclude illiterates were vetoed by Taft and Wilson, but such a bill was finally passed over Wilson's veto late in 1917. Immigration had already greatly decreased as a result of the war, so the new law has not yet received a thorough test, but, though not very stringent, it will undoubtedly serve to exclude many undesirables, particularly from southern European countries and Russia. In the past more than half the immigrants from those countries have been illiterates.

The most serious of all race problems is still that of the negro, though relatively it is less serious than formerly. There was a period in which alarmists pictured the African race as reproducing so rapidly that it would swamp the white population. The census figures show, however, that this is not likely to happen. According to the census of 1870, which was defective on this subject, the total number of persons of African descent was 5,392,172. In the next forty years the colored population increased to 9,827,763. In the same period the ratio of colored population compared with the whole population decreased from 13.5 to 10.7 per cent. In 1790 the negroes made up 19.3 per cent of the population. The fact is that though the negro birth-rate is high, their death-rate much exceeds that of the white race; furthermore, their number is not increased to any extent by immigration. On the other hand, the theory sometimes propounded that the negroes will die out and disappear is also unlikely to be realized —at least not within many centuries. It is true that pneumonia, tuberculosis, and venereal diseases are alarmingly prevalent among them; nevertheless, they continue to increase, and only when their number becomes stationary or begins to decline will it be reasonable to predict their ultimate extinction. However, the pure African type is already rapidly disappearing. This is due, in part, to white trespasses across the color line, though it

The Negro Problem.

seems to be beyond question that direct infusion of white blood into the race is relatively less than formerly. Mulattoes, however, are constantly intermixing with the pure-blooded blacks, and it is not improbable that in the course of a few generations the genuine black will be as extinct as the dodo and that this will result even should all sexual relations between Caucasians and Africans cease. It is likely, however, that the tendency known among anthropologists as "reversion to type" will tend to keep the negroes in America decidedly Ethiopian in features and characteristics.

From the point of view of geographical distribution the most important changes taking place are slight tendencies toward concentration in the "black belt" in the South, and toward herding in towns in all parts of the country but especially in the North. In such States as Louisiana, Mississippi, South Carolina, and Alabama, counties in which the ratio of blacks to whites is five to one, or even eight or nine to one, are not uncommon. But this state of affairs is by no means a new development. In New England almost 92 per cent of all the negroes live in urban centres. In the South the negroes are not moving townward quite so rapidly as are their white neighbors. Their most sensible leaders advise them to stick to the soil and to avoid the more strenuous competition of cities and the undesirable quarters into which they are usually crowded. An influx of Southern negroes into the North is constantly taking place, and this movement was accelerated during the Great War because of the increased demand for labor. However, despite this influx, the relative rate of increase of the negro population in the North is slower than in the South, for the death-rate in the North is abnormally high, while the birth-rate is relatively low. Nearly nine-tenths of the colored race is still concentrated in the sixteen former slave States, and the negro continues to be in a special sense "the Southerner's problem." His presence has tended to prevent any considerable immigration of Europeans into the South, and to keep that section mainly agricultural in occupation.

In spite of the "war amendments" the position of the negro in the United States continues, generally speaking, to be one of decided inferiority. In the South "Jim Crow laws" draw the "color line" against him on trains, on street-cars, in schools, theatres, hotels, and other such places. Economically, too, his position both in the South and in the North is, generally speaking, one of decided inferiority, though many members of the race have won financial independence.

Inferior Position.

The negro's outlook for the future appears pessimistic or optimistic, according to the angle from which the subject is regarded. When we recall, however, that negroes as slaves were generally thieves, that most had little more conception of true family life than the beasts of the field, that they were almost universally unable to read or write, and that when they became freedmen they were "turned loose naked, hungry, and destitute to the open sky," we cannot escape the conclusion that in half a century they have really made wonderful progress, economically, morally, and mentally. Few people realize the number of decent, self-respecting negroes who lead honorable lives, for unfortunately we usually judge the white race by its great men and the black race by its members who get into the police court. Despite narrow-visioned opposition to negro education on the part of many Southerners and some Northerners, two-thirds of the race are now able to read and write, and there are tens of thousands who have enjoyed the advantages of a college or normal-school education. In 1910 negroes owned property of a value estimated at $750,000,000, including 220,000 farms.

Race Progress.

Among negroes there are two schools of opinion as to what should be done concerning the assertion of their rights. One school, the chief leader of which was Booker T. Washington, takes the view that negroes should acquire property and education, cultivate habits of thrift and sobriety, and fit themselves for citizenship before becoming too insistent in demanding their "rights." Washington himself performed a great work in uplifting his people, and the inspira-

Two Schools of Opinion.

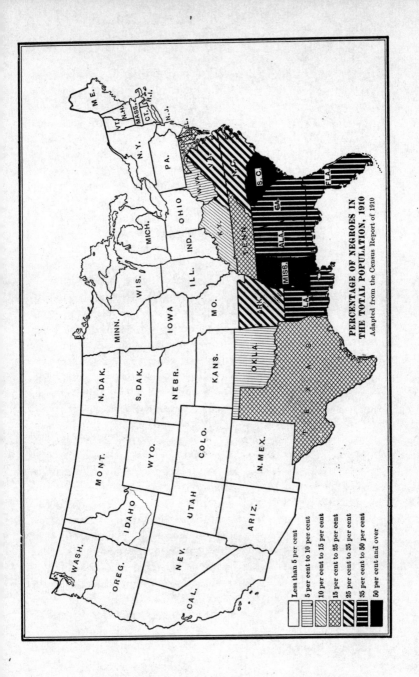

PERCENTAGE OF NEGROES IN
THE TOTAL POPULATION, 1910
Adapted from the Census Report of 1910

Less than 5 per cent
5 per cent to 10 per cent
10 per cent to 15 per cent
15 per cent to 25 per cent
25 per cent to 35 per cent
35 per cent to 50 per cent
50 per cent and over

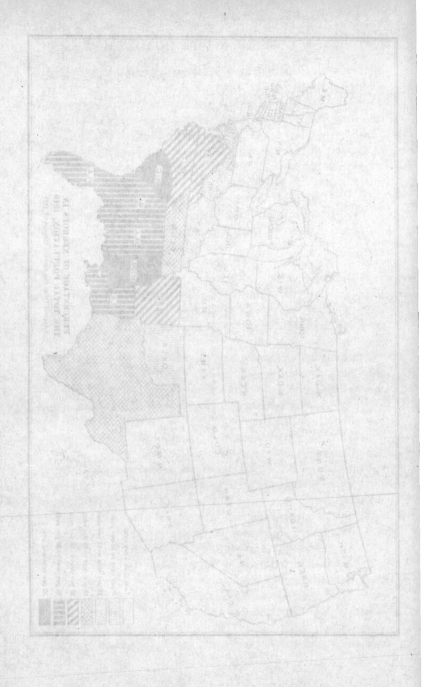

tion of his life will last for generations. The other school, of which Doctor W. E. B. Du Bois is the foremost advocate, holds that negroes should persistently demand every legal and constitutional right. Some even advocate complete social equality, including the right of intermarriage.

Southern whites are still determined that the negroes shall remain strictly apart. Most still favor keeping them in an inferior "place." Some would not even permit them to be educated; others think they should be given the sort of education that will make them economically efficient; only a comparative few realize that, just as do white men, they need broad training that they may develop leaders for their race. Fortunately more and more Southerners are giving the great problem really serious study; are asking themselves what should be done. "How shall we take these ten millions of shiftless, improvident, unmoral, inefficient child-men of an alien race and convert them into desirable citizens?" writes a Southern educator. "With individual exceptions, the negro population rests like a great black blight upon the South. It can not be removed, and the only chance is to train the race to do intelligent, honest work—to be economically efficient. Booker Washington has pointed the way, the one best both for the negroes and the whites, but it is a big undertaking—one that makes every other social problem of our people seem simple."

Attitude of Southern Whites toward the Race Problem.

A historian ought not to suppress uncomfortable facts, and it is undeniable that the treatment of negroes forms a blot on America's fair fame. In parts of the South they are kept in a state of practical serfdom; in all cities they are herded into unsanitary districts; they are denied equal opportunities for advancement; and not infrequently they are maltreated and murdered by brutal mobs. It is true that individual negroes, by fiendish assaults on white women, now and then rouse white men to frenzy, but statistics show that only about a fifth of the lynchings of negroes are because of the "usual crime." Burning at the stake is never justifiable under any circumstances, and it is undeniable that

Race Riots and Lynching.

in race riots scenes of horror have been enacted that are a disgrace to American civilization. Such scenes are sadly out of place in a nation that proclaims itself the special champion of liberty and justice, and which enlists in a crusade to make "the world safe for democracy."

Perhaps the most encouraging sign of progress is the increasing number of men of broad sympathies and vision who realize the truth of Booker Washington's wise declaration that you cannot keep a man down in a ditch without staying in the ditch with him. Among the wisest men of both races there seems to be a growing concensus of opinion that the two races should be kept separate, that there should be race distinctions but not race discrimination—or oppression. Everything done to uplift the negro mentally and morally tends also to uplift his white brother.

An Encouraging Sign.

In colonial days and even later the use of strong drink was almost universal. Ministers of the gospel openly drank with members of their flock, and not infrequently "went under the table with them." Even George Washington for some years had a distillery on his plantation, while Abraham Lincoln, as a grocery clerk, sold whiskey over the counter like any other commodity. But the evils of strong drink gradually aroused many thoughtful people to the need of restricting or abolishing the traffic. In the '50's a strong anti-liquor wave swept over the country; and, largely as a result of the eloquence of Neal Dow, one State, namely Maine, adopted permanent prohibitory legislation. But the reforming impulse spent its force, and for a generation prohibition seemed to make little concrete progress, while its advocates were the butts of much ridicule. Even many men who were not drinkers objected to prohibition as "sumptuary legislation" that interfered with "personal liberty." Furthermore, the constant influx of immigrants, most of whom had been accustomed to the use of intoxicants since childhood, helped to strengthen the opponents of restriction. The manufacture and sale of distilled and malt

The Liquor Problem.

liquors and of wines came to be an immense and extremely profitable industry employing hundreds of thousands of persons.

However, the agitators continued their work unceasingly. Leaders of the old parties generally strove to keep the subject out of politics. Despairing of persuading existing political organizations to take up the cause, some of the more radical reformers, in 1872, as already described, founded a national Prohibition party. Thereafter this party entered every presidential contest, but it never carried a single State, and its highest vote was only 270,710, polled in 1892. However, it kept the subject agitated. Other powerful agents in the same work were the Women's Christian Temperance Union and the Anti-Saloon League, both of which waged unceasing battle against what they called the "Rum Power." Gradually restrictive legislation, especially local-option laws, were put on the statute-books of all the States, while before the end of the century Kansas joined Maine in the dry column.

The Prohibition Movement.

The liquor interests fought desperately to beat down prohibition sentiment, and spent vast sums in influencing elections and legislatures. In cities they employed all sorts of reprehensible methods to prevent the enforcement of Sunday-closing laws and other regulations, for it was the policy of those behind the traffic to keep territory as thoroughly "saturated" as possible. Theirs was invariably a corrupting influence in politics, while many saloons were operated in close co-operation with gambling-houses, the white-slave traffic, and such evils. Gradually the very sordidness of the liquor business antagonized millions, while millions of others came to believe that the business involved a great economic loss to society and ruined the lives of multitudes— not only of drinkers themselves but of their wives and children. An increasing number of business men came to see that drinkers were, generally speaking, less dependable, less efficient, much more likely to cause accidents than were non-drinkers, and many business establishments adopted a policy of employing only teetotalers or those practically so.

Growing Opposition to the Traffic.

In the South, where drink was responsible for many horrible crimes perpetrated by the negro population, prohibition found particularly fertile soil, and in the first decade of the new century several of the Southern States abolished the sale of intoxicants, though some permitted the importation of liquor for individual use. Early in 1913 prohibition took a decided step forward by the enactment, over President Taft's veto, of the Webb bill, forbidding the shipment of liquor into a dry State in violation of a State law. In consequence the stamping out of "boot-legging" and "blind tigers" was rendered less difficult. At this time nine States, namely, Maine, Kansas, West Virginia, Tennessee, Georgia, Mississippi, North Carolina, North Dakota, and Oklahoma, had adopted State prohibition. The total population of these States was 14,695,961, while more than 30,000,000 other persons resided in districts made dry by local-option laws.

Progress of Prohibition.

Thenceforth prohibition swept forward like a prairie fire. By the end of 1917 twenty-six States had entered the dry column. In that year Congress enacted a prohibitory law for the District of Columbia, forbade the shipment of liquor, except for medicinal purposes, into any dry State, and submitted to the States a prohibition amendment. The distillation of intoxicating beverages had already been prohibited by the President as a war measure, and brewers had been ordered to keep the alcoholic content of their beer below $2\frac{1}{2}$ per cent. Subsequently Congress enacted a law under which the President proclaimed that after July 1, 1919, the country should be "dry" until the end of the war. Meanwhile the liquor interests had combined for a final stand. But public sentiment constantly grew more hostile, and the fact that breweries and distilleries were largely owned by persons of German blood undoubtedly reacted unfavorably against the traffic. Before the end of January, 1919, all but four of the States had ratified the amendment, which provided that the manufacture and sale of intoxicants for beverage purposes must cease after January 16, 1920. Legislation to carry the amendment into effect was

War-Time Prohibition.

Prohibition Amendment Adopted.

passed by Congress in the fall of 1919. As a forlorn hope the liquor interests attacked the constitutionality of both the amendment and of the act enforcing it, but, in a decision handed down in June, 1920, the Supreme Court upheld both.

It is certain that difficulty will be met with in enforcing prohibition in some localities; it is equally certain that the abolition of the liquor traffic will result in a tremendous saving to Economic Saving. the American people. It is estimated that the total consumption of liquor in a single year exceeded 2,000,000,000 gallons, that the average consumption for each man, woman, and child amounted to over 22 gallons, and that the total cost to the consumer amounted to from $1,500,000,000 to $2,000,000,000. The greater part of this money was spent by working men, who could ill afford such expenditure. Under prohibition much of this money will still go for inutilities of one sort or another, but a vast deal of it will go for the purchase of more food, clothing, school-books, and shoes for wives and children.

Prohibition means the loss of large revenues to national and local governments; it also means fewer paupers, fewer criminals, fewer cases of insanity. Wherever prohibitory laws are enforced comparatively little use is found for jails and Other Effects of Prohibition. workhouses. A jurist who was for many years a police and criminal judge in one of the large cities of the country estimates that fully 70 per cent of all cases that came before him prior to the enactment of prohibition were directly due to strong drink, while a large part of the remainder were indirectly due to that cause.

In all ages woman has usually occupied a decidedly inferior position in the world. In primitive society woman, being physically weaker than man, was condemned to do all the drudgery; and when her lord and master felt so inclined he beat her with his fists or war-club, and there was no "cop" or "bobby" to say him nay. Man hunted, fished, fought, and sat about at ease; while his mate performed all the real work, built the rude shelters, gathered berries and nuts, brought in the game that had been killed, tanned skins or wove clothing of bark or fibre, and carried the household goods, the babies, and perhaps the weapons of her lord on the trail. Even to-day among savage peoples women are often practically slaves. In New Britain, for instance, they must do all the work, which is so hard that they become prematurely old; and if they offend their husbands they are in danger of being killed and eaten.

Inferior Position of Woman in Primitive Society.

Among the Romans and a few other ancient peoples woman occupied a reasonably high position, but after the break-up of the Empire her position became decidedly less favorable. The canon law condemned her to a position of decided inferiority; many of the church fathers, including the Apostle Paul, emphasized her dangerous character; and in the minds of many holy and impeccable monks she was considered an ally of Satan himself.

In Ancient and Mediæval Times.

By the time of the settlement of America woman's position in England had improved somewhat. If a single woman of mature age, her legal rights were almost equal to those of a man, though she had no political rights and was at a great disadvantage in the matter of inheritance. A married woman, however, was virtually under the domination of her husband, who enjoyed the right to chastise her for certain offenses, even "with whips and clubs," a privilege of which many a brutal Briton took full advantage. The husband had an estate in any land belonging to his wife and might alienate it without her consent; he was also entitled to take possession of any movables that she owned on marriage or that might subsequently come to her, and he could do with them as he thought proper. Not until the last half of the nineteenth century did Parliament annul the law giving the husband full ownership of his wife's property and permitting him to seize her wages even after he had deserted her. As regards the marriage bond and other matters, the law was all with the husband. No English woman ever attempted to secure a divorce until 1801.

In England.

In colonial times woman's position in America was somewhat better than in the England of the corresponding period, yet in 1848, seventy-two years after the Declaration of Independence, the members of the first Woman's Rights Convention, held at Seneca, New York, complained that "the history of man is a history of repeated injuries and usurpations on the part of man toward woman, having in direct object the establishment of an absolute tyranny over her"; that he has never allowed her the right to share in the making of laws to which she must submit; that "he has made her, if married, in the eyes of the law, civilly dead"; that "he has taken from her all her right in property, even to the wages she earns"; that she is compelled to obey her husband as her master, "the law giving to him power to deprive her of her liberty, and to administer chastisement"; that "he has monopolized nearly all profitable employments"; that he has given "to the world a different code of morals for men and women"; and that "he has endeavored, in every way he could, to destroy her confidence in her own powers, to lessen her self-respect, and to make her willing to lead a dependent and abject life."

First Woman's Rights Convention, 1848.

The woman's movement in America dates from this Seneca convention, and the declaration of independence then issued by such pioneers as Lucretia Mott, Mary N. McClintock, Martha C. Wright, and Elizabeth Cady Stanton will stand as one of the landmarks of progress. It took courage in those days to enlist in such a movement, for the prevailing attitude toward it was one of derision, and ridicule is often harder to fight than force. Newspapers headed their accounts of the convention with such phrases as "Insurrection among the Women," and "Reign of Petticoats," and declared that the convention was composed of "divorced wives, childless women, and sour old maids." It is significant that many women joined in the gale of laughter at the expense of their own sex. To persuade such women to take the movement seriously was to require generations of educational work—a task not yet completed.

Pioneers in the Work of Emancipation.

When Harriet Martineau visited the United States in 1840 she found only seven kinds of work open to women—namely, teaching, typesetting, household service, needlework, work in book-binderies and cotton-mills, and keeping boarders. There was not a single woman physician or lawyer, and it was not until 1852 that a woman was ordained in the ministry, though in the Quaker and Shaker sects they were permitted to exhort.

Woman's higher education was almost totally neglected until Troy Seminary, the first institution for their higher education that was aided by government funds, was founded in 1821.

Higher Education for Woman. Twelve years later Oberlin, the first coeducational college, opened its doors. Even as late as 1870 the number of women college students was very small. To-day more than 100 institutions devote their entire time to such students. There are about 350 coeducational institutions of higher learning, including most of the Western colleges and State universities; even conservative Harvard and Columbia make provision for women students. In the school year 1913–14 about 117,000 women and girls were attending universities, colleges, and technological schools, and about 11,000 received degrees.

Women have forced their way into almost every kind of work and profession. In 1910 about 20 per cent of the persons employed in manufacturing were females of 16 or over, and there were about 2,000 women journalists, 3,500 women preachers, and 7,000 women doctors, besides immense numbers in teaching, the civil service, commerce, and other pursuits. There were women mayors and women county clerks, and in 1916 a woman, Jeannette Rankin of Wyoming, was elected a member of the federal House of Representatives.

Women in Professions.

The transformations thus wrought tended to make women less dependent on man and to increase their intelligence, but it also brought many difficult moral and economic problems, one of these being the minimum living wage for female bread-winners. It was partly in order to help solve these problems that the women were demanding the ballot.

New Problems.

Meanwhile the statutory discriminations against woman were disappearing and she was even obtaining political rights. In 1869 Wyoming Territory and in 1870 Utah Territory granted the suffrage to women. Congress withdrew the right in Utah in 1887, but equal suffrage was incorporated into the constitutions of both Utah and Wyoming when they attained statehood. In 1893 Colorado and in 1896 Idaho entered the equal-suffrage column. Many other States also permitted women to vote in school and other special elections. For a decade or more there was a lull in interest, then a great impetus was given by the suffragette agitation in England. Slowly the movement gained momentum, and eastward resistlessly the course of suffrage took its way. In 1912 the Progressives openly declared for it. The old parties evaded the direct issue in 1912, but by 1916 most of their leaders were beginning to see a "great light," and the platforms of both declared for equal suffrage but favored enfranchisement by State rather than federal action. By 1916 seven more States —Oregon, Washington, California, Arizona, Nevada, Montana, and Kansas—had conferred full suffrage rights on women, while Illinois permitted them to vote for presidential electors and for certain local officers. In 1917 the great State of New York joined the procession, reversing a contrary verdict rendered two years before.

Woman Suffrage.

In many other States, however, suffrage was defeated during these years, and leaders of the movement sought eagerly to secure nation-wide suffrage by federal action. As early as 1869 agitation had been begun in favor of the "Susan B. Anthony amendment," which provided that the right to vote should not be denied or abridged "on account of sex." From about 1913 onward constant pressure was maintained on Congress to submit this or other amendments to the States. Some enthusiasts even resorted to "picketing" the White House and to the use of other extreme measures similar to those made familiar by their suffragette sisters in England. Early in 1918 the suffrage amendment passed the House of Representatives, but later in the year it was defeated in the Senate, though a change of one vote

A Suffrage Amendment Submitted to the States.

would have given it the necessary two-thirds. Finally, in the extra session of 1919, the amendment was submitted to the States. By April, 1920, it lacked only one State of the necessary three-fourths.

Meanwhile Great Britain and other foreign countries have conferred the suffrage on women, and it seems safe to predict that the complete triumph of the cause will not be long delayed

The Future. in the United States, and that the last relics of woman's inequality will be swept from the statute-books. It is certain that some of the results of suffrage will prove disappointing to enthusiastic supporters; equally certain that the United States will never return to the old inequality.

The full story of developments in education during the last half-century would of itself require a bulky volume. The system of public elementary education already in existence in the

Elementary Education. North was expanded and improved and was further developed in the South, where in some States its existence prior to the war had been more or less rudimentary. In many States the number of persons over ten years of age unable to read and write had been reduced by 1910 to a fraction of 1 per cent; in South Dakota, Wyoming, and Washington to only two-tenths of a per cent. Yet there were in the United States more than 5,500,000 persons over ten years of age who were illiterate. Over 2,000,000 of these were negroes, 1,650,361 were of foreign birth, and most of the rest were Southern whites. The percentage of illiteracy was much the highest in the South, rising as high as 7.9 per cent in Texas.

Comparatively speaking, secondary and higher education made much greater strides than elementary education. The public high school is almost wholly a development of the last

Secondary and Higher Education. half-century, while the expansion of higher education has been one of the marvels of the age. In 1920 there were far more college graduates than there were high-school graduates in 1865. Coeducation, which was formerly hardly thought of, had almost become the general rule. Few of the colleges of 1865 were much more than academies, while graduate work was hardly attempted at all. For years thereafter students desiring to do advanced work were obliged to go abroad for such training, most of them going to Germany. But in time graduate faculties were developed in American institutions, and now a number of our universities equal, if they do not surpass, any others in the world. Public appropriations and immense private gifts combined to produce a total sum far exceeding any ever invested in higher education in any other country.

Yet the last word had not been said regarding education in any field. Fads followed one another almost as fast as fashions change in feminine apparel, and the new ideas were not always wiser than the old. But it was to be hoped that something permanent would ultimately develop out of this constant state of flux. Observers often became impatient with educational vagaries, but perfection is rarely attainable in human affairs, and, when all was said, the sum of educational results spelled the salvation of the republic.

Fads in Education.

Only a reading nation can govern itself, and Americans are perhaps the greatest readers in the world. The development of education, cheaper methods of making paper, especially out of wood-pulp, improvements in printing-presses, the invention of stereotype plates, of the monotype, and of the linotype, all have combined with other causes vastly to increase the use of the printed word. The expansion of advertising has transformed and multiplied newspapers and magazines. In 1882 a single volume of 1,442 pages sufficed for the titles of articles published up to that time in the important magazines of the English-speaking world. But so rapid was the development of magazines thereafter that the years 1905-9 alone required a book of 2,491 pages, and the greater part of this increase had been in America. A mere list of the newspapers and magazines published in the United States, together with a few facts concerning their character, management, and circulation, filled in 1917 more than 1,000 large, closely printed pages. Books, too, fell from the press like autumn leaves, though, generally speaking, Americans read newspapers and magazines rather than books. Of the

Vast Expansion of the Publishing Business.

books in most demand, by far the greatest number were works of fiction. Close observers said that automobiles and moving-picture shows were tending to decrease reading of all kinds.

Notwithstanding the progress of education, the expansion of publishing, and the vastly greater financial rewards of authorship, creative literature had probably retrograded rather than advanced. With the death in 1916 of James Whitcomb Riley there disappeared from the literary stage the only poet then living of large reputation, yet few critics would assign him a place in the same rank with Lowell, Bryant, Whittier, Longfellow, or even Holmes, all of whom were still writing at the close of the Civil War. However, there were many successful novelists, and some of distinguished merit, such as William Dean Howells, Henry James, Winston Churchill, Edith Wharton, Margaret Deland, James Lane Allen, Booth Tarkington, John Fox, and Owen Wister, though it might be doubted if any one of them would ultimately be given as high a rank as Hawthorne, who died in the last year of the Civil War. Of American writers of his day, Mark Twain probably enjoyed the widest reputation, and it seems safe to predict that he will have a place among the great humorists of all ages. Theodore Roosevelt wrote many books on a great variety of subjects. His style is vivid and picturesque, he lived and knew the things of which he wrote, and he described better than any other man of his time certain phases of American life which will be of interest to future generations.

Literature.

In imaginative literature decidedly the greatest progress was made in the realm of the short story. Before the Civil War the only short-story writers with a national reputation were Hawthorne and Edgar Allan Poe, who is generally credited with having created or at all events fixed the principles of this order of composition. In the next period the form was adopted by writers of such varied talent as Henry James, Cable, Harris, Bunner, Edith Wharton, Mary Wilkins Freeman, and many others, and so developed as to make the short story the department of English literature in which primacy of American achievement was undisputed.

The Short Story.

In recent years a whole host of such writers have sprung up, and some of them, such as Jack London, "O. Henry," Morgan Robertson, and Richard Harding Davis, may be said to have mastered their art to a degree that entitles them to classification with their foremost predecessors. One has only to compare the magazines of the '70's and '80's with those of the '90's and the new century to realize how wide-spread among our authors has expertness in this branch of literature become.

In historical writing, if the subject be regarded as a science, there has been a real advance. A great number of meritorious monographs have been produced, while there has been much publishing of original sources. Few recent historians, however, possess the literary gift, and from this point of view the older writers must be given the palm, though Fiske, McMaster, Mahan, Rhodes, and Thayer have worthily upheld standards created by Prescott, Motley, and Parkman. Though there is more studying of history than formerly, few people, comparatively speaking, read history for pleasure.

Scientific History.

In other forms of art the most notable progress was made in the cultivation of American taste rather than in the production of great names. Generally speaking, Americans of the Civil War period were deplorably backward in such matters, and travellers from abroad smiled at the varied manifestations of American crudity in painting, music, and architecture in spite of the tradition by no means extinct of Allston, Stuart, and Copley and of our excellent colonial building. But foreign travel, world's fairs, and other influences opened to discerning eyes the compelling power of the beautiful, and many Americans deliberately set to work to correct our national deficiencies along artistic lines. Art museums were established in many large cities, and these helped to bring about a truly wonderful transformation.

Development of Artistic Taste.

With higher appreciation has come greater encouragement to artistic endeavor, and much work of a high order, comparable with that of contemporary Europe, has been done. In painting, Chase, Sargent, Lafarge, Abbey, and many others achieved high reputations, but the most original American artist was

Painting. James A. McNeill Whistler, most of whose work, however, was done in Europe. In addition, many artists won fame and fortune as illustrators, and we could ill spare the spirited pictures of Frederic Remington, who preserved for posterity certain phases of Western life—bronchos, Indians, cowboys. In some respects, in fact, Remington was the most distinctively American of all our artists. For the higher forms of music we still look mainly to Europe, but there have been many successful composers of popular music, while "ragtime"—based on negro melodies—won favor of a sort, both at home and abroad.

The most distinctive forms of American architecture were the log cabin, the sod hut, and the sky-scraper, all of which were more notable for utility than artistic merit. In 1865 there were

Architecture. comparatively few really notable buildings in the United States, but by 1919 the country contained some of the finest in the world. In the matter of domestic architecture a wonderful transformation was wrought. Some colonial homes were really beautiful, but in the Civil War period there was a distinct retrogression in such matters. The war-time millionaire was likely to build "for himself enormous wooden mansions in many colors, surmounted by wooden cupolas and towers and battlements, and adorned with a maze of wooden pillars representing what someone cleverly styled 'the jigsaw renaissance,' while his lawn was adorned with cast-iron statuary painted to resemble bronze." That age is now past, and in both town and country the traveller sees many mansions and country estates in which the skill of architect and landscape-gardener have combined to produce harmony of form and color and give pleasure to the most critical eye. Even the homes of the middle class are built and furnished with a taste almost totally lacking fifty years ago.

In theoretical science great strides had been made, but America still lagged somewhat behind Europe. In applied science, however, Americans were unsurpassed, and the Yankee still lived up to his old reputation as an inventor. Thomas A.

Applied Science.

Edison, a veritable "wizard" in producing new devices, alone took out over 900 patents for inventions, including the incandescent light, the phonograph, and the kinetoscope, or moving-picture machine. Bell produced the telephone, Browning automatic firearms, and Holland and Lake perfected the submarine. In fact, there was hardly a field of human endeavor in which American inventive genius did not originate some device or improvement. The adoption of these and foreign inventions did much to transform life in many of its aspects. Merely to mention electric lights, electric motors, telephones, and automobiles is sufficient to indicate some of the revolutionary changes which half a century of invention has produced.

But of all inventions of recent times the most spectacular was the work of two brothers, Wilbur and Orville Wright of Dayton, Ohio. These young men, the sons of a bishop of the

The Airplane.

United Brethren Church, owned a small bicycle-repair shop, but they became interested in the subject of aviation and sought to invent a heavier-than-air flying-machine. Other men of reputation—for example, Maxim in England and Professor Langley of the Smithsonian Institution in America—were also making experiments along the same line; but people generally thought the problem insolvable, and classed any one who tried to build a "flying-machine" as a crank or lunatic. The Wright brothers, therefore, faced much ridicule, but they did not give up, though at one time they were so financially embarrassed that they were compelled to accept assistance from a devoted sister.

The perseverance of genius finally had its reward, and on December 7, 1903, at Kitty Hawk, on the sandy coast of North

A Great Triumph.

Carolina, Wilbur Wright made the first successful man-flight in a heavier-than-air machine in history. His machine remained in the air less than a minute, and flew less than three hundred yards, but the possibility of flight had been proven and progress thereafter was rapid. In November, 1904, he flew three miles in four minutes and a half, and in October, 1905, he remained in the air thirty-eight minutes and made a circular flight of twenty-four miles. In 1909, taking with them improved machines, the brothers visited Europe, where interest in aviation was much more intense than in America, and were received as conquering heroes. Later they were accorded high honors in America, and their home town made humble amends for once having laughed at them. Unfortunately Wilbur Wright died in 1912 before he could enjoy to the full his well-earned honors and prosperity, but his brother continued the work. Thus far their invention has found its chief place in war, but much use will doubtless be made of it in times of peace.

Another field in which Americans won fame was that of geographical discovery. In the early '70's Henry M. Stanley, a naturalized American, attracted world-wide attention by finding Livingstone, the British missionary and ex- Exploration. plorer who had been lost to sight in the interior of Africa. Later Stanley penetrated westward to the headwaters of the Congo and followed that river to the sea, thus completing the first crossing of the "Dark Continent." Yet later he helped found the Congo Free State and rescued Emin Pasha. Lieutenant Frederick Schwatka, Lieutenant A. L. Greely, and various others did notable work in Arctic exploration, but the supreme achievement of all was that performed by Lieutenant Robert E. Peary of the navy.

Peary first entered the field of Arctic exploration in 1886, when he made a reconnoissance of the great Greenland "ice cap." The work fascinated him, and for more than twenty Robert E. years he devoted himself to hyperborean explora- Peary. tion and to attaining the supreme goal of all Arctic exploration, the North Pole. Among his achievements from 1891 to 1905 were the discovery of Melville Land and Heilprin Land and the determination of the insularity of Greenland, the northern point of which he named Cape Morris K. Jesup, after one of the promoters of his work. In 1905 he sailed northward in the stanch steamer *Roosevelt*, expressly built for him by the Peary Arctic Club, and the next year, with dog-sledges, passed all previous records and attained 87° 6' north latitude, the "farthest north" ever reached up to that time by man, or only 203 miles from the Pole. There he was turned back by starvation and impossible seas of ice.

But Peary was not satisfied. The great ambition of his life had not been realized. On July 6, 1908, therefore, he once more set sail in the *Roosevelt* on his eighth Arctic quest. He was then fifty-two years old, and he knew that he must succeed on this trip or leave the great prize to younger men. But through years of experience he had learned the best methods of Arctic travel—and fortune smiled. The *Roosevelt* battled her way safely through the ice-pack to Cape Sheridan, in Grant Land, and there the party wintered. Early the next year the explorers, accompanied by Eskimos, set out northward with dog-sledges over the frozen sea. On April 6, 1909, after overcoming indescribable obstacles, the foremost party, consisting of Peary, his faithful negro helper, Matthew Henson, and four Eskimos penetrated to the boreal centre and "nailed the Stars and Stripes to the Pole."

The Pole Reached, April 6, 1909.

Some days before the *Roosevelt* reached Labrador and Peary flashed his great news to civilized centres, the world was startled by a cablegram from Lerwick in the Shetland Islands to the effect that another American, Doctor Frederick A. Cook, had reached the Pole on April 21, 1908, a year before Peary. Many people were misled by Cook's story, but it ultimately developed that he was a monumental impostor, who had not only sought to deceive the world with regard to discovering the Pole but had also falsely claimed to have reached the top of Mount McKinley, the highest point in North America. For a time the true discoverer's laurels were somewhat dimmed by Cook's claim to priority, but presently the facts came out. The world then perceived that Peary's heroic twenty years' quest had been crowned with deserved success, and that he had won a passport to immortality.

A Gigantic Hoax.

At the time of entering the war against autocracy the republic was by far the richest of nations, and, with the exception of Russia, the most populous of civilized nations. The war served merely to increase its material superiority over its rivals. Its shadow loomed ever larger across the narrow world; there seemed no bounds to its possible achievements.

A Boundless Future.

In less than a century and a half America had grown from a weak and thinly inhabited state into a leviathan among states. It had disappointed the predictions of its enemies and surpassed the fondest hopes of its friends. Yet there were unlovely aspects in its complicated life, which had drifted far from the simplicity of earlier days. Not all the ideals of its founders had been realized. Probably some of them never will be realized, for perfection in human institutions is rarely found except in dreams. Some features of its development had taken forms not contemplated by the "Fathers"; it may be that the "Fathers" would not be proud of some of the results of their handiwork. Yet, despite obvious blemishes, it is doubtful whether in any other country human beings have ever attained so high a degree of material well-being, political and intellectual liberty, and general happiness.

But the future will not all be easy sailing. The very vastness of the republic has increased the difficulty of its problems. The interests of section clash with section, and those of class with class, and the task of reconciling these diverse interests taxes the ingenuity of statesmen. The very government itself has grown so complicated that sometimes it seems almost on the point of breaking down. The war has proved expensive beyond all past imaginings, and a vast debt has been incurred which future generations must help to bear. The high cost of living, social and economic discontent, and the contagion of the world-wide ferment have created a spirit of unrest that causes grave concern. But, unlike the Russians, Americans have had long years of experience in self-government, and it is improbable that they will swing far from safe moorings.

In times like these it is well for men to reflect that institutions are constructed slowly, and that it is much easier to tear down than to build up. To that which is good in our institutions we should hold fast with a firm grip, for it is the priceless heritage of all the ages.

SUGGESTIONS FOR FURTHER READING

The following list does not purport to be an exhaustive bibliography. Readers desiring to investigate yet further should consult J. N. Larned, *Literature of American History* (1902); Channing, Hart, and Turner, *Guide to the Study and Reading of American History* (1912); and the bibliographies in vols. 22–27 of *The American Nation : a History* (28 vols., 1903–1918), edited by A. B. Hart. The proceedings and debates in Congress for the years 1865–1873 are in the *Congressional Globe*, and from 1873 onward in the *Congressional Record*. Presidential messages are printed in J. D. Richardson, *A Compilation of the Messages and Papers of the Presidents* (10 vols., many editions). Much of value can be gleaned from the *American* (after 1875, *Appleton's*) *Annual Cyclopedia* (1861–1902) and from contemporary periodicals. In seeking material in magazines the student should, of course, consult *Poole's Index to Periodical Literature* (1882 and many supplementary volumes) and *Readers' Guide to Periodical Literature* (1910–   ).

CHAPTER I—THE AFTERMATH OF WAR

W. A. Dunning, *Reconstruction, Political and Economic* (1907), chaps. I–II; one of the best short books about the Reconstruction period. J. W. Burgess, *Reconstruction and the Constitution* (1902), chaps. I–II; particularly valuable on the legal and political aspects of the period. J. F. Rhodes, *History of the United States from the Compromise of 1850 to the Final Restoration of Home Rule at the South in 1877* (7 vols., 1893–1906), vol. V, pp. 344–465, 556–560; contains one of the most complete accounts of Reconstruction. E. P. Oberholzer, *A History of the United States since the Civil War* (1 vol., pub. 1917), vol. I, chap. II; covers the period 1865–1868, and is in some respects the best book on these years. W. L. Fleming, *Documentary History of Reconstruction* (2 vols., 1906–1907), vol. I, pp. 9–102, 315–383; contains much valuable original material, and the editor supplies interpretative comment and a list of references. C. H. McCarthy, *Lincoln's Plan of Reconstruction* (1901), sets forth exhaustively Lincoln's Reconstruction policy. Sidney Andrews, *The South since the War* (1866), was written by a Northern newspaper correspondent who investigated Southern conditions. Mrs. Roger A. Pryor, *Reminiscences of Peace and War* (1904), contains an interesting account of post-bellum conditions in the South from the standpoint of the wife of a prominent Southerner. Similar in character are Mrs. C. C. Clay, *A Belle of the Fifties* (1904); Susan D.

Smedes, *Memorials of a Southern Planter* (1900); and Myra M. Avary, *Dixie after the War* (1906). Philip A. Bruce, *The Rise of the New South* (1905), is especially valuable on the economic side. G. W. Williams, *History of the Negro Race in America* (2 vols., 1883), gives a negro's view of his race's history.

CHAPTER II—PRESIDENT JOHNSON'S PLAN OF RECONSTRUCTION

Dunning, *Reconstruction, Political and Economic*, chap. III and pp. 55–59. Burgess, *Reconstruction and the Constitution*, chap. III. Rhodes, *History of the United States from the Compromise of 1850*, vol. V, pp. 516–540, 555. Oberholzer, *A History of the United States since the Civil War*, vol. I, chap. I. Fleming, *Documentary History of Reconstruction*, vol. I, pp. 105–117, 273–312, 163–196. James Schouler, *History of the United States, 1783–1877* (7 vols., 1913), vol. VII, pp. 1–47. James G. Blaine, *Twenty Years of Congress* (2 vols., 1884–1886), vol. II, pp. 1–15, 34–50, 56–111; partisan and not always accurate, but often useful and suggestive because written by a prominent participant in many of the scenes described. S. S. Cox, *Three Decades of Federal Legislation* (1885), pp. 346–364; the work of a prominent Democrat and forms a good antidote to Blaine's history. D. M. DeWitt, *The Impeachment and Trial of Andrew Johnson* (1903), contains a history of the Johnson administration and is perceptibly hostile to the radicals. Gideon Welles, *Diary of Gideon Welles* (3 vols., 1911); the author was a member of Johnson's cabinet, and he sets down unreservedly the happenings from day to day as well as his own opinions. For some of the speeches on the Reconstruction question see Alexander Johnston and James A. Woodburn, *American Orations* (new ed., 1897, 4 vols.), vol. IV, pp. 129–148.

CHAPTER III—CONGRESS TAKES CONTROL

Dunning, *Reconstruction, Political and Economic*, chaps. IV–VII. Burgess, *Reconstruction and the Constitution*, pp. 42–206. Rhodes, *History of the United States from the Compromise of 1850*, vol. V, pp. 541–625. Oberholzer, *A History of the United States since the Civil War*, vol. I, chaps. III, VII. Fleming, *Documentary History of Reconstruction*, vol. I, pp. 118–153, 197–240, 397 *ff*. Blaine, *Twenty Years of Congress*, vol. II, pp. 111–384. Cox, *Three Decades of Federal Legislation*, pp. 365 *ff*. Schouler, *History of the United States*, vol. VII, pp. 47–123. DeWitt, *The Impeachment and Trial of Andrew Johnson*. S. W. McCall, *Thaddeus Stevens* (1899), is short but worth consulting. More exhaustive is J. A. Woodburn, *The Life of Thaddeus Stevens* (1913). W. D. Foulke, *Life and Public Service of Oliver P. Morton* (2 vols., 1899); a good biography of one of the most forceful figures of the period. Frederic Bancroft, *William H. Seward* (2 vols., 1900); the best biography of Seward. The student will also find material of value in F. W. Seward, *Seward at Washington* (1891). Carl Schurz, *The Remi-*

niscences of Carl Schurz (3 vols., 1907–1908), contains an account of the author's Southern investigations. E. L. Pierce, *Memoirs and Letters of Charles Sumner* (4 vols., 2d ed., 1894). *Senate Executive Documents, 39th Cong., 1st Sess.: No. 2* contains reports of Schurz and Grant on Southern conditions; *No. 43* contains that of Truman. See also Johnston and Woodburn, *American Orations*, vol. IV, pp. 149–188.

CHAPTER IV—MEXICO, ALASKA, AND THE ELECTION OF 1868

Dunning, *Reconstruction, Political and Economic*, pp. 124–135, 151–163. Burgess, *Reconstruction and the Constitution*, pp. 206–213, 299–303. Rhodes, *History of the United States from the Compromise of 1850*, vol. VI, pp. 179–213. Oberholzer, *A History of the United States since the Civil War*, vol. I, chap. VIII. Blaine, *Twenty Years of Congress*, vol. II, pp. 385–421. Cox, *Three Decades of Federal Legislation*, pp. 617–624. Schouler, *History of the United States*, vol. VII, pp. 123–143. Bancroft, *William H. Seward*. Pierce, *Memoir and Letters of Charles Sumner*. Edward Stanwood, *A History of the Presidency* (new ed., 2 vols., 1916), vol. I, chap. XXIII; contains an account of every presidential election down to 1916. H. H. Bancroft, *History of Mexico* (6 vols., 1883–1888), vol. VI, pp. 1–332, contains an account of French intervention in Mexico. See also Percy F. Walker, *The French in Mexico* (1914). J. B. Moore, *A Digest of International Law* (8 vols., 1906); a valuable compilation, contains an account of the French interference in Mexico. F. Bancroft, *William H. Seward*, vol. II, chaps. XL, XLII, describes the course of the American Government with regard to the French in Mexico, and deals also with the purchase of Alaska. The career of Grant down to his presidency is best told in his *Personal Memoirs* (2 vols., 1886), and in Hamlin Garland, *Ulysses Grant* (1898). For the financial issues of the campaign consult D. R. Dewey, *Financial History of the United States* (1903 and many later editions); W. C. Mitchell, *History of the Greenbacks* (1903); and Hugh McCulloch, *Men and Measures of Half a Century* (1888), written by Johnson's secretary of the treasury.

CHAPTER V—THE FRUITS OF RECONSTRUCTION

Dunning, *Reconstruction, Political and Economic*, chaps. XI, XIII, XIV, XVI, XVII. Burgess, *Reconstruction and the Constitution*, chaps. XI–XII. Rhodes, *History of the United States from the Compromise of 1850*, vol. VI, pp. 236–243; VII, pp. 74–174. Fleming, *Documentary History of Reconstruction*, vol. II, pp. 1–404. Schouler, *History of the United States*, vol. VII, pp. 144–154, 168–178, 243–261. Cox, *Three Decades of Federal Legislation*, pp. 451–577. J. S. Pike, *The Prostrate State* (1874), is a Northern man's description of the lurid carnival of misrule in South Carolina. H. A. Herbert, editor, *Why the Solid South ?* (1890); a collection of essays by various authors dealing with the Reconstruction period in the South; very partisan but worth consulting. Under the general oversight of Professor W. A. Dunning of Columbia, a number of valuable monographs dealing with Reconstruction in individual States have been written. Among these are J. A. Garner, *Reconstruction in Mississippi* (1901); W. L. Fleming, *Civil War and Reconstruction in Alabama* (1905); J. G. de R. Hamilton, *Reconstruction in North Carolina* (1914); Charles W. Ramsdell, *Reconstruction in Texas* (1910). Walter Allen, *Governor Chamberlain's Administration in South Carolina* (1888), defends in great detail the career of the last carpet-bag governor of South Carolina; while J. S. Reynolds, *Reconstruction in South Carolina* (1905), treats the whole reconstruction period in that State from the standpoint of a Southern partisan. The story of the Ku-Klux movement is told by J. C. Lester and D. L. Wilson, *Ku-Klux Klan, Its Origin, Growth, and Disbandment* (new ed. edited by W. L. Fleming, 1905); an excellent short account is given in W. G. Brown, *The Lower South in American History* (1902), chap. IV.

CHAPTER VI—FOREIGN RELATIONS AND THE LIBERAL REPUBLICAN MOVEMENT

Dunning, *Reconstruction, Political and Economic*, pp. 163–173, 190–202. Rhodes, *History of the United States from the Compromise of 1850*, vol. VI, pp. 343–377, 412–440. Burgess, *Reconstruction and the Constitution*, pp. 264–268, 305–327. Blaine, *Twenty Years of Congress*, vol. I, pp. 458–536. Stanwood, *A History of the Presidency*, vol. I, chap. XXIV. Schouler, *History of the United States*, vol. VII, pp. 161–168, 194–220. J. B. Moore, *History and Digest of the International Arbitrations to Which the United States has been a Party* (6 vols., 1898); a valuable compilation which contains a full account of the *Alabama* claims. On this subject the student will also do well to consult C. F. Adams, "The Treaty of Washington," in *Lee at Appomattox, and Other Papers* (1902); J. C. B. Davis, *Mr. Fish and the Alabama Claims* (1895), written by the American agent at Geneva; and John Morley, *Life of Gladstone* (3 vols., 1903), vol. II, pp. 393–413. Schurz, *Reminiscences*, vol. III, pp. 338–353, contains a sketch of the origin of the Liberal Republicans. W. A. Linn, *Horace Greeley* (1903), tells the life story of the Liberal Republican and Democratic candidate. George S. Boutwell, *Reminiscences of Sixty Years* (1902), was written by a member of Grant's cabinet. Albert B. Paine, *Thomas Nast, His Period and His Pictures* (1904), contains an account of the fight against the Tweed Ring, and of the campaign of 1872.

CHAPTER VII—THE END OF AN ERA

Dunning, *Reconstruction, Political and Economic*, chaps. XV–XXI. Burgess, *Reconstruction and the Constitution*, chap. XIII. Stanwood, *A History of the Presidency*, chap. XXV. Fleming, *Documentary History of Reconstruction*, vol. I, pp. 405–455; Schouler, *History of the*

United States, vol. VII. Rhodes, *History of the United States from the Compromise of 1850*, vol. VII, pp. 1–73, 175–291. Cox, *Three Decades of Federal Legislation*, pp. 636–668. Blaine, *Twenty Years of Congress*, vol. II, pp. 537–589. C. R. Williams, *Life of Rutherford B. Hayes* (2 vols., 1914). John Bigelow, *Samuel J. Tilden* (2 vols., 1895), contains a long account of the campaign of 1876. The various aspects of that campaign are set forth exhaustively in P. L. Haworth, *The Hayes-Tilden Election* (1906). For further material concerning the New South and the race problem the student may consult E. G. Murphy, *Problems of the Present South* (1904); J. L. Mathews, *Remaking the Mississippi* (1909); E. A. Alderman and A. C. Gordon, *Life of J. L. M. Curry* (1911); Ray S. Baker, *Following the Color Line* (1908); G. S. Merriam, *The Negro and the Nation* (1906); Thomas N. Page, *The Negro, the Southerner's Problem* (1904); W. E. B. Dubois, *The Souls of Black Folk* (1903); Booker T. Washington, *Up from Slavery* (1901); H. W. Grady, *The New South* (1890); Bruce, *The Rise of the New South*.

CHAPTER VIII—THE PASSING OF THE WILD WEST

F. L. Paxson, *The Last American Frontier* (1910), contains in small compass some of the salient aspects of the passing of the Wild West. Katherine Coman, *Economic Beginnings of the Far West* (1911), an excellent work but containing comparatively little material on the period after the Civil War. F. J. Turner, *Significance of the Frontier in American History* (in American Historical Association's *Annual Report* for 1893), an essay which did much to promote the study of Western history. J. P. Davis, *Union Pacific Railway* (1894), the best account of the building of the first transcontinental. E. V. Smalley, *The Northern Pacific Railroad* (1883), tells the story of the Northern Pacific. Oberholzer, *A History of the United States since the Civil War*, vol. I, chaps. V–VI; a good summary of Western conditions at the end of the Civil War. Richard I. Dodge, *The Plains of the Great West* (1877), written by an army officer who spent many years on the border; an absorbing book on the "Wild West" at the time it was passing into history. Indian campaigns in the West are described in Nelson A. Miles, *Personal Recollections and Observations* (1896); George A. Custer, *My Life on the Plains* (1874); Philip H. Sheridan, *Personal Memoirs* (1888); Henry Carrington, *Ab-sa-ra-ka, Land of Massacre* (1878), contains a history of the Indian wars from 1865 to 1878, and also a description of frontier life; John F. Finerty, *Warpath and Bivouac* (1890), by a correspondent who witnessed some of the campaigns against the Sioux. The best account of the Custer massacre is given by Captain E. S. Godfrey in his article "Custer's Last Battle," in *Century Magazine*, vol. 43 (1892), pp. 358–384. The "Story of the West Series," edited by Ripley Hitchcock, deals in a popular way with salient features of Western life; among the volumes may be mentioned C. H. Shinn, *Story of the Mine* (1896); Cy Warman, *Story of the Railroad* (1903); and Emerson Hough, *The Story of the Cowboy* (1897). Theodore Roosevelt, *Ranch Life and the Hunting Trail* (1888, etc.), embodies some of the author's own experiences.

Robert P. Porter, *The West from the Census of 1880* (1882), is a convenient résumé. Hubert H. Bancroft, *West American Historical Series* (39 vols., 1875–1887), deals mainly with an earlier period of Western history, but some of the volumes are of value on our epoch. Seymour Dunbar, *A History of Travel in America* (4 vols., 1915), contains much interesting material on the history of transport problems in the West, and also on the Indian question. See also Henry Inman, *The Old Santa Fé Trail* (1898).

CHAPTER IX—AN INTERLUDE

Edwin E. Sparks, *National Development, 1877–1885* (1907), covers in more extended form the same period as this chapter. James F. Rhodes, *History of the United States from Hayes to McKinley, 1877–1896* (1918), chaps. I–X; a volume that continues the story from the point where the author's larger work stops. Williams, *Life of Rutherford B. Hayes*, vol. II, chaps. XXVII–XXXII. John W. Burgess, *The Administration of Rutherford B. Hayes* (1915). Stanwood, *History of the Presidency*, chaps. XXVI–XXVII. Edward Stanwood, *James G. Blaine*, (1905). On the spoils system the student will find material in C. R. Fish, *Civil Service and the Patronage* (1905); Lyon G. Tyler, *Parties and Patronage* (1888); James Bryce, *The American Commonwealth* (1893), vol. II, chap. LXV; Dorman B. Eaton, *Government of Municipalities* (1899); George W. Curtis, *Orations and Addresses* (3 vols., 1893), vol. II, p. 477; Theodore Roosevelt, *Theodore Roosevelt: an Autobiography* (1913), chap. V; J. A. Woodburn, *The American Republic and Its Government* (1903); and Edward Cary, *George William Curtis* (1895). On the Chinese question see George F. Seward, *Chinese Immigration in Its Social and Economical Aspects* (1881); Richard Mayo-Smith, *Emigration and Immigration* (1890); J. A. Whitney, *Chinese and the Chinese Question* (1888). On financial questions see Dewey, *Financial History of the United States*; A. D. Noyes, *Thirty Years of American Finance* (1898); A. S. Bolles, *Financial History of the United States* (3 vols., 1883–1886); F. W. Taussig, *Tariff History of the United States* (1905); J. Laurence Laughlin, *Bimetallism in the United States* (1897). John Sherman, *Recollections of Forty Years in the House, Senate, and Cabinet* (2 vols., 1895), contains much valuable material on political and financial questions.

CHAPTER X—THE CHANGING ORDER

Sparks, *National Development*, especially chaps. II–V, XVIII. Rhodes, *History of the United States from Hayes to McKinley*, pp. 13–97, gives a detailed account of the railway strike of 1877, and of the Molly Maguires. On the labor question see also T. V. Powderly, *Thirty Years of Labor* (1889), written by the head of the Knights of Labor in this period; C. D. Wright, "An Historical Sketch of the Knights of Labor," in *Quarterly Journal of Economics*, vol. I (1887), pp. 137–168; M. A. Aldrich, "The American Federation of Labor," in American Economic Association's *Economic Studies*, vol. III (1898), no. 4; R. T. Ely, *The Labor Movement in America* (1890); John Mitchell, *Organized Labor* (1903). On the development of American industries see J. M. Swank, *History of the Manufacture of Iron* (1897); W. J. Mitchell, *Story of American Coals* (1897); T. M. Young, *The American Cotton Industry* (1903); M. T. Copeland, *The Cotton Manufacturing Industry of the United States*, in *Harvard Economic Studies*, vol. VIII (1912). See also Edward W. Bryce, *Progress of Invention in the Nineteenth Century* (1900). The rise of the first trust is traced in detail in Ida Tarbell, *History of the Standard Oil Company* (2 vols., 1904), a work widely read at the time of its publication. A shorter and more friendly account is G. H. Montague, *Rise and Progress of the Standard Oil Company* (1903). On the railroads consult F. H. Dixon, *State Railroad Control* (1896); B. H. Meyer, *Railway Legislation in the United States* (1903); A. T. Hadley, *Railroad Transportation* (1890); and Frank H. Spearman, *The Strategy of Great Railroads* (1904). C. D. Wright, *The Industrial Evolution of the United States* (1895), is helpful but inadequate. Richard T. Ely, *Studies in the Evolution of Industrial Society* (1903), throws much light upon the subjects considered in this chapter. Katherine Coman, *Industrial History of the United States* (1905), is an excellent but brief book. The stirrings of industrial and social discontent appear in Henry George, *Progress and Poverty* (1879), a famous treatise advocating the "single tax" on land; in Edward Bellamy, *Looking Backward* (1888), a widely read novel; and in *The Breadwinners* (1884), published anonymously but written by John Hay.

CHAPTER XI—THE RETURN OF THE DEMOCRACY

Rhodes, *History of the United States from Hayes to McKinley*, chaps. XI–XIII. H. T. Peck, *Twenty Years of the Republic* (1906), chaps. I–II, IV; a readable but not always trustworthy volume. Davis R. Dewey, *National Problems* (1907), chaps. I–VIII, especially strong as regards economic questions. Many of Cleveland's public utterances are given in G. F. Parker, *Writings and Speeches of Grover Cleveland* (1892). Grover Cleveland, *Presidential Problems* (1904), deals mainly with his second administration. On the tariff question see Taussig, *Tariff History of the United States ;* and Edward Stanwood, *American Tariff Controversies in the Nineteenth Century* (2 vols., 1903). On the railway question see Meyer, *Railway Legislation in the United States ;* E. R. Johnson, *American Railway Transportation* (1903); and W. Z. Ripley, *Railway Problems* (1907). An account of the trial of the Chicago anarchists is given in Frederick T. Hill, *Decisive Battles of the Law* (1907), pp. 240–268. Matilda Gresham, *Life of Walter Quinton Gresham* (2 vols., 1920), purports to give an "inside" account of the Republican convention of 1888 and of some phases of the campaign, but should be used with caution. See also Stanwood, *History of the Presidency*, vol. I, chaps. XXVIII–XXIX.

CHAPTER XII—THE SECOND HARRISON

Rhodes, *History of the United States from Hayes to McKinley*, chaps. XIV–XVII. Dewey, *National Problems*, chaps. IX–XV. Peck, *Twenty Years of the Republic*, chaps. V–VI. Stanwood, *History of the Presidency*, vol. I, chaps. XXVIII–XXX; and S. B. McCall, *The Life of Thomas Brackett Reed* (1914), chaps. X–XV. On the tariff question consult Taussig, *Tariff History of the United States;* and Stanwood, *American Tariff Controversies in the Nineteenth Century.* On the trust question see A. M. Walker, *History of the Sherman Law* (1900); J. W. Jenks, *The Trust Problem* (1900); Tarbell, *History of the Standard Oil Company;* and Henry D. Lloyd, *Wealth against Commonwealth* (1898). Robley D. Evans, *A Sailor's Log* (1901), contains an account of the Chilean difficulty; the author was in command of the *Baltimore.* For a first-hand description of Samoan affairs see Robert Louis Stevenson, *A Footnote to History : Eight Years of Trouble in Samoa* (1891). Mary H. Krout, *Hawaii and a Revolution* (1899), and E. J. Carpenter, *America in Hawaii* (1898), describe the overthrow of Liliuokalani's power. On this and other diplomatic questions consult also John W. Foster, *American Diplomacy in the Orient* (1903), and J. B. Henderson, *American Diplomatic Questions* (1901). For the rise of Populism see F. L. McVey, *The Populist Movement*, in American Economic Association *Studies*, vol. I (1896), no. 3.

CHAPTER XIII—HARD TIMES AND FREE SILVER

Rhodes, *History of the United States from Hayes to McKinley*, chaps. XVIII–XX. Dewey, *National Problems*, chaps. XIV–XX. Peck, *Twenty Years of the Republic*, chaps. VII–XI, and McCall, *The Life of Thomas Brackett Reed*, chaps. XVI–XIX. Theodore E. Burton, *Financial Crises and Periods of Industrial and Commercial Depression* (1902), contains an account of the chief periods of depression down to 1902. H. Vincent, *The Story of the Commonweal* (1894), is a history of the Coxey movement. W. J. Ashley, *The Railroad Strike of 1894* (1895), deals with the chief labor trouble of the period, and analyzes the report made by a federal commission which investigated the strike. For the injunction issue see W. H. Dunbar, *Government by Injunction*, in American Economic Association *Studies*, vol. III (1898), no. 1; and F. J. Stimson, *Modern Use of Injunctions*, in *Political Science Quarterly*, vol. X, pp. 189–202. On the Hawaiian question consult Krout, *Hawaii and a Revolution ;* Carpenter, *America in Hawaii ;* Henderson, *American Diplomatic Questions ;* Foster, *American Diplomacy in the Orient.* President Cleveland's *Presidential Problems* contains a detailed defense of his bond-issue policy, and also of his course with regard to Venezuela. On the latter subject see also W. F. Reddaway, *The Monroe Doctrine* (1898). Gresham, *Life of Walter Quinton Gresham*, defends Gresham's course as secretary of state. On the currency question the free-silver view was set forth in a popular way in W. H. H. Harvey, *Coin's Financial School* (1894). A reply to it was published in Horace White, *Coin's*

Financial Fool ; or the Artful Dodger Exposed (c. 1896). Less partisan discussions will be found in A. B. Hepburn, *History of Coinage and Currency in the United States* (1903); J. L. Laughlin, *History of Bimetallism in the United States* (4th ed., 1897); and H. B. Russell, *International Monetary Conference* (1898). Bryan's view of the election of 1896 is set forth in his *The First Battle* (1897). The story of how McKinley was nominated and elected is told in Herbert Croly, *Marcus Alonzo Hanna* (1912), and in C. S. Olcott, *The Life of William McKinley* (2 vols., 1916). See also Stanwood, *History of the Presidency*, vol. I, chap. XXX.

CHAPTER XIV—THE WAR WITH SPAIN

Latané, *America as a World Power* (1907), chaps. I–IV. Peck, *Twenty Years of the Republic*, chap. XIII. The diplomacy of the war is set forth in French E. Chadwick, *The Relations of the United States and Spain ; Diplomacy* (New York, 1909), an exhaustive book; and E. J. Benton, *International Law and Diplomacy of the Spanish-American War* (1908). For naval aspects see George Dewey, *Autobiography of George Dewey* (1903); John D. Long, *The New American Navy* (2 vols., 1904); A. T. Mahan, *Lessons of the War with Spain* (1899); W. S. Schley, *Forty-five Years under the Flag* (1904); R. D. Evans, *A Sailor's Log* (1901); and French E. Chadwick, *The Relations of the United States and Spain ; the Spanish-American War* (1911). The last is, upon the whole, the most adequate treatment of naval events, and is almost equally authoritative on the military side. For other books dealing with the campaigns on land see R. H. Davis, *The Cuban and Porto Rican Campaigns* (1898), written by a war correspondent; Joseph Wheeler, *The Santiago Campaign* (1898), by a prominent actor in the campaign; and Theodore Roosevelt, *The Rough Riders* (1899), an extremely vivid and picturesque work. See also Roosevelt's *Autobiography* (1913), chap. VII.

CHAPTER XV—"IMPERIALISM"

Latané, *America as a World Power*, chaps. V–X. Peck, *Twenty Years of the Republic*, chap. XIV. A vivid account of the war against the Filipinos will be found in Frederick Funston, *Memories of Two Wars* (1912), written by the officer who captured Aguinaldo. Dean C. Worcester, *The Philippines : Past and Present* (2 vols., new ed., 1914), is by an author who was familiar with the islands before the American period and who subsequently was a member of the Philippine Commission; it favors the retention of the islands. James A. Leroy, *The Americans in the Philippines* (2 vols., 1914), is a work of high merit, but the death of the author found it uncompleted. Charles E. Elliott, *The Philippines* (2 vols., 1917), was written by a former justice of the Philippine Supreme Court, and is especially good on the institutional side. Arguments against retaining the islands will be found in Carl Schurz, *The Policy of Imperialism* (1899); George F. Hoar, *No Power to Conquer Foreign Nations and Hold Their People against Their Will* (1899), a pamphlet; Edward Atkinson, *Cost of War and Warfare from 1899 to 1902* (1902); James H. Blount, *The American Occupation of the Philippines* (1912); and Maximo M. Kalaw, *The Case for the Philippines* (1916), a plea for independence by a native writer. W. F. Willoughby, *Territories and Dependencies of the United States* (1905), contains a description of the organization of governments in the insular possessions. See also Carl Crow, *America and the Philippines* (1914), and F. C. Chamberlin, *The Philippine Problem* (1913). A summary of affairs in the insular possessions is given in *Annual Reports of the Secretary of War, 1899–1903*, published in a single volume. See also Leo S. Rowe, *The United States and Porto Rico* (1904). For the election of 1900 consult Edward Stanwood, *A History of the Presidency*, vol. II, chap. I. On China and the "open door" consult Thayer, *Life of John Hay* (2 vols., 1915), vol. II, chap. XXVI. W. A. P. Martin, *Siege of Pekin* (1900), tells the story of the Boxer movement from the standpoint of a missionary. For the career of McKinley in these years and his death see Olcott, *Life of William McKinley*, and Croly, *Marcus Alonzo Hanna*.

CHAPTER XVI—"BIG BUSINESS" AND THE PANAMA CANAL

Peck, *Twenty Years of the Republic*, chap. XV. Latané, *America as a World Power*, chaps. IX–XVI. Stanwood, *History of the Presidency*, vol. II, chap. II. In his *Autobiography* Roosevelt tells the story of his life in an interesting way, and deals with many aspects of his administration. There have been many other biographies of Roosevelt, most of them uncritical. See F. E. Leupp, *The Man Roosevelt* (1904); J. A. Riis, *Theodore Roosevelt, the Citizen* (1904); J. L. Street, *The Most Interesting American* (1915); C. G. Washburn, *Theodore Roosevelt; the Logic of His Career* (1916); and W. R. Thayer, *Theodore Roosevelt: an Intimate Biography* (1919). Much light on the events of these years is thrown by *Theodore Roosevelt and His Time—Shown by His Own Letters*, edited by Joseph B. Bishop, in *Scribner's Magazine*, beginning September, 1919. On the trust and railroad questions see B. H. Meyer, *History of the Northern Securities Case* (1906); John Moody, *The Truth about the Trusts* (1904); Gilbert Montague, *The Trusts of To-day* (1904); Tarbell, *History of the Standard Oil Company*; H. S. Haines, *Problems in Railroad Regulation* (1911); W. Z. Ripley, *Railroads: Rates and Regulation* (1912); Frederick N. Judson, *The Law of Interstate Commerce and Its Federal Regulation* (1906); and William H. Taft, *The Anti-Trust Act and the Supreme Court* (1914). *Documentary History of American Industrial Society* (11 vols., 1910–1911), edited by John R. Commons and others, is a valuable storehouse of information concerning industrial matters, labor, etc. On the Panama Canal consult, Willis F. Johnson, *Four Centuries of the Panama Canal* (1906); M. W. Williams, *Anglo-American Isthmian Diplomacy, 1815–1915* (1916); Forbes Lindsay, *Panama and the Canal To-day* (new ed., 1913); L. Hutchinson, *The Panama Canal and International Trade Competition* (1915); E. R. Johnson, *The Panama Canal and Commerce* (1916).

C. Lloyd Jones, *The Caribbean Interests of the United States* (1916), is sufficiently indicated by its title. On this subject see also F. A. Ogg, *National Progress* (1918), chaps. XIV–XV. An account of foreign affairs in Roosevelt's "first" term is given in Thayer's *Hay*, vol. II, chaps. XXVIII–XXXII. Chapter XXVIII deals with the "German Menace," and tells the story of Roosevelt's Venezuelan ultimatum; a detailed statement on the last subject by Roosevelt himself is printed in the appendix.

CHAPTER XVII—ROOSEVELT'S "SECOND" TERM

Ogg, *National Progress*, chaps. I–IX. Stanwood, *History of the Presidency*, vol. II, pp. 141–212. The best general work on conservation is Charles R. Van Hise, *The Conservation of Natural Resources of the United States* (1910). See also C. E. Fanning, *Selected Articles on Conservation of Natural Resources* (1913); Gifford Pinchot, *The Fight for Conservation* (1911); Roosevelt, *Autobiography*, chap. XI; and P. L. Haworth, *America in Ferment* (1915), chaps. II–III. On the trust problem see references cited for preceding chapter. On the trouble with Japan consult K. K. Kakawami, *American-Japanese Relations* (1912); Sidney L. Gulick, *The American-Japanese Problem* (1914); H. A. Millis, *The American Japanese Problem* (1914); and Amos S. and Suzanne Hershey, *Modern Japan* (1919), chap. XVII. See also biographies of Roosevelt cited for preceding chapter.

CHAPTER XVIII—THE NEW WEST

Paxson, *The Last American Frontier*, chap. XXII. Sparks, *National Development*, chaps. XV–XVI. Joseph Schafer, *A History of the Pacific Northwest* (new ed., 1918), pp. 240–307. On Reclamation see R. P. Teele, *Irrigation in the United States ; a Discussion of Its Legal, Economic, and Financial Aspects* (1915); W. H. Olin, *American Irrigation Farming* (1913); W. E. Smythe, *The Conquest of Arid America* (1900 and later eds.). The last tells the history of reclamation from the standpoint of a leader in the movement. For a short account see F. A. Ogg, *National Progress*, pp. 107–113. On Alaska consult A. W. Greely, *Handbook of Alaska* (1909); and *Report of Alaska Railroad Commission* (1913).

CHAPTER XIX—THE REVOLT OF THE PROGRESSIVES

Ogg, *National Progress*, chaps. IX–XI. F. W. Taussig, *The Tariff History of the United States* (6th ed., 1914), contains a discussion of the Payne-Aldrich Act. I. M. Tarbell, *The Tariff in Our Times* (1911), tells the story of the tariff question from the Civil War onward, and is strongly anti-protectionist. The controversies over conservation can best be studied in the files of such periodicals as *The Outlook*, *Collier's Weekly*, and *The Review of Reviews*. See also Pinchot's *Fight for Conservation*. On our changing institutions see Herbert Croly, *The Promise of American Life* (1909), advocates a stronger nationalism and is a book of much distinction; Theodore Roosevelt, *The New Nationalism* (1910); Frank J. Goodnow, *Social Reform and the Constitution* (1911), emphasizes the cramping effects of a written constitution; W. L. Ransom, *Majority Rule and the Judiciary* (1912), deals with alleged reactionary tendencies of the courts; Walter E. Weyl, *The New Democracy* (1912), a notable book that is strongly progressive in tone; Nicholas M. Butler, *Why Should We Change Our Form of Government?* (1912), is a conservative's view of our institutions. On "direct government" see E. P. Oberholzer, *The Referendum, Initiative, and Recall in America* (new ed., 1911); D. F. Wilcox, *Government by All the People* (1912); W. B. Munro (ed.), *The Initiative, Referendum, and Recall* (1912), contains articles by Roosevelt, Woodrow Wilson, and others; C. A. Beard and B. E. Schultz (eds.), *Documents on the State-Wide Initiative, Referendum, and Recall* (1912); A. H. Eaton, *The Oregon System* (1912); J. D. Barnett, *Operation of the Initiative, Referendum, and Recall in Oregon* (1915). Interesting governmental experiments in Wisconsin are described in Charles McCarthy, *The Wisconsin Idea* (1912). Recent experiments in city government are set forth in E. S. Bradford, *Commission Government in American Cities* (1912). On the rise of progressivism see S. J. Duncan-Clark, *The Progressive Movement* (1913); Herbert Croly, *Progressive Democracy* (1914); Weyl, *The New Democracy;* William E. Walling, *Progressivism and After* (1914), a Socialist's view; and B. F. DeWitt, *The Progressive Movement* (1915). On election of 1912 consult files of the magazines, *The American Year Book* for 1912, and *The New International Year Book* for 1912. Some of Roosevelt's speeches are gathered in his *Progressive Principles* (1913). The gist of those by Wilson may be found in *The New Freedom* (1913), edited by W. B. Hale. For the life of Wilson see H. J. Ford, *Woodrow Wilson, the Man and His Work* (1915); and W. B. Hale, *Woodrow Wilson ; the Story of His Life* (1912). On the campaign see also Haworth, *America in Ferment*, chaps. XIV-XV; and Robert M. LaFollette, *Autobiography* (1913), strongly anti-Roosevelt. The various platforms are given in Stanwood, *History of the Presidency*, vol. II, appendix.

CHAPTER XX—THE "NEW FREEDOM" AND "WATCHFUL WAITING"

Ogg, *National Progress*, chaps. XII-XXI. On the Underwood Act see F. W. Taussig, *The Tariff Act of 1913*, in *Quarterly Journal of Economics*, vol. XXVIII, 1-30; H. P. Willis, "The Tariff of 1913," in *Journal of Political Economy*, vol. XXII, pp. 1-42, 105-131, 218-238; H. R. Mussey, "The New Freedom in Commerce," in *Political Science Quarterly*, vol. XXIX, pp. 600-625. On the Federal Reserve Act see H. P. Willis, "The New Banking System," in *Political Science Quarterly*, vol. XXX, pp. 591-617; O. M. W. Sprague, "The Federal Reserve Banking System in Operation," in *Quarterly Journal of Economics*, vol. XXX, pp. 627-644; T. Conway and E. M. Patterson, *The Operation of the New Bank Act* (1914); and H. P. Willis, *The Federal Reserve* (1915).

On the trust question consult W. H. S. Stevens, "The Trade Commission Act," in *American Economic Review*, vol. IV, pp. 840–856; W. H. S. Stevens, "The Clayton Act," in *American Economic Review*, vol. V, pp. 38–54; A. A. Young, "The Sherman Act and the New Anti-Trust Legislation," in *Journal of Political Economy*, vol. XXIII, pp. 201–220, 305–326, 417–436; E. D. Durand, *The Trust Problem* (1915); and W. H. S. Stevens, *Unfair Competition* (1917). A good description of Mexico under Diaz is given in P. F. Martin, *Mexico of the Twentieth Century* (2 vols., 1907); more sensational is J. K. Turner, *Barbarous Mexico* (4th ed., 1914); C. W. Barron, *The Mexican Problem* (1917), deals largely with economic questions; Mrs. E. L. O'Shaughnessy, *A Diplomat's Wife in Mexico* (1916), consists of letters written from the American embassy in 1913–14; R. Batchelder, *Watching and Waiting on the Border* (1917), describes patrol work along the Mexican frontier. See also John Reed, *Insurgent Mexico* (1914). Of the vast number of books and pamphlets dealing with the Great War only a comparatively few are of any real value. Several helpful collections of diplomatic documents on the origin of the war have appeared, among them being J. B. Scott (ed.), *Diplomatic Documents Relating to the Outbreak of the European War* (2 vols., 1916). See also E. C. Stowell, *The Diplomacy of the Great War of 1914* (1915). A useful book on the origins of the conflict is W. S. Davis, *The Roots of the War* (1918). Of German propagandist books designed to influence American opinion good examples are Hugo Münsterberg, *The War and America* (1914); and E. von Mach, *What Germany Wants* (1914). J. M. Beck, *The Evidence in the Case* (1914), weighs the conflicting testimony and decides against Germany. The course of the war can be followed in the files of *Current History* and other magazines. Of the many histories Frank H. Simonds, *History of the World War* (5 vols., 1915–1920), is one of the most illuminating. A. F. Pollard, *A Short History of the Great War* (1920), is a good brief account. America's lack of preparedness is discussed in F. L. Huidekoper, *The Military Unpreparedness of the United States* (1915). Pleas for preparedness are made in Theodore Roosevelt, *America and the World War* (1915); Francis V. Greene, *The Present Military Situation in the United States* (1915); and Leonard Wood, *Our Military History, Its Facts and Fallacies* (1916). Light on our diplomatic relations with Germany is thrown in J. W. Gerard, *My Four Years in Germany* (1917), and the same author's *Face to Face with Kaiserism* (1917). A detailed history of those relations is given in John B. McMaster, *The United States in the World War* (2 vols., 1918–1920), vol. I, chaps. I–XII. President Wilson's course in foreign affairs is defended in E. E. Robinson and V. J. West, *The Foreign Policy of Woodrow Wilson, 1913–1917* (1917), which contains his speeches on foreign affairs and some of the chief diplomatic papers; and by George Creel, *Wilson and the Issues* (1916). Wilson's course is severely criticised in Theodore Roosevelt, *America and the World War* (1915), and *Fear God and Take Your Own Part* (1916); in Munroe Smith, "American Diplomacy in the European War," in *Political Science Quarterly*, vol. XXXI, pp. 481–518; and in *Addresses of Elihu Root on International Subjects* (1916), pp. 427–447.

Materials for the Study of the War (1918), compiled by Albert E. McKinley, contains selections from President Wilson's addresses, a topical outline of the war, prepared by S. B. Harding, statutes relating to the war, and other features, including a bibliography. For the election of 1916 consult magazines and newspapers, *The American Year Book* for 1916, and *The New International Year Book* for 1916.

CHAPTERS XXI–XXII—AMERICA AND THE GREAT WAR

For America's part in the Great War we are still largely dependent upon newspaper and magazine accounts. The student may consult the files of such magazines as *Current History, The Outlook, The Review of Reviews, The Independent, The World's Work,* and *The Literary Digest.* Extended accounts are given in *The American Year Book* for 1917 and 1918, and *The New International Year Book* for 1917 and 1918. McMaster, *The United States in the World War,* and Simonds, *History of the World War,* are both meritorious. John S. Bassett, *Our War with Germany* (1920), is a short account, containing comparatively little about military operations. Of the more "popular" histories may be mentioned Francis A. March, *History of the World War* (1919); and Richard J. Beamish and Francis A. March, *America's Part in the World War* (1919). Robert R. McCormick, *The Army of 1918* (1920), was written by a member of Pershing's staff. E. Alexander Powell, *The Army Behind the Army* (1919), deals with America's war preparations in an interesting but uncritical way. Frederick Palmer, *America in France* (1918), brings the story of American participation down to the early stages of the battle of the Meuse. The same author's *Our Greatest Battle* (1919) describes the American drive down the Meuse Valley to Sedan. E. C. Peixotto, *American Front* (1919), is sufficiently indicated by its title. F. Maurice, *How the War Was Won, or the Last Four Months* (1919), was written by a former director of military operations of the British General Staff. William F. Sims, *The American Navy in the War* (1920), is a judicious account of American naval participation by the admiral in charge. General Pershing's final *Report* is given in *Current History* for January and February, 1920. Erich von Ludendorff, *My War Memories* (2 vols., 1919), gives a German version of the war, and is written by the real German commander-in-chief during the last two years. It lacks frankness and also minimizes America's part in the final outcome.

CHAPTER XXIII—THE PEACE CONFERENCE

For the Peace Conference we are even more dependent upon newspaper and magazine accounts. The student may consult the files of the magazines mentioned under the preceding heading, also *The American Year Book* for 1919 and *The New International Year Book* for 1919. E. B. Krehbiel (compiler), *Paris Covenant for a League of Nations* (1919), contains an analytical summary of the covenant and the text in full. Stephen P. Duggan, *League of Nations* (1919), contains the covenant in an appendix. Viscount Grey, E. S. Talbot, Sir Julian Corbett, and others, *The League of Nations* (1919), is a collection of essays setting forth the views of a number of prominent Englishmen. Economic aspects of the treaty are discussed in J. L. Garvin, *Economic Foundations of Peace* (1919), and John M. Keynes, *The Economic Consequences of the Peace* (1920); the last was written by the representative of the British treasury at the Peace Conference, and severely criticises the treaty. E. J. Dillon, *The Inside Story of the Peace Conference* (1920), is very critical of the completed work.

CHAPTER XXIV—A GOLDEN AGE IN HISTORY

Of general works dealing with contemporary conditions one of the most valuable is James Bryce, *The American Commonwealth* (revised ed., 2 vols., 1910), perhaps the most notable book ever published about America. H. G. Wells, *The Future in America* (1906), is thought-provoking. Herbert Croly, *The Promise of American Life* (1909), is a book of much merit. See also E. A. Ross, *Changing America* (1912); Hugo Münsterberg, *The Americans* (1904); John G. Brooks, *As Others See Us* (1908); P. L. Haworth, *America in Ferment* (1915); and Peck, *Twenty Years of the Republic*, chap. XVI. On the concentration of wealth see Charles B. Spahr, *The Present Distribution of Wealth in the United States* (1896); Thorstein Veblen, *The Theory of the Leisure Class* (1899); Max West, *The Inheritance Tax* (revised ed., 1908); Andrew Carnegie, *The Gospel of Wealth* (1900); Frederic Mathews, *Taxation and the Distribution of Wealth* (1914); R. T. Ely, *Studies in the Evolution of Industrial Society* (1903); Gustavus Meyers, *History of the Great American Fortunes* (3 vols., 1911); and W. I. King, *The Wealth and Income of the People of the United States* (1915). On the subject of immigration H. P. Fairchild, *Immigration* (1913), takes a strong stand in favor of restriction; F. J. Warne, long a student of the problem in an official capacity, also advocates restriction in *The Slav Invasion* (1904), and *The Immigrant Invasion* (1913). Emily G. Balch, *Our Slavic Fellow Citizens* (1911), is more favorable to immigration; while Isaac A. Hourwich's *Immigration* (1912) seems written to combat exclusion tendencies. In *The Immigrant Tide* (1909), and in *On the Trail of the Immigrant* (1907), E. A. Steiner, himself foreign-born, tells in readable fashion the story of the experiences of incomers in search of a home. *The Promised Land* (1912), by the Russian Jewess Mary Antin (Mrs. A. W. Grabau), is a romantic account of the author's own experience. Sidney L. Gulick, *The American-Japanese Problem* (1914), and H. A. Millis, *The Japanese Problem in the United States* (1915), are sufficiently described by their titles. On the race problem see Ray S. Baker, *Following the Color Line* (1908); Thomas Nelson Page, *The Negro, the Southerner's Problem* (1904); Booker T. Washington, *Up from Slavery* (1901); G. T. Stephenson, *Race Distinctions in American Law* (1910); W. E. B. Dubois, *The Souls of Black Folk* (1903); and *The Negro's Progress in Fifty Years*, a collection of articles by several authors, in *Annals of the American Academy of Political and Social Science* for September, 1913.

Tuskegee Institute publishes annually a survey of race progress in *The Negro Year Book*. On the woman's movement see Eugene A. Hecker, *A Short History of Woman's Rights* (1910); Susan B. Anthony and Ida Husted Harper, *History of Woman's Suffrage* (4 vols., 1881–1902); William I. Thomas, *Sex and Society* (1907); James N. Taylor, *Before Vassar Opened* (1914), an account of the early days of feminine education in America; Annie M. MacLean, *Wage-Earning Women* (1910); and Edith Abbott, *Women in Industry* (1910). Admiral Peary tells the story of his final triumph over obstacles in *The North Pole* (1910). See also his *Nearest the Pole* (1907), and *Northward Over the Great Ice* (1898).

INDEX